International Real Estate Handbook

“This invaluable reference source for professionals will undoubtedly prove every bit as indispensable to the individual. Anyone seriously considering buying or selling a home abroad would do well to follow its advice to avoid the many pitfalls of the property maze.”

Jill Keene,
Editor, International Homes magazine

“The International Real Estate Handbook is a great reference book, summarizing in a concise way the relevant information concerning the acquisition, sale and transfer of real estate in a number of important countries. It will be a very useful tool for the advisors of wealthy and internationally mobile individuals.”

Professor Dr. Hans Rainer Künzle,
University of Zurich; Partner, KENDRIS, Zurich

“This book provides you with all the information you need concerning investing in properties abroad: it not only reviews the whole real estate acquisition process, from the search to the financing, but also gives a lot of tips and checklists. A must buy if you are thinking about investing in real estate abroad.”

Ángel Serrano,
Manager International Clients, Deutsche Bank SAE

Christian H. Kälin • Andrew J. Taylor

International Real Estate Handbook

Acquisition, ownership and sale of real estate
Residence, tax and estate planning

5th Edition • Revised and Expanded

IDEOS

ZURICH • LONDON • HONG KONG • NEW YORK

Published by Ideos Publications Ltd. in Zurich.

For general information on our other products and services please visit: *ideospublications.com*

All books published by Ideos Publications are also available as eBooks.

The CIP Catalogue record for this book is available from the British Library.

ISBN (Paperback): 978-0-9927818-3-5

ISBN (Hardback): 978-3-9524052-6-0

ISBN (eBook): 978-0-9927818-4-2

Data correct as at 1 January 2015

Contents

List of Tables

About the Editors

Christian H. Kälin is a Swiss lawyer and Partner at Henley & Partners, as well as the Chairman of the firm's Global Executive Committee. He is one of the pioneers and leading specialists in residence and citizenship planning. He advises key clients as well as governments in those areas, is a frequent writer and speaker on these issues and is regularly quoted in the international media. He is the author of the Global Residence and Citizenship Handbook, editor and one of the co-authors of the Switzerland Business & Investment Handbook as well as numerous other publications. He is a member of the Governing Board of the Investment Migration Council.

Andrew J. Taylor is a leading authority in strategic international real estate advisory for private clients and Partner at Henley & Partners. After finishing at the BC Institute of Technology for Business and Marketing Management, and forming a solid foundation with leading real estate corporations, he lived in several countries and worked in many real estate markets before merging his own successful firm with Henley Estates and later becoming the Vice-Chairman of Henley & Partners.

Authors of the Individual Chapters

International Chapter
Christian H. Kälin
Henley & Partners
Zurich

Andrew J. Taylor
Henley & Partners
South Africa

Austria
Mag. Dr. Peter Madl and Dr. Michael Lagler
Schönherr Attorney's at Law
Vienna

The Bahamas
John F. Wilson
McKinney, Bancroft & Hughes
Nassau

Belgium
Dirk Reynders, UBS AG
Alain Van Geel/Claudine Bodeux, Tiberghien Lawyers

Canada
Alexander Sennecke
Baldwin Sennecke Halman
Toronto

Croatia
Mia Jug-Dujaković
Attorney at Law
Split

Cyprus
Yiannos Trisokkas
Henley & Partners
Cyprus

France
Donald Manasse
Donald Manasse Law Offices
Nice

Ireland
Duncan Grehan
Duncan Grehan & Partners
Dublin

Italy
Doris Reichel
Studio Legale Reichel
Milan

Malta
Adrian Camilleri
Malta

Monaco
Donald Manasse
Donald Manasse Law Offices
Monaco

Montenegro
Dr. Wolfram Zeihe and Ivan Raičević
Prelevic Law Firm
Podgorica

Portugal
Cristina Dein
Dein Advogados
Lisbon

Spain
Philipp Kirchheim
Marimón Abogados
Barcelona

St. Kitts & Nevis
Andrew J. Taylor
Henley & Partners
South Africa

Jackie Hunkins
JHT Law & Consultancy Firm
Nevis

Switzerland
Christian H. Kälin
Henley & Partners
Zurich

UK / England & Wales
Mustafa Hussain/Nicholas Warr/Elaine Dobson
Taylor Wessing LLP
London

US / Florida
Claudio Riedi
Tew Cardenas
Miami

About This Book

This book presents general information on the most important questions concerning the acquisition, ownership and sale of private real estate. It is designed as a guide and reference for lawyers, tax consultants, asset managers, private-client advisors in banks, family offices and other advisors dealing with the acquisition, ownership and sale of privately used real estate in an international context. It is of course also addressed to private individuals who wish to acquire and own real estate abroad.

The focus on the select countries particularly relevant to this sector, and the use of concise and precise language, reflects its character as a handbook and reference source. In particular, the authors have endeavored to express the terms and concepts involved as transparently as possible in order to make them easily accessible to those without a legal background. Footnotes are dispensed with for the sake of clarity.

The address section includes the various international offices and contacts for Henley & Partners, the global leaders in residence and citizenship planning.

This book can in no way substitute legal, investment or other advice. The publisher and authors therefore unreservedly exclude any liability for losses or damages of any kind – be these direct, indirect or consequential – which may result from the use of this book or the information it contains. Although the publisher and authors have undertaken great care in preparing this book, they obviously cannot guarantee its correctness and completeness, and the explanations and strategies contained herein may not be suitable for your situation.

Any comments and suggestions, praise and criticism will be gratefully received. If you feel that a particular topic or country should be added to this volume, please let us know. We will be happy to recompense any useful information with a complimentary copy of the next edition of this book.

How To Use This Book

The book is divided into a general section and individual country sections. The general section covers all the criteria which should generally be considered by anyone wishing to acquire or own real estate. The individual country sections explain the details of acquisition, forms of ownership, taxes and inheritance law up to residence and domicile which are specific to that country. The book also contains contact information, checklists and overview tables, making it an excellent reference source.

The book has a systematic structure, and the contents of the various country sections have an identical layout so that the same matters in each country section can always be found under the same titles or subtitles.

The comprehensive checklist in the general section offers a systematic approach to the most important points to be considered when acquiring real estate. In addition, each country section contains country-specific checklists which are designed to supplement the general checklist and contain the most important points to be considered when acquiring real estate in the respective country.

Overview tables are inserted at various points. They make no claim to completeness and are designed to give the user an overview of key sectors and to facilitate comparisons.

A bibliography, i.e. a selection of more comprehensive and specialized publications, is included at the end of each section. It is more or less extensive depending on the country and the available literature.

At the end of the volume a comprehensive index of key words allows a systematic search for terms.

Henley & Partners: The Global Leaders in Residence and Citizenship Planning

The production of this book has been made possible by the generous sponsorship of Henley & Partners – the global leaders in residence and citizenship planning.

Over the years, Henley & Partners has emerged as the world's leading firm specialized and focused in this particular area of practice. International residence and citizenship planning has itself become a major topic among the increasing number of internationally mobile entrepreneurs, as well as many wealthy individuals and families, who are interested in looking at alternative residence and citizenship solutions.

Henley & Partners is the preferred partner of the world's most established private clients, and also has specific knowledge and experience of the acquisition of alternative citizenship through qualifying investments, in many cases these qualifying investments are real estate.

Henley & Partners provides the most efficient service to those with busy schedules by taking full responsibility for a client's international residence and citizenship affairs. The preservation of time is their renowned value, and they are committed to delivering reliable and professional service in the shortest possible time.

Residence planning and related tax planning for private clients involves finding solutions for individuals and families who move internationally, own property in different countries and who often have complex international situations and requirements. In this regard, they work closely together with leading tax and estate planning lawyers, and our combined services cover real estate structuring, tax, immigration and citizenship law, international private law, and more.

For many years, Henley & Partners have organized the Global Residence and Citizenship Conference, which is the most important such event in the world. It is held annually around November in different locations each year. To check for the program of the next conference and to benefit from early registration discounts, please visit *henleyglobal.com/events*

For more information about the firm please visit *henleyglobal.com*

Impact

Besides governments and government agencies, Henley & Partners typically advises very wealthy individuals and families, successful Entrepreneurs and investors, top-level managers, artists, and celebrities. Without a doubt, we and our clients are among the most privileged people in the world.

An important distinguishing feature of our firm is our substantial commitment to help those who are less fortunate. This commitment dates back to its roots and is today expressed mainly through the Henley & Partners Foundation. It operates quietly but very effectively.

While several of the firm's partners are themselves involved in important philanthropic work, for many years Henley & Partners as a firm has committed large parts of its yearly global profits to support humanitarian projects. This substantial commitment is further strengthened by the fact that all projects benefit directly from it and are administered by volunteers within the firm or associates in the countries where we operate. Furthermore, several of our clients have become important sponsors of our projects.

Most of the projects are focused on helping children in need. For example, more than 120 million children around the world are without any formal education or schooling, and many more have only very limited access to education. With rare exceptions, they never have the chance to improve their lives, and those children who are born poor tend to die poor. We therefore believe that one of the most significant contributions we can make to humankind is to help those who cannot help themselves, in particular underprivileged children.

In addition, we also fund other significant projects of local, national or international importance, such as youth entrepreneurship initiatives, reforestation, and our partnership with UNHCR. We support

UNHCR's global refugee registration activities with a contribution of over USD 1 million and further advocacy to assist UNHCR's resource mobilization efforts.

If you would like to know more about our
humanitarian initiatives, or if you would like to support them,
please contact the Henley & Partners Foundation at
foundation@henleyglobal.com

Acknowledgements

This publication arose from the idea and need to produce a first-rate, up-to-date and useful international handbook of residential real estate, simply because nothing of this kind had been attempted before. The original publishers, *Orell Füssli* of Switzerland, concurred with this idea, and so did the publishers of this present English edition, *Ideos Publications.* They and the editors are now pleased to present this edition to interested readers. A great deal of specialist knowledge, work and effort has gone into this project, and it has certainly proved worthwhile. As an expression of its overall concept, this volume can unquestionably be seen as a pioneering achievement. The authors, editors and publisher hope that our readers share this viewpoint as well as their enthusiasm for the project.

We would like to express our sincere thanks to all those who have contributed to the book. Special thanks are due to *Nicole Koen*, who was principally responsible for coordinating the authors, and *Amanda Philp*, who managed the launch of this edition. Furthermore, we would also like to thank all the co-authors as well as *Ideos Publications.* Thanks to their professional support, they have also contributed significantly to the successful publication of this book.

Christian H. Kälin
Zurich, June 2015

Andrew J. Taylor
Cape Town, June 2015

PART 1

General Principles

General Principles

Key Aspects of International Real Estate

by

Christian H. Kälin

Henley & Partners Switzerland AG
Henley Haus
Klosbachstrasse 110
8024 Zurich
Switzerland

Telephone +41 44 266 22 22
christian.kalin@henleyglobal.com

Andrew J. Taylor

Henley & Partners South Africa (pty) Ltd
Henley House
Building 9, Fairways Office Park
Somerset West
Cape Town 7130

Telephone +27 21 850 0524
andrew.taylor@henleyglobal.com

1 Introduction – Real Estate Abroad

Many people no longer limit the horizon of their activities and aims to the borders of their own country. New transport and communications media, the political stability and integration of Europe, cross-border activities, prolonged stays in foreign countries and the acquisition of real estate abroad are an expression of this trend. In particular, the last of these – in the form of vacation homes, second homes or a new main domicile – is gaining in interest and importance within Europe and worldwide. The ongoing integration of the European Union, in particular the free movement of persons and capital as well as the single European currency, has made its contribution to the growing trend for foreign nationals to acquire real estate abroad, above all in southern Europe. European countries such as France, Italy, Portugal, Spain, the UK and more recently Switzerland, due to newly relaxed foreign owner-restrictions in Andermatt, are among those most favored by foreign buyers who seek a mild climate, a more relaxed lifestyle and recreational surroundings. However, interest is increasingly extending to destinations such as the Caribbean, Croatia, Malta, Montenegro on the Adriatic, The Bahamas and elsewhere, and even cooler regions such as Canada, Ireland and Sweden are popular.

The acquisition and ownership of real estate across borders raises legal and tax issues, and problems may occur where their full extent is unknown by purchasers. Private acquisitions of real estate are not infrequently made without any accurate knowledge of the legal, tax and economic background. Even if quality of life and personal use are paramount motives for the purchase of non-commercial real estate, the acquisition of property is always a capital investment. Value maintenance and capital growth as well as aspects of fiscal and inheritance law will accordingly play an important role. So it is important to clarify these key framework conditions before acquiring real estate in order to be protected from unexpected legal and tax consequences. Although this applies to real estate in general, it is particularly true for property located abroad.

The acquisition of real estate abroad must clearly be approached with particular care by buyers without sufficient legal and possibly linguistic knowledge, but this should not deter them from trying. Nevertheless, it is generally advisable to play safe by consulting lawyers, tax experts, architects and trustworthy real estate agencies familiar with local conditions. The costs incurred will almost always be more than offset by the smooth and correct handling of the procedures involved.

Other countries have different habits – and different legal systems. This applies quite particularly to real estate and fiscal law, which may assume very different forms in various countries. So foreign acquirers of real estate cannot let themselves be guided by their native feeling for what is right, but must inform themselves in an unprejudiced way about the circumstances prevailing locally. Still, the acquisition of real estate is quite safe in most countries as long as certain basic rules are observed.

Ownership of land and property satisfies a basic human need for a home and shelter, and to acquire a piece of real estate in an attractive location is equivalent to gaining a certain quality of life. At the same time, it means acquiring an asset that almost always retains its value, and in most cases gains in value over a longer period of time. However, it is important to observe certain important principles here, and understand the market conditions.

2 Finding The Right Property

2.1 Brokers, real estate agents and developers

In every country, many players are involved in the real estate sector. A great deal of money can be earned and lost in this business but few, if any, qualifications or other professional or personal preconditions are generally required to take part in it, with the exception of a few countries which are governed by strict guidelines such as Canada and the US. Corresponding care must therefore be taken, as there are some agents, brokers, general contractors and promoters whose business methods cannot be called respectable.

Real estate brokers

Real estate brokers and agents are found throughout the world. Whereas some countries, such as the US, require authorization to be a real estate broker/agent, other countries exercise no supervision at all, so that absolutely anyone can try their hand at the business. The services offered by a broker may also vary greatly. In some countries, the broker or agent does almost everything for the buyer, including drawing up the contract, administrative work, completion of tax forms etc. Often, however, the broker does no more than bring the buyer and seller together and, at most, accompanies the transaction as far as the notary or a selected lawyer. As a rule, brokers receive a commission only when a purchase actually takes place. If no sale results, they go away empty-handed. That's why brokers are interested in rapid closure and accordingly tend to urge prospective customers to buy. However, good brokers always have an overall consulting service for their client in mind and endeavor to describe the prospective property in relatively objective terms. Good brokers also tend to have an extensive portfolio of properties from which to select the most suitable for their client. However, the fact that the broker is commissioned by the seller and usually receives his fee from the latter in practice tends to produce a bias in favor of the seller's interests – although this is contrary to the rules of the profession and often also infringes the legal obligation to neutrality. As a buyer, therefore, one should always maintain a certain distance and communicate this reserve clearly.

The business of a real estate broker for privately used real estate normally has a strong local orientation. Brokers tend to limit their activities to a particular city, province or region. In some small countries, however, brokers may extend their activities over the whole country (for instance in the Caribbean or Malta). Larger real estate brokers may have an extensive network of branches and their activities can extend over several regions or even across the whole country. However, their individual offices obviously have a local orientation. Franchise companies are also expanding across the world, especially from the US. They comprise a number of autonomously managed and independent real estate brokers who present a united brand to the outside world and apply uniform standards for marketing, quality assurance etc. Only in the luxury segment is a certain level of internationalization observed, although here too the leading brokers continue to be specialists with a strong local presence. Some companies with an international scope of operations thus offer luxury real estate worldwide via exclusive networks of brokers.

Real estate dealers

In contrast to brokers, who essentially merely bring buyer/s and seller/s together and receive a commission for this service, real estate dealers act as buyers and sellers on their own behalf. The buyer must be even more careful in this case, as a real estate dealer who wants to sell a property now acts completely in his/her own interest and also tends to urge the buyer to make a quick closure. In addition, there is obviously a danger that the dealer may try to take advantage of an unsuspecting buyer, for instance by concealing important facts about the property. In this case it always makes good sense to call in an independent expert (such as a reputable broker, real estate expert or lawyer with experience in real estate) in order to do a valuation or inspection of the property.

Developers

The term developer refers to a kind of general contractor responsible for the overall realization of real estate projects. The developer is usually the owner of a piece of land which is ready for development and handles all the building work up to the marketing and final handover of the individual properties. Buyers must exercise the greatest caution when buying property from a developer for various reasons. Firstly, the developer is obliged to complete specific project phases within certain periods of time, which may lead to the use of somewhat more aggressive sales methods. Moreover, the buyer may incur an extensive financial risk by buying the property on the basis of a mere plan, i.e. before any building work has been started or while this is still in progress. New or un-developed properties should only be acquired from very well established and reputable developers, as poor build quality and failure to deliver what is promised in plans (especially within set budgets) is a frequent shortcoming of inexperienced developers. Corresponding guarantees are indispensable.

2.2 How to recognize a reputable real estate professional

The reputability of a real estate professional cannot be determined from any specific paradigm or perfect model. However, a number of indications may allow a conclusion to be drawn one way or the other. Although these seem obvious to many readers, experience shows that it is nevertheless important to make oneself aware of this time and again.

Reputable brokers, real estate dealers and developers will always be distinguished by a professional, reserved manner. Professional associations whose members comprise real estate brokers, architects, surveyors, developers etc, are found in all countries. Depending on the organization, the selection criteria for membership usually guarantee a certain quality standard. Moreover, it makes sense to find out how long the relevant broker, real estate dealer or developer has been established. Anyone who has already been in business for many years, possibly at the same address, would normally merit a positive valuation. You should also ask openly for references and not neglect to check them. A real estate professional should be honest, clear and understandable. Their approach should not leave you feeling pressured, but rather informed, allowing you to make an educated decision. It is always worthwhile to sign an agreement with a buying agent where they are compensated by you on success, and nullifies them from earning commission from the seller. Extra compensation can then be offered once a property is found, based on a negotiated price. An agreement such as this ensures your representative is acting with your best interests in mind, as their advice will not be motivated by additional compensation available from certain properties.

2.3 Key criteria to note when looking for real estate

Although common knowledge, it is nevertheless worth stressing that location is the most important factor in the selection of any piece of real estate. Quite apart from the present circumstances, special care must also be taken to check how the environment may change in future. So it is not immaterial if projects for constructing freeways, airfields, power lines, waste dumps or similar major developments are planned in the area. One should also know in which construction zone the building plot and its surrounding plots are situated (might a neighbor add another storey to his property and in so doing obscure the marvelous lake view?). The best way to be quite sure about these factors is to buy an existing property in surroundings which are already well developed and in which re-zoning is unlikely. If there are still many undeveloped plots of land around a property, it is hard to estimate how the surroundings and perhaps the entire appearance of the locality may change. Many location factors must be considered, above all the quality of the local municipality. Thus the way in which this quality is likely to change in a positive way in the future is of critical importance for any gain in the value of the property. This will be explained in greater detail further on. Also, the quality of the location within the municipality where the property is situated is important. Is the house located on a quiet street in a quiet area? Where are the nearest shops, bank, post office, schools and kindergartens, high schools, evening classes, restaurants and sports facilities? Are there cultural facilities nearby? How easily can the property be reached by public transport? Where is the nearest national or international airport? Where is the nearest rail station? What are the connections like? How far is it to the nearest highway or freeway access? How close is the nearest healthcare facility, and where are the nearest major hospitals? These are the questions that you need to ask your broker, and ask them to acquire reports and information for your review.

These questions concerning the infrastructure are of central concern to anyone interested in acquiring real estate and their answers have a corresponding effect on price levels. In general, properties situated in largely rural localities with a modest infrastructure are much less in demand and are correspondingly harder to re-sell. In contrast, properties in locations offering an extensive infrastructure immediately command higher prices. In the case of "bargains", a poor infrastructure is often a major reason for the relatively low price. And although the same demands are not necessarily made on infrastructures around vacation residences, where a rural idyll away from the hustle and bustle of the city is often sought, considerations of this kind are nevertheless just as important as for a principal residence. The ideal for many people is likely to be a property in a very quiet location in idyllic surroundings, but nevertheless close to a town and an international airport. And it is precisely properties of this kind which represent the ultimate luxury and attract the relatively highest prices worldwide.

If interest focuses on the maintenance and growth potential of a property's value, it should be noted that owner-occupied residential properties often tend to be a poor investment in real terms – i.e. when adjusted for inflation. At any rate, the return is worse than is generally assumed, as real estate tends to be considered a very secure and, above all, inflation-proof investment. However, the most important factor in maintaining and increasing the value of residential real estate is not its current location quality but potential positive changes, i.e. the improvement of location quality. Such improvements are often the result of expanding residential areas, especially in the periphery of larger cities, and of associated infrastructure improvements in transport links and shopping facilities. However, the expansion of the infrastructure can also have a negative impact on location quality, such as the construction of new freeways or the extension of airports and the associated changes in flight paths. The latter can have an impact dozens of kilometers away from the actual location of the airport.

In making an estimate of the future potential growth in value of a property as far as possible, it is always worthwhile clarifying the planned and future development of the residential area in which it is located as well as any changes in local infrastructure in advance of purchase.

Important aspects of the property itself are the size and shape of the plot, the orientation of the building and its exposure to sunlight, the view as well as the extent to which it is overlooked by neighbors. Exposure to wind plays a significant role in many areas (the Mistral in southern France, for example), causing salt corrosion etc. A secluded outside patio can be very attractive, but excessive exposure to wind can make conditions quite disagreeable outside the house. Tranquility is also important, and noise, especially from busy roads and airports, should not be underestimated. Intrusive odors also represent an important factor (proximity to paper factories, pig farms, food-processing establishments etc.). Exhaust emissions must also be considered. In view of the pollution from fumes, it is important to be sufficiently far away from filling stations, covered car parks and busy roads. Likewise, one should be sufficiently far away from pylons/high-tension lines and mobile phone network antennas. It is also necessary to be aware of possible risks of accidents. For instance, industrial or other installations may represent a considerable risk (chemical factory, nuclear power plant, liquid gas tanks, cyanide warehouse of a metal-processing plant etc.). Given a choice, a prospective buyer would obviously opt for property located a sufficient distance from installations of this kind.

Where buildings are constructed on a slope, excessive water pressure and thus damp masonry may be a problem. Any danger of natural hazards must also be clarified. Landslides, avalanches, earthquakes, forest fires as well as flooding, tidal waves and tornadoes may present considerable risks in certain areas. The situation and construction of the property must be carefully considered to estimate the real risks.

Certain special features must be considered in the case of rural properties as well as of historical properties and properties located by rivers, lakes and close to the sea. These will be discussed in separate chapters.

What about access and access authorization? Is there a public road leading to the property, or only a private road? Is snow clearance an issue in winter?

Security must not be neglected either. How frequent are burglaries in the area where the property is located? Is the house very isolated? Is there a need for a burglar alarm? Are there any neighbors and trustworthy persons who can keep an eye on the house when the owner is absent? Might there be a need for a private surveillance service?

The most varied criteria must then be considered as regards the building itself. They include the size and configuration of the rooms and ancillary premises, the number of bathrooms, potential for additional fittings and extensions (for instance, can the attic be extended?), construction quality of the building, heating insulation, energy consumption, heating system (a necessity in a country like Spain if the property is to be used all the year round). Penetration of moisture (e.g. in the case of old walls, damp subsoil or sloping situations) can constitute a major problem which may not be easy, or indeed possible, to solve. The condition of the roof is a major consideration, and pest damage – not only in the attic – is by no means unusual in many countries. The technical equipment of the house and the various installations must also be carefully examined. What is the state of the electrical installations and the plumbing? Are telephone lines, internet connections, ISDN/ADSL, cable TV connections, a satellite dish all present? What kind of water supply and waste-water disposal facilities are present? What kind of heating system is in place? In the case of oil heating, the potential environmental risk means that the oil tank must not be placed directly on or in the soil outside. It should be located in the cellar or other separate building and be equipped with a protective trough. One should also check whether the heating installation and the oil tank have been regularly maintained.

In the case of a swimming pool, it is also of interest to know whether it has been regularly maintained. What is the condition of the pool? Is there potential for extension? Would this require approval?

It is important to ensure sufficient sound insulation, including against footfall sound, especially in apartments and condominiums. To check this out in practice, it is best to spend several days in the building or – more realistically – to have the sound insulation inspected by an expert who can accurately measure it.

Prestige elements such as a sauna, swimming pool, tennis court, parking facility or a direct lakeside location naturally increase the value and thus the price of a property. Any historical importance of the building, a very exclusive location or the fact that it has been built by a celebrated architect can have a significant effect on the price of the property.

High quality and well-maintained properties which are not too large, in good-to-excellent locations, particularly those close to large cities, in regions with a promising future in terms of residential development, with practical interior designs and appropriate fittings are always sought after. Such properties are correspondingly easier to resell and offer above-average potential for value growth.

When searching for a property, one should ideally already apply criteria which will be of significant interest to future buyers as it will improve re-sale potential.

2.4 The valuation of real estate

The value of real estate is always subjective. This makes an objective valuation difficult, and there is never anything like a "right" value, but only value bands which may be justified on both objective and subjective grounds. The price for a specific property is fixed precisely only when the buyer and seller agree on it at the sale. However, this is merely a momentary value.

The property announcements in the local press and in specialized publications like property magazines give an initial overview of the price level of comparable local properties. As brokers almost always represent the sellers, their pricing information and recommendations must be taken with due caution. It is much better to be advised by an independent expert, for example a chartered surveyor, a lawyer familiar with the relevant market, or a local architect.

In the case of larger, older or special properties, such as historical buildings, it is wise to commission an assessment by an expert (surveyor, architect or civil engineer). The associated costs, depending on the detail of the assessment, the size and location of the property and the country, normally range between USD 1,500 and USD 20,000, and represent a sound investment in most cases. It may even be worthwhile obtaining a second opinion, especially if the initial appraisal was made by a potentially biased party.

It is very important to find a suitable expert who can appraise the property on objective criteria and analyze its market value as realistically as possible. A suitable expert should possess local building knowledge as well as experience in the type of real estate to be assessed. In the case of older properties, and especially of historical buildings, it is important that the condition of the building and any need for renovation be examined and realistically assessed. Professional surveyors perform a valuable service here, as these questions can hardly be answered by a buyer unfamiliar with local circumstances.

There are various different real estate valuation methods. In past- or cost-based methods, the original building costs are extrapolated to their current value via a suitable index and annual hypothetical amortizations are concurrently calculated. The land value is also determined. In contrast, future-oriented methods are based on the revenue value or on discounting future revenues. However, market or cross-comparison methods are of particular relevance for private, owner-occupied real estate. The price of the property being assessed is then determined on the basis of the latest prices of comparable properties. This method is also used intuitively by a layman when comparing different properties.

When buying from developers, it is important to understand construction costs to ensure a realistic and fair price is being offered. When the difference between the cost of land/construction and purchase price is minimized, it will add protection against a future drop in price at re-sale.

3 Ownership of Real Estate

3.1 Possession and ownership

Non-lawyers often confuse the terms possession and ownership, so it's worth briefly clarifying what these two terms, which originate in property law, mean in most legal systems. Possession entails the actual control over a physical object (such as an automobile, a shovel or a house) with the intent to have and to exercise such control. A tenant who lawfully rents a house on the basis of a rental agreement from the owner and therefore has real power to use it is consequently the possessor of the house (for the duration of the rental). In contrast, ownership means the fully comprehensive power of disposal and complete dominion over a property, including the right to transfer it to others. Ownership is of course often associated with possession, and these two legal powers often coincide. However, it is important to distinguish between them, as such a distinction may be relevant under certain circumstances.

3.2 Different forms and types of ownership

Sole ownership of real estate is possible in all legal systems of interest. A sole owner has maximum comprehensive power of disposal and legal control over a piece of real estate within the scope of the prevailing legal and factual limits. As a rule, various forms of shared ownership are also possible, especially joint and condominium ownership. The different forms and types of ownership existing in various countries are explained in the respective country sections. Some jurisdictions additionally allow separate ownership rights to the land and the buildings standing on it, resulting in split ownership. This is particularly the case for the right to build which exists in some jurisdictions.

3.3 Encumbrances, easements, covenants and mortgages

Ownership can be encumbered and restricted in various ways. In addition to contractual agreements, which apply only between the contractual parties, all jurisdictions allow various rights relating to property, which are generally applicable and can in most cases also be entered or noted in a land or ownership register or in the title deeds. In contrast to comprehensive ownership rights, these imply restricted control over or rights to a property. Restricted property rights limit ownership to the encumbered property and to this extent take precedence over comprehensive ownership rights.

There are essentially four types of restricted property rights, although several different designations for them are found in various jurisdictions. Thus personal easements or personal servitudes depend on the entitled person and normally end at the death of the person/s whom it benefits, or in case of legal entities being beneficiaries, after some period set by law. A classical example is the right of usufruct which exists in various forms. There are also various forms of easements on property, or real servitudes. These involve a servient and an entitled property. The respective owner of the servient property must tolerate certain interventions by the respective owner of the entitled property (such as right of way or right of passage) or restrict the exercise of his ownership right in a certain way (e.g. not build higher than one storey). Real charges on property have been handed down from feudal times and still exist in some countries. They obligate the owner of the property not only to exercise tolerance, but to perform a certain action, for instance to supply a certain amount of grass or to pay an annual land rent. However, it is now usually possible to be released from a real charge by paying a redemption fee. To secure claims and to mobilize the value of a property, virtually all jurisdictions also include various forms of liens and mortgages (real estate security interests).

So, it is very important to check before every acquisition whether the property to be acquired is encumbered with any easements, charges, restrictive covenants, liens or mortgages. Such rights may be significant and may often greatly restrict the enjoyment or use of the property. The existence of such encumbrances may also have considerable effects on its value and future appreciation.

3.4 Protection of ownership, proof of ownership and registration

Private property is guaranteed in all the countries considered here by their respective laws and usually even at a constitutional level. In countries such as Germany and Switzerland, a land register allows the exact ownership relationships and encumbrances of properties to be determined at any time, and a relatively high legal security prevails. However, title to ownership cannot be quite so easily proved in some other countries. For instance, in the US, it is even usual for acquirers to secure themselves in this regard by means of a title insurance.

4 Purchase and Sale of Real Estate

Table 1. Overview: real estate market in selected countries

	Types and forms of ownership	Usual financing by credit institutes	Usual rental duration for residential real estate	Rental payments	Security due from tenant for residential rental	Usual deposit at purchase
Austria	Sole ownership, co-ownership, apartment ownership, building right	Up to 80% of the estimated value, subject to financial soundness	Agreed by contracting parties, usually between 3 – 10 years	Monthly in advance	Up to three months' rent in form of a bank savings book or a bank guarantee	100% at signing
The Bahamas	Sole ownership, co-ownership, apartment ownership, timesharing, leasehold, trusts	Up to 75% of the market value	Residential rental usually 1 year. Leasing: longer term	Monthly	Typically 2 months' rent	10%
Belgium	Sole ownership, co-ownership, joint ownership with right of accrual, apartment ownership, joint tenancy, timesharing, building right	Up to 80% of the market value or the sale price.	Residential rental 9 years	Monthly in advance	Residential rental: 2 months' rent	5 – 10%
Canada	Sole ownership, co-ownership, joint ownership, condominium ownership, timesharing, leasehold, trusts	Up to 75% of the market value. For foreign nationals: 65%	According to use. One year and thereafter month to month	Payment due at beginning of each month	Leasehold: Rent for the first and last months	5%

	Broker's commission[1]	Land register and notaries' fees	Purchase taxes	VAT on new buildings	Annual property and wealth taxes	Capital appreciation taxes as % of appreciation
Austria	Max. 3%, possible from both buyer and seller, i.e. max. total of 6%	1.1% land registry fee, authentication costs, 1 – 3% attorney's fees	Real Estate Transfer Tax 3.5%	20%	Ca. 1% of assessed value, no wealth tax	Capital gains tax for natural persons 25%. For corporations normal corporate income tax of 25% and dividend withholding tax of 25%
The Bahamas	6% for developed, 10% for undeveloped building plots	2.5% of the real-estate value (lawyer's fee)	2 – 10%; VAT at a rate of 7.5% is payable for commercial property; the transfer of vacant land and the sale of a dwelling are exempt	VAT at a rate of 7.5% is payable with respect to construction costs	Real estate tax varies, however approx. 1 – 2% of the market value	None
Belgium	3 – 5%	0.05 – 5% notary fees	Registration tax upon purchase : 5% – 12.5%	21%	Annual tax as percentage of cadastral value No wealth tax	No tax for main residence. No tax if sold after 5 years[2] Other: 16.5% – 33%
Canada	3 – 6%	Notaries in Quebec, otherwise lawyers: either hourly fee or flat rate	Varies by province, mostly between 0.5 and 1.5%	Varies from province to province[3]	Land tax: varies greatly[4] No wealth tax	Ca. 25% of the appreciation

	Types and forms of ownership	Usual financing by credit institutes	Usual rental duration for residential real estate	Rental payments	Security due from tenant for residential rental	Usual deposit at purchase
Croatia	Sole ownership, co-ownership, joint ownership, apartment ownership, building right	Up to 75% of the market value	No specifications	Payment due at beginning of each month	Depends on the contractual relationship and the conditions	10%
Cyprus	Sole ownership, co-ownership, joint ownership, apartment ownership, leasehold	70 – 80% of the market value	Agreed by contracting parties, usually between 2 – 5 years	Monthly in advance except if otherwise agreed between the parties	Up to one months' rent	10 – 20%
France	Sole ownership, co-ownership, joint ownership with right of accrual, apartment ownership, joint tenancy, timesharing, building right	Up to 100% of the market value or the sale price. Foreign nationals: max. 70%	Residential rental at least 3 years	Monthly in advance or quarterly	Residential rental: 2 months' rent or one month rent if quarterly payment	5 – 10%
Ireland	Sole ownership, co-ownership, apartment ownership, timesharing, leasehold, trusts	Up to 90% of the market value	Residential rentals 1 – 3 years. Leasing: 25 years are standard. The contract is renewable every 5 years. Leases of up to 999 years are possible	Monthly in advance for residential rentals. Quarterly in advance for commercial rentals.	Depends on the contractual relationship and the conditions. 1 month would be standard	10%
Italy	Sole ownership, co-ownership, joint ownership, apartment ownership, timesharing, inherited building right	Up to 75% of the market value	Four years with automatic extension by another 4 years. Shorter-term contracts may be agreed	Monthly in advance. Other modes of payment may also be agreed	1 – 3 months	10 – 30%

	Broker's commission[1]	Land register and notaries' fees	Purchase taxes	VAT on new buildings	Annual property and wealth taxes	Capital appreciation taxes as % of appreciation
Croatia	2 – 5%	€35 land register registration fee, €10 signature authentication by notary	5%	22%	Vacation home tax €0.7– 2/m[4] usable area, depending on position and infra-structure. No wealth tax	Maximum 45% [5]
Cyprus	3%, except if otherwise agreed by the parties	3% – 8%, depending on the value of the property sold	Stamp duty fee from 1.5% to 2% depending on the contractual purchase price (max. fee is €20,000)	19%. A reduced VAT rate of 5% applies in certain cases.	6% –9% depending on the value of the property	20% – 35% for physical persons 12.5% for legal persons
France	5 – 10%	0.825 – 5%	Purchase tax: 5.09% plus notary fees of around 7%	20%	Land tax and living space tax (varies from place to place)	No capital appreciation tax for main residence; non-residents depending on whether EU or non-EU – 19% plus 15.5% social charges
Ireland	1.5 – 2.5%	Each party pays its own lawyers' fees as agreed, usually 1% of the property value	Stamp Duty 1 – 2%	13.5%, but included in the purchase price	None	20 – 40%
Italy	2 – 3% if only one intermediary, possibly 5% for an exclusive broker	€2,500 – 10,000, varies greatly depending on real estate value and notary	2 – 12%	4 – 22%	Land tax: between 0.4 and 0.7%, referred to cadastral value. No wealth tax	None

	Types and forms of ownership	Usual financing by credit institutes	Usual rental duration for residential real estate	Rental payments	Security due from tenant for residential rental	Usual deposit at purchase
Malta	Sole ownership, co-ownership, joint ownership, apartment ownership, timesharing	75 – 90% of the market value, depending on the bank	Rentals before 1995: terminable only in specific restricted circumstances. Rentals arranged after 1995: by free agreement	Quarterly	One months' rent	10%
Monaco	Sole ownership, co-ownership, apartment ownership	50 – 70% of the market value	By free arrangement, usually 1 – 3 years	Quarterly	3 months	10%
Montenegro	Sole ownership, co-ownership, joint ownership and common hold.	40 – 50% of the market value	negotiable	Monthly	not common, but some rental payments may need to be paid in advance	5 – 10%
Portugal	Sole ownership, co-ownership, joint ownership, apartment ownership, timesharing, building right	60 – 80% of the estimated value	2 years	Monthly in advance	1 – 3 months' rent	10 – 40%
Spain	Sole ownership, co-ownership, condominiums, time-sharing, usufruct, heritable building right, leasehold (land rent)	Up to 60 – 70% of the market value or the sale price	Up to a maximum of 3 years (mandatory for the landlord), plus optional 1 year	Rent and charges to be settled monthly in advance	One months' rent, further securities can be requested; usual up to six months' rent	5 – 10%
St. Kitts and Nevis	Freehold, share of freehold, joint tenancy, tenancy in common.	40 – 50% of the bank's determined valuation	No specifications	Payment due at beginning of each month	One or two months' rent	US $10,000 non-refundable if part of a citizenship application or 10%

	Broker's commission[1]	Land register and notaries' fees	Purchase taxes	VAT on new buildings	Annual property and wealth taxes	Capital appreciation taxes as % of appreciation
Malta	3% to 5%	1%	Conveyancing fee 5% plus €250 for authorizations	15%	None	35%
Monaco	Purchase: 8%[6] Leasing: 10% of the first year	Registration and notary costs ca. 9%	Ca. 9%, 7.5% being registration fees and stamp duties, 1.5% notary fees	19.6%	None	None
Montenegro	3 – 5%	€15 Land Registry fees; €70 – €5,000 Notary Fees	19% VAT for 1st sale of new built residential property; 3% on market value on other sales	19%	0.1% – 1.0%	9%
Portugal	3 – 6%	Notaries' and land register fees ca. €300 minimum	Property acquisition tax 6.5%.[7] Statutory duties 0.8%	None; 23% on building materials and works contracts	0.3 – 0.8%; blacklisted offshore companies 7.5%	28% for non-residents
Spain	Usually 3 – 5%	Ancillary purchasing costs ca. 2 to 3% maximum	Property acquisition tax, the rate depending on the region (6 – 10%)	10%	Local tax IBI 0.3 – 1.1% on cadastral value; wealth tax 0.2 – 2.5% on cadastral value or acquisition value, the highest	Max. 3.7% of the cadastral value per year; max. 20 years. Must be distinguished from capital gains tax where rate is 20% for non-residents from 2015 on
St. Kitts and Nevis	5 – 10%	1.17%	5.2% on properties classed as a condominium, 12.2% on land and all other property	17%	Annual Property Tax 0.2% on the value	0%

	Types and forms of ownership	Usual financing by credit institutes	Usual rental duration for residential real estate	Rental payments	Security due from tenant for residential rental	Usual deposit at purchase
Switzerland	Sole ownership, co-ownership, joint ownership, apartment ownership, building right	60 – 80% of the market value, 50% for investment objects	Leasing: normally 5 years, with renewal option for another 5 years	Monthly or quarterly in advance	Bank guarantee or up to three months' rent	10 – 15%
United Kingdom / England	Sole ownership, co-ownership, joint ownership, apartment ownership, leasehold, trusts	75 – 85% of the market value	Usually 1 – 3 years for residential rentals, otherwise anything between 5 and 999 years possible	For short rentals usually monthly, for longer rentals quarterly	For short rentals usually 3 months' rent	10%
United States / Florida	Sole ownership, co-ownership, joint ownership, apartment ownership, timesharing, leasing, tenancy by the entireties	For local residents up to 90%, for non-residents up to 70% of the market value	Negotiable in line with the tenant's requirements. 30-year leasing contracts are regarded as purchase contracts. Some cities prohibit short term rentals of less than 6 months	Monthly in advance	1 – 6 months' rent, depending on the credit-worthiness of the tenant; frequently waived	10% and more for residents; 30% and more for non-residents

1 Unless otherwise stated, the broker's commission is paid by the respective seller. Broker commissions are subject to VAT in most countries

2 Capital appreciation on land is only tax free after eight years

3 See calculation in Canada Chapter

4 For a house in Toronto valued at US$500,000, for instance, this tax is about US$12,000 including Provincial and Toronto land transfer taxes

5 There are no capital gains taxes in the following cases:
where the property was used as a residence for the owner's family
where the property was sold again more than three years after its acquisition
where the property was transferred between close relatives or divorced spouses

	Broker's commission[1]	Land register and notaries' fees	Purchase taxes	VAT on new buildings	Annual property and wealth taxes	Capital appreciation taxes as % of appreciation
Switzerland	2 – 4%	0.01 – 0.7% depending on the canton	1 – 3% depending on the canton	7.6% on building work	Wealth taxes 0 – 0.7% depending on the canton, plus property taxes; half the cantons 0.005 – 0.02%	Between ca. 25 and 70% depending on the canton and duration of ownership
United Kingdom / England	2 – 3%	Max. £800 land register fees, plus lawyer's fee	Up to 4% stamp duty. Up to £150 for data search at local authority	None (5 – 17.5% on reconstructions and extensions)	None	18 / 28%[8]
United States / Florida	6% developed; 10% undeveloped	None	Documentary stamp taxes, lawyers' fees, title insurance 2 – 5%	None	No wealth tax. Land taxes depend on various factors, approximation not possible.	10 – 28%[9]

6 Comprising 3% for the "buyer's broker" and 5% for the "seller's broker"

7 Property acquisition tax 0-10% depending on property value, nature of property and use, as well as incorporation of the buyer company in a tax haven; statutory duties 0.8%

8 Only for persons domiciled in the UK

9 Capital gains are taxed as regular income

4.1 How to proceed with a purchase

The buyer generally bears the greater transaction risk, as fittingly expressed by a principle of Roman law: *Periculum est emptoris*, or in other words: *Caveat emptor*. That's why certain precautions and clarifications are needed prior to every purchase in order to minimize risk. A long-term investment that ties up a lot of capital should be planned and carried out in a careful and rational manner. A property designed for private use should above all bring subjective pleasure to its users, and maintain and increase its value in objective terms, so careful clarification of these factors is most important.

1 **Start by renting.** Before purchasing, it is advisable to first rent a comparable property in a similar location for a while. Some time should also be spent in that area during the months that you intend to use the property in addition to months that you do not. This helps ensure there are no surprises later on.

2 **Viewing and detailed inspection of the property.** The best thing to do is to inspect the prospective property on several occasions at different times of the day and night (noise, the way the sunlight falls etc.) and if possible also at various times of the year.

3 **Consider the marketability of the property.** Special-interest real estate is often hard to re-sell. This applies to old mills, castles, houses with an unusual architectural style etc, as well as very expensive and very large properties. The market for such properties is very limited. In contrast, high-quality properties in good to very good locations, on not excessively large plots, in up-and-coming regions, will nearly always find buyers over the long term. Whoever lays value on marketability, i.e. on factors which will also be relevant at resale, will simultaneously take into account the factors important for preserving the value of the property.

4 **Observe real estate price cycles.** As property prices tend to follow cycles lasting several years, it makes sense to examine regional and recent price trends in the region in which the prospective real estate

is located. Hence, if the analysis shows that property prices have risen continuously over a decade, caution is called for, although an unbroken rise in prices does not necessarily mean that a slump will follow. On the other hand, we can generally assume that stabilization will follow several years of declining prices. However, it should be stressed that price trends can never be exactly forecast, and only a rough assessment can ultimately be made.

5 **Check the legal and tax situation.** Before a sales agreement or even a preliminary agreement is signed, all important legal and tax aspects must be clarified in detail. The checklists contained in this handbook set out all the key points.

6 **Purchase with the aid of one or several experts.** Depending on the country, place and circumstances, it may make sense to consult one or several experts when making the purchase. These may include a competent broker, an architect or engineer, a notary or a lawyer. In most cases, it is worthwhile for a buyer (or seller) unfamiliar with local circumstances to obtain advice from a competent source and have the purchase transaction checked. Further information on this point may be found in chapter 4.8.

4.2 The sales agreement (sale and purchase agreement)

The way in which real estate can be sold is sometimes subject to different rules, laws and regulations in various countries. Whereas a house can be legally sold via a short simple contract in Spain, indeed even by verbal agreement, many countries require a notarized contract and an entry in the land register before the purchase of real estate is legally valid.

Despite differences in legal systems and practices around the world, the key points which should be covered in a sales contract can be summarized as follows:

- A precise designation of the parties to the contract

- A precise designation and description of the property to be purchased (description of the property, notes, charges, easements, liens, other encumbrances, covenants and mortgages)
- The purchase price, mode and schedule of payment
- The time of transfer of ownership
- The time of transfer of rights and obligations, benefits and risks
- The security and interest on deposits, balance payments and funds held in escrow
- Payment of taxes due, especially of capital gains tax
- Warranty questions regarding title and material defects
- Settling existing contracts referring to the property (rental and tenancy agreements, insurance policies etc.)
- Any penalty clauses, forfeits and similar clauses
- Applicable law and jurisdiction

These are the most important points, but every sales contract should generally be negotiated and drawn up on an individual basis.

Nevertheless, standard form contracts are usual in some countries (e.g. the frequently used *FAR/Bar* standard contract in Florida). Although a pre-printed agreement is not suitable for all transactions, the *FAR/Bar* contract is well suited for the great majority of transactions involving residential real estate and even for commercial transactions. The same applies in several other countries. However, it is always advisable to consult a lawyer familiar with local practices and the local legal situation to at least review the sales agreement.

4.3 Restrictions on the sale/conveyance

The seller's power of disposal may be restricted for various reasons. If the seller is married, his/her disposal capacity is based on the matrimonial property regime that applies to him/her. It must therefore be clarified which matrimonial property regime the seller is subject to, and whether consent of the spouse is required. In many countries, the effects of the marriage, and thus any possible restrictions on the disposal of property, are based on the personal statute or *lex patriae* of the spouses, i.e. on the law of the country whose citizenship the spouses possess. The precise arrangements are a question of the international private law of the country in which the property is located. Many countries require the consent of the spouse for a valid agreement to be concluded if the sale refers to the matrimonial home of the spouses. In such a case, that spouse should be joined as a party to the contract and agree to the sale. To prevent possible fraud by the spouse who is the registered owner, the sales agreement should contain a confirmation that the other spouse has actually received separate legal advice before agreeing to the sale.

Furthermore, restrictions on minors and wards of court as well as contractual and legal pre-emption rights should be observed. A contractual pre-emption right or right of first refusal stipulates by contract that in the event of a sale, a particular named person has the right to acquire the property under the same conditions and the same price as would be offered to any other prospective buyers. Various legal pre-emption rights usually also exist, e.g. in favor of the municipality or the state. This is often the case particularly for historical buildings or those of particular cultural importance. Such rights may also exist in favor of lessees, neighbors etc. Current tenants often also possess a pre-emption right and could thus prevent a sale to another party. If a prospective property is rented or leased, extreme care must be exercised in its acquisition. It must be precisely clarified whether legal or contractual pre-emption rights exist and whether the property had been offered to the tenant or lessee as prescribed. In this context, it is worth mentioning the situation of a tenant who is aware of ongoing contractual negotiations between the owner and the prospective buyer. Although initially willing to leave the apartment voluntarily in return for compensation, he/she subsequently refuses to do so in violation of the agreement while attempting to obtain still higher compensation from the acquirer. As a rule, there is nothing that either the seller or the buyer can do against such unethical behavior by the tenant. In the interest of both parties, a tenant who enjoys pre-emption rights should firstly be offered the property so that all those concerned know where they stand after the legal period of notice has elapsed.

Finally, agricultural properties are subject to special restrictions in many countries.

4.4 Restrictions on acquisition

Analogously to such sales restrictions, some countries also impose restrictions on acquisition. The most significant of these are restrictions on the acquisition of real estate by foreign nationals. Whereas there are almost no restrictions of this kind in many of the countries we discuss here (such as in Canada, France, Portugal, Spain, the UK or the US), they are imposed by some countries, and range from minor restrictions and the obligation to obtain a permit, up to complete prohibition. Thus more or less strict acquisition restrictions apply in a number of countries including Austria, Croatia, Greece and Switzerland. The laws in some of these countries even stipulate draconian sanctions in the event of evasion. Thus in Switzerland, evasion of acquisition restrictions on foreign nationals leads to nullity of the relevant contracts, which may lead to a total loss of the foreign buyer's investment. On the other hand, other countries make it easy for such restrictions on acquisition to be bypassed via legal structures. Thus in Croatia, the obligation for foreign buyers to obtain approval – and the associated lengthy process of authorization – can be simply and legally avoided by setting up a Croatian company that acquires the real estate without the need for obtaining approval.

It is in any case essential to assure oneself before buying real estate that no sales or acquisition restrictions exist. If they do exist, the prospective buyer must clarify whether approval may be obtained, what the relevant conditions are, and how the obligation to obtain approval may impact a possible resale. It can also be worthwhile to check whether the approval obligation may be lawfully bypassed by means of a suitable legal structure. It must then be clarified with great care whether such a device is also accepted by the relevant authorities and is not classed as a structure established specifically to evade the law.

4.5 Other important points to consider when acquiring real estate

The following key points must be considered when acquiring real estate. However, other legal obligations and requirements may also impair rights to property ownership, depending on the country in question.

Capacity to act and entitlement of the seller

The seller's authorization to conclude contracts, and to transfer ownership in particular, follows from his status as the owner of the real estate. The person presenting himself as the seller must possess the unrestricted ownership of the real estate to be sold, and appropriate proof should be requested. The seller must be legally capable as well as authorized to dispose of the property. A seller is legally capable as long as he/she is not restricted in his legal capacity to act. Restriction of the seller's capacity to act may be due to various reasons. For instance it could be as a result of not yet being of an age to perform the sale. In this case, authorization by a legal representative or a ruling by a judge of the guardianship court must be submitted to allow the legal business to be carried out. Moreover, there must be no temporary legal incapacity or disallowance of business activity due to a criminal conviction. If the seller is married, it may not be possible for him/her to legally sell the matrimonial home without the consent of the spouse, or other restrictions based on the applicable matrimonial property regime may require involvement of the spouse.

If the seller is a legal entity (such as a company, foundation, etc), the legal capacity of its executive organ or the latter's representative must not be restricted. Ultimately, legal persons are always represented by natural persons, who sign contracts on their behalf. The same criteria naturally apply to these representatives as described above, i.e. they must possess full legal capacity. It must also be demonstrated that the legal person has authorized its legal representative to perform the sale, so that the sale can actually go through. If the purpose of a company does not expressly include the acquisition and sale of real estate, a decision by the owners (shareholders, stockholders of a limited company) is required in most countries, i.e. a decision by the managing board does not suffice. A restriction of the capacity to act by legal persons may also result from other circumstances, for instance if the company has gone into receivership. The authorization to perform legal business for the company then passes to the receivers. If a legal person is a contractual partner, special care must be taken with regard to the authorization or legal capacity of the persons acting on its behalf.

Third-party claims and unpaid taxes

Every buyer should acquire comprehensive clarity about the existence of any third-party claims which encumber the property. Various easements/servitudes, liens and other encumbrances on property, as well as lease and tenancy agreements, mortgages and unpaid taxes can have considerable effects on the possibility of acquisition, the value and resale possibility of the real estate. These risks can extend to everything which has any connection at all with the property. The seller need not necessarily intend any malicious concealment, but may simply have forgotten or overlooked something. In many cases – especially in the case of rural properties – the contracts in question will already have been concluded between the person owning the property before the current seller and the neighbors regarding matters such as rights of way and grazing rights. Even if such rights have not been recorded in a register, they may nevertheless be fully effective. For example, informal permission to let cattle graze on a particular meadow can over many years become a legally enforceable right of lease or even a restricted property right. It is consequently advisable in most cases, especially in the case of rural properties, to talk to the neighbors, the local authorities (such as members of the communal council) and other persons familiar with local circumstances in order to avoid unpleasant surprises.

If the seller has failed to pay bills from building tradesmen and contractors, the creditors can have a special building tradesmen's pledge or a lien entered in the land or ownership register in some countries. For the new owner, such pledges mean that his real estate is liable for payment of any outstanding bills. This must be borne in mind especially when acquiring a newly built apartment or house, and the seller must be requested to provide proof that no bills are outstanding.

The real estate may also be liable for capital gains and other taxes and duties not paid by the seller. In some countries, the taxes encumbering real estate have the character of a lien, i.e. the relevant real estate is directly liable for any unpaid taxes. Appropriate security for the buyer is thus absolutely necessary and may be arranged by means of a bank guarantee or by having a corresponding sum retained by a notary or lawyer.

Encumbrances and third-party claims are apparent firstly from the ownership or land register (where such a register exists), but they may also exist by law (e.g. the tacit rights of use or outstanding tax demands mentioned above) without being recorded in a register. Accordingly, the greatest care must be exercised in these matters. All existing encumbrances on and third-party claims to the property must be included in the sales agreement without fail and it must be agreed who bears or redeems which encumbrances and debts. Before every real estate acquisition, a current extract must be obtained from the respective ownership or land register, and it must be comprehensively clarified whether the property is liable to any encumbrances and third-party claims.

The lawyer called in to act as consultant in the acquisition of the real estate should clarify all outstanding matters to ensure which legally protected claims and rights of third parties may apply to the prospective property, and what entitlements the owners of neighboring properties may have. It is also important to view the property to be acquired, as this is a way to reveal those entitlements which cannot be determined from documents. If, for example, a path crosses the property, it may follow that the land is encumbered with a legally protected footpath, despite the fact that this right was not fixed in any document. A talk to the neighbors often helps to clarify such situations.

Provisions for protecting the environment, nature and cultural heritage

Environmental protection

Environmental protection is a sensitive issue in conjunction with real estate transactions and ownership, not least because environmental pollution in general must be cleaned up by the respective owner of the real estate if those who caused the pollution are unknown or unable to pay. This principle, applicable today in most countries, gives rise to delicate legal questions.

Some countries require former waste-disposal sites as well as other land polluted with noxious substances to be cleaned up (often at the costs of the actual owner of the property concerned) if they represent a risk of causing damage or creating a nuisance. It makes sense to clarify the situation even in countries with legislation for cleaning up polluted land. This is because the possible presence of noxious substances, whether below ground or in the building structure, has an impact on the value and resale potential of the property, and may even render it unsaleable. If relevant legislation exists, the authorities may demand that polluted land be cleaned at any time and not only within the scope of a building project. Environmental protection measures may have considerable impact, such as limitations of use, higher insurance costs, major additional expenditures as well as delaying building projects due to assessments, cleaning and waste-disposal measures. Possible claims by third parties, such as owners of neighboring properties polluted by hazardous substances, represent another problem. A few countries maintain registers of polluted land; however, a relevant check is often the only way of clarifying the exact condition of the land. As a rule, potential buyers are well advised to refrain from acquiring real estate polluted by hazardous substances or otherwise representing an environmental problem, as the associated risks are very difficult to estimate and are usually too high.

Protection of nature and cultural heritage

Although nature-conservation regulations generally have no impact on correctly zoned real estate, it is wise to clarify the situation if deemed appropriate. A more important factor is represented by restrictions relating to the protection of historical buildings. In most countries, the government or local authorities invest in the preservation of historical buildings at a local and national level, and keep records of this cultural heritage. Restrictions are normally noted in public registers or in the land register and often require mandatory official approval before any changes can be made. However, the authorities may also intervene in the case of a not yet classified building which may be deemed worthy of protection. Anyone acquiring historical real estate, which may be worthy of preservation, must include these eventualities in the clarification procedure. It may be worthwhile discussing any planned building projects in advance with the relevant authorities in order to avoid unpleasant surprises.

The other aspect of heritage preservation is that owners of protected properties may be eligible for state subsidies towards renovation and similar costs under certain circumstances.

Access to relevant records and documents

Today, most countries maintain some type of ownership register that records the existence and scope of private rights to real estate. These registers may be set out in diverse ways, and their legal status can vary greatly. However, the books of the relevant registering authority must always be viewed before making a final decision to buy on the basis of information supplied by the owner or seller of the prospective property. The result of viewing the relevant register is usually of decisive importance to the buyer. It allows him to determine firstly whether the seller in question is the lawful owner of the prospective property, and secondly whether this property is free of encumbrances or, what kinds of encumbrances exist (easements, mortgages etc.). Quite generally, the objection of being unaware of an entry in the register is normally invalid. It also makes sense to check various documents, especially the sales agreement that forms the basis of the seller's ownership, or agreements on easements, financing agreements etc. Another important point is proof of complete payment or securing of all taxes and duties by the previous owner, as the respective property and/or its owner are liable for unpaid taxes and duties in many countries.

Whoever buys an apartment or house which is attached to an owners association (e.g. relating to shared facilities of a residential property) must request copies of all relevant minutes and documents relating to the association, especially a copy of the minutes of the last general meeting, a list of expenditures, proof of the reserve fund and the name of the administrator. In particular, one should check whether the meeting has decided on any building works which have not yet been carried out or other larger expenditures.

Before every acquisition, the following must be checked by consulting the relevant register extracts and documents:

- Proof of the seller's lawful ownership and authorization to dispose of the property
- Proof of all existing encumbrances and claims on the property
- Proof that all taxes and duties have been paid by the seller
- Proof of any existing tenancy and lease agreements or of any corresponding negative declarations by the seller
- Where an owners association exists: minutes of the most recent meetings as well as confirmation that the seller has honored all his financial commitments to the association

Division of costs

It can never be precisely forecast at the time of signing the sales agreement when the actual transfer and complete payment will take place. Also, certain costs accrue up to the day of the transfer at the expense of the seller. Sales agreements consequently often contain clauses which divide up such costs between the seller and the buyer on a time basis. As a rule, this cost division is not exactly set until the transfer date has been fixed. The most common examples of such cost division refer to land taxes, insurance premiums for third-party liability (the property must always be covered), rental income, contributions to condominium or other owners associations and advance payments of maintenance costs.

It is also advisable for the buyer to assure himself that all invoices for electricity, gas, water, telephone, TV license fees etc, have been paid up by the previous owner up to the transfer date. Otherwise problems might arise when the property is re-registered.

4.6 Powers of attorney

It may be of advantage to use powers of attorney when dealing with a foreign notary, local authorities or lawyers, especially if the buyer is a foreign national and speaks the relevant language insufficiently or not at all.

Powers of attorney relating to transactions with real estate are subject to the law prevailing in the location of the relevant property, and a choice of law in this respect is usually excluded. Even if such powers of attorney do not require any particular format in some countries, those referring to property transactions usually require to be notarized. This also makes good sense quite generally for important business. Even if a choice of law were permitted (such as when the *lex patriae* of the grantor of the power of attorney were applicable), it is advisable for the power of attorney to be based on the local law in every respect. After all, the power of attorney must above all be recognized locally, where the real estate is located.

If the notarization is performed by a foreign notary, it will generally need to be legalized or authenticated. Most countries are party to the *Hague Convention of 5 October 1961, Abolishing the Requirement of Legalisation for Foreign Public Documents*, which requires the document bearing the signature and stamp of the notary to be provided with an apostille, on which a higher government authority supervising notaries confirms that the notary really is authorized to exercise his/her function. This is required so that the document will be recognized in the foreign country where the document will be used.

Powers of attorney may be granted in the form of a special or general power of attorney, and either as a power of attorney limited in time or as an enduring power of attorney. In most cases, a special power of attorney restricted to the purchase transaction is required.

4.7 Acquiring real estate through a holding structure

The most varied factors will dictate whether a property should be held via a company or other holding structure rather than directly. Certain features specific to various countries will be outlined here. Thus it is not uncommon in the US to hold real estate via a limited-liability corporation. In addition to any tax advantages, this is done especially for reasons of asset protection. In other countries, such as Switzerland, non-resident foreign nationals are prohibited in most cases from holding residential real estate via companies. The one exception is in Andermatt, which benefits from a unique full exemption to this law. The most varied regulations and reasons may exist in which a specific legal device may appear to be necessary, make sense, or no sense as the situation changes.

In general, the more expensive the real estate the more sense it will make to use a holding structure rather than buying directly in one's own name. It is debatable where to draw the line here, but in most cases a minimum value of USD 500,000 can be taken as a basis. Depending on the country and situation, however, this threshold may also be set significantly lower. This is the case in France when using the popular *Société Civile Immobilière,* or in Croatia, where the only straightforward way of acquiring real estate may be to establish a local holding company.

The larger and more valuable the property, the more important fiscal and succession-planning becomes, but also questions of asset protection and confidentiality play a role. It is often best to buy smaller properties directly in one's own name – or possibly under the name of one's children or other persons, depending on the inheritance law situation. The legal consequences in the event of succession can then be influenced by means of a will or other suitable legal instrument. In the case of larger properties the question arises whether it is worthwhile setting up a suitable legal structure, such as a company, to hold the property, or whether the same end cannot equally well be achieved by means of a will, transfers between living persons or other contractual arrangements.

When does it make sense to use a holding structure?

The use of a holding structure, such as a company, makes sense in many cases for legitimate reasons of fiscal and succession planning. In France, for example, it is certainly often a good idea to establish a French real estate company (*Société Civile Immobilière, SCI*) in order to achieve more flexibility with regard to the law applicable in the case of an inheritance. This is because exclusive application of French law is mandatory for directly owned real estate, whereas company shares are considered as movable assets and can accordingly be inherited with the testator's other movable assets. In the UK, it makes particular sense for a non-resident and/or non-domiciled owner to hold real estate via a (foreign) company rather than directly for tax reasons. For this purpose, companies are usually set up in countries where company taxes are nil or limited and annual maintenance costs are low. Such jurisdictions include the BVI, Jersey, Liechtenstein, Malta and Panama, where companies can be set up and maintained at low cost and with no or only limited local tax consequences. However, tax consequences may have to be taken into account depending on the country of residence of the company owner. So it is essential to clarify all circumstances and tax consequences carefully – including in the country where the company owner is resident.

It is also worth noting that corporate and other holding structures (such as private foundations and trusts) are still frequently recommended and also implemented despite failing to pass a thorough scrutiny by the relevant tax authorities – where such scrutiny takes place. Many countries have now extended the relevant tax laws with very extensive abuse regulations. If more than 50% of a company's assets consist directly or indirectly of real estate, that company will often be taxed as real estate. Thus the capital gains from the sale is also taxed on the same basis (and cannot simply accrue tax-free in a zero-tax country) when the responsible tax authorities discover the true nature of the transfer. Ultimately, many company structures are based on the transfer of company shares without the notification being made to the tax authorities. Although it is often highly unlikely that the tax authorities ever find out about the transaction, it cannot form the basis of a legal arrangement. The list of ways used in various countries to try and 'save' taxes, in some cases by means of complicated structures, could fill a whole volume. Only one thing is certain: in some countries and for larger properties it is certainly possible and makes good sense to save taxes and increase legal flexibility by setting up suitable holding structures. However, to do so requires international know-how and relevant country-specific knowledge, as well as extensive experience in connection with holding structures for real estate to be held by foreign nationals.

In addition to tax and succession-planning aspects, it is also desirable in certain cases for reasons of confidentiality and asset protection to hold real estate via the intermediary of a company rather than directly. The effective owner will then not appear in the ownership or land register.

When is it better to acquire real estate directly?

In many countries, such as Spain, France and Italy, it does not usually make much sense to acquire privately used real estate via a company, for various reasons. Firstly – for example in France – comprehensive regulations aim to prevent acquisition via the intermediary of companies and thus make such procedures more complicated – with the notable exception of the already mentioned domestic *SCI*. Secondly, this can even have tax disadvantages, as companies are often liable to higher capital gains tax than directly owned properties at a later resale. Furthermore, most companies (again perhaps with the exception of a French *SCI*) sometimes incur considerable administrative costs. In many countries it therefore makes more sense to acquire properties in the lower to middle price range directly in one's own name. However, careful planning is of particular importance in this case, and includes drawing up a suitable will or possibly acquiring the property in the name of one's children.

4.8 The execution of a real estate purchase transaction

The procedure involved in acquiring real estate differs from country to country, sometimes very greatly. Whereas it is generally unproblematic in a country such as France, the greatest care must be exercised in Italy. As the various jurisdictions apply diverse regulations with regard to contractual requirements and ownership transfer, only the most essential points have been summarized at this juncture.

In any sales transaction, a distinction must always be made between a new property still at the planning stage, and an already completed or used property.

In the case of new or still incompletely built properties, the purchase price is as a rule payable in advance with several instalments according to the progress of the building work. The buyer may therefore incur a considerable financial risk under certain circumstances, depending on the project developer. This can and should be secured by a suitable insurance policy or bank guarantee. In some countries, this form of security or insurance is mandatory (although this requirement is not always observed, for instance in Spain). Other countries have no legislation aimed at protecting the buyer. Due care must therefore be taken.

Although pre-printed standard-form contracts are easy to complete, they are usually designed to benefit the contractual party who has created them or suggested that they be used. On the other hand, balanced individual contracts are a frequent source of trouble. Insistence on an individually prepared contract may not only affect the mood of the contractual negotiations, but may also change the result decisively. Especially in the case of larger properties, it is essential to prepare an individual sales agreement appropriate to the situation with the aid of a competent lawyer. Nevertheless, standard-form contracts are usual and can be used with no problems in some places, such as Florida. There, such contracts are designed and published by the bar association and are prepared in a correspondingly fair and comprehensive manner. It should be checked in each individual case whether standard-form contracts are usual, who has published them and whether they seem to be appropriate in the individual case.

As the transaction risk involved in a purchase is usually greater for the buyer than the seller, the buyer should – independently of the seller or those persons associated with him (such as the broker) – have all documents relevant to the sale checked by a lawyer. As in all important transactions, trust is good, but security is better. Before and during the sales procedure, it must always be clear what guarantees are offered by the contractual parties so that what has been promised and agreed in a contract can also be executed – if necessary by the agency of the courts. So it usually makes sense to conclude a preliminary agreement – assuming this is permitted by the relevant jurisdiction – in order to obligate the seller to conclude the sales agreement and if necessary also to enforce his declaration of intent via a court if necessary.

The buyer should always take care to ensure the necessary security either by means of provisional registration (where possible) or of an appropriate guarantee by the seller. Some countries allow a provisional entry of the acquisition in the land or ownership register in order to secure the buyer's rights vis-à-vis third parties. This is done to safeguard the interests of the buyer and is to be recommended if available. The same purpose is also served, alternatively or additionally, by requiring the seller to set up a bank guarantee to the amount of the purchase price. It must run until the ownership rights of the buyer have been definitively entered in the relevant ownership register or the title deeds have been issued.

In most countries, the sales agreement – which may be drawn up privately or by a notary – is entered in a public register, usually known as the land or ownership register, in order to ensure public access to proof of purchase. The buyer should always insist on immediate conclusion of a notarial sales agreement and on his name being entered as the owner in the relevant register.

For the safe conclusion of a real estate transaction, it is advisable to consult an expert, and not only in the event of difficult questions. His fee will be a fraction of the damage that could result from improper or careless action.

4.9 Defects and warranty claims

All jurisdictions make a distinction between legal and material defects. Legal defects are those which affect the ownership rights to the property. Thus a legal defect exists if the seller is not the real owner of the property, or if the property is encumbered with a mortgage or right of use unknown or undisclosed at the time the contract was concluded. Also, if other legal obligations exist for which the property is liable, easements and encumbrances of all kinds, or claims by someone with a stronger entitlement (e.g. in the case of a double sale by the former owner) etc. As a rule, the seller is liable vis-à-vis the buyer to ensure that the property is free of legal defects. Depending on the type and severity of the defect, the buyer can in general be entitled to a reduction of the purchase price, to withdraw from the agreement or to claim compensation for damages.

Material defects are those present physically on the property, such as a leaky roof, peeling paint etc. Material defects can be further distinguished into patent defects, which would involve a visible deterioration of the property, and latent defects, which only an expert may discover upon inspection. A concealed defect on the other hand would in most cases constitute a fraudulent misrepresentation and would normally give the buyer the right to claim that the contract is void.

In practically all jurisdictions, the seller is generally liable for both legal and material defects. However, relevant warranty claims always lapse after a certain time. A buyer should always try to safeguard himself against possible obligations associated with the property and any undiscovered defects such as environmental pollution. In contrast, the seller has an interest in limiting any warranty claims after conclusion of the contract. For used properties, any warranty by the seller is, as a rule, waived in the sales agreements. In most cases, therefore, only maliciously undisclosed defects can justify damage compensation claims.

4.10 Key points that a seller should consider

The seller is the contractual party who normally bears the lower risk. However, he/she should also observe a number of important points.

From the viewpoint of the seller, it is particularly important that the purchase price is paid in full or secured before or concurrently with the transfer of ownership. This may be done for instance by means of a promise to pay, transfer of a bank check or a deposit with a notary. A direct bank transfer is in general not recommended for practical reasons, because as a rule, to protect the interests of both parties, the purchase price should be paid immediately upon the signing of the notarial sales agreement. If the buyer has to sell his previous home to pay for the acquisition, special care must be taken, as it must be certain that the he/she really can sell the property and thus secure the funds required for the acquisition of the new house. A definitive form of security, for instance by means of an irrevocable bank guarantee, is essential in this case.

Generally, too, the seller should check whether the buyer has received financing approval from his/her bank before breaking off negotiations with other prospective buyers or making other arrangements in the assurance that the sales agreement will indeed be concluded.

In many jurisdictions, the observance of contractual or statutory time limits is an absolutely basic condition for the correct fulfillment of a contract. If one of the contractual parties (for instance the seller) is delayed, therefore, the other party may under certain circumstances be released from his/her contractual obligations and may possibly also claim compensation for damages. So both parties are well advised to observe all agreed or legally stipulated time limits to the letter.

The seller must also ensure that he/she can produce all authorizations (e.g. consent of his/her spouse) needed for the purchase, as failure to do so would delay the transaction.

Moreover, in most countries the seller is obliged to inform the buyer of any defects. As a rule, the seller must also inform the buyer of the existence of any pre-emption rights. Often, the seller is liable to a comprehensive obligation for information and disclosure and bears corresponding liability to the buyer. So it is advantageous to clearly indicate any defects in the sales agreement, for purposes of later evidence. Accordingly, it is essential for the seller to settle all questions of liability in the agreement in detail. In general it is recommended, wherever possible, to exclude all liability by the seller from the agreement (this is also usual for second-hand real estate in most countries). This liability exclusion should be comprehensive and expressly include liability for legal and material defects, error and damage compensation, as far as this is permissible on the basis of the local law. In any case, care must be taken to ensure that the sales agreement contains no guarantees which the seller is unable to satisfy. If the seller makes any representations or warranties, a carefully drafted sales agreement will limit the warranties and representations to the period of time the seller has owned the real estate and exclude the periods of ownership by previous owners.

The seller should also note who is responsible for which fees, taxes and lawyers' or notaries' fees. In many cases, notaries' fees and transfer taxes are divided on a 50/50 basis, but this division is ultimately a matter for negotiation. Lawyers' costs are usually borne by the party commissioning the lawyer. However, the seller is always responsible for paying capital gains tax.

If real estate is sold together with furniture (especially valuable furniture, for example antiques that belong to a historic property), the purchase price may be split (property/furniture) and as a consequence the taxes may be somewhat reduced as most taxes are only calculated based on the purchase price of the property, and not on the furniture.

In most cases, the seller is also liable to pay the broker's commission. This varies between 2% and 10% of the sale price in different countries and is usually subject to value added tax (where such a tax exists). It should be noted that it is only in a seller's interest to conclude an exclusive agreement with a single broker in justified exceptional cases, in particular for expensive properties where confidentiality is important. As a rule, however, it is more advantageous to commission several brokers with the sale in order to maximize the exposure of the property. However, it is also important to understand that agencies and brokers under a non-exclusive listing agreement will sometimes simply add your property to their website, and only passively introduce your property to prospective buyers. There is no harm in maximizing the exposure of your property by engaging all brokers and agents available, although the seller will usually find this extremely time-consuming. In some cases, it is wiser to secure an exclusive agreement with a single firm that will more actively promote and sell your property. An exclusive agreement such as this should be considered if the firm has no real competition, and/or the contracting firm agrees to appoint subagents with a commission sharing arrangement. If done properly this will still ensure maximize exposure while the seller maintains one point of contact. Such exclusive agreements normally cost the seller a slightly higher commission rate, however, it saves time and energy and could result in a quicker sale, as the contracting firm usually commits to active marketing due to the alleviated risk over non-exclusive agreements where a 3rd party company could sell the property before them.

Further, the seller should from the outset find out precisely what other costs for which he is liable may be involved in the sale, i.e. which will be deducted from the sale price, and what tax consequences the sale may have. The property acquisition taxes which are levied everywhere are, as a rule, borne by the buyer. However, if they cannot be collected from the buyer, they may in some countries be charged to the seller. This is particularly relevant when the seller remains resident in the same country.

When apartments or houses belonging to an owners association (e.g. concerning the shared amenities of a condominium) are sold, the amount of any reserve or renovation fund must be determined, as this can have an effect on the sale price.

4.11 Checklist: acquisition of real estate

The following checklist offers a systematic approach to clarifying all essential factors (due diligence) which must be taken into account when acquiring real estate.

The location

Location is the first and most important factor to be considered when selecting a property. In addition to the current circumstances, it should be noted how the environment may change in future. A future positive change in a location is the most important factor for the potential growth in value of real estate.

- Location quality of the local municipality
- Position within the municipality
- Changes in location quality to be expected in the mid to long-term
- Orientation of the building (north/south, east/west)

- Sunlight exposure of the building, balconies, terraces, gardens – during all seasons
- Climatic situation: does the climatic zone meet expectations? Consult tables of average monthly temperatures, air humidity and rainfall
- Wind exposure: how frequently and strongly do winds blow in this location? Perhaps consult a relevant wind atlas. Winds such as the *Bora* in Dalmatia or the *Mistral* in France can considerably impact on comfort in outside areas
- If the house is on a slope, may water pressure have an impact, is there danger of landslides, avalanches etc.
- Level of groundwater table: relevant in particular with regard to basements and cellars, but also if it is desirable to have one's own well, for example on a country estate
- View: is the view safe from obstruction by subsequent building?
- Is it overlooked by neighbors?
- Size and shape of the property
- Access: asphalted, concreted, gravel, dirt track?
- Is access possible in winter? Is there winter service? Who clears the snow?
- Waste disposal service
- Noise (roads, airports, rail lines etc.)
- Smells (paper factories, pig farms, food industry etc.)
- Sufficient distance from filling stations, covered car parks and heavily used roads (exhaust and noise emissions)
- Sufficient distance from pylons/high-tension lines and mobile phone network antennas
- Proximity to shopping facilities, banks, post office
- Proximity to schools and kindergartens, secondary and higher schools, evening class venues

- Sports facilities
- Cultural facilities
- Public transport: can the property be reached by public transport? Where is the nearest national or international airport? Where is the nearest rail station? How good are the connections?
- Links to road and freeway network
- Basic healthcare
- Extended healthcare: where are the nearest major hospitals?
- Existing or planned future projects for the construction of freeways, airports, high-voltage power lines, transmission equipment, power plants, waste disposal tips, factories or other major public or private projects?
- Existing or planned future projects for changing flight paths of nearby airports?
- In which construction zone is the property located? Existing or planned future projects for other buildings in the vicinity?
- Is the property located in a protected area?
- Major accident risks: are there any industrial or other plants in the vicinity which may pose a risk (chemical plant, nuclear power plant, liquid gas tank, cyanide store of a metal-processing factory etc?)

Building materials and building quality

- Size and distribution of main and ancillary rooms
- Fitting and extension options
- Architecture
- Construction of the building (masonry, concrete, wood)
- Quality of the materials used
- Windows (wood, plastic, aluminum)

- Energy consumption
- Thermal insulation (is a heat insulation certificate needed/available?)
- Footfall sound/soundproofing (especially important for apartments)
- Penetration of moisture (e.g. old walls, sloping location)
- Condition of the roof
- Pest damage (e.g. termites)
- Asbestos contamination (old tiles, insulation materials, etc.)
- Lead contamination (old, decaying paints, plumbing, etc.)

It is often advisable to call in a building expert familiar with the local building standards in order to correctly assess the condition of the property.

Interior design

- Standard and equipping of kitchen, bathroom, showers, toilets
- Quality of the materials used
- Design and interior architecture (e.g. color and concept)
- Wheelchair access: is the house also suitable for elderly or handicapped people?
- Special details

Installations and household technology

If certain installations are absent or need renovating, what would the installation or renovation cost? How long will the work take? Are approvals required?

- Electrical installations
- Sanitary installations; connection to the water supply
- Heating: what heating system is used? In the case of oil heating, it is important to note if the oil tank is outside (environmental risk)

- Have the heating system and oil tank been regularly serviced?
- Telephone connection, internet connection / ISDN /ADSL
- Television reception, cable TV, satellite dish
- Swimming pool: has it been regularly serviced? What is the condition of the pool? Can it be extended? Does this need approval? Are there water usage restrictions?

Security

- Are burglaries frequent in the area?
- Is there an alarm system, and is it working?
- Is the property sufficiently illuminated?
- Are all outer doors sufficiently secured?
- Are all windows, day shafts and balcony doors, shutters and roof windows secured against intrusion?
- Is there a need for security doors or security windows?
- Are power and communications lines secure from sabotage?
- Are there any neighbors or trustworthy persons who can keep an eye on the house during your absence?
- Is there a need for a private surveillance service?
- Danger of natural hazards (forest fires, flooding, storms, avalanches etc.)

Legal questions concerning the real estate and its acquisition

- In what building zone are the property and its neighboring properties located?
- Can construction activity be expected on the neighboring properties? If so, how extensive will it be (e.g. building height)?
- Distances between the houses

- Is there room for extensions, and would approval for an extension / rebuilding be issued?
- Might the house or parts of it have been built illegally? Possibly check the building permits
- Is the seller really the lawful owner (land register extract, proof of ownership)?
- If a real estate holding company is acquired, it should be scrutinized in detail. It may be more secure for the buyer not to acquire company shares but to buy the property from the company
- Is the seller married, or is he/she cohabiting? Is approval by the spouse or cohabiting partner required?
- What rights, easements, servitudes etc. exist in favor of the property?
- Are there any easements, servitudes, liens, charges or other encumbrances on the property?
- Have all duties and taxes been paid in full by the previous owner?
- Inspection of the most recent and earlier tax statements for real estate taxes and other duties
- Do contractual pre-emption rights exist?
- Do legal pre-emption rights exist (e.g. in favor of tenants, neighbors or the state)?
- Are there any restrictions concerning environmental, nature or heritage protection?
- Could pollution of the soil constitute a hazard? If so, the property should be checked accordingly. A check is in any case recommended for larger properties
- How will the property be used in future? Depending on its use (e.g. as a guest house), official approval may be required (does it already exist or is it available?)
- In which name or possibly company is the property to be purchased? (See below: Legal questions on structuring real estate ownership)

- The property purchase transaction should be handled only by a competent notary or lawyer. The functions of notaries vary in different countries, and use of a notary or lawyer may be mandatory
- After the sales agreement has been concluded, the acquisition must be entered immediately in the land or ownership register
- In the case of condominium or other ownership which involves membership in an owners association, it is important to request copies of the statutes and all regulations, the minutes of the most recent general meeting, the most recent annual accounts or list of expenditures, the key to expenditure distribution as well as the name of the administrator. In particular, a check must be made as to the rights and obligations incumbent on the individual owners as well as on the administration and whether the meeting of the owners association has decided on building work which has not yet been carried out
- Secondary assurances and evident matters should also be confirmed in writing by the contractual partner
- In the event that a lower sale price than the actual price is specified on the sales agreement in order to reduce the tax burden, the risks should be assessed. Such action is illegal in all countries

Legal questions on structuring real estate ownership

- Should the property be acquired under one's own name, or should a company be used as an intermediary?
- Are other, possibly more complex, holding constructions possible and useful?
- Advantages and disadvantages of using a company as an intermediary in the country in which the property is located
- Advantages and disadvantages of using a company as an intermediary in the country in which the buyer is resident
- Acquisition in one's own name or together with one's spouse? Note that there are various kinds of joint ownership rights possible in different countries

- Acquisition in the children's names (or skipping of one generation)?
- In the event of acquisition in the children's names, should a right of residence be retained?
- In the event of acquisition via a company, should a local or an offshore company be used?

Renovations and building-law restrictions

- Is reconstruction and extension permitted?
- Heritage and monument protection regulations
- Requirements of the fire and police services
- What does partial or complete renovation cost?
- Are good local construction companies and reliable tradesmen available?
- Is it possible to carry out the renovation work oneself without coming into conflict with local construction companies or the law?

Taxes

- One-off real estate acquisition taxes
- Recurring real estate and income taxes related to the real estate
- With regard to income taxes on rental income, is it possible to offset borrowing interest and other expenses against rental income?
- Inheritance and gift taxes
- Capital gains taxes on a future sale (possible different scenarios if property is held directly vs. through a company)
- Have all previous taxes been paid by the seller?
- In the case of change of residence: total tax burden? Is pre-immigration tax planning advisable?

Inheritance law aspects

- Which inheritance law applies? Is a choice of law possible?
- What impact does the matrimonial property regime have, and can this be used in inheritance tax planning?
- International estate planning (use of wills, gifts, trusts, foundations etc.)
- Possible acquisition of the property in children's names

Various

- Home-contents' insurance, possibly buildings' insurance, additional insurance policies (see chapter 10.1)
- If there is a private well or spring, can this be used privately? Do communal charges exist?
- How are foreign nationals accepted in the area? Do many foreign nationals already live in this area?
- Think of resale. From the standpoint of potential value growth, properties in areas in which the location quality is likely to improve in the future are to be preferred

5 New Buildings and Purchasing from a Developer

Planning and building one's own house can be an extraordinarily satisfying experience, but it can also end in great frustration and disappointment. This is even truer in a foreign country. Whoever hopes to build their own house abroad must be particularly aware that special rules apply in the construction trade – and those rules are different abroad.

In every country, it is possible to find an architect and commission the necessary experts to build a new property according to plans prepared by oneself or the architect. However, this approach inevitably requires relevant legal and practical advice so that various agreements can be drawn up and mutually coordinated. It should also be noted that deadlines and costs often overrun even in the best, most professionally managed building projects, leading to greater or lesser frustration for the principal. Architects are normally paid for providing their services in a reasonably competent and diligent manner. Unless agreed otherwise, the principal normally has the responsibility of reviewing the designs and reporting any errors or requirements for re-design, unless the agreement with the architect or general contractor clearly stipulates that the architect or contractor guarantees the design and proper execution or it was agreed to deliver a turn-key construction. It is therefore important that in any agreement the risk for inappropriate design or construction clearly lies with the architect or general contractor.

In view of complex building standards and the diversity of offers in the construction trade it is often wise to engage a highly experienced architect as well as an independent advisor who really represents the interests of the principal vis-à-vis both the architect and the various building contractors. Such an advisor may also be called in on an ad-hoc basis, i.e. merely in the event of important decisions.

It is usually much easier to buy a new building from a developer. However, special rules must be noted here too. The buyer essentially acquires the land from the developer together with a building which is still to be constructed. Specific contractual conditions are then mandatory in some countries. There may even be special laws aiming principally to protect the buyer of the property. The latter must also note various particularities, especially as regards the manner in which the purchase price is paid, questions of warranty, release from encumbrances (such as the mortgage used to finance the development) and the risk involved in completing the buildings. Key factors include the building schedule and the securing of the purchase-price payment. If a forced contractor or contractors are imposed then design, land and construction cost should be agreed before committing non-refundable funds or deposits.

It is usual for the purchase price to be paid in accordance with the progress of the building work, for example as follows:

- 10% deposit
- 15% foundations
- 20% when walls are done
- 15% when core and shell is closed
- 15% after cabinetry and fittings
- 15% on full completion
- 5% hold back / snagging

In some countries it is usual to retain 5% of the total price for warranty work. This is also a good idea in those places where it is not usual.

Unfortunately, developers and general contractors are only rarely called to account by the courts for overrunning deadlines. So the risk of such delays, which may be very unpleasant for the principal, is correspondingly high.

It should also be noted that many developers, i.e. sellers of new real estate, are financially not very strong. So unless one deals with a reputable, financially sound and well-managed company the buyer may also incur a considerable financial risk from this standpoint. If a developer becomes insolvent, deposits may be lost and warranty claims may no longer be asserted. So here too it is essential to ascertain exactly what kinds of guarantees are offered, who is actually guaranteeing it, and to be aware of the worst-case scenario.

Local authorities virtually everywhere have considerable freedom in granting building permits – this applies at least to all more or less densely populated areas. So a prospective builder will usually be bound by more or less strict regulations. It is obvious that building cannot begin until appropriate building approval has been granted. If approval is needed it is advised to acquire such approval before finalising a transaction to avoid disappointment or refusals. It makes sense to start planning as early as possible and to submit the application for approval at an early stage. Prospective builders are also strongly advised to discuss their project in advance with the responsible authorities, as well as with any neighbors who may be affected, and to comply with their requests wherever possible. The applicable legal situation must clearly also be considered. Some countries require the use of a qualified architect. In any case, it will be impossible to dispense with the services of an architect as well as other specialists in order to deal with all the questions and problems arising in connection with the project.

The building work should be accurately documented throughout the building process. Successful claims against warranties and to enforce the correction of building defects depend in such documentation and will need to be compared to the initial order and the successful completion of work notification. Disputes often result from insufficiently documented supplementary orders which had been awarded without any separate cost estimates and in some cases without being clearly drawn-up.

6 Reconstruction and Renovation

Most buyers acquire a used property. This may be in a good or very good condition and the new owners might be able to move in straightaway. However, buildings with an old structure may need or could benefit from reconstruction or renovation before the new owners can reasonably be expected to live in them.

It is often possible to acquire a substantial old house with considerable land around it surprisingly cheaply. However, such properties have their price when it comes to renovating them and making them comfortably habitable again. In most cases, such renovation work not only takes up a lot of time but also a lot of money. Retiling a large roof alone might equate to the entire initial purchase price of the property. The costs of laying a damp course, renovating the electrical installations and plumbing, assuring thermal insulation, renewing the windows, floors, etc., should not be underestimated either.

So, when buying an old property that needs renovation, it is absolutely necessary to call in a surveyor, architect or construction engineer, and obtain a report assessing the condition of the building. Besides a general evaluation of the structure, walls, roof, etc., issues such as possible asbestos contamination in old tiles and insulation, or lead contamination due to decaying paints, plumbing etc. should be carefully addressed. Often in older houses wooden structures such as the roof, beams, etc. are affected by xylophagous insects (e.g. termites). Although such checks cost money, it often saves unpleasant and very expensive surprises.

The availability of reliable tradesmen and other specialists needed for a reconstruction or renovation job is often a major concern for a foreign property owner. In many countries, especially in the south of Europe, artisans are good and relatively inexpensive. There is also no lack of well qualified and experienced architects and other specialists who may have to be called in for particular projects. Although tradesmen may also be available elsewhere, they can be relatively expensive (for instance in Switzerland), or very scarce (as in the US or Sweden). As a result, owner-occupied properties there tend to be maintained and renovated by the owners themselves.

Tradesmen everywhere are normally happy to do work without an invoice and be paid in cash, (especially in countries such as Italy, Spain and Greece, but elsewhere as well). A considerable proportion of privately commissioned artisan work can be carried out without payment of VAT, and is usually a considerable amount. Apart from the fact that this practice counts as tax evasion, it is also disadvantageous for the customer. If no invoice is issued, the expenditures cannot be accounted to the value of the property in the event of a later resale and the capital gains tax works out correspondingly higher. This may be unimportant in the case of maintenance work and smaller renovations; however it could well be relevant for larger rebuilding projects.

7 Rental and Tenancy

For a prospective buyer, it is a very good idea to rent a similar property in a comparable location for a while before purchasing. Local and internationally specialized agencies offer a broad range of vacation apartments and houses which may be rented on a daily, weekly or monthly basis.

Many second homes are rarely used and remain empty for many months of the year. So for an owner of a second home, it is obvious to ask whether it makes sense to rent out such a property, at least for limited periods. The answer always depends on your cash flow and intentions. Temporary rental is not worthwhile in most cases, as the time and costs involved are relatively large (administration, cleaning, wear and tear of furniture by careless tenants etc.), and the net revenue is subject to substantial tax in most countries (Antigua and Barbuda, The Bahamas, Croatia and St. Kitts and Nevis are notable exceptions). For these reasons it is important to understand your annual expenditure and how much income is possible, then based on the above decide if it is worthwhile. However, if you are not concerned about a negative cashflow for the property, and wish it to stay in perfect condition, it is best not to rent it out.

Whereas some countries have practically no relevant tenants' protection legislation, and a tenant can be evicted from a rented property at practically any time (for example in Florida), other countries have tenants' protection laws which may be very rigorous. In some circumstances, they may offer tenants a position almost as secure as that of owners (e.g. in France, Spain, Sweden and some other European countries). So it is wise to check carefully before any rental how extensive the local tenants' protection laws are. In some cases, this may be a good reason not to pursue a rental option. On the other hand, rental agreements not designed for permanent residence, especially those relating to vacation homes, usually come under the category of general rental conditions and are not subject to rigorous tenants' protection regulations as for normal residential real estate. Before deciding to rent, it is in any case wise to find out exactly what legal stipulations would apply to the tenancy and, especially from a practical standpoint, what ways exist of terminating the lease against the tenants' wishes and evicting them from the rented property.

Standard-form contracts are often used to conclude rental agreements, and specific forms are sometimes mandatory for giving notice. Payment of rental security amounting to between one and six months' rent is usual and also makes a lot of sense from the landlord's standpoint. The security sum is often paid to the landlord or into a special rental security account at a bank.

7.1 Checklist: Rental and leasing agreements

The following list sets out the key points and clauses which should form part of every rental agreement:

- A precise description of the property, its location plan, inclusive of all buildings, parking spaces, interior fittings, living area etc. Separate plans may also be annexed to the rental agreement
- Prepare house rules when renting out residential property
- Key data (signature date, start of rental, start of payment, expiry date)
- Time of handover of ownership
- The agreed rent and an itemized list of all costs, such as taxes, to be borne by the tenant
- Regulation of insurance policies and insurance costs
- Regulation of cases of damage (deferment of rental payments; obligation to carry out repairs)
- Tenant's liability
- Repairs and maintenance
- Regulations concerning subletting
- Provision of security by the tenant
- Contract extension/options
- Possible formula for calculating the rent
- Notifications (method, addresses)

- Lawyers' costs (in favor of the prevailing party in litigation – this is particularly important in the US, where the prevailing parties normally have to bear their lawyers' fees themselves)

8 Succession and Gifts

The ownership of real estate abroad also involves questions of international law and taxes relating to inheritances and gifts. Depending on the country in which the assets are located, different rules concerning inheritance and various taxation laws will apply. In earlier times, a foreigner's estate fell automatically to the state in some countries (such as in France up to 1819). This is obviously no longer the case. Nevertheless, cross-border inheritance and gifts are often relatively complicated matters, and international inheritance law is one of the trickier legal domains. Thus French inheritance law continues to make life difficult for foreign owners of real estate because property located in France is subject exclusively and compulsory to French law. There is no choice of law. This means, among other things, that inheritance contracts are recognized only to a limited degree if at all, and that a surviving spouse is considerably disadvantaged. However, such a disadvantage may be mitigated or even avoided by suitable legal instruments such as a will, a gift or other arrangements during the testator's lifetime. In contrast, other countries such as Italy and Spain permit properties located there to be inherited on the basis of the laws of the testator's country of citizenship *(lex patriae),* i.e. according to for example English law if the deceased was an English citizen.

The applicable rules will depend on the country concerned. Before acquiring property abroad, a prospective buyer is well advised to check a number of points:

- Exactly which law is applicable
- Whether a choice of law is permitted
- What inheritance taxes are payable
- Whether there are any ways of reducing or even avoiding inheritance taxes by means of suitable legal instruments or holding structures

By being aware of these questions even before the purchase, one can take appropriate steps to make favorable arrangements in terms of inheritance law and possibly save considerable taxes and costs. A detailed check of the relevant circumstances is always worthwhile.

Two central questions arise in such cases:

- Applicable law: what inheritance law is applicable to the foreign property – can the applicable law be determined by a choice of law or by the intermediary of a suitable holding structure?
- Inheritance taxes: where and to what extent is inheritance tax payable in the event of a testator's death – can this tax be reduced or even avoided by suitable measures?

8.1 International inheritance law

In the case of cross-border real estate ownership, i.e. when the owner lives in a different country from that in which his property is located, the laws of both countries must be considered. This applies especially to inheritance law. The interplay and delimitation between various national inheritance laws is the province of international inheritance law. Two questions are of primary importance here: which authorities or courts are responsible for handling an inheritance case, and which law is to be applied? The question also arises as to which law should apply to the form of a testamentary disposition. In order to answer these questions, the relevant national laws which regulate national and international private law must be consulted. International conventions must also be considered, especially the *Hague Convention of 5 October 1961 on the Conflicts of Laws Relating to the Form of Testamentary Disposition*. The *Hague Convention* stipulates that a testamentary disposition shall be valid as regards its form when it has been drawn up to comply either with the law of the testator's home country, of the place where it is drawn up, or in the case of real estate, of the place where the property is located. Other conventions which may be relevant are the *Convention of 2 October 1973 concerning the International Administration of the Estates of Deceased Persons*, the *Convention of 1 July 1985 on the Law Applicable to Trusts and their Recognition*, as well as the *Convention of 1 August 1989 on the Law Applicable to Succession to the Estates of Deceased Persons.* For more information about these conventions, see the homepage of the *Hague Conference on Private International Law* at *hcch.net*

Furthermore, one will need to consider the new *European Succession Regulation*, which applies in the European Union to estates of decedents dying after 16 August 2015. Under this regulation, the succession laws of the country where the decedent was last habitually resident applies, in principle, to their worldwide estate. For example, if a US citizen domiciled and habitually resident in New York owns real estate in Spain, from a European perspective New York law should apply to the worldwide estate, including the French property. Under New York law, however, inheritance of real estate is always governed by the situs law, and also this conflict of law rule would be recognized from a European perspective: this renvoi to Spanish succession rules, including Spanish forced heirship rules, will be accepted under the new *EU Succession Regulation.* But the new rules also allow a choice of law of the succession laws of a testator's home jurisdiction. In the case of a choice of law, only the internal succession law of the chosen jurisdiction will be applied (in this example: New York, excluding thereby Spanish forced heirship rules). The principles established by the *EU Succession Regulation* and in particular the choice of law possibility will be particularly relevant also for situations within the EU, for persons domiciled in one country owning property in another.

The inheritance law of many countries is based on the principle that an estate cannot be divided (the principle of unity of the estate), i.e. if the testator is a foreign national and owned local property, then foreign inheritance law applies. However, some legal systems make the application of local law mandatory to real estate located in their national territory (e.g. in France, where French law applies exclusively and necessarily to all immovable property located in France, and a choice of law is excluded). This may lead to division of the estate. This principle of scission is followed by most common law as well some civil law jurisdictions. One part of the estate (movable property) is then subject to the law of one country, and the other part (immovable property, e.g. the house in France) to that of another. If one owns property in a state that applies the principle of scission, separate wills should be made for the different parts of property. In many cases, however, the problem may be bypassed by setting up a suitable company structure. That is because if a property is held through a company, the company shares count as movable property (just like cash, bank accounts, jewelry etc.), and are subject to the law of the testator's last domicile.

In some circumstances, a choice of law is possible (e.g. in Spain), and in particular, with regard to Europe, once the new *EU Succession Regulation* comes into force. Meanwhile, in many countries (e.g. in Italy), however, the *lex patriae* of the testator generally applies, i.e. the law of the country whose citizenship the deceased possessed. So if an Australian decedent leaves a property in Italy, Australian inheritance law will also apply to it. If a will exists, its contents will take precedence: if no testamentary disposition exists, the inheritors designated on the basis of Australian inheritance law will inherit. For the transfer of ownership of a property abroad, however, legal procedures require the application of the foreign law, and relevant responsibility rests with the foreign authorities and courts. The foreign authorities may consequently be confused by unfamiliar documents. In general, land registry officials, notaries and even judges are sometimes bewildered if they are suddenly confronted in the course of their daily work with the law of another country and foreign documents. So it is often advisable to draw up a suitable will for the foreign property which satisfies the legal requirements of the country in which it is located. Intestate succession applies if the testator has left no or an invalid testamentary disposition, the entire estate was not divided up in the will, or the testamentary inheritor has predeceased the testator, has renounced his inheritance or is unworthy of receiving it. So it is always advisable to make a testamentary disposition. As already mentioned, its specific form will depend on the requirements of the relevant legal system.

Inclusion of the property or parts of it in a property holding company, a trust or a family foundation may in certain circumstances offer a suitable means of efficient succession planning. In any event, expert advice should be sought in these matters to avoid costly complications in the case of an international inheritance situation.

8.2 Matrimonial property regime and inheritance law

Questions of inheritance law may also involve issues of matrimonial property law and, in particular, questions as to which matrimonial property regime applies. The matrimonial property regime selected by the spouses when they got married, or at their first matrimonial domicile, is recognized in most countries. This has a corresponding effect on the situation of married testators with respect to inheritance law. (As spouses are subject to a specific property regime according to their national law, the law applicable at the time of the marriage or the law of their first matrimonial domicile is given priority in case of an inheritance). This means that the assets which are actually to be included in the estate will depend on the relevant matrimonial property regime. It follows that the careful selection of a suitable matrimonial property regime may allow succession planning in favor of the surviving spouse, which might not have been possible purely from the standpoint of the applicable inheritance law.

8.3 Forced heirship provisions

Whereas on the civil law dominated European continent, the testamentary capacity of the testator tends to be more or less restricted by forced heirship rules which provide for reserved portions of close relatives; testators in the common-law, Anglo-American legal sphere are largely free to order their estate as they wish. However, foreign real estate located in a country with no forced heirship can be inherited with exclusion of the forced heirship of the testator's home country – which remains valid – only under certain preconditions. This is particularly the case when the main residence has been moved abroad specifically for this purpose. In many cases, an international change of domicile is the only way of bypassing forced heirship provisions in a legally effective way. The same end may in some cases be achieved with the aid of suitable structures, such as private foundations or trusts. However, this involves a very sophisticated area of international estate planning. It should be approached only by suitably qualified and experienced specialists, as all too often structures are set up in this context which cannot hold up against challenges in a court.

8.4 Gifts

Real estate may also be transferred as a gift, and here too corresponding formalities must be observed (the written form being the minimum requirement in most cases). However, higher transfer taxes (gift taxes) usually apply for transfers due to inheritance. So it may make more sense to arrange a transfer between living persons as a sale rather than a gift. In this context it should be noted however that a purchase at an intentionally low purchase price is known as a mixed gift, which may have an effect on the tax consequences. If the purchase price is purely symbolic, the contract is normally considered as a pure gift.

9 Taxes and Charges

The principle that real estate is taxed where it is located applies on an international level. However, the asset value or any income from real estate may additionally be taxed at the owner's domicile. In the worst case, double taxation may be incurred. This may mean that for example wealth taxes are charged on the real estate in country A where it is located, and that the real estate is included, not exempted, in the calculation of the net wealth of the owner resident in country B, where he is being taxed on his total worldwide wealth, including the real estate located in country A.

9.1 One-time taxes and charges on purchase

The purchase of real estate generally involves considerable transfer taxes (in the form of land or document transfer taxes, stamp duties, etc.) which may well exceed 5% of the purchase price, in some countries even more, for instance up to 11% in Greece. The purchase of new real estate normally incurs no transfer tax, but is subject to a sales tax or Value Added Tax (VAT) in many countries. VAT rates are usually higher, around 20% in most European countries, but lower VAT rates often apply for new buildings.

In general, land transfer taxes are charged only on the price of the land and buildings, i.e. exclusive of any movable property. If a furnished house is sold, it is in most cases permissible to list the price of the furniture separately in the contract so that only the part of the purchase price relating to the land and buildings is specified in the taxable property sale. This often allows the total purchase price and the associated land transfer taxes (as well as other fees depending on the purchase price such as notary fees) to be legally reduced to some extent.

As a rule, notary and registry fees are also payable. However, both their structure and amount vary greatly in different countries. Whereas registry fees and often notary fees too are specified by the law, in some countries notaries have considerable discretion in setting their fees. Consequently, notary fees for a property of a particular value may vary greatly. By requesting a cost estimate from the notary, the prospective buyer can obtain a clear idea of the costs involved and avoid unpleasant surprises later on. If a lawyer is also called in, lawyers' fees will also be due. Here too it makes good sense to obtain an estimate in advance. In some countries, lawyers work strictly on the basis of hourly fees plus out-of-pocket expenses. However, in many cases a one-off fee can also be arranged, which usually comprises a certain percentage (as a rule 1% to 3%) of the transaction value. In most common-law countries (such as in The Bahamas, England and the US), property transactions are handled exclusively by lawyers and almost no notary costs are involved. However, the lawyers' costs are then correspondingly higher.

9.2 Annually recurring taxes and charges

In addition to unavoidable annual real estate taxes, which are levied in some form or other in almost every country (except, for example, in

Malta, which has no annual charges of any kind on property), any revenue is also regularly taxed as income if the property is rented. As a rule, however, maintenance and similar costs can then be set off against the taxable income. Some countries levy income tax on what is known as an own rental value, i.e. an income is calculated which would be obtainable in the event of rental, and this fictitious income is then taxed. Some countries additionally levy wealth taxes, which can constitute up to 1.5% and more of the value of the property. In Spain, for instance, the maximum tax rate on larger assets is 2.5%, which is very high in an international comparison. In contrast, many countries have no general wealth tax, but merely charge such taxes on property in the form of land or real estate taxes.

9.3 Capital gains tax

In most countries, the owner of real estate is liable to pay taxes on any value increase or capital gains resulting from the sale. These capital gains taxes often decline in proportion to the time which the property is held. Sometimes different tax rates are applied depending on whether the property is held or sold by a private person or a company. This will have to be considered where holding structures are set up.

It is advisable to carefully retain all invoices and receipts for costs incurred during the period of ownership for renovation and maintenance work, as any expenditure for value-increasing investments can usually be deducted in calculating the capital appreciation.

9.4 Inheritance and gift taxes

Whereas US real estate is taxed at a rate of up to 55% at transfer to the inheritors, countries such as The Bahamas, Italy and the canton of Schwyz in Switzerland charge no inheritance taxes at all. Except for Italy, which has abolished inheritance taxes altogether, rates of inheritance tax can be very high in the EU. Even if the inheritance takes place between spouses and close relatives, if the testator is the direct owner of the property, inheritance taxes can quickly rise to 20 or 30%

Table 2. Succession laws and inheritance taxes in selected countries

Country	Uniform inheritance law[1]	Divided inheritance law[2]	Applicable inheritance law based principally on: Actual domicile	Nationality	Legal domicile
Austria	x			x	
The Bahamas	x		x		
Belgium		x	x		
Canada		x	x		
Croatia	x			x	
Cyprus		x			x
France		x	x		
Ireland		x			x
Italy	x			x	
Malta	x		x		
Monaco		x		x	
Montenegro	x			x	
Portugal	x			x	
Spain	x			x	
St. Kitts and Nevis	x		x		
Switzerland	x		x	x[3]	
United Kingdom / England		x			x
United States / Florida	x		x		

1 Uniform inheritance law = the same law applies to movables and real estate

2 Divided/split inheritance law = different laws apply to movables and real estate

3 If the foreign national domiciled in Switzerland expressly stipulates application of the law of his home country

4 Renvoi: The applicable law makes provision for remission to the referring law or further remission to a different foreign law

5 Relatively broad terms are used for the sake of legibility. As a rule, however, it can be assumed that the term "nearest relatives" refers to children and spouse and the term "other relatives" to parents and siblings

6 Inheritance taxes are a regional competence and vary largely. Spouses are completely exonerated from inheritance taxes on the main residence in Flanders and the Brussels Capital Region, and partly in the Walloon Region

7 Children, spouse, direct descendants or forebears, adopted children and parents

8 Only on real estate. Movables are not taxed

Country	Need a renvoi be considered?[4]	Is there a forced heirship?	Maximum tax rates in % on inheritance for[5]		
			Spouses and closest relatives	Other close relatives	Unrelated persons
Austria	Yes	Yes	0	0	0
The Bahamas	No	No	0	0	0
Belgium	Yes	Yes	30[6]	65	80
Canada	No	No	0	0	0
Croatia	Yes	Yes	-	5	5
Cyprus	No	No	-	-	-
France	Yes	Yes	40[7]	45	60
Ireland	Yes	Yes	20	20	20
Italy	Yes	Yes	4	6	8
Malta	Yes	Yes	5[8]	5[9]	5[9]
Monaco	Yes	Yes	0[17]	8	16
Montenegro	Yes	No	0	3[10]	3[10]
Portugal	Yes	Yes	0	10	10
Spain	No	Yes	40.8[11]	64.8[11]	81.6[11]
St. Kitts and Nevis	No	No[12]	0	0	0
Switzerland	Yes	Yes	0[13] – 11%[14]	0[15] – 23.1[13]	0[14] – 54.6[13]
United Kingdom / England	No[16]	No	40	40	40
United States / Florida	Yes[17]	Yes	55[18]	55	55

9 In the case of both tax-free inheritance and the donation of real estate, certain taxes are payable for the transfer from testator to inheritors or from donator to donees as recorded in the land register. If this does not involve the main residence, these mortgage and land-register taxes do not exceed 3%

10 Standard transfer tax applies to inheritance

11 Maximum tax rates, depending on the size of prior assets (max EUR 4,020,770) and the multiplier referred to them; nonetheless, the autonomous regions foresee substantial reductions from case to case. New legislation underway after ECJ judgement in September 2014

12 Possible by using a trust

13 Most cantons, including canton Schwyz

14 Canton of Geneva

15 Canton Schwyz

16 The UK does, however, have legislation providing for dependants who have not been adequately provided for

17 Florida law allows renvoi to be legally excluded

18 Tax-free allowances of up to USD 1 million for spouses of US residents

of its market value. In the event of inheritance to unrelated persons, they can easily reach 60% (in France) and in extreme cases even over 80% (such as in Spain, where the highest tax rate for inheritance to wealthy unrelated persons is 81.6%). The higher the value of the estate and the more distant the kinship, the higher is the inheritance tax. Spain also has the interesting peculiarity of taking into account not only the value of the estate and the degree of relationship, but also the wealth of the inheritor. This may in certain circumstances lead to the enormous maximum tax rate of 81.6%. So it should always be determined before buying who is to be the owner of the foreign property. Depending on the circumstances, various options are available, such as setting up a holding structure or direct acquisition of the property in the names of the children.

Even for real estate in the medium price range, it makes sense to make suitable legal arrangements to reduce or avoid foreign inheritance taxes within the framework of international estate planning. This can often be done, and it is worthwhile carefully checking out each case individually.

9.5 Other taxes and charges

In most countries, various lesser taxes and duties are payable at acquisition, but also annually. They include smaller stamp duties for documents, sewage connection charges (which can be considerable, for instance in Switzerland), garbage removal charges, and connection charges for cable TV which in some countries can also have a tax-like character, such as the UK 'TV Licence', payable by everyone that owns a TV or a computer that can view TV channels or movies.

Other charges may include costs for fire or buildings insurance. These are not mandatory in many countries, so it is at the discretion of the owner to take out such a policy or not. In other countries, however, every property owner is obliged to conclude such an insurance policy.

If the activities of a private real estate investor exceed the limits of "normality", in many countries there is a risk of being considered as a property dealer for tax purposes. In such a case, all revenues from the property inclusive of sales profits count as earned income and are liable to the usual income tax, which may be very high. However, this will obviously not apply to a one-time purchase of a privately used property.

9.6 Incorrect (lower) statement of sale price on the sales agreement

The basis for calculating real estate transfer taxes and capital-gains taxes is normally the purchase price documented in the purchase deed (such as a sales agreement authenticated by a notary). This offers a tempting way of 'saving' taxes by stating a lower sale price on the sales agreement. However, such action constitutes tax fraud and can lead to considerable sanctions, depending on the country concerned. Nevertheless, it continues to be common practice in countries such as Spain and Italy and in some cases the other party to the agreement will even insist on it.

This practice not only evades part of the real estate transfer tax usually payable by the purchaser, the seller also 'saves' taxes on the appreciated value of the property. In addition, the difference to the real purchase price not declared in the sales agreement is often paid in untaxed money, which represents another motive for this practice in addition to tax evasion.

Sometimes – for instance in Spain and Italy – it may even be quite impossible to acquire a property without such illicit payment, as the seller is only willing to sell to someone who is prepared to pay part of the purchase price illicitly. This preference on the part of the seller may also be linked to the fact that he too had paid part of the price illicitly and would now have to pay considerably higher capital gains tax if he were to put the true sales price on the agreement.

Quite apart from the fact this practice is illegal in most countries, and leads not only to fiscal risk but also in some cases to considerable criminal sanction, it involves more disadvantages than advantages, above all for the buyer.

A particular problem, which should not be underestimated, concerns the handover and time of transfer of the cash. Should the money be transferred when the preliminary contract is signed, at the notarial authentication of the main agreement or only when the property changes hands? If the sales agreement is not fulfilled, any illegal subsidiary arrangements can be unfortunate for both buyer and seller. A purchase in which the declared price does not correspond to that actually paid is generally considered a fictitious transaction, which is invalid in most countries, and leads to corresponding complications if any contractual claims are asserted. Thus if the buyer should wish to pursue litigation against the seller, either for building defects or in connection with the title, the responsible court will as a rule at most sentence the seller to reimburse the documented and registered purchase price. Normally no evidence is admitted which shows the purchase price to be any other than the official one. The buyer should also note that an officially lower purchase price leads to a higher capital gain at a later resale and thus to correspondingly higher capital gains tax – unless the seller finds another prospective buyer who is willing to pay part of the sale price illicitly.

In the case of acquisition from a legal entity, such as a company, this illegal practice can also be risky in the event of the latter's bankruptcy. In most countries, if the purchase price specified in the official sales agreement differs significantly from the market value of the property, the receiver can contest the sales contract and possibly even reclaim the property. In the worst case, the buyer would have to register his bankruptcy claim at the price specified in the official sales agreement, or alternatively consider the option of notifying the tax authorities of his own tax evasion, because the buyer actually paid a higher purchase price.

9.7 International taxation and avoidance of double taxation

Any tax liability is always based on the tax law of each individual country, i.e. a specific country will always assert its right to impose tax with respect to a particular matter (such as property, income, license earnings etc.) within its borders. As long as the person concerned does not cross the borders of a particular country and maintains no tax-relevant relationships beyond its borders, only the tax laws of that country are applied.

However, by crossing national borders, for instance by acquiring real estate in another country, a buyer also becomes liable – at least in part – under the fiscal laws of this other country. The question then immediately arises of the delimitation of the rights to impose tax between these two countries, because double taxation then becomes a threat. The buyer can be taxed firstly by the tax authorities of the country of his or her residence, which in most countries means unlimited tax liability based on global income and (in some countries) assets. But he or she can also be taxed by the country in which the real estate is located on the basis of the limited tax liability based on the ownership of real estate. So it often happens that parts of the assets (such as the real estate in the other country), or of the income, will in principle be taxed by two countries, i.e. the same part of the assets or income is subject to double taxation unless a delimitation is affected. This can be done on the basis of national law (by means of provisions in the law limiting tax liability). For instance, although Switzerland basically taxes the global income and assets of persons who have their tax residence in Switzerland, real estate assets located abroad are exempt from Swiss taxation. However, such national regulations are relatively rare, and to avoid double taxation in an international context as far as possible, double taxation agreements (DTAs) have been concluded between many countries.

Double taxation agreements

Double taxation agreements are bilateral state treaties which delimit the tax-imposition rights between two countries and take precedence over national legislation. The aim of such treaties is to avoid double taxation by preventing incomes, assets and in some treaties also inheritances and gifts from being taxed twice. An extensive worldwide network exists of agreements regarding income and wealth taxes. In contrast, relatively few agreements concern inheritance and gift taxes.

For real estate, DTAs generally apply the following taxation principle: real estate is taxed as an asset and any revenues deriving from it is taxed as income in the country in which the real estate is located. The other contracting state (in this case the country of residence of the real estate owner who is liable to unrestricted taxation there) must either exempt the real estate from its own taxation or credit the taxpayer with the taxes imposed by the other country.

One may always consider that the owner of real estate in a high tax jurisdiction may be a company based in a low-to-no tax jurisdiction. Depending on the DTA between the two nations, the sale or transfer of an asset normally triggers capital gains tax in the jurisdiction of the asset. Therefore the sale of an owning company in a low-to-no tax jurisdiction may be more logical then a physical transfer of real estate in a potentially high tax jurisdiction, and considerable tax savings could be possible, depending on the jurisdictions involved. As tax law and DTAs change frequently it is always important to acquire current and professional tax advice prior to make and investment or purchase.

Imputation method / tax credits

The DTAs of relevance here often apply the imputation method. The real estate located abroad is then tax-liable in both countries, i.e. in the state of residence and the state of where the real estate is located, although the former credits the taxpayer with the tax already collected in the latter. This means that the taxpayer will always be liable to the higher tax rates applicable. This shall be illustrated by means of an example: a person resident in state A who is liable to unlimited tax owns property in state B which he lets. His net revenue from the rental may be USD 100, which would be taxed in state B at 25%. State A levies tax of 35% on the same income of USD 100, but credits the USD 25 already paid, so that only the additional 10% of the income derived from the rental revenue is taxed in state A. The taxpayer is consequently not taxed twice on the same income, but ultimately pays the higher tax rate of state A. However, if the tax rate in state A was also 25%, then state A would impose no further tax on the relevant income.

Exemption method

In the exemption method, the taxation right is assigned exclusively to the state in which the property is located and the residence state must exempt the corresponding income or assets from taxation. However, in most cases a saving clause as to tax progression (exemption with progression) is applied. This means that in the overall taxation of the taxpayer, the state of residence may apply the tax rate which would be applicable to the taxpayer's income or assets if his income or assets located in the treaty state were to be added to these. This saving clause thus affects only those taxpayers whose taxable income or assets are not already subject to the highest progression bracket of income or wealth tax. It is irrelevant to those who already pay at the top tax rate.

Splitting debts and debt interest

The DTAs do not deal with the question of splitting the debts and debt interest encumbering a property between states. Practically all states accept debts and debt interest on the basis that the mortgage and debt interest encumbering a particular property are subtracted from the corresponding market value or revenues and only the respective net asset value or net income is taxed. Switzerland is an exception to this rule, as it applies a quota-based exclusion of global debts and debt interest (as a ratio of Swiss to global assets), so that double deductions or deduction gaps can naturally result with respect to Switzerland.

Combating tax evasion

In addition to avoiding double taxation, DTAs increasingly also serve to combat tax evasion. The contracting states thus agree on extensive exchange-of-information clauses. It is worth noting that some of the countries which interest us here have introduced special taxes or reporting requirements on foreign companies which hold local real estate (e.g. France, Spain). Exemption is usually possible only if the foreign company is domiciled in a country which has concluded a DTA containing extensive information-exchange clauses with the country in which the real estate is located.

The *Organization for Economic Co-operation and Development (OECD)* has published a model double taxation agreement which acts as a reference for most DTAs applicable between contracting states. After various partial revisions between 1992 and 2000, the *OECD Steering Committee* has now ratified a further update of this agreement. A significant and relevant change is that *Article 13* now includes a stipulation about the sale of shares of a company whose main asset(s) is real estate. Also, *Article 27* was added; it concerns mutual help between states in collecting tax.

The new stipulation in *Article 13 (4)* is as follows: *"Gains derived by a resident of a Contracting State from the alienation of shares deriving more than 50% of their value directly or indirectly from immovable property situated in the other Contracting State may be taxed in that other state."*

This new stipulation will be considered in future double taxation agreements or in renegotiations of existing agreements and should be accordingly borne in mind. If property is acquired abroad via a company, it is certainly advisable to consult the domestic law both of the country in which the property is located and of the owner's country of residence, and in particular any relevant double taxation agreements. These agreements may diverge from the *OECD* model agreement in significant points concerning these issues.

Table 3. Overview of personal taxation in selected countries

Country	Maximum tax rates in % Income	Capital gains	Wealth	Inheritance/ gifts[1]	Number of double taxation agreements concluded	Assessment[2]
Australia	45	45	0	0	42	***
Austria	50	25[3]	0	0[4]	61	***
Bahamas	0	0	0	0	-	*****
Belgium	50[5]	33[6]	0	30 – 80[5]	92	**
Canada	49.53[7]	24[8]	0	0[9]	55	***
Cayman Islands	0	0	0	0	-	*****
Croatia	40	12	0	5	57	****
Cyprus	35	20	0	0	52	*****
Finland	49	32	0.9	13- 32	56	*
France	49.6	34.5[10]	1.8	45 - 60	108	*
Germany	50.05	25	0	30 - 50	76	*
Greece	45	45[11]	0.8[12]	40	21	***
Hong Kong	15	0	0	15 / 0	1	****
Hungary	16	16	0	21 - 40	54	***
Ireland	48	30	0	20	42	****
Italy	12.5[13] - 43	20	0	4[14] / 8[15]	71	***
Japan	50[16]	52[17]	2.1	50	45	*
Jersey	20	0	0	0	-	*****
Malta	35[18]	12[19]	0	5	65	*****
Mexico	30	30	0	0	27	***
Monaco	0	0	0	16[20]	2[21]	*****
Montenegro	9 - 15	9	0	3	42	****
Netherlands	52	25	0	20-40	79	*
New Zealand	33	0	0	0 / 25	27 (3 not in force yet)	***
Portugal	48	28	0	0-10.8	46	**
Singapore	20	0	10	10 / 0	47	****
Spain	52	20 24	2.5	40.8 - 81.6	83	**
Sweden	56.6	30	0	30	83	*
St. Kitts and Nevis	0	0	0	0	22	*****
Switzerland	23.5[22] -45.5[23]	3 - 60	0.4 -0.7[24]	0 - 54.6[25]	52	****
United Kingdom	50[26]	28	0	40	118[27]	****
United States	39.6	15[28]	0	55	64	**

1 The first number designates the maximum tax rate for spouses and children, the second number the maximum tax rate for unrelated persons. If different tax rates apply for inheritances and gifts, the figures before the dash refer to inheritance, after it to gifts

2 Assessment of the total tax burden on foreign nationals taking up residence, including all tax planning options: * = Tax desert ***** = Tax paradise

3 For real estate properties which were acquired as of 31 March 2002 or later

4 Real estate inherited is subject to land transfer tax at the rate of 2% for closest relatives and 3.5% for others

5 Plus additional taxes at municipal level: 0 - 4.5% and social contributions (13.07%)

6 Capital gains are in general exonerated if they are realized within a normal management of an estate

7 Ontario, on income over CAD 220,000

8 Capital gains: 50% of capital gains taxed at the applicable tax rate

9 There is no inheritance tax, but capital gains tax is charged as per the day of death

10 Capital gains resulting from the sale of listed shares, if acquired after December 31 2012, are taxed equally to the general tax brackets. If the listed shares being sold were acquired on or before 31 December 2012, the gain is subject to a 0.2% tax on the sales price

11 Capital gains derived from the sale of real estate acquired after 1 January 2013 are subject to a final 20% tax payable by the seller, adjusted for length of ownership

12 Only on real estate assets

13 On interest earnings from foreign bonds

14 In the case of tax-free inheritance or donation of real estate, certain taxes are payable for entry of the transfer in the land register from the testator to the inheritor, or from the donator to the donee. If this is not the testator's main residence, these mortgage and land-register taxes total 2%

15 Gifts between spouses and relatives of up to fourth degree (cousins) are tax-free

16 Total of national, regional and municipal taxes

17 If the property is already resold five years after acquisition

18 For foreign nationals with residence permits: taxation limited to 15% of income transferred to Malta

19 Relating to immovable property only, otherwise the standard income tax applies to the capital gain

20 Only on assets in Monaco

21 With France and Luxembourg

22 Cantons of Zug and Schwyz

23 Canton of Geneva

24 Wealth taxes vary between the cantons

25 Canton of Geneva (unrelated persons)

26 For foreign nationals under certain conditions only on UK income

27 Some countries have more than one DTA with the UK, 118 represents the number of countries that have any form of DTA with the UK

28 On assets held for over 12 months before liquidation

10 Insurance

Incidents involving new and reconstructed buildings can lead to considerable liabilities for the principal. The latter is normally liable for any damages which may be caused by his building project, usually in a causal sense, i.e. also without fault. If the principal wishes to shift liability to the causal agent, he will first have to find the latter and then prove negligent conduct. The principal's liability risk must consequently be covered by a suitable insurance policy. It is also advisable to consider cover for unpredictable damage during the building phase, as unfinished buildings are at particular risk. Damage to the building itself is covered by the builders' liability insurance. In addition, cover can be arranged for existing buildings and movables as well as for costs for clearance, inspection for damage and reconstruction.

Upon completion of the building work or acquisition of a completed building, building damages insurance is absolutely necessary and is even mandatory in many countries. Suitable cover must also be arranged for the owner's causal liability associated with the property. It must furthermore be ensured that the household effects contained within the building are sufficiently insured – against damage by fire, water, etc. as well as burglary. Normal household effects' insurance does not cover rare or expensive objects such as jewelry or works of art sufficiently, if at all. Special valuables or art cover should therefore be arranged for them. Finally, the risk arising from financial obligations should not be neglected either. Life or loss-of-earnings insurance may also be advisable to provide security in the event of death or disability.

10.1 Checklist: Insurance

The following risks should be checked and suitably insured:

- Liability consequences of the principal: principal's liability insurance
- Damage by the elements to the still incomplete building: buildings' insurance and builders' liability insurance

- Damage by fire, water, etc. to the completed building: building damages insurance
- Liability of property owner: homeowner's insurance
- Household effects contained in the building: household effects' insurance
- Particularly expensive objects such as jewelry, objets d'art, valuables or art
- Financial obligations of the owner (especially with regard to bank loans): whole or term life insurance, loss-of-earnings/income replacement insurance

11 Financing

Real estate is generally considered as an asset retaining its value over the long term, so that building societies, banks and other financial institutions usually grant mortgages of up to 80% of the current market value, in some countries even up to 100%, against corresponding collateral. As a rule, however, this applies only to property buyers or owners living in the same country who can demonstrate sufficient income. Foreign buyers of real estate often find that opportunities for local financing are severely restricted, and in many cases a maximum of 50% loan-to-value applies. Depending on the country concerned, few lenders are willing to grant foreign property owners corresponding loans. On the other hand, banks in some countries (for example in Spain) grant relatively generous mortgages to foreign owners too.

However, banks in the buyer's home country tend to be even less willing to finance properties located abroad, unless a substantial private banking relationship is leveraged.

Property can also be financed by means of leasing. However, this is far more usual for commercial properties such as office buildings, industrial premises etc. than for private houses and apartments. In a leasing transaction, the owner of the property acts as the lessor who lets the lessee have the use of the property in return for remuneration. The latter may obtain 100% financing for this purpose. As a rule, leasing agreements can be concluded with a buy option.

With regards to vacation homes, it should be pointed out that they should be seen essentially as consumer goods and should consequently be largely financed from one's own funds wherever possible. On the other hand, financial planning and tax aspects may often make some degree of borrowing advisable.

11.1 Checklist: External financing

- Amount and specific conditions
- Amount of own funds required
- Interest rate: the interest rate can be arranged to be either fixed or variable. Various interest-stage and interest-plateau models are also available
- Bank charges and other ancillary costs
- Term, amortization and other conditions. In some countries it can make sense from a tax viewpoint to maintain a high mortgage and amortize it indirectly
- To secure the loan, there are usually several different ways of setting up a suitable lien or mortgage on the property which acts as collateral
- Some countries (such as the US) require title insurance
- In some countries, the payout of loans is taxable

12 Special Real Estate

12.1 Timeshares (timesharing) and fractional ownership

Instead of acquiring a vacation home as a sole owner, and then letting it stand empty much of the year, it can make good sense to share the property with other interested parties. Although this is basically a good idea, many providers of timesharing services have acquired a bad reputation, and not without reason. In most cases, this is because they offer over-priced projects and often market them by using aggressive sales methods. Acquirers of timeshares are frequently swindled out of their money as a result of false information about the possible utilization to be expected and excessive maintenance fees. They may even lose their entire investment if a vacation resort remains unfinished. It is frequently suggested that timesharing rights are a kind of capital investment which appreciates in value and can be resold. And yet often no entry is made in the land or ownership register, so the buyer has no security in the event of bankruptcy, and in most cases no real resale market exists, and resale value is almost always less than the purchase amount. Great care must accordingly be taken by prospective acquirers.

For this reason, various countries – in the US, the state of Florida is exemplary in this respect – have introduced regulations aimed at preventing such exploitation of the timesharing concept. Thus providers of timeshares in Florida are liable to extensive disclosure requirements, so that the risks of a purchase must be made apparent and the buyer is clearly informed that he has a ten day right of withdrawal from the contract. The *American Resort Development Association* (*ARDA*) has also published a code of ethics for the US. In Europe, an EU timesharing directive has been in existence since 1994, but has not been implemented in all countries. It stipulates that sellers must provide comprehensive information and make provision for withdrawal rights for the buyer as well as for additional protective regulations.

Forms of timesharing and fractional ownership

There are several different forms of timesharing and fractional ownership. In most cases, a share is acquired in an ownership association in conjunction with a temporary utilization/occupancy right which is entered in the land or ownership register. This may also be called deeded or real timesharing. In some timesharing agreements, however, no such utilization right is entered in the ownership register but a right to a timeshare is secured merely by contract. This is known as non-deeded or contractual timesharing and is in reality closer to a long-term rental or accommodation contract with full pre-payment of the rent. In a number of countries (for example in Switzerland) real timesharing is not possible because the law does not actually allow real estate ownership to be divided up into various periods of use calculated over the year. However, arrangements to this effect in contract and company law are usually permitted. This leads to another form of timeshares that consists of the acquisition of company shares or participation rights in a similar legal entity which in turn permits utilization of property held by that legal entity. This form of timesharing is often called cooperative timesharing, vacation club or incorporated timesharing. The companies can for example be organized as stock corporations whose shareholders acquire shares or other participation units for which residential-rights points are distributed. Also worth mentioning is that trust structures are not infrequently set up to complement real timesharing arrangements. Trusts play an important role above all in the English-speaking world which generally uses various forms of trusts. In trust structures, the acquirer is a trust beneficiary and not a holder of real ownership.

The costs of timesharing

Even if a provider is above board, the question must be asked whether timesharing is really worthwhile, as it almost always works out much more expensive than a hotel stay or package tour. Equally, it fails to offer the comfort of one's own four walls assured by full ownership or the option of using the property at any time.

A utilization right in a timeshare is usually acquired by paying a certain initial purchase price. Its amount depends on diverse factors, such as the location and facilities of the property and the season for which the utilization right applies. It has no upper limit but usually costs up to some USD 25,000 per week. However, regular annual maintenance fees must be paid in addition to this. These can be quite considerable, depending on the property. It should also be noted that they are regularly increased in line with cost-of-living criteria. If services such as final cleaning are retained, service charges are also incurred. If a client does not wish to take his vacation in the same place every year, he should consider membership of an exchange network. There are two main providers in this market, both based in the US: Interval International and RCI. In most cases, membership is acquired right at the start with the rest of the package and is also used as a sales argument. However, exchange-pool membership also incurs annual membership fees which must be added to the running costs.

The best way of obtaining a timeshare under relatively attractive conditions is via the second-hand timeshare market. Agents specializing in this business can be found especially in the US, but also for example on the Caribbean island of St. Martin. Elsewhere, especially in Europe, there is almost no market for second-hand timeshares. Shares of incorporated timeshare companies which distribute dividends in the form of residence-rights points for vacation properties can also be acquired second-hand rather than new. Such shares are even offered via newspaper advertisements. As a rule, the price obtainable on the open market is well below the initial sales price, which is also a clear indication that timesharing tends to be overpriced.

12.2 Historical real estate

A chateau in France, a historical country estate in Andalusia or an apartment in the old center of Venice is the ultimate dream of many. Residential properties with a long history are indeed something special, with their own charm and romanticism. Old walls, wooden beams and floors of natural materials often hold great appeal for many prospective buyers.

However, old masonry in particular can give rise to considerable problems and costs. Dampness, poor insulation, rotten attic timbers, a leaking roof, antiquated electrical and sanitary installations and much else can mean expensive renovation and maintenance work.

In extreme cases, a house may be beyond repair because of insalubrious conditions – such as excessive decay and mold or asbestos contamination – and should really be pulled down. However, this need not be the case, and solidly built dwellings, such as all-wood chalets in the Alps, are often exemplary in terms of residential quality and biological factors.

In any case, historical properties should never be bought until they have been examined by a specialized architect or construction engineer. Surprises lurking in the attic, cellar, or even behind a newly painted wall, may be just too major and unpleasant. The fee charged by the architect for an assessment (typically between USD 2,500 and USD 15,000 depending on the property) is very reasonable in comparison.

In most countries that are of interest here, historical real estate is protected in some way, and preservation regulations may even encumber the property with major restrictions. Every item of renovation or alteration work, no matter how minor, may require approval from the relevant authorities. This can be a very laborious procedure in some countries. However, that need not be the case. For example, hundreds of historical buildings in France are not protected. Before acquiring historical real estate, however, it is important to check exactly what restrictions apply. On the other hand, the owner may well be able to claim state subsidies for (usually very expensive) renovation work. In any case, the legal framework conditions and restrictions should always be examined carefully and should be completely clear to the prospective buyer before buying.

12.3 Rural and agricultural real estate

Rural properties such as a farm or an olive grove usually suffer from the same problems as historical ones in terms of masonry, preservation orders and similar factors. However, prospective buyers of such real estate should be aware of many other points. They include the question of their earlier use. Thus buildings which were formerly used as animal stalls or as shelters for shepherds or farm laborers and are sold today as rustic homes were never designed for residential purposes.

Access is often difficult and maintenance of a track leading across rough ground may be troublesome and expensive. Other points to consider are a supply of fresh water and a means of removing sewage, as remote properties are rarely connected to the public water supply and sewage systems. It can also be difficult to obtain a telephone line and electricity supply. Real estate located in agricultural zones are nearly always subject to relatively extensive building prohibitions or restrictions, and any utilization rights by neighbors and other questions of neighbors' rights must be clarified before a purchase is made. Safety aspects must not be neglected either in the case of remote properties. Poorly secured properties which are not under surveillance in the absence of their owners are preferred targets for burglars. And finally it should not be forgotten that agricultural land must be suitably tended. This may be done by the neighbors in many cases, but such arrangements must be organized and usually have to be supervised.

Although the acquisition of agricultural real estate - such as olive groves in Andalusia, a vineyard in Piedmont or a country estate in England - is essentially comparable to the purchase of any other real estate, special care must be taken due to the peculiarities of agricultural use. In political terms, agricultural land has long been treated as a special case in virtually all countries, but especially in Europe, and this largely continues to apply. Laws passed in favor of farmers frequently encroach upon the rights of residential and commercial tenants. A buyer of agricultural real estate must take this particularly into account. Decades-old rights of neighbors, such as grazing rights, are often in place. They may not be recorded in any register but nevertheless have full validity and can be enforced if necessary. Special tax allowances or state subsidies are often available for farmed land. Not infrequently, special restrictions on acquisition by foreign nationals continue to apply.

The purchase and sale of agricultural real estate may involve contact with unfamiliar stipulations of the local laws, often with deep roots in the history of the country. Agricultural properties may also be subject to various regulations, such as hunting and fishing rights, which may be important in a particular case. So the purchase and sale of such real estate usually takes much more time than other real estate, and such transactions often require special knowledge and experience.

Moreover, particularly larger agricultural estates may be regarded as an enterprise and often there are employees that permanently work and sometimes live on the estate. The buyer would then need to consider employment-law aspects and may have to assume an employer's liability to continued wage payment, pension contributions, insurance payments and the like. He/she would then have to decide whether to keep employees on after the acquisition and may even have an obligation to do so under local employment law. Such cases must be examined on the basis of the relevant legal stipulations as well as concrete employment contracts and agreements so that the obligations passing to the buyer can be evaluated from a legal standpoint.

12.4 Vineyard properties

As a special form of agricultural real estate, vineyards require particular knowledge in viticulture and oenology. Accordingly, at least for the purchase of larger vineyard properties, vineyard experts, oenologists, specialised architects and surveyors, nursery gardeners and vineyard planners should be involved.

Regarding the vineyard in general, in a number of countries, permits are required for vineyards above certain acreage. Classification of origin is available in countries such as France, Spain and Italy and may be of interest for the prospective buyer. For example in France, the *INAO (Institut National des Appellations d'Origine)* issues certificates which will confirm the *AOC* classification of wines.

A land survey controls the exact planted surface area before the sale. The resulting computerised document is also used for the day-to-day running of the vineyard (for example spraying). The sanitary condition of the vineyard is checked to detect possible diseases and problems, and the climatic risks (in particular, hail, frost, and flooding) are estimated via empirical data and maps identifying sensitive areas.

There are specific regulations in most countries regarding the buildings and installations on the property, such as vinification plants, cellars, offices, shops and houses. Regulations include provisions regarding asbestos and other pollutants, surface area of the building and possibility to enlarge existing facilities, the water quality of wells if the property is not connected to the public water supply, termites and other xylophagous insects, etc. When the buildings are large, it is important for a surveyor to carry out a check of the main structures.

Regarding vinification plants in particular, attention must be given to the conformity of the installations to local regulations, especially concerning work safety and electrical installations. Appropriate conformity certificates and reports must be attached to the sales agreement. Also the constantly changing regulations concerning the treatment of effluents and the growing problem of chloroanisoles must be verified. A comprehensive list of equipment mentions its condition as well as the possible securities, guarantees, leasing agreements, etc.

If the vineyard produces significant quantities of marketable wine, in other words it is operated as a real business, the goodwill of the business is the most delicate factor to measure in the estimation of the overall value of the property. Very often, the quality and reliability of the business will depend on the owner and therefore no guarantee can be made on the value of the business in this manner. It is nevertheless essential to check the sound protection of the trademarks sold, in this case the trademark of the estate or the château.

As wine is a living product, a complete qualitative control (wine-tasting coupled with laboratory analysis and maturing tests) is essential in all transactions. Although a contradictory evaluation does not free the seller completely, it increases the security and clarifies the operation. In addition to the stock, the standing crops correspond to the expenses engaged by the seller with a view to the future harvest which will be to the benefit of the buyer.

Unless there is a special agreement, the takeover of the estate usually implies the takeover of all existing staff. On the day of the sale, the legal situation of the employees must be up to date (remuneration, bonuses, sick leave and paid holidays) and any risk of litigation clearly announced to the buyer.

Often, when an estate contracting to a cooperative cellar is sold, the buyer does not wish to carry on this contract. In this case, the buyer's position must be clearly and precisely stipulated in writing before the sale at the risk of having to pay cancellation fees in conformity with the regulations of the cooperative cellar. A written agreement before the sale will ensure the financial consequences are minimised.

Because of comprehensive tenant protection regulations in many countries, a leased estate with a tenant is normally difficult to sell. In the case of a sale, the owner must pay attention to the deadlines and the form of the notification for the ending of the lease in order to disengage himself from his tenant farmer without financial consequences (compensation for the tenant farmer) because in the case of a sale, in many countries a considerable amount (for example in France, up to 30% of the value of the property) can be allocated to the tenant farmer as an indemnity for termination. The calculation is determined by the quantity and the nature of the investments carried out by the tenant farmer on the estate.

With the purchase and sale of a vineyard, the interests of the seller are usually very different from those of the buyer. This will greatly affect purchase price calculation as both sides must set prices of the various assets being sold. For example, the buyer will want to optimise the redeemable values (equipment, plantation) whereas the seller will want to reduce them as these assets are often already depreciated. On the other hand, the seller may aim to maximise the value of his main residence whereas the buyer may prefer to minimise it.

A vineyard purchase transaction, from the provisional sales agreement to the signature of the final contract, usually takes four to six months. The transaction must be formalised by experts qualified in their respective fields of competence. Lawyers, accountants and bankers must verify and validate, amongst other things, the title deeds, the release of mortgage and other encumbrances, the notifications to neighbors and organisations benefiting from a pre-emption right (government, commune, etc.), easements, the annual accounts and balance sheets of the vineyard operation, the guarantees of assets and liabilities (when there is sale of company shares) and the execution of contingency clauses.

12.5 Properties located near water

A location close to or with a view of water is often sought after for vacation homes, perhaps directly adjoining a sea, lake or river. However, properties located close to water are liable to particular problems. Especially in the case of still waters such as lakes, considerable nuisance from gnats and midges must be expected in the summer months or in warmer climate zones throughout the year, and the vicinity of such waters generally encourages pests. A pleasant summer's evening in the garden can be considerably disturbed. Certainly there are various mechanical and chemical ways of limiting this nuisance, but their use is not always pleasant. Secondly, water can be a danger from various standpoints. Rivers and lakes can burst their banks during floods, and coastal flooding as well as hurricanes in certain subtropical and tropical regions can be a serious hazard to buildings and people. The possibility of sudden devastating waves caused by earthquakes must also be considered. In some countries, such as New Zealand, the danger of tsunamis is a real one and is taken very seriously. In many parts of the world there were good reasons not to build directly next to the water in the past, but rather to seek out more elevated locations further inland.

In areas close to the sea it should also be noted that salt air tends to ravage building materials. Metal parts in particular corrode very quickly. Window fittings which function perfectly when a new owner moves in can be defective after only a short time. Prospective builders of a property in the vicinity of the sea should make sure to use appropriate materials. In most cases, certain types of wood should be used, special paints are required and the right architecture is also important. It is essential to call in an expert familiar with local building traditions, irrespective of whether a new property is being built or an existing one acquired.

13 Private Islands

by
Farhad Vladi, PhD, Vladi Private Islands, Hamburg

The thought of a private island conjures up dreams and wonderful fantasies: your own untouched piece of land completely surrounded by water where you can enjoy the isolation and beauty of nature. In earlier centuries, islands were perceived as hostile isolated places, utilised as sites for prisons or remote locations of exile and banishment. The only other "positive" purpose they served was to save shipwrecked sailors from drowning!

Then with the paintings of *Gauguin* which captured the enchantment of distant tropical islands, and with Stevenson's book *Treasure Island*, islands came to signify places of freedom, exoticism and secret desires. Today, for people living under modern-day stress, islands symbolise a further desire: a longing for peace and fulfilment, and a retreat to pure nature and the rhythm of the simple life without all the worries of modern life. In today's civilised world, the desire for a private island is becoming very popular.

Due to technological progress, islands are no longer cut off from civilisation. On the contrary, islands are becoming much more accessible. Through development of technology such as solar energy, prefabricated homes, desalination systems as well as mobile phone networks and the Internet, the advantage of mainland property as opposed to island property has almost disappeared.

Many celebrities have taken the initiative and have secured their own oasis of tranquillity: for example the shipping magnate Onassis with his island Scorpios in the Ionian Sea in Greece, Rockefeller with island groups in the Caribbean, which he then devoted to nature conservation, actors such as Nicolas Cage (The Bahamas) or Tony Curtis (Canada), artists such as Diana Ross (Pacific Ocean) or the entrepreneur Richard Branson who offers his Necker Island in the British Virgin Islands for rent.

Although some private islands for sale, for example in the Caribbean, have been developed into luxury refuges (and have corresponding price tags), not all private islands represent extreme wealth. Most private islands sales take place in the region of USD 150,000 to USD 350,000. Despite different budgets, all island buyers have one characteristic in common: they are individualists and lovers of nature.

Irrespective of the fact that certain countries such as India, the Philippines or the Seychelles restrict or forbid the purchase of private islands by foreigners, the following criteria have proven to be important when considering the purchase of a private island.

13.1 The most important criteria for the purchase of a private island

Infrastructure on the mainland

The distance to the mainland or to another inhabited island should not be too long, for example, 1 km to max. 5 km. The mainland should offer the necessary infrastructure such as roads, parking areas, access to a grocery store, services, and road connections to the next airport, plus electricity and telephone connection possibilities. For some islands the journey by boat from the island to the mainland is often easier than that on land from a remote ranch or forest property to the next village. The potential owner of a private island should be aware that good infrastructure on the nearby mainland is an essential prerequisite.

Absolute ownership essential

The investment in a private island is a capital investment for which maximum security is imperative. The private island owner must ensure that he receives the documentation in his or her own name from the property registry or registry of deeds and that the ownership title is free and clear. Only good ownership titles are insurable and give the potential to earn profit through possible appreciation. This does not apply to leasehold titles.

Construction possibilities on the island

Islands, similar to most other property, have value only if they can be used. Potential owners should avoid islands designated as conservation area for birds or any other nature reserve. Instead, the island must have planning and building permission. It is therefore important that the buyer has confirmation that a building permit is readily available or that a building permit is attainable before signing an agreement and conclusion of the purchase and sale transaction. The buyer should request for this to be one of the conditions for purchase outlined in the agreement. Local legal experts can provide advice on applying for, and obtaining, a building permit.

Appearance of the island

Of course, the island must have natural appeal and offer such features as woodlands, beaches, cliffs, and several coves, one of which should be protected and of suitable depth to anchor a boat. Drinking water must be available on the island and a healthy flower, plant and tree vegetation must also be apparent so that the overall appearance is a positive one.

Geographical location

A private island should be bought only in areas which are politically stable, in countries where a safe legal system and reliable judiciary is in place. A pleasant climate is also important. These criteria help narrow down the choice and also determine the price.

13.2 The cost of a private island

There is a serious selection of private islands around the globe and price generally ranges from around USD 30,000 to USD 130,000,000 and beyond depending primarily on location, size and infrastructure. For instance, with USD 30,000 you can acquire a small private undeveloped island off the east coast of Canada, or for USD 160 million you can have 110 acres just 20 minutes from the highly demanded tourist destination of Phuket in Thailand. For USD 10,000,000 you could own a six acre island within the Florida Keys with a sizable modern home. Otherwise, USD 15,000,000 can buy you an eight acre tropical island in The Bahamas, surrounded by two white sandy beaches and including a state-of-the-art home, three guest houses, a personal five boat marina, fitness centre, and dive centre. Numerous Caribbean islands are already developed with large luxurious villas and more than sufficient space for staff accommodation, and some even have airstrips for your private jet.

For approximately USD 7,500,000 you could acquire an island in the Mediterranean near Monaco with a large harbour for your yacht and a medieval tower. USD 5,000,000 will buy a large, 22 square kilometres island in New Zealand, somewhat isolated but with a sheep farm and lodge with magnificent views. For USD 745,000 you could purchase an undeveloped island in the Caribbean off the coast of Belize only two hours from largest barrier reef in the Western Hemisphere and widely known as one of the best diving areas in the world. For USD 350,000 you could savour the views from the terrace of your own island home over the famous castle of Gripsholm in Sweden. For USD 200,000 one of the prettiest islands off the east coast of Canada, only a few minutes by boat from a popular tourist resort, can be acquired. Lastly, for USD 30,000, a small private island with a summer cabin, also off the east coast of Canada, could be yours.

13.3 After the purchase

There is more to the purchase of an island than just a carefully thought out transaction. Like every other property, an island must also be managed and properly maintained in the future. In this respect one can retain a property management company or manage the property oneself. The annual costs that need to be considered depend on such factors as taxes, insurance, and the costs for a caretaker. However, in the case of most privately owned islands, the employment of a caretaker who would reside on the island is not necessary. In most cases, a manager is sought on the nearby mainland. Often one can employ a fisherman, who sails by the island daily and can keep an eye on the property for a reasonable monthly salary. Additionally, an hourly wage is paid for actual work done. Such a person normally also acts as the local contact person.

If an island is uninhabited and is held solely as an investment for future development or resale, then virtually no other expenses are incurred. In such cases, nature is the best and most convenient manager.

In the case of construction, one must ensure that a valid building permit is granted, in which case the availability of electricity must be determined. This is possible either via underwater cable or generator or by solar or wind generated power on the island itself. A careful cost analysis prior to implementation is normally advisable.

In many areas prefabricated houses are also available. Often, prefabricated houses on an island are only 10% more expensive than those on the mainland. They have the advantage of being structurally approved, and the parts are delivered and, circumstances permitting, helicopters can also help transport them. The costs of prefabricated homes are less than one may think, often around USD 1,500 per square metre.

Drinking water is an important issue. In most cases, there is rainwater underneath the surface of an island, i.e. groundwater which has seeped through and which floats on top of the lower-lying salt water. If this amount of water is not sufficient, for example because more than one home or even a hotel requires supply, then one must purchase a desalination system. For the smallest such system that can produce 300 litres an hour (1,800 per day) one needs to spend approximately USD 7,500; or for close to 300 litres an hour (6,800 per day) some are available for around USD 10,000. Larger and more sophisticated models can cost from USD 50,000, however choosing a smaller system and operating a dual-unit water system is normally recommended, as it protects from unit failure and two smaller units are more energy efficient then one larger system.

In addition, one should definitely include in one's budget a boat, a car or small truck on the mainland and a small site on the mainland with a boat house, storage and garage.

14 Citizenship via Real Estate Acquisition in St. Kitts and Nevis, Antigua and Barbuda, and Cyprus

Antigua and Barbuda, St. Kitts and Nevis, and Cyprus are three of the countries that allow legal citizenship to be granted based on an investment into real estate. In all cases the whole procedure from submitting a citizenship application up to its conclusion, i.e. the issue of the Citizenship Certificate and a passport, usually takes about three to six months. Successful applicants are subsequently issued with a passport like any other citizen, allowing them to enter over 130 countries without a visa. While the qualifying real estate investment in Cyprus is at least EUR 2.5 million, holding citizenship in Cyprus provides your family European Union citizenship and the right to live, work, and study in any of the 28 EU countries.

Aside from the financial benefits you acquire from real estate investments, owning a residence in the country of your citizenship provides further advantages and should be considered when the possibility to acquire citizenship exists. Tax residence in a tax friendly country is extremely important for optimizing your tax structures. Having a residence for instance in St. Kitts or Antigua, with a mailing address and utility bills in your name, provides the needed tools to enhance your international tax planning capabilities, and provides the highest level of privacy for your international business and banking affairs.

Advantages of Alternative Citizenship

Dual citizenship and thus a second passport offer various advantages, particularly in terms of personal freedom, security and flexibility. As a citizen of two different countries, one has a 'second homeland' to which one can return at any time. Citizens of Cyprus, St. Kitts and Nevis, and Antigua and Barbuda can of course travel, work and settle there whenever they wish.

St. Kitts and Nevis as well as Antigua and Barbuda are among the most beautiful islands of the Caribbean. They are politically and economically stable and virtually free of crime – thus offering an ideal environment for a second residence. Citizenship secures the right to move to one's second home at any time and set up one's main residence there. This is open to every citizen at any time, without the need for a visa or residence permit, by right of settlement.

The St. Kitts and Nevis, Antigua and Barbuda and Cyprus passports all allow visa-free travel to more than 130 countries, including Ireland, Switzerland, the UK, most European countries and many others. It may well be asked, however, why a holder of a US or EU passport, which allows visa-free access to many countries around the world, should additionally acquire a passport from one of these countries. There are several answers to this question. In the first place, geopolitical constellations repeatedly arise which may make it difficult or impossible for an US or EU citizen to obtain a visa for a particular country. Increased terrorist activities also imply the danger of attacks and kidnappings, especially of tourists who are citizens of certain EU countries, the US and some other countries. So holding a second citizenship and a passport of a small country which is insignificant in terms of world politics may even save one's life. Barriers to entry and leaving, aircraft hijackings, armed conflicts and terrorism are all situations in which a second passport can be extremely useful if not vital. Dual nationality is a kind of insurance. One hopes that it will never be needed, but if the insured event occurs, the insurance must already have been concluded, as it would be too late to take it out after the event. It may also happen that one's passport is unavailable, perhaps because it has been submitted for extension, has been lost or had to be sent off to a consulate for a visa application. If one wants or needs to travel urgently to another country in such a situation, this would be impossible without a second passport.

For good reasons, many wealthy individuals, important personalities and international business people who are active worldwide have opted for a second citizenship and passport. In an unsettling, ever-changing world, acquiring an alternative citizenship is a wise decision and an investment for the future. Making an active decision with regard to citizenship and residence options gives more personal freedom, privacy and security. It also returns countless other benefits for life.

15 International Changes of Residence

Most owners of real estate abroad sooner or later consider the option not only of using it occasionally as a vacation home or second residence, but of possibly setting it up as their principal residence. Anyone thinking seriously about moving their main residence abroad faces a series of questions which are not always easy to answer. Right at the outset, it should be clarified whether it makes fundamental sense in view of one's personal situation to transfer one's residence, i.e. the center of one's activities, to another country. In view of the oppressive fiscal and increasingly burdensome regulatory environment in some high-tax countries such as Canada, France, Germany, the Netherlands, the UK, the US and others, a move of domicile to a country with a milder tax regime will be an interesting option for many people. It often offers the only alternative to reducing their tax burden significantly in a legal manner. However, one is well advised not to move abroad for tax reasons alone.

15.1 Immigration law and tax residence

With some exceptions, such as Croatia or Switzerland, many countries (including Canada, France, Spain, the UK, the US, etc.) allow foreign nationals to acquire real estate with no restrictions or special formalities. However, the acquisition of real estate in most countries does not imply a right of residence or permanent settlement. In fact, such investments have little if any relevance to immigration requirements. Thus any foreign national may easily acquire real estate in the US and anyone with sufficient funds and of good character may enter the US (with or without a visa depending on their citizenship). However, anyone wishing to live and settle there must first obtain a residence permit. Unlike most countries, the US does not allow financially independent persons who wish to simply spend their retirement in, say, Florida, to obtain such a permit on this basis. The alternative is to seek out other ways, in particular the US EB-5 Investor Immigration Program as it provides residence to persons who invest at least USD 500,000 into a government approved project; or by acquiring a simple business visa which, depending on the situation, is actually quite difficult to obtain. Although residence in the US may seem attractive, it is critically important to understand that physical residence in the US is locked together with fiscal tax residence. Therefore absolute worldwide taxation must be considered for those thinking of residing in the US, and it is widely seen as a poor choice of residence for wealthy individuals or families.

However, it is relatively easy for financially independent persons who do not need to work, but live from their investments or a pension, to obtain a residence or settlement permit in most countries. For example Belgium, Cyprus, Portugal, Switzerland and the UK grant financially independent foreign nationals a residence permit (not citizenship) as non-employed persons. Requirements range from an investment of EUR 250,000 in real estate in Portugal to an investment of GBP 2 million in the UK. All applicants must prove that they have a clean criminal record by submitting a police certificate of good conduct or an extract from a central criminal register confirming that they are not recorded in it. Some countries also insist on proof of suitable accommodation before they issue a residence permit, while others allow you to arrange this after the permit has been issued.

EU citizens have the freedom to settle anywhere within the European Union with no restrictions. So anyone who holds EU citizenship and consequently an EU passport can move within the EU, for instance from the UK to a country such as Ireland, Portugal or Spain without any immigration restrictions. Since 1 June 2002, the same also applies to financially independent EU citizens who wish to reside in Switzerland (see the explanations in the country chapter on Switzerland) and vice-versa.

Americans, Australians and Canadians, among others, in most cases have traceable ancestry in Europe. If the ancestry is not too far back, it may be possible for them to re-acquire the citizenship of their ancestors. For example, an Irish-born grandparent, or a grandparent from Poland or Lithuania, may be the basis for a successful claim to Irish, Polish or Lithuanian citizenship and – as a result - to an EU passport. In Croatia, it is possible reclaim citizenship with any level of Croatian ancestry, which is even more relevant since Croatia joined the EU in July 2013. And as discussed in chapter 14.1, dual or multiple citizenships offer numerous benefits beyond the option of residing in the country of citizenship (and in case of citizenship of an EU country, of residing throughout the EU).

15.2 Change of residence under tax law

Tax residence

The location of a main or secondary residence can have considerable effects, particularly in the sphere of fiscal and inheritance law. This question will not concern those who use their house in the south only for a few weeks during the year, but anyone who wishes to live regularly for half a year in another country must look seriously into questions of legal domicile and especially of tax residence. For those who do not need to work for a living and have sufficient funds, the right of residence presents no problem in most countries. However, anyone who spends more than three months in a particular country without working should at least be aware of the question of tax residence. Whoever regularly spends more than six months of the year in their second home will almost always be considered as tax domiciled there and will thus normally be liable to pay tax on an unlimited basis, which in most countries means taxation of worldwide income. By choosing a country with a mild tax climate for a main residence, a taxpayer can considerably reduce his burden quite legally and effectively without the need for complex tax planning. The Bahamas, Croatia, Ireland, Malta, Monaco, Panama, Switzerland and the UK are attractive destinations in this respect. So a change of residence may well be worthwhile not only for climatic reasons but also from the standpoint of taxation.

Exit taxes and extended income taxes

The main problem with moving one's tax domicile to another country, especially one with low taxation, is that some high-tax countries have taken steps to discourage such moves, namely by introducing a form of exit tax such as in Canada or the US, or an extended income tax regime, or a combination thereof. Germany is an interesting example. Its *Foreign Transactions Tax Act (Aussensteuergesetz)* lays down special tax rules to make moves abroad fiscally less attractive. Thus, significant (>1%) participations in companies held by German citizens are almost inevitably taxed upon emigration, and unrestricted German tax liability may continue to apply despite a move abroad, although the taxes payable in the country of domicile (if any) are then credited. The result is that, besides the payment of an exit tax, the higher German tax level is ultimately retained, at least during a certain period (usually between five and 10 years). Many other high-tax countries impose similar conditions. It is possible to mitigate – or in some cases even completely bypass – such taxation by appropriate structuring before, during and after a move abroad. However, this almost always requires the taxpayer to make a clean break with the former country of residence and to strictly avoid any links with it such as maintaining a second home there, making frequent visits or longer stays on its territory etc. These conditions can be tough for many expatriates and should be carefully weighed against the tax advantages such a radical change in one's life will bring.

In this context it should be noted that on 11 March 2004 the *European Court of Justice* rendered an interesting and potentially very significant judgment concerning exit tax which is imposed in France on holders of substantial participations who give up their residence and move abroad. The court ruled that these French tax provisions restrict the freedom of movement (*Art. 43* of the *EC Treaty*). Given this decision regarding France, it is foreseeable that for example Germany's even stricter exit tax rules will also be qualified by the EU as contrary to the principle of freedom of movement. This decision will in all likelihood have a significant impact on the continued existence of exit taxes provided for in the legislation of many other EU countries, and opens a new perspective with regard to emigration from European high-tax countries to lower-tax countries within the EU.

Double taxation agreements

It was already noted in the context of international tax law with regard to real estate that bilateral agreements to avoid double taxation of persons resident in contractual states exist between many countries. These agreements are particularly relevant to a taxpayer who moves abroad, as they concern the determination of his tax residence. Whereas ownership of property abroad usually implies limited tax liability by this real estate in the foreign country, a move abroad always affects tax residence and has considerable consequences on tax liabilities. Inheritance and gift taxes, which depend primarily on the testator's last residence, may also be relevant. If a taxpayer who moves abroad has considerable income and assets, experience shows that the tax authorities concerned are particularly interested in where he is tax resident, as this leads in most countries to unrestricted tax liability.

It may happen that two countries – according to their respective tax laws – simultaneously consider a particular taxpayer as fiscally resident and unrestrictedly tax liable. This could result in him being taxed on his global income and possibly also on his assets by both countries on the basis of their domestic tax regimes. But, if a double taxation agreement exists between the two countries, it will decide where the taxpayer is fiscally resident and thus liable to unrestricted taxation, and which country is to merely apply restricted taxation – namely on any assets or income located within its territory.

Residence in one of the two contractual states is the precondition for the application of the relevant double taxation agreement and all claims on its protection. The agreement lays down precise rules to determine in which of the two contractual countries a taxpayer is deemed to be fiscally resident. They are known as tie-breaker rules and in the majority of double taxation treaties they follow the *OECD Model Convention*.

Accordingly, most double taxation agreements define the country of fiscal residence as the place where the taxpayer has his permanent home. If he has homes in both countries, the crucial point is where his personal and/or economic activities are centered. His habitual place of sojourn is then in third place, and citizenship is considered only in fourth place. If the tax residence cannot be determined on the basis of these criteria, it is decided by mutual agreement between the countries concerned.

Double taxation agreements can also be useful in terminating tax residence in the country of emigration more quickly. So where someone no longer wishes to count as a UK tax resident, for instance to avoid paying capital gains tax, UK domestic law stipulates that certain taxes apply up to five years even after moving abroad. But if they move their tax residence to a country which has a suitable double taxation agreement with the UK, such as Belgium, they can bypass such domestic tax regulations and reduce the period during which certain UK taxes still apply after a change of residence.

However, in the absence of a double taxation agreement between the previous and new country of residence (such as when moving for example from the Netherlands to Monaco), only the respective domestic fiscal regulations apply. These are generally stricter – at least for high-tax countries – i.e. it is more difficult to terminate one's former fiscal residence. In order to avoid continuing to pay tax on one's global income and possibly assets there too, often all links to one's former country of fiscal residence must be severed, and even then sometimes certain extended taxation applies for some time after emigration.

15.3 Inheritance law and inheritance taxes

Moving permanently to another country can also have considerable effects on the applicable laws regarding inheritance, and on inheritance taxes. Depending on the country in which one sets up new residence, this can bring either advantages and tax savings, or disadvantages and a higher tax burden. Some jurisdictions permit different asset dispositions in the event of succession to the estates of deceased persons (e.g. no forced heirship, greater testamentary freedom, but in other cases stricter forced heirship regulations apply). As inheritance taxes in many countries are only charged if the decedent had his last or primary residence (domicile) there, a change of residence of a person expecting to bequeath substantial wealth may lead to considerable tax savings for the heirs. Other countries however charge inheritance taxes if the inheritors are residents, and some countries, for example Germany, combine both systems. Thus German regulations consider not only the decedent's last place of residence; but also whether the inheritor lives in Germany. So any inheritors living in Germany and wishing to avoid paying tax on the inheritance they receive would also have to consider moving their own residence to somewhere offering more favorable tax conditions.

A similarly difficult situation exists for US citizens, who are subject to inheritance (estate) taxes on the basis of their citizenship regardless of their place of residence; in other words, even if a US citizen moves his or her residence abroad, this does not change anything with regard to his or her US inheritance tax liability. Moreover, a US citizen is subject to gift taxes on gifts of assets made during his life in excess of the applicable lifetime and annual exemptions. For a US citizen, the only way to escape US Federal estate and gift tax liability is to relinquish US citizenship.

Finally, it should be noted that, as a principle of international tax law, real estate is generally subject to inheritance tax in the country where the property is located. Therefore, if one's wealth primarily consists of real estate located in countries which have high inheritance tax rates, a change of residence may have little or no effect on the inheritance tax due.

15.4 International health insurance

International health cover is an extremely important topic for anyone thinking of moving abroad, and yet it is scarcely considered by many people and hardly mentioned at all by advisors. Admittedly, it is not the job of a lawyer specializing in international inheritance law or an international tax advisor to also know about insurance, and especially about international health insurance. There is consequently relatively little specialist competence in this sector available to private clients. Most advisors and insurance brokers worldwide with such expertise merely represent a single insurer. Only very few offer more than a small number of products or are able to provide really comprehensive advice.

Trying to find ideal health cover is no easy task even without moving abroad, but it is of particular importance when moving to another country or even staying there for a limited period. The risks of sickness and accident must be covered comprehensively in an international context in order to avoid unpleasant surprises. A few important points must be considered in view of the wide choice of diverse solutions and different insurance products.

Anyone who lives or works abroad, runs a company or retires there should arrange insurance cover that is as extensive as possible and applicable around the world. Health insurance in particular should allow the patient to choose his preferred doctor and hospital with as few restrictions as possible, and ideally none at all.

A question of residence

In the event of a temporary stay abroad with no change of residence, basic state insurance usually assures at least minimum cover within Europe in emergencies. In addition, almost all local health insurers offer the option of comprehensive cover for sickness and accident via private supplementary policies, even for temporary stays abroad. Before moving abroad definitely, however, it is useful to check out the insurance options in detail, from free choice of doctor and hospital to medication cover, as previous health policies normally terminate with a move abroad. In addition, unbroken insurance cover must be assured during the actual process of moving.

Comprehensive cover with a free choice of doctor and hospital worldwide is strongly recommended in most cases. This is because even in many developed countries the public healthcare system satisfies only minimum requirements and it is essential to seek out private hospitals to ensure competent medical treatment. There is no alternative to comprehensive insurance cover for anyone thinking of moving to, say, The Bahamas or the US, or to a developing country. Many countries have good local private health insurers, and some of them also offer international cover and a free choice of doctor and hospital. Although such a local insurer usually represents the least expensive solution, it is rarely the best one. It should be stressed that virtually all insurers with a local or national scope of activity in the relevant country will only accept policyholders who are actually resident in the country. Anyone who leaves the country again will normally lose his/her insurance cover, which can become an insoluble problem with increasing age. It is also difficult to obtain a truly international and unrestricted free choice of doctor and hospital in many places. So the ideal insurance policy will be independent of residence and duration of stay and will also guarantee fully comprehensive cover as far as possible. Most local insurers offer only unsatisfactory solutions if at all, and very few offer private health insurance which can be concluded or retained even when the policyholder lives abroad. So it is vital to check these important aspects, and in most cases it is worthwhile consulting an independent insurance advisor specializing in international health insurance.

Free choice of doctor and hospital, worldwide cover

Although an extensive choice of private health insurance schemes with an international scope is available worldwide, only very few can really be recommended. When comparing the various offers, it is important not merely to look at a specific insurance product but also at the financial soundness and reputation of the insurer, as well as the latter's experience in international health insurance. The insurance product which best satisfies the individual requirements must then be considered.

Private health insurers are not obliged to accept everyone. So anyone who is already over 55 years of age or is not perfectly healthy has little chance of obtaining private health insurance and still less comprehensive insurance with international cover. For this reason in particular, it is advisable to check out the insurance situation in detail before moving abroad. It may make sense to change over to an international health insurance scheme several years before a planned or possible move abroad in order to be assured of the necessary flexibility later on. Even if no transfer of residence is planned, but one wishes to be optimally insured against sickness and accident, a detailed review of all the options is worthwhile. It may even be of benefit to take out international health insurance in this case.

Anyone staying abroad frequently or planning to move abroad permanently should arrange insurance cover independently of residence and sojourn – i.e. inclusive of any subsequent moves abroad or even a return home at a later stage. Such cover will ideally permit an unrestricted choice of doctor and hospital worldwide.

Checklist: International health insurance

In selecting suitable health insurance, care should be taken to consider the following points:

- Worldwide cover at attractive premiums. It is also important to consider premiums in higher age brackets
- Free choice of physician and hospital worldwide without restrictions
- No restrictions on the policyholder's residence and duration of stay, even in the event of a later permanent return to the home country
- Guaranteed lifelong policy renewal, even in the event of a later change of residence, or illness of longer duration etc.
- Efficient processing in the event of a claim
- Multilingual emergency telephone service manned around the clock throughout the year

- Choosing an insurance company which is well known and has a good reputation as well as broad experience in the domain of international health insurance

15.5 Other types of insurance

Many factors which apply to health insurance are also relevant to other kinds of insurance. However, they are less critical for the latter because property, personal liability and similar cover can usually be arranged or modified at any time irrespective of the age and state of health of the policyholder, i.e. also at a later stage. And in complete contrast to health insurance, it is often best to conclude this kind of insurance policy directly with a local insurer. However, it makes sense to clarify certain issues before actually moving in this case too.

For every insurance policy, it is important to check whether the cover continues to apply indefinitely after a move, only for a short time or expires immediately. It should also be checked whether any kind of restrictions apply, for instance in a geographical sense (such as motor vehicle insurance). It is always advisable to clarify these matters in writing via letters to the respective insurers. Then, in the event of damage claims later on, the insurer's comments or commitment can be indubitably demonstrated. An individual confirmation on the insurer's letterhead is also better than mere reference to the insurance conditions, as these may change and will always offer scope for discretionary interpretation. A policyholder is best assured by an unequivocal inquiry addressed to the insurer and an unequivocal reply which can be insisted on.

As already mentioned, it usually makes sense or may even be mandatory to conclude insurance policies for items such as household effects, motor vehicles, private liability, jewelry or objets d'art locally in the new country of residence. In some cases, however, such as for vacation homes, art collections or jewellery it may also be wise to arrange insurance in one's home country or via an international insurer. Special insurers with worldwide operations are particularly relevant for items such as larger and expensive furnishings or art.

15.6 Financial and estate planning

Anyone transferring their residence abroad will find that various parameters of their personal financial and estate planning will also change. Having previously been oriented to the legal and fiscal situation and general framework conditions prevailing in the home country, these must now be revised to cover conditions abroad.

Anyone who moves to a part of the world dominated by the Euro should readjust to this as now the local reference currency rather than the US Dollar, Sterling, Australian Dollar, etc., and vice-versa. It may, however, still make good sense to retain investments in other currencies. As a rule, a move of a person's regular activities to a new currency zone will also lead to different weighting of the currencies in their personal investment portfolio and will require a re-think of their financial planning and asset management arrangements. It may well be wise to consult a specialized investment advisor familiar with cross-border issues.

A move abroad also offers the opportunity for more flexible pension planning, as capital tied to government-regulated pension funds can often be released. Previous retirement provisions may have to be reorganized, liquidated or taken out prematurely (e.g. life insurance policies, pension claims, tied-up assurance funds etc.). It is particularly important to consider withholding taxes when receiving payouts from pension institutions and any tax concessions when drawing any benefits in the form of pensions or capital payouts. As a rule, different costs of living also change the provision requirement and usually make it necessary to adapt one's cash planning strategy.

A move will also require careful examination of previous estate planning or succession structures (partnerships, foundations, trusts, family holding companies and the like). Here too, considerable scope may be available for optimization depending on one's destination. Thus anyone moving for example to Antigua and Barbuda, The Bahamas, Ireland, Malta, St. Kitts and Nevis or the UK can structure their assets by means of suitable succession structures so that they are transferred without restrictions and in many cases also in tax-neutral form to freely designated inheritors. The situation will be quite different when moving to a country such as France or Spain, although here too various opportunities for optimization usually exist. In any case, existing estate-planning strategies should be checked and their adaptation to the new conditions and opportunities examined. Professional support is usually indispensable in this domain too.

It is also important to include the aspect of asset protection, especially in the US. In view of the peculiarities of the American legal system, which is characterized by a relatively low threshold of civil litigation, suitable measures to avoid excessive exposure of one's personal assets are indispensable. When moving to other countries too, it may make sense to structure at least some of one's assets – perhaps including real estate – so that they are safe from seizure. Suitably designed asset protection trusts as well as specially structured Swiss annuities and life insurance policies are available for this purpose.

16 Bibliography

Bärtels Andreas: Bäume und Sträucher für mittelEuropäische und mediterrane Gärten, Verlag Eugen Ulmer, Stuttgart 1991

Bauman Robert: The Complete Guide to Offshore Residence, Dual Citizenship and Second Passports, The Sovereign Society, Waterford 2001

Benedict Bert / Anderson Gordon: The Essential Homebuilder's Sourcebook, BNI Building News, 2001

Betten Rijkele: Income Tax Aspects of Emigration and Immigration of Individuals, IBFD Publications, Amsterdam 1998

Bird Richard / Slack Enid: International Handbook of Land and Property Taxation (Elgar Original Reference S.), Edward Elgar, Aldershot 2004

Blake Fanny: A Place in the Sun: Favourite Destinations. A guide to buying your dream home in Spain, Italy, Portugal and France, Channel 4 Books, 2003

Bolz Norbert / Ehlers Ernst-August / Grune Jörg / Korth H.-Michael / Moritz Joachim: Grundstückserwerb und Besteuerung von Nichtresidenten in Spanien, Aktuelles Steuerrecht, Special Volume 7, Richard Boorberg Verlag, Stuttgart 2002

Brueggeman William B. / Fisher Jeffrey: Real Estate Finance and Investments, 11th edition, McGraw-Hill, 2001

Cadman D. / Topping R: Property Development, Spon Press, London 1995

Cahiers De Droit Fiscal International: Tax Treatment of Transfer of Residence by Individuals (IFA Cahiers S.), International Fiscal Association, Kluwer Law International, 2002

Chao Sheau-yueh: Internet Resources and Services for International Real Estate Information, Oryx Press, Westport 2001

Coutalides Reto (Editor) / Ganz Roland / Sträuli Walter: Innenraumklima, Werd-Verlag, Zurich 2002

Corporate and Individual Taxes: Worldwide Summaries, Edited by PwC PriceWaterhouseCoopers, John Wiley & Sons, Chichester, 2003

Davey Charles: The Complete Guide to Buying Property in France: Buying, Renting, Letting and Selling, Kogan Page, London 2004

Davey Charles: The Complete Guide to Buying Property in Spain: Buying, Renting, Letting and Selling, Kogan Page, London 2004

Jeremy Davies: The "Which?" Guide to Buying Property Abroad, Which? Books, 2004

Drexel Thomas: Mediterrane Häuser und ihre Gärten. Griechenland, Portugal, Spanien, Italien: richtig kaufen – gekonnt renovieren – landschaftsgerecht gestalten, Callwey, Munich 2001

Ferid Murad / Firsching Karl / Dörner Heinrich / Hausmann Rainer: Internationales Erbrecht, Loseblatt-Quellensammlung mit systematischen Darstellungen des materiellen Erbrechts sowie des Kollisionsrechts der wichtigsten Staaten, Verlag C. H. Beck, Munich

Förster Hartmut: Praxis der Besteuerung von Auslandsbeziehungen. Typische Fallgestaltungen für Personen- und Kapitalgesellschaften im In- und Ausland, 2nd edition, Luchterhand, Munich 2003

Frank Susanne: Bauträgerrecht in Europa, Mitteilungen des Bayerischen Notarvereins, der Notarkasse und der Landesnotarkammer Bayern, March/April 2001, p. 113 ff

Friedman Jack P. / Harris Jack C. / Lindeman J. Bruce: Dictionary of Real Estate Terms, 6th Edition, Barron's Educational Series, Hauppauge NY, 2004

Gadow Sandy: The Complete Guide to Your Real Estate Closing: Answers to All Your Questions – From Opening Escrow, to Negotiating Fees, to Signing the Closing Papers, McGraw-Hill, 2002

Grandjean Etienne: Wohnphysiologie. Grundlagen gesunden Wohnens, Verlag für Architektur Artemis, Zurich 1973

Grotherr Siegfried: Handbuch der internationalen Steuerplanung, 2nd edition, Verlag Neue Wirtschafts Briefe, Herne 2003

Grotherr Siegfried / Herfort Claus / Strunk Günter u. a.: Internationales Steuerrecht, 2nd edition, Erich Fleischer Verlag, Osnabrück 2003

Gulbenkian Paul / Badoux Ted: Entry and Residence in Europe: Business Guide to Immigration Rules, John Wiley & Sons, Chichester 1997

Hayton David: European Succession Laws, Jordans, Bristol 2003

Heinl Leo J.: Immobilien kaufen im Ausland, Walhalla Verlag, Regensburg, Bonn 1998.

Henrich Dieter / Schwab Dieter / Nagel Andrea: Familienerbrecht und Testierfreiheit im Europäischen Vergleich, Verlag Ernst und Werner Gieseking, Bielefeld 2001

Herfurth Ulrich: Immobilienerwerb in Europa, Economica Verlag, Bonn 1998

Hines M. A.: Investing in International Real Estate, Quorum Books, Westport/London 2001

Hinks John / Cook Geoff: The Technology of Building Defects, Spon Press, London 1997

Hodgkinson Liz: The Complete Guide to Buying Property Abroad, Kogan Page, London 2003

Hodgkinson Liz: The Complete Guide Letting Property, Kogan Page, London 2004

The Homebuilder's Handbook: The Ultimate Guide to Sourcing Building Materials and Services, Ascent Publishing, 2004

Igoe Mark / Howell John: Buying a Property: France, Cadogan Guides, London 2002

Isphording Stephan: Der ideale Grundriss, Callwey Verlag, Munich 1997

Kälin Christian H.: Global Residence and Citizenship Handbook, 4th Edition, Revised and Expanded, Ideos Publications, New York/London/Zurich/Hong Kong, 2014

Kälin Christian H.: Switzerland Business and Investment Handbook, 3rd Edition, Revised and Expanded, Orell Füssli Verlag AG, Zurich, 2010

Kälin Christian H.: Internationales Immobilienhandbuch, 3rd Edition, 3. überarbeitete und erweiterte Auflage, Orell Füssli Verlag, Zürich, 2009

Koch Wilfried: Baustilkunde, Orbis Verlag, Munich 1994

Karp James / Klayman Elliot I. / Gibson Frank / Mthembu-Salter Lindiwe: Real Estate Law, 5th Edition, Dearborn Trade Publishing, Chicago 2003

Kroiss Ludwig: Internationales Erbrecht. Einführung und Länderüberblick, Verlag C. H. Beck, Munich 1999

Leisse Bernhard: Holz natürlich behandeln, Oberflächen im Haus färben, schützen, pflegen, C. F. Müller Verlag, Heidelberg / Alembik Verlag, Braunschweig 1994

Losh John Brian (Editor): Who's Who in Luxury Real Estate, John Brian Losh, Inc., Seattle 2003

McCluskey William: Property Tax: An International Comparative Review, Ashgate Publishing, 1999

Mehlin Günther / Germann Albrecht / Kownatzki Ralf: NatursteinLexikon, Callwey Verlag, Munich 2003

Nicholson Dawn / Layman Richard P. / Williams Robert Lee: International Private Wealth: Tax Planning in the UK and the US, Tolley Publishing, 2004

O'Grady Sarah: The Complete Guide to Buying & Selling Property. How to get the best deal on your home, Kogan Page, London 2004

Parnham Phil / Rispin Chris: Residential Property Appraisal, Taylor & Francis, London 2000.

Paradis fiscaux et opérations internationales. Pays et zones à fiscalité privilégiée, Mesures antiévasion, Editions Francis Lefebvre, Paris 2002

Pownall Katy: No Going Back - Buying Abroad: Making a New Life in the Sun, Time Warner, 2004

Renouf Norman / Howell John: Buying a Property: Spain, Cadogan Guides, London 2002

Rostron J.: Dictionary of Property and Construction Law, Spon Press, London 2001

Sandner Siegfried / Weber Ulrich: Lexikon der Immobilienwertermittlung, Bundesanzeiger, 2003

Scarrett D.: Property Valuation, Spon Press, London 1991

Schmitz-Günther Thomas: Lebensräume, Der grosse Ratgeber für ökologisches Bauen und Wohnen, Könemann, Cologne 1998

Schneider Ulrich / Knoblauch Harald: Bauchemie, 5th edition, Werner Verlag, Düsseldorf 2001

Schöllhorn Peter: Irgendwo im Süden, wo es warm ist ... Vorruhestand und Ruhestand im Ausland, Deutsche Schutzvereinigung Auslandsimmobilien e. V., Freiburg im Breisgau 2000

Schöllhorn Peter: Sicherheit und Versicherungen für Auslandsimmobilien, 2nd edition, Deutsche Schutzvereinigung Auslandsimmobilien e.V., Freiburg im Breisgau 2003

Scholz Wilhelm / Knoblauch Harald / Hiese Wolfram: Baustoffkenntnis, 14th edition, Werner Verlag, Düsseldorf 1999

Scognamiglio Donato: Methoden der Immobilienbewertung, Hauseigentümerverband Schweiz, 2002

Smith C.G. / Pearce E.A.: The World Weather Guide, 3rd edition, Helicon Publishing, Oxford 1994

Sous Maria Constança Dias Urbano: Das Timesharing an Ferienimmobilien in der EU: eine rechtsvergleichende Studie unter Berücksichtigung der Timesharing-Richtlinie (94/47/EG), Nomos Verlagsgesellschaft, Baden-Baden 1998

Steiner Claus: Immobilienfinanzierung in den Ländern der Europäischen Gemeinschaft. Ein Überblick, Fritz Knapp Verlag, Frankfurt am Main 1990

Tessenow Heinrich: Hausbau und dergleichen, Vieweg Verlagsgesellschaft, Wiesbaden 1998

Tolley's International Handbook of Corporate and Personal Taxes, Butterworths Tolley, 2003

Tonner Klaus: Das Recht des Timesharing an Ferienimmobilien, Verlag C. H. Beck, Munich 1997

Torpey John: The Invention of the Passport. Surveillance, Citizenship and the State, Cambridge University Press, Cambridge, 2000

Weise, Stefan (editor): Beck'sches Formularbuch Immobilienrecht, C. H. Beck, Munich 2001.

Weise, Stefan (editor): Beck'sches Formularbuch Immobilienrecht, Supplement to the 1st edition, C. H. Beck, Munich 2003

Williams Martha R. / Ventolo William L.: Fundamentals of Real Estate Appraisal, 8th Edition, Dearborn Trade Publishing, Chicago 2001

Youngman Joan M. / Malme Jane H.: An International Survey of Taxes on Land and Buildings, Kluwer Law International, Amsterdam 1994

Zullinger Jürg: Umbauen & modernisieren, Ueberreuter Verlag, Vienna 2001

PART 2

Individual Countries

17

Austria

Republic of Austria
Republik Österreich

by

Mag. Dr. Peter Madl

Dr. Michael Lagler, LL.M.

Schönherr Attorneys at Law
Schottenring 19, A-1010 Vienna
Austria

Telephone: +43 1 534 37 – 50231
Facsimile: +43 1 534 37 – 66231

m.lagler@schoenherr.eu
p.madl@schoenherr.eu
schoenherr.eu

Peter Madl is a Partner at Schönherr Attorney's at Law in Vienna and was admitted to the bar in Austria in 1990. His practice areas are real estate and IT. He was educated at the Vienna University of Economics and Business (Mag. rer. soc. oec. 1987) and the University of Vienna, Austria (Dr. iur. 1983). Peter is the author of articles and books on real estate law, IT law, private law and product liability and is lecturer at the Law School of the Vienna University where he holds lectures on International Real Estate Transactions and at the Vienna University of Economics and Business. He speaks German, English and French.

Michael Lagler is a Partner at Schönherr Attorney's at Law in Vienna and was admitted to the bar in Austria in 2001. His practice areas are real estate, corporate real estate (M&A), energy, outsourcing and CEE Business Law. He was educated at the University of Salzburg (Mag. iur. 1994, Dr. iur. 1996); Pallas Consortium, Nijmegen, The Netherlands (LL.M. 1997). He has authored various articles relating to real estate and CEE Business Law and is also the co-author of the Handbuch des internationalen GmbH-Rechts. He speaks German and English.

17.1 Introduction

Located in the southern part of central Europe, Austria has a total area of 83,879 square kilometers and is composed of nine independent federal states. The total population of Austria in 2014 was 8.5 million, with 1.8 million people living in Vienna, Austria's largest city and capital. Austria is a well-developed country with a generally strong economy and one of the highest standards of living in Europe. Major industries in Austria include tourism, construction, vehicles and parts, food, chemicals, timber and wood processing.

The main statutes in relation to real estate transactions are the *General Civil Code*, the *Land Register Act*, the *Laws on the Acquisition of Land by Foreigners and Acquisition of Agricultural and Forestry Land* of the nine federal states, the *Tenancy Act* and the *Act on Brokers*.

The acquisition of specific types of land, such as agricultural and forestry land, and the acquisition of real estate by foreigners are restricted by the *Laws on the Acquisition of Land by Foreigners and Acquisition of Agricultural and Forestry Land* (*Grundverkehrsgesetze*) of the nine federal states.

Regulations for investment funds have existed in Austria since 1963. However, these rules apply only to mere investment funds in securities. To establish regulations for investment funds investing in real estate, the Austrian Parliament enacted the *Real Estate Investment Fund Act* (*Immobilien-Investmentfondsgesetz*) in 2003, which regulates, *inter alia*, in which assets the real estate fund may invest, which entities are entitled to administer a real estate investment fund, the appraisal of assets, prospectus, supervision and tax treatment etc.

17.2 Real estate ownership

Different forms and types of ownership

General

Generally the *General Civil Code* (*ABGB*) follows the principle, '*superficies solo cedit*'. This means that the proprietor of land also owns buildings erected and located thereon, which are solidly connected with the ground (exceptions: building rights and superedifices).

Furthermore, acquisition of real estate requires both title (e.g. purchase contract) and modus by registration with the Land Register (*Grundbuch*).

Sole ownership and co-ownership

Besides sole ownership (*Alleineigentum*) entitling the owner to make use of the substance of and the proceeds from a property, Austrian law recognizes co-ownership of two or more persons (*Miteigentum*), which can be created, *inter alia*, by agreement. Fractions of the ownership right, not the real estate itself, are divided among the co-owners. Accordingly, each co-owner can dispose of the ownership right to the extent of his portion thereof at his own discretion (e.g. pledge, sale). Each co-owner has the right to participate in the earnings of the jointly owned real estate and the obligation to bear costs and expenses in proportion to his or her ownership interests.

Condominium

The condominium (*Wohnungseigentum*) is regulated by the *Condominium Act* (*Wohnungseigentumsgesetz 2002 - WEG*) and grants a co-owner of a real estate the exclusive right to exclusively use a certain unit, such as an apartment, business premises or parking space, in a building located thereon. The creation of condominium is based, on a written agreement by all co-owners, a judgment decision or a division of marital savings. The unit connected with a condominium can be transferred and inherited.

Right to build

A right to build (*Baurecht*) is the transferable and inheritable right of one or more persons to construct (permanent) buildings on or beneath the surface of a certain piece of land. Rights to build are regulated in the *Building Right Act* (*Baurechtsgesetz*) and may be granted for a period of not less than 10 and not more than 100 years. The holder of the building right is owner of the erected building, but not of the land on which such building is located. The building right can be transferred, encumbered, and divided. The building right is deemed to be immovable property and is registered separately (with its own lot number) in the Land Register.

Superedifice

A superedifice (*Superädifikat*) is a non-permanent construction built on another person's property with the intention that it should not always remain there. Accordingly, the ownership of the building and the ownership of the land are assigned to different persons. Thus, the constructor of the building must obtain the right of use from the owner of the relevant land before starting to erect the building. Superedifices are deemed movable property even if constructed in a solid manner. Therefore, transfer of title and other rights regarding a superedifice do not require registration with the Land Register. The proprietorship in superedifices is transferred by depositing the relevant contract with the *Document Deposit Register* (*Urkundenhinterlegungsregister*) at the competent district court.

Timesharing

According to the *Directive 94/47/EC*, which was implemented by way of the *Timesharing Act* (*Teilzeitnutzungsgesetz - TNG*), timesharing is the right to use a piece of real estate, usually a vacation home, on a recurring basis during a specified period. Timesharing can have different forms, such as co-ownership or usufruct. Another possibility is the acquisition of shares of a company owning real estate.

Easements, charges, covenants and mortgages

Easements in general

Easements are regulated by the *General Civil Code* and are limited rights *in rem*, which grant the right of use of a property in favor of another real estate (*Grunddienstbarkeit*) or a person (*persönliche Dienstbarkeit*). The right to use a property is granted by the owner of such property. As beneficiary *in rem*, the holder of an easement has an absolutely protected legal position, which may be asserted vis-à-vis any other party as soon as the easement has been enrolled in the Land Register.

Scope and term of an easement

The scope of an easement depends on the content of the underlying title (e.g. an easement contract), in particular the foreseeable purpose of the easement. To become a right *in rem*, easements must be registered in the Land Register. The beneficiary is responsible for the establishment and the maintenance of the subject-matter of the easement.

An easement expires *inter alia* by destruction of the servant real estate, by lapse of time (if the easement is limited with respect to time), by abandonment or confiscation. In addition, easements may expire within 30 years due to non-use or within three years if use is hindered by measures set by the owner of the servant real estate (e.g. blocking a right of way with a locked door).

Real easements, personal easements, explicit easements

Real easements must be distinguished from personal easements. In the case of real easements, the easement belongs to the owner of a specified real estate, the "dominant real estate". Personal easements are the right of usufruct or the right of abode and are connected to a person. The acquirer of real estate (where a third party obtains easement rights) also assumes any non-registered easements, if they are evident so that the existence of an easement may be assumed, in particular by visible construction or other visible signs of use.

Charges on land

Charges on land (*Reallasten*) are encumbrances of real estate obligating the owner of the real estate to perform recurrent services, e.g. payment of annuities, etc.

Restraints on alienation and encumbrance

Austrian law recognizes statutory, jurisdictional and contractual restraints on alienation and encumbrance of real estate (*Veräußerungs- und Belastungsverbote*). Statutory restraints may apply where construction or refurbishment of real estate is totally or partly financed by public funds. In such case, the disposal of the property is generally subject to prior approval by the relevant authority. Contractual restraints on alienation and encumbrance are only binding among the contracting parties, except in case the restriction was agreed to operate in favor of parents, children or spouses and is registered with the Land Register.

Leases

Leases under Austrian law must be distinguished from leases *in rem*, as they are known in Anglo-Saxon law. In Austria, leases are classified under the law of contracts and not under the law of real estate. They do not constitute an encumbrance on real estate, but constitute a mere contractual relationship between lessor and lessee. As a matter of principle, a lease will not be terminated by the sale of the real estate after the object of lease has been handed over to the lessor. However, the new owner can terminate the lease under the legal notice period irrespective of the term originally agreed.Only if the lease contract is subject to the Tenancy Act or if it is registered in the land register is the new owner also bound by the original agreement or the lease period and the notice period.

A lease contract can be registered as an encumbrance in the *C-folio* of the relevant Land Register entry for a specific period of time with a waiver of the termination right for a certain period. In case of a transfer of the real estate, the new owner is then obliged to take over the lease contract as concluded with the prior owner. According to the registration of the lease the payments of the lessee made in advance are secured vis-à-vis the new owner.

Liens and mortgages

A mortgage (*Hypothek*) is a pledge of real estate. The creation of a mortgage is subject to a mortgage agreement (*Pfandbestellungsvertrag*), which must be drawn up in writing. The signatures of the parties to the contract have to be duly notarized by a notary or a court to allow an entry in the Land Register.

The mortgage agreement may be made in the form of a notarial deed and may contain a clause which certifies that the mortgage agreement establishes an executory right. Thereby, the bank is enabled to enforce the mortgage immediately in enforcement proceedings without the necessity of prior court proceedings in order to obtain a final and enforceable judgement for enforcement proceedings.

Mortgages have to be registered in the Land Register in order to become fully effective; particularly with regard to third parties. While a legal transaction involving real estate is not registered, the party to the contract has only a contractual claim for performance against the other contracting party.

It is possible and common practice to register more than one mortgage in respect of one piece of real estate. The ranking is established in general in the order of the date of filing of the application for registration of the mortgage with the Land Register. Changes in ranking are possible upon duly notarized approval by all parties involved. The proceeds of a sale of an encumbered real estate are distributed among the secured creditors in the order of their rank.

Protection of ownership, proof of ownership and registration

Land Register

The Land Register (*Grundbuch*) covers the real estate of a district and is kept by the district court of the district where the property is situated. It is held on an electronic database that is publicly accessible, e.g. to notary publics, attorneys and banks. Excerpts can either be obtained from any district court or in electronic form from other institutions having access.

The Land Register consists of the general ledger (*Hauptbuch*) and archives (*Urkundensammlung*). The general ledger contains a Land Register enclosure (*Grundbuchseinlage*) for each existing surface area, which also includes an estate's lot number (*Einlagezahl, EZ*).

The individual enclosure contains three parts (folios):

- A-folio (*Gutbestandsblatt*), which covers two departments, in the first department (the A1-folio), properties are registered with their respective lot number and disposition of use and size; the second department (the A2-folio) contains the rights and encumbrances (e.g. clearance areas) connected with the real estate (e.g. easements on the entitled property, write-offs, public restrictions and burdens)
- B-folio (*Eigentumsblatt*), which contains details about the proprietorship structures
- C-folio (*Lastenblatt*), which shows encumbrances on the real estate, in particular mortgages, easements, real burdens, prohibitions of sale or encumbrances, etc.

Principle of registration

Under Austrian law, any grant, transfer or limitation of rights pertaining to real estate generally has to be registered in the relevant Land Register in order to become effective *vis à vis* third parties. Therefore, e.g. a proprietorship in real estate may – except in the case of adverse possession, inheritance, merger and demerger (universal succession) – only be transferred on grounds relating to a legal title (e.g. purchase contract) by registration in the Land Register (*Einverleibung*). As long as a legal transaction involving real estate is not registered, the party to the contract has only a contractual claim for performance against the other contracting party.

Principle of good faith

Every person may fully rely on the correctness and completeness of Land Register entries. As in other jurisdictions, any person relying in good faith on information contained in the Land Register is protected against third party claims, even if the registered information turns out to be inaccurate or incomplete.

Principle of predecessor in title

Title to real estate may only be acquired from the registered predecessor. By way of exception, acquisition of title from a non-registered person is possible if the chain of transfer of title is proven from the last registered owner to the ultimate buyer.

Principle of priority

According to the principle of priority, the ranking order of multiple registrations for a certain property is determined by the date of filing of each application with the relevant Land Register court (first come, first served). This principle is particularly significant for the registration of mortgages and other encumbrances.

Registration procedure

The beneficiary of a registration must file an *application for registration* (*Grundbuchsgesuch*) with the competent district court. Depending on the nature of registration, specific documents supporting the granting, transfer or limitation of rights to be registered must be attached (e.g. contract regarding title). Certain real estate transactions require the form of a notarial deed. In all cases, however, the signatures of the parties involved must be duly notarized. Furthermore, where real estate is purchased by foreigners, the application must be accompanied by a certificate or notification of the land transfer authority approving the registration and, in the case of transfer of ownership, a confirmation of the tax authority (or the notary or an attorney at law) must be submitted to the Land Register, verifying the payment of the land transfer tax and the registration fee due.

The application must be submitted electronically and all supporting documents must be uploaded to a database from where the courts can download the documents. The upload of documents and the electric filing can be done by notaries or attorneys at law.

17.3 Purchase and sale of real estate

The sales agreement

General

According to the principle of private autonomy, parties may establish a contractual relationship at their free discretion within the framework of *bonos mores* (*Gute Sitten*). A contract is concluded by the expression of the mutual consent of the parties, either simultaneously by both parties or by the acceptance (*Annahme*) of a prior offer (*Angebot*).

A preliminary agreement (*Vorvertrag*) under Austrian law is an agreement which exclusively provides the obligation to enter into a particular agreement at a later date. Each party may only demand the conclusion but not a specific performance of the main contract.

An option granting one party the right to enforce a determined agreement in content is comparable to a preliminary agreement. However, due to the fact that contractual obligations are directly created upon exercising the option, the other party may demand specific performance.

A *Punktation* is an agreement which contains only the essential provisions of a contract. Although a *Punktation* is more of a framework than a complete contract, it is considered binding, and the parties may claim specific performance of the contract.

Material requirements of a sales agreement

The conclusion of a sales agreement is preceded by the consent of the parties to the essential parts of the agreement. The sales agreement must designate the parties, the real estate and the purchase price or the method of its calculation.

Furthermore, the seller has to formally approve the registration of the buyer in the Land Register. The seller usually grants this consent (*Aufsandungserklärung*) in the sales agreement, although it may also be expressed in a separate document. The agreement to register must be made in writing and certified by a district court or a notary public. These formal requirements do not affect the validity of the agreement, but are required for the registration in the Land Register. Therefore, oral agreements or side agreements are valid and binding upon the parties.

Other terms customary for real estate purchase contracts are representations and warranties (relating, for example, to encumbrances and third party rights, to the zoning of the real estate and building regulations, environmental issues, administrative and corporate approvals, taxes, etc.), the agreement concerning the acceptance of encumbrances, the appointment of an escrow agent, and the obligation to register priority notices. In many cases, the prospective buyer obliges the seller to deliver to him (or to the trustee under the agreement) a ranking order of the intended sale (*Rangordnung der beabsichtigten Veräußerung*), a decree executed in only one counterpart safeguarding that no entry in the register affected by the potential seller may precede the purchase by the buyer. Such a decree is valid for one year.

Governing law and jurisdiction

The parties are free to choose the law governing the contract and the court that shall have jurisdiction over any disputes relating to the contract. As far as rights *in rem* concerning real estate located in Austria are concerned, Austrian law is, however, mandatory. Furthermore, any disputes concerning such rights *in rem* mandatorily fall within the jurisdiction of the Austrian courts.

Restrictions on sale and acquisition

Restrictions under family law and matrimonial property regime

According to the *Act on International Private Law* (*Internationales Privatrechtsgesetz*), questions of matrimonial property law are in principle to be regulated according the legal order that was expressly chosen by the spouses (party autonomy). If the spouses have not chosen any legal order, the matrimonial property issues are to be regulated according to the statute that was applicable for the legal effects of marriage at the time of the wedding. If the parties are nationals of Austria and of another state, then Austrian citizenship will take precedence.

As far as matrimonial property is concerned, the law regulates two types of matrimonial property regimes, namely the separation of property (*Gütertrennung*) and the community of property (*Gütergemeinschaft*).

Austrian law prefers the regime of separation; therefore, if the spouses did not provide for any agreement on their matrimonial property, the regime of separation will be applicable. According to the separation of property regime, each spouse retains sole ownership to the property that he/she brought into the marriage and will be the sole owner of what he/she will acquire or inherit during marriage.

If a marriage is dissolved by either divorce or invalidation, the property that has been acquired by the spouses during their marriage is divided according to the rules of the *Matrimonial Act* (*Ehegesetz*) without regard to ownership.

A marriage contract (*Ehepakt*) is a contract in the form of a notarial deed on the regulation of the matrimonial property regime between the spouses. It replaces or modifies the legal matrimonial property regime of separation of property.

Options and rights of pre-emption

If a real estate is subject to a pre-emption right (*Vorkaufsrecht*), the owner of the real estate has to offer the real estate first to the beneficiary of the right of pre-emption at the terms and conditions agreed with a potential buyer. The pre-emptor may exercise his right within 30 days otherwise it expires. Provided that pre-emptive rights are registered with the Land Register, a transfer of the real estate in violation thereof is null and void. Generally, the right of pre-emption is not transferable and not inheritable.

Another subsidiary agreement to the purchase contract is the agreement on a re-purchase right (*Wiederkaufsrecht*). If the real estate is subject to a re-purchase, the seller of the real estate has the right to re-purchase the real estate according to the terms and conditions agreed in the former purchase contract. The right can only be granted when a property is sold and can neither be transferred nor bequeathed. Furthermore, it cannot be subject to execution.

By registration in the Land Register, the re-purchase right can be enforced against the buyer as well as against third parties subsequently acquiring the real estate from the buyer.

Additionally, parties to the sales agreement can agree to resell (*Rückverkaufsrecht*) the real estate. In this case, the buyer has the right to request the seller to purchase the real estate for a specified price. This right is not transferable or inheritable either.

Agricultural real estate

The land transfer laws of the federal states restrict the purchase of specific types of land, such as agricultural and forestry land, in various ways. These laws mainly apply to the maintenance of agricultural areas in certain regions. Under these acts, the acquisition of certain rights, such as ownership, right of usage (usus fructus; *Fruchtgenuss*), building rights or long-term leases with respect to real estate used for agricultural and forestry purposes requires prior approval by or, in certain cases, notification to the competent land transfer authority (*Grundverkehrsbehörde*) for Austrian as well as for foreign buyers.

Restrictions regarding acquisition of properties by foreigners

The acquisition of real estate by foreigners is restricted by the *Laws on the Acquisition of Land by Foreigners and of agricultural and forestry land* (*Grundverkehrsgesetze*) of the federal states. This, depending on the respective state, is also true for the acquisition of certain rights like usufruct (*Fruchtgenuss*), building rights or long-term leases.

In almost every federal state of Austria, foreigners are required to obtain a permit (prior approval) from the land transfer authority in order to purchase land. This also applies for companies where a foreigner is a majority shareholder.

Under many *Land Transfer Acts*, the acquisition of shares or the increase of shareholdings in an Austrian limited liability company or partnership is subject to the prior approval of the land transfer authority if this company or partnership owns real estate located in the relevant states. Some states do not apply restrictions to companies whose majority shareholder is an Austrian company controlled by a foreigner. Therefore, a foreign investor may avoid having to obtain a permit by setting up two companies, one of which is the majority shareholder of the company purchasing the real estate.

Under all *Land Transfer Acts*, *EEA/EU* citizens and companies are treated like Austrian citizens/companies. Also Swiss citizens (but not Swiss companies) are treated like Austrians.

Furthermore, in certain municipalities which the law qualifies as preserved regions (*Vorbehaltsgemeinden*), an approval by the land transfer authority must be obtained even by Austrian citizens acquiring real estate for the purpose of establishing a second domicile.

Various restrictions are also set forth in the *Federal Act on Urban Modernization* (*Stadterneuerungsgesetz*). The acquisition of land which is located in what are known as 'clearance areas' (*Assanierungsgebiete*) designated by states or municipalities is restricted thereunder. The municipality is granted a pre-emptive right in regard of such land.

Further important preconditions for buying real estate

Capacity and entitlement of the seller

Minors (persons under 18) are especially protected by law. Real estate belonging to a minor may only be sold if this is necessary or if the advantages prevail. Further, such transactions require a tutelage court approval.

Third-party claims and unpaid taxes

Encumbrances on the real estate, in particular mortgages, easements, charges on land, prohibitions of sale or encumbrances, etc. should be checked before purchase by obtaining a register excerpt and visiting the premises to be purchased. Furthermore, an agreement concerning the assumption and deletion respectively of encumbrances should be inserted in the purchase contract. An inspection of the Land Register is therefore absolutely essential.

For special public encumbrances (such as the annual real estate tax) and the operating expenses due to the management company of a condominium. Austrian law recognizes legal mortgages that take absolute priority over all other registered encumbrances.

Provisions for protecting the environment, nature and cultural heritage

Several sources of environmental law, which encompass, more or less, public law as well as private environmental regulations have to be observed. In Austria, there are a number of environmental laws, including:

- Water Rights Act (*Wasserrechtsgesetz*)
- Waste Management Act (*Abfallwirtschaftsgesetz*)
- Contaminated Sites Act (*Altlastensanierungsgesetz*)
- General Civil Code (Allgemeines Bürgerliches Gesetzbuch)
- Trade Act (*Gewerbeordnung*) and its implementing ordinances
- Act on Presentation of Energy Performance Certificate (*Energieausweis-Vorlage-Gesetz*)

In general, the legislation follows the "polluter pays principle", which maintains that the person who caused the contamination is primarily responsible for repairing the damage or at least paying for the decontamination.

However, property owners who have not caused any contamination can also be held liable under certain circumstances.

The *Contaminated Sites Act* (*Altlastensanierungsgesetz*) provides that contaminated properties must be listed in a *Register of Potentially Contaminated Sites*. The Governors of the states are obliged to inform the *Federal Ministry for Environmental Affairs* about potentially contaminated sites that have been detected within their states. However, this information is listed in the aforementioned register for information purposes only and has no significant legal relevance. Moreover, absence from the list may under no circumstances provide proof that environmental burdens do not exist on a particular piece of land.

Acquisition of real estate that is protected as historic buildings or monuments may be restricted under Austrian law. Protected historic buildings and monuments in Austria are listed in a special register kept by the national monument authority at the *Federal Ministry of Education, Art and Culture*. Furthermore, they are shown in the Land Register. Buildings owned by the state, federal states, municipalities and other public entities are assumed to be protected until the monument authority explicitly confirms they are not. Therefore, an inquiry with the monument authority is recommended.

According to the *Act on Presentation of Energy Performance Certificates*, the seller or the lessor is obliged to present and hand over an energy performance certificate which is not older than 10 years to the buyer or lessee respectively.

Access to relevant records and documents

According to the principle of good faith, which may be of great consequence in legal proceedings, and to obtain general information about the real estate, it is advisable to search the publicly accessible Land Register, especially its general ledger and archives. It is advisable to inspect the real estate itself in order to identify obvious defects. The exact topographical location of the real estate is shown in the cadastral map as well as in the site plan. As soon as a piece of land has been entered by the land surveying office (*Vermessungsamt*) in the electronic cadastral map, the size and location of a real estate are fixed and no *bona fide* acquisition of land is possible (e.g. if the fence is already on the ground of the neighbour).

Information about corporations, partnerships and sole proprietorships may be obtained from the *Commercial Register* (*Firmenbuch*). In general, any person may rely on the accuracy of the information in the commercial register, unless proven otherwise. The commercial register is accessible online. An excerpt from the commercial register can be obtained also from the courts as well as from public notaries and attorneys.

Key points that a seller should consider

Under the sales agreement, the seller is obliged to sell and transfer title to the designated real estate to the buyer. It is therefore necessary to describe the real estate as well as the fittings and furniture in as much detail as possible.

Provisions relating to warranties are significant for both contracting parties.

The costs arising in connection with the execution of the sales agreement and the registration of the agreement and all taxes, stamp duties, and other charges imposed in connection with the execution and registration in the Land Register are usually borne by the buyer. This should be stated in the sales agreement. Both seller and buyer are liable to pay land transfer tax to the tax authorities.

The purchase price is usually withheld by a trustee until registration in the Land Register. Depending on the structure of the deal, parts of the purchase price may be withheld or secured by bank guarantees for possible warranty claims.

According to the *Insurance Contract Act* (*Versicherungsvertragsgesetz*), by passing title to the real estate, the rights and duties under an insurance contract will vest in the seller as long as the seller holds title, and they will pass to buyer upon registration. Both seller and buyer are liable to pay premiums for the current premium period. As long as the insurer has not been notified of a change of title, it may still release the insured sum to the seller without having any additional obligation towards the buyer. The buyer may terminate the policy within one month after title was registered in the Land Register, notwithstanding any contractual provisions to the contrary.

The execution of a real estate purchase transaction

The execution of a real estate purchase transaction involves the following steps:

- A search of the Land Register and building authority
- Inspection of the real estate to identify obvious defects, possibly with a building engineer or architect, in order to check the conformity of the building with its building permits and to check whether there are indications for unregistered easements
- Drafting of the sales agreement by an attorney or a notary public
- Negotiating with banks in the case of debt financing
- The conclusion of the contract and certification of the signatures by a district court or a notary public
- Registration of ownership (and mortgage) with the Land Register; transfer of title to the new owner

The attorney or notary public acting as the escrow agent must inform the buyer about the escrow provisions of the relevant notary or Bar Association of the federal state, especially with regard to the deposit of the purchase price on the escrow account. It is common practice that the purchase price is transferred to the seller once the buyer is registered in the Land Register.

Legal fees are governed by the *Attorneys' Tariff* (*Rechtsanwaltstarif*) and the *Autonomous Guidelines for Attorneys' Fees* (*Autonome Honorarrichtlinien*) issued by the *Austrian Bar Association*. However, with a few exceptions, attorneys may freely negotiate their fees with their clients, with the *Attorneys' Tariff* and the *Autonomous Guidelines* serving only as a guideline. Thus, for on-going consultation, client and attorney may agree on an hourly rate or a flat fee. However, it is generally prohibited to take over a case on a pure contingency fee basis.

According to the *Act on Brokers* (*Maklergesetz*), real estate agents are entitled to a commission upon execution of the contract as follows:

- Purchase or sale of real estate or condominium:

  3% of the purchase price, provided that the purchase price is above EUR 36,336.42. If the purchase price falls short of this amount, the commission rate increases to 4%

- Residential and commercial lease agreements:

  Commission of the tenant of up to three months' rent for commercial leases and up to two months' rent for residential leases

Powers of attorney

Both seller and buyer may issue a power of attorney to other persons, vesting them with authority to conclude a sales agreement. In this case, the power of attorney must be established with regard to the actual sales agreement and certified by court or a notary public. If foreigners are involved, the signature of the notary public must be superlegalized in most countries by affixing an Apostille pursuant to *The Hague Convention*.

Financing

Acquisition of real estate is often bank financed, where a mortgage is granted in favor of the bank. Depending on the lender's credit standing, banks may insist on the registration of the mortgage with the Land Register. It is possible to establish a mortgage in the form of an enforceable notarial deed, so that the bank may enforce the mortgage without the necessity of prior court proceedings in order to obtain a valid title for enforcement proceedings.

Purchase through a company.

Real estate can also be purchased, possessed and leased by legal entities, such as stock companies and limited liability companies or by partnerships, such as general partnerships or limited partnerships, as well as by private foundations.

The costs for the formation of the company must be considered, whereby the minimum share capital of, for example, a limited liability company is EUR 35,000. At least one half of the share capital must be paid up upon foundation or in assets (contribution in kind).

Similarly, foreign legal entities and partnerships with their corporate seat outside of Austria or legal entities that have their corporate seat in Austria but are controlled by foreigners, are able to purchase real estate as long as it is not restricted by the *Laws on the Acquisition of Land by Foreigners* of the federal states.

Warranty claims

Sales contracts on real estate frequently contain warranties relating to possible statutory liabilities of the buyer and/or defective or faulty performance of the seller.

The statutory warranty period for real estate is three years from the handing over (for factual defects) or from when the possibility arose to detect the fault (for legal defects); it can be extended or abbreviated by mutual agreement. Real estate contracts often provide for different warranty periods, depending on the issue warranted. The buyer must notify the seller of defects or defective performance within the relevant warranty period. If the seller does not accept the defect, the buyer has to sue in order to prevent the claim from becoming statute-barred. Six months after handing over, the buyer bears the burden of proof that the defect has existed when possession was transferred. Furthermore, buyer may claim damages in case of negligent or willful breach of contract.

17.4 New construction, rebuilding and renovation

Zoning law and construction permits

Building law, regional planning law and zoning regulations are subject to legislation of the federal states of Austria. The laws of the federal states vary in detail, but follow the same basic principles.

Zoning plan and building regulations

The building laws of the federal states provide for the basic material and procedural rules for regional development and building constructions. Based on these rules, each municipality enacts a zoning plan (*Flächenwidmungsplan*) and building regulations (*Bebauungsbestimmungen*) governing the development of certain areas of the municipality (e.g. building areas, recreation areas, industrial areas etc.), providing for the permitted use and maximum measures of construction to be respected in these areas.

Building permit

Prior to the construction of a new building, it is generally necessary to obtain a building permit (*Baubewilligung*). The *Building Acts* list the cases when a building permit has to be obtained exhaustively. Construction work may not be carried out before the permit has been granted and has become effective. Furthermore, a building permit is appurtenant to the property. Thus, the building permit is also effective vis-à-vis the successive owner of a property, even if it was granted to his predecessor. Such a building permit grants the right to carry out the building project underlying the application.

Neighbours whose piece of land directly borders the land on which the construction takes place are parties to the administrative proceedings; they may raise objections against the entire construction or parts thereof. If they have raised timely objections in the proceedings, they are entitled to appeal the building permit.

Architect's and building contracts

Architect's contracts should be concluded in writing, with detailed information about the construction work and fees, liability for infringement of copyright, terms for the implementation of the construction, right to change the building after erection without the consent of the architect, etc. Moreover, it is recommended to obtain proof of existing pecuniary damage liability insurance as the legal minimum is pretty low.

The responsibilities usually assigned to an architect are:

- Basic evaluation and drafting
- Planning for the purpose of the building permit
- Obtaining of the building permit
- Detailed planning of the implementation of the project
- Obtaining, verifying and assessing offers
- Arranging local building supervision to manage the realization of the project
- Ascertaining deficiencies, listing of the warranty periods

Completion of construction and formalities

Notification of completion

The completion of a construction project must be notified to the building authority (*Fertigstellungsanzeige*), which must be accompanied by the relevant certificates and a statement of the architect certifying the compliance of the building with the building permit.

Operating permit

According to the *Trade Code* (*Gewerbeordnung*), a localized plant that is operated for commercial reasons requires an operating permit from the local trade authorities. Environmental protection in particular, as well as the protection of neighbours from external influences such as noise and dirt, shall be prevented. The Trade Authority issuing the permit usually imposes a number of conditions in order to protect the environment or neighbours, which the owner of the plant or the factory must fulfill during operation. The operating permit is appurtenant to the plant. Therefore, such decrees authorize and oblige not only the current operator of the plant but also his legal successors.

This permit must be obtained before the start of the construction works.

Deficiencies and warranty claims regarding new construction

The conclusion of a wide-ranging building contract should be the basis for the successful assertion of defects *or deficiencies in construction* and warranty claims. *Austrian Standards* (*Ö-Normen*, e.g *Ö-NORM B2110*) have been established, which contain appropriate contract templates, but the parties are free to agree whether or not to use these templates.

For the successful assertion of defects *or deficiencies in construction* and warranty claims, a detailed documentation of the progress of construction work must be prepared. Furthermore, the work as ordered and work results must be compared. In the majority of cases, a lack of documentation of additional orders will result in disputes.

Building Development Contract Act

Building development contracts are contracts on the acquisition of property or leasing rights to buildings, condominium apartments and office space which are not yet built or which will be subject to rigorous renovation. The *Building Development Contract Act* (*Bauträgervertragsgesetz*) protects the buyer vis-à-vis the developer, and provides, *inter alia*, for a withdrawal of the buyer's offer, provision of security against losses, appointment of an escrow agent and a 2% retainer for the warranty period of three years.

Building development contracts must be made in writing and contain certain minimum information relating, *inter alia*, to the subject matter of the contract, the consideration and the date on which the consideration is payable, the latest date of delivery, encumbrances, if any, assumed by the buyer, designation of a security for the buyer's payments to the developer and nomination of an escrow agent.

The developer must designate a security for all repayment claims the buyer may have under the building development contract. The security may be an *in personam* security (guarantee, surety, insurance), a lien on another real estate, a bank, insurance company or a public entity or a payment schedule, which follows the progress of the construction of the building. If no *in personam* security is provided, an attorney-at-law or a notary public must be appointed as escrow agent.

The application of the *Building Development Contract Act* cannot be waived by consumers; businessmen are free to waive its application.

17.5 Rental and tenancy

Rental and leasing agreements

Austrian laws regarding leases are highly restrictive. Lease agreements for residential and business purposes are mainly governed by the Tenancy Act (*Mietrechtsgesetz*). The Tenancy Act does not apply to real estate leased in connection with the tourist industry, parking houses, warehouses, employee housing, leases for a definite period not exceeding six months and apartments used for recreation, houses with not more than two separately leasable objects of lease (top-floor apartments erected after the erection of the building do not count). If the premises are part of a building newly erected without public funds after 30 June 1953, only parts of the Tenancy Act will be applicable.

Regulations on protection of tenants and rent control

The Tenancy Act intends mainly to protect the lessee's interests. Therefore, court decisions under the Tenancy Act are restrictive, especially with regard to regulated rent for specified types of leases, the conclusion of leases for a limited period of time and notice of termination given by the lessor. The provisions of the Tenancy Act are mandatory and, with a few exceptions, cannot be waived or otherwise modified to the disadvantage of the lessee. The Tenancy Act deals, *inter alia*, with the duties of lessor and lessee, the limitation of lease payments (*Mietzins*), the limitation of operating costs (*Betriebskosten*) and maintenance contributions (*Erhaltungsbeiträge*), the termination of contracts (*Kündigung*), compensation (*Entschädigung*), administrative procedures to determine the lease owed (*Mietzinsfestsetzung*), procedures to settle disputes, etc.

Contracts which fall under the Tenancy Act only in part are subject to only some of the Act's regulations, such as regulations on the termination of contracts.

Term and termination

In general, lease contracts entered into for an indefinite period may only be terminated by the lessor for the specific reasons listed in the Tenancy Act. The lessor may only terminate an agreement for good cause, such as the lessee's default of payments despite a reminder, a substantially detrimental use of the demised premises by the lessee, etc. Other reasons for termination except those mentioned above may only be valid if the agreed reasons are comparable to the ones provided for by law, otherwise they are void and unenforceable. On the other hand, the lessee may terminate the agreement at any time without cause. Jurisdiction in most cases tends to be in favor of the lessee. Therefore, lease contracts on commercial and residential space are frequently entered into for a definite term, to avoid the termination provisions, which clearly favor the lessee, applying.

Lease payments

Generally, the parties are also free under the Tenancy Act to agree on the amount of rent payable, provided that as of the day the parties enter into the lease agreement the lease payment is adequate for the relevant category (type, condition, location, maintenance) and the size of the leased object. Apartments in buildings erected before 1953 with a size of up to 130 m^2 are subject to a complex system of rent control. Typically, it is agreed that lease payments are adjusted from time to time, usually according to the *Austrian Consumer Price Index*. It is common practice upon conclusion of the lease agreement for the lessee to provide a security for future lease payments (usually a bank guarantee).

According to the Tenancy Act, the lessee of business premises in buildings erected before 1953 has to notify the lessor of any changes in the lessee's enterprise or ownership structure. Such substantial changes do not constitute good cause based on which the lessor may terminate the agreement, but the lessor may increase the rent to market price.

Stamp duties

In Austria, a written lease agreement is subject to a stamp duty payable to the Austrian tax authorities at a rate of 1% of all rental payments (including operating costs and VAT) payable by the lessee to the lessor during the term of the lease. With indefinite term contracts, stamp duty is calculated on the basis of three annual rental payments. For fixed term contracts, stamp duty is calculated on the basis of a maximum of 18 years (for apartments the maximum is three years). The signed contract must either be submitted to the tax authority before the 15th of the second month after signing or the lessor has to calculate the stamp duty himself and transfer the amount directly to the tax authority. Typically, stamp duty is borne by the lessee, but the parties are free to agree otherwise. However, parties are jointly liable towards the authority.

17.6 Succession and gifts

Applicable law and jurisdiction

The legal consequences of a succession *mortis causa* depends on the personal statute (nationality) of the testator at the time of his death. If probate proceedings take place in Austria, the transfer of the heir and liability for debts of the estate must be considered and determined according to Austrian law. Probate proceedings concerning properties located in Austria must be conducted before an Austrian court.

Fundamentals of the succession and gift/donation laws of Austria

Succession is determined by the will of the testator, an inheritance contract or by legal succession in case no testamentary disposition was made. Wills are valid in Austria if they are written by hand and provide for the appointment of an heir (without witnesses). Wills in the handwriting of another person or in typing are also valid. They require the presence of three witnesses to the will, of which only two have to be present at the same time and confirm (only) the identity of the testator with their signatures.

Intestate heirs are spouses and, in the 1st line, children and their descendants, in the 2nd line parents, siblings and their descendants, in the 3rd line grandparents, parents' siblings and their descendants, and, finally, in the 4th line the first great-grandparents. If there are children and further descendants a spouse is entitled to inherit one third of the estate; a spouse is entitled to two thirds if there are parents and their descendants, or if there are grandparents. Children and the spouse are forced heirs who are entitled to a mandatory share, which consists normally of half of the statutory share in the inheritance for each of these persons. If there are no children, the testator's parents are entitled to this mandatory share; their claim is normally only one third of the statutory share in the inheritance.

17.7 Taxes and charges

One-time taxes and charges on purchase and new constructions

Purchase/acquisition taxes

Most transactions for the purchase of domestic pieces of land *inter vivos* by purchase or other agreements, such as exchange deals which create a claim for a transfer of title (obligation *ex contracto*), trigger land transfer tax under the *Land Transfer Tax Act 1987 (Grunderwerbsteuergesetz 1987)*. This is also true for the acquisition of property by expropriation, forced sale, or adverse possession, for example. Land transfer tax is also levied where 100% of the shares of a corporation owning real estate are transferred or where unification in one hand (of either an individual or legal entity) of 100% of the shares of a corporation occurs.

The tax base is generally the value of the compensation such as the purchase price, exchange performance, highest bid in forced sales, indemnification for expropriation, but also other factors accepted by the buyer, such as payments or outstanding mortgage. If there is no compensation or if the compensation cannot be determined, the tax base is the market value of the land. If the transfer of land occurs within the close family, the tax is assessed from three times the standard value (*Einheitswert*), an assessed value for tax purposes, which is calculated in accordance with the Valuation Law (*Bewertungsgesetz*), however is never more than 30% of the market value. Three times (or in some cases two times) the standard value is also the basis in case of certain corporate measures like mergers, demergers, etc. The standard value of real estate is quite often considerably lower than its market value.

Land transfer tax amounts to generally 3.5% of the tax base, or 2% if purchased by the spouse/partner or a 1st degree relatives of the ascending line and up to the 2nd degree of the descending line. Tax arises with the creation of the obligatory claim to transfer the title. The persons involved in the acquisition are liable as joint and several debtors.

Therefore, it is advisable that the purchase agreement defines which party bears the tax, which is normally the buyer. The tax return must be filed with the *Tax Office for Stamp Duties (Finanzamt für Gebühren, Verkehrsteuern und Glücksspiel)* by the 15th day of the second month following the calendar month in which the tax liability was incurred. The tax is due one month after service of the assessment notice (if assessed by the Tax Office) and at the date of filing of the tax return in case of self assessment respectively.

A buyer may only be registered as owner in the Land Register if his request contains a so-called tax clearance certificate (*Unbedenklichkeitsbescheinigung*), a confirmation which is issued by the tax office that the land transfer tax been paid, or a statement of self-assessment of a representative. Attorneys-at-law and notaries may, as party representatives of the person liable to tax, calculate themselves the land transfer tax for acquisitions and issue a statement of self-assessment.

Value Added Taxes

Sales proceeds on pieces of land within the meaning of the *Property Tax Act* are exempt from Value Added Tax. Entrepreneurs may treat (opting-in) transactions concerning land as taxable whereby the general VAT tax rate of 20% would apply. If so, input taxes on the purchase and the erection of the building are deductible.

Currently, the rate of statutory Value Added Tax in Austria amounts to 20% and is due also on rent and operating expenses for business premises and offices. For residential property the special tax rate is 10% of the rent and operating expenses. Under lease contracts on business premises let to tenants who are exempt from VAT for their services (like banks, insurance companies and doctors) the landlord is not entitled to opt to VAT and loses the input VAT for these premises.

Real estate registration and notary charges

The actual registration of the transfer of ownership triggers a registry charge of 1.1% whereby the tax base corresponds in nearly all cases to the same amount on which land transfer tax would be assessed. Upon registration of a mortgage in the Land Register, a registration fee at a rate of 1.2% of the secured amount has to be paid by the applicant. Further, according to the *Act on Court Fees and Judicial Administration Taxes 1984* (*Gerichts- und Justizverwaltungsgebührengesetz 1984*), a lump sum fee of currently EUR 42.00 is payable on all filings for registration with the Land Register.

In general clients may agree with the attorneys on the fee whereby, *inter alia*, lump sum fees or hourly fees are admissible. If there are no prior arrangements, attorneys bill their clients for real estate transactions according to the Act on *Attorneys' Tariffs* (*Rechtsanwaltstarifgesetz*). However, they may also choose to calculate their fees according to the *Act on Notaries' Fees* (*Notariatstarifgesetz*), whereby the fee is mostly calculated as a percentage of the purchase price (plus VAT and cash expenses), and is negotiable between 1% and 3%, depending on the expected work load and the purchase price. The costs for drawing up the purchase agreement and entering the buyer in the land register are usually borne by the buyer.

Only notaries and district courts are authorized to perform the simple procedure of notarizing signatures along with the verification of the undersigned's identity; this involves minor costs.

Recurring taxes and charges

Real estate tax

Land, including agricultural and forestry assets, real estate and business premises, is subject to land tax (*Grundsteuer*) calculated on the basis of the standard value. The rates vary among the municipalities, which have the right to tax.

Parcels of land without buildings or constructions are subject to a federal duty on land value (*Bodenwertabgabe*) at a rate of 1% of the standard value minus EUR 14,600 per year. No such tax accrues in cases where the standard value does not exceed the amount of EUR 14,600.

Income tax

Individuals are subject to personal income tax and legal entities are subject to corporate income tax. The income concept and the profit concept, developed for purposes of assessment of the personal income tax, apply to corporate income taxation as well. Therefore, with some exemptions, profits are computed in the same way for purposes of personal income tax and corporate income tax.

The *Income Tax Act* (*Einkommenssteuergesetz*) distinguishes seven categories of income; one of these is income from rental and commercial leasing. The overall concept of rental and leasing is not strictly defined but includes both rental and leasing of immovable assets as well as, for example, earnings from the use of an entirety of movables. The taxable income is generally computed on the basis of the receipts less expenses. Special rules apply for expenditures made for repair to a building in any particular year. Whereas expenses for ongoing repairs are tax deductible immediately, expenses for repairs leading to an increase in the building's value are deductible only over a period of 10 to 67 years rather than in the year the expenses have been incurred. Certain expenditures for (re)building are tax deductible only over a period of 15 years. Finally, as far as income generated in the category of rental and commercial leasing relates to income from agriculture, industry and commerce or an independent profession, it is added to the relevant category of income when computing income from these sources.

Annual income tax

up to	EUR	11,000				0%,
from	EUR	11,000	to	EUR	25,000	36 %
from	EUR	25,000	to	EUR	60,000	43.214286 %
for any further income						50%

Personal use of premises is considered own consumption. Premises that are used personally, for example apartment houses, are reduced by fictitious rental proceeds corresponding to the personally used surface, which must fulfill the criteria for arm's length dealings. This personal use also means that the depreciation rates are reduced by analogy. Although the owner-occupier does not actually have to pay himself rent, the fictitious receipt thereof is subject to tax. It is advisable to consult a tax adviser.

Companies and other legal entities are subject to corporate income tax (*Körperschaftssteuer*). The income tax rate for corporations is 25%. The minimum corporate income tax for Austrian limited liability companies amounts to 5 % of the minimum share capital, therefore to EUR 1,750 per year. Corporate income tax law does not distinguish seven different kinds of income. Upon distribution of dividends a further 25% dividend withholding tax accrues which brings the tax burden to 43.75%.

Net wealth taxes

Net wealth tax was entirely abolished in Austria with effect as of 31 December 1993.

Capital gains taxes

Sales transactions concerning pieces of land and other rights are subject to income tax. Only the permanent residence which has been held for a certain period (the immediately preceding two years or five years in the last 10 years) is exempted.

Any increase in value from the sale of real estate will be taxable; from year 11 onwards the income is reduced by 2% p.a. up to maximum 50% to compensate capital gain due to inflation. Income tax accruing on the capital appreciation is 25%. However, the tax payer can opt to include this income in his total income and thus come to a lower rate.

As sales of real estate by individuals which held real estate as private investments have been tax free after a holding period of 10 years until 31 March 2012, there is a complicated system to avoid inadequate burdens to persons who bought the real estate before 1 April 2002.

The calculation and payment of this capital gains tax is necessary that the buyer may be entered in the land register.

This capital gains tax does basically not apply to companies which are subject to corporate income tax.

Other taxes and charges

Certain documentary stamp duties are levied on various legal transactions concluded in written form.

Incorrect (lower) statement of sale price on the sales agreement

Incorrect (lower) statement of sale price on the sale agreement is uncommon in Austria. One reason for that fact may be the relatively low (compared to other jurisdictions) land transfer tax of 3.5% or 2%. However, this may increase due to the fact that natural persons have to pay income tax on the capital gain in cases of a sale since 2012. Where real estate is purchased together with movables, the purchase price should be divided to prevent the amount for movables being added to the taxable base.

Tax offences are punishable according to the provisions of the *Fiscal Crimes and Penalties Act (Finanzstrafgesetz)* and may be subject to imprisonment, fines, forfeiture or compensation for lost value.

International taxation

Although the more recent double taxation treaties Austria has concluded follow the *OECD-Model Convention*, deviations exist, and the relevant treaty must be consulted in any event. Generally, income from immovable property including income from leasing of real estate may be taxed in the state where the property is located. Income from the alienation of real estate may be taxed in the state in which such property is located. Income from the alienation of any other property is generally taxed only in the contracting state where the seller is a resident.

According to tax treaties covering also inheritance tax, inheritance taxes are assessed by the state where the real estate is located. Industrial and commercial property of a permanent establishment is taxed by the state where this establishment is located. Other property is taxed by the state where the deceased had his residence on the day of his death whereby this state is entitled to apply a tax rate that would be applicable to the total amount of inheritance.

17.8 Immigration law and tax residence

Entry, residence and settlement of foreigners

There are no border controls when entering Austria from a Schengen Area country. Border-crossing documents are only required at EU external borders, specifically borders of countries which are not party to the Schengen treaty. EU nationals may reside and establish themselves for an unlimited period in Austria. The *Foreign Nationals Act* (*Fremdengesetz*) provides that other nationals have to obtain a residence permit from the authorities and, under certain conditions, also a work permit.

Tax residence

Unlimited tax liability applies to those natural persons whose residence or habitual place of abode is in Austria. Unlimited tax liability includes all domestic and foreign income. Residence within the meaning of Austrian tax laws is where someone has a home, suggesting that he will keep and use the home. Tax law therefore refers to objective circumstances; objectively noticeable circumstances suggesting that there is an intention to keep and use the home are required; a subjective intention alone is not sufficient. The habitual place of abode is where someone resides and the circumstances indicate that he does not just temporarily stay at this place or in this country. Unlimited tax liability applies to any actual residence in Austria that lasts for more than six months. In this situation, the first six months are also taxable. As a result, a person may have multiple residences, but only one habitual place of abode at any given time.

Limited tax liability for natural persons who have neither a residence nor a habitual place of abode in Austria includes, *inter alia*, income from agriculture and forestry operated in Austria and income from rental and commercial leases if the real estate is located in Austria or registered in a public ledger or register or is exploited within the scope of a domestic permanent establishment. These persons are also liable to tax on income from speculative transactions involving domestic pieces of land subject to the provisions of civil law regarding pieces of land and on capital assets obtained from domestic real estate ownership.

International double taxation for residents of Austria

Austria has entered into double taxation treaties with more than 90 countries, among others with Australia, Canada, the UK and the US. These tax treaties, which are generally closely modeled after the *OECD-Model Convention*, apply either the exemption method or the tax credit method. Some apply a mixed method for avoiding double taxation. In the meantime, there are also a number of EU Directives on double taxation, which must be observed.

Nationals of Member States of the European Union or a state to which the *Treaty on the European Economic Area* applies and who have neither a residence nor their habitual place of abode in Austria are treated as taxpayers with unlimited tax liability upon request if and to the extent they have special income subject to limited tax liability. This applies only if at least 90% of their income for the calendar year is subject to Austrian income tax or if their income not subject to Austrian income tax is less than EUR 11,000. Domestic income, which may only be taxed up to a certain limit under a tax treaty, is not considered as not subject to Austrian income tax in this context. The amount of income not subject to Austrian income tax must be proven by submission of a certificate of the competent foreign tax office.

17.9 Checklist: Real estate in Austria

- Search of the Land Register as to registered encumbrances
- Inspection of real estate as to obvious defects and obvious encumbrances
- Review of zoning ordinances (dedication of land), building regulations, excerpt of the cadastral map, monument preservation and urban development matters
- Identification of restrictions on transferability and (non-) registered encumbrances
- Existence of construction permits and permits to use
- Examining of material contracts to be adopted or terminated, such as lease agreements, agreements with abutters, utility agreements (gas, electricity, heating), property management contracts, agreements on refurbishment, etc.
- Financial and tax matters (e.g. unpaid taxes, prevention of land transfer tax if possible, etc.)
- Environmental considerations (contamination and other environmental issues – asbestos, oil residues, storage)
- Search in the Register of Potentially Contaminated Sites
- Insurance
- Litigation (third party claims, restitution claims of former owners, etc.)
- Drafting of the sales agreement by an attorney or a notary public
- Conclusion of the contract and certification of the signatures by a district court or a notary public
- Negotiating debt financing with banks
- Deletion of encumbrances, if any
- Registration of ownership with the Land Register

17.10 Bibliography

Arnold Wolf-Dieter / Arnold Nikolaus: Kommentar zum Grunderwerbsteuergesetz 1987 (loose-leaf-edition), ORAC-Verlag, Wien 2011

Artner Stefan / Kohlmaier Katharina (editors): Praxishandbuch Immobilienrecht, Linde Verlag, Wien 2014

Bovenkamp Helene, et al: Immobilienbesteuerung NEU Abgabenänderungsgesetz 2012, 2. Auflage, MANZ-Verlag, Wien 2013

Dirnbacher Wolfgang: Das Mietrechtsgesetz (MRG) 2013 idF ZVG, ÖVI-Verlag 2013

Dirnbacher Wolfgang: WEG: Das Wohnungseigentumsgesetz idF der Wohnrechtsnovelle 2009, ÖVI-Verlag, Wien 2009*Doralt Werner / Ruppe Hans-Georg:* Grundriss des Österreichischen Steuerrechts, MANZ-Verlag, (Band 1: 11. Auflage, Wien 2013; Band 2: 7. Auflage, 2012)

Hausmann Till / Vonkilch Andreas: Österreichisches Wohnrecht Kommentar MRG und WEG, (loose-leaf-edition), Springer-Verlag, Wien

IMMOLEX: Fachzeitschrift für Immobilienrecht, MANZ-Verlag, Wien 1998-2014

Kallinger Winfried / Gartner Herbert / Stingl Walter: Bauträger & Projektentwickler (Praxishandbuch), 6. Auflage, MANZ-Verlag, Wien 2011

Kodek Georg: Kommentar zum Grundbuchsrecht samt Ergänzungsband, MANZ-Verlag, Wien 2009

Koziol Helmut / Bydlinski Peter / Bollenberger Raimund: Kurzkommentar zum ABGB, 4. Auflage, Verlag Österreich, Wien 2014

Koziol Helmut / Welser Rudolf: Grundriss des bürgerlichen Rechts, 13. Auflage, MANZ-Verlag, Wien 2006+2007, Band 1 und 2

Pachler Hannes / Uhl Reinhard: Grundverkehrsrecht für die Praxis, LexisNexis ARD ORAC, Wien 2011

Prader Christian: Mietrechtsgesetz und ABGB-Mietrecht mit Anmerkungen, Literaturangaben und einer Übersicht der Rechtsprechung, 4. Auflage, MANZ-Verlag, Wien 2013

Prader Christian: Wohnungseigentumsgesetz 2002, 4. Auflage, MANZ-Verlag, Wien 2013

Rainer Herbert: Handbuch des Miet- und Wohnrechts (loose-leaf-edition), MANZ-Verlag, Wien

Rummel Peter: ABGB-Kommentar, 3. Auflage, Band 1 (2004) und 2 (2002/2007), MANZ-Verlag, Wien

Stingl Walter / Nidetzky Gerhard: Handbuch Immobilien & Steuern (loose-leaf-edition), MANZ-Verlag, Wien

Takacs, Peter: Grunderwerbsteuergesetz mit Erläuterungen und einer ausführlichen Übersicht der Rechtsprechung der Höchstgerichte, 5. Auflage, MANZ-Verlag, Wien 2009

Würth Helmut / Zingher Madeleine / Kovanyi Peter: Miet- und Wohnrecht, MANZ-Verlag, 22. Auflage, Wien 2009 (Band I) und 2011 (Band II)

18

The Bahamas

Commonwealth of The Bahamas

by

John F. Wilson

McKinney, Bancroft & Hughes
4 George Street
Mareva House
P.O. Box N-3937
Nassau
The Bahamas

Telephone: +1 242 322 4195
Facsimile: +1 242 328 2520

jfwilson@mckinney.com.bs
mckinney.com.bs

John Fritzgerald Wilson is a partner in the Bahamian law firm of Mckinney, Bancroft & Hughes specializing in commercial litigation, shipping and trust and Private Client work. In addition to his authorship of the Bahamas chapter in The International Real Estate Handbook, he has written extensively on a number of Bahamian law topics in his area of practice; he is the contributing author of the Bahamas chapter in the most recent publication of Carter-Ruck on Libel and Privacy published by Buttersworth and was the first non-English Barrister to appear as lead counsel before the Judicial Committee of the Privy Council in its first-ever sitting outside London in The Bahamas in 2006.

18.1 Introduction

In 1492 when *Columbus* landed in the 'new world' at the Bahamian island of *Guanahani* (later renamed *San Salvador*), he discovered a world already inhabited by Lukku-Cairi, or island people. The Lucayans, who were Amerindians, are understood to be the original Bahamians who came to the Americas by way of the land bridge that once joined Alaska with Siberia. Artifacts from burial sites have been retrieved giving testimony to the existence of early Lucayan communities throughout The Bahamas. In 1647, after periods of occupation by Spanish and French settlers, English settlers from Bermuda seeking religious freedom would populate The Bahamas and claim them for Great Britain.

The Bahamas archipelago spans 100,000 square miles extending southeast from Florida in the United States of America to northern Hispaniola.

The Bahamas is noted for being one of the oldest parliamentary democracies in the Western hemisphere, enjoying peaceful and stable governance for close to 300 years. Accordingly it is one of the safest and most stable international locations for investments. During 1972, the Bahamian people intimated their desire to become independent from the UK and on 10 July 1973, under the leadership of Lynden Oscar Pindling and the Progressive Liberal Party (PLP), full independence as the Commonwealth of The Bahamas were achieved. Today, The Bahamas remains a member of the Commonwealth of Nations.

The legal system in The Bahamas is based upon the English legal system with the notable exception that The Bahamas has a written constitution. The Constitution of The Bahamas provides for an independent Bahamian judiciary. Generally the judicial system in The Bahamas follows the English common law. Additionally, there is a large body of local statutes, which together with the common law constitutes the laws of The Bahamas.

There are three levels of courts in The Bahamas: the Magistrates Court which determines small claims; the Supreme Court which has unlimited jurisdiction in civil and criminal matters; and The Bahamas Court of Appeal which is the highest court sitting in The Bahamas and hears appeals from the Supreme Court. The Privy Council in London is the final court of appeal. Judges in The Bahamas are appointed by the Governor General.

The legal currency of The Bahamas is the Bahamian dollar. The US dollar is however widely accepted and treated by merchants on par with the Bahamian dollar. Within the banking system conversion of foreign currency including US dollars to Bahamian and the reverse are subject to an official rate of exchange fixed by the Central Bank of The Bahamas. The Central Bank's buying and selling rates for US dollars from/to commercial banks are USD 1.00 = BSD 1.00 and USD 1.00 = BSD 1.0025, respectively, and at par for cash transactions.

18.2 Real estate ownership

Different forms and types of ownership

The primary forms of real estate ownership in The Bahamas include fee simple, leasehold, life estates, co-ownership, joint tenancy, tenancy in common, condominium, future interests and timesharing.

Easements, charges, covenants and mortgages

Easements

Easements in The Bahamas generally take the form of rights of way or easements of support in connection with multi-unit buildings with common support walls. Section 6 of the *Conveyancing and Law of Property Act 1909*, chapter 138 of the *Statute Laws of The Bahamas Revised Edition 2000*, has the effect of passing to the transferee of land the benefit of existing liberties, privileges, easements, rights and advantages which appertain to the land conveyed, or are reputed to appertain to it, or which are, at the date of the conveyance, enjoyed with the land.

Licenses

Grants of licenses to allow another party to utilize or pass over land in circumstances which would typically amount to trespass in Bahamian law are not uncommon. These can normally be found where a beach front property owner wishes to allow a neighbouring property owner access to the beach but does not wish to burden his property with a legal easement.

Restrictive Covenants

Restrictive covenants generally arise in the context of subdivision developments and condominiums and are imposed to regulate land use. In Bahamian law the burden of restrictive covenants binds succeeding owners of the property and is deemed to run with the land.

Liens

The primary liens and charges affecting real estate ownership in The Bahamas are as follows:

Judgments

The Supreme Court Act 1996, chapter 53 of the *Statute Laws of The Bahamas* provides that every judgment entered in the Supreme Court of The Bahamas, against any person, shall operate as an equitable charge upon every estate or interest (whether legal or equitable) in all land to or over which the judgment debtor at the date of entry or at any time thereafter is or becomes beneficially entitled or entitled to exercise a power of disposition for his own benefit without the assent of any other person. A charge imposed by section 63 of the *Supreme Court Act* shall take priority over all other mortgages or charges affecting the land other than a mortgage or charge registered under the provisions of the *Registration of Records Act 1928* prior to the date of the entry of the judgment or any further advance made under the security of a charge or mortgage registered prior to the judgment provided that the security allows for the mortgagee or chargee to make further advances.

Condominium contributions (common expenses)

Any unpaid contribution due from the owner of any condominium unit under the provisions of the *Law of Property and Conveyancing (Condominium) Act 1965,* chapter 139, shall constitute a charge upon the unit in priority to all other encumbrances on the unit except a charge under section 25(1) of the *Real Property Tax, Act 1969*, chapter 375.

Mortgages

Mortgages (both legal and equitable) duly recorded in the *Registry of Records (Registrar General's Department)* pursuant to the *Registration of Records Act 1928,* chapter 187, are afforded priority over subsequently recorded documents dealing with the same security. A security created under a mortgage is subject to the overriding charge created under section 25(1) of the *Real Property Tax Act 1969*, chapter 375.

Protection of ownership, proof of ownership and registration

Title to land and registration

The transfer of a legal title in land in The Bahamas is affected by the valid execution of a deed by the grantor. At present there is no mandatory system of land registration in The Bahamas. The *Registration of Records Act 1928,* chapter 187, provides for the voluntary registration of documents and names of parties to a transaction, but is not a system of land registration. However, all instruments recorded in the *Registry of Records* in Nassau pursuant to the provisions of the Act are afforded priority over subsequent instruments purporting to deal with the same interest except in the case of fraud. Additionally, it should be noted that the recording of an instrument in the *Registry of Records* creates a permanent record of the transaction in the event that the original title deeds are lost or destroyed.

Title Search

As there is no system of land registration in The Bahamas, in order to ensure that clear title to property is being acquired, a purchaser should have the title to the subject property researched and certified by a local attorney; or alternatively, should secure title insurance from a local title insurance company. It is not customary local conveyancing practice for a vendor to produce an abstract of title in relation to his property, although the parties to the transaction can stipulate otherwise in the Agreement for Sale. Unless otherwise agreed, a vendor in The Bahamas is only obliged to show a good and marketable title to his property commencing with a good root of title at least 30 years old. Prior to completing a sale, all real estate taxes due must be paid and all required permits or validating permits (if necessary) must be obtained.

18.3 Purchase and sale of real estate

The sales agreement

The *Statute of Frauds Act 1799*, chapter 154, stipulates that any contract or agreement dealing with the disposition of an interest in land must be in writing. Consequently under Bahamian law an oral agreement for the sale of land is not specifically enforceable. A properly executed agreement for the sale of land has the effect of transferring the equitable estate in the subject property to the prospective purchaser while the vendor retains the legal estate until completion. Accordingly it is recommended that where the completion of a property sale transaction is delayed, the Agreement for Sale be registered pursuant to the *Registration of Records Act*.

Restrictions on sale and acquisition

Restrictions under family law and matrimonial property regime

Previously, under Bahamian law, a wife acquired a right to dower in all real estate owned by her husband. Consequently on the sale of any real estate owned by a married man, it was necessary for a wife to renounce her right to dower in the subject property before clear title could pass to the purchaser. The Bahamian Parliament has since replaced a wife's right to dower with a spousal right of occupation in the matrimonial home, with the passage of the *Inheritance Act, 2000*, chapter 116. It should be noted that doubts have arisen as to whether or not the right to dower has been effectively abolished and at the moment there remains a degree of uncertainty in Bahamian law on this issue.

Options and pre-emption rights

A vendor can, by a written agreement, grant to an intended purchaser a right of pre-emption. This gives the intended purchaser the right to call upon the vendor to contract to sell the subject property to the owner of the pre-emptive right. This is based entirely in common law.

Agricultural real estate

There are no discernible agriculture estates in The Bahamas.

Restrictions regarding acquisition of real estate by foreigners

The *International Persons Landholding Act 1994,* chapter 40, (IPLA) was enacted to encourage non-Bahamians, as defined in the Act, to acquire real estate in The Bahamas. The Act sought to remove past onerous restrictions placed on the international investor and replaced them with a more investor friendly regime. Pursuant to the IPLA, a non-Bahamian can purchase or acquire an interest in a condominium or property for use by him as a single family dwelling, provided the property is less than two contiguous acres, subject only to an obligation to register the purchase or acquisition with *The Bahamas Investments Board* (Investment Board). This, and all applications made under this Act, are facilitated by the Bahamas Investment Authority (BIA). It should be noted however that a failure to register the acquisition with the Investment Board will render null and void any attempt to record the conveyance in respect of the transaction. In all other circumstances, unless a non-Bahamian has been granted permanent resident status in The Bahamas, he must obtain a permit from the BIA in order to acquire an interest in real estate. Failure to obtain a permit renders the acquisition null and void in the absence of the issue of a validating permit in relation thereto upon application to the BIA.

Further important preconditions for buying real estate

Capacity and entitlement of the vendor

Under Bahamian law, in order to enter into a binding contract, a party must be over the legal age of majority i.e. 18 years or over, and mentally competent. The only contracts which can bind a minor or a mentally disordered person are contracts for necessaries and a contract of any other nature entered into by a minor or a mentally disordered person is voidable.

Any legally incorporated entity can hold land in The Bahamas. The *Companies Act 1992,* chapter 308, provides that where a company has been removed from the Register of Companies, all its property immediately vests in the *Treasurer of The Bahamas.* Consequently, a company which has been struck off the Register would have no capacity to enter into an agreement for the sale of any land titled in its name in The Bahamas. As such, it is necessary that a company selling real estate is in good standing with the *Bahamian Companies Registry.*

Third party claims and unpaid taxes

The primary third party claim affecting the ability of a vendor to sell real estate would be the claim by a judgment creditor (see chapter 18.2). To protect against such a claim, a cause list search should be carried out at the *Bahamian Supreme Court Registry* to ensure there are no judgments on record affecting the vendor. Additionally, the cause list should be examined to ensure that the property being sold is not the subject of any proprietary claim by any third parties.

Where there is outstanding real estate tax due (see chapter 18.7), a new owner cannot pass clear title to any subsequent purchaser until the unpaid taxes have been satisfied. To guard against such an eventuality, a purchaser's attorney should insist on the vendor's attorney providing an assessment from the real estate tax office which confirms that there are no outstanding real estate taxes due in respect of the subject property.

Provisions for protecting the environment, nature and cultural heritage

The primary legislation enacted for the protection of the environment includes *The Bahamas National Trust Act 1959*, chapter 371, the *Conservation and Protection of the Physical Landscape of The Bahamas Act 1997*, chapter 260, the *Antiquities Monuments and Museums Act 1946*, chapter 51, and the *Coast Protection Act 1968*, chapter 204. There is currently no legislation specifically directed at the preservation of Bahamian cultural heritage, although some provisions of these Acts do touch on cultural aspects.

In The Bahamas, *The Bahamas Environment Science and Technology Commission* (BEST) is charged with the responsibility of ensuring that there is a coordinated and concerted effort to protect, conserve and manage the environmental resources in The Bahamas. It is generally a pre-condition of any large-scale real estate development in The Bahamas that a favourable environmental report is obtained (see also chapter 18.4). Environmental matters are also administered and monitored by the Ministry of Environment and Housing.

Access to relevant records and documents

The Bahamas does not have a system of land registration. Consequently all title deeds in the chain of title should be carefully vetted by a prospective purchaser's attorney. Additionally, a search of the Registry of Records should be undertaken to ensure that there are no other conveyances or transactions recorded in respect of the property to be purchased which would affect title to the property. The *Department of Physical Planning* should be consulted to ensure that the property is in an approved subdivision.

Key points that a vendor should consider

When selling real estate, a vendor should always ensure that it is clearly stated in the offer and any resulting agreement for sale whether the price is a net or gross price. A net price refers to the prices that the vendor expects to receive in his hand after payment of all closing costs. A professional appraisal should be obtained so as to ensure that the sale price accurately reflects the market value of the property. In The Bahamas it is the obligation of the purchaser to ensure that the property is fit for its intended use, however a vendor cannot materially misrepresent the features of the property to the purchaser. The vendor should also check to make sure that real estate tax payments (see chapter 18.7) on the property are current as any outstanding amounts will have to be paid prior to closing.

The execution of a real estate purchase transaction

The first step that a potential vendor or purchaser should take is to retain the services of a licensed real estate broker. Under the provisions of section 4 of the *Real Estate (Brokers and Salesmen) Act 1995*, chapter 171, no person may engage in the practice of real estate business without a license. Therefore it is important to ensure that any real estate broker retained is properly licensed under the Act. Secondly, once a purchaser or potential property is identified the sales contract or *Agreement for Sale* will have to be prepared. Most licensed brokers have standard form real estate contracts at their disposal but it is still preferable that a lawyer is retained either to draft or review the contract. See chapter 18.7 for customary professional charges on real estate transactions.

Powers of attorney

In The Bahamas the law applicable to powers of attorney is found in the *Powers of Attorney Act, 1992*, chapter 81. A power of attorney must be signed and sealed by the donor of the power and provision is made under the Act for the recording of the power with the Registrar.

The Act also provides for the creation of enduring powers of attorney which survive the subsequent mental incapacity of the donor. Contracts executed pursuant to a valid power of attorney are binding on the donor of the power; this includes any contracts for the sale of land.

Financing

The primary sources of obtaining real estate financing in The Bahamas are banks and insurance companies. While *Credit Unions* also provide some limited financing options, these are usually restricted to members. In order to process a loan application for the purchase of real estate, a bank will typically require evidence of employment, an executed agreement for sale and a current appraisal report on the subject property. Where the applicant is a non-Bahamian, in addition to the foregoing, a bank will often request proof of residence status. As non-Bahamians must secure approval from the *Central Bank of The Bahamas* to borrow funds from a bank in the jurisdiction, evidence of *Central Bank* approval for the loan is usually required at the time the loan application is being processed.

Purchase through a company

In The Bahamas there are two distinct forms of corporate entities: companies formed under the *Companies Act* and those formed under the *International Business Companies Act 2000,* chapter 309 (IBC Act). IBC Act companies are specifically designed for the international investor. Real estate can be held by either type of company but in every case where the beneficial owner is a non-Bahamian, it will be necessary for the company to obtain approval from the *Central Bank* for the purchase. Incorporating a company in The Bahamas is a relatively simple and uncomplicated exercise. All that is required is the proposed name of the company and the required fee which is typically USD 2,000, inclusive of professional fees. An incorporator must of course be vetted in accordance with the appropriate procedures.

Warranty claims

In The Bahamas, warranty claims generally refer to breaches of contract which would not result in a repudiation or termination of the contract. In contracts for the sale of land however, there is no implied warranty covering defects of quality, the governing rule being *caveat emptor.* While a vendor is not bound to call a purchaser's attention to patent defects of the property, he must nonetheless deliver property corresponding to the description in the contract. An express warranty that a property is free from defects will found an action for breach of contract if the property is not in fact free of defects. A vendor may not conceal patent defects from a purchaser as this would be regarded as fraudulent.

As to legal defects of title there is an implied obligation on a vendor to deliver good and marketable title to the property sold. This implied obligation only applies to legal defects and does not apply to physical defects. A legal defect is one which affects the vendor's ability to pass on a good title to the property sold.

18.4 New construction, rebuilding and renovation

Zoning law and construction permits

Given the peculiar characteristics of the islands of The Bahamas, including its archipelagic nature and size, it will be readily appreciated that the practice of zoning is not as one would be accustomed to in larger cosmopolitan areas. In The Bahamas the zoning of any particular section or area of The Bahamas is governed by the Planning and Subdivision Act, 2010.

The stated purposes of this Act include providing for land use planning based on land use designations and zoning, the promotion of sustainable development in the environment and the protection and conservation of the natural and cultural heritage of The Bahamas.

All development, which term includes the construction and alterations of buildings and the adjustment of property lines, must be carried out in accordance with the Act and approval of the Town Planning Committee established by the Act. In particular, except for in limited circumstances, all development, approvals and zoning must conform to Land Use Plans developed by the Department of Physical Planning.

The Act further provides for the adoption of National Land Use Development Policies on matters which relate to land use planning which are of national interest. Land Use Plans are to be in line with any National Land Use Development Policies.

Environmental protection

Environmental protection in The Bahamas is primarily governed by the *Conservation and Protection of the Physical Landscape of The Bahamas Act 1997,* chapter 260. The Act considers impacts to the physical landscape including the filling up of wetlands, areas commonly known as natural ponds, drainage basins and blue holes, excavation and landfill operations, the removal of sand, dunes or stones from beaches and coastlands. It should be noted that this list is not exhaustive and the Act and accompanying Regulations should be carefully consulted. Under the Act, where any construction works have the potential to impact the physical landscape of The Bahamas, approval of the responsible Minister must first be obtained. Where prior Ministerial approval is not obtained, the offending party is liable to a fine of up to BSD 10,000. The fine can be increased in the case of repeat offenders. Additionally, the Act allows for the imprisonment of an offender for three to six months.

With regard to the construction industry, the Act applies to excavations for large scale luxury residential developments, the development of tourist attractions and facilities as well as the excavation for canals or other purposes connected therewith. However the restrictions under the Act do not apply to excavations related to small, individual construction projects. Such projects include excavations for swimming pools, septic tanks, rainwater tanks, trenching for building foundations or other building operations approved under the *Buildings Regulation Act.*

The Planning and Subdivision Act also addresses matters concerning the environment and the control of development related thereto.

Architect's contracts and building contracts

Professional architects in The Bahamas primarily use the *American Institute of Architects* standard form contracts for building projects. These standard form contracts, *inter alia*, make provision for the commencement and completion of building projects, periodic payment of the contract sums, general conditions regarding the supply of materials, subcontracting of works, and govern the general administration of the project.

Completion of construction and formalities

On completion of any building works, the *Ministry of Public Works* must conduct a final inspection of the works and issue an Occupancy Certificate. This inspection is undertaken by the Buildings Control Officer. However during the course of the works, at several set stages, an inspection must be undertaken by the Buildings Control Officer who will either approve the works or require the builder to bring the works into conformity with the requirements under the *Building Code*. The requirements to comply with the set stages for inspection are the same for new construction projects, renovations, alterations and extensions to existing buildings (see paragraphs 301 and 304 of the *Building Code*).

In The Bahamas building projects are required to undergo the following:

- Foundation inspection
- Piling inspection
- Column inspection
- Structural column inspection
- Tie beam inspection
- Structural beam and slab inspection

- Structural framework inspection
- Roof inspection
- Plumbing inspection
- Special inspection relative to the particular works being undertaken
- Electrical inspection
- Any other inspections the *Buildings Control Officer* may deem necessary

The timing of each inspection is designated in the *Building Code*. The builder must give the *Buildings Control Officer* at least 48 hours notice to attend and conduct his inspection.

Deficiencies and warranty claims regarding new construction

There are no statutory provisions that specifically address deficiencies and warranty claims in connection with building works. Defects and deficiencies are left to the parties to address in their contract. The large majority of Bahamian building contracts contain a clause which requires the contractor to rectify all defects which may appear during a fixed period. Where the contract makes no such provision for defects, the law of negligence and or common law principles apply. Similarly certain warranties are also normally included as provisions of the contract. These normally relate to warranties as to quality of materials and workmanship.

18.5 Rental and tenancy

Rental and leasing contracts

A tenancy in The Bahamas may be classified as a fixed term tenancy, a periodic tenancy, a tenancy at will or a tenancy at sufferance. A tenancy may be created orally and there is no legal requirement that a lease be in writing. The law relative to tenancies in The Bahamas is contained in the *Landlord and Tenant Act 1799*, chapter 161; the *Landlord and Tenant (No.2) Act 1799*, chapter 162; the *Conveyancing and Law of Property Act 1909*, chapter 138; the *Distress for Rent Act 1872*, chapter 164; the *Distress for Rent (No. 2) Act 1799*, chapter 165; and the *Rent Control*

Act, chapter 163. Subject to express agreement, the intending lessee is not entitled to call for any deduction of the freehold or leasehold estate under a contract to grant or assign a term of years. Acquisition of leasehold interest by non-Bahamians is subject to the provisions of the *IPLA.*

Regulations on protection of tenants and rent control

Protection of tenants

There is no general statutory regime established to protect tenants. Such protection as exists is afforded to a tenant by virtue of the common law. Examples of the protections granted to tenants under the common law include the covenant for quiet enjoyment and the obligation that notice be given where the tenant is required to vacate. There are a few exceptions however, where statutes reinforce common law principles created for the protection of tenants. An example can be found in section 24 of the *Rent Control Act*, where landlords are mandated to maintain the rented or tenanted premises in good repair and adequate for occupation.

Rent control

Legislation affords some protection to tenants with regard to the amount of rent they may lawfully be charged. The *Rent Control Act* protects tenants who reside in premises with a value of BSD 75,000 or less. Where the value of the premises exceeds the abovementioned amount the Act is inapplicable. Under the *Rent Control Act* a landlord may not charge more than a prescribed percentage of the annual declared or assessed value of the premises. The prescribed percentage currently stands at 20%.

18.6 Succession and gifts

Applicable law and jurisdiction

Where a foreign national who is resident in The Bahamas dies in The Bahamas without having made provisions for the disposition of his/her estate either in The Bahamas or elsewhere, his estate may be distributed in accordance with the guidelines established in section 4 of the *Inheritance Act.*

Fundamentals of the succession and gift/donation laws of The Bahamas

Fundamentals of succession

In The Bahamas, the law of succession was extensively revised in 2002. The revision abolished colonially inherited practices including *tenancy by the curtsey*, dower, and all other then existing modes, rules and canons of descent and of devolution by special occupancy or otherwise of real or personal estate. In place thereof, three associated statutes were created to govern the law of succession in The Bahamas. The assembly of statutes were the *Inheritance Act 2002,* chapter 116; the *Wills Act,* chapter 115; and the *Probate Act 2011*. The *Inheritance Act* provides an alternating system of succession when a person dies intestate. The *Wills Act* governs the creation of wills in The Bahamas, the necessary formality requirements, and the recognition of wills created outside The Bahamas. It should also here be noted that a subsequent marriage after the creation of a Bahamian will invalidates the earlier will. In such circumstances, it would be advisable for the will to be reaffirmed or restated. The third Act, the *Probate Act* deals with situations where an administrator must be appointed over a deceased's estate.

Intestate succession

The *Inheritance Act* sets out the general guidelines regarding intestate succession. Where an intestate dies leaving a spouse and no children, that spouse inherits the entire estate; where an intestate dies leaving a spouse and one child the estate is shared equally between them. If an intestate dies leaving a spouse and more than one child, the statute provides that one half of the estate vests in the spouse while the children share equally in the remaining half. Where an intestate dies leaving no surviving spouse and only children remain, the estate is divided equally among his children. Similarly where an intestate is only survived by his grandchildren, the estate is shared equally among them. If there are no children, grandchildren or spouse remaining, the law directs its attention to the parents of the intestate or alternatively to the siblings, nieces and nephews, grandparents, or aunts and uncles of the intestate in that order. Where no such person exists of any of the above descriptions, the estate will devolve upon the next of kin.

Intestate succession also applies in circumstances where a person "leaves a will but dies intestate as to some beneficial interest in his real or personal estate" (*Inheritance Act 2002*, section 2).

Creation of a Bahamian Will

Under the *Wills Act 2002*, an individual's freedom to choose to create a will is not affected. Although it is recommended that a non-Bahamian execute a Bahamian will to govern the devolution of any property within The Bahamas, it should be noted that each situation is dependent on its particular circumstances and the desires of the testator. Part 4 of the *Act* expressly makes provisions for wills executed outside The Bahamas. Consequently, if a subsisting will currently complies with all necessary formalities of the territory where the testator was either a national, domiciled or resident at the time of its creation or complies with the formalities of the territory in which it was executed, it is likely that the Bahamian courts will give effect to its provisions. One provision should be given special note however. Where a will purports to deal with immovable property, the device ought to conform to the law of the territory where the property is located. The Act makes provision for such circumstances where the testator, not domiciled in The Bahamas, wishes for the devise to be subject to Bahamian law (see section 7 of the *Wills Act 2002*).

Under the *Inheritance Act*, irrespective of any other law, provision is made to prevent a surviving spouse from being evicted from the matrimonial home. Section 24 expressly entitles a spouse not otherwise entitled by virtue of a testamentary devise, to remain in the matrimonial home he or she was residing in at the time of the spouse's death.

However this benefit extends only during the surviving spouse's lifetime or until terminated by marriage. Section 25 extends this right of occupation to the minor children of the marriage, thereby ensuring that they are housed on the death of the parent. Apart from the above provisions, there are no forced heirship rules dictating who may receive testamentary bequests.

Donations

The law does not regulate donations in The Bahamas. Subsequently persons and private corporations are free to make such charitable gifts and donations they may deem fit.

18.7 Taxes and charges

One-time taxes and charges on purchase

Purchase/acquisition taxes

There are no purchase/acquisition taxes in The Bahamas, save for the payment of stamp duty and Value Added Taxes as outlined below.

Sales taxes (Value Added Taxes)

Value Added Taxes with respect to most goods and services will be introduced as of 1 January 2015 at a rate of 7.5%. Value Added Taxes will not be payable on the sale or rental of a dwelling or the transfer of vacant land.

Real estate registration and notary charges

Under the provisions of the *Stamp Act, 1925*, chapter 370, stamp duty is payable on, *inter alia*, the following instruments:

	Instrument	Stamp Duty
1.	Every deed of Conveyance, assignment or transfer of realty or personalty where the amount or the value of the consideration:	
	does not exceed BSD 20,000	4% of the amount or value of the consideration
	exceeds BSD 20,000 and does not exceed BSD 50,000	6% of the amount or value of the consideration
	exceeds BSD 50,000 and does not exceed BSD 100,000	8% of the amount or value of the consideration
	exceeds BSD 100,000	10% of the amount or value of the consideration
2.	Every deed of exchange or realty or personalty shall be liable to stamp duty on the amount or value of the consideration, whichever is greater	See scale rate above
3.	Every lease:	
	where the lease is for a term not exceeding 7 years	2% of the annual rent reserved
	where the term of the lease exceeds 7 years but is less than 10 years	3% of the annual rent reserved
	A lease in excess of 10 years is treated as a conveyance and stamp duty is chargeable on the value of the lease or the consideration, whichever is greater	
4.	Every mortgage or transfer of mortgage or realty or personalty or both, for every BSD 100 or fraction thereof. It should be noted however that the transfer of a home mortgage or of a home mortgage combined with other domestic loans from one licensed lending institutions to another shall be exempted from stamp duty on the instrument of transfer	BSD 1.00
5.	Every re-conveyance of realty or personalty or both to a borrower or mortgagor only, for every BSD 100 or fraction thereof	BSD 0.10

Notary fees

There are no standardized rates for notary services. Generally, notary fees will be based upon the nature and number of documents to be notarized with a premium being charged for travelling expenses if applicable.

Annually recurring taxes and charges

Real estate tax

Under the provisions of the *Real Property Tax Act 1969*, chapter 375, real estate tax is payable annually on all real estate specified in the Act (subject to certain exceptions). All outstanding taxes levied pursuant to section 25(1) of the Act, shall constitute a first charge upon the property for which the tax is unpaid for so long as the tax remains payable. The rate of tax is dependent on the assessed market value of the property.

No real estate taxes are levied in the city of Freeport, the port area on the island of Grand Bahama.

	Description Of Real Estate	
1.	Upon that part of the market value which exceeds BSD 250,000 but does not exceed BSD 500,000	0.75% of the market value of the property per annum
2.	Upon the part of the market value which exceeds BSD 500,000	1% of the market value of the property per annum provided that the maximum annual tax shall not exceed BSD 50,000
3.	Upon that part of the market value which does not exceed BSD 7,000	BSD 100 per annum
4.	Upon that part of the market value which exceeds BSD 7,000	1.5% of the market value of the property per annum
5.	Upon that part of the market value which does not exceed BSD 500,000	1% of the market value of the property per annum
6.	Upon that part of the market value which exceeds BSD 500,000	2% of the market value of the property per annum

**All rates outlined herein for Owner Occupied property are effective as of 1 January 2013*

Income tax

There is no income tax payable in connection with income from real estate in The Bahamas. Indeed, there are no direct income taxes at all.

Net wealth taxes

There are no net wealth taxes in The Bahamas.

Capital gains taxes

There are no capital gains taxes in The Bahamas.

Inheritance and gift taxes

There are no inheritance and gift taxes in The Bahamas.

Other taxes and charges

Real estate sales commission

Depending on the terms of the sales agreement a real estate sales commission may be payable where a real estate agent is involved in the transaction. Sales commissions charged by real estate agents range begin at 10% of the value of the consideration for undeveloped land and 6% of the value of the consideration for developed land.

Legal fees

The general fee scale used to assess legal fees by attorneys in The Bahamas in connection with conveyancing transactions is as follows:

- 2.5% of the consideration for the first BSD 500,000
- 2% of the consideration for the next BSD 500,000
- 1% of the consideration for transactions over BSD 1 million up to BSD 3 million

Incorrect (lower) statement of sale price on the sales agreement

The effect of intentionally quoting an incorrect/lower statement of the sales price on an agreement for sale is to commit a fraudulent act that deprives the Bahamian Government of stamp duty which the parties are obligated to pay pursuant to the provisions of the *Stamp Act*. Accordingly the Stamp Act stipulates that the full purchase price be quoted in the transaction documentation (section 22 of the *Stamp Act 1925*). A breach of the provisions of the *Stamp Act* may result in the imposition of fines ranging between BSD 50 to BSD 200. Alternative penalties under the Act include imprisonment.

International taxation

Due to the absence of direct income taxes, there are no operative principles of international double taxation in The Bahamas.

18.8 Immigration law and tax residence

Entry, residence and settlement of foreigners

Generally The Bahamas welcomes persons desiring to be resident in the islands. The primary statute governing this area is the *Immigration Act 1967,* chapter 191. The Act categorises persons entitled to enter into The Bahamas into six main groups. These include Bahamian citizens; permanent residents; members of the diplomatic corps; persons employed by the Bahamian government; spouses and children of persons in the previous categories; and persons that immigration officials are authorised to treat as so entitled. With particular reference to residential status, persons are categorised as either:

- Permanent residents
- Spousal residents
- Resident cardholders
- Holders of work permits

An applicant for permanent residence should be over 18 years old, of good character, in good health, mentally and physically and must declare the intention to reside permanently in The Bahamas. Also, given that permanent resident status may be granted with the condition that the applicant not engage in gainful employment, such applicant must also satisfy the *Immigration Board* that he is able to maintain himself in The Bahamas as well as any accompanying dependants. An application for residence may be declined if the applicant is not perceived as offering or adding some benefit or enrichment to Bahamian society. Once granted, residence status continues for the duration for the applicant's lifetime unless revoked.

The Immigration Act also contemplates situations where an applicant seeking permanent residence is married. In those circumstances an endorsement may be made on the permanent resident's certificate reflecting that fact. Alternatively, application may be made for a resident spouse permit (Regulation 3, *Immigration Regulations*) which grants the spouse of a permanent resident equivalent resident status.

Pursuant to section 11 of the *International Persons Landholding Act, 1994,* chapter 40, a non-Bahamian who owns a home in the islands is entitled to apply to the *Director of Immigration* for an *Annual Home Owner Resident Card.* This card allows the applicant, his spouse and minor children to enter and remain in The Bahamas for the duration of the permit unless otherwise prohibited. While the holder of an *Annual Home Owner Resident Card* does not become a resident, he is given leeway to enjoy what may be a second home without having to relocate permanently.

The provisions of the *Immigration Act* do not distinguish between skilled and unskilled employees. Section 30 of the *Act* allows for the grant of a work permit to persons already possessing resident status in The Bahamas. A work permit may also be granted to individuals, allowing them entry into The Bahamas to undertake a particular job. The work permit issued may specify the occupation the holder is authorized to perform. Where work permit holders who have been permitted entry into The Bahamas to perform a specific work function are no longer employed by the entity that required their services, the work permit is revoked, thereby removing the permit holder's authorization to remain in the jurisdiction.

Tax residence

The Bahamas is primarily a 'tax-free' jurisdiction. In that regard there are no income taxes, whether personal or corporate, no sales taxes, no gift taxes and no inheritance taxes. Therefore, permanent residents do not need to comply with any rules or pre-requisites to be resident for tax purposes.

Historically, the system of taxation in The Bahamas is such that an estimated 65% of the government's revenue is generated through custom import duties, however with the introduction of Value Added Tax the country's reliance on custom import duties will be reduced. Additionally, stamp duty is payable on certain instruments and transactions, including the sale of real estate. The government generates further revenue by assessing an annual real estate tax, which is subject to certain exemptions and is based on the assessed value of the property. A nominal departure tax is payable at every port, via air or sea, as persons leave the jurisdiction. Various transactional and filing fees are also a means of revenue for the government. Examples of such fees include business license fees, and annual corporate registration fees. Both Bahamian and non-Bahamian residents are required to pay the applicable taxes and fees.

International double taxation for residents of The Bahamas

In the wake of the Organisation for Economic Co-operation and Development initiatives of recent times, The Bahamas has entered into a number of *Tax Information Exchange Agreements* with a number of countries including Canada, the UK and the US. These agreements provide for cooperation between states in tax matters including the exchange of information for tax purposes.

18.9 Checklist: Real estate in The Bahamas

- Real estate acquisition by foreigners requires both *Investment Board* approval or registration, and *Central Bank* approval for the purpose of bringing money into the country for purchase and to repatriate sale proceeds on any future sale (investor status)
- A real estate purchase by a non-Bahamian must be registered or a permit obtained in advance of purchase under the *International Persons Landholding Act*
- A purchaser has to undergo verification procedures under the *Know Your Customer* guidelines
- A title search should be carried out by a lawyer
- The purchase of title insurance is recommended
- Stamp duties upon purchase can be considerable, therefore it is sensible to calculate in advance the amount payable
- If required, an application should be made for an *Annual Home Owner Resident Card*. The card does not give the holder resident status but during the validity of the card facilitates entry into the country for the holder, his spouse and minor children

18.10 Bibliography

Craton, Michael: A History of The Bahamas, Collins, 1968

Dupuch, S.P.: The Bahamas Handbook, Etienne Dupuch Jr. Publications Ltd. Nassau, 2004

Knowles, Sir Leonard: Bahamian Law of Real Property, The Nassau Guardian, Nassau, 1989

Statute Laws of The Bahamas Revised Edition, Juta & Co. Ltd., 2000

19

Belgium

Kingdom of Belgium

Koninkrijk België/ Royaume de Belgique/ Königreich Belgien

by

Alain Van Geel & Claudine Bodeux*

Tiberghien Lawyers
Tour et Taxis
Havenlaan/Avenue du Port, 86C, B.419
1000 Brussels
Belgium

T: +32 2 773 40 00
F: +32 2 773 40 55

info@tiberghien.com
tiberghien.com

Dirk Reynders

Senior Wealth Planner Benelux
UBS AG
Rue de la Confédération 2
1211 Genève

T: +41 22 375 68 55
F: +41 22 375 30 58

dirk.reynders@ubs.com
ubs.com

**The authors would like to thank Mr Guillaume Delfosse for his kind assistance*

19.1 Introduction

Belgium has become popular for foreign real estate investors, in part because the EU's headquarters are based in Brussels. Although its surface area of 30,528 km^2 makes Belgium a small country, its location has made it Europe's economic and urban nerve center.

Property prices are relatively cheap compared to other European countries. However, the Belgian property market is strongly influenced by the economy and prices tend to constantly fluctuate. The building sector faced the 2008 crisis in a relatively better way than the Belgian economy as a whole and much better than the building sector in other European countries.

Brussels is one of the main property markets in Belgium. Therefore, prices are higher than in the rest of Belgium. Belgium is a popular expat destination and has several communities of foreign nationals living in Brussels, Wavre, Overijse, Waterloo, Rhode-St-Genese, Genval, Rixensart and La Hulpe, as well as in the university towns of Leuven and Louvain-la-Neuve.

Property investors will find plenty of reasonably priced, comfortable accommodation options available in Belgium. All types of housing are to be found, from town houses to furnished, unfurnished and luxury apartments, villas and estates.

In Belgium there are no restrictions concerning real estate acquisition, both residents and non-residents may purchase real estate.

19.2 Real estate ownership

Different forms and types of ownership

Real estate in Belgium may be owned in many different forms. Belgian property law is based mainly on the *Belgian Civil Code* (BCC). The influence of Roman law is still present.

Under Article 544 of the BCC, property includes the absolute right of use, enjoyment and alienation of a thing, to the extent its use is not contrary to compulsory rules.

In Belgium, real property ownership is governed by the principle of accession. Under this principle, the owner of a plot of land normally owns the property and all that is attached to it. The plot of land's owner thus becomes the owner of anything built on this plot of land and of any improvement or transformation made to the building, regardless of the identity of the person constructing the building and/or owning the building materials.

Besides property, real rights include usufruct, easements and two specific land rights: a building right (*droit de superficie / opstalrecht*) and a long lease right (*droit d'emphytéose / erfpachtrecht*)

When property is transferred from one owner to another (such as a result of a sale or a legacy) the property right transferred to the new owner remains the same and cannot be different to the previous owner's right. Thus, if a burden or obligation exists on a property right, such as a real right, that burden or obligation is also transferred.

The rule about the transfer of property by agreement is that the right of property is transferred as soon as the agreement is made, without any other formality. Possession of the property need not even be transferred. For real estate, however, the transfer of property as regards third parties can only be established after an entry in the Belgian Mortgage Deed registry.

Joint ownership

The BCC recognises three types of joint ownership (Article 577-2 sq. BCC):

- Free joint ownership, which occurs when two or more persons acquire real estate together

- Occasional ownership, which occurs when ownership of real estate is inherited by more than one person
- Forced joint ownership, which occurs when the parties involved are obliged to remain in joint ownership for a specific period of time

For real estate divided between different entities with separate owners, a memorandum of association (*acte de base / basisakte)* determines which parts of the buildings are common and which are private and how they are managed. The joint owners form together an association that has a legal personality and that represents the joint-owners towards third parties (Article 577-5 BCC).

Condominium

Condominium complexes, of the kind that might include a swimming pool or a gym are (almost) non-existent in Belgium.

This situation is probably a consequence of the fact that home security is not a major issue in Belgium. Although minor break-ins do occur in some neighbourhoods (especially in the larger cities), such crimes are rarely violent and the installation of a simple alarm system is often sufficient to deter potential criminals.

Building right (le droit de superficie / opstalrecht)

A building right is a right *in rem* of a maximum of 50 years' duration that allows its holder to own buildings, works or plants constructed on land belonging to another party. For the duration of his/her right, the holder is the sole owner of such assets: they may use, enjoy or demolish them provided that they returns the land in the condition in which they received it. At the expiry of the right, the holder is entitled to claim compensation for the actual value of the plants, works or buildings they have constructed.

Long lease (le bail emphytéotique / erfpachtrecht)

A long lease is a right *in rem* giving the right of use of real estate that belongs to the lessor in exchange for a yearly remuneration (*canon)*.

It is a right granted for a period from 27 to 99 years. The lessee may exercise all the rights attached to the use of the real property provided that the property's value is not reduced.

Usufruct (le droit d'usufruit / recht van vruchtgebruik)

Usufruct is a right *in rem* that gives its holder the use of a property that continues to belong to the bare owner and puts the holder under the obligation to preserve the property's substance (i.e. its fundamental structure and form).

The usufruct may not last longer than the life of the life tenant or, if the beneficiary is a legal entity, for more than 30 years.

Timesharing

Timesharing has never been popular in Belgium and is almost non-existent.

It is regulated by the law of 28 August 2011, implementing the *EU Directive 2008/122* on the protection of consumers in respect of certain aspects of timeshare, long-term holiday products, re-sale and exchange contracts.

Easements, charges, covenants, liens and mortgages

Easements (servitude / erfdienstbaarheid)

The BCC defines an easement as a real right that burdens a property to the benefit of another property (Article 637 BCC). The principle behind easements is to limit the disadvantages of the division of land in general. They aim to recreate a balance that was lost by dividing the land.

Some of the most common easements include the right of passage, the right to have sufficient light/view, and a limit upon a building's height.

An easement will always encumber a property to the benefit of another property and never to the benefit of a person. It is therefore described as a continuous and additional real right. Continuous here refers to the fact that the easement will exist as long as both properties exist. Contractual easements can however be limited to a certain period. 'Additional' means that this right is linked to the property and in principle will always pass on when the property is transferred, even if the easement was not mentioned in the sales deed.

Belgian legislation (Article 639 BCC) distinguishes between three different types of origins for easements: by natural location (e.g. the right for a higher located property to have water run down over a lower located property); by law (e.g. the prohibition to build next to a military airport); and by men. For this last category, three different ways of creating such easements are distinguished: by agreement; by open and notorious use for 30 years; and by a material deed from a former owner of two connecting properties before the properties were divided.

Easements that are created by an agreement between property owners exist legally from the moment that there is a (verbal) agreement between the parties concerned. Easement enforceability against third parties requires the easement to be registered in the Belgian Mortgage Deed registry.

Prerogative (privileges / voorrechten)

A prerogative is a security right that is attributed to a creditor because of the special nature of their debt claim (Article 12, *Law on Mortgages*). In the case of multiple creditors, this right grants a privilege to the creditor that allows them to be the first to have their claim paid out, even before the creditors that have a mortgage upon the particular property.

A prerogative can only be created by law. Belgian law has created different types of prerogatives. Most prerogatives are linked to movable assets but some prerogatives are linked to specific immovable property, for example the prerogative given to the unpaid seller of an immovable property.

A prerogative does not attribute a direct claim to a certain asset. The prerogative is limited to the money value. If the asset (e.g. an immovable property) is sold then the prerogative holder will be the first to be paid with the price received from the sale.

A prerogative on an immovable property needs to be registered in the *Mortgage Deed* registry to be enforceable against third parties (Article 29 *Law on Mortgages*).

Mortgages

The *Law on Mortgages* (Article 41) defines a mortgage as a real security right on (linked) immovable property for the appeasement of an agreement. A property becomes designated for the security of a debt without the owner losing control over the property.

There are four main characteristics of a mortgage. First, a mortgage is always linked to immovable property. Second, a mortgage is an accessory right of the secured claim. It will always be linked to this claim. If the claim no longer exists, nor will the mortgage. If the claim is transferred, so will the mortgage. Third, it creates a 'right to follow' (*droit de suite / volgrecht*). That means even if the property is transferred to a third party, the property will remain a security for the claim to which it is an accessory. Finally, a mortgage is indivisible. A part-payment of the claim will not reduce the nature of the mortgage. The mortgage, in terms of all the rights and obligations arising for all parties involved, will remain as a whole until the claim is fully paid.

A mortgage always needs to be registered in the Mortgage Deed registry to be enforceable.

There are three ways a mortgage can be created (Article 43 *Law on Mortgages*): by law; by agreement; or by will.

A conventional mortgage can be created for any type of valid claim, and even for possible future claims. In the past, Belgian banks, when attributing a loan for a piece of real estate, have sometimes tried to take a mortgage not only for the initial loan but also for all possible future loans or debts that the client may have with the bank. To prevent possible abuses of this system a specific law was created in 1995 for mortgage loans.

Protection of ownership, proof of ownership and registration

In principle, under Belgian law a sale is "perfect" when there is an agreement on the object and the price.

However, contracts concerning rights on real estates should take place by a notarial deed, signed in front of a notary and deposited in the notary's Minutes. The notary will verify the registry's documents to determine whether any other transfer of title has been registered for the same property, indicating that the seller is no longer the owner, and whether there are liens, encumbrances, or servitudes on the property. If the registry lists other notarial acts as having been registered for the same land, the notary can request copies of them to analyse fully the existing ownership rights.

The mortgage deed will then be sent to the Mortgage Office (*Bureau de la Conservation des Hypothèques / Hypotheekkantoor*), a branch of the Treasury Department, to be registered in the Mortgage Deed registry.

19.3 Purchase and sale of real estate

The sales agreement

Under Belgian law (Article 1583 BCC) a purchase is concluded when there is an agreement on the object and the price, meaning that even a non-written agreement is binding upon the parties concerned, although in practice, proof of such a verbal agreement may be difficult to provide.

Such an agreement could form the basis of a request in law for specific performance, meaning that a court could order the execution of the verbal agreement. Such a court order can be registered in the registry thus making such a purchase enforceable against third parties. In some cases such a specific performance order could have unexpected consequences and so it is more common in such cases to demand the agreement's termination with compensation for damages.

Once an agreement has been reached, the purchase is concluded and the property's ownership is legally transferred. This transfer is however not yet enforceable against third parties. To obtain such protection the purchase must be registered in the registry (Article 1 *Law on Mortgages*). This registration must be made within a three month period, meaning that the registration rights must also be paid within this period.

This rule often causes lots of practical problems. For instance, often the buyer still needs to receive a loan before s/he can effectively buy the property. If a purchase agreement has been reached and the buyer has not yet managed to receive the loan, the purchase still must be registered within three months and the registration rights must be paid. Only if a purchase agreement is annulled by a court decision may it not be registered.

To avoid these types of problems in practice, notaries or real estate agents always work with 'preliminary' contracts (often called *compromis de vente / verkoopscompromis*) that contain a certain number of suspensive conditions. Only if all the suspensive conditions are met, for example if a loan has been granted, then the purchase agreement itself will enter into force. The four month period will therefore only start after all the conditions are met.

Whatever name is given to such preliminary contracts, they will be regarded as a sales contract if there is an agreement on the object and the price.

Real estate agents will often propose pre-printed standard forms of agreement. There are significant differences amongst such standard form contracts and both parties should be very careful about the terms and conditions these contracts contain. It is recommended that such a contract is reviewed by a lawyer or notary prior to signature.

The unilateral promise and the bilateral promise

The unilateral promise (*promesse unilatérale de vente / eenzijdige verkoopsbelofte*) is similar to an option to purchase. The seller grants the buyer the right to purchase the property for a predetermined price. The buyer must exercise the option to purchase within a specified period of time. If the option is exercised the purchase is complete.

It is legally possible for the seller to ask for compensation for the unilateral promise. In such a case the buyer needs to pay a deposit to the seller when the unilateral promise is granted. If the buyer does not exercise the option within the given period then s/he will lose his/her deposit.

The bilateral promise (*promesse synallagmatique de vente / wederzijdse verkoopbelofte*) must be distinguished from the unilateral promise. Technically, the bilateral promise is the equivalent of a sale. The binding force of the bilateral promise is stronger than the unilateral promise inasmuch as the bilateral promise can be enforced as an actual sale before the courts by way of specific performance. There would only be a difference between a bilateral promise and an actual sale if one or both parties have suspensive conditions linked to their promise.

The sales deed (l'acte de vente/verkoopsakte)

As mentioned above, a preliminary contract needs to be followed by a notarial deed within a four month period.

The notary needs this period to verify the property's situation at the registry of deeds and obtain information from any registered creditors concerning the amounts required to discharge any outstanding mortgages. The notary will also need to check several environmental issues and possible pre-emptive rights. These matters can vary considerably from one region to another.

The sales deed will include the full identity of the parties, the price, the description of the property being sold, the legal warranties and specific conditions and the property's history over the last 30 years. The sales deed thoroughly describe the complexities of the transaction. It may also specify a date different to the signature date concerning the right to occupy the property.

The notary will register the sales deed at the registry, which puts all third parties on notice that the transfer has taken place. Notaries have a legal monopoly over the registration of such deeds.

Restrictions on acquisition and conveyance

Restrictions under matrimonial law and matrimonial property law

If the seller is married, his/her disposal capacity is based, amongst other things, on dispositions of matrimonial law and his/her matrimonial property regime.

Choice of law

There is no possibility of choice of law under the *Belgian Code of Private International Law* (CPIL).

The applicable matrimonial law will be determined by the actual (common) residence of the spouses.

In accordance with CPIL, there is a limited choice of applicable matrimonial law.

Applicable matrimonial law

Under Article 215 BCC, one of the spouses cannot sell (lend or rent) the family home (defined as real estate acquired privately, i.e. by natural persons and not through a legal entity such as a company).

Applicable matrimonial property law

The Belgian default regime is the regime of common property of marital gains. If the spouses do not make an explicit choice before they marry then this regime will apply. It is possible to change the marital regime during the marriage if the applicable procedures are followed (Articles 1392, 1394-1396 BCC). Since same-sex marriages are permissible in Belgium, the same regimes apply to these marriages too.

Legal regime of community of marital gains

Under this default regime, there is a common property and each spouse also has his/her own separate property.

Assets and Debt

Assets that belong to each spouse's separate property include the assets each spouse owned at the time of the celebration of the marriage and strictly personal goods (such as clothes and jewellery). Pensions, gifts, inheritances or bequests acquired during the marriage also are each spouse's separate property. Community property includes the spouses' professional income, income from separate property, assets given to both spouses jointly or to one of them with the specification that it should be common. Besides these specific types of property, it is presumed that all other assets, unless proven to be separate property, are community property.

The rules concerning debts are similar to those concerning assets, as set out above (Articles 1406-1407 BCC).

Management

The spouses are equal under the law. Each spouse manages his/her separate property independently. The community property is managed according to the rule of concurrent management (Article 1416 BCC). Each spouse can exercise management powers on his/her own and can, for example, let or rent (for a period not exceeding nine years) a common real estate (with the notable exception of the family home). There are two exceptions to this management of the community property. The first exception concerns professional activities. The second one is joint management for certain acts that are seen as important. This exception encompasses, among other things, the sale of common real estate or borrowing money and taking out a mortgage.

Regime of separation of property (Articles 1466-1469 BCC)

This regime, which must be agreed explicitly by a marital contract, reduces the estate consequences of a marriage to a minimum. Under this regime, everything is separated: assets, debts and management. Each spouse has his/her own separate property and there is no community property.

Full community property

These types of marital contracts are modifications of the legal regime. The spouses adopting a community property regime may not derogate from the management rules or the rules concerning creditor's rights towards the legal regime. Moreover, professional revenues always have to be part of the community property. Besides these requirements, the spouses enjoy a large degree of freedom in how they contract their marital regime.

Legal cohabitation (the relationship of cohabitation)

Belgium does not only recognize marriage between two persons of the same sex but also the legal partnership or the relationship of cohabitation.

The registration of the written contract of cohabitation can only take place in Belgium if, at the time such contract is entered into, both partners have their joint habitual residence in Belgium.

Every legal partner has his/her own separate property (or 50% of the undivided property). There is no community property.

The family home can only be sold or rented with the consent of both partners.

Accretion clause and *Tontine*

These two concepts are mostly used in situations where unmarried couples jointly acquire real estate that will be used as the couple's dwelling. Although these concepts have no legal basis, they are widely-accepted in legal practice. A *tontine* is an agreement under which two or more persons jointly acquire an asset and under which the survivor becomes the owner of whole the asset. All the parties to the agreement must have an equal chance of acquiring the assets. The acquirers obtain their rights directly based upon the acquisition agreement. A *tontine* can therefore never be agreed upon without the involvement of the initial owner/original seller. This is the reason why people often prefer an accretion clause.

An accretion clause implies that all the participants in the clause agree that upon the realization of a certain event, often the death of one of the participants, the part of one participant is added automatically to the part(s) of the other participants. As is the case with a tontine, all the parties to the agreement must have equal chances of acquiring the asset. The asset's seller is not part of the accretion agreement. Both in case of a tontine or an accretion clause, the part that is acquired by the surviving party will not be part of the predeceased party's estate. The asset will be treated as the survivor's property following the conclusion of the original agreement in which the asset was jointly acquired.

Split purchase of usufruct and bare property with accretion at the time of death of the usufructuary

Usufruct automatically accretes to the bare property at the time of death of the beneficiary of the usufruct. A split purchase can be advantageous. For example, if parents buy the usufruct of a house, the children buy – with their own funds - the bare property. Upon the parents' death, the usufruct will automatically and without further taxes accrete to the bare property held by the children. In this respect, it is advised to pay careful attention to certain "fictions" applicable under inheritance taxes that could lead to tax liability.

Options and pre-emption rights

Pre-emption rights are legal or contractual rights to purchase land or property before anyone else.

In Belgium a large number of different options and pre-emption rights exist. Federal or regional governments, municipalities, provinces and semi-governmental entities may all have a right of pre-emption regarding a real estate property acquisition.

Information in this respect is not always easy to find. Based upon their general advice and information obligations, a notary has the duty to check if there is a pre-emption right regarding a specific property before they can execute the purchase deed. If a pre-emptive right exists, notification of the intended sale must be given and the holder of the pre-emptive right has the right to buy the property. In principle, the property should be bought at the same price and upon the same conditions as was agreed by the original buyer.

Agricultural real estate

Regulatory power over agricultural issues has been transferred by the Belgian Federal government to the three Regions. Each of the Regions has issued specific rules regarding agricultural real estate and forests. There are different options and pre-emption rights that are accorded to different regional semi-governmental entities.

Agricultural land can often be purchased, exchanged or rented from these entities.

Restrictions regarding the acquisition of real estate by foreigners

Foreigners may freely buy land in Belgium. There are no specific restrictions upon acquiring immovable assets or upon obtaining loans from either Belgian or foreign banks. There are however significant tax regime differences depending upon whether the taxpayer has his/her tax residence in Belgium or abroad (see below).

Capacity and entitlement of the seller

The parties must be capable of acting with full legal capacity for their consent to be validly given and for a sale to be valid.

In principle, every major (an adult over the age of 18 in Belgium) has full legal capacity except if a statute or a judgment expressly provides otherwise. For a minor (under the age of 18 in Belgium) to validly sell, their legal representative or parent must act on their behalf and court approval will be required.

Adults who become physically or mentally incapacitated, and so are unable to manage their own property, can be placed under a type of legal guardianship or their property be put under temporary administration.

For actions such as the sale of real estate, the temporary administrator will have to seek a special authorization from the competent judge.

In September 2014, Belgium enacted a new regime concerning incapacity.

Power of Attorney

A power of attorney can be given to a third party. It is advisable to pass the power of attorney before a notary.

The power of attorney can be specific and limited in time or general.

The representation of legal entities

Companies are in principle fully capable of acting, in the same manner as natural persons. The issue that arises for contracting parties is mainly the company's valid representation. How could a third party be sure that they are actually contracting with the company itself and not with the natural person signing the contract?

The company's power of representation usually belongs to a company's director or board of directors.

In a company without legal personality, any restriction upon this power of representation is enforceable against a third party; that means that it is for a third party to assure themselves that the natural person claiming to represent the company has the actual authority to do so. In a company with a legal personality and without limited liability, such restrictions are enforceable against third parties as soon as they are published in the *Belgian Official Journal*. Both hypotheses may lead to uncomfortable situations in practice.

Therefore, the law provides for the so-called *Prokura-system* in companies with legal personality and limited liability, i.e. that contractual limitations of the power - both internally or externally - of the directors, are not enforceable against a third party in any event but only in a case where it is clear that the third party should be aware of such a restriction. In other words, third parties should know or find out know the legal division of responsibility within a company.

In a public company limited by shares (*SA/NV*), legal representation should be collegiate as well as the decision itself. However such a company's *Articles of Incorporation* may allocate the power to represent the company to one or more directors in particular. Such a delegation is enforceable against third parties and again any limitation upon this power can never be invoked against third parties.

Third party claims and unpaid taxes

The search at the *Registry of Deeds* prior to completion will reveal whether there are outstanding mortgages, judicial liens or tax liens. The notary will ensure at closing that any mortgages and liens are discharged.

In the case of a mistake, this will probably be deemed professional negligence and the notary will be liable.

The notary will also check whether there are unpaid taxes and will automatically withhold such unpaid taxes from the amount that is ultimately paid to the seller.

Provisions for protecting the environment, nature and cultural heritage

Environmental protection

Environmental issues are a competence of the three Regions in Belgium. The rules therefore vary from one region to another. The applicable environmental protection regulations must be respected when requesting planning permits. They are more relevant to developments, whether industrial or residential, rather than to building individual homes.

Protection of cultural heritage

The protection of cultural heritage and monuments used to be a competence split between the Federal and Regional governments. Since 1 July 2014, this competence has been completely transferred to the three Regions.

Protected property can still be sold but there are certain obligations imposed on the owners of such properties. They have a duty to maintain and protect the property.

Changes to the protected property are in general allowed and are strictly regulated. Owners of protected property can on the other hand often benefit from subsidies and tax advantages.

Access to relevant records and documents

The records of the registry of deeds are in principle not publicly accessible. Certain information can however be obtained.

In the local registry office certain information is publicly accessible, such as the owner of a property, the property's history of previous owners, the cadastral income and the cadastral section. To obtain such information, specific application forms must be used. Property owners can also obtain a copy of the registry document (but not the official document).

In the regional head office, official documents can be requested. Again, official application forms must be used.

Key points that a seller should consider

While the seller must inform the buyer of any hidden defects of which s/he is aware, real property is usually sold on an 'as is' basis. Defects can relate to the buildings or land itself and also to legal issues regarding property, for example the absence of documents relating to building permits. The seller's liability in this respect will be more important if the seller is a professional in the real estate business. The deed should describe any apparent defects in the property so that the buyer cannot deny having been informed about them.

The seller must also inform the buyer of all easements that encumber the property.

Before a property can be sold, the seller must obtain a certain number of documents and certificates. Some of these documents will be obtained by the notary that will execute the purchase deed. Other documents and certificates must be obtained by the seller at his/her own cost, for example an energy efficiency certificate or a technical approval of the building's electrical circuits.

The execution of a real estate purchase transaction

Once there is an agreement as to the purchase price and other conditions then a preliminary contract will be signed subject to suspensive conditions. In practice such a contract will usually be drafted by a notary or a real estate agent.

Afterwards a purchase deed must be signed and the registration duties paid within a four month period. In practice it usually takes three to four months before the purchase deed is signed. That time-period allows the notary to obtain the necessary documentation (such as the registry documents, certificates regarding zoning regulations and certificates regarding soil pollution).

Notaries in Belgium may act for both parties without such representation being considered a conflict of interest. However either party may always select his/her own notary, without the other party being entitled to refuse. The presence of an additional notary in the transaction does not increase costs because the notaries will divide the fees.

The cost of purchase (notarial fees and registration costs) is, by custom, paid by the buyer.

At the moment the preliminary contract is signed a deposit of 10% is usually paid.

The real estate agent (l'agent immobilier / vastgoed makelaar)

Any person habitually acting as a real estate intermediary and receiving commissions for doing so must be licensed and insured. The real estate agent must also have a third party bank account (*compte tiers / derdenrekening*) to receive the client's funds. This is a specific kind of bank account that clearly indicates that the money in this account is not owned by the bank account owner.

The real estate agent must have a mandate from the seller to show property to potential buyers. If the buyer has instructed the agent, then a mandate to search for property is necessary. The agent may only claim a commission if the transaction is completed. However, the contract can specify that a commission is due if the agent has found a candidate buyer that has made a genuine bid. Such a bid must be made in writing.

The mandate may be exclusive or non-exclusive. It should detail, among other things, the property, the selling price, the amount of commission, and whether or not the mandate is exclusive.

The mandate must be limited in time. For an exclusive mandate, the period cannot exceed six months, although it can be renewed.

The agent is responsible for informing the client of a property's market value, particularly where the client is selling at a price considerably lower than usual price for the area.

The agent's commission is freely negotiable. The seller's commission is generally between 3% and 5% (plus 21% VAT).

The notary (le notaire / de notaris)

There are approximately 1,500 notaries in Belgium. The notary is a ministerial officer appointed by the government. Notarial fees are fixed and not ordinarily negotiable. The notary's participation is necessary for any transfer of title to property (other than for transfer by the government or by auction). Only the notary may register the transfer documents at the registry of deeds (and is necessary to give notice to third parties of the transfer).

It will be the notary's responsibility to verify that the seller has good title and that any outstanding liens or mortgages can be discharged with the purchase price. The notary will most commonly receive and hold both the initial deposit and the purchase price on a third party account until such a discharge takes place. Sometimes the price can also be paid outside the notary's accounts, although such a step is not recommended. Where separate notaries act for the buyer and seller, the fees will be divided between them and there will be no extra cost for the buyer.

The notary owes the client and the parties, if he is the sole notary, a duty of confidentiality and the duty to advise them of all the risks inherent in a transaction. The notary must verify the parties' identities and their capacity to act. The notary must also make a declaration to the appropriate financial intelligence unit (CTIF /CFI in Belgium) whenever the origin of funds for any transaction appears to be suspicious. The notary may not advise his/her clients of those suspicions.

The notary will pay the registration taxes for each sale and will therefore demand that the buyer pays, on top of the purchase price, the registration taxes and fees prior to completing the transaction.

Powers of attorney

To sign a notarial deed using a power of attorney, the powers of attorney must be given in a separate notarial deed. This can happen using a foreign notary's deed.

The power of attorney must clearly specify the property and may set limits as to the price (for example "not less than a certain amount" without specifying the actual sale price eventually agreed).

Financing

It is very common to obtain bank financing for a property transaction. Belgian banks will lend to non-residents and foreign banks may loan and obtain mortgages on Belgian properties.

The loan will typically be secured by a mortgage. Generally this mortgage will be for the amount borrowed with an increase of 10 to 20% for certain "accessories" such as the costs of foreclosing and interest arising if there is a foreclosure. However, since the registration cost of the mortgage will be a percentage of the entire amount secured, the cost of such accessories will increase the overall cost.

The lender may be satisfied, in rare cases, with a promise to mortgage rather than a mortgage itself, although such a promise will not secure the bank's loan, since other borrowers may then register a lien and have precedence over the bank.

Mortgage loans are commonly concluded for periods between 10 to 30 years. A mortgage loan can have a fixed or variable interest rate. Variable rates can only be changed at predetermined moments, such as every year or every five years. Mortgage loans of up to 100% of the value of the purchased property have been granted in the past. In recent times a percentage of 80% is more likely.

As the foreclosure procedure is cumbersome and requires a sale of the property at auction, lenders will not be satisfied in securing the value of the property alone and so will also want to verify income stream(s) to determine whether the borrower can make the mortgage repayments. Ordinarily, the monthly mortgage repayment should not be more than 33% of the borrower's monthly net income.

Mortgage loans often provide a tax advantage. This issue used to be a Federal competence but was recently transferred to the Regions.

As well as loans covered by a mortgage, other types of loan are also possible. A fairly common alternative is a loan (often called a "Lombard" loan) guaranteed by a pledge on deposits or on an investment portfolio (referred to as "pledged assets"). Generally these kinds of loan do not give a tax advantage. They are mostly concluded for shorter periods (such as for between one month to five years) and are easy renewable. The interest rates and administrative costs are far lower than those on a mortgage loan.

In general, no capital repayments are made during the loan period and only interest is repaid. This arrangement enables the borrower to invest the pledged assets and generate a financial leverage. As long as the return on investment remains higher than the interest cost of the loan it is financially attractive to keep the loan. If the loan cost exceeds the return on investment then the loan can easily be repaid using the pledged capital.

For these types of loans the amount loaned is not linked to the value of the purchased property but to the value of the pledged assets.

Purchase through a company

There is no single solution for every type of real estate investment in Belgium. Whether an asset deal or a share deal is optimal will depend on the nature of the investor, its objectives and the characteristics of the investment project.

Most large investments are structured via special purpose companies (so each project has its own company).

Capital gains on shares are often either not or only taxed in a limited way in Belgium (see below). Contrary to what happens in the case of an asset deal, the purchaser will not benefit from any step-up on the asset, which will keep the tax value it previously had. The purchase price for the shares of a company owning real estate is usually determined, taking into account a discount of 50% of the standard corporate income tax rate (i.e. 16.995%) on the hidden capital gain.

Defects and warranty claims

Warranty claims favouring the buyer

Every seller has the obligation to deliver and transfer the sold property to the buyer. This obligation also contains the duty to deliver the property as defined in the purchase agreement and to deliver the accessories of the sold property (e.g. the easements). If the seller does not fulfil his/her obligation to the buyer then the buyer has the right to seek specific performance.

The seller also needs to protect the buyer against eviction (*garantie en cas d'éviction / vrijwaring voor uitwinning*) (Article 1626 BCC). The seller has to protect the buyer against attacks against their ownership rights. This obligation entails protection against the seller's own actions (for example if a seller sells a house twice to different persons) and also against the actions of third parties (for example given where it is discovered that a rental agreement exists for the property).

The seller will be liable for defects preventing or reducing the possible use of the property or making the property unfit for its intended use. First, the buyer has an obligation to check for existing defects that could be discovered by a typically attentive person. If such a defect is discovered then the buyer may request either a price reduction or a cancellation of the purchase itself. The request for either should be filed within the shortest available time following the defect's discovery. Secondly, the seller is liable for hidden defects that could be discovered at the moment of transfer. Such a petition should also be filed within the shortest available time after discovery.

Warranty claims favouring the seller

Just as the seller has an obligation to deliver the purchased property, so the buyer has an obligation to accept the transfer. However in practice, it is more difficult for a seller to file a claim for specific performance if the buyer refuses to accept the transfer. A seller would be more likely to seek an annulment of the purchase and to ask for damages.

A seller who has not been fully paid has a particular type of interest or right in the property. This particular situation means that if the buyer goes bankrupt and the property is put into a forced sale then the seller would be the first to be paid with the sale proceeds. To exercise this particular type of interest or right, the seller must register his/her prerogative in the registry.

If the seller discovers that they have sold the property for a price less than 7/12th of the property's market value, the seller can ask that the sale be rescinded. The request must be presented within two years of the sale and proof of the market value must be presented by three experts named either by the parties or by the court. The buyer can choose to pay the remainder of the "just" price or return the property to the seller and receive the price paid in return.

19.4 New construction, rebuilding and renovation

Construction zones and construction permits

All regions and municipalities in Belgium have divided their territories into different zones, such as building, agricultural, forestry and industrial zones. The question of whether a building can be constructed on a particular piece of property and if so, what type of building (such as a house or factory) depends first of all on the zone in which the property itself is situated.

Such urban structuring plans are in general set up for longer periods of time and are not easily changed by a Region or a Municipality.

Building permit (permis de construire / bouw vergunning)

A building permit is required to construct a new building or modify an existing building concerning its use, volume, exterior aspect or number of floors. Modification of the interior layout of a building does not require a permit unless it will modify the use to which the building is put, modifies the number of floors, or modifies the structural composition of the house.

Demolition also requires permission. Certain works require only a preliminary notification *(déclaration préalable / meldingsplicht)*. Adding a swimming pool, whether covered or not, may require a notification rather than a permit depending upon its design.

A permit request is filed with the Municipality by the property owner or his/her representative. The use of an architect is usually not required if the foreseen modifications or new building(s) do not require a building permit, although this situation is not always the case. It is advisable to check the situation first with the Municipality. If a building permit is required then an architect will be needed.

If a permit is granted, work must begin within a two year period and must not be interrupted for more than two years. The construction work must also have reached a certain level of completion within a three year period.

The architect

A person may only practice as an architect if s/he is a member of the *Order of Architects*. Any works requiring a building permit must be based on a plan prepared by an architect who defines the place of the building(s) on the land, the volumes, layout, colours and materials.

The owner's contract with the architect is not a mandate from the owner to the architect. The architect will require a specific power of attorney to carry out additional tasks such as signing building contracts on the owner's behalf or paying the contractors.

The architectural contract should accurately describe the architect's role in relation to the project: it may go from the conception of the building to its receipt by the owner and cover some or all of the steps in-between.

The architect has a permanent obligation to advise and assist his/her client. The architect may be charged with directing the works, and with supervising them. The architect's fees are freely negotiable, although the Order publishes "suggested fee" schedules. The fees may be fixed (*forfait*) or based on a percentage of the cost of the works, or a mixture of both. For constructing a new building the range of percentages is often between 6% and 9% of the cost of the works (excluding VAT). The architect must have professional liability insurance.

The building contract (des marches / aannemingen)

Belgian legislation does not provide an exact definition of a building contract. It is however often defined as an agreement where one party (the master builder) charges another party (the contractor) to complete a task by means of material and intellectual actions without the contractor having the power to represent the master builder or being in a subordinate role.

Contractors need to be registered in Belgium. The use of non-registered contractors can have very serious consequences for the master builder. For instance a master builder that works with non-registered contractors becomes responsible for certain social and tax debts of the non-registered contractor.

Contractors have, to some extent, a 10 year liability for the work they have done.

If there are at least two different contractors that are used for the building then a safety coordinator must be appointed.

The Home Construction Law

The *Home Construction Law* (HCL; often called *loi Breyne / wet Breyne*), applies to agreements that transfer the property of a house or apartment that is yet to be constructed or is under construction; or contain the obligation to construct or deliver such an immovable property (if the house or apartment will be used by the buyer to live in or work and live in and the buyer has to make several payments before the building is finished).

The HCL is a typical consumer protection law that is interpreted very broadly.

All agreements that fall under the scope of the law must have several specific pieces of information concerning matters such as the price, way of payment, delivery date.

Under the HCL, the normal 10 year liability for contractors is extended to the building developer (Article 6 HCL) who has sold the yet-to-be-built house to the buyer. This is a very important protection for the buyer.

Upon the building's completion, it is formally accepted by the owner. The 10 year guarantee is triggered by this receipt or acceptance of the building by the owner. At the formal handing over, all reservations about the construction and appearance are preserved in a minute or *procès-verbal de reception / process verbal van aanvaarding* that is signed by all the parties. An individual buyer would be advised to have an independent architect or expert present during this process.

The ten year guarantee

The law provides that all the contractors, building developers, the architect and their sub-agents involved in a particular construction project are liable for 10 years, following the owner's acceptance of the building, for any defect in the works that could affect the building's solidity or any essential elements that would make the building unfit for its intended use. That warranty does not cover minor defects. Case-law construes "works" widely so that, for example, a swimming pool or a support wall are included. Renovations will also be covered by the 10 year guarantee.

It is important to verify that the insurance actually covers the type of work done by the contractor. Thus a general policy does not necessarily cover work on swimming pools. The insurance will continue its validity even when the contractor goes bankrupt or otherwise ceases to work, provided that it was in force when the work commenced.

19.5 Rental and tenancy

General rules

Rent is a type of contract that is very strictly regulated in Belgium. The general rules applicable to all types of rental agreements can be found in Articles 1714-1762 BCC. These general rules are not binding for parties that wish to conclude a rental contract. The parties can decide certain rights and obligations in the contract that deviate from these general rules. However if a rental contract does not express a specific deviating rule then the general rules will apply.

Apart from these general rules, Belgian law has created specific rules for certain kinds of rental agreements (for example, contracts concerning a property that is used as the main residence by the tenant, or as a commercial rent or as social housing). The rules that are set out in these specific laws are, in principle, binding for the parties concerned.

When looking at a rental agreement it is of the utmost importance to first determine which set of rules are applicable. In this respect, the wording used in the contract is not important. It is the actual factual situation that will determine the applicable legislation.

If the general rules apply then a rental contract can either be for a determined period of a maximum of 99 years or for an undetermined period. Contracts for a determined period cannot be terminated by a unilateral decision of one of the parties, unless such action is foreseen in the contract. Contracts for an undetermined period can at all times be terminated by the unilateral decision of either of the parties, if a termination period of one month is given. Both types of contract can at all times be ended by the mutual consent of all parties concerned.

All contracts for a period of more than nine years need to be registered in the registry.

Unless otherwise determined in the rental contract, sub-renting is permitted without the proprietor's consent.

The sale of a rented property does not terminate a rental contract. However the important question remains about how far the specific details of a rental contract are enforceable against the buyer. The answer to this question depends on different aspects of the particular purchase and is not always very clear. It is possible to include a specific clause in the purchase agreement determining that the buyer will fully respect the existing rental agreement.

Contracts concerning property that is used as a main residence by the tenant

In 1991 a specific section of the *House Renting Law* (HRL) was included in the Belgian Civil Code (after Article 1762 BCC). This section applies to all rental contracts where the tenant (a natural person) uses the rented property as his/her main residence. Whether or not the property is used as a main residence by the tenant is a factual discussion. A person's domicile is in this respect an important but not determining criteria.

The use of the property as a main residence has to be with the consent of the owner. Such a consent can be given either expressly or silently. A simple contractual clause that a property cannot be used as a main residence is not allowed (Articles 1§1 and 2 HRL).

The HRL has several very specific rules that deviate from the general rules and are mainly for the protection of the tenant.

In general, a rental contract that is subject to the HRL will always be for a predetermined period of nine years. At the end of that period the contract will not automatically end. It will be renewed for a period of three years unless a termination letter was sent at least six months' in advance.

Unilateral terminations of the rental contract are possible but are strictly regulated and vary depending upon whether the tenant or the landlord wishes to end the contract. Even terminations by mutual consent are strictly determined and not always possible.

A rental contract that is subject to the HRL needs to be registered at the registry.

Sub-renting a property that is used as a main residence is in principle not allowed. Under certain circumstances partial sub-renting could be allowed but only with the landlord's consent.

If the property is sold the buyer will, in principle, need to respect the existing rental contract.

Commercial rent

In 1951 a specific section of the Commercial Rent Law (CRL) was included in the Belgian Civil Code concerning commercial rental contracts. This section applies to a rental contract if the following cumulative conditions are met: the rental contract must concern the rent of an immovable property that is mainly used for a small commercial or craft enterprise and this use is with the landlord's explicit or implicit agreement.

The main principles of the CRL are similar to those of the House Renting Law. The rules apply to factual situations where various different cumulative conditions are met regardless of how the parties have named the contract. The rules mainly provide for the tenant's protection.

The minimum rental period that must apply is for nine years. Unilateral termination of the contract by the landlord is only possible in a very limited number of situations. Unilateral termination by the tenant is more flexible. Early termination by mutual consent is possible but is also strictly regulated. It needs to be done either in an authenticated deed or before a Judge. At the end of the initial nine year period the tenant remains highly protected and they have the right to demand an extension of the contract (Article 13 CRL).

Sub-renting is in principle allowed but can be limited in the rental contract.

If the property is sold there are different situations possible depending upon whether the rental contract has a fixed date or not. The buyer has very limited possibilities to terminate such a contract.

19.6 Successions and gifts

Applicable succession law and jurisdiction

The *Belgian Code of Private International Law* (CPIL) determines the law applying in the area of succession and inheritance.

Article 79 CPIL permits a person to designate the law that will apply to that person's (entire) estate. That designation must be expressed in a declaration that is in the form of a will. The deceased only has limited choices s/he can make about this designation.

In the absence of a valid choice of law, the succession or inheritance is governed by the succession law of the legal jurisdiction in which the deceased had his/her habitual residence at the time of death (unless it can be demonstrated that s/he clearly had closer connections with the law of another jurisdiction than the jurisdiction of his/her habitual residence at the time of death).

The courts of the deceased's last domicile have primary jurisdiction.

A distinction can be made between the Law of Succession and the Law of Donations as the latter includes Donations *inter vivos* and Wills even though both branches of the law are often applied together in practice. As an example, making a donation or making a will should take the rules of the disposable portion into account, with those rules belonging to the Law of Succession. On the other hand, the heirs have to restore to the beneficiaries of the donor's estate the donations and the legacies that were given to them by the deceased person unless otherwise provided.

Fundamentals of the succession and gift/donation laws of Belgium

1. Intestate succession

Heirship based on partnership or blood relation

In the absence of a will, only blood relatives and the surviving spouse will inherit. A legal cohabiting partner also has limited inheritance rights. A distinction is made based on whether there is a surviving spouse.

Inheritance in the absence of a surviving spouse

There is an order in which blood relatives inherit:

- First order: children, grandchildren and so on
- Second order: parents, brothers and/or sisters of the deceased
- Third order: parents, in the absence of brothers or sisters of the deceased; grandparents and so on
- Fourth order: collaterals, other than brothers and sisters (e.g. aunts, cousins)

Relatives of one order exclude relatives of the next order. Within an order, the persons closest to the deceased will inherit. The closeness is calculated by the "degree" (Articles 737-8 BCC). The inheritance rights of the collaterals are restricted to the fourth degree (Article 755 BCC). No such restriction exists for the descending and ascending line.

Inheritance in the Presence of a Surviving Spouse

The devolution of the succession will depend on the marital property regime of the spouses. When one of the spouses dies, the marital property regime must be settled first. It is only after settling the marital property regime that the succession can be dealt with. The inheritance rights of the surviving spouse depend on the presence of other heirs (Article 745 BCC). If there are descendants (typically children or grandchildren) present, the surviving spouse's inheritance rights encompass the usufruct on the entire estate. The descendants' inheritance rights will be determined by the rules set out above (Inheritance in the Absence of a Surviving Spouse); so instead of inheriting the full property, their rights will be limited to the bare property of the estate.

In the presence of other heirs, the surviving spouse receives the full property of the deceased spouse's half in the community property. As a consequence, when one spouse dies, the surviving spouse receives full ownership of the community property. The survivor will be given one half as a result of the settlement of the marital property regime and another half as a result of the settlement of the succession. The surviving spouse will also receive the usufruct of the separate property of the deceased spouse. If there are no other heirs, the surviving spouse will receive full ownership of the entire estate. Heirs may prefer full ownership instead of bare ownership or usufruct. The BCC makes it possible for heirs to request conversion of their usufruct or bare ownership into full ownership (the procedure and conditions are set out in Article 745 BCC).

Inheritance rights of the surviving legal cohabiting partner (Article 745 BCC)

Legal cohabitants who survive their deceased partner have limited inheritance rights. A surviving legal cohabitant who is not a descendant of the deceased inherits the usufruct of the immovable asset that was used as the family dwelling during the period of cohabitation, regardless of any other heirs that have inheritance rights relating to the deceased's succession. If the cohabitants rented the asset that was used as the family dwelling, the surviving cohabitant, who is not a descendant of the deceased, has the right to the dwelling's rent. All other heirs are excluded of this right.

Restitution (rapport / inbreng)

All gifts made by the donor/deceased to persons who have inheritance rights in the deceased's estate are presumed to be an advance on the deceased's inheritance. When the donor dies, these donees / heirs must effectively restitute (or return their counter-value) their gift into the estate. This mechanism is in place to treat all heirs equally. However, it is possible for the donor to explicitly state that a gift does not have to be restituted at the time of death.

Will formalities and enforceability of foreign wills

Belgian law allows three types of wills: the holograph will, the public will, and the international will.

Holograph will

A holograph will is a will in its most simple form. It must be written by hand by the testator (maker of the will), mention the date on which it has been written and duly signed by the testator (Article 970 BCC).

Public will

A public will is an instrument drawn up by a notary in the presence of two witnesses or an instrument drawn up by two notaries (Article 971 BCC). A public will is subject to specific formal requirements for formal deeds and public wills. This type of will must be read to and signed by the testator.

International will

The rules concerning this type of will are set out in *the Convention Providing a Uniform Law on the Form of an International Will of 26*

October 1973 (the Convention). The international will consists of both a private document and formal deed drawn up by a notary. This type of will is made in writing and does not have to be written by the testator themselves. It may be written by hand or by any other means. The testator must declare in the presence of two witnesses and a notary that the document is the testator's last will. The testator must sign the will (on each page and at the end of the will), unless the testator is unable to sign, in which case the reasons for this situation must be explained. The notary attaches a formal document to the will to certify that the formalities prescribed in the Convention have been taken into account.

Validity of foreign wills in Belgium

Regarding the validity of foreign wills in Belgium, the *Convention of October 5th 1961 on the Conflict of Laws Relating to the Form of Testamentary Dispositions* applies. A testamentary disposition is valid as to its form if it complies with the local law:

- Of the place where the testator made it, or
- Of a nationality possessed by the testator, either at the time when they made the disposition, or at the time of their death, or
- Of a place in which the testator had their domicile either at the time when they made the disposition, or at the time of their death, or
- Of the place in which the testator had their habitual residence either at the time when they made the disposition, or at the time of their death, or
- To the extent that immovable property is concerned, of the place where such property is situated

It is important to note that testamentary dispositions made only in oral form by Belgian citizens that only have Belgian nationality will not be recognized.

Forced heirship

"Reserved Portion" and "Disposable Share"

Belgian estate law contains forced heirship rules. Some family members, such as the children, surviving spouse and, in some cases, parents and grandparents, have an entitlement to a fixed share in the deceased's estate. Forced heirs cannot be excluded from the inheritance. Even if the deceased excludes a forced heir from the inheritance by will, this heir will be able to claim the portion to which they was entitled by means of a reduction claim. To calculate the portion to which these protected heirs are entitled, the so-called "reserved portion," the fictitious hereditary mass or total must be determined. The reserved portion will include both the assets present in the estate of the deceased at the time of death and also lifetime gifts made by the deceased. Debts of the deceased will be deducted from this total. This system is intended to protect the forced heirs. In this way, the deceased cannot leave forced heirs with nothing at the time of his death by giving away all their assets during their lifetime. Hence, the deceased will only be able to dispose freely of a part of their estate, the so-called "disposable share."

Reduction claim

If the deceased has made too many gifts during their lifetime and/or too many bequests in the will, the forced heirs will be able to claim a reduction of anything that exceeds the disposable share. The fictitious hereditary mass is calculated (assets present at the time of death plus gifts made during the lifetime of the deceased minus the deceased's debts). On this basis, the disposable share is calculated. If the bequests and/or gifts exceed this disposable share, reduction can be claimed. First, bequests will be reduced and, if this is insufficient to satisfy the forced heirs, gifts will be reduced, starting with the most recent gift.

2. Gifts inter vivos

In principle anyone who is capable of making disposals can freely give away their goods taking into account the rule of the disposable portion (see above).

To protect the family and to promote legal security, any deed containing a donation *inter vivos* has to be made by a deed executed before a notary.

However, some exceptions exist. Moveable and tangible goods can be bequeathed by a simple transfer to the beneficiary without a notarial deed being required (*don manuel*). It is also possible to make an indirect donation i.e. intending to give something away through a neutral deed. This last example refers to any deed that does not show the intention to give something away (for example, a mere bank order without any further communication). These indirect donations are totally legal and valid.

Between spouses, gifts made in a prenuptial settlement are, in principle, irrevocable, while gifts made between spouses during their marriage, other than by marriage contract, are r evocable *ad nutum*.

Spouses married under a community property regime can only make gifts of community assets by mutual consent. A gift of community assets made by only one of the spouses can be contested by the other.

19.7 Taxes and charges

One-time taxes and charges on the purchase of existing constructions of on the transfer of new constructions

Real estate transfer taxes

Transfer of real estate

Transfer of the ownership of real estate in Belgium generally triggers real estate transfer tax (*droit d'enregistrement / registratierecht*), which is generally payable by the purchaser.

The tax is based on the actual sale proceeds. However, the tax authorities may adjust the price upwards if the actual sale price is deemed to be below market value. This adjustment must take place within two years after the transfer.

When the real estate is transferred together with a mortgage or other type of loan, registration duty will be payable on the full value of the real estate and not on its value net of the amount borrowed.

At the time of writing, the general tax rate is 10% in the Flemish Region and 12.5% in the Brussels and Walloon Regions. Under specific conditions, the tax can be reduced to 5% in the Flemish and Walloon Regions and to 8% in the Brussels Region if the real estate is acquired for resale by a real estate professional.

On the transfers of rights *in rem* (e.g. a long lease or a building right) a registration duty of 2% applies.

Real estate transfer tax is normally not payable in cases where the transfer of real estate is subject to VAT. In such cases only a fixed amount of EUR 50 is due.

Transfer of shares in corporations

In general, the transfer of shares in companies owning Belgian real estate does not trigger any registration duties.

Sales taxes (Value Added Tax, TVA/BTW)

Sale of real estate

The transfer of real estate is generally VAT exempt (subject to registration duties).

However, a transfer of a new building can be subject to VAT. If VAT is applicable, there is an exemption for the real estate transfer tax. A building is considered "new" until 31 December of the second year following the year of the building's first use or occupation.

VAT is applicable under the following scenarios:

- The new building is sold by a professional building company (a company whose professional activities cover real estate transactions).

For professional building companies, VAT is automatically applicable to the sale of a new building

- The new building is sold by a VAT taxable person, not being a professional building company, or a non-VAT taxable person. In such a case, the seller has the option of selling the real estate with VAT. Certain specific formalities must be fulfilled (including making a preliminary declaration and/or a special VAT return)

If VAT has to be applied for the building's sale, VAT is also due on the land upon which the building stands, provided that this land is transferred at the same time and by the same person.

If VAT is applicable, in general, the standard rate of 21% applies. Reduced rates apply for certain real estate transactions in connection with social housing (6%) and the social sector (12%).

Any change in the use of the real estate property within a 15 year period requires a pro rata adjustment of the input VAT claimed upon purchase (a sale of real estate property without VAT within this period will trigger a VAT adjustment).

Renovation and transformation work in connection with real estate is subject to a five year adjustment period.

No VAT is applicable and no VAT adjustment is required if the transfer of real estate is part of a VAT neutral transfer of a going concern.

The transfer of shares in corporations is VAT exempt.

Renting/leasing of real estate

The lease of real estate is in principle VAT exempt, without the right to recover input VAT. Belgian VAT law does not provide for an option to tax the lease of real estate.

There are several exceptions to this VAT exemption:

- Immovable lease (a lease contract with an option to purchase the real estate at the end of the agreement). The application of VAT on immovable leases is subject to specific conditions (including the contract's content and length). It should be noted that under Belgian VAT law both operational and financial lease agreements qualify as a supply of services
- Hotel services
- Provision of accommodation in holiday camps
- Letting of sites for the parking of vehicles
- Letting of warehouses
- Letting of real estate in connection with the exploitation of harbours, airports and navigable rivers
- Letting of permanently installed tools/equipment or machinery

VAT grouping

Under Belgian VAT law there is an option to establish a VAT group between taxable persons for VAT purposes if there is a financial, organizational, and economic link. Within a VAT group, intra-group supplies and services are disregarded for VAT purposes. A VAT group can be an adequate alternative to cover negative VAT adjustments in connection with intra-group real estate transactions and renting/leasing operations.

Real estate registration and notary charges

As mentioned above, rights in real estate must be recorded in the Belgian land register as such rights only come into existence upon registration.

Generally the buyer pays for the notarial charges and the administrative costs related to the purchase deed. The notarial charges are fixed by the *Royal Decree of December 16 1950* and are identical for all notaries. The cost of the charges depends on the type of deed. There are fixed and proportional fees. The proportional fees are regressive.

Annually recurring taxes and charges

Real estate tax

Belgian real estate is subject to a real estate withholding tax (*précompte immobilier / onroerende voorheffing*) levied annually. The real estate tax is based on the deemed rental income (*revenu cadastral / kadastraal inkomen*) of the real estate, as assessed by the Belgian tax authorities at a given reference date (i.e. 1 January 1975).

To obtain the basis for calculating the tax, the deemed rental income on 1 January 1975 is multiplied by a revaluation index, which is determined on an annual basis.

The effective rate of tax usually varies from 30-40% of the indexed deemed rental income of the property, depending on its exact location.

If the property is used for business purposes (by individuals or companies), the real estate tax is deductible as a business expense.

For specific cases, a real estate tax exemption is possible.

Income tax (impôt sur les revenus / inkomstenbelasting)

Personal income tax

Personal income tax is subject to a progressive tax rate (so the assessment year 2015 refers to the income in calendar year 2014, with local municipality surcharges excluded). Currently, personal income tax rates are as follows:

- From EUR 0.01 up to EUR 8,680: 25%
- From EUR 8,680 up to EUR 12,360: 30%
- From EUR 12,360 up to EUR 20,600: 40%
- From EUR 20,600 up to EUR 37,750: 45%
- Above EUR 37,750: 50%

Income from real estate is in principle taxed at the progressive tax rate, either based on a deemed rental income (*revenu cadastral / kadastraal inkomen*) or on the actual rental income received.

As a general rule, capital gains realized by individuals who have not used the real estate for business purposes are exempt from income tax.

Expatriate executives enjoy an attractive tax status in Belgium.

Corporate income tax

The standard corporate income tax rate is 33.99%. If the amount of taxable income does not exceed EUR 322,500, the following progressive tax rates apply:

- From EUR 0.01 up to EUR 25,000: 24.98%
- From EUR 25,000 up to EUR 90,000: 31.93%
- From EUR 90,000 up to EUR 322,500: 35.54%

There is no specific tax rate for real estate investments.

Companies may deduct a notional interest deduction in Belgium from their taxable profits. The deduction is also granted to non-resident companies regarding their Belgian permanent establishment or immovable property (or related rights) located in Belgium.

The deduction is based on the company's equity, subject to certain adjustments. The notional interest deduction rate applicable for assessment year 2015 (financial year 2014) is 2.63% (+0.5% for small and medium sized enterprises (SMEs) – with the criteria to be determined on a consolidated basis). Excess notional interest deduction cannot be carried forward. However, a transitory regime applies to notional interest accumulated up to and including assessment year 2012. While this "stock" remains available, its use is restricted.

Furthermore, distributed profits qualifying for the participation exemption received by Belgian companies are exempt from taxation.

However, an amount equivalent to 5% of a corporation's dividend income is treated as a non-deductible business expense. Therefore, 95% of the dividend income received is effectively tax-exempt. The excess dividend received deduction may be carried forward. This regulation applies to dividends that are paid by domestic or foreign corporations.

To qualify for the participation exemption, several conditions must be met (such as a minimum participation, a minimum detention period and a minimum taxation of the distributed profits).

It should also be noted that changes of ownership (directly or indirectly) of a corporation can cause the loss of the exemptions or deductions described above, if the takeover cannot be justified on sound financial or economic grounds. The taxpayer has the right to ask for a ruling on this issue.

Recently, Belgium introduced a so-called Fairness tax. The Fairness tax is a separate corporate tax assessment of 5.15% on distributed profits (dividends) that have not been effectively taxed as a result of the notional interest deduction and/or the deduction of Tax Losses Carried Forward (TLCF). SMEs (as determined on a consolidated basis) are not subject to the Fairness tax.

The Fairness tax is a kind of minimum tax. It is only due if (i) dividends are distributed during the concerned financial year and (ii) notional interest deduction and/or carried-forward tax losses are used to (partially) reduce the corporate income tax base. The Fairness tax is not deductible for corporate income tax purposes.

Belgian tax law has no concept of tax consolidation for corporate income tax purposes.

Dividends distributed by Belgian companies are generally subject to a withholding tax at a rate of 25%. A withholding tax of 15% may, under certain conditions, apply to SMEs (with the criteria determined on a consolidated basis).

In accordance with the *European Parent-Subsidiary Directive of July 23, 1990* (90/435/EEC), modified by the *Directive of December 22, 2003* (2003/123/EC), dividends are exempt from withholding tax provided the parent company:

- Has a legal form mentioned in the Directive's annex or a similar legal form in a jurisdiction with which Belgium has concluded a double tax treaty providing for the required exchange of information
- Has its tax residence in Belgium, a Member State of the European Union or is subject to a double tax treaty
- Is subject to corporate taxation or similar taxation without the benefit of a specific beneficial regime different to the normal taxation rules
- Holds, at the moment of the attribution of the income, a participation of at least 10% of the share capital of the distributing company for an uninterrupted period of at least one year
- The minimum participation has not been subject to any collateral or a stock lending arrangement. If the one year period has not expired yet then withholding tax relief is provisionally granted

Tax depreciation of real estate

Land is not depreciable. Buildings used for business purposes are depreciable based on the asset's acquisition or production cost.

The common depreciation rate (straight line rate) for business real estate is 3% per annum. Industrial buildings can be depreciated at 5% per annum. Some items of expenditure on the building can be separately depreciated (e.g. central heating, air conditioning, lifts). Depreciation rates vary from 10% to 33% of the purchase price depending on the type of equipment involved.

In most cases depreciation is made using a straight line rate. However, provided the taxpayer does not rent the building to third parties, the taxpayer is entitled to a double-declining depreciation on a reducing-balance basis up to a maximum of the double of the straight line depreciation (with an absolute maximum of 40% of the acquisition price).

No depreciation is allowed for real estate held as private property (i.e. for non-business purposes).

An exceptional tax effective write-down is possible when the asset is exceptionally impaired due to technical, technological or economic conditions.

Real estate transaction: asset deal or share deal?

The real estate investor can acquire Belgian real estate by way of an asset deal (i.e. the direct acquisition of real estate) or a share deal (i.e. the acquisition of a corporation that owns real estate).

a Asset deal

If an investor purchases a Belgian real estate property, the respective book-values of the assets transferred are stepped-up to the level of the acquisition cost paid by the investor. The seller on the other hand, realizes a capital gain equivalent to the difference between the purchase price and the tax basis of the assets. Depreciable assets are depreciated over their useful lives.

As stated above, land is not subject to depreciation. Furthermore, capital gains can benefit from deferred taxation if all conditions are met (see below). For other tax consequences (such as RETT and VAT) see the relevant paragraphs.

b Share deal

The book-values of the assets and liabilities at the level of the target company remain unchanged. For other tax consequences (RETT, VAT, etc.) see the relevant paragraphs.

Deduction of acquisition and financing costs

a Thin-cap rules applicable to interest payments

In Belgian tax law, the following limitations regarding the deductibility of interest payments should be observed and monitored.

For Belgian tax purposes, a 5:1 debt-equity ratio applies if interest is paid by a company to:

- A beneficial owner who is either not subject to income tax or who is, for the interest concerned, subject to a tax regime that is significantly more advantageous than the common Belgian income tax regime. (It should be noted that common tax regimes applicable to companies established in another EEA member state are deemed not to be significantly more advantageous than the common Belgian income tax regime)

or

- a beneficial owner who is a (directly or indirectly) related company

If a loan is guaranteed by a third party or is funded by a third party which partly or wholly bears the risk related to the loan, the third party is deemed to be the beneficial owner of the interest, provided the guarantee or the funding has tax avoidance as its main purpose.

If the debt-equity ratio is not respected, the interest deduction is disallowed to the extent that the amount of the loans to the parties in these two instances exceeds five times the sum of the fiscal paid-up capital (at the end of the taxable period) and the taxable reserves (at the beginning of the taxable period).

There are several exceptions to this thin-cap rule. Bonds and other publicly issued securities are excluded, as well as loans granted by banks and other financial institutions. Furthermore, it does not apply to loans contracted by movable leasing companies and companies whose main activity consists of factoring or immovable leasing within the financial sector (being companies that are under permanent prudential control) and to the extent these funds are effectively used for leasing and factoring activities.

Furthermore, the thin-cap rules are not applicable to companies whose main activity is the execution of PPP projects obtained in accordance with public procurement legislation.

A 1:1 debt-equity ratio applies to interest payments made by a Belgian company to a foreign company that has the role of a managing director or member of the board (or has similar functions as those executed by a managing director) of a Belgian company. The interest deduction would be disallowed and dividends are deemed to be distributed to the extent that the amount of the loan exceeds the sum of the paid-up capital (at the end of the taxable period) and the taxable reserves (at the beginning of the taxable period). The same rule applies for the part of the interest paid to such beneficiaries that exceeds market interest rates.

Interest paid or attributed to non-residents or foreign establishments that are not liable to income tax or are subject to a significantly more favourable tax regime than the Belgian tax regime are not deductible.

In such situations, interest is only deductible if the taxpayer shows that the payment corresponds to a normal business transaction and that the amount is not abnormally high. The taxpayer is entitled to ask for a ruling on this issue.

Interests on loans that are not contracted with Belgian financial institutions are deductible only to the extent that the interest rate is not higher than the market rate.

b Withholding tax on interest payments

Interest paid to (non-resident) companies is subject to a withholding tax at a rate of 25%.

In accordance with the *European Directive of June 3 2003* (2003/49/EC), interest and royalties paid or attributed by a Belgian company are exempt from withholding tax, provided the beneficiary is a Belgian company or a company of a Member State of the European Union, and the companies are affiliates. The companies are affiliated if one of them holds, directly or indirectly, at least 25% of the share capital of the other company at the moment of attribution or payment of the income. The same exemption applies when, at the moment of allotment or payment of the income, a third company of the European Union has fully owned a direct or indirect participation of 25% of the share capital of both the companies for an uninterrupted period of at least one year. The beneficiary of the income must have fully-owned or enjoyed the usufruct of the stock, rights or goods in respect of which the income arises and that such stock, rights or goods were, in the period during which the income arises, at no point under the assets of a permanent establishment of the beneficiary situated in a third state.

The latter exemption is not applicable to income from real estate certificates, regarding the allotment or payment of the income wholly or partly-related to the realization of the underlying property.

Furthermore, dividend or interest payments to non-resident companies can be subject to a withholding tax at a limited rate due to double-tax treaties. Belgium has concluded many comprehensive treaties for the avoidance of double taxation.

Other exemptions from the withholding tax on dividends and interest paid by Belgian companies are available.

c Acquisition costs and financing fees

Acquisition costs and financing fees can be regarded as business expenses or charges if they are directly or closely connected with the conduct of a business.

Deductible business expenses or charges are those that were incurred or borne by the taxpayer to obtain or retain taxable business income under the *Belgian Income Tax Code* (BITC), Article 49. They must actually be paid or borne during the taxable period or be booked as certain and fixed liabilities. Their authenticity and amount must be proved.

Fiscal consolidation (the creation of a tax group for corporate income tax purposes) is not possible in Belgium.

Business losses

The tax losses of a company or an individual using real estate for business purposes may in principle be offset against all other sources of income and gains arising in the current taxable period. Losses may also be carried-forward for an indefinite period.

Losses cannot be carried-back.

Direct or indirect change of a corporation's ownership can cause the forfeiture of tax loss carry forwards, if the takeover cannot be justified on sound financial or economic grounds. The taxpayer is entitled to ask for a ruling on this issue.

Furthermore, there are restrictions on loss carry-forwards on the occasion of a merger.

Net wealth tax

There is no wealth tax as such under Belgian law.

Capital gains taxes

Capital gains on real estate

As a general rule, capital gains realized by individuals who have not used real estate for business purposes are exempt from income tax.

There are however a number of exceptions:

- Capital gains realized on the disposal of land transferred within eight years from the acquisition (or within three years if acquired by gift if the transfer occurs within eight years of the original acquisition by the donor). These capital gains are taxed at a rate of 33% in the case of a disposal within five years from the acquisition and at 16.5% on the hypothesis of a disposal after this period of five years

- Capital gains realized on the disposal of buildings transferred within five years from the date of the acquisition (or within three years if acquired by gift if the transfer occurs within five years of the original acquisition by the donor) or on the disposal of buildings constructed on land acquired if the construction of the building started after five years from the acquisition by the taxpayer or the donor and if the alienation takes place within five years after the date of the first occupation or rental of the building. These capital gains are taxed at a rate of 16.5%
- Capital gains that arise from speculative operations that cannot be considered as "normal management of private property" are always taxable (regardless of the date of acquisition and transfer). These capital gains are taxed at a rate of 33%.

Capital gains realized by individuals who use real estate for business purposes are always subject to tax at the general personal income tax rates. However, the taxation of the gain may be subject to deferral under certain conditions (which is similar to the conditions of deferred taxation for companies).

Capital gains on real estate realised by companies are subject to the standard corporate income tax rate.

A withholding tax is applicable on the capital gain realised by non-residents on the transfer of real estate. Such withholding tax is withheld by the notary when completing the notarial deed.

Deferred taxation regarding capital gains on real estate

Capital gains tax on the sale of real estate may be deferred both by companies and by individuals who use the real estate for business purposes by reinvesting the proceeds into other depreciable assets, provided the real estate has been held for more than five years and the sale proceeds are reinvested within three years (being reinvestment in depreciable assets other than buildings, ships or aircrafts) or within five years (for buildings, ships or aircrafts). Furthermore, the capital gain must be made unavailable for distribution by recording it as an unavailable reserves account.

If these conditions are met, the corporate or personal income tax on the capital gains will be deferred over the period during which the reinvested assets are being depreciated.

Capital gains on shares

Capital gains from the sale of shares held by individuals are, in general, exempt from personal income tax. Under certain conditions such capital gains can be taxable as business income at the general personal income tax rates or as 'miscellaneous income' at 16.5% or 33%.

Capital gains are fully tax exempt for capital gains realized by SMEs (that are determined on a consolidated basis) on shares held for an uninterrupted period of more than one year as far as the legal taxation condition is met. Capital gains realized by companies other than SMEs are taxed at 0.412% if the conditions set out above (concerning the minimum holding period and taxation condition) are met.

If the legal taxation condition is fulfilled and the minimum holding period of one year is not observed, the capital gain will be subject to tax at a rate of 25.75%. Taxation at the standard corporate income tax rate of 33.99% applies to capital gains on shares if the legal taxation condition is not met (regardless of the holding period of the shares).

Losses on the sale of shares and write-downs to impaired values are not tax deductible.

Inheritance and gift taxes

Registration duties

Registration duties are due on certain deeds or transactions. These deeds or transactions must be presented to the local tax collector of VAT, Registration and Domains, who records these duties in a register and collects the tax at the same time.

The principal relevant instances in which the deed or transaction is registered include the following:

- Notarial deeds (within 15 days); if a deed has to pass before a notary to be valid, e.g. for some gifts (see above) registration will be obligatory too
- Deeds regarding the transfer (sale, gift, contribution) of real estate situated in Belgium (within a four month period)
- Written contracts of letting, subletting or assignment of leases of real estate located in Belgium (within a four month period). Verbal tenancy agreements are not subject to registration tax

Sales of real estate located in the Brussels-Capital and the Walloon Regions are registered at the rate of 12.5% while in the Flemish Region these operations are taxed at a rate of 10%.

The tax is calculated on the purchase price and the charges that may not be less than the normal market value. However, the basis of the taxation may be reduced in several circumstances, notably for a dwelling. If an individual sells a residential building and then buys another one (both being situated in the Flemish Region), the registration duties paid for the first acquisition are deducted from the registration duties due for the second acquisition.

A reduced rate is granted for sales of real property that is not sold by public auction and that is sold by certified deed to persons who buy real estate for business purposes with a resale intention. In the Flemish and the Walloon Regions, the tax rate amounts to 5%. In the Brussels-Capital Region the tax rate amounts to 8%. The property acquired in this manner must be resold by certified deed at the latest by 31 December of the tenth year following the date of the deed of purchase. If this condition is not fulfilled, a supplementary duty has to be paid.

For rental agreements, a duty of 0.2% is due. A 2% duty applies on building rights and long lease contracts.

Gift tax is imposed in Belgium on the registration of a written document in which a gift is granted. With respect to real estate situated in Belgium that is transferred by way of gift, registration is always required. In contrast, movable property given without a written document and gifts of real estate located outside Belgium are not subject to the Belgian gift tax.

The gift of an immovable asset is subject to progressive tax rates similar to those applicable for inheritance tax (see below). It depends on the relationship between the donor and the recipient and there are differences in the three Regions. In all three Regions, it goes from 3% to 30% above EUR 50,000 between spouses and in a direct line.

However, a gift of movable assets between spouses and in favour of children and other descendants are subject to a much more advantageous fixed tax rate of 3% (3.3% in the Walloon Region) and or 7% (5.5% in Walloon Region).

Each Region also provides for specific exemption or advantageous tax rates in certain circumstances, such as gifts to certain kinds of foundations or non-profit companies. It is worth noticing that, among those favourable regimes, the gift of family enterprises is subject, under strict conditions, to a tax rate of 0% in the Flemish (where this gift is also exempted from any registration tax) and the Walloon Regions and 3% in the Brussels Region.

Mortgage duties are levied on the registration of mortgages and liens on real estate. This duty is not to be confused with the registration duty of 1%, which is due on the deeds of loan, granting a loan, or transfer of a claim, secured by a mortgage on real estate situated in Belgium. The mortgage duty as such amounts to 0.3%. Mortgaging thus costs 1%

for the registration tax, 0.3% for the mortgage duty plus the notary's fees and expenses.

Inheritance taxes

Belgium has two types of inheritances taxes: "estate duties" due to the death of Belgian residents and "estate transfer duties" due to the death of non-Belgian residents. As well as for registration duties, the Regions are competent to change the rates, the taxable base and the exemptions. Belgian inheritance taxes are due irrespective of the fact that the devolution is by law, will or matrimonial contract.

The applicable law will be determined by the fiscal residence of the deceased at the moment of death. If the deceased had been resident in more than one Region during the five years preceding the moment of death, then it will be the Region where the deceased was resident for the longest time.

If the deceased, at the moment of death, was resident in Belgium, inheritance taxes are levied on the deceased's worldwide net property, i.e. all goods comprising the estate (movable and immovable, situated in Belgium or abroad), less debts.

If, on the other hand, the deceased, at the moment of death, was resident abroad, inheritance taxes are levied on the Belgian gross real estate, i.e. on the Belgian real estate only and without any deduction of debts. It is most uncertain whether this prohibition of deduction of debts will stand the test of conformity with EU non-discrimination rules. A comparable Dutch provision has been considered as discriminatory by the Court of Justice of the European Union's Advocate-General (*Barbier* case).

Furthermore, it is important to underline that, in addition to the goods included in the estate, certain goods are fictitiously considered as forming part of the estate. One example is any gifts made by the deceased in the three years prior to death and that are not subject to Belgian gift taxes. These gifts will then fictitiously be considered as a legacy and be subject to inheritance taxes.

Normally assets must be valued at their normal market value on the day of the deceased's death.

The heirs and legatees (beneficiaries of real estate property), even if they are living abroad, must file a return within five, six, or seven months (depending on the country where the deceased's death took place) for the purpose of collecting inheritance taxes. The taxes are then payable within a two month period following the due date for filing the return.

The applicable progressive tax rates depend upon the relationship of the beneficiary to the deceased and the region where the deceased was resident.

In all three Regions, the tax rate varies from 3% to 30% above EUR 50,000 between spouses and in a direct line.

By way of an example, see the applicable table in the Brussels Region between spouses and in a direct line.

	Tax rate	**Overall due tax**
Up to EUR 50,000	3%	-
EUR 50,000 to EUR 100,000	8%	1,500
EUR 100,000 to EUR 175,000	9%	5,500
EUR 175,000 to EUR 250,000	18%	12,250
EUR 250,000 to EUR 500,000	24%	25,750
Above EUR 500,000	30%	85,750

Especially for high wealth inheritances or for inheritances other than in the direct line or between spouses, Belgian inheritances taxes are rather high. This situation can be mitigated through the use of several mechanisms such as:

- A gift of company shares (eventually keeping the usufruct of the given goods)
- Bringing goods (making it attractive for movable assets) into a general partnership without legal personality or a limited partnership with legal personality whereby the donator is nominated as the director

- Using a Belgian private foundation. The assets are handed over to the foundation in exchange for certificates. Subsequently, the "naked" property of the certificates is donated to the beneficiaries, the donator is the beneficiary of the income of the certified assets and keeps control over the property as the foundation's director
- Time-consecutive gifts of real estate (each three year period) to benefit from the application of the reduced tax rates (e.g. 3% to 9%)

Each Region has specific rules for the non-taxation of the part of the family home that is acquired by the surviving spouse. For example, in the Flemish Region the usufruct of the family home inherited by the surviving spouse will not be subject to estate duties.

Trusts are unknown under Belgian law. They are nevertheless recognized in Belgium, though the tax consequences of such as "vehicle" are intensively discussed. According to the Belgian tax administration, distributions by a discretionary trust (as opposed to "fixed interest" trusts) to beneficiaries upon the settlor's death will be subject to inheritance taxes, but only at the moment of the distribution.

Other taxes and charges

Some municipalities impose specific taxes on buildings not used for residential purposes, e.g. commercial buildings, on parking offices, on parking places, on second residences or on deserted and empty buildings. These taxes vary considerably from location to location. The taxes on deserted and empty buildings are generally calculated according to the extent (in square metres) of the potential occupation.

Incorrect (lower) statement of the sale price on the sales agreement

Belgium tax law has severe penalties if an incorrect (typically lower) statement of the sale price is mentioned in the sales agreement. Each notarial deed mentions the sanctions.

Supplementary real estate transfer tax and fines (potentially doubling the initial tax charge) can become due. Furthermore, criminal sanctions are possible.

If the conventional price is lower than the market value, the market value should be mentioned in the notarial deed. Real estate transfer tax will be levied on the market value. Sanctions can be imposed for stating an incorrect market value.

International taxation

The Belgian tax treaties allocate the right of taxation to the *situs* country of the property.

As indicated above, investing in real estate in Belgium could thus trigger (limited) tax liability in Belgium.

19.8 Immigration law and tax residence

Entry, residence and settlement of foreigners

The basic principle is that a visa is required for citizens coming from outside the European Union (as well as the European Economic Area and Switzerland). A second principle is that any stay longer than for three months requires a residence permit.

European Union and EEA citizens

Any European Union and EEA citizen wishing to reside for more than three months in a member country must request a residence permit. The following documents will be required in Belgium: a valid identity card or passport, three photos, recent proof of a residential address (lease and utility contracts), work contracts or statement of means of support. European Union citizens who are employed in France and wish to transfer their residence there can obtain a 10 year residence permit, if their home country provides a reciprocal right to do so. No work permit is required. The same applies for Swiss citizens.

Non-European Union citizens

Citizens of countries that are not members of the European Union must apply for a visa to reside in Belgium on a short- or long-term basis. This visa can be obtained at a Belgian embassy or consulate.

If the stay is for less than three months, the citizen must go to the municipal authority responsible for that citizen's place of residence within three days of arrival (unless s/he is staying in a hotel). Otherwise, a residence permit should be obtained from the municipal authority within eight days of arrival in Belgium.

To work in Belgium, citizens from countries that are not members of the European Union must hold a work permit. There are three types of work permit depending on whether the citizen wishes to acquire self-employed or employee status. There are additional requirements related to the Belgian social security regime.

The requirements under this heading are not applicable for Swiss residents.

Tax residence

Criteria

Belgian tax laws usually consider a person to be tax resident if they are an "inhabitant of the Kingdom". This means that the taxpayer has their domicile or "seat of wealth" in Belgium. Those two notions should be distinguished from each other. The domicile for tax purposes should not be confused with the legal domicile. The tax domicile refers to a factual notion, characterized by a certain permanence and continuity though, for example, the seat of wealth. The seat of wealth refers not to the place were the assets are located but to the place where the assets are managed.

The taxpayer is presumed to be an "inhabitant of the Kingdom" when they are inscribed on the national register or when married, if their household is established in Belgium.

Corporations are deemed to have their tax residence in Belgium when their seat, their principal establishment or their seat of direction or management is located in Belgium.

When anyone is considered as a tax resident in Belgium and another country with which Belgium has entered into a tax treaty, those treaties usually contain tie-breaker rules to determine the fiscal residence of the taxpayer for that purpose.

Non-resident tax liability

Non-resident tax applies for a non-resident individual, i.e. individuals (including certain foreign, diplomatic and consular agents) who do not have their principal abode or their centre of economic interests in Belgium; as well as to non-resident companies i.e. all corporations or institutions, whether or not having a legal personality, that do not have their registered office, main establishment or place of management in Belgium and also foreign states or their political subdivisions.

The non-resident tax liability is then limited to Belgian source income as listed in Article 228 of the *Belgian Income Tax Code* (BITC), which includes:

- The income from real estate located in Belgium, the proceeds from letting furnished real estate located in Belgium, and also capital gains realized on Belgian land
- The income from movable property paid by a natural or legal person who has tax residence in Belgium
- All profits and gains made through the permanent establishment of a foreign corporation
- The income from activities performed in Belgium by the members of the liberal professions, by directors and liquidators
- The salaries and wages paid by a natural or legal person or by the permanent establishment of a foreign company located in Belgium (the salaries and wages paid for activities carried on abroad are exempted)
- Extraordinary profits made in Belgium (such as speculative profits)

Non-resident individuals may carry out business in Belgium as a sole Entrepreneur through a Belgian permanent establishment or as a partner of a Belgian partnership (a Belgian partnership basically constitutes the permanent establishment of the partners in a partnership).

Income derived from the activities listed in Article 228 BITC is subject to income tax at the same rates as apply for resident taxpayers.

International double taxation for residents of Belgium

Agreements concerning taxation of income and capital have been concluded with about 80 countries to avoid double taxation. These treaties are patterned after the OECD draft treaty and deviate from this model with respect to specific issues.

The jurisdiction of tax is allocated according to the following rules.

The residence country has jurisdiction to tax all types of income unless the treaty provides otherwise. When a treaty allows the source country to tax the income, then Belgium, as the residence country, must exempt such income. Exemption is granted to individual residents subject to a reservation of progression. Dividend, interest and, in some treaties, royalties may be taxed both in the source country and in the residence country. Belgium, as the residence country, allows corporate taxpayers the dividend received deduction and grants a tax credit with respect to interest and royalties.

These are important exceptions and the applicability of such treaties should always be examined on a case-by-case basis.

Under most treaties, the application of an exemption is not dependent on an effective taxation in the source state. On the other hand, certain treaties such as those with Japan, Malaysia, the UK and the US contain a *subject to tax clause* whereby an effective taxation is required to benefit in Belgium from the exemption.

Double taxation treaties with respect to inheritance taxes have only been concluded with France and Sweden.

19.9 Checklist: Real estate in Belgium

- Selection of the type of property sought:
    - Residential or commercial
    - Urban, agricultural, holiday home
    - Speculative purchase, investment purchase, own use
- Take into account considerable tax and legal differences between regions
- Determination of manner of purchase, whether through a company or in the individual's name
- Selection of appropriate real estate agent in accordance with the general market serviced (high-end, middle-range, low-end, agricultural, holiday home, or commercial)
- Visits to real estate
- Selection of notary
- Offer to purchase
- Signature of a purchase contract, often called *compromis de vente / verkoopscompromis*, binding the parties together with a 10% deposit payment held in the name of the notary or agent
- Specific attention to suspensive conditions in the purchase contract
- If an apartment or property in a subdivision, review the condominium statutes and annual running costs and works voted on by the existing property owners that may be charged to new owners
- If a company, the same as above and an additional due diligence investigation of the company, the property and of its beneficial owners
- If works are required on the property, determination whether the works will be authorized by the managing agent of the building and the local municipality

- Conclusion of the transfer of ownership to the notary within a four month period after signing the purchase contract and payment of the purchase price, fees and registration taxes to the notary following the notary's verification of the respective powers of the buyer and seller to act and of clear title on the property and additional certificates
- Registration of the transfer at the property registry and payment of registration fees is then made by the notary

19.10 Bibliography

Tiberghien (coll.), "Belgian Taxation, an outline", 2003

Tiberghien (coll.), "Manuel de Droit Fiscal 2013-2014", *Kluwer*, Waterloo, 2014

Bocken (H.), De Bondt (W.), "Introduction to Belgian Law", Brussels, *Kluwer Law International*, 2001

De Page H., Dekkers R., "Traité élémentaire de droit civil belge, V", Brussels, 1975

Deblauwe (R.), "Summary of Belgian inheritance and gift taxes", Brussels, 1988

Dekkers (R.), Dirix (E.), "Handboek Burgerlijk Recht, Deel II Zakenrecht, Zekerheden, Verjaring", Antwerpen, *Intersentia*, 2005

Faes (P.), "Belgian income tax law: principles and practice", Chichester, *Wiley & Sons*, 1995

Herbots J.H., "Bijzondere overeenkomsten", Leuven, *Acco*, 2002

Vandenberghe H., "Voorrechten en hypotheken", *L. Wouters*, 2002

Vanneste F., Vandenberghe, H., Hamelinck P., Kokelenberg J., "Zakenrecht", Gent, 1984-1994

20

Canada

Canada

by

Alexander Sennecke, MA, LLB

Baldwin Sennecke Halman LLP
25 Adelaide Street East – Suite 900
Toronto, ON M5C 3A1
Canada

Telephone: +1 416 410 2113
Facsimile: +1 416 410 9423

asennecke@sennecke.com
bashllp.com

Alexander Sennecke has over 27 years' experience representing German speaking clients doing business in Ontario and Canada with a special focus on German-Canadian cross border corporate, commercial, real estate, estates and litigation matters. His representative work involves providing set up and ongoing legal advice to subsidiary corporations in a broad range of industries and advising high net worth investors in all aspect of their corporate and real estate investments. He also acts as general counsel for real estate investment syndicates and property managers and developers.

Alexander regularly participates as a speaker on various topics at "Doing Business in Canada" seminars conducted by the Canadian Embassy, the German or Austrian Chambers of Commerce and the German Canadian Lawyers Association.

20.1 Introduction

Canadian real estate law has its roots in the British feudal and post feudal system starting with the *Quia Emtores* in 1290. This statute of King Edward I, also called *Statute of Westminster III*, set the legal framework which established conditions of land use, land possession and the sale and purchase of real estate in the realm of King Edward I. Today the full bundle of all real estate use, possession and ownership rights and conditions is called "fee simple" ownership of real estate.

The *Constitution Act 1867* confirmed Canada as a constitutional monarchy, with Her Majesty Queen Elizabeth II as the Head of State.

In 1982, with the enactment of the *Canada Act,* England enabled Canada to enact its own constitutional law, the *Canadian Constitution Act, 1982* and the *Charter of Rights*. The Queen of England is still the Head of State of Canada. Furthermore, the institution of a constitutional Monarch grants the federal Crown and the provincial Crown all powers in connection with freehold real estate, including the right of expropriation.

In 1930, Ontario passed legislation that provided for persons engaged in the trade in real estate to register as a real estate broker. Today, it is not possible to act as a real estate broker/agent in Canada without meeting provincial or territorial statutory requirements including the registration of the real estate broker and salesperson/agent, the disclosure of the agency relationship, and also the agent's right to sue for commission or other remuneration for services rendered as an agent in connection with a trade in real estate. Historically, the relationship between a salesperson (the agent) and an owner (the principal) was based on the agent offering his assistance to the owner to sell the owner's real estate (immovable property). However, we now find across Canada a highly regulated and pervasive system of listing agents listing real estate for sale with the local Real Estate Board's Multiple Listing System (MLS), and buying agents working with the listing agents to conclude an agreement for the purchase and sale of real estate between a buyer (purchaser) and a seller (vendor). The system has recently been relaxed somewhat, following a challenge by Canada's Competition Bureau over the restricted nature of access to MLS; since 2010 buyers have now been able to have an agent list real estate for sale on MLS without having to purchase the agent's full complement of services. This has allowed for greater flexibility in pricing and service options for vendors wishing to use the MLS.

The listing agreement is usually a standard form prepared by the local Real Estate Board and is based on the *common law* principle that an agent is authorized by the principal to provide certain services on his behalf, but must also include certain information that is prescribed by provincial and territorial statutes. One of the most significant aspects of this system of cooperative open listing information (which is not directly accessible to the general public) is that, in most instances, the buyer agrees that the broker is to be compensated through the listing broker as provided for on the MLS system.

This arrangement has led to a very effective system based on professional conduct and mutual respect among real estate brokers/agents, and has made it possible for listing brokers to charge a maximum of 6% commission of the sale price for the purchase and sale of residential properties, and more or less in a range between 2% to 10% if the real estate is a rural property, such as a cottage or farm (not more than 10%), or an industrial or commercial property (not less than 2%).

In Canada, real estate brokers generally try to cooperate with lawyers. It is the responsibility of a lawyer to give legal advice in connection with all aspects of a transaction involving real estate and to ensure that the monetary arrangements have been fulfilled and that each party has completed the covenants in the agreement of purchase and sale, including the transfer of title to the immovable property. Lawyers in Canada used to provide to their clients a formal opinion with respect to the conveyance of the title of the immovable property, but this is now more and more undertaken by way of title insurance. A lawyer's report will deal with all aspects of the transaction including the conveyancing services performed by the lawyer on behalf of his client. Only in Quebec are notaries involved in the closing of real estate transactions. In the rest of Canada, notaries have a limited role as commissioners of affidavits or providing authentication of documents.

Lawyers (also known as barristers and solicitors) are retained by their clients pursuant to a retainer agreement which will outline the legal services to be performed by the lawyer and will confirm the fee arrangement. This may be a fixed fee based on a percentage of the purchase price or may be based on a time spent basis, with the lawyer setting out his hourly rate plus disbursements. These generally include photocopy charges, long distance charges, courier charges, search fees, plus *Goods and Services Tax* (GST), or in those Provinces that have combined the Provincial sales tax with the Federal sales tax, *Harmonized Sales Tax* (HST), and other applicable charges including title searchs, government registration fees and title insurance fees.

20.2 Real estate ownership

When England divided the colony of Quebec into Upper Canada and Lower Canada, the *Constitutional Act, 1791* stated that all future land grants from the *Crown* in Upper Canada were to be in free and common soccage. Even today all land is owned, in theory, by the *Crown* in the right of the applicable province/territory, and individuals do not hold absolute private ownership in land. It is necessary to review the original *Crown* patent which may contain conditions and reservations such as the rights to minerals, timber and road and shoreline allowances as well as the bed of navigable water or streams running on the land.

Different forms and types of ownership of real estate

The owner's interest in immovable property is documented in his legal title to the land and any structures thereon and may be separated into two basic categories: (1) that of an estate in fee simple or freehold title; and (2) that of a leasehold estate or leasehold title. Furthermore, whereas an estate in fee simple is an absolute grant in perpetuity, a life estate is a disposition of immovable property designed to provide for a succession of persons, such as the present and future members of a family. The life estate comes to an end upon the death of the life tenant, and exclusive possession reverts back to the original grantor or passes to another person. Similarly, leasehold title estates provide that a tenant or lessee has the exclusive right of possession subject to certain contractual terms and conditions, and this may run from year to year or month to month or for a fixed term.

The fee simple interest is the legal estate and includes certain equitable rights. Whereas a legal estate is a right *in rem* (enforceable against the whole world), an equitable estate is a right *in personam* (enforceable only against a limited number of persons). Equitable interests in immovable property may be enforced against the owners of legal title and include such interests as easements, encumbrances, statutory charges and liens, options and rights of first refusal, restrictive covenants, and rights of way. This multitude of interests in real estate allows for the creation of various structures in ownership that generally may be determined by agreement among various parties, but also are regulated by law.

Whereas an interest in real estate may be owned in "sole ownership", or "in trust" for a beneficiary, or "to uses", an interest in real estate may also be owned concurrently by multiple parties in the form of a "joint tenancy", a "tenancy in common", or a co-operative ownership or a partnership ownership, or also more regulated forms of ownership such as a condominium or time sharing, or even in the form of a more recent investment structure known as a *Real Estate Investment Trust* (REIT).

During his or her lifetime, an owner of immovable property may transfer his or her ownership interest either by agreement of purchase and sale or by way of an *inter vivos* gift, and upon a person's death title will pass to the estate of the deceased either intestate or by testamentary grant. Title may also be transferred by possession, operation of law or court order.

A condominium combines both individual ownership and shared ownership. The concept of a condominium is well-known and was introduced in Ontario in 1967. Today, almost 40% of new construction in Toronto is in the form of a condominium development. Ontario introduced a significantly revised statute, the *Condominium Act*, governing condominiums in December 1998. All provinces and territories in Canada have their own specific condominium legislation; however, they generally follow the principles set out in the Ontario legislation. A buyer of a condominium unit in effect owns a fee simple estate in the unit as well as a fee simple estate as a joint tenant of such common areas as parking or recreational facilities, lobbies and hallways, elevators, foundations, common walls and roofs as well as a share in the capital of a condominium corporation that manages the condominium development. Most of the changes introduced by the Ontario legislation deal with expanded possibilities for condominium structures and improve the disclosure requirements enhancing consumer protection.

Upon entering into an agreement of purchase and sale, a buyer of a condominium is entitled to receive a *Current Disclosure Statement*. This statement will contain specified information including: a table of contents; details regarding the legal structure and organization of the condominium; a statement as to whether the proposed units and common elements are to be registered in the *Ontario New Home Warranties Plan Act*; a budget statement; a statement setting out the fees or charges, if any, that the condominium corporation is required to pay to the declarant or any other person; and other prescribed information. A buyer, having received the disclosure statement, has a period of 10 days to review the material and decide whether he/she wants to proceed with the purchase.

Easements, charges, covenants and mortgages

Potential claims that may form a charge against the ownership of real estate are commonly known as liens, but other encumbrances may arise, for example, upon bankruptcy or by way of a writ of execution filed with the sheriff.

In some jurisdictions in Canada, an interest in real estate may be acquired by way of adverse possession. Adverse possessory rights may be claimed by an adjoining owner, if he can demonstrate that for a 10 year period he has occupied the land and this was not disturbed or challenged during this time by the owner of the land. A permanent easement, in turn, may be acquired if, for a period of 20 years, without consent, an adjoining landowner makes use of certain interest in land; for example, a right to drain water across a neighbour's land or a right to have a roof extended over the neighbour's property. Easements may also be created by agreement; for example, an owner of land may grant his neighbour a right of way over his land.

Easements are frequently used to regulate such common uses as mutual driveways, common party walls, access to lake frontage, or utility easements which may provide for hydro lines, gas pipes, underground sewer or water lines. Restrictive covenants are frequently used in land development agreements.

Another form of encumbrance of the interests of an owner in real estate are security interests, either in the form of a mortgage/charge registered against the title of the real estate or a security interest in certain personal (moveable) property which may be registered pursuant to the provincial *Personal Property Security Act* (PPSA).

Protection of ownership, proof of ownership and registration

The first registry system in Canada was created in 1795 by the parliament of Upper Canada. Today, this system of municipal public land registry offices is still in place; however, with the development of microfilm technology and the internet, it is now possible in certain jurisdictions to access the applicable land registry system electronically rather than physically attending at the land registry office.

The registry system requires that a 40 year search of past registrations in relation to a particular piece of land must be conducted each time before a property is transferred. In 1885, Ontario introduced the land titles system which, rather than producing an inventory of instruments affecting title, is a system whereby the local land titles municipal office issues a statement as to the title registered in connection with a certain parcel of land.

With the introduction of the land titles system, which is based on the *Torrens Title System* developed in the 1850s in Australia and which is also used in most western provinces of Canada, a government guarantee of title provided easy access and certainty with respect to identifying ownership and any other rights that may affect the title to the property. The land titles system maintains a general register wherein all dealings affecting a parcel of land are recorded, as well as a leasehold register, a highway register, the *Trans Canada Pipeline* register, a powers of attorney register, the execution book and a register under the *Condominium Act*.

Although the land registry systems are maintained by local government offices, they still require that legal instruments be prepared and registered by the public. This process is generally described as a conveyance and is conducted by lawyers, with the assistance of paralegals and conveyancers. However, before an interest in real estate is conveyed by a seller to a buyer, the parties must have reached an agreement in writing to do so. Usually, a contract for the sale of real estate precedes the conveyance of the legal title to the buyer. There are in effect two distinct stages involved in a transfer of an interest in real estate: (i) first, the agreement between the parties that determines the interests that are to be transferred; and (ii) second, the conveyance of that interest by way of registration in the local registry office.

20.3 Purchase and sale of real estate

The sales agreement

The *common law* of contract is the basis for a transaction involving an interest in real estate. An offer/agreement of purchase and sale is usually negotiated until one party's offer is accepted by the other. Only when an offer has been accepted without changes will an agreement or contract have been formed. A contract does not exist until there has been a definite offer and an unconditional acceptance of the offer communicated by the offeror to the offeree. Before a court will find that an agreement is enforceable, it will require that the parties have concluded their negotiations and settled not just the price but all terms of their agreement.

Another essential element of the formation of the agreement is that it must be in writing. All provinces and territories have re-enacted the English *Statute of Frauds* legislation except Manitoba, which has repealed the Statute, and British Columbia, which has its own legislative scheme. The British Columbia legislation recognizes the possibility of part performance and demands less in terms of an agreement reduced to written form. There are no formal requirements with respect to execution other than the requirement that signatures of individuals must be witnessed. It is accepted practice that offers and the acceptance thereof may be sent by facsimile or other electronic means.

There is no legal requirement that a seller and buyer deal directly with each other. Agreements, in the *common law* jurisdictions, are not concluded before a notary. Instead, the process of presenting offers, especially for residential properties, is managed by real estate agents; and before a seller and buyer are about to conclude an agreement they also involve their respective lawyers.

Restrictions on sale and acquisition

All standard form agreements deal with certain statutory restrictions that limit a seller's ability to sell his/her real estate, which include family law issues, control of subdivision provisions and the residence status of a seller.

Restrictions under family law and matrimonial property regime

In Ontario and the other provinces and territories in Canada there are certain family law requirements with which spouses must comply before they can transfer or encumber an interest in a matrimonial home. The *Family Law Act (Ontario)* provides that each spouse has an equal right of possession in the matrimonial home, irrespective of registered or beneficial ownership. Furthermore, a spouse has a special possessory right in the matrimonial home which is triggered on marriage breakdown or on the death of one of the spouses.

Options and pre-emption rights

Section 15 of the standard form agreement of purchase and sale used in Ontario contains a further statutory limitation regarding the disposition of real estate. Ontario introduced the *Planning Act* in 1946, providing that local planning boards (now committees of adjustment or land division committees) were to decide upon applications to sever existing lots of land, particularly in rural areas; whereas municipal councils were given the power to enact zoning by-laws to regulate the use of land within developed areas. Effectively, in the event that an owner wishes to convey a parcel that is not within the prescribed conveyances of the *Planning Act*, it will be necessary to obtain a consent or severance. Similar restrictions were also introduced in the other provinces of Canada.

Aside from the above-noted statutory restrictions on the disposition of an interest in real estate, it is possible that the granting of an option to purchase or a right of first refusal or a right of repurchase may also operate as a restraint on the alienation of immovable property. In effect, upon the buyer electing to exercise the option, the option agreement becomes an agreement of purchase and sale.

Rights of first refusal differ from options as the seller is not obligated at any point to offer the property and, if the property is offered, the buyer is not obligated to accept the offer. Therefore, first rights of refusal are contractual, but do not create an interest in real estate, although they may be regarded as having similar attributes to an interest in real estate. Only upon the triggering event which gives rise to the right does a first right of refusal convert to an option, and it is at that time that an equitable interest in real estate is created.

Agricultural real estate

Many rural properties in Canada are not connected to a municipal water system, and it is therefore necessary to determine whether well water meets certain minimum requirements: regarding the quality of the water or its potability; the pressure of the water flow; the capacity of the well and the overall operational efficiency of the well. Local health authorities will provide testing facilities to determine potability, and it is possible to inquire whether the local health authority has issued any orders regarding a well.

Restrictions regarding acquisition of real estate by foreigners

Five out of the ten Canadian provinces do not have any restrictions with respect to filing requirements or ownership of real estate by foreigners. Quebec and Prince Edward Island have filing requirements. The western provinces, Manitoba, Saskatchewan and Alberta, have filing and ownership restrictions. For example, in Manitoba, only a Canadian citizen or permanent resident or a qualified permanent resident who intends to become an eligible individual within two years after acquiring farmland interest is permitted to purchase an interest in farmland. In Saskatchewan, non-residents cannot own or acquire aggregate farm lands with an assessed value for municipal tax greater than CAD 15,000, excluding any assessment for buildings and similar improvements; and in Alberta, the registrar can refuse to register a land transfer if it is not accompanied by a statutory declaration containing prescribed information.

In addition, *Crown land* may not be sold to non-Canadian citizens or non-Canadian corporations.

Further important preconditions for buying real estate

Capacity and entitlement of the seller

In Canada, lawyers generally get involved in real estate transactions at an early stage and commonly assist sellers in the negotiation and conclusion of listing agreements and provide legal advice to the seller and buyer in connection with the offer/agreement of purchase and sale.

The seller's lawyer has certain responsibilities such as preparing the transfer, statement of adjustments, direction regarding the payment of funds, responding to requisitions submitted by the buyer's lawyer and receiving payment of the purchase price on closing from the buyer in consideration for giving the transfer of the real estate to the buyer's lawyer so that he can attend to the registration on the title to the real estate. Lawyers have a duty to act in the best interest of their clients. Therefore, a lawyer acting for a buyer will not only search and give an opinion as to the title of the real estate, but will also conduct extensive due diligence on behalf of the buyer.

Having completed the title search, reviewed the adjoining lands, obtained an execution certificate and searched for any personal property security registrations, a buyer's lawyer must also satisfy himself as to the corporate authority of a corporation selling property as well as the authority of an attorney acting under a power of attorney. Most standard form agreements of purchase and sale provide for the execution of the agreement to be signed, sealed and delivered in the presence of a witness. The requirement of a seal stems from the old English *common law* requirement that a corporation executed a document not only by the authorized signing officer providing his signature but also by affixing the corporation's seal to the document. This *common law* rule has been changed in Canada. All business corporation legislation in Canada provides that a corporation need not execute an agreement by affixing its corporate seal. Pursuant to the indoor management rule a corporation cannot deny a contract if it was signed by an officer or otherwise-authorized person in the ordinary course of the corporation's business.

The phrase 'authorized signing officer' is only descriptive and does not confirm that the person has authority to sign for the corporation. The statement "I have authority to bind the corporation", together with the individual's title, is sufficient.

Contrary to the practice in continental Europe, the execution of legal documents in Canada (except Quebec) is not conducted before a notary. Lawyers may upon application also become notaries. In the *common law* jurisdictions in Canada, notaries, when having an affidavit sworn before them, are required to administer an oath and satisfy themselves as to the genuineness of the signature and the identity of the deponent.

In Ontario, a buyer is required to file with the transfer or real estate an affidavit of residence and value of consideration Form 1 – *Land Transfer Tax Act*. A seller is required to deliver certain statutory declarations in connection with the possession of the real estate or other matters. A buyer's lawyer may be authorized to sign on behalf of the buyer the land transfer tax affidavit; however, if closing documents are sent to persons residing in Europe the documents may be sworn as follows: (1) before an officer of any of the Canadian diplomatic of consular services who must impress the stamp of the office held on the document; or (2) a notary who must impress the official stamp on the document.

The Ontario form of affidavit is rather unique, and the usual statement of a notary confirming that he knows or has identified the party and saw the party sign the document is not acceptable for registration purposes. The notary should sign as "witness", and the stamp of the notary should be placed underneath his signature.

A trustee who holds real estate may disclose the fact of the trust by using the word "trustee" or "in trust" after his name; however, it is possible that the trust relationship is not disclosed in order, for example, to conceal the identity of the beneficial owner or to avoid the real estate vesting in a minor.

An extra-provincial license is required for a corporation incorporated in a foreign jurisdiction to carry on business including the ownership of real estate in most provinces in Canada including Ontario.

Third-party claims and unpaid taxes

All municipalities in Canada assess and tax owners of real estate. Arrears in realty taxes take priority over any other encumbrances registered on title to real estate and if, after more than three years, an owner of real estate in Ontario has not paid the real estate taxes, the local municipality may proceed by public auction to sell the real estate. It is, therefore, standard conveyancing practice that, before a transaction involving real estate is completed, a search letter is sent to the treasurer of the municipality asking for a tax clearance certificate.

The buyer's lawyer must ensure that the outstanding arrears in realty taxes and penalties to the date of closing are paid by the seller, or he must obtain an undertaking of the seller's lawyer to pay any taxes owing, pursuant to which the seller's lawyer will undertake to deduct the taxes owing from the balance of the purchase price due on closing and remit payment to the treasurer of the municipality. Realty taxes are a significant cost of ownership of real estate. In Toronto, for example, the assessment of realty taxes was changed from a historical valuation to a fair market valuation which significantly increased the realty taxes payable by owners of properties located in areas of the city that were developed some time ago.

Another important statutory lien and charge upon the interest of real estate of an owner or occupant/tenant is the charge for services such as water, gas and in some jurisdictions hydroelectricity supplied for the use on such real estate by a public utility. A lien for public utilities has the same priority as municipal taxes. Furthermore, the *Corporations Tax Act* provides for a lien for arrears of Ontario corporation taxes which may be enforced in the same manner as a writ of execution.

There are other statutory liens and charges that may affect the title to real estate, such as a contractor's right to register a lien, and a buyer is well advised to consult with his lawyer to obtain a complete understanding of the statutory liens that may arise with respect to his/her particular transaction.

Provisions for protecting the environment, nature and cultural heritage

Another area of concern to a buyer is the statutory obligations that may arise as a result of the condition of the immovable property. In particular, the *Environmental Protection Act* provides that no person shall discharge into the natural environment any contaminant, and no person responsible for a source of contaminant shall permit the discharge into the natural environment of any contaminant from the source of contaminant, in an amount, concentration or level and excess of that prescribed in the regulations.

Although the potential liability arising out of environmental contamination is limited in residential or farm areas, it is of great concern in dealings with commercial properties. Most provincial statutes dealing with environmental protection provide that the test for liability may be not just limited to the owner but may also extend to the person who has or has had charge, management or control of a substance. The *Environmental Protection Act* defines the responsible person as the owner, or the person in occupation or having the charge, management or control of a source of contaminant. The potential for liability that may arise in the case of environmental contamination is therefore not restricted to legal ownership but, in the case of a corporation, can be extended to parent companies being responsible for their subsidiaries on the basis that the parent company controls the actions of the subsidiary. Furthermore, the statutory provisions provide a potential for liability for directors and officers who authorize, acquiesce or participate in an environmental offence.

Many rural properties in Canada, including farms and cottages, are not connected to municipal water management systems; prior to the purchase of such properties additional searches are therefore necessary to determine, for example, whether the water of a well meets specific minimum requirements and if the septic system was properly installed.

Access to relevant records and documents

The agreement of purchase and sale obligates a seller to convey ownership or title to the interest in real estate sold to the buyer. The buyer will want to ensure that title is good and marketable. It is a matter of disclosure and negotiation as to what encumbrances, if any, a buyer will accept in connection with the seller's title.

Ontario prides itself on being the first jurisdiction in the world that has a land registry system in place that functions entirely by way of a paperless electronic registry called *Teraview Electronic System*, also known as *E-Reg*. The foundations for *E-Reg* were put in place in 1970 with the introduction of the *Land Registry Information System*, also known as *Polaris*. The objective of *Polaris* was to provide for a province-wide system of electronic registration using a *Property Identification Number* (PIN) to locate a particular parcel of land that may be accessed over the counter or from the internet through the *Teraview* website. The conversion process from the registry system to the land titles system is almost completed but for certain remote or rural areas of Ontario.

E-Reg is a paperless system where documents are created, submitted and maintained as well as registered online electronically. In order to facilitate a closing electronically, lawyers are licensed to have access to *Teraview*, and are entitled to make the necessary statements of law in a document and, upon completeness, the document is released for registration by the respective lawyers. The process is structured in the form of the escrow closing, the terms of which describe a specific protocol and process pursuant to which the respective lawyers will proceed with the closing of the transaction.

Another important aspect of the conveyance of real estate is the delivery of a survey which gives the purchaser a complete review of the land and structures on the land as mapped by a surveyor and is an essential document not only for the buyer but also for the creditor holding a mortgage or charge; however, the information contained in a survey must be carefully reviewed and in the event of conflicting information regarding boundaries, for example, a legal opinion should be obtained.

A buyer of real estate in Ontario may seek compensation as a result of a defective title as follows: (a) on the basis of a lawyers professional negligence under the *Lawyers Professional Indemnity Fund*; (b) on the basis of an error or omission on the title registry under the *Land Titles Assurance Fund*; or (c) on a contractual basis pursuant to a title insurance policy. More and more, title insurance is obtained by a purchaser of real estate in lieu of a lawyer's formal opinion on the status of the title, and covers losses incurred by the purchaser due to defects to the property's title that existed at the time of purchase but were unknown to the purchaser.

Key points that a seller should consider

All standard form agreements of purchase and sale expressly provide that time is of the essence, entitling the parties to performance of the terms and conditions of the agreement within a specified time. As a result, a failure to comply with an obligation within the time provided is a fundamental breach entitling the other party to treat the agreement as at an end. If both parties agree that the specified time cannot be met, some standard forms authorize the seller and buyer or their respective lawyers to agree in writing to an extension. In the event no such agreement is forthcoming, the non-defaulting party that wishes to pursue an equitable remedy of specific performance must demonstrate that, as of the specified time, it was ready, willing and able to complete the transaction in accordance with the terms and provisions of the agreement of purchase and sale. A tender is not necessary if there is clear evidence that the defaulting party is not in a position to close the transaction. The alternative to a claim for specific performance is a claim for liquidated damages or a forfeiture of the deposit.

The execution of a real estate purchase transaction

It is recommended that a buyer avail himself of the right to inspect the property before closing. Lawyers will conduct the closing and prepare in anticipation of a closing a closing memorandum. Before the *E-Reg* system, lawyers or their respective conveyancers were required to meet in the land registry office on the date of the closing. The purpose of the personal attendance was to exchange all documents, for the seller's lawyer to receive keys and the balance due on closing and the buyer's lawyer to attend to the registration of the transfer and any mortgage documentation. The delivery of payment of the balance due on closing in the form of certified cheque or bank draft against keys would be subject to a short escrow pending confirmation of the registration numbers of the documents registered.

Provided the lawyers have exchanged the appropriate closing documentation, the closing can proceed subject to confirmation as to the receipt of the closing funds. The Canadian banking system does not facilitate the transfer of funds on an immediate confirmed basis, and therefore funds are usually sent by the buyer to the buyer's lawyer in trust, enabling the buyer's lawyer to forward the funds to the seller's lawyer's trust account in time for confirmation of receipt by the seller's lawyer on the date of closing. The terms of the escrow are summarized in an *acknowledgement and direction* which is signed by the client, authorizing the lawyer to complete the transaction and register the same electronically.

Prior to closing, the seller's lawyer will prepare a *statement of adjustments* identifying the purchase price and deposit as well as adjustments in relation to realty taxes, utilities and any other items such as rental deposits or financing. The seller will also provide a direction regarding the balance due on closing which will be forwarded by the seller's lawyer to the buyer's lawyer to issue the closing funds. After closing, the seller's lawyer will provide his client with a trust ledger statement identifying the receipt and disbursements of the closing funds from the buyer's lawyer in accordance with seller's direction regarding the disbursement of same. The buyer's lawyer will advise the client of the balance due on closing as well as the payment of the land transfer tax and his fee and disbursements.

Powers of attorney

If a seller wishes to authorize the execution of a document to be registered in a land registry office, then he may execute a power of attorney appointing another person as his "attorney" to execute documents on his/her behalf. Powers of attorney may be drafted to remain effective even if the grantor becomes incapable of acting for him/her. A power of attorney in Ontario must be executed by the grantor and witnessed by at least two witnesses and include a statement confirming that the witnesses are not the attorney, the spouse of the attorney or the grantor or a child of the grantor. Other provincial statutes provide for similar statutory forms of powers of attorney. Powers of attorney may be registered in the local land registry office general register. Powers of attorney do not survive the grantor's death, as the attorney has no more power or capacity to act than does the grantor. A power of attorney must include specific language to enable the attorney to offer and accept or negotiate an agreement of purchase and sale or otherwise deal in real estate in order to be effective in connection with real estate transactions. To do this a power of attorney may give the attorney the authority to deal with real estate generally and does not need to specifically identify the real estate to which it pertains, although a grantor may wish to limit the authority in such a manner.

Financing

Most buyers of real estate finance the purchase by way of arranging financing either with a private or institutional lender. Canadian banks will provide a loan of generally up to 75% of the value of the residential property, provided it is occupied by the owner as his ordinary residence and the owner can show sufficient income to service the mortgage payments. A person who intends to borrow money will submit an application for an approval of a loan to a lender. The lender will issue approval of the loan in the form of a commitment letter which will set out the contractual relationship between the borrower (mortgagor) and the lender (mortgagee) and provide for confirmation of the principal amount of the loan, the negotiated interest rate, the monthly payments, the period over which the loan is amortized, the maturity date at which time the amount of the principal outstanding must be repaid and fees charged in connection with the loan. A loan may be drawn for a specific period of time or may be open. Furthermore, a loan to an individual that does not contain a prepayment privilege is repayable any time after five years provided the borrower pays three months interest.

A buyer of real estate who does not have sufficient income or is not resident in Canada may find it difficult, if not impossible, to obtain financing from a Canadian institutional lender.

Commercial properties are generally financed up to 60% of the value of the property providing the income of the real estate is sufficient to cover the mortgage payments. Personal guarantees from non-resident borrowers are generally not required as Canadian institutional lenders look primarily to the real estate located in Canada as security for the loan.

A lender will not issue a loan commitment to a borrower without having obtained its own independent appraisal of the real estate.

In Ontario, with the introduction of the *Land Registration Reform Act*, a registration of a charge/mortgage is an encumbrance on the legal estate of the chargor/mortgagor.

A lender who secures his loan by way of registration of a charge/mortgage against the title of the real estate of the borrower has certain mortgage remedies. The rights and obligations of a lender (chargee/mortgagee) and that of a property owner (chargor/mortgagor) are best discussed with a qualified lawyer. Generally, a mortgagee has the right to enforce his security either by way of a power of sale proceeding which would obligate the mortgagee to provide an accounting to the mortgagor and obtain the best price on the market or to proceed by way of foreclosure which would entitle the mortgagee to realize on the equity of redemption, ultimately becoming the owner of the real estate.

Purchase through a company

Non-residents of Canada are subject to Canadian tax only in respect of their income from employment in Canada, business carried on in Canada, disposition of taxable Canadian property (capital gains) and certain types of income of a passive nature (interest or rental income).

For Canadian tax purposes, a limited partnership is not a taxable entity. The income or loss of the limited partnership is determined at the level of the limited partnership in accordance with Canadian tax rules, as if it were a separate person, but the income for tax purposes is allocated to the limited partner at the year end of the limited partnership and taxed in the hands of the non-resident earning Canadian income from immovable property located in Canada.

The general partner of a limited partnership, being an Ontario corporation, is subject to Canadian tax on its worldwide income. However, the general partner may not have any income and may not be allocated any profits. It will be required to file at the very least a "nil" corporate tax return.

Therefore, investing directly or as a limited partner may be more preferable than through a corporation because direct ownership or the limited partnership structure permits Canadian rental income to be taxed only once in the hands of the individual or limited partner(s). If howver a corporation is incorporated in a province or pursuant to the *Canada Corporations Act*, a second level of tax arises on distributions by the corporation to its shareholders: firstly the tax payable by the corporation; and secondly the withholding tax on the dividend paid to the non-resident shareholder. It should be noted that the combined tax payable may however be more advantageous than the single tax payable by the non-resident who invests in real estate located in Canada directly, and therefore an investor is well advised to review the various options with a legal and accounting specialist.

A non-resident investor must also consider the consequences arising upon the disposition (including the deemed disposition upon death or a gift) of an investment in real estate located in Canada. Therefore, before investing in Canadian real estate, one must consider not only the benefits of limiting personal liability, the level of taxation of income and capital gains, but also estate planning issues.

Subject to the registration requirements, if the investor is a foreign corporation, this may provide additional tax or estate planning advantages.

Warranty claims

Standard form agreements of purchase and sale will not only set out certain conditions that are fundamental to the completion of the agreement of purchase and sale but will also provide for certain representations and warranties.

Representations are statements of fact that are important information that may have induced the buyer into entering into the agreement. Standard representations relate, for example, to the condition of the building on the immovable property or the availability of a permit with respect to a dock or boathouse in connection with the purchase of a cottage.

A fraudulent misrepresentation will entitle the defrauded party to damages and/or a rescission of the agreement. A negligent misrepresentation made outside the written contract will not succeed unless there are special circumstances where a material false statement was made carelessly and there was a significant reliance by the other party on the statement which resulted in a loss.

A warranty is a covenant that would entitle a buyer to damages only and not to rescind the agreement. For example, most standard form agreements provide for a warranty with respect to whether a building has been insulated with insulation containing urea formaldehyde, which warranty survives and does not merge on the completion of the purchase transaction. A carefully written agreement of purchase and sale will limit the warranty to the period of time the seller has owned the property and exclude the ownership of the building by previous owners.

Buyers will try to protect against potential liabilities; for example, with respect to any environmental contamination, which may not be discovered during the due diligence period; whereas sellers seek to limit any post-closing obligations. Similarly, a buyer will request an unqualified representation and warranty with respect to regulatory issues such as compliance with rent control legislation or tax assessments; whereas a seller will try to limit the representations and warranties to limited statements within his/her personal knowledge.

Lawyers and real estate agents, following the introduction of the *Proceeds of Crime (Money Laundering) and Terrorist Financing Act* in 2006, are now required to obtain representations regarding the seller's and purchaser's identity or corporate status and the *E-Reg* system requires a warranty as to the identity of the parties to a transaction involving real estate in Canada.

A buyer may also wish to protect himself against the existence of a patent defect which would involve a visible deterioration of the structure of the building or roof as well as defective windows or doors. The *common law* doctrine of *caveat emptor* would be successfully argued if a visible inspection by a reasonably competent person would have revealed the defect. Latent defects, which are problems only an expert may discover upon inspection, may also prove problematic for a buyer to raise in order to rescind an agreement. A concealed defect however does give the buyer the right to claim that the contract is void.

20.4 New construction, rebuilding and renovation

Zoning law and construction permits

In Ontario, as in most other provinces, land is subdivided by way of a registered plan of subdivision. When a municipality enters into a development agreement with a developer/builder, the municipality will impose certain conditions on the approval of the plan of subdivision. Generally, developers/builders will pay the charges in connection with the installation of services such as water mains, sewers, streetlights and sidewalks, as well as services to the building itself. The purchaser of a new building is not required to pay for such charges unless this is explicitly provided for in the agreement of purchase and sale.

Prior to any new construction, restoration, or expansion and extension respectively a building permit must be obtained. The *Building Code Act of Ontario* contains regulations regarding security, fire protection and building admissibility and is based on the *National Building Code of Canada*.

Currently, new construction of condominiums accounts for almost 65% of the total new construction in the Greater Toronto Area with about 130 condominium towers currently under construction. In December 1998 Ontario amended the legislation for condominiums significantly. The amendments strengthen consumer protection by requiring improved disclosure The purchaser of a condominium shall receive a declaration from the condominium corporation containing certain statements, including details about the legal structures and organization of the condominium owner, a schedule containing the budget, a schedule of actual fees and charges. After receiving the declaration of disclosure the buyer may examine the documents for a 10 day period and determine either to continue with the purchase or not.

Architect's contract and building contract

In Canada the services of both a professional design consultant and a general contractor are recommended to ensure proper completion of the construction of a new building. The relationship between the owner, the design consultant and the general contractor may be negotiated and agreed upon in the form of a simple letter agreement or set out in detail using a standard form agreement. Architects and engineers are professional service providers subject to a professional code of ethics, educational and licensing requirements administered by provincial self-governing associations.

An owner may enter into separate agreements with an architect or engineer respectively. The process of the construction of a building starts with the initial design phase, during which the design consultant prepares preliminary drawings which are used for purposes of the selection of a contractor. Thereafter, the design consultant will prepare complete design and construction specifications and usually administers the progress and completion of the construction work including periodic inspection of the work, certification of progress payments and substantial performance of the work.

However, the services of the design consultant and the work performed by a general contractor are not always easy to determine. In effect, design professionals do not have to guarantee their services and are merely required to exercise reasonable judgment, competence and diligence. For example, the responsibility to review the design documents and report any errors or requirements for redesign may rest with the owner unless the contract with the contractor clearly stipulates that the contractor assumes a design risk or guarantees the work to be performed within a turn-key/build to suit contract. It is, therefore, important that the agreement with the contractor clearly allocates the risk for inappropriate design or construction methods to the contractor and should also provide for a unit price for any additional work that may be required.

Architects and engineers carry professional liability insurance providing coverage for circumstances where they failed to exercise reasonable care in providing such services as: preparation of drawings and specifications; acting as payment certifier; interpreting requirements of the construction contract and judging performance thereunder; and acting as decision maker in disputes. However, architects and engineers generally do not carry the complete control of the construction work and have therefore usually limited their responsibilities to a limited supervision and inspection of the contractor's work.

Completion of construction and formalities

In Ontario, as well as the other provinces of Canada, general contractors as well as any other supplier of materials or services to a construction project are able to enforce payment of any outstanding amounts by registering a lien against the title to the real estate. Ontario introduced its *Construction Lien Act* in 1983, setting rules designed to protect persons who supply services and materials to construction projects. A person who performed any work or services or furnished materials for a construction project will be entitled to register a lien within a period of 45 days once a certificate of substantial completion issued by an architect or engineer or the owner personally confirming substantial performance/completion of the construction of the building has been published.

A lien claimant is required to commence an action within a 90 day period after the work has been substantially completed in order for the lien to remain on title, and if after two years no other action has been taken, an owner may apply for the vacation of the certificate of action and a discharge of the lien. Therefore, in order to protect his/her interest in the land, an owner should insist that no payments be made to a general contractor while liens are registered against the real estate. The cost of the removal of any liens should also be the responsibility of the general contractor.

A further requirement provided for by the *Construction Lien Act* is the requirement that a certificate for payment of holdback monies be issued. The holdback amount is 10% of the amount owing until all liens have expired (i.e. 45 days after publication of the certificate of substantial performance). If a lien has been registered, the owner must retain sufficient funds to cover the lien and any costs associated therewith. The standard form construction contract provides that holdback monies be placed in a joint account which obviously creates certain difficulties for the owner, if he wishes to set off any holdback funds from claims he may have against the general contractor.

The construction of new buildings is regulated pursuant to a building code which sets minimum construction standards. These standards provide for efficiency in construction and the safety of a building. Prior to the construction of a new building or any changes to an existing building the owner of the property must obtain a building permit from the building department of the local municipality. Building officials will inspect the construction of a building prior to occupancy and may issue work orders should there be outstanding work to be completed. Once the work is completed, notice must be given to the chief building official, and following an inspection, an occupancy certificate is issued enabling the owner take possession of a new or renovated part of a building. Prior to purchasing a new building the purchaser should obtain a building clearance certificate to ensure that there are no outstanding work orders.

Deficiencies and warranty claims regarding new construction

A buyer of a new house will require the general contractor to fulfill the obligations of an owner under the *Construction Lien Act*, to act as the constructor under the *Occupational Health and Safety Act*, and qualify under the *Ontario New Home Warranty Program*. In Ontario all builders/general contractors/developers must register under the program. The Ontario statute requires each seller of a new house to warrant that the house:

- Is constructed in a good and workmanlike manner, free from defects in material
- Is fit for habitation and is constructed in accordance with the *Ontario Building Code*
- Is free from major structural defects as defined by the regulations, and "such other warranties as are prescribed by the regulations." Under the *Ontario New Home Warranty Program* a certificate of completion and possession will be issued to the buyer which will form the basis of a warranty claim

20.5 Rental and tenancy

All provinces and territories in Canada have passed legislation providing for comprehensive regimes governing the relationship between landlord (lessor) and tenant (lessee) both in the residential and, to a lesser degree, commercial context.

Rental and leasing agreements

Whereas the terms of a residential tenancy are subject to the comprehensive regime set out in Ontario in the *Residential Tenancies Act* (with similar legislation also passed in the other provinces and territories of Canada), the rights and obligations of commercial landlords and tenants are mainly a matter of contract (*common law*). Most agreements of purchase and sale involving the purchase of a residential, commercial, industrial or retail property containing leased premises will set out numerous representations by the seller which must be reviewed by the buyer (and/or his lawyer) during the due diligence process in order to satisfy him/herself that the assignment of a lease is completed with the parties having a comprehensive understanding of the rights and obligations between landlord and tenant. The most common form of confirmation of the basic terms of a lease is by way of an estoppel certificate. The buyer will rely on the representations provided by the tenant in the estoppel certificate to determine that there is no dispute between the landlord and tenant with respect to the terms and conditions of the lease.

In Ontario, the *Commercial Tenancies Act* provides for certain minimum rights and obligations between a commercial tenant and landlord (many may be over-written by agreement between tenant and landlord). For example, a landlord may terminate a commercial tenancy for non-payment of rent on the 16th day after the day rent was due. Alternatively, a landlord may seize a tenant's property contained within the rented premises and may dispose of the seized property within five days without advance notice if not otherwise provided for in the lease.

Most residential or commercial leases are negotiated by way of offers to lease which contain the most important terms and conditions of the lease. A more formal lease is completed upon occupancy of the leased premises by the tenant. The offer to lease will focus on the following essential matters: a definition of the leased premises; the identification of the parties; the determination of the rent; the term of the lease; the commencement date; and such other material terms that may be particular to the relationship between the landlord and tenant (for example, leasehold improvements).

Regulations on protection of tenants and rent control

Ontario introduced its first rent control legislation in the mid-1960s. Until the *Tenant Protection Act* was introduced in 1997, landlords were not in a position to increase rent beyond a prescribed rate. The current legislation in Ontario, the *Residential Tenancies Act*, replaced the *Tenant Protection Act* in 2006 and allows a maximum yearly price increase based on the change in Ontario's Consumer Price Index, which in 2014 was 0.8%. Landlords may apply to increase rents above the guideline on the basis of major renovations or repairs or other improvements to the rental premises, extraordinary increases in taxes or utility charges or for security costs related to the rental premises. If a tenant leaves the premises, then the rent that was negotiated no longer applies and a landlord is free to charge market rent. Rent increases are only possible after the expiry of a 12 month period and must be delivered by written notice to the tenant 90 days prior.

Security of tenure applies to residential tenants, with a landlord able to end a tenancy via two basic methods: either during the term of the tenancy, on the basis of termination for a cause, or at the end of the term, for no fault reasons. An immediate termination of a tenancy is possible, for example, for non-payment of rent, illegal activity, disturbance, over-crowding or substantial interference with the rights of the landlord or other tenants.

A tenancy may only be terminated at the end of the term on no fault grounds if the landlord requires possession of the premises for his or her own use. In the event that a tenancy is not renewed by an agreement between the landlord and the tenant, the tenancy continues on a month to month basis.

Any dispute between a landlord and a residential tenant is determined before the *Landlord and Tenant Board* which has the power to either mediate or adjudicate disputes between landlords and tenants. In order to terminate a tenancy early with cause (such as non-payment of rent, damage rented premises or illegal activity) a landlord must first provide notice of the intent to terminate to the tenant, and may then apply to the *Landlord and Tenant Board* for an order of termination/eviction.

20.6 Succession and gifts

Applicable law and jurisdiction

Private international law provides that succession to moveable property is governed by the law of the last domicile of the deceased. Succession to immoveable property is governed by the law of the place where the real estate is situated.

All provinces and territories in Canada, including Quebec, have passed legislation dealing with the formal requirements of making a last will and testament (Will). The English requirement that a Will be in writing and must be executed by the testator and two witnesses has been uniformly adopted by the Canadian provinces and territories.

Any person who is mentally competent and at least 18 years old may act as a witness to a Will. However, beneficiaries or spouses of beneficiaries should not act as witnesses. The executor (estate trustee) is competent to witness a Will provided he/she is not a beneficiary. It is not necessary that the testator and witnesses initial each page of the Will. It is, however, necessary that the testator sign at the end of the Will in the presence of the two witnesses and the two witnesses both sign after the testator in the presence of each other. Standard practice is for the testator to initial each page of the Will and for at least one witness to sign a statutory declaration verifying the execution of the Will.

A holograph Will written in the testator's own handwriting and dated and signed by the testator does not require a witness and is recognized in most of Canada.

In Canada, court offices have a system of safe keeping of original Wills. However, this service is not widely used and a more likely location for the safe keeping of an original Will is with a lawyer, with a copy being kept by the client in a safety deposit box. An executor may be informed by a testator of his appointment and may also be given a copy of the testator's Will.

It is also possible to enter into an International Will, which conforms to the requirements of the *Uniform Law on the Form of International Will*, as adopted by the 1973 Diplomatic Conferences on Wills in Washington, D.C.; note, however, that British Columbia, Quebec and the Territories have not adopted this convention. In order to meet the requirements of formal validity, an International Will must be in writing and the testator must sign the Will in the presence of two witnesses and at least one witness must attest to the execution of the Will.

All provinces and territories in Canada have passed legislation dealing with the conflict of laws and provide for the recognition of foreign Wills. However, only Ontario, Manitoba and Newfoundland have extended recognition of Wills made in the foreign jurisdiction to include not only the disposition of moveable property but also immoveable property.

Fundamentals of the succession and gift/donation laws of Canada

Canadian laws, as they relate to estate matters, are very different from the laws of continental Europe, and this may lead to some unforeseen complications especially if real estate is part of the estate of the deceased. Therefore, any buyer/owner of real estate in Canada is well-advised to familiarize him/herself with some of the more common forms of estate planning, including a disposition of real estate either by *inter vivos* gift, declaration of trust, an assignment to a joint tenant or a last will and testament.

A gift is an irrevocable transfer of property by a donor to a donee for no consideration, with the intention that the donee owns the property. Although there is no required form, a written deed of gift should identify the donor making the gift, the donee accepting the gift and provide for the irrevocable transfer of the real estate for no consideration.

A donor may gift real estate during his lifetime not only for estate freezing or income splitting purposes but also to minimize or avoid estate administration requirements including probate court fees. The donee, in effect, acquires the real estate at the same cost as the donor's proceeds which are deemed to be equal to the fair market value of the real estate.

Trusts are most commonly created by a written declaration of trust which provides that a settlor (the owner of the property) transfers the property to a trustee to hold the property for the benefit of a beneficiary (the *cestui que trust*). The trustee may therefore hold the legal title to the real estate for the benefit of an undisclosed beneficiary. The trustee has the duty, enforced by courts of equity, to use his nominal ownership and control of the trust property for the benefit of the *cestui que trust*.

A joint tenancy involves the registration of the ownership of real estate in the names of two or more persons as joint tenants. Jointly held real estate has the benefit of not forming part of the estate of a deceased person; instead, the surviving joint tenant becomes the sole owner by reason of survivorship.

The *Civil Code of Quebec* to some extent follows the continental European statutory codes by providing that every successor may accept a succession and become an heir inheriting all the rights and obligations of the deceased. The successor has six months in which to decide to accept all the assets and debts of the deceased. Quebec follows the civil law principle that the opening of a succession is the legal principle pursuant to which property is transmitted to the deceased heirs which coincides with his or her date of death. The role of the liquidator (estate trustee) is to liquidate the succession, and in the event there is no will, the selection of the liquidator is done by the heirs. The liquidator will determine the content of the succession and pay the debts of the deceased.

The other provinces, which are *common law* jurisdictions, follow a different regime. For example in Ontario, section 2 of the *Estates Administration Act* provides that when a person dies in Ontario, all his property vests in the person's personal representative (also referred to as an executor, administrator or estate trustee) to pay debts and distribute the remaining estate to the beneficiaries. All real estate situated in Ontario, whether owned by a person resident or domiciled in Ontario or not, must be administered in accordance with the Ontario statutory regime.

In Ontario it is necessary to obtain probate (i.e. a certificate confirming the appointment of an estate trustee), if the value of the real estate is more than CAD 50,000, or if the title to the real estate is registered in the land titles system, or if there is an intestacy.

In order to obtain probate, the Will must have been executed in the manner and form required by the Will statute of the province. When a person dies without leaving a Will, upon application by an interested person to the court, an administrator will be appointed to perform the duties and responsibilities of the estate trustee. The estate trustee must pay all debts and distribute the property of the deceased in accordance with the provincial succession laws.

Canadian succession laws do not recognize a minimum entitlement [i.e. there are no forced heirship provisions]. However, if a person dies intestate and only his spouse survives leaving no issue, then the surviving spouse is entitled to the entire estate. Where a person dies intestate and leaves a spouse and one child, the spouse is entitled to a preferential share of CAD 200,000 (in Ontario) and to one-half of the remaining property with the child entitled to the other half; where there is more than one child the spouse is entitled to one-third of the remaining property and the children share the other two-thirds with the issue of a predeceased child taking the child's share *per stirpes*.

In Canada, spouses are protected by a statutory community of property regime which is subject only to the terms of a domestic agreement. In effect, the rights of a testator to provide for the distribution of his/her estate is unlimited (in most provinces) and the special rights of the surviving spouse or those of dependants who require support are limitations on the testator's freedom of testamentary disposition.

The surviving spouse must decide within six months of the death of the deceased spouse, to elect an equalization share pursuant to section 5(2) of the *Family Law Act* or accept the dispositions in the Will of the deceased spouse or accept the entitlement on intestacy. The transmission of the real estate as provided for in the Will or pursuant to an intestacy would be carried out by the estate trustee and the surviving spouse would be entitled to a cash equalization payment if he or she elected his or her share of the net family property and this was more than had been provided for in the Will or intestacy. Only if both spouses maintain a common habitual residence outside of Ontario do the provisions of the *Family Law Act* not apply.

The other statutory limit on the distribution of an estate in Ontario (and other provinces) is that if the deceased does not provide adequately for the support of his dependants, the court in Ontario has broad power to order that provisions be made out of the estate of the deceased for such support.

A *certificate of appointment of estate trustee* does not contain a complete detailed list of the value of the estate of the deceased. In order to obtain a complete inventory of a deceased's estate and confirmation regarding the receipts and disbursements of capital and revenue it is possible for a beneficiary to obtain an order for a statement of assets or further particulars. An estate trustee may be required "to render a just and full account" before the Ontario court which will confirm the following:

- The allocation of receipts and disbursements of capital and revenue
- The original assets of the estate at the time of death and any investments made by the estate trustee
- Any fees, compensation and taxes paid and the distribution of the capital and revenue of the deceased's estate

In the event that the estate trustee does not provide a complete and satisfactory accounting, beneficiaries may force the passing of the accounts of an estate.

Upon making an application for a certificate of appointment of estate trustee, the estate of the deceased will be required to pay, not only the fees of the estate trustee and professional fees, but also an estate administration tax (probate court fees). In Ontario, the tax is based on the gross value of the deceased's assets: the amount of tax payable under the issuance of an estate certificate for which application is made after 7 June 1992 is:

- CAD 5 for each CAD 1,000 or part thereof of the first CAD 50,000 of the value of the estate
- CAD 15 for each CAD 1,000 or part thereof by which the value of the estate exceeds CAD 50,000

A non-resident who owns real estate in Ontario that is registered in the land titles registry system may make a Will dealing specifically with a testamentary disposition of real estate in Ontario and thereby limit the estate administration tax that will be payable on the application to the court for a certificate of appointment of estate trustee to be based on the net value of the real estate situated in Ontario. Therefore, if, for example, the value of the real estate is CAD 1 million, the estate administration tax that must be paid to the Minister of Finance of Ontario at the time of the issuance of the certificate by the court is CAD 14,500.

The probate court fees in other provinces of Canada are also calculated pursuant to the value of the estate and vary from province to province with Quebec being the most attractive at a flat rate of CAD 45 regardless of the value of the estate. The fees on an estate of CAD 1 million in the other provinces are as follows:

Alberta	CAD 400
British Columbia	CAD 13,650
Manitoba	CAD 7,000
New Brunswick	Min. CAD 1,417 plus up to 1/3 of 1%
Nova Scotia	CAD 15,778.45
Newfoundland	CAD 5,055
Prince Edward Island	CAD 4,000
Saskatchewan	CAD 7,000

In Ontario, a trustee is entitled to "such fee and reasonable allowance for the care, pains, and trouble, and the time expended in and about the estate as may be allowed by a judge of the *Superior Court of Justice*. The

Ontario rates of compensation for an estate trustee as set by the Ontario court are equal to 5% of the gross value of the estate; based on 2.5% of the revenue and capital receipts and 2.5% of revenue and capital disbursements. Where there are ongoing trusts the compensation for "care and management" is based on a fee of 0.4% per annum allocated on the basis of ⅔ to the capital account and ⅓ to the revenue account. It is not unusual for professional estate trustees to negotiate higher compensation.

An estate trustee may be required to retain the services of various professional advisors including the assistance of a lawyer. The estate trustee has the overall responsibility for the administration of the estate. The duty of a lawyer may be required to assist the estate trustee in almost all aspects of the administration of the estate including the filing of court documents and transfer documents in the land registry/titles system.

20.7 Taxes and charges

One-time taxes and charges on purchase

Both the federal government and the provincial governments impose taxes that may be applicable at the time that a transfer of real estate is registered.

Purchase / acquisition taxes

In Ontario, Section 3 of the *Land Transfer Tax Act* provides that the prescribed rate of tax is payable on a "disposition of the beneficial interest in land". Not included is a vesting of land in a trustee pursuant to a will or a transfer of beneficial interest arising from the death of the registered owner. In order to determine the value of the consideration for purposes of calculating the land transfer tax, a buyer must file with the deed/transfer an *Affidavit of Residence and of Value of the Consideration.* The prescribed rate of tax for the disposition of land except single family residential properties is 0.5% of the first CAD 55,000, 1% of the next CAD 195,000 and 1.5% of the balance of the value of the consideration over CAD 250,000. For properties containing one or two single family residences there is an additional 0.5% tax on the balance of the value of the consideration over CAD 400,000.

The tax payable for a single family residence with a value of consideration of CAD 500,000 would be:

0.005 x 55,000 + 0.01 x 195,000 + 0.015 x 250,000 + 0.005 x 100,000 = CAD 6,475.

As of 1 February 2008 the City of Toronto levies a *Municipal Land Transfer Tax* to be paid in addition to the taxes levied by Ontario at the time of the deed registration of the conveyance of property. The prescribed rate of tax for the disposition of land containing one or two single family residences is 0.5% of the first CAD 55,000, 1% of the next CAD 345,000 and 2.0% of the balance of the value of the consideration over CAD 400,000.

The Toronto portion of land transfer tax that would be payable for a single family residence in Toronto with a value of consideration of CAD 500,000 would be:

0.005 x 55,000 + 0.01 x 345,000 + 0.02 x 100,000 = CAD 5,725.

The total tax would be CAD 5,725 (Toronto tax) plus CAD 6,475 (Ontario tax) = CAD 12,200.

Overview: Real estate transfer taxes in the Provinces[1]

Province	Land Transfer Tax	Other Taxes
Alberta	0%	A registration fee in the amount of CAD 50 plus CAD 1 for every CAD 5,000 of the value of the conveyance/mortgage
British Columbia	1% on the first CAD 200,000 of the market value and 2% thereover	
Manitoba	0% on the first CAD 30,000 0.5% between CAD 30,000 and CAD 90,000 1.0% between CAD 90,000 and 150,000 1.5% between CAD 150,000 and 200,000 2.5% over CAD 200,000	
New Brunswick	0.5% on the greater of purchase price and assessed value	
Newfoundland	0%	A registration fee of CAD 100 + 0.004 x of the value of the conveyance/ mortgage
Northwest Territory	0%	Registration fee is CAD 1.50 per CAD 1,000 of the land value up to a land value of CAD 1,000,000, then CAD 1 for every CAD 1,000 thereafter - registration fee is CAD 1.00 per CAD 1,000 of the mortgage value, with a minimum fee of CAD 80
Nova Scotia	0.5% - 1.5%	Harmonized Sales Tax of 13% payable on purchase of the new building, commercial properties and on purchase of wasteground
Nunavut	0%	Registration fee is CAD 1.50 per CAD 1,000 of the value of land up to a land value of CAD 1,000,000, then CAD 1 for every CAD 1,000 thereafter The registration fee is CAD 1.00 per 1,000 of the mortgage value, with a minimum fee of CAD 80
Ontario	For a single-family house 0.5% on the first CAD 55,000 1% between 55,000 and CAD 250,000 1.5% over 250,000 plus 0.5% on the remaining sum over CAD 400,000	

[1] Moderate registration fee between CAD 50 and CAD 100 per document are raised by land registries. Legal services are based on hourly fees or flat rates based on the transaction value

Province	Land Transfer Tax	Other Taxes
Prince Edward Island	1%	Value of the deed of conveyance/mortgage CAD 0 to CAD 9,999 CAD 77.25 CAD 10,000 to 19,999 CAD 103 CAD 20,000 to 49,999 CAD 154.55 CAD 50,000 to 99,999 CAD 231.80 CAD 100,000 to 149,999 CAD 309.10 CAD 150,000 to 199,999 CAD 386.40 over CAD 200,000 CAD 463.65
Quebec	0.5% on the first CAD 50,000 1% between CAD 50,001 and 250,000 1.5% over CAD 250,000	
Saskatchewan	0%	0.3% of the value of the conveyance
Yukon	0%	Per CAD 1,000 over CAD 25,000, CAD 0.25

Sales taxes (Value Added Taxes)

On 1 January 1991, the federal government introduced the *Goods and Services Tax (*GST*)* which applies to goods and services provided in Canada. The GST is calculated at a rate of 5% of the value of the goods and services and is also applicable to the sale of real estate situated in Canada subject to certain exempt supplies of real estate. For example, the sale of used residential real estate is exempt.

In Ontario, Nova Scotia, New Brunswick, Prince Edward Island and Newfoundland and Labrador the GST has been combined with the respective provincial sales taxes to form the *Harmonized Sales Tax* (HST), with rates ranging from 12-15%; in Ontario the HST is 13%. British Columbia had previously implemented the HST, but this ceased to be effective on April 1, 2013. In these provinces the full HST is applied to the sale of real estate, but Ontario offers a rebate of up to CAD 24,000 and Nova Scotia offers a rebate up to a maximum of CAD 1,500. New Brunswick and Newfoundland and Labrador do not offer HST rebates.

HST rebates for new housing purchases

Province	Maximum HST Rebate	Threshold Maximum Rebate is Reached
Ontario	CAD 24,000	CAD 400,000
Nova Scotia	CAD 1,500	CAD 100,000
New Brunswick	n/a	n/a
Newfoundland and Labrador	n/a	n/a
Prince Edward Island	n/a	n/a

Real estate registration and notary charges

Lawyers' fees in Canada are determined on a *quantum merit* basis taking into consideration the time and effort required and spent; special skill and services provided; and may also take into consideration the value of the real estate, the results obtained and any other special circumstances. Most lawyers in Ontario will charge an hourly rate for general real estate services. For the transfer of real estate lawyers (or notaries in Quebec) may enter into a fixed fee arrangement. Upon registration, local land registry offices charge minimal document registration fees, for example, less than CAD 100 per document in Ontario.

Recurring taxes and charges

Realty tax

In January 1998, Ontario changed its realty tax assessment to a system based on the current market value of the real estate. The *Municipal Property Assessment Corporation* is a municipal corporation that works with the local municipalities to establish the municipal realty taxes payable by owners of real estate located in Ontario. For example, the owner of a residence valued at CAD 500,000 will be required to pay in mid-Toronto approximately CAD 5,000 (which includes approximately CAD 1,750 educational tax) in annual realty tax. Similar municipal realty tax assessments are applicable throughout Canada.

Income tax

Canada taxes individual's resident and corporations incorporated in or controlled and managed from Canada on their worldwide income. Non-residents are taxed only on Canadian sourced income. The *Income Tax Act* does not contain a definition of residence. An individual will be deemed to be a resident in Canada for the entire year, if the individual "sojourns" in Canada for 183 days or more in a year. Part 1, Division E of the *Income Tax Act* sets out the computation of the marginal rates payable by individuals. The provincial income tax rates are also based on various marginal rates.

2014 Combined federal and provincial personal top marginal tax rates

Jurisdiction	Regular Income / (%) over CAD 136,270
Alberta	39.00%
British Columbia	43.70% (and 45.80% over CAD 150,000)
Nova Scotia	46.50% (and 50.00% over CAD 150,000)
Ontario	46.41% (and 47.97% over CAD 150,000 and 49.53% over CAD 220,000)
Quebec	44.75%
Non-resident	42.90%

2014 Federal/Ontario personal tax brackets

Taxable Income	Federal Tax	Add Ontario Tax
CAD 43,953 or less	15%	5.05% on first CAD 40,120
CAD 43,95442,708 to CAD 87,907	22%	9.15% on next CAD 40,122
CAD 87,908 to CAD 136,270	26%	11.16% on next CAD 69,758
CAD 132,406 or more	29%	12.16% on next CAD 70,000, plus 13.16% over CAD 220,000

If a non-resident decides to acquire an indirect interest in Canadian real estate through a Canadian corporation the income of the non-resident controlled corporation will be taxed as follows:

2014 General corporate income tax rates (including non Canadian controlled)

Jurisdiction	Investment Income/ Combined Rate
Basic Federal	15.00%
Alberta	25.00%
British Columbia	26.00%
Ontario	26.50%
Nova Scotia	31.00%
Quebec	26.90%

Net wealth tax

Neither Canada nor the provinces and territories impose a wealth tax on individuals. Some Canadian provinces and also the federal government levy a capital tax on large corporations. The calculation of the taxable capital differs from province to province and applicable rates are being reduced to nil.

Capital gains taxes

A non-resident person who disposes of "taxable Canadian property" as defined in the *Income Tax Act* is required to file a Canadian tax return to report the disposition of the real estate and pay tax on any resulting taxable capital gain. The capital gain is calculated using the value of consideration on the sale less the original purchase price (adjusted cost base) and any expenses. In October 2000, the inclusion rate of a capital gain was reduced from 66% to 50% so that currently only 50% of the capital gain is included in the taxable income. A non-resident who disposes of real estate in Canada will be subject to tax on the taxable gain on the same basis as if resident of Canada.

Any capital gain arising on the disposition of a principal residence by a resident individual taxpayer is exempt from tax under the *Income Tax Act*. Interest payments and other expenses including improvements are not deductible from the taxpayer's income.

When a non-resident person disposes of *taxable Canadian property*, which includes all real estate situated in Canada, as well as shares in a corporation (subject to public corporation exemptions), then section 116(1) of the *Income Tax Act* requires the non-resident person to give notice of the disposition to the *Canadian Revenue Agency* (CRA) and the person so disposing of the taxable Canadian property is required to obtain a certificate from the *Minister of National Revenue* in the following cases:

- The corporation's assets include immovable property in Canada
- The distribution from an estate to a non-resident beneficiary
- The value of the estate is more than 50% derived from immovable property in Canada

In order to receive the certificate a non-resident seller must remit with the notice of disposition 25% of the amount, if any, by which the proceeds of disposition of the taxable Canadian property exceeds the adjusted cost base of the property immediately before the disposition. Expenses of disposition, such as legal fees or real estate commissions, cannot be used to reduce the portion of the capital gain which is subject to the withholding tax calculation. If the *Minister of National Revenue* does not issue a certificate, then the buyer is personally liable for payment of 25% of the purchase price which must be remitted to the *Minister of National Revenue* within 30 days after the end of the month in which the taxable Canadian property was acquired.

The cost base of real estate excluding the land may be depreciated at a rate of 4% per annum and any depreciation claimed in connection with the income producing real estate is subject to recapture on the sale of the real estate.

The deceased taxpayer is deemed to have immediately disposed of the real estate before death and any accrued capital gains on such property is subject to tax to be reported by the estate trustee in the final tax return.

Inheritance and gift taxes

The Canadian income tax regime taxes income and the capital gain on a disposition of property. There is no tax based on a person's wealth or a gift or inheritance. The transfer of real estate to a close person for proceeds less than the fair market value, or the transfer of real estate to any person by way of gift, or the transmission of real estate as a result of an inheritance are all transactions that are deemed to occur at fair market value. Therefore, a gift of real estate is subject to capital gains tax based on a deemed disposition at fair market value. Similarly, a transmission of real estate as a result of death does not trigger any gift or estate tax; instead, there is a deemed disposition at fair market value resulting in a capital gains tax payable by the estate of the deceased.

Other taxes and charges

All applicable taxes and charges have been discussed above.

Incorrect (lower) statement of sale price on the sales agreement

If a person transfers real estate at less than fair market value, then section 69(1) (b) of the *Income Tax Act* deems the transferor to have received proceeds of disposition equal to the fair market value of the real estate at the time of transfer. There is no corresponding adjustment to the cost base of the transferee. In the case of a gift or inheritance, the tax will be payable by the donor or the deceased's estate and the donee/beneficiary has the benefit of the increased cost base. This requirement for transactions to occur at fair market value leaves no opportunity for transactions to be structured to reduce or avoid capital gains taxation.

In principal, the tax-payer is entitled to benefit from the best possible tax advantages. In September 1988 Canada enacted the *General Anti-Avoidance Rule*. The Canadian tax regulations impose tax consequences that depending on the circumstances may provide that a transaction is deemed to be a willful avoidance of tax payments. In November 2001

Canada enacted regulations against terrorism and money laundering in compliance with the *Criminal Code* and other statutory provisions. Under the *Proceeds of Crime (Money Laundering) Act* a reporting obligation requires the expert, such as an accountant, legal advisor, estate agent or securities broker to notify the committee of any suspicious transactions.

International taxation

Canada has entered into reciprocal tax treaties for the avoidance of double taxation with many countries. Information regarding these tax treaties may be obtained at the *Canada Department of Finance* website, *fin.gc.ca*. Canada entered into these tax treaties with the main objective to avoid double taxation either by providing for tax credits or exemptions. The scope of the tax treaties is based on the *OECD Model Treaty* of 1977 which provided that the application of a tax treaty is determined by residence and not by nationality. The taxes covered are both taxes on income and on capital. The tax treaties provide for a more or less uniform treatment of non-resident investors in real estate situated in Canada.

Pursuant to the tax treaties, if a non-resident person derives rental income from a rental operation the net rental income will be taxed "in the State where immovable property is located" at the applicable progressive rate of tax. A different federal and provincial tax rate is applicable depending on whether the non-resident entity is an individual, corporation or trust and on the amount of the income. A non-resident person that receives income from the rental of immovable property that is located in Canada is subject to withholding tax under Part XIII of the *Income Tax Act* at the rate of 25% of the gross rents received. The Canadian resident payer has an obligation to withhold and remit the tax.

Under Canadian tax law, a non-resident receiving rental income may reduce the withholding tax of 25% on the gross rental income by making an election and providing an undertaking to file an income tax return and pay tax under Part I of the *Income Tax Act.* The non-resident, in effect, is entitled to pay the applicable tax on the net rental income as if he or she were resident in Canada.

Income in the form of interest and dividends received by a non-resident is subject to Canadian withholding tax and relief from double taxation under the tax treaties is available.

Subject to certain exemptions interest income paid by a Canadian borrower to a non-resident lender is subject to a 25% withholding tax. The Canadian borrower is subject to personal liability as well as interest and penalties for failure to remit to the *Canada Revenue Agency* the withholding tax. Applicable tax treaties provide relief from double taxation by reducing the basic withholding tax rate of 25% on interest income to up to 10%.

Withholding taxes in the basic amount of 25% on dividends paid by a Canadian corporation to a non-resident shareholder may be reduced by a tax treaty to 5%. In order to qualify for the reduced withholding tax rate of 5% the non-resident shareholder must control at least 10% of the voting shares of the Canadian corporation paying the dividends.

20.8 Immigration law and tax residence

Entry, residence and settlement of foreigners

Canada's immigration policies and procedures have been designed with the following objectives in mind: (1) to attain the country's demographic goals; and (2) to enrich and strengthen the multicultural fabric of its society. Every year the *Minister of Citizenship and Immigration* issues immigrant targets based on the three main immigration categories: (i) economic immigrants (2014: 165,046); (ii) family class (2014: 66,666); and (iii) refugee claimants (2014: 23,277) and other immigrants (2014: 5,338) for a total of 259,020 landings in 2014.

Temporary visitors to Canada from certain specified countries are required to obtain a temporary resident visa. Citizens of other countries, including European Union members and Switzerland, are exempt from the temporary resident visa requirement. The foreign national will be entitled to remain in Canada as a visitor for a period of up to six months unless an immigration officer makes a determination of an applicable shorter period which is normally notated in the foreign national's passport at the time of entry.

Foreign nationals who seek to engage in international business activities in Canada without directly entering the Canadian labour market do not need to obtain a work permit. The *Immigration and Refugee Protection Regulations* (Regulations) specifically identifies the following persons as business visitors:

- A person purchasing Canadian goods or services for a foreign business or receiving training in respect of such goods or services
- A person receiving or giving training within a Canadian parent or subsidiary of the corporation that employs them outside of Canada if any production of goods or services that results from the training is incidental
- A person representing a foreign business for the purposes of selling goods for that business if the person is not engaged in making sales to the general public in Canada

Under the Regulations, a foreign national may seek to engage in international business activities in Canada without directly entering the Canadian labor market only if:

a The primary source of remuneration for the business activities is outside Canada; and

b The principal place of business and actual place of accrual of profits remain predominately outside Canada

In 2014, the Government of Canada announced significant reforms to the Temporary Foreign Worker Program and introduced the International Mobility Programs.

The Regulations provide the authority for officers to issue work permits on the basis of a Labour Market Impact Assessment (LMIA) from Employment and Social Development Canada (ESDC). ESDC has the broad authority to evaluate several factors in assessing the impact on the Canadian labour market. These include traditional factors such as wages and working conditions and the availability of Canadians or permanent residents to do the work in question, as well as whether skills and knowledge transfer would result from accepting the foreign worker, and whether the work is likely to create other jobs for the benefit of Canadians or permanent residents.

Intra-company transferees may apply for work permits under the general provision of the Regulations if they:

- Are currently employed by a multi-national company and seek entry to work in a parent, a subsidiary, a branch, or an affiliate of that enterprise
- Are transferring to an enterprise that has a qualifying relationship with the enterprise in which they are currently employed, and will be undertaking employment at a legitimate and continuing establishment of that company (18–24 months can be used as a reasonable minimum guideline)
- Are being transferred to a position in an executive, senior managerial, or specialized knowledge capacity
- Have been employed continuously (via payroll or by contract directly with the company), by the company that plans to transfer them outside Canada in a similar full-time position (not accumulated part-time) for at least one year in the three year period immediately preceding the date of initial application

In January 2015, CIC introduced an Express Entry system to manage applications for permanent residence under:

- The Federal Skilled Worker Program
- The Federal Skilled Trades Program
- The Canadian Experience Class

Express Entry is the first step to immigrate to Canada under the included programs. Potential candidates can complete an Express Entry profile at any time. There is no deadline to complete a profile and no limit on the number of candidates that will be accepted into the pool.

Anyone who is accepted into the Express Entry pool could receive an Invitation to Apply for Permanent Residence. Draws to invite candidates to apply will take place regularly over the course of each year. CIC will pick only the top candidates, no matter when they were accepted into the pool.

If an applicant is invited to apply, he or she will have sixty days to submit a complete Application for Permanent Residence online. The Express Entry system comprises two steps:

1 Online Profile

Potential candidates complete an online Express Entry profile. This is a secure form that they use to provide information about their:

- Skills
- Work experience
- Language ability
- Education
- Other details that will help CIC assess them

Those who meet the criteria of one of the federal immigration programs listed above will be accepted into a pool of candidates.

Anyone who does not already have a job offer supported by an LMIA, if the candidate needs one, or a nomination from a province or territory, must register with the ESDC Job Bank. The Job Bank will help connect Express Entry candidates with eligible employers in Canada.

It should be noted that entry into the Express Entry pool does not guarantee that a candidate will be issued an Invitation to Apply (ITA) for permanent residence. Invited candidates still have to meet eligibility and admissibility requirements under the Immigration and Refugee Protection Act.

2 Invitation to Apply

The highest-ranking candidates in the pool will be invited to apply for permanent residence. Candidates will be ranked using a point-based system called the Comprehensive Ranking System (CRS). Points are awarded using the information in their profiles. Candidates will be awarded points for:

- A job offer, and/or
- A nomination from a province or territory (PT), and/or
- Skills and experience factors

A candidate can get additional points for:

- A job offer supported by an LMIA
- A nomination by a province or territory

Candidates with a *qualifying offer of arranged employment* or *a PT nomination* are awarded an additional 600 points in the CRS and are normally invited to apply at the next eligible round of invitations, subject to the PT's overall nomination space and Citizenship and Immigration Canada's (CIC) ministerial instructions for each round.

These additional points may make a candidate rank high enough to be invited to apply at the next drawing of candidates. If an applicant is invited to apply, he or she will have sixty days to submit an online application for permanent residence.

CIC strives to process the majority of complete applications within six months. Candidates can stay in the pool for up to 12 months.

Someone who does not get an ITA within twelve months of submitting an Express Entry profile may submit a new profile. If he or she still meets the criteria, he or she can re-enter the pool. This will prevent backlogs and ensure quick processing times.

On 19 June 2014, the *Economic Action Plan 2014 Act* (Bill C-31) became law. This resulted in the termination of applications in the backlog of the federal Immigrant Investor Program (IIP) and federal Entrepreneur Program (EN). IIP and EN applications were terminated if an immigration officer did not make a selection decision before 11 February 2014. For those applications that were terminated, CIC will return the application fees paid by the applicants. CIC has set up a central task force based in Ottawa to handle the process.

In January 2015, CIC introduced a new Immigrant Investor Venture Capital (IIVC) Pilot Program in order to attract experienced business immigrants who can actively invest in the Canadian economy, stimulating innovation, economic growth and job creation.

The requirements of the IIVC Program are as follows:

Personal Net Worth

- A personal net worth of CAD 10 million or more. The net worth must have been acquired through lawful, private sector *business or investment activities*
- Personal net worth acquired by inheritance or in the value of the applicant's primary residence will not count towards the personal net worth requirement

Proof of Personal Net Worth

- CIC will require applicants whose applications can be considered for its second stage review to obtain a due diligence report at their expense from one of the designated service providers

- The due diligence report is an independent examination and validation of the applicant's past business or investment experience, source of funds and personal net worth

Non-guaranteed investment

- An at-risk investment (non-guaranteed) of CAD 2 million in the IIVC Fund
- If the applicant is one of the immigrant investors approved under this program, he or she will be required to enter into an agreement with CIC committing a sum of CAD 2 million to the IIVC Fund for approximately 15 years
- The investment is an at-risk investment. Accordingly, there is no guarantee of a return and it is possible that the applicant could lose some or all of his or her investment.

Language Skills

- The applicant must prove his or her proficiency in English or French in all four language abilities (speaking, reading, listening and writing), take a language test approved by CIC; and meet the minimum language levels of *Canadian Language Benchmark* (CLB) 5 in either English or French for all four language abilities

Education

- The applicant must have a completed Canadian post-secondary degree, diploma or certificate of at least one year, or a foreign equivalent, as validated by an original ECA report from a CIC-designated organization. The ECA report must indicate that the applicant's completed foreign education credential is equal to a completed Canadian post-secondary education credential of at least one year

However, if the applicant is able to demonstrate that he or she has a personal net worth of CAD 50 million or more acquired through lawful, private sector business or investment activities, the applicant may request an exemption from the education requirement.

Since its inception in January 2015, there were a number of closures and re-openings under the IIVCP. The most recent re-opening of the Program took place in May 2015.

CIC will accept applications from 25 May to 30 December 2015, and will process the first 60 complete applications. CIC will also accept up to 60 additional applications that will be placed on a waiting list. The Program may close earlier if 60 immigrant investors are approved for permanent residence, or once 60 applications are in process and 60 applications are on the waiting list.

Below is a general step-by-step description of the sequence of events from the day that a qualified immigrant applicant develops an interest in Canada to the day when he/she obtains permanent residence:

1 Exploratory visit to Canada by the person intending to immigrate to Canada

2 Visit government authorities in the province of destination

3 Filing of application for permanent residence at Canadian visa post abroad

4 Interview by Canadian visa officials

5 Medical examinations for the applicant and family

6 Background clearance (police/criminal record)

7 Seek advice on Canadian immigration, tax, family and business law

8 Issuance of immigrant visa, valid for 12 months from the time of medical examination

9 Implement pre-landing tax planning measures

10 Prepare a list (in duplicate) of all personal effects to be brought into Canada, including those brought in at the time of landing and those which are to follow at a later date

11 Arrival at port of entry and processing of permanent residence

Upon arrival in Canada, the immigrant applicant will be greeted by an officer from the *Canada Border Services Agency* (CBSA).

The officer will ask to see the immigrant applicant's passport and other travel documents.

At the Canadian Port of Entry, the applicant must have the following:

- Valid passport and/or travel documents
- Confirmation of Permanent Residence (COPR) and/or his or her permanent resident visa. The officer will make sure that the applicant is entering Canada before or on the expiry date shown on his or her COPR
- Proof that the applicant has the funds to support the applicant and his or her family after he or she arrives in Canada

If the applicant is not inadmissible and there are no problems when he or she arrives, the officer will allow the applicant to enter Canada as a permanent resident. The officer will also confirm the new permanent resident's Canadian mailing address. The new Permanent Resident Card will be mailed to the permanent resident at this address.

Once the immigrant has landed and obtained a Permanent Resident Card, he or she is eligible:

- To work in Canada
- To apply in person for a social insurance number at a local Service Canada or to mail an application to Service Canada
- To register with the provincial health insurance plan
- To apply for a new provincial driver's licence

In order to maintain permanent resident status, there are few requirements that the permanent resident must fulfill. One requirement is the residence obligation. The permanent resident must live in Canada for at least two years within a five year period. During this time, the permanent resident must be physically in Canada.

The two years may not need to be continuous. An officer can confirm if the permanent resident's time in Canada counts when he or she does one of the following:

- Re-enters Canada
- Applies for a Permanent Resident Card
- Applies to be a Canadian citizen

Time spent outside Canada may also count towards the two years if the permanent resident is:

- Travelling with his or her spouse or partner who is a Canadian citizen
- A child travelling with a father or mother who is a Canadian citizen
- An employee of (or under contract to) a Canadian business

It may also count if the permanent resident is:

- Travelling with his or her spouse or partner who is a permanent resident and works full-time for:
    - A Canadian business, or
    - The public service of Canada or a province
- A child travelling with a father or mother who is a permanent resident and who works full-time for:
    - A Canadian business, or
    - The public service of Canada or a province
- An employee of (or under contract to) the public service of Canada or a province and he or she is on a full-time assignment to:

- A position outside Canada
- A partner business outside Canada, or
- A client of the Canadian business or the public service outside Canada

Tax residence

There are potentially three bodies of law that a person coming to Canada as a permanent resident will have to consider:

- The income tax rules of the person's country of origin
- The Canadian tax rules
- Any applicable international tax treaty between Canada and the person's country of previous residence/citizenship

The timing of becoming a resident of Canada for purposes of Canadian tax laws is a question of fact. A person may be deemed to be a Canadian resident and consequently taxable on his worldwide income, if he sojourns in Canada for more than 183 days. In order to determine residence other factors such as the location of the permanent home, the social and economic ties, the residence of a spouse and dependants as well as the time spent in Canada must be taken into consideration. The citizenship of the person and the fact that the person entered Canada as a permanent resident are not relevant with respect to determining residence under Canadian tax law. Upon becoming a Canadian resident, a person will be deemed to acquire all of his capital property at a cost equal to the fair market value of the property. Therefore, the immigrant is well-advised to obtain valuations with respect to his capital property (other than taxable Canadian property) held at the time of becoming a Canadian resident.

Canada taxes individual resident and corporations incorporated in or controlled and managed from Canada on their worldwide income. Non-residents are taxed only on Canadian sourced income. The *Income Tax Act* does not contain a definition of residence. An individual will be deemed to be a resident in Canada for the entire year, if the individual "sojourns" in Canada for 183 days or more in a year. *Part 1 Division E* of the *Income Tax Act* sets out the computation of the marginal rates payable by individuals. The provincial income tax rates are also based on various marginal rates.

Upon emigration from Canada the ceasing of the tax residence in Canada will trigger a deemed disposition of the property owned by the departing taxpayer; however the deemed disposition rule in section 128.1 (4) (b) of the *Income Tax Act* does not apply to real estate situate in Canada.

International double taxation for residents of Canada

Upon to entering Canada as a permanent resident, a person used to be able to transfer income-producing assets to a foreign trust and thereby not be required to pay Canadian tax on the income of those assets for a period of up to five years. With the passing of the 2014 Federal Budget on 11 February 2014 the immigration trust has been eliminated.

20.9 Checklist: Real estate in Canada

- The quality of public schools may vary significantly and other infrastructure aspects such as travel connections and shopping facilities may also be an important criteria in selecting a suitable location for a home
- Most purchases of residential real estate in Canada begin with the assistance of a real estate broker/agent who is a licensed member of a local real estate board. The broker will expect for his services a commission of the total purchase price. Generally the listing agent will split a 6% (or less) commission (sale of residential property) on a 50/50 basis with a cooperating agent
- Lawyers will not only also assist with respect to the negotiation of agreements of purchase and sale but once the agreement has been accepted in writing (this may be done by fax or other electronic form) the purchase and sale transaction will be subject to certain due

diligence and once the conditions have been waived the transaction will be closed by lawyers (or notaries in Quebec) ensuring that title to the real estate is registered in the name of the buyer in exchange for the payment of the purchase price

- Prior to the closing, the buyer's lawyer will search for all forms of possible encumbrances on the title including realty taxes, unregistered liens, easements and utility charges
- On the closing date, upon payment of the closing funds, the ownership and any third party interests in the real estate will be registered by the buyer's lawyer in the public registry system administered by local land registry offices
- When registering a transfer of land, for example in Ontario, the buyer is required to pay land transfer tax in the amount of approximately 1.5% of the purchase price
- There are no estate or gift taxes in Canada. Instead a transfer (disposition) of real estate is regarded as a taxable event and if the seller's (donor's) cost base exceeds the fair market value of the real estate, then 50% of the capital gain (deemed capital gain in the case of a gift or inheritance) is subject to tax
- Canada taxes capital gains and a non-resident must provide on closing a S*ection 116 Certificate* or give an undertaking to file the application to obtain same within 10 days after the closing, or the buyer must hold back 25% of the purchase price and remit the payment of the tax to the CRA

20.10 Bibliography

Balfour, Derek Mendes Da Costa: Property Law, Edmond-Montgomery, Toronto, 1982

Burn, Edward and Cartwright, John: Cheshire and Burn's Modern Law of Real Property, 18th ed., Oxford, London, 2011

Donahue, Quinn & Grandilli: Real Estate Practice in Ontario, 7th ed., LexisNexis, Toronto, 2011

Feeney, Thomas G.: Feeney's Canadian Law of Wills, 4th ed., Butterworths, Toronto, 2000

Hogg, Peter W.: Constitutional Law of Canada, 5th ed., Carswell, Toronto, 2007

Rintoul, Margaret E.: The Practitioner's Guide to Estate Practice in Ontario, 5th Edition, LexisNexus, Toronto, 2012

Salvatore, Bruce, Carter, Craig R., Perell, Paul M.: Agreements of Purchase and Sale, Butterworths, Toronto, 1996

Ziff, Bruce H.: Principles of Property Law, 6th ed., Carswell, Toronto, 2014

21

Croatia

Republic of Croatia
Republika Hrvatska

by

Mia Jug-Duјaković, dipl.iur.

Attorney at Law
Ispod ure 3
21000 Split
Croatia

Telephone: +385 21 343 972
Facsimile: +385 21 321 028

attorney@lawcroatia.com
lawcroatia.com

Mia Jug-Dujaković is an Attorney at Law with an office in Split, Croatia, working closely with Henley & Partners in Croatia. As part of her legal practice she represents and advises Croatian and foreign individuals and companies particularly in real estate, commercial and tax law, as well as residence and citizenship.

21.1 Introduction

The Republic of Croatia is a parliamentary democracy situated in the heart of Europe, being part of Central Europe as well as the Mediterranean. Becoming a member of the EU on 1 July 2013 set new challenges as well as new opportunities for further development of Croatia within the common market of the EU. The tourism industry, with its breath-taking natural landscape and cultural heritage, is steadily expanding each year through private and public sector investment.

The population of Croatia is about 4.3 million. The capital is Zagreb with the largest population of 800,000, followed by Split and Rijeka. Croatia is somewhat larger than Switzerland and has 5,835 km of spectacular coastline on the Adriatic Sea - 1,777 km on the mainland coast and 4,058 km of island coast. Of the 1,185 islands, only 66 are inhabited. This coast is considered to be one of the most beautiful in Europe with innumerable bays, inlets, coves and beaches. Most islands receive more than 2,600 hours of sunshine per year. As well as a beautiful coast and countryside, Croatia has a very rich culture and many historical sites including Pula, Split, Korčula, Trogir, Hvar and Dubrovnik. There are five *UNESCO* World Heritage sites on the Adriatic coast alone.

Croatia is a member state of the EU and a member of the *UN*, *WTO* and *NATO*. It is expecting to join the Schengen Area in the coming years. Croatia has a legal system similar to the civil law of other continental European countries such as Germany, Austria and Switzerland. In recent years the legal system has been undergoing a reform to align with the requirements of the EU. Croatia has a three tiered judicial system made up of the Municipal Courts, County Courts and the Supreme Court. Misdemeanour courts, commercial courts and administrative courts rule on their specific areas, and the Constitutional Court rules on cases regarding the Constitution. The official language is Croatian; however English, German and Italian are widely spoken.

Croatia is a country with generally high taxes, but it offers opportunities to people with certain types of income, e.g., bank interests and certain types of capital gains. In addition to the charming, well preserved landscape and rich historic heritage, these fiscal advantages make Croatia an attractive location for European residence.

21.2 Real estate ownership

Ownership of real estate is provided for in the *Ownership and Other Property Rights Act* and the *Land Registers Act*.

Special laws may limit and remove ownership rights (subject to recovering their market value) in order to protect national interests and safety, to protect nature or the environment and health, and may limit ownership rights with regard to the use and exploitation of goods of particular national interest (e.g. objects of particular cultural, historical or economical importance). These include the following Acts: *Defense Act, Environment Protection Act, Nature Protection Act, Agricultural Land Act, Waters Act, Forests Act, Maritime Domain and Seaports Act, Cultural Heritage Protection, Preservation Act, Roads Act* and the *Expropriation Act* which provides for the removal of ownership rights when this is a matter of national interest. As well as the above, ownership rights are also limited by stipulations of the *Ownership Act* which provides for neighbour's rights.

Different forms and types of ownership

Co-ownership

Unlike individual ownership, co-ownership is ownership of several owners over a single piece of property in its relative (ideal) parts. Each co-owner may freely dispose of his part, in other words, he may alienate, encumber, etc., at any time. When a co-owner sells his part of a property, the remaining co-owners have no right of first refusal (right of pre-emption), unless it is agreed otherwise. Each co-owner may demand the dissolution of co-ownership at any time; he may not waive his right to dissolution in advance, but may validly contract limitations to the right to dissolution. The way of dissolution is usually a matter of agreement, however, if co-owners cannot agree, the dissolution is ruled upon by a court of law in a non-contentious procedure.

Joint ownership (joint tenancy)

Joint tenancy is the ownership by several persons over a single piece of property by shares that are not relatively (ideally) determinable; but are determinable never the less. Unlike co-ownership, joint owners may not dispose of their shares by a legal transaction *inter vivos*, and may only transfer it to another joint owner. Property that is jointly owned by several persons may be subjected to material-law disposal only if all of the joint owners agree (unanimously). Joint ownership frequently exists in hereditary communities.

Condominium

Condominium is the ownership over a particular part (flat, business premises, garage or parking lot) of co-owned property which consists of land with a building on it or the right to build a building. Ownership over a particular part of a property is indivisibly connected with the appropriate (ideal) part of the property to which it refers.

Ownership over a particular part of a property is established by the written consent of all of the property co-owners and afterwards by the entry in the land register as a right connected to a particular co-owned part of the property. Condominiums may also be established in the procedure of partition (dissolution) of a co-ownership, in which the co-owners agree to limit their co-ownership rights by connecting a certain ideal part of the property with ownership over a particular part of the co-owned property.

Timesharing

Timesharing is rare in Croatia. Only a couple of hotels are part of the world's biggest timesharing exchange systems (R.C.I. and I.I.). The Consumer Protection Act regulates protection of the purchasers in respect of contracts relating to the purchase of the right to use immovable properties on a timeshare basis. Such contracts should be notarized.

Right to build

The right to build is a property covenant referring to another person's land, authorizing its holder to build his own building on such land and the land owner is obliged to allow this. The holder/owner of the right to build is also the owner of the building which was constructed based on the right to build. Once established, the right to build is transferable by legal transactions like any other real estate, and the ownership over the building is also transferred with it. It is recorded by a double entry in the land register, both as a property covenant, and as a particular land register entity in a new file.

Easements, charges, covenants and mortgages

Personal easements

Personal easements are special rights over somebody else's property, on which basis a certain person is entitled to the use of the property in a certain way. These are a) the usufruct, b) the right to use, and c) the right of residence. Unlike material easements, personal easements are normally divisible rights (e.g. a co-owner may establish a personal servitude over his ideal part). Personal easements are non-transferable (they are bound to the beneficiary) and non-inheritable (they expire with the death of the holder, unless they are established to the benefit of heirs as well). In this case we can only consider the non-transferability of rights, and not the non-transferability of performing the content of the personal easements rights (e.g. beneficiary of a personal easement may lease the property). The personal easement right is established only by a legal transaction (contract, testament).

Usufruct

The purpose of usufruct is to enable particular persons to commercially utilize things without them becoming their property. The usufructuary right may exist in relation to assets, real estate and also to properties that are creating a profit. A common form of this right is the lifetime usufruct (e.g. a father leaves property to his children, and the wife has the lifetime right of using the property).

The usufructuary right is strictly a personal right and cannot be transferred by inheritance. However, the implementation of the contents of this right can be transferred to third persons. For instance a real estate that is subjected to this right may be rented to a third person. If the usufructuary right expires, then the right to implementation of this right by a third person also expires. The right of usufruct does not end with the sale of the real estate if it is registered in the land register in favor of the entitled person. The entry in the land register is the condition for establishing the right of usufruct. Without the entry this right does not exist.

Right of residence (habitatio)

The right of residence is another non-transferable personal easement, which gives the entitled person a right to live in someone else's building or to use a part of it for living purposes. If the object of this right (e.g. an apartment) is sold, then the right of residence remains if it was registered in the land register. This principle applies to all personal easements.

Real servitude

Real servitude is the right of the owner of a real estate (dominant property) to use the real estate of another owner (servient property) for the need of his real estate. The owners of dominant and serving properties must be different persons, and it must always relate to two different properties. A real servitude is registered to the favor of the respective owner of the dominant property and charged to the respective owner of the serving property, and is always connected to the real estate, whoever its owner may be. The real servitude can be established by a legal transaction (contract, testament), by a court decision (inheritance, probate procedure, in the procedure of division of the co-ownership), by national authority (expropriation procedure) or directly by law (adverse possession and inheritance). When acquired by a legal transaction, the contract must be in writing, and the signatures must be notarized, because only in this way can the entry of this servitude be registered in the land register.

Real servitudes can be divided into land servitudes (the road servitude, the water servitude, the pasture servitude) and city and home servitudes (the right to lean the weight of the building in question upon another), the right for a window in another's wall, the right to have part of your own building or device upon another's property (balconies, signboards, antennas, electrical installations, etc.), the right to take waste-water over another's land (the servient property), etc.

Charges

A charge is the right over another's property, authorizing the beneficiary to demand the owner of certain real estates to perform certain periodic actions (giving and acting, in contrast to easements where the acting consists exclusively of suffering and omission). The responsibility for the execution of these actions lies with the respective property owner to the maximum value of the property, as well as with the person who owned the property at the time of the establishment of the charge to the maximum value of his entire personal assets. The charge is a personal right and expires with the death of the beneficiary. The right is transferred to the holder's heirs only if this is explicitly contracted.

Liens and mortgages

Liens encumber property for payment of a debt, claim or obligation. Objects of the lien can be movable or immovable property as well as rights which are usable and/or have monetary value. The lien is the security for a debt or an obligation. To secure a debt or obligation, a lien can be established over a property and over property rights; this can be done voluntarily by contract or in form of a court record; in the form of an agreement made before a notary public; by court order; or by law (statutory).

If a lien is statutory or in the case of voluntary and court enforced liens, the creditor, before enforcing his claim, must obtain a court order (enforcement order). Litigation can be avoided in cases of voluntary court and voluntary notary liens, where the document (court record, notarized agreement) of establishing such a lien is itself an enforceable document.

A lien over real estate can be established only as a mortgage on an individual property, on an ideal part of property or on several properties together. A claim secured by a mortgage can only be enforced in court.

Fiduciary transfer of ownership

Besides the lien, another important institute is the securing of a claim by fiduciary transfer of ownership which is exercised on the basis of an agreement (contract) between the owner of the property and the creditor, where the title to the property is conveyed to the creditor, with the intention of securing a certain creditor's claim against the previous owner or a third person. The contract must be made in the form of a court record, a notarized document, or as a solemnized private document made before a notary public.

Unless otherwise agreed, the debtor is authorized to use the real estate whose title is transferred to the creditor while the creditor is not authorized to sell or encumber the real estate. If the creditor sells or encumbers the property contrary to the contract on securing the claim, such a sale or burdening is legally valid but the creditor is responsible to the debtor for damages.

A contract which would allow the creditor to keep the property if the claim is not settled when due cannot be made in advance. When a claim becomes due, the creditor and the debtor may agree that the creditor is to receive alternative settlement. If the creditor does not agree to the alternative settlement, he is authorized to sell the property to settle his claim, and this can be done either in court or out of court through a notary public or an authorized sales agent. If the creditor does not settle his claim from the property sale proceeds, he may settle it by selling other assets or rights owned by the debtor.

It is important to point out that the transfer of title for security and for the return of property following settlement of the claim, is not subject to payment of property transfer tax.

Protection of ownership, proof of ownership and registration

Real estate can be acquired by a legal transaction, by inheritance, by court order and by force of law. When the acquisition is made by a legal transaction (which must be done in writing before a notary public) ownership is acquired by registration in the land register. Ownership of real estate which is not registered in the land register is acquired by deposit of a certified document, which is suitable for the entering the title in the land register. An heir acquires ownership over an inherited property at the moment of exercising the succession, that is, at the moment of death of the legal predecessor. However, in order to obtain the entry of his right in the land register, the heir must wait until probate has been completed and the inheritance order becomes legally valid. With the acquisition by a court order or by order of another responsible authority (administrative authority) the title is acquired at the moment when the court or other document becomes legally valid. Ownership by force of law is acquired when all of the legal conditions are fulfilled. The most common cases of acquisition of property by force of law are: adverse possession and building on another's land.

The procedure for registering real estate ownership is regulated by the *Land Register Act*. The land register is deemed to show both the actual and the legal status of real estate. Therefore a person who proceeds in good faith and with trust of the land register, not knowing that it is incomplete or different to the true status of the property, is protected by law. In the case of the multiple sale of a property by the owner, the ownership will be acquired by the person who was the first to request the entry into the land register. Therefore it is in the best interest of each property acquirer to apply for registration as soon as possible after conclusion of the sales agreement, because of the rules over the protection of trust in the correctness and completeness of the land registers.

21.3 Purchase and sale of real estate

The sales agreement

The sales agreement is to be made in writing. The signature of the party whose rights are to be transferred, charged, removed or limited (which is usually the seller) is to be authenticated by a notary public. If the agreement imposes certain liabilities upon the buyer as well, his signature must also be authenticated (e.g. if the buyer's rights are to be limited by stipulating the seller's right of first refusal).

In order to acquire title after the conclusion of the sales agreement, the buyer must place a request for entry of the title with the district court which has jurisdiction over the real estate. The delivery of the real estate into the possession of the buyer is not a condition for the acquisition of the title.

Restrictions on sale and acquisition

Restrictions under family law and matrimonial property regime

Spouses may have their personal and marital property. Personal property is property that a spouse had at the moment of contracting the marriage as well as all of the property acquired during the marriage on another basis (inheritances, gifts, etc.). Marital property is property acquired by the spouses during their marriage. Spouses are co-owners of their marital property in equal parts. However, if only one spouse is entered in the land register, the third party will rely on the entry in the land register. Therefore it is strongly recommended to register marital property after its acquisition.

In marriages where one spouse is a foreign national, foreign laws may be applied to their marital issues since it is a marriage with international characteristics. Such a marriage is subjected to whichever foreign law the spouses select. However, this does not apply if the spouses married in Croatia and have a joint residence in Croatia, particularly since in such a case the law relevant to their personal and marital issues, i.e., the *Family Act of the Republic of Croatia*, excludes the application of foreign laws in such a situation. The same applies to property issues of common-law marriage partners.

Options and pre-emption rights

The right of pre-emption is the right of a certain person to whom the owner of real estate must offer this real estate first in case of a (re)sale. The right of pre-emption may be on the basis of law or a contract. The pre-emption right may be entered in the land register.

A contractual right of pre-emption exists when the buyer commits himself by a special regulation in a contract that he will offer the bought property first to the seller under the same conditions and at the same price in the case of the eventual resale. The contractual right of pre-emption can be agreed upon with a maximum duration of five years starting from the day of the conclusion of the contract. In the case of a violation of the right of pre-emption, cancellation of the legal transaction can be demanded with a subjective period of six months and an objective period of five years under certain conditions.

A legal right of pre-emption is for example shown in the *Law on Protecting and Preserving Cultural Properties*. The seller of any cultural property (as well as a mediator in such a sale) is to advise the buyer that the object of the sale is a protected cultural property, and that it shall be first offered to the authorities (i.e. The Republic of Croatia, Municipality, City, and County). Only if they decline to exercise their pre-emption right may the property be sold to another person. The owner is obligated to inform all of these institutions of his intention to sell. If no reply is received within 60 days, the owner can sell the cultural property to another person. This means that before conclusion of the sales agreement, the buyer has to check whether the owner informed all of the pre-emption right holders, otherwise he exposes himself to the risk of possible contract annulment. A foreign person may also purchase such property, but will require consent from the *Ministry of Foreign Affairs*. The duration of the legal right of pre-emption is unlimited. There are no other forms of pre-emption rights.

An option to buy must be made in writing either in the form of a pre-agreement without deposit, or in a form of non-refundable deposit (*kapara*) agreement.

Agricultural real estate

Agricultural real estate is of national interest and enjoys special protection. Agricultural properties are used, protected and administered in accordance with the *Agricultural Land Act*. Fields, gardens, meadows, pastures, orchards, olive groves, vineyards, fish ponds, reeds and marshlands are considered as agricultural properties, as well as any other land that can be used for agricultural production. Foreign legal and physical persons cannot acquire agricultural real estate, unless otherwise stated by an international treaty.

Restrictions regarding acquisition of real estate by foreigners

When acquiring real estate in Croatia, foreign nationals must fulfil the following prerequisites: with the acquisition of real estate by inheritance mutual reciprocity is presumed; with the acquisition of property by a legal transaction mutual reciprocity is required as well as a resolution of a court or an administrative authority and the consent of the *Minister of Justice*. A foreigner can thus become a real estate owner in Croatia, if the laws of the country of his citizenship permit Croatian citizens such a possibility under the same conditions. The reciprocity in different capacity and depending on the kind of real estate that is intended to be acquired exists for the citizens of following countries: Argentina, Belarus, Canada, Chile, Japan, Malaysia, Norway, New Zealand, Paraguay, Turkey and the US. Citizens of Australia, Bosnia and Herzegovina, South Africa and Switzerland can become direct owners of real estate only if they have permanent residence in Croatia. However there is still the possibility to acquire property indirectly through a Croatian company.

Even if there is reciprocity and consent, foreign legal and physical persons cannot acquire agricultural land (*Agricultural Land Act*), real estate in protected nature areas (*Nature Protection Act*) or forests and forest land (*Law on Forests*).

Citizens and legal persons from EU member states can acquire ownership of real estate under same requirements as Croatian citizens and legal persons. This does not apply to agricultural land or protected nature areas.

If a foreign person inherits excluded areas, instead of acquiring the title, they will be entitled to indemnification as if the real estate had been expropriated.

The procedure for obtaining the consent of *the Minister of Justice* can take up to six months. Upon definite permission only a relatively small deposit should be paid, usually 10% of the purchase price.

Further important preconditions for buying real estate

Capacity to act and entitlement of the seller

A physical person becomes legally competent at the age of 18 and can make legal transactions independently.

People with limited legal competence are adults whose legal capacity to act has been partially taken away by a court order after their coming of age. Persons with no legal competence are minors (i.e. younger than 18) as well as adults whose legal competency was taken away by a court order (e.g. because of a mental disorder). However a minor older than 16 becomes legally competent by marriage or becoming a parent.

All legal transactions related to the properties of people with limited competence and persons with no legal competence must be in the form of a notarized document and must be approved by the *Social Welfare Center* (the public institution for family legal protection). The fact that the person has no legal competence must be registered in the land register (if such a person is the owner of real estate) and must be made public. Whoever buys real estate from such a person (notwithstanding such a note in the land register) exposes himself to the risk of having such a legal transaction annulled. If there is no such note registered, rules of trust in the truthfulness and completeness of the land registers apply.

If the seller is a company, the sales agreement must be signed by the director or other authorized person. Accordingly, it is very important to check whether the person(s) signing for the company are actually authorized to do so and may legally bind the company. For a Croatian company, this may be verified by obtaining an up-to-date extract from the commercial register.

Third-party claims and unpaid taxes

A person is still entitled to the real estate if the land register was trusted in good faith but it failed to show the existence of any third party rights, charges or restrictions. Exceptionally, the person acquiring the real estate does not enjoy the protection of trust in the completeness of the land registers regarding those rights, charges and restrictions which exist in law (statutory), and which do not need to be registered in land registers.

Unpaid taxes do not represent an obstacle to registering the title into the land registers and therefore the land register office is obligated to permit the execution of the entry even if the taxes were not paid, provided that all of the other conditions for title registration are fulfilled.

However, in the case where taxes are not paid within the required period, the tax authority may enforce collection by seizing funds, selling company shares, assets or real estate, etc. As a condition for a delay of tax payment, the revenue office can also ask for collateral, e.g. a bank guarantee, movable property lien, mortgage, etc. However, after the title is transferred, the new owner of the real estate is not responsible for the unpaid tax liabilities of the previous owner.

Provisions for protecting the environment, nature and cultural heritage

The coastline is classified as general property (public domain) and, therefore, cannot be subject to ownership regardless of whether it concerns native or foreign persons. Real estate of particular cultural, historical or economic importance is under special national protection. Their acquisition is equally complicated for nationals and foreigners.

Access to relevant records and documents

The land register is public and contains documents regarding the existence and legal status of real estate. Land registers are maintained by municipal courts that have special land registry offices. Land registers and their transcripts enjoy public trust and have the power of evidence of public documents. The land register consists of land register sheets. Only one real estate is registered on each sheet (a land register object). A land register sheet consists of three listings: A (List of Properties), B (Ownership listing) and C (Encumbrances). For each cadastral district a land register is maintained, in which real estate that lies in that cadastral district is registered. However, the land register data often does not correspond to the cadastral data or to the actual ownership or possession rights.

Land registers are open to the public. Anyone can demand inspection of a land register and receive excerpts and copies of it. For an extract from a land register, the average waiting time is about eight days, however, in some courts it is available on the same day. A person requesting an extract from a land register must bring HRK 20 in duty stamps. The party must know the number of the land register sheet in which the real estate is registered, or, if not knowing this, he must know the number of the property or the building as well as the name of the cadastral district in which the real estate is registered. The number of a plot and/or other relevant data one could check in the Cadastral Office.

An extract from a land register can be obtained to show the status of the whole land register object (general excerpt) or for the part of the land register object (special excerpt). For instance, if the real estate is co-owned by several persons, the general excerpt from the land register would show all of the co-owners, while a special excerpt would only refer to the information on the portion owned by one of the co-owners. An extract could also display all registries' entries prior to the actually registered ownership (history excerpt). The Land Register is also available online, but the data is unofficial, and can be only used for informative purpose. The law regulates the Land Register which should allow getting official excerpts online in the near future.

Requirements for restitution and outdated land registers

The reason for the out of date condition of Croatian land registers and requirements for restitution goes back to the previous political system, when expropriations were made and when a privately owned house could be built on community owned land, which in turn resulted in separation of the land from the building. The situation is made complicated by the fact that many owners acquired properties either by inheritance or other statutory means and became owners but never registered their property in the land register. Thus, it is often the case that a person registered in the land register passed away a long time ago or has already sold the property in question a long time ago. In those cases, the new owners simply failed to register the transfer of title in the land register. The situation is complicated even further by the fact that in certain cases, registration in the land register can take up to a few years. However, this long period can be overcome by administrative measures which enable the full utilization and disposal of properties within a reasonable time. New regulations require the computerization of land registers, therefore improvements are already underway.

The restitution of real estate that has been expropriated under the former political system is enabled by a law of 1 January 1997 which regulates the return of real estate to those original owners who were expropriated by nationalization, confiscation or by other measures under the earlier system. However, Croatian citizens had to submit the request by 30 June 1997, and foreigners by 5 January 2003, otherwise they lost their right for restitution.

Due to the possible problems regarding requirements for restitution and outdated land registers, the title should be checked and an excerpt from the land register requested to ascertain whether a clean title can be acquired prior to the purchase of any real estate in Croatia. If this is not the case, the acquisition of real estate is not recommended.

Key points that a seller should consider

Above all, it is essential for the seller to know that the payment is guaranteed. All payments should be made through the bank or office of a lawyer or notary, and this can be done in a relatively simple manner.

Broker commissions are usually paid by the seller and are normally between 2% and 3% of the sale price. However, a broker commission can also be required from the buyer in cases where a real estate search order was requested. Broker commissions can be freely negotiated by the parties concerned, and it is usually between 2-5% of the purchase price.

The execution of a real estate purchase transaction

After a foreign national has signed and certified the sales contract and obtained consent from the *Ministry of Justice*, the real estate purchase procedure can be completed. It is customary that at the moment of entering the agreement and before obtaining the Ministry's consent, the buyer pays a deposit directly to the seller or, preferably, to an attorney or notary in escrow. After receiving permission from the Ministry, the buyer has to pay the remainder of the agreed purchase price as well as the transfer tax under the tax authority decree and he should immediatelly apply for registration of the title in the land register. The acquisition of property takes place when the new owner is entered in the land register.

It is strongly advisable that when a house or other building is bought, an architect or building engineer checks that the building has all the correct building documents and permits and that the measurements of the building adhere to those in the building documents and permits; and if the building was built prior to 1968, that it has a usage permit for the building and that the actual measurementss of the building adhere to the usage permit issued. The seller is obliged to hand over complete building documents and permits to the buyer.

When advertising a building for sale the seller is obliged to obtain an Energy certificate for the building. If you are the seller, not having an energy certificate for the building is punishable by law and strict monetary punishments are applied.

Most real estate agencies also offer advice in this area; however, it is strongly recommended that the entire purchase procedure be executed with the assistance of a reputable attorney and a professional tax advisor.

Powers of attorney

The real estate sale agreement can also be signed by an authorized person. The signature of the seller and authorized person must be authenticated by a notary public. The signature of the buyer and authorized person must only be authenticated if the agreement imposes some liabilities on the buyer.

A special power of attorney is valid until revoked or until the buyer's title is registered. A general power of attorney may not be more than 12 months old at the time of title registration application.

A power of attorney which is issued abroad must be legalized. The land register office will also permit the entry of private and public documents if they are authenticated in the way prescribed by international treaties or laws. The *Croatian Act on Legalization of Documents in International Traffic* prescribes that public documents issued abroad can be used in Croatia only if they were authenticated by the *Croatian Ministry of Foreign Affairs* or a Croatian diplomatic or consular mission abroad.

If a document originates from states which are co-signatories of the relevant Hague convention, legalization with an apostille is sufficient. If a document comes from a state with which Croatia entered a treaty on document acknowledgement, it is necessary that such document is authenticated in accordance with the regulations of the signatory state. Further authentication is not necessary. The same rules also apply if Croatian documents are to be used abroad.

Financing

The most frequent way of financing is a mortgage loan obtained from a local bank. However, only recently have some banks in Croatia made this kind of financing available to foreigners. More options for financing are available if a person has permanent residence or employment in Croatia.

Purchase through a company

A legal entity, both Croatian or foreign, can also be a real estate owner. However, the same restrictions apply to foreign companies as to foreign individuals; therefore it is generally not advisable to use a foreign company for the purchase of real estate in Croatia. It is usually much better to transact the acquisition through a Croatian company which may however be fully owned and controlled by foreign persons. This procedure eliminates the obligation to request consent for the purchase from the Ministry of Justice, so the acquisition of real estate can be realized much faster. In addition, by using a domestic company it is also possible to legally avoid payment of transfer tax upon the acquisition and with each subsequent resale of the company.

The two most commonly used company forms in Croatia are the Limited Liability Company (LLC, *društvo s ograničenom odgovornošću – d.o.o.*) and the corporation (*dioničko društvo – d.d.*). The members of a LLC and the shareholders of a corporation can be foreign or Croatian legal and physical persons. Only physical persons, either Croatian or foreign, can be managing directors. The minimum share capital required for the establishment of an LLC company is approximately EUR 2,600, while the capital required for the establishment of a corporation is approximately EUR 26,000.

Recently, a new form of Limited Liability Company has been introduced and is regulated under the name Simple Limited Liability Company. A Simple LLC can have no more than three members of the company, and one member of the board of the directors. The minimum share capital required for the establishment of a Simple LLC company is approximately EUR 1.33. The costs of incorporation are also minimized.

Warranty claims

In a case where the seller has sold the same real estate several times, the title will be acquired by the buyer who, in good faith, was the first to request their entry in the land register. However, the buyer who was not the first to apply for title registration but was the first to obtain the possession of the property may exceptionally demand deletion of the entry of the buyer who was the first to apply for registration if this buyer knew that ownership of the same real estate had been already transferred to someone else, or if this buyer did not act in good faith. In such situations, the damaged party (if he cannot arrange entry in his name or his entry is deleted, although he acted by trusting the land register) is entitled to dissolution of the contract and compensation from the seller who sold the real estate several times.

In general, all contracts should be kept safe in case there is a reason for legal dissolution or if the contract should in any way be proven invalid.

The buyer of a real estate is also entitled to demand dissolution of the contract and payment of damages if for example, the actual surface area of the acquired real estate is smaller than what was registered in the land register.

For used real estate any warranties regarding physical defects are normally relinquished by the seller in the sales agreement. The seller is however responsible for any hidden defects for a period of two years if the buyer was not aware of these defects, but the defect must be reported within two months after a defect is discovered, and in contracts between companies seller is however responsible for any hidden defects for a period of six months if the buyer was not aware of these defects, but the defect must be reported immediately after a defect is discovered. This period can be longer but must be agreed in the sales agreement.

21.4 New construction, rebuilding and renovation

Area planning, building permits and construction

Area planning, building permits and construction are regulated by two laws, the *Act on Area Planning and Construction Act*. Each intervention in the area (construction, rebuilding, and renovation) is to be performed in line with planning documents, special regulations and based on a requested permission. The zone permission is an administration act that is given on the basis of area planning documents which comprise of the *Strategy and Regional-Planning Program of the Republic of Croatia* and regional plans (the County regional plan, Regional plan for special areas, City and Municipal plan, general and detailed town planning). The responsible administration is obligated to issue a zone-permit within 30 days from the date that the correct application was filed and that the required documents from other administrative authorities (consents, etc.) were obtained. Zone permission is valid for two years from the date of issue if an application for a building permit is placed within that time, or if construction work has begun, for which (in accordance with the special directions) no building permit is required.

The validity of the zone permission can be extended for two more years providing that there is no change to the regional-planning documents on which the original issue was based.

Construction work can be commenced only with a final building permit. Zone permission is required only in exceptional cases. Simple structures and simple building works as defined by the *Regulation on Simple and Other Buildings and Works* can be built either without any documents or permits or just with a major project (garages, storage rooms, tool houses, pool up to 100m^2 etc.). The authority responsible for issuing the above mentioned permits is obligated to issue the permit within 30 days after receipt of the correct application. Acquired permits will cease unless the works started within two years from the date of issue. In exceptional cases, this period can be extended for two more years.

Owners of neighbouring lands are also parties in the zone or other permit issuing procedure. This means that they have the right to lodge an appeal after the issuance of the permits; therefore the building program can be considerably delayed. In such a case, the investor to whom a zone or a building permit was issued must wait until the administrative authority of the second instance (the responsible ministry) decides over the objection; that is, until the zone or the building permit becomes final.

Architect's and building contract

It is common practice that a building contract is made with the building contractor while a building supervision and control contract is made with a certified person. The building contract is a contract whereby the contractor commits to erect a certain building or to carry out certain work on an already existing object, and the investor commits to pay the contractual price. The making of such a contract is always preceded by the so-called preliminary actions (producing the project documentation, obtaining the building permit, etc.).

The project documentation (preliminary plans, main plans and working plans) is to be made by a duly authorized person – an architect, who is usually also commissioned to supervise and inspect the construction works and to obtain the building permit along with all of the required approvals. Relations with the architect are set by a contract, and his fees are contracted in line with the official rate of the *Croatian Chamber of Architects and Building Engineers.*

The building price can be contracted as a unit price (e.g. per m^2) or as a total price (a single amount for the entire structure). The law allows changes to the price even when it is contracted as fixed. If the parties do not contract the price as variable, the law allows the contractor to increase the price if the prices of elements on which the contracted price is based increase (e.g. building material price increase) between the start and the fulfilment of the contract. The building contract may also contain a 'turn key' clause, meaning that the contractor is to furnish all works independently and to deliver the finished object to the investor. In this case, the contracted price also includes the sum for all unpredictable works. If the price significantly increases above the contracted one, the investor may terminate the contract.

Completion of construction and formalities

The completed building may be used after the responsible authority has delivered *utilization permission* for its use. The utilization permission is given after a technical examination. Furthermore, an acceptance protocol is to be prepared before moving in. The acceptance protocol is to be signed by both the buyer and the seller. With new condominiums, all owners must sign an agreement in regard to building maintenance which will regulate how high the monthly maintenance and reserve payments should be and who should be responsible for organizing the maintenance, etc.

Deficiencies and warranty claims regarding new construction

The contractor is obligated to guarantee to the investor permanent supervision over the work and inspection of the materials used. The contractor and the designer are responsible for rectifying any construction and quality defects; the contractor is responsible for the execution and the designer for the building plans. The investor and his legal successor may claim against defects within 10 years from the acceptance of the building. It makes no difference whether the claim concerns hidden or obvious defects. This time period can be neither waived nor limited in the contract.

21.5 Rental and tenancy

Rental and leasing agreements

A lease agreement is to be made in writing and signed before a notary public. The person leasing the property is obligated to submit the lease agreement as well as all of the changes with respect to the rent details to the local authority and the responsible revenue office. The person leasing the property has a lawful lien on furniture and other movables belonging to the tenant and members of his household in case of overdue rent or damage compensation. The person leasing the property can retain these movables until the owed rent or compensation is paid.

The same rules also apply to land leases. Land rental is subject to the *Agricultural Land Act*, but only in cases where the State leases land that is in its ownership. Rental of private land is subject to general rental and lease regulations.

Regulations on protection of lessees and rent control

There are no special regulations on the legal protection of tenants. However, they are entitled to enter the lease agreement in the land register.

21.6 Succession and gifts

Applicable law and jurisdiction

As already mentioned, foreign citizens can acquire real estate in Croatia through inheritance and gifts under the assumption that mutual reciprocity exists.

The *Conflicts-of-Law Act* contains stipulations on applicable laws and court jurisdiction in the matters of succession in cases where this is not regulated by bilateral international treaties and conventions. Therefore, this Act rules that inheritance is subjected to the laws of the state in which the testator was a citizen at the time of death and that the capacity for creating a testament is subjected to the law of the state in which the testator was a citizen at the time of making his will. However, the estate of a foreigner consisting of real estate located in Croatia is in the exclusive jurisdiction of the Croatian courts. When applying stipulations on applicable laws, it is important to point out that an authorized court in Croatia is obligated to establish the contents of any foreign material law which is to be applied. Also, parties in the court proceedings (heirs) can submit a public document which discloses the contents of the foreign law.

With regards to inheritance by foreigners, special restrictions regarding certain matters ruled by special laws (agricultural land, forests, etc.) are to be borne in mind. If such special regulations rule that foreigners cannot have or acquire title to real estate, this means that upon the death of a predecessor holding title to such real estate, the heirs cannot acquire title by succession, but would be entitled to the reimbursement of its market value.

Fundamentals of the succession and gift/donation laws of Croatia

Legal (statutory) succession

Statutory heirs are divided into the following orders: heirs of the first order, which include the decedent's descendants, the decedent's adopted children and their descendants as well as the decedent's spouse. They all inherit equal portions. Heirs of the second order include parents of the decedent, the spouse as well as the siblings and their descendants. Decedents without descendents are succeeded by their parents and spouse. Decedent's parents inherit together one half of the estate (to be shared equally) while the spouse inherits the other half. If both parents died before the decedent, the spouse inherits the whole estate. If the decedent did not have a spouse or the spouse died before him, the decedent's parents inherit the whole estate, shared in equal parts. If one of the decedent's parents died before the decedent, the part which would have been inherited by that parent is inherited by the surviving parent. The third order of succession consists of the decedent's grandparents while the fourth order of succession consists of the decedent's great grandparents. Any decedent who did not leave behind any descendents, parent or a spouse is succeeded by his grandparents.

Succession by will

There are several types of last wills and testaments: personal testament, witnessed testament, judicial testament, and international testament. It must be noted that stipulations on international wills were added to the *Succession Act* and that Croatia is co-signatory to the *Hague Convention on the Conflicts of Laws Relating to the Form of Testamentary Dispositions*, concluded 5 October 1961, and that all co-signatory states recognize, with regard to this form, wills made in line with the Convention and the laws of the co-signatory states.

According to Croatian inheritance regulations, the testator is not completely free in managing his property in his last will and testament. In other words, there is a circle of people to whom the testator must leave part of his estate. These are the so called obligatory heirs. Obligatory heirs are the testator's children and adopted children along with their descendants and the testator's spouse. The testator's parents, adoptive parents and other predecessors are only considered as obligatory heirs if they are permanently incapable of working or if they do not have sufficient means to survive.

Gifts/donations

Gifts are subject to the provisions of the *General Civil Code*. A gift is a contract whereby the donor gives something to the beneficiary voluntarily and without compensation. Any transferable article or right can be a subject of a gift. A gift contract may be revoked, for example because of the donor's subsequent impoverishment, ingratitude of the beneficiary, breach of maintenance liability, etc.

A gift contract without simultaneous delivery of possession of the given thing (e.g., promise to donate or donation at the moment of death) must be in the form of a notary document. In a gift with simultaneous delivery of possession, no special contract form is required. However, if the object of the gift is a piece of real estate, the contract must be made in writing and the donor's signature must be notarized. The gift contract on real estate property, depending on the content of obligations taken over by parties has to be signed in a prescribed form.

21.7 Taxes and charges

One-time taxes and charges on purchase

Real estate transfer taxes

There are two kinds of transfer taxes that apply, depending upon the type of real estate and upon who the seller is. Generally, newly built structures are charged at 25% Value Added Tax (see the following section), while other real estate is charged at 5% real estate transfer tax.

Type of Real Estate	Status of Previous Owner	Tax
Land	Not relevant	5%
Older structure (built before 31/12/1997)	Not relevant	5%
New structure	VAT exempt	5%
New structure	Not VAT exempt	25% and 5%

Every transfer of real estate in Croatia is subject to real estate transfer tax – whether by purchase, exchange, inheritance, gifts, release of real estate from company assets, the acquisition of real estate in a procedure of winding up or bankruptcy, the acquisition on the basis of court order or by another authority, as well as all other kinds of real estate property acquisition by other persons. All agricultural, building and other land is taxable; all business and other buildings built prior to 31 December 1997 are acquired and taxed in accordance with the *Real Estate Transfer*

Tax Act, regardless of who sells them; all used and newly built real estate disposed of by persons who are exempt from VAT (individuals, banks, insurance companies, etc.); as well as all further transfers of newly built real estate properties initially acquired by persons exempt from VAT who, therefore, could not have reclaimed the paid VAT.

Real estate transfer tax is paid by the acquirer of the real estate – domestic or foreign individuals or legal entities. However, the seller of the real estate is responsible for the payment of transfer tax as well as the buyer in cases where he agreed to take over the obligation for the payment of the tax in the purchase agreement. The assessment of the amount of real estate transfer tax is based on the market value of the real estate at the time of its acquisition. The tax office is authorized to determine the market value of real estate.

Tax exemption occurs in some cases of inheritance, donation and other acquisitions without payment: persons acquiring certain parts of a property upon the termination of a co-ownership or upon the distribution of jointly owned real estate; acquisition by the decedent's or the donator's spouse, descendants, ancestors and adoptive children; persons acquiring real estate under a lifetime support agreement and who are successors of the first degree related to the person disposing of the real estate; acquisition by former spouses when settling their property matters in divorce proceedings. Bringing real estate into a company as a contribution in kind is not taxable.

Tax liability occurs at the moment of concluding a contract or other legal transaction by which real estate is acquired. The real estate acquirer is to declare the tax liability to the tax office holding jurisdiction over the real estate within 30 days of concluding the contract. The real estate acquirer must pay the due tax within 15 days from the receipt of the tax demand.

The real estate acquirer may reclaim the tax paid if the real estate title transfer is terminated with the agreement of both parties within 60 days from conclusion and before the new owner is registered in the land register, or if such contract is terminated or annulled by the court.

Sales tax (Value Added Tax)

Value Added Tax (VAT) is regulated by the *Value Added Tax Act* and the *Value Added Tax Rules*. The regular VAT rate is 25% and payable only on the value of a newly built building, or a used building for which the VAT was already paid if disposed of by a business VAT payer. When such buildings are bought by a non-business individual, VAT must be paid by the buyer at 25% of the building value plus the transfer tax to the amount of 5% of the land value. Each possible subsequent sale of such real estate is taxed at the 5% transfer tax only.

The rule is, therefore, that if real estate was charged with the 5% transfer tax when sold for the first time, it will remain within this tax regime for any subsequent transfers. This rule is not applicable with regards to VAT, because real estate taxed with 25% VAT remains in this taxation regime only when sold between businesses which are VAT registered. So, for instance, if real estate that was previously within the VAT regime is acquired by a non-business individual, then such real estate passes into the 5% taxation regime also for each subsequent sale.

Real estate registration and notary charges

Upon concluding a real estate sales agreement, the seller is to have his signature authenticated by a notary public. Registrations in the land register and the transfer tax payment procedures require six copies of the contract. The notary fee for signature authentication is HRK 47.5 (approximately EUR 7). The fee for the land register entry is HRK 250 (EUR 35).

Recurring taxes and charges

Real estate tax

A special holiday home tax is payable by all legal and physical persons who own a holiday home. Every building or a part thereof used occasionally or seasonally is considered to be a holiday home. Taxes on holiday homes are between HRK 5 - 15 (EUR 0.70 - 2) per annum per square meter of the effective area of the holiday house. Holiday home tax rates are set by the town or the municipality and will depend upon location, age and infrastructure. The persons responsible for the payment of the holiday home tax have to submit all data concerning their holiday homes to the responsible tax office by 31 March each tax year. Holiday home taxes are payable within 15 days of the receipt of the tax bill.

Apart from the holiday home tax, no other land or real estate tax is levied in Croatia.

Income tax

Physical persons residing in Croatia pay taxes on income obtained world-wide. Persons who are not resident in Croatia only pay taxes on the income generated in Croatia (limited tax liability). Income tax is payable at the following rates:

- 12% on income from dividends of more than HRK 12,000 per year
- 12% on income from leasing or renting real estates or movable property
- 12% on income from insurances
- 40% on income from interest (if this is considered business activity of the subject)

On all other income:

- 12% up to HRK 2,200 per month
- 25% on any additional income between HRK 2,200 - 8,800 per month
- 40% on any additional income which is more than HRK 8,800 per month

It is to be noted that with the taxation of real estate rental income, there is an allowance of 30% of the income, so the effective tax rate amounts to only 8.4%. When letting property to tourists, this allowed expense amounts to 50% and thus the effective income tax rate for renting out holiday real estate is only 6%.

Income tax is increased by a municipal surtax which is calculated as percentage of income tax, with rates depending upon the place of residence. For example, the municipal surtax in the capital Zagreb is 18%, in Split 10%, in Rijeka 12%, in Dubrovnik 15% and on the island of Hvar, 0%.

Among others, the following income is tax exempt:

- The first HRK 2,200 per month
- Interests on savings deposits of domestic and foreign currency with banks, saving banks and saving and lending associations, interests to securities issued in line with the special law
- Receipts resulting from insurances and liabilities, unless the premiums were tax-deductible expenses

Corporate income tax is payable at a unified rate of 20%. There is a set of fiscal privileges for companies in certain areas, in free trade zones as well as for foreign direct investments.

Net wealth tax

There is no net wealth tax in Croatia.

Capital gains tax

Capital gains tax is payable at the rate of 25% on the income received from real estate acquisition or takeover of ownership rights.

Capital gains tax is not payable on gains resulting from:

- Disposal of financial assets (such as shares, bonds, other securities, etc.), unless this is the business activity of the taxpayer
- Disposal of real estate provided:
    - The real estate was used as the residence of the owner or his dependants, or

- The real estate was sold at least three years after its acquisition, or
- If the disposal is exercised between spouses or first degree relatives and other close family members, or between divorced spouses

The sale of more than three properties of the same kind within a five year period is considered to be a business activity and is taxable by the usual income tax rates.

Inheritance and gift taxes

Inheritance and gift tax payers are physical and legal persons who acquire taxable property on Croatian territory free of charge either by succession, as a gift or in another way. If an heir waives the inheritance or cedes it in the probation procedure, the inheritance and gift taxes are payable by the person who inherited or ceded such property.

Inheritance tax is payable at the rate of 5% on cash and receivables, securities and assets worth more than HRK 50,000 (EUR 6,750). The 5% real estate property transfer tax is levied in the case of the inheritance of real estate.

Inheritance and gift taxes are not payable by spouses, blood relatives in direct line, and the decedents or the donor's adoptive children and adopters.

Other taxes and charges

Taxes on vacant cultivatable agricultural land, tax on unused industrial or commercial real estate and taxes on vacant building land have been abolished by the decision of the Constitutional Court.

Visitor's tax is payable by owners of holiday homes or apartments in tourist areas and by all persons staying in that home or apartment. Visitor's tax is between HRK 2 - 7 per person/night, depending upon the season and the tourist resort category.

Incorrect (lower) statement of sale price in the sales agreement

Stating a price lower than the actual price in the sales agreement usually has no effect on tax liability. The responsible tax office will estimate the market value of the real estate at the time of the conclusion of the contract and calculate the tax based on such estimation.

The practice of stating a lower sales price than the actual price paid is illegal and not recommendable, but it is sometimes used in order to lower the VAT when purchasing a new property. Besides this, the illegally lowered purchase price can result in a higher capital gains tax in some cases, e.g. if the real estate is sold within three years of acquisition.

International taxation

If income is received by foreign tax payers domiciled or residing in a country with which Croatia has entered a double taxation agreement, the regulations of that agreement are applicable.

Croatia has entered into 57 agreements which avoid double taxation. The countries with which these agreements were signed include Canada, Ireland, Switzerland and the UK, among others.

If income from renting or sale of real estate is received by, for instance, British, Canadian, Irish or Swiss residents, such income is taxed exclusively in Croatia.

21.8 Immigration law and tax residence

Entry, residence and settlement of foreigners

Foreigners can enter Croatia with a valid passport and an appropriate visa. Citizens of EU member states as well as citizens of Andorra, Ireland, Lichtenstein, Monaco, Norway and Switzerland, among others, can enter Croatia with an identity card or another document that proves identity and citizenship. Citizens of Australia, Canada, the US and some other countries are also permitted to stay in Croatia without a visa for up to three months. Foreigners that have residence in the Schengen area or have Schengen visa C or D temporarily don't need a visa to enter Croatia. However, any person entering Croatian territory should, within 24 hours, report the stay to the police department unless they are staying in a hotel or hospital or with a person providing accommodation services.

Foreigners wishing to stay in Croatia as tourists for longer than 90 days must apply for a temporary residence permit. A temporary residence permit is issued for periods of up to 12 months, upon presentation of evidence of accommodation, non-criminal record, medical insurance, necessary financial means and has proved the reason for temporary residence. The procedure takes about four weeks. This residence permit is renewable annually.

Foreigners wishing to start a holiday home or room rental business should establish a company in Croatia and request a temporary residence permit, if they want to stay in Croatia for longer than 90 days. If they want to hold the position of managing director, they must request a permit for residence and work. Permits for residence and work are issued for periods of up to 12 months upon presentation of incorporation documents and fulfillment of other conditions. This procedure takes about four weeks.

Permanent residence can be granted to a foreigner who has stayed in Croatia with a temporary residence permit for a period of not less than five years continuously.

Croatian citizenship may be acquired by origin, by birth in the territory of the Republic of Croatia and by naturalization. While the naturalization conditions are generally rather restrictive, it is relatively easy to acquire Croatian citizenship for persons of Croatian origin.

Tax residence

A person is deemed to be a Croatian tax resident if he has accommodation at his disposal in Croatia, either owned or rented, continuously for at least 183 days in one or two calendar years. The actual period of stay in this accommodation is not relevant. This definition of fiscal residence in Croatia may be very attractive to foreigners having income that is not taxable (bank interests, capital gains) or with an income that is taxable at low rates (gifts), and who wish to be Croatian residents but do not want to have to stay physically in Croatia for a minimum number of days.

Alternatively a person is deemed to be a tax resident in Croatia if he stays in Croatia for at least 183 days in one or two calendar years, under the condition that he/she indicates that the stay is not a temporary one.

Persons with fiscal residence in Croatia are generally taxed on their worldwide income (unrestricted tax liability), however important exemptions apply (bank interests, capital gains) while persons residing abroad are taxed only for the income generated in the Republic of Croatia (limited tax liability).

International double taxation for residents of Croatia

If a person comes from a country with which Croatia has signed the agreement on avoiding double taxation, including Canada, Ireland, Switzerland, the UK and the US amongst others, his status is determined in the following way:

The person is deemed to be a resident of the country of his permanent residence, and if resident in both countries, he will be deemed to be a resident only of the country of closer personal and economic relations (center of vital interests). If the country of the center of vital interests cannot be determined, he will be deemed a resident of the country in which he stays for at least 183 days a year.

21.9 Checklist: Real estate in Croatia

- During the selection of real estate, usually with the help of a real estate broker or a real estate agency, a consultation with a tax advisor and a reputable attorney is highly recommended for examination of the property documents in the land registers and for providing a real estate sales contract, even if these services are offered by some real estate agencies. Special detailed care should to be taken due to the changes to the political system and expropriations in the past; the risks of unclear title or possible demands and restitution claims from former owners are found on many properties in Croatia
- After comprehensive examination, authentication of the sales contract takes place before a notary and pre-payment of a deposit (10%) to the escrow account of the attorney or notary as well as payment of the brokerage commission (2% - 5%)
- The attorney applies to the *Ministry of Justice* for purchase consent. After receiving the consent, the attorney transfers the deposited amount to the seller, and the buyer pays the remaining amount of the agreed purchase price. The attorney applies for registration of the real estate in the land register and the buyer receives proof of title. Caution: the passing of property title only takes place through entry in the land register
- The seller of a cultural property (as well as a mediator in such a sale) is to advise the buyer that the object of the purchase is a cultural property and that it must be offered to the authorities first due to their right of pre-emption

22

Cyprus

Republic of Cyprus
Κυπριακή Δημοκρατίαby
Kıbrıs Cumhuriyeti

Yiannos Trisokkas

Henley & Partners Cyprus Ltd
Spirou Kiprianou Avenue
No. 9, Office 301
3070, Limassol
Cyprus

Telephone: +357 2531 1844
Facsimile: +357 2531 1770

yiannos.trisokkas@henleyglobal.com
henleyglobal.com

Yiannos Trisokkas is Managing Partner of Henley & Partners Cyprus. He graduated from the American Academy in Larnaca, a private American Institute in Cyprus, majoring in Accounting, Mathematics and Economics. Yiannos has worked in the real estate market in Cyprus since 2002. Local independent consultants and international law firms have used his local expertise to establish their network and operations in Cyprus and to develop business relationships with high net worth individuals. This has made him a valuable consultant and partner to various developers, estate agents, law firms and financial services providers. Yiannos is active in his community and takes participating involved in local charities and anti-cancer society organizations.

22.1 Introduction

Cyprus is an island in the Mediterranean Sea and covers an area of 9,250 square kilometres, with a population of approximately 865,900 inhabitants. Cyprus's capital is Nicosia and it is the third largest island in the Mediterranean after Sicily and Sardinia. Cyprus was a British colony until 1960, when the island became an independent republic. The form of state is a Presidential Republic. As a result of British Rule, the English legal system was introduced in Cyprus and many laws were enacted in an effort to import the doctrines of common law and equity in Cyprus. After independence in 1960 the English legal system was largely preserved. English jurisprudence is closely followed and all statutes regulating business matters and procedure are based essentially on English Laws.

The current applicable laws are:

- The Constitution of the Republic of Cyprus
- The laws retained in force by virtue of Article 188 of the *Constitution*
- The principles of Common Law and Equity
- The Laws enacted by the House of Representatives

Cyprus has been a full member of the EU since 1 May 2004 and therefore European law supersedes Cyprus law in cases of conflict. Since 1 January 2008, Cyprus has used the Euro as its official currency. Cyprus is also signatory to many international Treaties and Conventions.

22.2 Real estate ownership

Different forms and types of ownership

Land registration in Cyprus is controlled by the Department of Lands and Surveys, the Government Department which provides services related to all rights associated with immovable property, land surveying, registration, transfer and mortgage of immovable property, ownership of land and evaluation of immovable property.

The *Immovable Property (Tenure Registration and Valuation) Law, Cap. 224* is the main law regulating the rights over immovable property, provides for and recognizes the following forms of ownership:

Freehold

The freehold interest includes immovable property which according to section 2 of the *Immovable Property (Tenure, Registration & Valuation) Law, Cap. 224* is defined as follows:

a Land

b Buildings and other erections, structures or fixtures affixed to any land or to any building or other erection or structure

c Trees, vines, and any other thing whatsoever planted or growing upon any land and any produce thereof before severance

d Springs, wells, water and water rights whether held together with, or independently of, any land

e Privileges, liberties, easements and any other rights and advantages whatsoever appertaining or reputed to appertain to any land or to any building or other erection or structure

f An undivided share in any property hereinbefore set out

A registered person is considered to be the undisputed owner and his title to ownership is absolute, subject to the Lands and Surveys Department Director's power to correct errors or omissions and to the inherent power of the courts to order an amendment. The land and any buildings on it are registered together and are inseparable for title purposes, specifically, the owner of the land owns any buildings on it.

Further, private ownership of immovable property extends to the surface of the land, beneath the surface and above the surface to the extent that it is reasonably necessary for enjoyment of the land. However, ownership does not extend to minerals.

As stated above, immovable property may consist of one or more plots and be held by two or more persons in undivided shares. Each undivided shareholder is entitled to sell his undivided shares subject to the other undivided share holder's option to purchase his shares at the price achieved. The property may be partitioned upon agreement reached between all co-owners. The partition, either by division of the plots in smaller parts without a breach of the provisions for minimum extends provided by the Law, or by partition of the whole plot, may be registered in the names of the co-owners with the Department of Lands and Surveys which shall then issue a separate title to each co-owner for the property or part of the property allocated to him/her.

Leasehold

In Cyprus there are two broad categories of leases, (a) the contractual lease, the terms of which are freely negotiable between the parties; and (b) the statutory lease which relates to properties controlled by the *Rent Control Law, No. 23/83.*

There are no legal restrictions in regards to the length of lease and this is usually determined in the lease agreement between the parties. The same applies with any renewals thereof. Upon signing of the Lease Agreement and during the term of the lease the tenant has the possession, occupation and enjoyment of the premises, provided that he complies with the terms of the said agreement. The tenant is usually responsible for paying the utility bills, and the landlord the taxes and levies imposed to owners of properties. Upon termination or expiration of the Lease Agreement, the tenant is obliged to deliver the free possession of the premises in the state and condition they were at the commencement of the tenancy, unless the owner accepts any conversions and/or alterations of the said premises. Any sublease of the leased premises without landlord's consent is prohibited.

Commonhold (commonly owned buildings)

According to the provisions of *Law 6(I) of 1993* that amended the *Immovable Property (Tenure Registration and Valuation) Law, Cap. 224*, "a jointly owned building" is a building consisting of at least five units, even if it belongs mainly to one owner. Every commonly owned building is registered as such with the Department of Lands and Surveys. A commonly owned building consists of the units and the commonly owned property.

According to *Law 6(I) of 1993*, "Unit" means a storey or part of a storey, a room, an office, an apartment, a shop or any other part, or space of a commonly owned building which may be appropriately and conveniently possessed and enjoyed as a complete, separate and self-contained unit for any purpose. Every unit of a commonly owned building is registered separately as a private property with the Department of Lands and Surveys.

Further, "commonly owned property" means every part of a commonly owned building which has not been registered as a unit (it includes, among others, the common parts of the building such as common-use areas, staircases, roof, electrical installation, plumbing system, engine room and lifts) and belongs to, is possessed by and enjoyed by all the unit owners in undivided shares.

The owners of all units contained in the commonly owned building participate in the expenses, which are necessary for the insurance, maintenance, repair, restoration and management of the commonly owned building. The proportion of the share of each joint owner in the expenses is prescribed by the Regulations which provide for the control, operation, management, administration, use and enjoyment of the units. The regulations are deposited at the Department of Lands and Surveys of the District where the commonly owned building is situated. Where no Regulations have been prepared, the standard regulations provided in section 38KA of *Immovable Property (Tenure Registration and Valuation) Law, Cap. 224* apply.

According to the Law, every commonly owned building must have a Management Committee for the regulation and management of its affairs that acts on behalf and for the benefit of the owners of the units. The committee has legal capacity and may enter into contracts with regards to any matter concerning the maintenance and management of the commonly owned building. It can also sue and be sued with regards to any matter concerning the commonly owned building.

Easements, charges, covenants, liens and mortgages

An easement is a right granted to a person over a property owned by another person and is usually acquired:

- Upon grant from the owner of the property: the owner (the grantor) can give another person an easement over his property. Such grant requires an agreement between the parties and the grant must be made in writing including the details of the parties involved, the particulars of the properties and detailed description of the right so granted. An application for the registration of the easement can be filed at the Department of Lands and Surveys and the right will be recorded against the title of the property

- By reservation upon the transfer of property: upon selling of a property from one person to another, the seller may withhold such right (in the form of life interest or occupancy of a property) for himself. Such reservation shall be stated in writing and it will be recorded against the title of the property upon registration of the transfer of the property

- Upon compulsory acquisition of a right of way: where a property is for any reason surrounded completely by other properties in such a way as to be deprived of the necessary access to a public road or where the existing access is insufficient for the proper use of the property, the owner may claim to obtain a right-of-way through the adjacent properties upon on payment of reasonable compensation. The Director of the Department of Lands and Surveys then decides, based on the particularities of each case and his decision may be contested by each of the parties, via an appeal procedure. The Director of the Department of Lands and Surveys has the power to determine and/or vary the position and/or direction of any existing right-of-way, channel, watercourse, stream or any other similar right upon submission of an application by the owner of the servient or dominant property. An easement ceases to exist if is not exercised for a continuous period of 30 years or where it has been abandoned by the beneficiary. Further, if a new public road is registered or any other access is created after registration of a right of way then the owner of the servient or dominant property is entitled to request the abolition of such right

With regards to charges, covenants, liens and mortgages, the terms Encumbrances and Prohibitions (as referred to in the *Immovable Property (Transfer and Mortgage) Law 9/65*), are used to describe all impediments which render impossible the transfer of a property. The most common are the following:

- *Deposit of Contract of Sale of Immovable Property* under *The Sale of Land (Specific Performance) Law No. 81(I)/2011)*: the deposition of the contract of sale with the Registry of the Department of Lands and Surveys is deemed as an encumbrance to the land because the Seller (who is the owner of the land where a specific property is constructed) is actually barred from selling the said property to any other purchaser or using it for his own benefit
- *Registration of an Interim Order* issued under the *Civil Procedure Law, Cap. 6*: this order can be issued by any Court upon application by a Plaintiff in a legal action for recovery of debt or damages, prohibiting the Defendant in such an action from alienating and/or charging the whole or a part of his immovable property that is sufficient to satisfy the claim of the Plaintiff in case he obtains a final judgment in his favour. The said interim order may remain in force until the issuance of a final judgment or for as long as the Court may decide and may be cancelled or amended only upon an order of the Court. It can be also withdrawn by the applicant

- Registration of a judgment made under sections 53 – 62 of the *Civil Procedure Law, Cap.6*, (known as a Memo): where a creditor has obtained a Court judgment against a debtor ordering him to pay a specific amount of money to him, then the creditor can apply to the Department of Lands and Surveys and register a charge against any immovable property registered in the name of the judgment debtor so as to secure payment of the judgment debt; a Memo remains in force for 10 years from the date of first registration of the judgment and may prolonged by a Court Order for a further period not exceeding 10 years each time
- Mortgage on property created under the *Immovable Property (Transfer and Mortgage) Law 9/65*: a mortgage is a voluntary, temporary and conditional encumbrance of a property as a security for the performance of an obligation or repayment of an existing, future or contingent liability. It is to be noted that mortgages are accepted only if the property/ies to be mortgaged is/are free from encumbrances. An unlimited number of subsequent mortgages may be constituted. Mortgage registration fees are calculated on the amount of the mortgage debt. The mortgaged property may be released from the mortgage upon payment of the debt. It is also possible for a share in the said property to be released against partial payment of the mortgage debt. The mortgagee may transfer the mortgage registered in his favour to another person, provided that this is not prohibited in the contract of mortgage.

Protection of ownership, proof of ownership and registration

The protection of ownership is safeguarded by the provisions of the *Constitution of Cyprus*, as one of the fundamental human rights. Non-Cypriots who own property in Cyprus enjoy all property rights which are available to Cypriot citizens. All transactions with regards to immovable property are conducted through the Department of Land and Surveys which has exclusive responsibility and provides means and instruments, amongst others, for the ownership, registration, transfer, and mortgage of immovable properties. The Registry of the said

Department is unique in that by its function all rights in land are defined and secured and all transactions relating to immovable property are protected. In Cyprus, Title Deeds (also known as *Certificates of Registration of Immovable Property*) issued by the Department of Land and Surveys are a definite proof of ownership. Title Deeds contain information with regards to the registered owner the size and location of the property and its unique file number.

According to the *Immovable Property (Transfer and Mortgage) Law 9/65*, every title of immovable property can be transferred by a voluntary act from one person to another provided that receipts of payment of Immovable Property Tax, Capital Gains Tax, Sewerage Board Tax, Town Rates and Communal Rates for the property under transfer are produced to the Department of Land and Surveys. Both parties must appear either in person or by agent. The procedure for acceptance is completed upon the calculation and the payment of the transfer fees by the purchaser to the Lands and Surveys Department.

With regards to transactions where the seller is not allowed to immediately transfer the acquired property into the name of the purchaser even though payment of the consideration has been made, the *Sale of Land (Specific Performance) Law 81(I)/2011* applies and safeguards such a purchaser. According to the provisions of this law, by lodging a copy of the contract of sale with the Land and Surveys Department's Registry within a specified time limit of six months from its signing, the purchaser has the right to seek "specific performance" of the terms and conditions of the contract. The term "specific performance" means the registration of the property in the name of the purchaser, with a Court Order, issued when the seller refuses or fails to comply with her/his contractual obligations. By lodging the contract with the Land and Surveys Department, the Purchaser is deemed to be the Beneficial Owner of the specific property that is described in the Contract of Sale. This means that the Seller is barred from selling the said property to any other purchaser or using it for his own benefit. Furthermore, the fact that the deposited Contract of Sale can only be withdrawn with the purchaser's consent offers maximum security.

22.3 Purchase and sale of real estate

The sales agreement

The sale of properties with deeds in Cyprus is regulated by the *Immovable Property (Transfer and Mortgage) Law 9/65*. For the sale of a certain property, a Contract of Sale is signed between the parties, providing for the sales price, time of transfer etc., and as soon as the Seller produces to the Department of Lands and Surveys receipts of payment of Immovable Property Tax, Sewerage Board Tax, Municipality Tax and Capital Gains Tax, and the Purchaser pays the relevant transfer fees, the transfer of the property is completed.

With regards to the sale of properties without title deeds (mainly properties that form part of a development where the issuance of separate Title Deeds for the specific properties is not yet completed) the *Sale of Land (Specific Performance) Law 81(I)/2011* applies. According to the provisions of this law, a contract of sale will be signed between the parties without the need to provide any receipts to the Department of Lands and Surveys in order for the transaction to be completed. There will not be an immediate transfer of the property due to the lack of separate title deeds. Instead, the Contract of Sale shall be duly stamped and lodged with the Registry of the Department of Lands and Surveys within a time limit of six months from signing for specific performance purposes and the provisions of the to the *Sale of Land (Specific Performance) Law 81(I)/2011* will apply.

Properties with title deeds may be re-sold following the procedure regulated by the *Immovable Property (Transfer and Mortgage) Law 9/65* as described above.

With regards to the re-sale of properties without title deeds this can be affected in two ways:

- Cancellation and Release Agreement: this procedure was mainly followed before the enactment of the *Sale of Immovable Property (Specific Performance) Law, No. 81(I)/2011* and required the cooperation of the original vendor in order for the procedure to be completed. The first purchaser has to cancel his contract of sale with the Vendor by signing a Cancellation and Release Agreement. The said Cancellation and Release Agreement must include the sale price and also the name of the new purchaser, and to stipulate that the sales price is to be received by the first purchaser. Then, the new purchaser has to sign a new Contract of Sale directly with the original vendor (who is the registered owner of the land where the property sold is situated and the only one eligible to sign a contract of sale). The first purchaser shall pay any Capital Gains Tax. Finally, the Contract of Sale between the vendor and the first purchaser will be withdrawn, and the Contact of Sale between the vendor and the new purchaser, duly stamped, shall be simultaneously lodged to the Lands and Surveys Department Registry. According to section 3(1)(c) of the *Sale of Immovable Property (Specific Performance) Law, No. 81(I)/2011* the time for lodging the new Contract of Sale to the land registry is limited to six months from signing. Following this procedure, the new purchaser is deemed to be the Beneficial Owner of the property sold and as soon as the separate title deeds are issued to the property, it will be transferred to his name

- Assignment Agreement: the enactment of the *Sale of Immovable Property (Specific Performance) Law, No. 81(I)/2011* that entered into force on 1 August 2011 replaced the previous legislation, regulating the specific performance of Sale Contracts and aims to expedite the procedure of sale of such properties

According to this law, the first purchaser may assign his rights deriving from the Contract of Sale to a third person, either with or without consideration, by signing an Assignment Agreement. This Assignment Agreement can be concluded without the consent of the original vendor and should be lodged with the Lands and Surveys Department Registry within two months of its signing, provided that the original contract has already been lodged at the Registry.

The Assignment Agreement is binding on the original vendor and by lodging it at the Land Registry Department the Assignee is granted the same protection as that provided by the *Sale of Immovable Property (Specific Performance) Law, No. 81(I)/2011* to the first purchaser. According to this law there is no obligation on the first purchaser to pay any transfer fees. The transfer fees will be paid directly by the second purchaser as soon as the title deeds are issued. The only obligation of the first purchaser is to pay any Capital Gains Tax arising from the sale.

Either of the two alternatives may be followed as per the parties' choice. The differences between the two procedures are: (a) in the case of the Assignment Agreement, the first purchaser may assign all his rights and obligations under his Sales Contract with the original vendor to the new purchaser, without seeking the permission of the original vendor, something that was not possible prior to the enactment of the *Sale of Immovable Property (Specific Performance) Law, No. 81(I)/2011* when the cooperation of the original vendor was a prerequisite in order for the transaction to be completed and (b) the new purchaser will acquire the property with the same legal status when it was initially purchased by the first purchaser. This means that the Assignment Agreement will have priority over any encumbrances registered against the property after the deposition of the initial contract of sale. Accordingly, the assignment of rights is most preferable between the parties as it offers more security to the Purchaser than the previous regime.

Agricultural real estate

The acquisition of agricultural land in Cyprus is, in principle, similar to the purchase of any other piece of land.

Acquisition of immovable property by foreigners

The *Acquisition of Immovable Property (Aliens) Law, Cap. 109*, deals with the acquisition of immovable property in Cyprus by aliens. According to Section 2 of the above law, an "alien" means any person who is not a citizen of the Republic of Cyprus, and includes alien-controlled companies, foreign companies and a trusts in favour of an alien, but does not include:

- A non-Cypriot citizen
- An alien wife of a citizen of the Republic, not being separated from her husband under a decree of a competent Court
- A citizen of a member state of the European Union
- A corporate body formed in accordance with the law of a member state and having its registered office, central administration or principal place of business within a state of the European Union

According to Section 3 of the *Acquisition of Immovable Property (Aliens) Law, Cap. 109*, no alien may acquire immovable property in Cyprus, other than by reason of death (mortis causa), without the prior permission of the Council of Ministers, after written application has been made on a specified form. The authority of the Council of Ministers to grant permits is vested to the District Officers to whom the relevant applications are submitted.

Grant of permission is required for the following:

- The purchase of freehold property
- Leases exceeding 33 years
- The acquisition of shares in a company which is duly registered as a legal entity in Cyprus and which owns immovable property in the Republic, if such acquisition itself or in conjunction with other shares already held by aliens in that company, would turn such company into an "alien controlled" company
- The formation of a trust in favour of a an alien which involves, wholly or partly, the leasing of immovable property under the provisions of a lease for a period exceeding 33 years or a shareholding in an alien controlled company

It should be noted that the above-mentioned legal exception, "other than by reason of death," means that an alien may acquire immovable property in Cyprus without permission from the Council of Ministers, if they has inherited it as a legal heir or if it has been bequeathed to them as a legatee in a Will.

Normally permission is granted to *bona fide* aliens to acquire a flat or a house or a piece of land not exceeding three donums (about 4000 m^2) for the erection of one house for use as a residence only by the purchaser and his family. The application should be submitted after the contract of sale is signed and must be accompanied by certain supporting documents. In the meantime, the purchaser can take possession of the property without restriction and live in it or rent it out as he is the legal owner of the property according to the law.

Key points that a seller should consider

Despite the fact that the law does not regulate how expenses are allocated between the contracting parties, it is custom that the seller completes Form N.270 (*Declaration of Transfer of Immovable Property*), and also pays the Immovable Property Tax on the property under sale, the Capital Gains Tax, the Sewerage Board Tax, the Municipal Tax or Communal Rates, and presents all relevant receipts to the Department of Land and Surveys on the day of transfer. The seller is also obliged to release the property from any mortgage or other encumbrances. The Purchaser has to pay the Stamp Duty for the Contract of Sale, the fees for lodging the same to the Registry of the Department of Land and Surveys, the VAT and the transfer fees upon acceptance of the transfer by the Land and Surveys Department. Any remaining balance from the purchase price (in the case of staged payments) must be paid simultaneously with the completion of the transfer.

Powers of Attorney

All transactions with regards to immovable property in Cyprus can be done in person or by proxy. Any person may appoint an agent to perform acts on their behalf. With regards to acts relating to immovable property, a power of attorney must be presented. The signature of the Principal (the person granting the power of attorney) must be duly certified by any Certifying Officer or the President of the Community Council or the Mukhtar. If it is signed abroad, it must be certified by a Consular Officer of the Republic of Cyprus. The power of attorney musty also be duly stamped. The Stamp Duty payable for a special power of attorney (granting power for specific transactions) is EUR 1.71 and for a general power of attorney (it can be used for any transaction) is EUR 5.13. A power of attorney is valid as long as the principal is alive, mentally competent and has not revoked it.

Disabled persons such as mental patients, and all other persons, who by law have been deprived of the right to execute legal acts (minors, bankrupts, companies under liquidation etc) are under lawful agency and their agents are determined by law and/or appointed by a competent Court. Any such guardian and/or agent may act on behalf of the disable person provided that he/she presents a Court Order for his/her appointment.

22.4 New construction, rebuilding and renovation

Construction zones and construction permits

The *Streets and Buildings Regulation Law, Cap. 96*, in conjunction with the *Town and Country Planning Law, 90/1972*, defines the development and building control system of Cyprus. The promotion and control of development in Cyprus is achieved through the implementation of the following four types of published Development Plans that are provided in the *Town and Country Planning Law, 90/1972*:

- The Island Plan is a statement of the broad national strategy in the area of regional spatial planning with strong links to overall national economic and social policy and refers to the whole of the island. To date, no Island Plan has been published due to the continuing Turkish occupation of a large proportion of national territory
- Local Plans cover all major urban and urbanised areas of the island and contain, a broad range of provisions which refer to a wide variety of types of development, infrastructure networks, standards, quantitative limitations and intensities of development, as well as areas of exceptional importance and areas lagging behind in terms of physical and economic development

- Area Schemes are more detailed Development Plans and contain policy measures and provisions. They define special measures, projects, opportunities, sets of incentives and other provisions, and directing major new development to specific locations
- The Policy Statement for the Countryside is a legally binding document which defines the planning strategy and detailed policies for the control of development and the protection of the environment. It concerns the entire territory of the State where neither a Local Plan nor an Area Scheme is in force. The British Sovereign Bases areas and the part of Cyprus under Turkish military occupation are also excluded

The Minister of Interior is designated by law as the competent Planning Authority for the preparation of Local Plans and Area Schemes.

Planning Approval

Before the commencement of any development it is necessary to obtain a planning approval from the Planning Authority. The same applies for the conversion of premises and/or the relevant building/construction works.

In accordance with the *Town and Country Planning Law 90/1972*, development is defined as:

"The carrying out of building, engineering, mining or other operations in, on, over or under immovable property, or the making of any material change in the use of any building or other immovable property".

In certain cases prescribed by the law, the Planning Authority is obliged to ensure that the submission of an application for planning approval has been adequately publicised. The relevant procedure intends to inform the public and in particular those citizens who may be affected by any proposed development in a timely and reliable manner so that any views and representations may be submitted to the Planning Authority before decision making.

The Planning Authority has the power to examine, in certain cases, an application for planning approval through a departure from the provisions of the Development Plan. Such cases are an exception to the rule and the use of such a procedure will need to be adequately justified.

Every citizen has the right to appeal against a decision of the Planning Authority within a period of 30 days from the date of notification of the planning decision, in the following cases:

- Refusal of planning
- Granting of planning approval with conditions attached which in the applicant's view are onerous or unnecessary
- Failure to take a decision with respect to an application and to notify the decision to an applicant within the specified time period
- Serving of an enforcement notice, provided that the terms specified by the Law are met
- Refusal to grant a certificate of commencement of works

The right to appeal ensures a person's right to have her/his application reviewed, by a body other than the one which took the initial decision. The Planning Appeals are examined by a Ministerial Committee based on the provisions of the applicable Development Plan and other material considerations related to the development. If the decision of the Ministerial Committee is not to the applicant's satisfaction, the latter has the right to lodge an appeal before the Supreme Court of Cyprus.

Building Permit

Once a Planning Approval has been issued, an application needs to be submitted to the relevant Building Control Authority (normally the Municipalities or the Community Councils) for the issuance of a Building Permit. Applications for a Building Permit should in general be in conformity with the issued Planning Permit, the provisions of the *Streets and Buildings Regulation Law, Cap. 96*, relevant Regulations, and the Building Authority. Through this application, the structural stability of the building, the provision of public services, health and safety, the fire adequacy of the building, sewage and drainage, energy performance of buildings etc. will be checked.

Partition Permit

Simultaneously with the application for the issuance of Building Permit, an application for the issuance of a Partition Permit should also be submitted. This is normally sought when more than one unit is going to be built in a certain plot and it enables the relevant authorities to sub-divide the specific properties in order for a Title Deed to be issued for every property comprising the development.

Final Approval Certificate

Once the construction of the premises is finished, an on-site inspection by the Building Authority, is carried out to inspect whether the premises have been built in accordance with the Town Planning and Building Permits issued for their construction. If the premises are not built according to the permits, a revised Building Permit Application shall be filed. The same applies for the conversion of premises and/or the relevant building/construction works. Following the inspection, a Certificate of Final Approval is issued by the Building Authority.

In cases of development of multiple units a Certificate of Approval for the Partition Permit is also required, once the Partition Permit has been issued. The procedure is similar to the the issuance of the Certificate of Final Approval.

Title deeds

Soon as the Certificate of Final Approval (and Certificate of Approval of the Partition Permit where applicable) is issued, an application should be submitted to the Department of Lands and Surveys for the issuance of Title Deeds for the premises.

It should be noted that if building works are commenced without a Planning and/or a Building Permit, or in the case of severe discrepancies with the terms of the said Permits, then a Demolition Order may be issued by the Court, upon application by the relevant authorities, requiring the demolition of the building.

22.5 Rental and tenancy

Property leases in Cyprus are normally governed by the provisions of *Contract Law, Cap. 149*. According to article 77 (1) of the *Contract Law, Cap. 149*, contracts relating to leases of immovable property that exceed one year are valid and enforceable only if they are expressed in writing and signed by the parties concerned in the presence of at least two witnesses who are competent to contract and subscribe their names as witnesses. Oral lease agreements are valid for tenancy periods less than one year.

However, if a building was constructed prior to 31 December 1999 and is situated within a controlled area designated in the law then the lease is governed by the provisions of the *Rent Control Law 23/1983* that aims to protect tenants against eviction under certain circumstances. When the initial rental period has expired or was terminated by the landlord but the tenant still occupies the premises, he becomes a statutory tenant and can only be evicted when the grounds specifically stipulated in the law are met. Statutory tenancy also means that any increase of rent cannot exceed the maximum provided by law (currently fixed at 4% per year). The *Rent Control Law 23/1983* does not apply to non-Cypriots renting properties in Cyprus (EU members are treated as Cypriots). It should be noted that there is no VAT payable on the leasing of immovable property in Cyprus.

According to the provisions of Sections 65A – 65IE of the *Immovable Property (Tenure, Registration & Valuation) Law, Cap. 224*, any agreement for the lease of immovable property with an unexpired term of at least 15 years may be registered with the Department of Lands and

Surveys. The registration should be made within three months from signature of the contract of lease. Upon signing of the leasehold and throughout its duration, the lessee holds the right of possession of the property and the landowner holds only the naked ownership of the property. Third country (non-EU) nationals may not take a lease of immovable property for a period exceeding than 33 years without prior permission from the Council of Ministers.

22.6 Successions and gifts

The law of succession in Cyprus is comprised in the *Wills and Succession Law, Cap. 195*, which deals with both Wills and intestacy; the *Administration of Estates Law, Cap. 189*, which deals with execution of wills and administration of estates; and the *Probates (Re-Sealing) Law, Cap. 192*, which deals with the sealing of probates or letters of administration granted by a court in the UK or any other Commonwealth country by Cypriot courts.

Cypriot succession law, irrespective of whether a person was domiciled in Cyprus (i.e. his permanent residence was in Cyprus and he had an intention to spend the rest of his life in Cyprus), does not regulate any immovable property which is situated outside Cyprus, but regulates the immovable property which is situated in Cyprus irrespective of where the domicile of the deceased is found. It also regulates all the movable property anywhere in the world of the deceased who has a Cypriot domicile.

On the death of a person, his estate will pass as a whole to his heirs. According to Section 21 of the *Wills and Succession Law, Cap. 195*, a person may distribute his estate according to the law of succession, or by drafting a Will. It is to be noted that persons domiciled in Cyprus may not dispose of the whole of their estate by Will if they have a surviving spouse, children or both. This restriction does not apply to any person if he or his father was born in the UK or in most other Commonwealth countries apart from Cyprus, as they are allowed to dispose the whole of their estate as to their wishes. The restrictions on the freedom of testamentary disposition were imposed for the benefit of the family of the testator. The disposable portion is calculated as follows: (a) if the deceased leaves a spouse, children or both, the disposable portion is ¼ of the net value of his estate; (b) if the testator has no children or descendants of children but leaves a spouse or parent then the disposable portion is ½ of the net value of his estate; and (c) if the testator has no children, no descendants of children, no surviving spouse or a parent then the whole of his estate may be distributed according to his Will.

In order for a Will to valid the testator must be over 18 years old and of sound mind and understanding. Both criteria must be satisfied otherwise the Will is considered to be void. Furthermore the Will has to be in writing and attested by two competent witnesses. According to Section 37 of the *Wills and Succession Law, Cap. 195*, a Will may be revoked by:

- A subsequent Will expressly revoking the former one
- By a subsequent Will inconsistent with the provisions of the former one
- By burning, tearing or otherwise destroying the same by the testator or by some person in his presence and by his direction, with the intention of revoking it

If a person dies intestate, then his estate will be distributed to his heirs by operation of law. The surviving spouse, if the deceased also left a child or a descendant of a child, is entitled to a share in the statutory portion of the deceased equal to the share of a child or descendant of a child. Where no child or descendant thereof has been left but there is an ancestor or descendant thereof within the third degree of kindred to the deceased, then the share of the surviving spouse is equal to ½ of the statutory portion. If no child nor descendant thereof, or any ancestor or descendant thereof within the third degree of kindred to the deceased has been left, but an ancestor or descendant thereof within the fourth degree of kindred to the deceased, the share of the surviving spouse is equal to ¾ of the statutory portion. Finally, if no child nor descendant thereof, or any ancestor or descendant thereof within the fourth degree of kindred to the deceased has been left, the surviving spouse is entitled to the whole share of the statutory portion.

There are no succession taxes as the Inheritance Tax has been abolished by the *Estate Duty (Amending) Law 74(I)/2000* concerning any person who passed away after 1 January 2000.

In Cyprus it is possible for immovable property to be donated and it is treated as a transfer for all intents and purposes. Donations from parents to children, whether married or not, between relatives or between persons related within the third degree of kindred, whether married or not, are exempted from the payment of Capital Gains Tax and reduced transfer fees rates exist.

When immovable property is transferred by way of gift to a company of which the only shareholders are related to the donor within the third degree of kindred, then after a lapse of five years from the day of transfer and provided that sufficient proof is submitted to the Director of Department of Lands and Surveys that the only shareholders of the company are the donor and his relatives, the amount of transfer fees paid at the day of the transfer is returnable to the company. According to Section 9 (2) of the *Department of Lands & Surveys Law (Fees and Charges) Cap. 219*, a sum equal to 4% on the assessed value of the property is deducted from the returnable amount. It goes without saying that the immovable property continues to be registered in the company's name at the time of return of the transfer fees.

22.7 Taxes and charges

Stamp duty payment

Upon the signing of a Contract of Sale, the purchaser is liable to pay a one-off stamp duty which relates to the contractual purchase price and payment is due within 30 days of signing, otherwise a fine will be imposed according to the *Stamp Law 19/1963*.

Contractual purchase price (EUR)	Stamp duty (%)
First EUR 5,000	0
From EUR 5,001 - to EUR 170,000	1.5%
Over EUR 170,000	2% with maximum total amount of stamp duty EUR 20,000)
Without fixed amount	EUR 35

Transfer fees

On transfer of the title deed of the freehold property and registration in the purchaser's name, the Land and Surveys Department will charge a one off transfer fee, which is based on the market value of the immovable property at the time of purchase and is always paid by the Purchaser. The rates are on a graduated scale and are calculated as follows:

Property value (EUR)	Transfer fee rate (%)
First EUR 85,000	3%
From EUR 85,001 to EUR 170,000	5%
Over EUR 170,000	8%

The Director of the Department of Lands and Surveys has the right to dispute the declared value (in the Contract of Sale) and adopt a market value of the property with the adopted valuation date being the date of purchase. For properties owned in joint names e.g. of a couple or two individuals, transfer fees are charged on 50% of the property value for each, providing an advantage for any property value exceeding EUR 85,430.07.

It is to be noted that sale-purchase contracts concluded between 2 December 2011 and 31 December 2016 which are subject to VAT will be exempt from the above transfer fees and those not subject to VAT will be eligible for a 50% exemption from the above transfer fees (subject to conditions).

Capital gains tax (*Capital Gains Tax Law*, No. 52/80)

Capital gains tax is levied at a fixed rate of 20% on both individuals and companies on gains from the disposal of immovable property situated in Cyprus including gains from the disposal of shares in companies which own such immovable property in Cyprus and are not listed on a recognised Stock Exchange.

The capital gain is calculated after deducting from the sales proceeds the initial acquisition cost and any additional expenditure or the market value as at 1 January 1980, whichever is the higher, inflated by the official Retail Price Index in Cyprus.

The following disposals of immovable property are not subject to capital gains tax:

- Transfer by reason of death
- Gift between relatives up to third degree of kindred
- Gifts to a company where the company's shareholders are members of the donor's family and the shareholders continue to be members of the family for five years after the day of the transfer
- Gifts by a family company to its shareholders (where all of its shareholders are member of the same family), provided such property was originally acquired by the company by way of donation. The property must be kept by the donee for at least three years
- Gifts made for educational or charitable purposes to a local authority or to any approved charitable institutions in Cyprus
- Transfers as a result of reorganisations
- Expropriations
- Exchange or disposal of immovable property under the *Agricultural Land (Consolidation) Laws*
- Exchange of properties, provided that the whole of the gain made on the exchange has been used to acquire the other property

The law provides for lifetime exemptions applicable only for individuals (not for legal persons) that are used for reducing / eliminating the taxable gain as follows:

Lifetime exemptions	(EUR)
For sale of own private residence (subject to certain conditions)	EUR 85,430
For sale of agricultural land by a farmer	EUR 25,629
For other sales	EUR 17,086

The above exemptions are granted only once for each taxpayer and not for each disposal. An individual claiming a combination of the above is allowed, subject to conditions, a maximum of EUR 85,430.

VAT payable on property

Since Cyprus accessended to the EU on 1 May 2004, VAT on properties was introduced. Properties for which an application for a town planning permit was filed before this date are exempted of VAT.

A reduced VAT rate of 5% applies to all contracts which were concluded as from 1 October 2011 onwards and which relate to the acquisition and/or construction of residences which are to be used as the primary and permanent place of residence for the next 10 years by the applicant (residents of the Republic or/and other EU member states). All contracts which were concluded before 30 September 2011 are subject to the current standard VAT rate and an eligible person should apply for a grant from the Tax Commissioner. VAT is not added on the sale price for the purposes of calculating the property transfer fees.

The application for a grant can be submitted to the Ministry of Finance in relation to residences for which a planning permission application has been submitted after 1 May 2004. Individuals who are citizens of the Republic of Cyprus or of any other EU Member State, who reside permanently in the Republic of Cyprus and who have reached the age of 18 at the time of application are entitled to this grant. As from 8 June 2012 eligible persons include residents of non-EU Member

States, provided that the residence will be used as their primary and permanent place of residence in the Republic.

The grant is given for residences whose total covered area does not exceed 275 m^2. The level of the grant is limited to 200 m^2. (For families with more than three children, the allowable total covered area increases by 15 square meters per additional child beyond the three children) and depends on the type of the property and on whether the house was constructed or purchased. The relevant legislation provides that the level of the grant will be adjusted annually for the increase in the Retail Price Index.

A person who ceases to use the residence as his primary and permanent place of residence before the lapse of the 10 year period must notify the Tax Commissioner, within 30 days of ceasing to use the residence, and shall pay the difference resulting from the application of the reduced rate and the standard rate of VAT attributable to the remaining period of 10 years for which the property will not be used as the main and primary place of residence.

Persons who make a false statement to benefit from the reduced rate are required by law to pay the difference of the additional VAT due, are guilty of a criminal offence and, upon conviction, are liable to a fine, not exceeding twice the amount of the VAT due, or imprisonment up to three years or may be subject to both sentences.

Inheritance tax

There is no inheritance tax since it was abolished by the *Estate Duty (Amending) Law 74(I)/2000* concerning any person who passed away after 1 January 2000.

Immovable property tax and local authority taxes and rates

Owners of immovable property located in Cyprus are subject to annual immovable property tax which is currently based on the market value of their property as assessed on 1 January 1980. The said tax is payable on 30 September each year. Physical and legal persons are both liable to immovable property tax.

The rate of taxation for the year 2013 and ongoing is as follows:

value of property (EUR)	annual property tax (%)
First EUR 40,000	6%
From EUR 40,001 to EUR 120,000	8%
From EUR 120,001 to EUR 170,000	9%
From EUR 170,001 to EUR 300,000	11%
From EUR 300,001 to EUR 500,000	13%
From EUR 500,001 to EUR 800,000	15%
From EUR 800,001 to EUR 3,000,000	17%
Over EUR 3,000,000	19%

Owners are also liable for other taxes imposed per annum to immovable properties such as municipal or village taxes, refuse collection, street lighting, sewerage etc. depending on the size of the property, the area etc.

22.8 Immigration law and tax residence

Immigration law

EU Citizens may enter, leave, travel and live in Cyprus and may also engage in any economic activity, under the same conditions as Cypriot citizens. With regards to non-EU citizens that seek to enter the Republic, for reasons other than immigration, an entry visa permit is required, to enter once or several times with the duration of each visit not exceeding three months in any half year, starting from the date of first entry. If the applicant needs to travel frequently to Cyprus for business purposes, for example, a multiple entry visa may be issued for a year, and in some cases for more than a year, but total visits must not exceed 90 days, starting from the first visit during each six month period.

Non-EU citizens that visit Cyprus for long-term purposes shall obtain special temporary permit, commonly referred to as a "Pink Slip". This type of permit can be issued for a period from one up to four years with the limitation of a total absence period of not more than four months. A non-EU citizen, who owns immovable property in Cyprus, automatically obtains "Pink Slip – Visitor" status. However, engagement in any form of business occupation is prohibited under the said status.

Third country nationals (non-EU citizens) can obtain immigration permits in the Republic of Cyprus provided certain criteria are satisfied. The most popular and attractive is the Category F immigration permit (under Regulation 6(2) of the *Aliens and Immigration Regulations*). This permit offers permanent residence in Cyprus and exempts the applicant from immigration entry procedures (there is no need to obtain any visas, residence permit renewals or re-entry permits) and is granted for an indefinite duration. The applicant needs to provide evidence that they have a secured annual income (such as a pension, dividends from investments, interest from deposits, rents etc.) of a sufficient amount to support themselves and their family whilst in Cyprus. If approved, the applicant will not be allowed to engage in any form of business profession or occupation. In cases where an applicant who satisfies the criteria of Category F additionally purchases immovable property in Cyprus at the price of EUR 300,000 or more, the application is fast-tracked and examined favourably by the authorities as the purchase proves the intention of the applicant to reside permanently in Cyprus.

The immigration permit category covers, besides the applicant, his spouse and children under the age of 18. The applicant and his family included in the Immigration Permit must visit Cyprus at least once every two years or else this status will be revoked.

Citizenship-by-Investment

Under Subsection (2) of Section 111A of the *Civil Registry Laws 141(I)/2002,* it is provided that the Council of Ministers may, under any conditions it determines as appropriate, allow the naturalization of foreign entrepreneurs. Therefore, according to the decision of the Council of Ministers dated 19 March 2014, a non-Cypriot citizen, who meets one of the economic criteria set in the above decision, may apply for the acquisition of Cypriot citizenship through Naturalization by exception. Acquiring Cypriot citizenship is similar to acquiring citizenship of any other EU country. As a Cypriot citizen, you have the right to live, work, and study in any of the 28 EU countries. The applicant must comply either with a single criteria or with a combination of the criteria. The investment, if made alone, must have a total value of EUR 5 million. In every case the applicant must have a clean criminal record and own a permanent privately-owned residence in the Republic, the purchase price of which must be at least EUR 500,000 plus VAT. The investment value can in some cases be only EUR 2.5 million, if grouped together with five other applicants for citizenship (managed by Henley & Partners).

For a single application, the economic criterion is an individual investment of at least EUR 5 million in:

- State bonds of the Republic of Cyprus
- Financial assets of Cypriot companies or Cypriot organizations (bonds / securities / debentures registered and issued in the Republic of Cyprus)
- Real estate, land development and infrastructure projects (residential or commercial developments, developments in the tourism sector or other infrastructure projects)
- Purchase or creation or participation in Cypriot businesses or companies
- Deposits in Cypriot banks for three years or deposits of privately owned companies or trusts (in which the applicant is the beneficiary owner)
- Impaired deposits in the Popular Bank due to the measures implemented after 15 March 2013 of at least EUR 3 million. In the case of impaired deposits of less than EUR 3 million, the applicant can apply after making additional investments

- Major collective investments of a total of five investors with total investments amongst them of at least EUR 12.5 million provided that each one invests at least EUR 2.5 million

Tax residence

All Cyprus tax resident individuals are taxed on all chargeable income accrued or derived from all sources in Cyprus and abroad. The tax year in Cyprus is the calendar year. Annual tax returns are filed by 31 December following the tax year.

Individuals and companies resident in Cyprus are liable to income tax in accordance with the *Income Tax Law 118(I)/2002* in respect of their worldwide income. An individual is tax resident in Cyprus if is present in the Republic for a period exceeding 183 days in a tax year. Individuals who are not tax residents of Cyprus are taxed on certain income accrued or derived from sources in Cyprus. However, non-tax residents having a permanent establishment in Cyprus may elect, if it is to their benefit, to be taxed in accordance with the provisions applicable to tax residents (the said choice may be made year-on-year). A company is resident in Cyprus, if its management and control are exercised in Cyprus.

A non-Cyprus tax resident company is taxed on income accrued or derived from a business activity which is carried out through a permanent establishment in Cyprus and on certain income arising from sources in Cyprus.

With regards to individuals the following income tax rates apply:

Chargeable income for the tax year (EUR)	Tax rate (%)
First EUR 19.500	Nil
From EUR 19.501 to EUR 28.000	20%
From EUR 28.001 to EUR 36.300	25%
From EUR 36.301 to EUR 60.000	30%
Over EUR 60.000	35%

The corporation tax rate for all companies is 12.5%.

The Law stipulates for various exemptions and deductions, provided certain conditions are satisfied.

Further, all companies registered in Cyprus must pay an annual levy of EUR 350 by 30 June of each year. In cases of group companies the total amount payable is capped at EUR 20,000. Non-payment of the levy may result the strike-off of a company of the Cyprus Company Registry.

Double Taxation Treaties

Cyprus has Double Taxation Treaties with many European and other countries. The main purpose of these treaties is the avoidance of double taxation of income earned in any of these countries.

22.9 Checklist: Real estate in Cyprus

- Legal Advice should be sought prior proceeding to any transaction
- An official search report with regards to the legal status of the purchased property shall be obtained by the Department of Lands and Surveys
- In case of an existing mortgage, a waiver from the Bank should be sought (i.e. a letter provided by the Bank stating that the mortgage creditor will remove the mortgage)
- Issuance of planning, building permits and final approval certificate should be checked
- In case of purchase of land then its possible development should be inquired
- A contract shall be signed containing provisions for the purchase price, terms of payment, full description of the property, date of delivery of the property, refund provision in case certain terms are not satisfied, warranty period (in case of new development), transfer date for the title deeds

- The Contract of Sale shall be duly stamped and lodged to the registry of the Department of Land and Surveys within six months from signing, for specific performance purposes. In case of Assignment Agreement this should be lodged within two months from signing
- In case of non-EU purchasers an application along with all necessary supporting documents for obtaining the permission of the Council of Minister shall be submitted
- Capital Gains Tax and any other fees, dues or taxes in respect of the property until the date of delivery of possession to the purchaser are exclusively paid by the seller
- Stamp Duty payment, VAT and transfer fees are paid by the purchaser

23

France

Republic of France
République Française

by

Donald Manasse

Donald Manasse Law Offices
2 rue du Congrès
06000 Nice
France

Telephone: +33 4 93 16 36 80
Facsimile: +33 4 93 16 36 81

manasselaw@rivieramail.com

Donald Manasse has more than 20 years experience representing clients in international transactions with a particular emphasis on matters having a connection with Monaco and France. He is a lawyer admitted to practice in New York and Connecticut, USA, and since 1986 in Nice, France. His Monaco office was authorized as a legal consultancy in 1989, as foreign nationals are not admitted to the Monaco bar. His principal areas of work are financial regulation, multinational litigation, representation of victims in fraud cases, structuring and advising on multinational investments; and languages include French, English, Italian, Russian, Flemish, Spanish and German.

23.1 Introduction

France is a world-leader in attracting foreign investors in real estate. With more than 544,000 km^2 in its continental area alone, housing some 60 million people, the country offers a widely varied landscape of property opportunities. From city apartments and office buildings to hill-top village houses, from historical chateaux to holiday homes on golf course developments, the real estate industry is well organized to receive the foreigner.

Property prices are as varied as types of property available, with relatively inexpensive investments still available in the rural regions not yet much discovered outside of France.

The system of property purchase is standardized throughout the country. Central to the system is the figure of the notary (*notaire)*. The notarial profession has the monopoly on receiving and registering acts that transfer title to real estate. Notaries are trained in the law, and are specialized in real estate, gift and inheritance law. Their professional liability insurance insures the good title for each transaction in which they participate. All funds paid to them (and to French lawyers or *avocats*) are guaranteed.

French property law and taxation relating to property transactions (other than local property and habitation taxation) are standardized throughout the country. Zoning and land-use issues will vary locally, however. So the foreigner purchasing in France should be aware of the tax consequences of the transaction that is being contemplated, both as regards the land transfer and as regards personal or corporate taxation. They should also be informed as to the use to which the land may be put, because non-respect of the zoning laws can be a criminal offence, and with increasing frequency French courts are ordering the demolition of constructions that do not respect or do not have proper building permits.

23.2 Real estate ownership

Different forms and types of ownership

Real estate in France may be owned in many forms. The most common are the equivalent of common law's fee simple or in joint ownership (*propriété indivise* or *indivision*), with or without a right of survivorship. Ownership rights may be divided between life estates (*usufruits*) and remainder interests (*nue propriété*). Long-term leasehold arrangements can be established. Multiple ownership in a common building, for example an apartment, will most frequently be in the form of condominium ownership (*copropriété*).

Ownership of property entails the absolute right of use and disposal as stated at Article 544 of the *Civil Code*, subject of course to applicable laws and regulations regarding appropriate use and construction which will apply in any particular area. Thus, quite apart from the provisions of the *Civil Code* that may generally apply, reference should be made to the *Code de l'urbanisme*; the *Code de la construction et de l'habitation;* the *Loi Littoral*, applying to seaside based buildings; the *Loi Montagne*, applying to buildings near the mountains; and to the zoning regulations adopted by the town having jurisdiction over the property concerned. Use will also be affected by whether land is considered to be in a fire or avalanche risk area.

Joint-ownership (l'indivision)

The term *indivision* refers to property that is owned in its entirety by more than one person. The ownership documentation will refer to a percentage of ownership for each *propriétaire indivis*. Joint ownership in this manner will afford all owners the right to use the property and to benefit from its use (for example the right to share rental income). If the joint-owners cannot agree on how the property is to be used, the matter can be referred for a judicial resolution. Unanimous consent is required for the administration or sale of the property. The joint owners may delegate the administration to one of the owners.

The essential principle is that no joint owner can be forced to remain in a joint-ownership situation. A division of the property and attribution to one or more of the various owners can be envisioned, and if there is no agreement or no possibility of such a *partage* then the property can be sold at auction (*vente par licitation*) and the proceeds divided.

Condominium ownership (la copropriété)

Ownership in condominium form is known as *copropriété*. The controlling statute is *Loi fixant le statut de la Copropriété des Immeubles Bâtis n° 65-557* of 10 July 1965, and the decree n° 67-223 applying it of 17 March 1967 which set out how *copropriété*s must be organized and run.

A *copropriété* will have private areas and common areas. The *règlement de copropriété* or *cahier des charges* is equivalent to the by-laws of the property association. It will set out the lot numbers for each of the privately owned areas in a building and the percentage of common areas that are owned by each lot owner. The percentage of ownership, usually expressed in *tantièmes* or in a fraction, the denominator of which will be multiples of 10,000), will determine the percentage of the common charges to be attributed to each owner.

Where the *règlement* is silent as to ownership, generally the access roads, the gardens, common equipment, roofs, corridors, and rights attached to them are commonly owned. A copy of the *règlement* will be given to each owner at purchase, and is binding on successive owners. It can be modified, but no modification resulting in an owner losing a property right or being assessed with additional charges beyond the percentage specified, can be passed unless there is unanimity of the condominium owners.

Management

The property owner's association (*le syndicat des copropriétaires*) will meet at least once every year to approve the prior year's accounts, approve the following year's budget, elect the managing board (*le conseil syndical*) of the building and select or confirm a property manager (*le syndic*). Normally in larger buildings this will be a professional property manager who holds the appropriate license.

The condominium, represented by the *syndic*, is a legal entity, a person before the law. It alone can sue on behalf of the apartment owners, and has the responsibility for the maintenance of the building. It will be liable for damages caused to individual co-owners or third parties.

The *syndic* is responsible for applying the condominium by-laws and for regulating the use of the common areas. He will manage the building, receive payment of common charges and hold funds, pay suppliers, subscribe insurance coverage for the building and for third party liability, account for funds received and with the agreement of the assembly, pursue defaulting payers in the courts.

The "Syndicat Des Copropriétaires"

The managing agent will convoke the annual assembly by registered mail. The documents sent will include the agenda of the meeting, the proposed budget and normally a proxy. While the law specifies that a proxy may be given to a third-party who is not an owner in the building, some by-laws will specify that only owners may receive proxies.

Each co-owner has a number of votes equal to his proportion of the property, unless the co-owner has a majority in which case his votes will be reduced to the aggregate number of the other owners. Most decisions are taken by a simple majority. Decisions outside the scope of everyday management require a greater majority, and under certain circumstances unanimity will be required. Minutes are kept and sent to the co-owners, who have two months to contest the assembly's decisions.

The right of construction (le droit de superficie)

The right of construction or building right (*droit de superficie)* confers a right to build on land owned by another. The owner of the right (*le superficiaire)* has rights on the buildings only, and not on the land. He may therefore rebuild the building, or add additional floors.

The "Concession Immobilière"

The *concession immobilière* is a contract by which the owner of real estate, built or unbuilt, confers its use to another person for a period of no less than 20 years, in return for an annual payment. Should the beneficiary build, then compensation is due to him at the end of the concession period.

Long-term lease (le bail emphytéotique)

The *emphytéose* is a long-term leasehold which confers a real estate right, and is signed before a notary. It can be mortgaged. The leasehold period can vary from 18 to 99 years. The tenant has the right to use the property during the period of leasehold. The system is generally used for construction and unless specifically specified, termination of the leasehold will imply that the landlord will own the buildings constructed without indemnification to the tenant.

Construction leasehold (le bail à construction)

The construction leasehold will commit the tenant to build, which is not the case in the *emphytéose*. The duration of the lease is the same (18 to 99 years), although a periodic rental will be due. At the end of the lease, the property reverts to the landlord. However, the contract can stipulate that title to the underlying land will be transferred upon termination.

The survivorship clause (la clause d'accroissement / pacte tontinier)

Where two or more persons purchase property jointly (in *indivision*) they can stipulate that upon the death of the first to die, the survivor (or survivors) will become the owner of the decedent's undivided property right. The transfer will trigger inheritance tax, unless the entire property has a value of less than EUR 76,000. The transfer at death will also be effective against children or parents of the decedent who would otherwise have a reserved portion of the decedent's estate, and for this reason has been in the past used by foreigners not wishing to submit their French property to French inheritance rules. However, it is generally disfavored today because of possible negative inheritance tax consequences.

Purchase of a life or remainder interest (la vente en viager)

The *vente en viager* is an often-used method of purchasing property rights. The owner sells the property, receiving a part of the sale price as payment (*le bouquet*) at the time of signature and the remainder as an annuity during the seller's lifetime. The seller may or may not remain in the premises, and this will affect the value of the annuity and of the *bouquet*. There may be multiple sellers, and the annuity will then be due until the death of the last survivor.

The annuity will be indexed for inflation, and will be registered as a lien on the property, so that non-payment will result in title to the property returning to the seller.

For the seller this is an effective form of estate planning, as the property will not be part of the estate at death, and thus will not be taxable. For the buyer, there is a reduced amount of capital due at closing. However, the final cost will depend on the longevity of the seller. Everyone in France remembers the story of *Jeanne Calment* who sold a studio apartment to her notary *en viager* when in her seventies, and survived the notary dying when she was past the age of 120 years.

Timesharing (la multipropriété)

Timeshare property ownership is regulated under the *Consumer Code* (*Code de la consommation,* Articles L. 121-60 and seq.). The definition is the contract offered to a consumer by a professional which directly or indirectly confers on the beneficiary the residential use of real estate for determined or determinable periods, during a minimum period of at least three years. Shares of companies conferring such rights are also included in the scope of the law. All contracts corresponding to this definition must comply with the legal requirements: the offer must be in writing and include no less than 12 specific details provided by law. The acceptance must also be written and return by registered mail. The consumer has a 10 day "cooling off" period during which he may withdraw. No deposit may be received before the expiration of the 10 day period. Violation of the provisions may not only result in civil liability but also in criminal prosecution.

Easements, charges, covenants, liens and mortgages

Easements

Real estate may be encumbered by restrictions on its use in the forms of *servitudes*. These most often provide for a right of access to a third party (usually a neighbor or a utility company), but they can also prevent construction on all or a portion of a parcel of entirely or limit the height of any building. A servitude is a right freely negotiated with the beneficiary and will "run with the land". It is created by a notarial deed registered at the registry of deeds (*Conservation des Hypothèques*) amd will reflect that one plot is encumbered (*fonds servant*) and that another benefits (*fonds dominant*) for the particular right or restriction.

Servitudes, and particularly rights of passage, may also be created by the open and notorious use of the land for a particular purpose for 30 years.

Servitudes may also exist by law, for example the requirement that no building be situated less than five meters from the boundary of the property or by the natural situation of the property (for example to allow the evacuation of rain water).

Usufruct (l'usufruit)

The life-estate is a right to use a property during the life of one or more people. It terminates at the death of the last *usufruitier* or life-estate holder.

The life-tenant can freely use the property, or rent it to third parties. If the property is commercial, a commercial rental requires the agreement of the owner of the remainder interest. The life-tenant is responsible for maintaining the property.

Right to occupy (le droit d'habitation)

French inheritance law now provides that a surviving spouse has the right to remain in the matrimonial domicile for the first year gratuitously. Following the first year, the surviving spouse may request to remain in the premises. If the domicile is a leased premise, the heirs must pay the rent for the first year. If the premises were owned by the decedent, the surviving spouse can now remain in residence for the remainder of their life, even where the children inherit.

The survivor must maintain the premises and must inhabit them: they may not be rented to third parties, unless the survivor requires institutionalization, in which case, the premises may be rented to generate income to pay for the retirement home.

Mortgages (les hypothèques, privilèges et suretés)

The mortgage of property takes different forms in French law, depending on whether it is formed by contract (by notarial deed), or by order of a court (*hypothèque conservatoire*). It is in all cases a measure to secure repayment of a debt and confers priority in accordance with the rank of the mortgage holder when there is a sale or auction of the property. It will permit the mortgage holder to force a sale of the property at auction, but will not allow the mortgage holder to take title of the property directly. The mortgage is a *privilège du vendeur* when it benefits a seller to secure an unpaid portion of the sale price. It is a *privilège de prêteur de deniers* when it benefits the entity, usually a French bank that has loaned funds to allow the purchase. The *privilèges* are less expensive to register than the *hypothèques*. Current case law however does not allow a foreign bank to register a *privilège de prêteur de deniers* but only a conventional mortgage.

Protection of ownership, proof of ownership and registration

While from a legal point of view, a sale is "perfect" when there is agreement on the object and the price, sale of real estate will actually take place by a notarial deed, signed in a single original, before one or more notaries, and deposited in the notary's "minutes." The deed will be sent to the registry of deeds for the area (the *Bureau de la Conservation des Hypothèques*), a branch of the Treasury Department.

The notary will verify the registry's documents to determine whether any other transfer of title has been registered for the same property, indicating that the seller is no longer the owner, and whether there are liens, encumbrances, or servitudes on the property. If the registry lists other notarial acts as having been registered on the same land, the notary can request copies of them to analyze fully the ownership rights that exist.

The registry is a public archive, and any person may request information or copies of registered acts or deeds. But only notaries may register acts there, with some exceptions. Attorneys at law (*avocats*) may register judicial mortgages and sales at judicial auctions, or legal challenges to title and the administration may register sales of property in which the government is involved.

Registration in the registry is not definitive proof that title is in the current owner. This proof may be established in any manner, through any written documents. Similarly, the holding of an *expédition* or certified copy of a title deed of the sale by which the current owner claims to have purchased will not be considered dispositive proof of current ownership. The registry serves, among other things, to give notice to third parties of the existence of an act concerning a property.

Proof of ownership is established by showing a continuous unbroken ownership of the property from preceding sellers to buyer for at least 30 years, the statutory period of limitation. The notary will relate in the deed or in its annex the ownership of the property in this manner, in order to provide the proof. The notary's professional liability policy insures good title. Thus there is no separate title insurance required in France.

23.3 Purchase and sale of real estate

The sales agreement

The *Civil Code* provides that a purchase in France is perfected when there is agreement on the object and the price, and thus even a non-written contract could be considered valid, although proof of the agreement may be difficult to provide. Such an agreement could form the basis for a request at law in specific performance. The existence of the lawsuit can be published at the registry of deeds, thereby preventing the sale of the property to a third party.

For this reason, no undertaking to sell or purchase should be granted, without including conditions precedent (*conditions suspensives*).

In practice, an offer to purchase will usually be drafted either by a lawyer, a notary or real estate agent, and will be accepted by the seller. The offer will be followed by a more formal preliminary contract that will either take the form of a *compromis de vente* (also called *promesse synallagmatique de vente)* or sale under conditions precedent, or of a *promesse unilatérale de vente* which is similar to an option to purchase.

The *compromis de vente* or *promesse unilatérale de vente* may be signed before a notary as an authentic act or deed, but this is not a requirement for validity. It may be registered with the tax office, and in the case of a unilateral promise (see below) it must be registered with the tax office within 10 days to retain its validity.

Property agents will often propose pre-printed standard forms of agreement. There are significant differences amongst these and both parties should be very prudent as to the terms contained. It is recommended that these be reviewed by a lawyer or notary prior to signature.

Since June 2001, all prospective buyers have a seven-day cooling off period during which they may retract their offer to purchase. No deposit may be requested during the seven-day period (with the exception of reservation deposits for new constructions), which begins on the day the buyer receives and acknowledges the contract to be signed. However, this consumer protection measure only applies to physical persons and not to companies undertaking to purchase, as was recently confirmed by the *Cour de Cassation* when it confirmed that a deposit of EUR 39 million made by Russian billionaire Mikhail Prokhorov was to be turned over to Mrs Lily Safra for the failed sale of a property in Villefranche-sur-Mer.

The Unilateral Promise (promesse unilatérale de vente) and the Bilateral Promise (promesse synallagmatique de vente)

The *promesse unilatérale de vente* is similar to an option to purchase. The seller grants the buyer the right to purchase against a deposit of a certain amount known as the *indemnité d'immobilisation*. The deposit is negotiable but in consumer transactions is customarily 10%. The buyer must exercise the option to purchase within a specified period of time, provided the conditions precedents are fulfilled. The customary conditions precedent are that there is proof the seller has good title, that there are no easements or servitudes burdening the property such as to reduce its value and that there are no mortgages or other liens greater than the purchase price. By law, the buyer is also entitled to withdraw if financing has not been obtained, unless the buyer has specifically waived that right in the preliminary contractual documents.

If the conditions precedents are fulfilled and the buyer does not purchase, he will lose his deposit and the seller is free to sell elsewhere. There can be no specific performance requested by the seller to force transfer of title. The buyer however can bind the seller to transfer title if he exercises the option in a timely fashion.

The *promesse synallagmatique de vente* must be distinguished from the *promesse unilatérale de vente.* Technically, the *promesse synallagmatique de vente* is the equivalent of the *compromis* or sale. The binding force of the bilateral promise is stronger than the unilateral promise inasmuch as the *promesse synallagmatique de vente* can be enforced as an actual sale before the courts by way of specific performance.

The *promesse*, whether unilateral or bilateral, can be a private document (*sous seing privé*) or by notarial deed (*acte authentique*).

The bilateral promise does not need to be registered to maintain its validity, whereas the unilateral promise must be registered at the tax office.

The sales deed (l'acte de vente)

The *acte de vente* will be prepared by the notary, who will have verified the situation of the property at the registry of deeds, and obtained information from any registered creditors as to the amounts required to discharge mortgages.

The *acte de vente* will recite the full identity of the parties, the price, the description of the property being sold, the legal warranties and specific conditions and the 30 year history of the property. It will be very thorough in describing the complexities of the transaction. It may stipulate a date different than the signature date for the right to occupy the premises.

Any preemptive rights existing in favor of the town or of the *SAFER* (a government organization having preemptive rights on agricultural land, the purpose of which is the development of agriculture) will have to be purged. The seller is also required to provide certificates as to the absence of asbestos, lead and termites in the buildings, and a report on the energy efficiency of the building, in addition to the analysis of risk (for earthquakes, fire and avalanches). A certified statement as to the surface area sold is required for most apartments.

The notary will register the *acte de vente* at the registry which will put all third parties on notice that the transfer has taken place. Notaries have the monopoly for registration of such *actes*. Thus while a transfer which is not by *acte authentique* can form the basis for a court decision to transfer title to property, no transactions on real estate in France take place without a notarial *acte de vente* unless the government is selling the property or if the property is acquired at auction.

Third parties are put on notice of the prior claim to title by registration at the registry of deeds.

Restrictions on acquisition and conveyance

Restrictions under family law and matrimonial property regime

Although the law of the place where property is situated generally controls the ownership of the property, the matrimonial law applicable to the person owning the property will have an effect on the ability to sell the property freely.

The French matrimonial regime, without a prenuptial contract, is the community property regime restricted to property acquired after the marriage (*communauté réduite aux acquêts*). Couples may choose the separate property regime, or a universal community property regime. In any event, however, a spouse will need the approval of the other to sell the matrimonial domicile.

France is a party to the *Hague Convention of 14 March 1978 on the Law Applicable to Matrimonial Property Regimes* (see *hcch.net*) regarding the applicable law in marital property. This allows foreign couples to adopt any one of the French regimes to govern their French real estate, even after their marriage. Failing such a choice, the French jurisprudence on conflicts of law will look to the place where the marriage took place and where the first matrimonial domicile was established to determine the matrimonial regime that is applicable.

The "Pacte Civil de Solidarité" or PACS

The *PACS* is a contractual arrangement for couples who wish to live maritally together, having some of the benefits of marriage with respect to taxes and laws on inheritance. It can be entered into by same sex couples. Where property is purchased after the registration of a *PACS*, it will be presumed to be undividedly owned 50% by each partner, unless the deed stipulates differently.

Options and pre-emption rights

Contractual rights of pre-emption

A third party can receive a preferential right to purchase property (*pacte de préference*). This can be part of the *acte de vente*, but there is no requirement that it be registered at the registry of deeds. The beneficiary of the right of preemption may sue to have a transfer in violation of that right set aside where he can show that the third party buyer had knowledge of the existence of the right of preemption and of the beneficiary's intention to exercise it, under current case law.

Statutory rights for tenants of leased premises

A residential tenant of unfurnished premises has a statutory right to purchase in the event of the refusal to renew his rental contract to allow the owner to sell. The tenant must receive formal notification from the owner, either by registered letter or by service from a bailiff, which will include information regarding the prospected sale: the sales price and other conditions of sale. The notice is equivalent to an offer to sell the apartment. The tenant must be given six months' notice that the landlord intends not to renew the lease and to sell the premises. The tenant has a two months period from the receipt of the notice to exercise his right to purchase, a period which is extended by an additional two months in the event the tenant must borrow to finance his purchase. If the tenant cannot complete at that time, the right of preemption is lost and the tenant must consider his lease terminated.

If the landlord then decides to sell at more advantageous conditions than those notified to the tenant these must be notified to the former tenant who has one month to accept and two months to complete.

Statutory right of pre-emption for governmental authorities

A municipality may have a right of pre-emption in cases of acquisition of a real estate property or of a property holding company (*société à prépondérance immobilière*). The information in this respect can be obtained from the *Mairie* of the town covering the property concerned. If the pre-emptive right exists, notification of the intended sale (*déclaration d'intention d'aliéner*) must be given, and the municipality may exercise its right during a two month period. The municipality may also offer a lower price, in which case the owner has a *droit de repentir* and may decide not to sell.

Agricultural real estate

There are no restrictions on foreigners seeking to purchase agricultural land. There is a statutory preemptive right in the *SAFER*, as mentioned above. Agricultural land can be purchased from the *SAFER*, who may also undertake to manage the agricultural exploitation for the owner.

Restrictions regarding acquisition of real estate by foreigners

Foreigners may freely buy land in France. There are no specific restrictions.

Further important preconditions for buying real estate

Capacity and entitlement of the seller

The parties must be capable of acting in order for consent to be validly given, and for a sale to be valid. The presumption under the *Civil Code* is that a party is capable of acting. A party must be of the age of majority (18 years of age in France, but the nationality of the seller will determine his or her majority). For a minor to validly sell, both parents must consent as well as the judge responsible for guardianship (*juge des tutelles*).

Adults who are placed under guardianship will be incompetent to act without the approval of their *tuteur* or guardian.

The representation of legal entities

A civil or commercial company becomes a "legal person" (*personne morale*) under the law once it is registered in the registry of companies. Although the corporate by-laws (*statuts*) may differ, in general the shareholders must consent for the sale of corporate real estate, particularly where these are the only corporate assets. Transactions of *SCIs* are exclusively civil, and their associates are jointly and severally liable for the company's debts. Associations formed under the law of 1901, which are the French equivalent of not for profit corporation, can act once they are registered at the *Préfecture*. The general assembly must decide on real estate transactions. *SCIs* are the most common form of company used for holding real estate (see later in this chapter).

Seller's title

A seller by law guarantees good title in property, even if the contract of sale says that no guarantees are given and unless the buyer had knowledge of the defect in title.

Third party claims and unpaid taxes

The search at the registry of deeds prior to completion will reveal whether there are outstanding mortgages, judicial liens or tax liens. The notary will ensure at closing that the mortgages and liens are discharged.

Provisions for protecting the environment, nature and cultural heritage

Environmental protection

The applicable environmental protection regulations must be respected in requesting planning permits. They are particularly relevant to developments, whether industrial or residential, rather than to the constructions of individual homes.

Protection of national monuments

Two types of protection exist for historic buildings. A site or building may be considered *inscrit* (or registered) on the list of historic monuments. It may also be *classé* as a historic monument.

Where the building is *inscrit* or registered the government may take measures to protect it from being altered or destroyed. Any modification or sale of the building must be notified.

Where a building is *classé* as a historical monument then it has been determined that its preservation is in the national interest. In that case any modification or sale is closely controlled. The government may subsidize work on the buildings in both cases, and certain tax relief is applicable. A relatively small number of *châteaux, manoirs* or *maisons de maître* are classed as historical monuments, and sometimes only part of the buildings (for example, a chapel) will be classed while the remainder of the estate is not.

Access to relevant records and documents

The records of the registry of deeds are public. They may be consulted only in writing, by requesting information on the appropriate forms, specifying the cadastral lot numbers in question. The registry document (*extrait hypothécaire*) will list all purchases and sales involving the land or apartment, all mortgages, and any lawsuits filed whose existence has been communicated to the land registry. Where it is a multiple dwelling building, the existence of condominium by-laws will be noted.

Any of the documents mentioned on the registry document may be requested from the registry, so that it is possible to obtain a copy of the preceding acts of sale, for example. The applicable zoning regulations and the existence of building permits can be verified at the municipal town planning office (*service de l'urbanisme*) or with the *Direction Départementale de l'Equipment* (*DDE*).

Prior to allowing the signature of an *acte de vente* a notary will also request a *note d'urbanisme* from an architect. This document, which will be appended to the *acte*, will explain the zoning situation, and whether there are any residual construction rights.

When an apartment is being purchased, additional documents requested will be the minutes of the meeting of the condominium association, and of the property manager, as well as of the budget. If the association has voted for major works that have yet to be carried out, this will be a financial charge on the members of the association. Although such charges remain the liability of the owner at the time the vote was taken, in practice the new owner will often be required to pay.

In all cases, it will be necessary to verify the amount of the *taxe d'habitation* (local occupancy tax) which applies to whoever occupies the residence on 1 January of any given year, and of the *taxe foncière* (local property tax). The *taxe d'habitation* is not adjusted at closing, while the *taxe foncière* will be shared by buyer and seller on a pro rata basis.

Key points that a seller should consider

The seller must inform the buyer of any hidden defects of which he is aware, but the buildings will usually be sold on an "as is" basis. The defects can relate to the buildings or land itself, and also to legal issues regarding property, for example the absence of documents relating to building permits. The seller's liability in these respects will be more important if the seller is a professional in the real estate business. The deed should relate any apparent defects in the property so that the buyer cannot deny having been informed. Real estate professionals who are sellers have a higher degree of responsibility.

It has become more usual to subject a purchase to a satisfactory survey, although the tendency is that while the seller is free to undergo the expense of a survey, the buyer will not accept to be bound until the survey results are known.

The execution of a real estate purchase transaction

Once there is an agreement as to the purchase price and other conditions, subject to conditions precedents, the parties may instruct notaries to go directly to closing, or may sign the *promesse unilatérale de vente* or *compromis de vente* stipulating the latest date on which completion is to take place.

Completion will normally be between six weeks and three months from the preliminary agreement. The time is necessary to allow the notary to obtain the necessary documentation (registry documents, certificates regarding zoning regulations, attestations regarding asbestos etc.).

Notaries in France may act for both parties, without this being considered a conflict of interest. However either party may always select his own notary, without the other party being entitled to refuse. The identity of the notary or notaries should be specified in every preliminary document signed, to avoid later misunderstandings. The presence of an additional notary in the transaction does not increase costs, because the notaries will divide the fees.

The cost of purchase (notarial fees and registration costs) is, by custom, paid by the buyer. If the buyer specifies in his offer that the purchase is made *acte en main*, this indicates that the seller will pay the registration costs. Such costs are approximately 7%, unless the transaction is subject to Value Added Tax, or made as a speculative purchase.

If a *compromis de vente* or *promesse unilatérale de vente* is signed, and the accompanying deposit, normally of 10%, is paid, the seller may not again promise to sell to a third party. "Gazumping", or the practice of holding a property out for a higher price, until completion, is not practiced in France once the parties have signed preliminary documentation. Among other reasons, the preliminary documentation may be registered at the registry of deeds, which will mean the seller cannot effectively sell the property on again. The buyer would bring an action to have the sale recognized as "perfect" and to have title transferred, which whatever its outcome, would prevent the seller from completing until all appeals were exhausted, effectively removing the property from the market.

The real estate agent (l'agent immobilier)

Any person habitually acting as a real estate intermediary and receiving commissions for doing so must be licensed and insured. The real estate agent must also have an account to receive client's funds which is fully guaranteed. The agent may not receive amounts in excess of his or her guarantee, which must be properly posted, so that potential clients are made aware of it.

The real estate agent must have a mandate to show property from a seller, but may work on a multiple listing basis, where one agent is properly mandated. If the buyer has instructed the agent, then a mandate to search for property is necessary. The agent may only claim a commission if the transaction completes.

The mandate may be exclusive or non-exclusive. It should list among other things the property, the selling price, the amount of commission, and whether or not it is exclusive. On standard mandates, a clause may often be included allowing an agent a commission even where completion does not take place, on the basis that an agreement exists on the "object and the price." Such a practice is controversial and need not be accepted by the client. If it is accepted, the client may find himself unable to undo a transaction that has somehow derailed prior to closing without paying a commission to an agent, impeding an amicable settlement between the parties.

The mandate must be limited in time, or it will be declared null.

The mandate will not authorize the real estate agent to oblige the client to sell or purchase, unless it says so. It must be of limited duration, and may, if non-exclusive, be cancelled unilaterally. Non-respect by an agent of the requirements may lead to prosecution or loss of license. The agent may not purchase the property himself while under mandate.

The agent is responsible for informing the client of a property's market value, particularly where the client is selling at a price considerably lower than normal for the area. The agent must also advise on defects in title or material defects of which the agent should have been aware as a professional, unless these were non-apparent and it is proven he did not have actual knowledge of them. He must verify that the persons giving the mandate are entitled to act, and where he drafts preliminary documents of purchase, he is responsible for their effectiveness. In short the agent has a *devoir de conseil*, an obligation to advise the principal for whom he is acting.

The agent's commission is freely negotiable. Seller's commission is rarely higher than 5%, plus VAT at 19.6%. The agent may request a commission from the buyer, which will not exceed 3%.

The notary (le notaire)

There are approximately 7,600 notaries in France. The notary is a ministerial officer appointed by the government. Their fees are fixed and not ordinarily negotiable. The notary's participation is necessary for any transfer of title to property other than by the government or by auction. Only the notary may register the transfer documents at the registry of deeds, giving notice to third parties.

It will be the notary's responsibility to verify that the seller has good title and that any liens or mortgages can be discharged with the purchase price. The notary most commonly will receive and hold both the initial deposit and the purchase price in his clients' account until such a discharge takes place, but the price can also be paid outside of his accounts (although this is not recommended). Funds held by the notary are entirely guaranteed. Where separate notaries act for the buyer and seller, the fees will be divided between them and there will be no extra cost for the buyer, the seller then paying no fees other than any costs involved in discharging mortgages (*mainlevée*).

The notary owes the client and the parties, if he is the sole notary, a duty of confidentiality and the duty to advise them of all the risks inherent in a transaction. He must verify the parties' identities and their capacity to act. The notary today must also make a declaration to the appropriate financial intelligence unit (*Tracfin* in France) whenever the origin of funds for any transaction appears to him to be suspicious. He may not advise his clients of his suspicions.

The notary will pay the registration taxes for each sale, and will therefore demand that the buyer pays, on top of the purchase price, the registration taxes and fees prior to completing the transaction. The notary must also collect and pay over the capital gains tax due on a transaction.

Powers of attorney

Notaries will generally require powers of attorney to be either notarized and apostilled, or signed before the French consul in a foreign jurisdiction. While the law does not strictly require it, it is customary particularly where the power of attorney is being used to sell.

The power of attorney must be specific as to the property and may set limits as to the price, for example, "not less than a certain amount", without stipulating the actual sale price eventually agreed.

Where companies purchase property, the power of attorney granted as a result of a shareholder's meeting need not be notarized, nor do the minutes of the meeting authorizing the purchase or sale.

Financing

It is very common to obtain bank financing for a property transaction. In fact all sales to consumers are subject to obtaining financing, unless the buyer specifically states in his or her own handwriting in the preliminary contract that financing will not be required. French banks will loan to non-residents and foreign banks may loan and obtain mortgages on French properties.

The preliminary purchase document will state that financing is to be obtained, the amount, the maximum interest rate acceptable to the buyer and the repayment period.

The loan will be secured by a *privilège* or *hypothèque* – a mortgage. Generally this will be for the amount loaned, increased by 10 to 20% for the "accessories" which are the costs of foreclosing and interest presumably due if there is foreclosure. However, since the registration cost of the mortgage will be a percentage of the entire amount secured, the accessories will increase the overall cost.

Banks may also request independent guarantees in the form of deposits pledged to cover a portion of the amount loaned. The lender may be satisfied, in rare cases, with a promise to mortgage rather than a mortgage itself, although a promise will not secure the bank, since other borrowers may then register a lien and have precedence.

Because the foreclosure procedure is cumbersome and requires a sale of the property at auction, lenders will not be satisfied to be secured with the value of the property alone, but will want to verify an income stream to determine that the borrower will make mortgage payments. Ordinarily, income should be three to four times more than the monthly mortgage repayment.

Under consumer law, the financial institution must make a clear offer in writing, which is to be valid for at least 30 days. The offer may not be accepted in the first 10 days following receipt. The offer must contain an indication of the *taux effectif global* (TEG), the actual interest and costs payable on the mortgage. Loans may have variable or fixed rates of interest, and where the interest is variable the TEG will be based on the applicable rate at the time of the making of the loan (for example, *Euribor*).

Completion must take place within a four month period from the acceptance of the loan offer.

Purchase through a company

Purchasing a French property through a company presents certain advantages, but also certain risks. The property investor will want to evaluate these carefully to ensure the advantages apply to his specific needs.

There is one main advantage for the foreign buyer. Ownership of shares of a property owning company is not considered under French inheritance law the equivalent to ownership of real estate. This means that when the owner of the shares dies, the shares will be considered "moveable" property under French law and will be subject to the law of the domicile of the decedent at death (or the law of the nationality of the decedent) but not systematically to French law (unless the decedent has in the meantime become a French domicile). From a practical point of view, the effect is that the civil law forced heirship provisions in favor of children or parents will not be applicable. It is important to note, however, that with a few exceptions resulting from specific tax treaties, the shares will be considered to be subject to French estate tax if the company assets are more than 50% composed of French real estate.

From 1 January 2012 shareholder advances made to companies owning property in France by non-residents are no longer deductible from the value of the assets owned by the company for purposes of calculating the wealth tax.

There are several disadvantages to purchasing through a company depending on the type of company involved. These will be discussed below.

The Société Civile Immobilière (SCI)

French law distinguishes between civil and commercial activity. Commercial activity is basically trading activity. Civil activity, in the context of property ownership, will include holding property for rental, or for the free use of the shareholders of a company.

The SCI is the most common type of company used to hold property. It requires no less than two shareholders, who hold parts not shares. No share certificates are issued. There is no minimum capital, and no requirement to file accounts.

The SCI is fiscally transparent, that is, any income it makes is attributed to its shareholders. However, the SCI may opt to pay corporate tax. This option is irrevocable and has a number of consequences, including on the calculation of capital gains tax liability on resale of property.

The SCI will be required to be registered at the company registry in order to be considered a legal entity. Once this is done and it has the *personnalité morale* (becomes a "person" before the law) it can sue or be sued, and may own property in its own name.

The company will have *statuts* that govern how it is to be run. These are the equivalent of the by-laws and memorandum and articles of incorporation. They will specify the capital, the address of the company, the corporate purpose, the number of shares, the names of the subscribing shareholders and the number of shares each will have, the duration (normally 99 years). The company's purpose clause should avoid a commercial connotation if the "civil" nature of the company is to be preserved. Thus the purchase and management of property is a civil objective, but the purchase and sale of property is a commercial one.

The company is represented or managed by one or more managing directors (*gérants*) who are chosen by the shareholders either in the statutes or by a general assembly. The *gérant* can be a foreigner, and need not be domiciled in France. The *gérant* can be revoked at any time, unless the statutes specify otherwise. The management has the power to bind the company for any acts which come within the corporate purpose and are not *ultra vires*. Third parties will not be considered to have notice of restrictions to the *gérant*'s authority in the statutes or in the minutes of the meeting appointing them. However, most careful notaries will require the approval of the shareholders in order to allow a *gérant* to dispose of all or a significant portion of the company's assets or to mortgage the property.

Limited liability companies may be shareholders of SCIs, but tax consequences will flow from such a choice.

Transfer of company shares

Any transfer of shares of the company will be registered both with the tax office at a cost of 5%, and with the registry of companies, and will in addition trigger capital gains tax liability. Failure to register will make the transfer not opposable to third parties, including the tax office.

One of the many tax reforms introduced in 2011 and 2012 makes it a requirement that any transfer of shares of a company that is predominantly a French property owning company (known in France as a *"société à preponderance immobilière"*) must now be registered with a French notary if the transfer is executed outside of France.

*SCI*s may be created without the participation of a notary. However, only a notary may act to contribute real estate to a company as part of the capital (*apport*). Transfer of *SCI* shares may take place without the intervention of a notary.

Annual costs

The costs of incorporation and annual management of an *SCI* are low, seldom more than EUR 3,000. It is recommended that *SCI*s keep annual accounts, and that an annual meeting of the shareholders be held to approve them, and to approve the management.

Unlimited Liability

The SCI is not a limited liability company. Each shareholder is liable for the company's debts, proportionally to his or her percentage of ownership of the company shares.

Tax obligations

The SCI will be required to file a tax form every year (Form 2072) listing the names of the shareholders and the identity and value of its French property. If no changes have taken place, then an exemption to the annual filing can be obtained.

Like all companies, foreign or French, owning property in France, the SCI must undertake to disclose to the tax office the identity of its shareholders, failing which an annual tax equal to 3% of the fair market value of any property held will be applicable.

Where the SCI is held by individuals and where it has not opted to pay corporate tax, the capital gains tax treatment of the sale of property will be the same as for individuals. Where the SCI is held by a corporation, this will not be the case.

Commercial company ownership

Property may also be owned through a *société en nom collectif* (SNC) or through the limited liability companies known a *société à responsabilité limitée* (SARL) or *entreprise unipersonelle à responsabilité limitée* (EURL), *société anonyme* (SA) or *société par actions simplifiée* (SAS). The latter two corporate forms are seldom used for individual property ownership as they are more adapted for larger businesses having commercial activities and are not included in the discussion below.

The SNC, EURL and SARL have a commercial activity and will be subject to annual corporate tax. The *gérants* of the SNC, SARL and EURL must either be citizens of a country that is a member of the European Union or have a *carte de commerçant* allowing them to do business in France. They need not be domiciled in France.

Transfers of shares of commercial companies other than SA and SAS will be subject to the same registration tax as for parts of SCI. Capital gains tax treatment on resale will be less favorable than for individuals or SCIs.

Ownership through foreign companies

All companies owning property in France directly or indirectly must either undertake at purchase to reveal the names of their shareholders, or make an annual declaration doing so, depending on the type of tax treaty existing between the company's country of origin and France, in order to avoid the above mentioned annual tax of 3%.

Companies incorporated or domiciled in countries not having a tax treaty with France will always be subject to the 3% annual tax, and may not be exonerated by declaring the names of the shareholders.

This is why all knowledgeable advisors in France will strongly discourage potential buyers from using any kind of non-treaty off-shore company when purchasing in France. If an SCI has an offshore company as a shareholder, then the percentage of ownership in the offshore company will be taxed at 3%.

The 3% tax will not apply to companies when less than 50% of their French assets are comprised of French real estate, or when the shareholder is public company, quoted on a stock exchange, or a pension fund.

The tax applies to ownership on 1 January of every year.

A commercial company owning property in France, whether French or foreign, will be required to file annual accounts every year. Unlike the SCI, granting gratuitous use of property held by a commercial property to a shareholder is considered an "abnormal act of management", and will create imputed income to the company. This "fictional" rental income must be declared in the annual corporate tax declaration.

The use of a foreign company to directly purchase property in France can only be recommended when the income or estate tax treaty between the country in which the company is resident and France presents particular benefits. Specialist advice is recommended to determine whether a foreign company may be used, on a case-by-case basis.

Defects and warranty claims

Warranty claims favoring the buyer

Every property transfer contains a warranty of good title (a guarantee that the new owner will not be evicted from the property). The property sold must be the same as that described in the preliminary contract, free of any flaws in title or defects known as "redhibitory defects" rendering the property unfit for use.

Where the property is an apartment, for one year following the sale the buyer has a right to have the apartment measured. If the square meterage is greater than 5% smaller that the surface area indicated in the *acte de vente* the buyer can claim a reduction in price.

The buyer is also protected against *troubles de fait* or *troubles de droit*: attacks against his ownership rights either in fact or at law, for example where it is discovered a rental agreement exists for the property.

The seller will be liable for hidden defects preventing or reducing the possible use of the property, or making the property unfit for its intended use. The buyer has an obligation to check for existing defects that could be discovered by an ordinarily attentive person. But where such a defect is discovered, the buyer may request either a reduction of price or a cancellation of the purchase. The petition for either should be filed within the shortest available time following discovery.

Warranty claims favoring the seller (la lésion)

If the seller discovers that he has sold the property for a price less than 7/12th of the market value, the seller can ask that the sale be rescinded. The request must be presented within two years of the sale and proof of the market value must be presented by three experts named either by the parties or by the court. The buyer can choose to pay the remainder of the "just" price or to return the property to the seller and receive the price paid in return.

23.4 New construction, rebuilding and renovation

Construction zones and construction permits

Regulations regarding construction of new buildings and modification of existing ones are codified in the *Code de l'urbanisme*. Local communes may enact zoning ordinances (*plan local d'urbanisme or* PLU*)* that will determine, amongst other things, the different zones for different types of development, thus whether land can be used for construction, and the size of buildings that may be constructed (what percentage of the land may be covered by construction).

Nearly all communes have enacted or are currently enacting a PLU, but as these may also be modified it is important to verify the current status in each commune. Different types of legislation will apply to construction other than zoning, for example rules regarding sanitation, historical preservation and security. The rules are independent of each other, thus a permit to build will not necessarily satisfy other required authorizations. It is not for example automatically a permit to demolish an existing structure.

Building permit (permis de construire)

No building may be constructed, and no modification as to the use, volume, exterior aspect or number of floors of an existing building may be made, without obtaining a building permit. Modification of the interior layout of a building does not require a permit unless it will modify the use to which the building is put, or modify the number of floors.

Demolition also requires a permit. Certain works require only a declaration or *déclaration préalable* – generally where no additional volume is being created or where the building does not create more than 20 square meters of additional volume on property containing an already existing building. Adding a swimming pool, whether covered or not, may, depending on the design for example only require a declaration rather than a permit.

The permit request is filed with the town hall (*Mairie*) by the property owner or his representative. The use of an architect is not required where the construction is being built for the owner and is smaller than 170 square meters, or in certain cases regarding agricultural buildings.

The request will be posted in the *Mairie* within 15 days of its receipt and will remain posted while the file is being examined. The *Mairie* must reply within one month informing the owner whether the file is complete and giving the date on which a decision will be taken, normally within two to three months of the receipt of the file but this can vary according to the size and importance of the project.

If the *Mairie*'s reply does not mention that additional information is required, or that failure to decide within the specified time does not constitute tacit agreement, then where no decision is taken at the expiration of the announced period, the permit is considered tacitly granted but it is recommended that the property owner requests written confirmation that no refusal has been decided.

The *Mairie* will also require the approval of the *Direction Départementale des Territoires* (*DDT*) or *Direction Départementale des Territoires et de la Mer* (*DDTM*) for the coastal French districts and of the *Architecte des Bâtiments de France* and of the *Architecte des Bâtiments de France* for various aspects of the permit.

If a permit is granted, work must begin within a two year period, and must not be interrupted for more than one year. The permit must be posted on site for the duration of the works (and a bailiff should establish existence of the posting on site or *affichage*) and in the *Mairie* for a two month period following issuance, to allow third parties to file oppositions to the legality of the permit with the administrative courts.

Architect's contract and building contract

Insurance is obligatory for both the contractor and the owner of a building being constructed or rebuilt. The owner's insurance is known as the *dommages ouvrage* while the builder's and subcontractor's insurance covers civil responsibility during the *garantie décennale* or 10 year period of liability.

Where the owner is building for his own use, then the *dommages ouvrage* insurance is not obligatory but it will nonetheless be requested should a sale be made during the 10 year period following completion of the construction, because the buyer will prefer to rely on the seller's own insurance contract for any defects that may appear rather than search for the contractors and their insurers years after they have left the site.

The Architect

A person may only practice as an architect if he or she is a member in good standing of the *Order of Architects*. Use of the title is otherwise a criminal offense. Any works requiring a building permit must be based on a plan prepared by an architect (*projet architectural*) which defines the place of the constructions on the land, their volumes and layout, their colors and materials. The architect retains certain intellectual property rights in the plans and in the executed building.

The architectural contract is not a mandate from the owner to the architect. He will require a specific power of attorney to carry out additional tasks such as signing building contracts on the owner's behalf or paying the contractors.

The architectural contract should be in writing, according to the rules of the *Order of Architects*, but the jurisprudence will allow its existence to be proven by other elements than a formal document. The contract should accurately describe the architect's mission in relation to the project: it may go from the conception of the building to its reception by the owner, covering all the steps in-between. The architect is then the *maître d'oeuvre* for the owner who is the *maître d'ouvrage*.

The architect has a permanent obligation to advise and assist his client. He may be charged with directing the works, and with supervising them. The architect's fees are freely negotiable, although the Order publishes "suggested fees" schedules. The fees may be fixed (*forfait*) or may be based on a percentage of the cost of the works, or a mixture of both. For example, the development of plans and preparation and filing of a building permit may be billed at a fixed cost, and the construction at a percentage of the cost of construction. The range of percentages is often between 8% and 10% of the cost of the works, Value Added Tax excluded. The architect must have professional liability insurance.

Depending on the complexity of the work, the owner and architect may decide to employ a quantity surveyor (*économiste* or *métreur*).

The building contract

The building contract follows the general provisions of French contractual law. Standard contracts that describe the works and the cost are often used. These can be found at *ogbtp.com* or *afnor.org* for example.

It is important to specify a precise time for completion, although this may depend on the granting or filing of a building permit. The contract may be for a fixed sum (*forfaitaire*) or it may specify that the cost may vary by defined percentages or be indexed. With a fixed price contract, the builder will be held to his bid, unless under the jurisprudence, some important extraneous and unforeseeable fact intervenes.

The contract for an individual home (contrat de construction de maison individuelle)

Precise consumer protection provisions apply to individual home contracts. These are codified in the *Code de la construction et de l'habitation.* Failure to include them in a contract makes the contract void and may result in criminal prosecution. The builder's responsibility will vary according to whether he has provided the building plans or not. They are applicable to any construction that will include up to two residential premises for the same owner.

The contract must be in writing, and the owner must receive it by registered letter, with all its annexes. He has a seven day cooling off period during which he may withdraw. It must include a complete description of the land on which the construction is to take place, and state that the owner may be assisted by a professional such as an architect. The contract must list the guarantee the builder provides that he will complete the works (through insurance or a bank guarantee – known as a *garantie de livraison*) or that he will reimburse funds received if he does not complete the works (*garantie de remboursement*), and make reference to the *dommages ouvrage* insurance obtained by the owner.

Other obligatory information includes the reference to the building permit, a technical description of the construction, the date on which the work will begin, and late delivery penalties (which cannot be inferior to 1/3000th of the price per day); the price and the stages of construction at which separate payments are to be made; and if there is bank financing, the amount the owner intends to obtain. If there are conditions precedent to the contract's validity (for example obtention of the building permit or financing), the contract must stipulate a date by which they must be fulfilled.

Certain clauses are considered invalid and will be given no effect (*clauses abusives*). These include any clause that require the owner to give the builder a mandate to obtain financing or that require the owner to prove he has requested financing of several institutions prior to returning the deposit.

The owner is entitled to retain 5% of the price for a period of one year following reception of the building. This retention can be substituted by a bank guarantee.

The builder can request payment during the works but the percentages are fixed by law. He can ask for no more than 15% before the work begins, 25% when the foundations are completed, 40% when the walls are completed, 60% when the roof is done; 75% when the windows and doors are installed and 95% at completion and reception.

Sale of building to be constructed (vente d'immeuble à construire)

In the *vente d'immeuble à construire* the seller undertakes to build a building on the land sold at a specified date. The contract can specify the sale will be completed when the building is delivered (*vente à terme*) or it can transfer the title to the land immediately.

The *vente en l'état futur d'achèvement* (VEFA), is the property transfer by which the seller undertakes to build and deliver, or renovate (*vente en l'état futur de rénovation*), all or part of a building on the land title whose title is being transferred. Construction may have begun prior to the sale. The VEFA is most used in sub-division developments and condominium sales. VEFA contracts must respect certain legal provisions, or will be considered null.

The reservation contract must specify the square meterage, the number or rooms, bathrooms and other services, its position in the building (if an apartment), the standard quality, the price and a delivery date, as well as conditions relating to financing of the purchase. There must be at least three originals, and the buyer must receive one in order for the seven-day cooling off period to commence. The deposit requested at reservation cannot be more than 5% if the building is to be completed within a year, 2% if completion is to take place within two years. No deposit may be requested if completion is not to take place within two years or more. Failure to respect these provisions can result in criminal sanctions. The deposit must be made to a notary or to a bank account in the buyer's name.

The notarial deed will require the buyer to pay the price of the land and to undertake the payment of the construction as it advances in amounts no greater than 35% when the foundations are completed, 75% when the roofing is done, and 95% upon delivery of the building. Completion of the construction is guaranteed either by independent bank guarantees or by a showing of sufficient assets and property sale in the development program, as well as by significant advancement in the construction at the time of sale, to ensure completion.

Upon completion of the construction, the building will be formally accepted (*réception*) by the owner. The insurance coverage is triggered by this reception of the construction. At the formal handover, all reservations about the construction and appearance are preserved in a minute or *procès-verbal de réception* which is signed by the participants. The individual buyer is well advised to have an independent architect or expert present during this process.

Completion of construction and formalities

Work must be finished prior to the expiry of the validity of the building permit. The permit will automatically expire if works are suspended for more than a year. Completion must be declared to the municipality within 30 days (*déclaration attestant l'achèvement et la conformité des travaux or DAACT*) with the authorized project manager or the architect that directed the construction certifying that the building conforms to the permit. The authorities are to visit the premises and deliver a *certificat de conformité* – a certificate that the building is conform to the permit – within three months after the delivered *DAACT* or within five months if the building is registered as a historical monument, is located in a protected area, or if the works were carried out in an area covered by a mining, technological or natural risk plan. After this time, the authorities cannot question the conformity of the works and are required to provide the certificate within 15 days, failing which they can be formally requested to do so. Consequently, in such a case the certificate is considered tacitly granted but it is recommended that the property owner requests written confirmation. The issuance of the certificate can be attacked by any third party having standing to sue.

A partial certificate of conformity can be issued where there is a building development of which the individual home or apartment building forms only one portion.

Deficiencies and warranty claims regarding new construction

Visible defects must be reported within one month. Structural integrity of the building is guaranteed for 10 years, and there will be independent insurance to cover that risk. The functioning of other elements of the construction and equipment, such as doors and windows, is guaranteed for two years from reception.

The ten year guarantee (garantie décennale)

The law provides that contractors, the architect and their sub-agents in the construction are liable for 10 years following acceptance for any defect in the works that can affect the construction's solidity or any essential elements that would make the building improper for its intended use. The warranty does not cover minor defects. The case law construes "works" widely so that swimming pools, supporting walls or tennis courts are included. Renovations will also be covered by the 10 year guarantee.

It is important to verify that the insurance actually covers the type of work done by the contractor. Thus a general policy does not necessarily cover work on swimming pools for example. The insurance will continue its validity even when the contractor goes bankrupt or otherwise ceases to work, provided that it was in force when the work commenced.

The two year guarantee (garantie de bon fonctionnement)

The builder, architect, engineer and their sub-contractors are liable for any defects in the equipment and fixtures (heaters, air conditions, windows and doors, for example). Most of these elements will also be covered under the manufacturer's warranty.

The one year guarantee (garantie de parfait achèvement)

The one year guarantee allows the owner to require the builder to correct the defects that were noted in the *procès-verbal de réception*, or that have become apparent since that time. The 5% sum retained on the amount of the works or the equivalent bank guarantee requested of the contractor serve to cover this guarantee.

23.5 Rental and tenancy

Landlord-tenant law is complex in France, and it is particularly protective of the tenant both in residential and in commercial leases. Expulsion of tenants is a lengthy and uncertain process, even in cases of non-payment, and government representatives may intervene to prevent the execution by the police of court orders to expel where they have determined it will create hardship.

Differences exist where a lease is made as a primary or secondary residence and when furnished or unfurnished. Commercial leases are automatically valid for nine years at the tenant's choosing, and failure to renew will require indemnification. Agricultural leases are governed by a separate Code (*Code rural et de la pêche maritime*) and have their own specificity.

Rental and leasing contracts

The rental agreement for residential premises should be in writing, but if a property owner accepts occupancy and rental monies without having a written agreement the landlord tenant relationship will be considered to exist, under the codified law (*law n° 89-462* of 6 July 1989) and conditions will be as specified in the law.

Clauses in a written contract that are illicit are considered at law as not having ever existed, (*clause réputée non écrite*) without necessarily invalidating the entire agreement. Such clauses would include imposing a particular insurance company or requiring the tenant to allow rent payments by automatic withdrawals from a bank account. Unfurnished residential leases must be for a period of at least three years, which is increased to six years if the property is owned by a company. The tenant may resiliate the lease if there is a change in his situation (loss of employment for example) by giving one month's notice and at termination, with three month's notice. The landlord must give six months' notice of his intent not to renew. He may not terminate the lease before the expiration, and he may not refuse to renew the lease unless he is selling the property or intends to use it for himself and his immediate family. The landlord may refuse to renew for non-payment of rent or a serious breach of the terms of the lease. Where the tenant is more than 70 years of age and can prove he has a minimum amount of income, the landlord cannot refuse to renew the lease without offering similar living accommodations elsewhere at a similar price.

Furnished and seasonal rentals are not subject to the law of 1989, and the provisions can be more freely negotiated.

Regulations on protection of lessees and rent control

The tenant's deposit may not be more than two months rent, if the tenant is paying on a quarterly basis, and one month's rent if the tenant is paying monthly. The tenant may choose which of the two is to apply. A common if questionable practice is to request an independent bank guarantee for additional sums of money to ensure payment of rent during the period it is estimated an expulsion would require.

Increases in rent at the expiration of the lease are linked to an inflation index. The landlord can propose a new rent amount, on the basis that the original rent paid is no longer equal to those for similar apartments. Where the tenant does not agree, an arbitration procedure exists to determine the appropriate amount that can be charged. *Decree n° 2012-894* dated 20 July 2012 limits the increase in rent in certain cities.

The portions of the common charges that can be recovered from the tenant are determined by government decree. The tenant will be required to pay provisional common charges together with the rent, and an accounting will be made at the end of the property owner's association fiscal year to determine whether sufficient common charges have been contributed by the tenant or whether, more rarely, a reimbursement is due. The tenant cannot be required, for example, to contribute towards the payment of construction works on the building.

The tenant whose lease is subject to the 1989 law has a preemptive right to purchase the property if the landlord decides to sell. He must receive notice of the terms and conditions of sale and given an opportunity to match any conditions agreed.

In commercial leases, the tenant may choose not to renew the lease every three, six and nine years. The landlord may not refuse to renew after the ninth year, without paying an indemnity equal to the value of the goodwill of the business (*fonds de commerce*). While the landlord continues to own the property (the walls or *murs*) the commercial tenant is considered to own the "commercial property" (*droit au bail*) which is an element taken into consideration for the evaluation of the business and which may be sold to third parties under certain conditions. An arbitration procedure exists for disputed rent increases in commercial leases.

23.6 Successions and gifts

Applicable law and jurisdiction

France applies the law of the decedent's domicile at time of death to his estate, with the exception of any real estate located in France, to which French succession laws will apply. The courts of the decedent's last domicile have primary jurisdiction, but French courts will accept jurisdiction in estates where French property is present, or where there is a French national who is an heir that has reserved rights under the *Code civil* provisions (a child or parent of the decedent).

Fundamentals of the succession and gift/donation laws of France

The French system of inheritance provides for forced heirship and reserved rights to children of the decedent, in equal shares. If there are no children then parents have reserved rights if one or both survive the child, in quarter of their child's estate. The surviving spouse's rights will depend on whether there were common children from the marriage, or children from a previous relationship of the decedent. If there are children-in-common, the spouse has a right at his or her choice, in a life-estate (*usufruit*) of all the assets in the estate or of the outright ownership of ¼ of the assets. If there are children born from a relationship with a person other than the surviving spouse, then the spouse has a right to the ownership of ¼ of the estate.

Where there are no children, but there are parents surviving, the spouse receives ½ of the estate and if there are neither parents nor children, the entirety. There is an exception where the decedent has inherited non-fungible property from his parents that remains in the estate. In that case, the decedent's siblings or their children will have a right to inherit one-half.

Any reserved heir and the surviving spouse may request that the *usufruit* be transformed into a guaranteed annuity under court order. The spouse however retains rights on the matrimonial domicile, which cannot be substituted by an annuity.

The surviving spouse has a right to remain in rented premises for one year, with the rents being reimbursed by the heirs. Unless the decedent has stipulated otherwise in a will, the surviving spouse has a right to remain in the principal matrimonial domicile, if this is owned by the decedent or jointly by the spouses, and retains the right to use the furniture for the remainder of his life.

A basic principle in French succession law is that any agreement on a future succession is null and void (*pacte sur succession future*). This means that reserved heirs cannot validly waive their rights in a person's estate before the person dies. Exceptions to this rule will allow fiduciary mandates or powers of attorney to survive the death of the principal for a limited period of time.

The statutory portion or reserved right of an estate is ½ if there is one child, $^{2}/_{3}$ for two children, and ¾ if there are three or more children. If there are no children, then each surviving parent has a reserved right of ¼ of the estate. To the extent that there is any freely available portion of the estate (*quotité disponible*) after the reserved heir's portions, then the testator is free to bequeath that as he chooses, by will or by donation prior to death.

French wills can be made in three forms: handwritten (holographic), authentic or mystic. The holographic will must be entirely handwritten, signed and dated by the testator. No other signatures may appear, and thus it must not be witnessed. The authentic will is dictated by the testator to a notary in the presence of witnesses. Although the procedure for the authentic will is cumbersome, particularly for foreign testators, the authentic will is less likely to be contested. The mystic will consists of delivering a sealed envelope containing testamentary dispositions to the notary in front of witnesses and declaring it to be the last will. Foreign wills are valid in France if they are executed in a form either that is valid in the country of which the testator is a citizen, or that is valid in the country where they were executed. If the will contains a provision that is contrary to French public policy (for example if the will ignores the forced inheritance rules) the bequests that violate the French rules will be modified to conform to French public order, but the will is not considered *a priori* null.

The holographic will should be deposited with a notary who will register its existence at the central registry of wills, but this is not a requirement for validity.

Heirs are vested in the property at the death of the decedent. The estate may be accepted, refused or accepted with the benefit of an inventory. The inventory allows the beneficiary to determine the assets and liabilities. The beneficiary is liable for inheritance taxes.

Gifts may be made by notarial deed, or by simply turning over the gift (*donation manuelle*). Gifts that reduced the value of a reserved heir's share of an estate may be called back through judicial procedures. However, gifts *inter vivos* made to reserved heirs will be taken into account to determine the reserved portion to which they are entitled.

The French succession laws will not apply to shares of companies that own property in France, if the decedent is not a French domicile. This is why the use of French *sociétés civiles immobilières* is an important aspect of French estate planning for persons owning French property.

23.7 Taxes and charges

One-time taxes and charges on purchase and new constructions

The accurate calculation of taxes and notarial fees due at closing is complex and contains many variants. Only the principal aspects are referred to in this section, and in general with approximate percentages. The notary is charged with collecting the fees and capital gains tax due at closing and paying them to the tax administration. An indication of the calculations is found at *pap.fr/argent/calculettes/frais-de-notaire*

Real estate transfer taxes

The general cost of a transfer of property for value (*mutation à titre onéreux*) including notary's fees is approximately 7%. This cost is by custom paid by the buyer unless the price is stated in the offer to be *acte en main* in which case it is understood the seller will pay. Registration of a security on the property to guarantee repayment of financing will add from 0.6% to 1.5% approximately depending on the type of security – *privilège* or *hypothèque*.

Notary's fees are not negotiable generally, although on large transactions the fee portion of the 7% may be subject to negotiation.

Sales taxes (Value Added Tax, TVA)

If the property was built less than five years prior to the transfer, Value Added Tax (VAT, French TVA) in the amount of 20% will be due by the seller. The buyer will therefore pay reduced notarial fees and reduced registration costs in the order of 2.5%. The reduced registration taxes and TVA will also apply to the first resale within five years of completion of a building.

A complete renovation or restructuring of an existing building may make a resale of the property subject to TVA, and it is therefore important to verify with an expert prior to committing whether the sale is subject to TVA or to ordinary registration costs.

Real estate registration and notary charges

The breakdown of registration taxes due at transfer is as follows: on top of the 4.8% registration tax and stamp duty, there is a 0.1% fee due as the *salaire du conservateur* or payment to the director of the *Title Registration Office*. The notary's fees are determined by law and contain a fixed and a variable amount based on the sales price. From EUR 16,777 the variable is of 0.825% of the sales price, on which *TVA* at 20% is paid.

Annually recurring taxes and charges

Real estate tax

Property tax (taxe foncière)

The property tax (*taxe foncière*) is due by all owners of property, whether the land has a building on it or not. This is a local tax imposed by the municipality in which the property is situated and will therefore vary in accordance with the commune's budgets. The amount of the tax should be verified prior to completion. The tax is assessed on a percentage of rental value of the property. When property is transferred, the buyer will undertake to pay a proportion equal to the days of the current year in which he will own the property. The tax is assessed in October of every year for the current year and it is not customary to request the seller, who will receive the tax bill for the current year in any event, to hold back the portion of the property tax which he will owe. Normally, the seller will pay the property tax and request the notary to have the buyer reimburse the pro rata portion.

Exemptions can be obtained for newly completed buildings, and for persons older than 65 with very reduced income. If the property is rented, the owner pays the property tax, and not the tenant.

Occupancy tax (taxe d'habitation)

Occupancy tax is levied on furnished residential properties. The tax is due by whoever occupies the property on 1 January of any given year. Unlike the property tax, no adjustment is made for it at completion of a transfer of property. Tenants will be liable for the *taxe d'habitation*. Partial or total exemption is possible where the occupant's income and age qualify him.

Income tax (impôt sur le revenu)

For non-residents, and subject to applicable double taxation treaties, only French source income is taxed. Income tax declarations are due at the end of the month of February for French residents and at different times of the year for non-residents depending on their location. For property owners, there exists an obligation to file an income tax return in the event of ownership of a secondary residence, because the French *Tax Code* applies the same obligation to residents even where there is no taxable income. The requirement is however seldom applied to non-residents who do not have French source income.

Residents in countries not having an appropriate tax treaty with France may be subject to taxation on imputed income equal to three times the fair market rental value of the property they have at their disposal in France (whether through ownership, tenancy or gratuitous use), unless they can show that they have paid a certain percentage of tax on their French income.

France applies a progressive income tax rate that will vary according to the number of persons and dependants in the "fiscal household" (*foyer familial*). More details may be obtained on the website of the Ministry of Finance (*impots.gouv.fr*).

Schedule of income tax rates for 2014 on 2013 income

Taxable income	Tax rate
Under EUR 6011	0%
From EUR 6011 to EUR 11,991	5.5%
From EUR 11,991to EUR 26631	14%
From EUR 26,631 to EUR 71,397	30%
From EUR 71,397 to EUR 151,200	41%
Above EUR 151,200	45%
Above EUR 250,000 for single taxpayer EUR 500,000 for couple	Additional 3% to 4% contribution exceptionnelle

Gratuitous use of real estate does not raise income tax issues for the individual. It will however create inferred income when a company owns the property (this is not the case with *SCIs*), and therefore if for example a shareholder has free use of a house there is an obligation to file corporate income tax returns based on the property's fair market rental value.

Net wealth tax (impôt de solidarité sur la fortune, ISF)

Wealth tax rates and exemptions were modified several times in 2011 and 2012. A reduced wealth tax rate, introduced in 2011, was modified as one of the first acts of a newly elected government in 2012.

Wealth tax is assessed where a fiscal household has assets valued more than EUR 1.3 million. For non-residents, the wealth tax is only applicable to French assets, and not to certain types of French financial investments and collectibles. Assets outside of France are only subject to the wealth tax after the fifth year of residence in France. Wealth tax is otherwise incurred on resident's worldwide assets. It must be declared annually and must include a description of real and personal property including automobiles and boats.

Schedule of wealth tax rates for 2013

Amount	Tax rate
Less than EUR 800,000	0%
EUR 800,000 to EUR 1,300,000	0.50%
EUR 1,300,000 to EUR 2,570,000	0.70%
EUR 2,570,000 to EUR 5,000,000	1%
EUR 5,000,000 to EUR 10,000,000	1.25%
More than EUR 10,000,000	1.50%

Capital gains taxes

When property is sold, or when shares of a company holding for more than 50% of its French assets or French real estate are sold, capital gains tax is due (subject to the appropriate tax treaties). Taxation of property either directly or through companies was modified in 2011 and 2012.

All property containing a building held for more than 22 years is not subject to capital gains taxation. From 1 September 2013, a reduction of 6% of the net profit is applied in the calculation of capital gains from the 6th to the 21st year of ownership and of 4% on the 22nd year so that no capital gains tax is due after 22 years. After the fifth year of ownership, a lump sum of 15% of the price of acquisition is applied to take into account works on property, but if greater amounts have been spent, then the real amount can be applied provided sufficient proof is provided (original estimates, invoices and proof of payment).,

Capital gains tax is levied at 19% of the result for residents of the European Union, 33.33% for non-residents and 50% for residents of states deemed "non-cooperative" in tax matters. In 2012, the rate was increased by a further 15.5% for social charges with a reduction over 30 years rather than 22 years. Capital gains tax and the social charges are paid at closing.

Unbuilt lots with building permit possibilities will be exonerated from capital gains tax after 30 years of ownership.

For residents, sale of a principal residence is excluded from capital gains taxation, provided it has been held for more than five years. Former residents can qualify for this exemption provided they can prove tax residence in France prior to completion. The first sale by residents of their second residence when they do not own their principal residence is not subject to capital gain tax if the proceeds of the sale are used within 24 months to purchase a principal residence.

Sales for amounts of less than EUR 15,000 are exempted from taxation. Amounts paid in gift or inheritance tax can be included for the calculation of capital gains.

For sales by companies (other than SCIs held by individuals) subject to corporate income tax, whether French or foreign, the capital gains calculation will not include the reductions based on the holding. On the contrary, the company will be considered to have benefited from a 2% per year depreciation deduction, whether or not the property has been rented, and therefore the tax basis will be reduced by that amount for every year of ownership, causing an increase in tax liability. The tax rate is the normal corporate tax rate on profits of 33.33%.

Any non-resident individual (except French and Monegasque nationals residing in Monaco and selling their properties in the Var and in the Alpes-Maritimes) or company selling property in France will be required to name a tax representative which will guarantee payment of any additional capital gains tax for the statutory period of the years in which the sale took place plus three years. The tax representative (or *représentant fiscal*) must be resident in France. Fiscal representation is a business in France, and the charge on the transaction will vary, from 1% to 0.3% depending on the size of the transaction. The cost of fiscal representation is deductible in calculating capital gains tax.

Inheritance and gift taxes

Inheritance and gift tax rates are identical. Rates vary in accordance with the relationship of the donor and beneficiary. Gifts and bequests between unrelated persons are taxed at 60%. Gifts and bequests between parents and children and between spouses benefit from exclusions and graduated rates. Gift taxes may be reduced by 50% depending on the donor's age.

The inheritance tax declaration is due within six months of death, if the decedent was a French tax resident and within one year if he was a tax resident elsewhere. The tax should be paid at the same time, or if it is difficult to value the estate, then a provisional payment should be made. Late payment can incur penalties of 40% and interest (at 0.75% per month).

The parent and child exclusion is EUR 100,000. There is no inheritance tax between spouses and PACS partners, whether resident or non-resident. These exclusions are applicable to gifts made in 15 year intervals.

Tax rates for inheritances and gifts

Between parents and children	Tax rate
Under EUR 8,072	5%
EUR 8,072 to EUR 12,109	10%
EUR 12,109 to EUR 15,932	15%
EUR 15,932 to EUR 552,324	20%
EUR 552,324 to EUR 902,838	30%
EUR 902,838 to EUR 1,805,677	40%
More than EUR 1,805,677	45%

Siblings	Tax rate
Under EUR 15,932	0%
Up to EUR 24,430	35%
More than EUR 24,430	45%
Family members up to the 4th degree included	55%
Other family members and unrelated persons	60%

Gifts and bequests of French property to charitable institutions will only be exempt if the charitable institution qualifies as a "*fondation d'utilité publique*" under French law, or if a tax treaty on gifts and estates exists and allows the exemption. It should not be assumed that because the foreign charity is qualified as a not-for-profit charitable institution in its home country, the French tax authorities will accept to exempt the charitable donation from 60% taxation. Inheritance tax treaties exist however that provide for recognition of foreign charitable institutions under certain conditions.

Other taxes and charges

Taxes on vacant apartments (taxe sur les logements vacants)

A special tax *(taxe sur les logements vacants)* is due on apartments vacant for more than two years as of 1 January of each tax year in towns that have more than 200,000 inhabitants, where the government has determined that there is an imbalance between the high demand for lodging and the insufficient supply. Cities include Paris, Lille, Bordeaux, Toulouse, Lyon, Montpellier, Cannes-Grasse-Antibes and Nice. The tax is paid by the owner.

Incorrect (lower) statement of sale price on the sales agreement

Declaring a lower price for of a property transfer in a notarial transaction is a criminal offence. Sellers may sometimes request this in order to lower capital gains tax and wealth tax exposure, and buyers may be tempted to lower the registration costs of a transaction, although this will increase their capital gains tax exposure on resale.

There are serious inherent risks quite apart from the method of making the undeclared payments. Penalties can be very substantial (interest at 0.75% per month on the undeclared portion and tax penalties of 50% and more).

The transfer deed will contain a declaration that the parties have not dissimulated the price. Notaries that knowingly accept an act containing an understated price may face serious criminal charges and incarceration.

International taxation

Ownership of real estate in France will not *per se* subject a foreign resident individual to income taxation in France. However, ownership of property by a foreign company will entail in most cases the existence of a permanent establishment in France and the requirement to file accounts and corporate income tax returns (*impôts sur les sociétés*) beyond the annual declaration of the identity of the shareholders (Form 2746, due on 15 May every year).

Income from French real estate is generally subject to French taxation, and if the property is worth more than EUR 1,300,000 and is unencumbered by debt, it will subject the owner to wealth tax.

Capital gains will be taxed by the country where the real estate is situated, and thus France will impose its capital gains taxation on sales, which, where double taxation treaties exist, will give the taxpayer a credit for French tax paid on their own home country taxation.

Income from property ownership, whether rental income or capital gains income, is generally taxed by the country where the property is situated. There are important exceptions and the applicability of the treaties should be examined always on a case-by-case basis.

23.8 Immigration law and tax residence

Entry, residence and settlement of foreigners

Two types of residence permits exist in France, the *carte de séjour* (short term) and the *carte de résident* (long term). The basic principle is that any stay longer than three months requires a residence permit, unless a visa has been issued allowing stays up to six months. Citizens of the European Union and the European Economic Area do not need visas in order to obtain residence permits.

European Union and EEA citizens

Any European Union and EEA citizen wishing to reside more than three months in a member country must request a residence permit. The following documents will be required in France: a valid identity card or passport, three photos, recent proof of a residential address (lease and utility contracts), work contracts or statement of means of support. European Union citizens who are employed in France and wish to transfer their residence there can obtain a 10 year residence permit (*carte de résident*), if their home country provides a reciprocal right to do so. No work permit is required. The same applies for Swiss citizens.

Non-European Union citizens

Citizens of countries that are not members of the European Union must apply for a visa to reside in France on a short or long term basis. The application is made, with certain exceptions, at the French consulate nearest the person's last place of residence. Once in France, application must be made for a short term residence permit (*carte de séjour*). Application may be based on offered employment in France. A work permit will be required in order to accept employment.

The application for a *carte de séjour* is filed with the *Préfecture*, although some municipalities will accept the applications. The documents required are similar to those required of European Union citizens, but a birth certificate, proof of recent residence and a medical certificate will also be requested.

The *carte de séjour* is valid for one year and can be renewed every year. Unlike the carte de resident it does not imply authorization to work in France. The *carte de résident* will be granted only to certain categories of individuals: spouses of French citizens, after one year of marriage; *carte de séjour* holders after three continuous years of residence. It is valid for 10 years and will be automatically renewed. A long term residence permit allows the holder to work.

Tax residence

French tax laws do not make the distinction between residence and domicile known in the UK, US and some other countries. The basic tax text is the *Code général des impôts* and its annexes, including the *Livre des procédures fiscales* which is a procedural text for the collection and verification of tax liability.

The *Code général des impôts* lists three criteria for tax residence in France. An individual will be considered a tax resident if he or she fulfills any one of the three following criteria:

- France is his principal home and place of sojourn, which means the family's usual place of residence. A person can have only one *foyer fiscal* and this means that if the person is living abroad but his wife and children live in France, and there is no decree of separation and divorce, he may be considered a French tax resident. The law does not specify a particular number of days that will trigger tax residence, although stays of more than 183 days per year will be a strong indication of evidence of residence. If the person cannot prove tax residence in another country that will be a very strong indication of French tax residence regardless of the number of days spent on French soil

- France is the place where an individual practices his or her principal profession
- France is the center of the person's economic interest – that is the main investments are made in France or the majority of income earned is French source

If the French authorities consider an individual to be a French tax resident, taxation will apply on worldwide income. Wealth tax will apply on worldwide assets after the fifth year of tax residence. Inheritance tax will apply on the worldwide assets at death. Even where double taxation treaties may exclude certain income from French taxation, it must be reported.

International double taxation for residents of France

France has entered into many bilateral income tax treaties and fewer estate and gift tax treaties. These will generally include non-discrimination provisions, and may apply to citizens or to residents of either country concerned. Taxation will vary in accordance to the nature and origin of the income concerned. Most double taxation treaties will eliminate the risk that a foreign property owner will be subject to the tax on imputed income equal to three times the fair market value of property. Income from property ownership, whether rental income or capital gains income, is generally taxed by the country where the property is situated. There are important exceptions and the applicability of the treaties should be examined always on a case-by-case basis.

23.9 Checklist: Real estate in France

- Selection of the type of property sought:
  - residential or commercial
  - urban, agricultural, holiday home
  - speculative purchase, investment purchase, own use
- Determination of manner of purchase, whether through a company or in the individual's name

- Selection of appropriate real estate agent in accordance with the general market serviced (high end, middle range, low end, agricultural, holiday home, or commercial)
- Visits to real estate
- Selection of notary or lawyer
- Offer to purchase accompanied by 10% deposit made to the name of a notary, lawyer or agent
- Signature of a preliminary contract (*promesse* or *compromis*) binding the parties and formalizing the deposit
- If an apartment or property in a subdivision, review of the *règlement de copropriété* (*Condominium Statutes*) and annual running costs (charges) and works voted by the property owners that may be charged to new owners
- If company, same as above, but additional due diligence investigation of the company, the property and of its beneficial owners
- If works are required on the property, determination if the works will be authorized by the managing agent of the building and the *Mairie*, as well as the *Architecte des Bâtiments de France*
- Conclusion of the transfer of ownership at the notary and payment of the purchase price, fees and registration costs as applicable, following verification by the notary of the power of the buyer and seller to act, and of clear title on the property
- If property, registration of the transfer at the property registry (effected by the notary) and payment of registration fees within one month of signature

23.10 Bibliography

Achour Dominique / Coloos Bernard: L'investissement immobilier, Le Moniteur 1993

Andrier Thierry: Les Sociétés Civiles Immobilières, Guide Pratique, Litec 2002

Avella Natalie: The French Property Buyer's Handbook, Harriman House, 2004

Davey Charles: The Complete Guide to Buying Property in France: Buying, Renting, Letting and Selling, Kogan Page, London 2004

De Vries Andre: Buying a House in France. Where and How to Do It, from Normandy to The Côte d'Azur, Vacation Work, 2003

Dutilleul François / Magois Bernard: Acheter ou vendre un bien immobilier, Dalloz 2001

Everett David: Buying and Restoring Old Property in France 2nd edition, Robert Hale, 1999

Gobert-Chéramy Pierre: Fiscalité immobilière des non-résidents, Litec 2002

Hampshire David / Watson Jim: Buying a Home in France 2003-2004, 4th edition, Survival Books, 2003

Igoe Mark / Howell John: The Sunday Times Guide to Buying a Property in France, Cadogan Guides, London 2002

Juilhard Philippe: Fiscalité internationale du patrimoine, Editions Formation Entreprise 2003

Laredo Joe: Renovating & Maintaining Your French Home, Survival Books, 2004

Lindsey Alan S.: Concise Dictionary of House Building Terms (Arranged by Terms), French-English, English-French, Hadley Pager, 2001

Lindsey Alan S.: Glossary of French Legal Terms, French-English, English-French, Hadley Pager, 1999

Lindsey Alan S.: Glossary of House Purchase and Renovation Terms, French-English / English-French, Hadley Pager, 2000

Medlow Rowena: French Property Buying Guide 2003, Merricks Media, 2003

Michèle Auteuil: Guide de l'immobilier, Maxima 2002

Parkinson Charles: Taxation in France 2004, Pannell Kerr Forster, 2004

Philippe Pambo / Pierre Lotte: Les clés de l'immobilier: Financement, acquisition, gestion et défiscalisation, Sefi 1998

Mémento Pratique Francis Lefebvre, Editions Francis Lefebvre: Urbanisme Construction 2012-2013, Gestion Immobilière 2012-2013

Fiscal 2012, International Series: France: Business law, Taxation, Social law, English 3rd Edition

Lamy Droit Immobilier, Editions Lamy 2012

Doing Business in France (summaries of and citations to selected laws in business, employment, securities, taxation, and other areas). By the Law Firm Moquet Borde Dieux Geens & Associés, Simeon & Associés. First published in 1983 (M. Bender), 2 volumes, looseleaf, updated with revisions

24

Ireland

Republic of Ireland

by

Duncan Grehan

Duncan Grehan & Partners
Gainsboro House
24 Suffolk Street
Dublin 2
Ireland

Telephone: +353 1 677 90 78
Facsimile: +353 1 677 90 76

mail@duncangrehan.com
duncangrehan.com

Duncan Grehan was admitted to practice in Ireland 1980 amd leads a small Dublin law firm of five solicitors. He was educated at Trinity College Dublin (MA; LL.B.) and Max-Planck-Institut for Private International Law, Hamburg. He speaks English, German and some French. The law firm carries on a general practice and is particularly active in property law, probate and inheritance law, commercial and injury litigation, insolvency, debt collection and the enforcement of foreign court Judgements. The team are German speakers with a niche in advertising and marketing law.

24.1 Introduction

The laws relating to property in Ireland derived from the social and political upheavals during the 17th, 18th and 19th centuries, with constant tension existing between tenants and absentee English landlords, who had acquired substantial tracts of land in Ireland as a result of confiscations and resettlements. This resulted in legislation governing the relation of landlord and tenant, the effects of which are still felt in many areas of modern law and practice today.

A large section of the *Irish Constitution* of 1937 is devoted to the protection of property rights. The Irish courts have increasingly turned their attention to the protection afforded by the *Constitution* to private property rights in property disputes.

Article 43.1.2° of the 1937 *Constitution* states:

"The State accordingly guarantees to pass no law attempting to abolish the right of private ownership or the general right to transfer bequeath, and inherit property."

Irish property laws are based on the laws of the UK. The most significant difference is that the Irish Republic has a written *Constitution* which preserves the right of private ownership.

Real estate values in Ireland increased exponentially during the 1990's and 2000's due primarily to the uncontrolled availability of credit, causing a bubble which burst in 2008 leaving capital values reduced by an average of at least 50%. There is currently an investors market, although the market has recovered somewhat throughout 2013 and 2014.

24.2 Real estate ownership

Different forms and types of ownership

There are several different interests which someone may hold in a property. The two main types are freehold and leasehold. A freehold property is the premier form of land ownership in the Anglo-Saxon world as the ownership of the property is absolute. It is followed by leasehold property, where the lease is for a set amount of time. A person may also have a future interest in property, through a gift or inheritance, where they will not be in possession of the property until some point in the future. A life interest in a property is also possible where the person has a right of residence in a property for the duration of their life.

Property can belong to one or several people; it may also however be held jointly or in common with others. All questions in relation to such property are regulated by way of private contract between the owners. Where no agreement can be reached, an application can be made to the court for directions to resolve the dispute on the basis of the usual provisions. The contract will normally deal with questions such as the maintenance of the property, its insurance and liability issues. Where property is held jointly, on the death of one joint owner, the share of the deceased will go to his lawful successors. Where the property is owned by way of tenancy in common, on the death of one of the owners the share will pass to the other owners.

The most usual form of property in Ireland is individual family homes, although in urban areas apartments and apartment blocks of one or more storeys are also common. Apartments are usually owned by individuals who enjoy common rights in the common areas, such as the garden and corridors, together with the other owners in the block. These common areas are generally held by a limited liability company of which each apartment owner holds a share. Properties which are set up for single or multiple lettings are also commonplace. The Multi Unit Developments Act, 2011 regulates the ownership and management of the common areas of multi-unit developments such as apartment blocks, and provides for the setting up of owners' management companies to manage such areas.

Timesharing is very uncommon in Ireland. *EC Directive 94/47/EC* on the protection of buyers in respect of timeshare agreements has been adopted into Irish law by *Statutory Instrument No. 204 of 1997 (Contracts for Timesharing of Immovable Property)*. The contract must be in writing and like all contracts in Ireland must contain the names and addresses of the parties to the contract, the completion date, the names of the people to whom a withdrawal notice should be sent and the price to be paid. In addition, the buyer is entitled to a cooling off period of 10 days from the time he/she signs the contract.

Only the owner of a property or such persons permitted by him can build upon it. In all cases the land and buildings remain one unit. The system of building rights and tenancies under a building lease in the continental European meaning of the terms do not exist in Ireland.

Easements, charges, covenants, liens and mortgages

There are many different types of easements affecting property in Ireland, e.g. fishing rights, rights of way, shooting rights, mining and quarrying rights. These rights in Ireland are called "*incorporeal hereditaments*". The person who possesses these rights usually has no right to the possession of the land under which the right is exercised. The exercise of these rights is covered in the absence of a contract under the laws of landlord and tenancy. However, *incorporeal hereditaments* can be registered in the *Irish Property Registration Authority* (which is discussed in detail in the next section) thereby ensuring that a purchaser of lands in the State can be certain to what rights exist over lands he is acquiring. The *Land and Conveyancing Law Reform Act, 2009* introduced an obligation to register any such easements which were previously unregistered. Originally the deadline for such registration was 1 December 2012 after which any rights would lapse, however that has now been extended to 1 December 2021. Failure to register the easement within the deadline could result in the person losing their rights.

The most commonly used method of raising money to buy a building or property is by arranging a loan from a bank or lending institution. This loan is secured by way of mortgage over the assets whereby the property is charged to the financial institution.

Under the *Registration of Title Act, 1964*, registered land (land registry land) may be mortgaged only by the registered owners by means of a charge. A charge involves no transfer of ownership to the lender, ownership remains with the owner and the lender only acquires rights over the property.

With unregistered land (i.e. property registered in the *Registry of Deeds*) the position up to 2009 was that the property was conveyed, leased or assigned by the borrower to the lending institution subject to the borrower's right to obtain the title back and have it vested in him once the loan is repaid. However, under the *Land and Conveyancing Law Reform Act, 2009* that method of mortgaging a property was abolished and now the property may only be mortgaged by means of a charge. The ownership of the property stays with the borrower and the mortgage is simply a charge against the property. A standard document called "a housing loan mortgage" was created by the Irish Banking Federation and the Law Society of Ireland for use for all residential property mortgages.

It is common to see property being sold by borrowers even where the property is subject to an existing mortgage. Normally after the sale of the property, the existing loan is repaid as soon as possible after closing from the proceeds of the sale. The seller's solicitor usually gives a written undertaking to complete all matters and discharge the loan.

In general terms the mortgage document is simple. It recites the date the mortgage is created, the name of the borrower, the details of the property (the address or land registry folio number) and that the borrower has agreed to repay the loan. The document also contains an agreement by the borrower to allow the registration of the charge as a "burden" on the property. It also refers to the Irish Banking Federation General Housing Loan Mortgage Conditions which are usually given to borrowers with their mortgage application documents.

Protection of ownership, proof of ownership and registration

There are two systems of registration currently in operation in Ireland both of which now fall under the "umbrella" name of the *Property Registration Authority*. The Registry of Deeds was introduced under the *Registration of Deeds (Ireland) Act, 1707* and was established for the purpose of giving priority to registered deeds (generally the document which transfers ownership of the property) and for the prevention of fraud in dealing with the transfer of ownership of land. It is now more commonly used in dealing with titles in urban areas. It is important to note that the registration in the Registry of Deeds is not compulsory. Registration is not necessary to transfer the title. Documents other than the purchase deed can be registered in the registry such as a contract for sale or an option to buy land. The Registry of Deeds has no responsibility for the effectiveness of the deed or other documents being presented to it for registration. This remains the sole responsibility of the parties preparing the documents. Therefore the registry does not guarantee ownership or good title. Since 1970 there has been a gradual, ongoing and continuous programme of movement away from the older system of recording Deeds in the Registry of Deeds to the more modern and comprehensive 'title registration' system provided through the land registry. When a Registry of Deeds property is being transferred it is now compulsory to register it in the land registry (as described below).

The second system of registration in Ireland is the land registry and this system is basically the alternative registration system to the Registry of Deeds. The present land registry system operates under the *Registration of Title Act, 1964*.

The land registry system is based on the boundaries of the particular property in respect of which the title is registered being shown on an *Ordnance Survey* map. When the title is registered in the land registry a *Folio* is opened. The *Folio* is the actual register and is set out in three parts:

- Part 1 gives the details of the property and specifies the map reference. It also specifies the area of the land
- Part 2 shows the title and the ownership
- Part 3 shows the burdens on the property and nature of burdens or mortgages, rights of way and easements registered

The *Property Services Regulatory Authority* maintains a property price register (*propertypriceregister.ie*) which details the purchase price of all residential properties bought since 1 January 2010.

24.3 Purchase and sale of real estate

The sales agreement

The contract for the sale and purchase of a property is prepared by the solicitors acting for the seller. *The Law Society of Ireland* has produced a standard Contract for Sale which is used by all solicitors in Ireland. The contract is drafted by the solicitor for the seller and contains a standard set of 51 general conditions, together with any applicable special conditions and additional details of the transaction which are set out below.

The first part of the agreement lists the parties, followed by an agreement between the parties setting out their names and addresses, the purchase price, the deposit (standard practice is that this is 10% of the purchase price), the closing date (being the date of completion of the transaction) and the interest rate payable in the event of a late closing. The parties to the contract sign this part when they are executing it. It also contains a provision for the spouse of the seller to provide their consent if it is a family home which is being sold.

The next part of the agreement deals with what is called "particulars and tenure". Essentially this provides details of the property being sold, however these details are taken from the title documents to the property and are not merely the postal address or a statement such as "three bedroom detached house". If the property is held as leasehold or freehold property it will be stated at this point.

A document schedule follows on from the particulars and tenure and identifies a list of documents which will be produced by the seller to show their title to the property. Copies of these documents are generally forwarded with the contracts for sale to solicitors for the buyer and the originals are then handed over on closing.

The second section of the sales agreement deals with special conditions to the sale. The standard Law Society contract includes three special conditions dealing with definitions, amendments to the general conditions and VAT. Special conditions can also be included for any matter dealing with the transaction and could include a condition dealing with anything about the title to the property and any title documents, a condition saying that the contract is subject to the buyer obtaining loan approval, a condition stating that the property is subject to a mortgage and the seller will discharge the same prior to closing, or a condition stating what items in the property are included in the purchase price. There are dozens of different special conditions which can be included as every transaction will of course have differing requirements.

The final part of the agreement sets out the general conditions which, as stated above, are standard and included in every contract. The general conditions correspond with the usual procedures which are accepted throughout Ireland by solicitors which have been approved by the Law Society of Ireland in consultation with the Construction Industry Federation, as well as the Royal Institute of Architects of Ireland. If a seller wishes to exclude a general condition then a special condition must be included explaining this. The more important general conditions would include conditions relating to title and conditions which relate to Planning Permission. Planning Permission is an authorization from the local authority in the relevant area to build a property or to alter a property. It is discussed in further detail at a later stage. The conditions also place an obligation on the seller to provide warranties in respect of the title and any Planning Permissions applicable to the property.

While contracts do not have to be notarized the signature of both the seller and buyer must be witnessed when they are signing. The contracts are not binding until both parties have signed and one copy has been returned by the solicitor for the seller to the solicitor for the buyer.

Restrictions on sale and acquisition

Restrictions under family law and matrimonial property regime

Since the introduction of the *Family Home Protection Act, 1976* there have been significant restrictions on conveyancing transactions dealing with matrimonial property. The chief purpose of the Act was to protect one spouse's interest in the family home (at the time this was targeted mainly at protecting the interests of a wife). Section 3(1) of the Act provides that where a spouse, without the prior consent in writing of the other spouse, purports to convey any interest in the family home to any person except the other spouse, then subject to certain conditions stated in the Act the purported conveyance shall be void. This section was at a later time limited by the *Family Law Act 1995* to six years from the date of the conveyance. It effectively means that if the spouse of the seller does not provide written consent to the sale or transfer of the family home, then the transaction is void provided an objection is raised within six years of the date of execution of the deed of conveyance. Generally in conveyancing transactions. a statutory declaration evidencing the position with regard to the property signed and sworn by both spouses before a commissioner for oaths or practicing solicitor is produced at the closing. Even in the event that a seller is not married it is common practice for him to swear a declaration stating this. Even in the event that a couple has divorced and one of the spouses is now selling the property, it is standard practice for a statutory declaration to be obtained from the other spouse, stating that the property is not a family home.

By virtue of Section 28 of the *Civil Partnership* and *Certain Rights and Obligations of Cohabitants Act 2010*, the requirement of obtaining consent prior to any conveyance of the shared home also applies to civil partners. A civil partnership can be entered by a same sex couple by registration and has similar implications as a contract for marriage. Non-owner cohabitants (whether same sex or opposite sex) acquire rights under the Act after they have been living with their partner in an intimate relationship for five years, or two years where there is a child or children of the relationship. The Act allows a financially dependent cohabitant or a civil partner to apply to court for certain remedies, including maintenance, property or pension adjustment orders, or provision from the estate of a deceased cohabitant.

Options and rights of pre-emption

In extremely rare circumstances a lease may contain a *covenant* where the buyer has to offer the property to a third party such as his landlord at the market value when the lease expires. Such leases are. However. very rarely found in practice. Legislation is also in place in Ireland which allows a local authority to compulsorily acquire property for a variety of purposes such as road widening, river drainage or the supply of utilities such as electricity. Compensation is payable by the local authority to the party whose property is compulsorily acquired.

In business properties where a lease is held for more than five years there is an existing right to renew the tenancy and to have the lease for an additional period of five years or more.

Agricultural real estate

The *Land Act, 1965* formerly imposed certain restrictions on transactions involving agricultural property. However that relevant section was abolished in November 2005 and no consents are now required for the transfer of agricultural real estate.

Restrictions regarding acquisition of real estate by foreigners

Again the *Land Act, 1965* formerly placed certain restrictions on the acquisition of real estate by foreigners. There are now no restrictions on the acquisition of real estate by foreigners since the relevant section in the Act was abolished in November 2005.

Further important preconditions for buying real estate

Capacity and entitlement of the seller

Property can only be disposed of by the registered full owner or the beneficial owner. The beneficial owner is the person entitled to be legally in possession of the property or entitled to obtain the benefit of the property. However, the instrument of transfer in all cases must be completed by the legal owner. The legal owner is the person who is entitled to be registered as the full owner of a given property.

In the event of a death of the registered owner the beneficiaries of his/her estate are entitled to the value of the property. However, an executor named under an Irish will is the person empowered to administer the estate and carry out the testator's wishes. It is the executor who would generally sell the property or transfer it to the beneficiaries in accordance with the terms of the testator's wishes.

Recent Irish legislation has placed increased obligations on the directors of companies in respect of filing accounts and compliance with the *Companies Acts, 1963 – 2014*. In the event that they do not comply with Irish tax or *Companies Office* obligations they may be deleted from the *Irish Companies Office Register* and thereby the capacity of the company to dispose of any assets would be extinguished and all its assets are vested in the State.

In relation to persons of unsound mind an application may be made to the High Court to have the person made a ward of court. In the event that a person is made a ward of court his/her assets are then deemed to be vested in the person appointed by the court. This person then has the power of sale. A minor is a person under 18 years of age and does not have capacity to act. Minors cannot conclude binding contracts of purchase or sale of properties and cannot conclude other dealings with land. As they cannot own land themselves, usually their parents or guardian will act as trustees in the administration of the land on behalf of their children until they reach the age of 18 or until the trust is dissolved. Trustees have a special duty of care for the trust property, the beneficiaries of the trust and for transfers of the property in trust. There is no statutory limitation period within which court proceedings for compensation must be commenced where fraud or breach of trust is alleged.

Third-party claims and unpaid taxes

Irish taxes fall into certain categories – income taxes, inheritance and gift taxes (including capital acquisitions tax as dealt with later) and capital gains tax. Capital gains tax can be a charge on property if it is left unpaid and a buyer therefore must seek a capital gains tax clearance certificate prior to completing a purchase if the purchase price exceeds EUR 500,000. This is generally in the form of a certificate from the Revenue Commissioners. In the event of taxes remaining unpaid, the Revenue Commissioners can take out a Judgment Mortgage on the property in question by which the sale of the property will be restricted for so long as the Judgment Mortgage has not been satisfied. The tax authorities and other creditors can in addition arrange for the registration of an entry in the applicable Folio of the land registry, a *lis pendens*, to the effect that any further transactions may not be processed without placing the person in whose favor the entry is made on notice. In this way the creditor can ensure that the owner of the property does not sell it to third parties without notice to the creditor.

Other encumbrances which may affect real estate usually take the effect of a mortgage where property is charged to a financial institution and the charge is registered in the land registry or *Registry of Deeds* and therefore the buyer will be on notice of these charges. Under the *Local Government (Charges) Act 2009* sellers also had to ensure a property which is not the principal residence of its owner was liable for the *Non Principal Private Residence Charge* (EUR 200 per annum). In addition every property was liable for the Household Charge under the *Local Government (Household Charge) Act 2011* which is EUR 100 per annum.

Under the *Finance (Local Property Tax) Act, 2012* a self assessed property tax was introduced from May 2013 onwards. Each residential property in the State is liable for property tax at a rate of 0.18% of the value of the property within certain "value bands" set out in the Act. The introduction of *Local Property Tax* (LPT) also abolished the *Non Principal Private Residence Charge* and the *Household Charge* however penalties and interest for non payment of those charges prior to 2013 continue to accrue and can be significant.

Provisions for protecting the environment, nature and cultural heritage

Irish law in relation to the protection of the environment was significantly changed by the implementation of the *Environmental Impact Assessment Directive (85/337/EC)* in 1989. The regulations which implemented the directive, the *European Communities (Environmental Impact Assessment) Regulations 1989*, have been amended several times since and most recently in 2011. The *Environmental Protection Agency* was also introduced into Irish law in 1992. *The Environmental Protection Agency Act, 1992* also listed several types of development where an integrated pollution control license is required before the development can begin. This is not relevant for a private residence.

Access to relevant records and documents

Searches are generally carried out by the solicitors for the buyer on the transfer of an interest in the property. In order for the buyer to be protected as a bona fide buyer for value it is a requirement that they carry out reasonable enquiries in advance of the transaction. Generally searches come in the form of a land registry or *Registry of Deeds* search on the title of the property. They will disclose details about the current registered owner, any charges on the property and whether the property is leasehold or freehold. Other searches include a judgments search against the seller, a Companies Office search if the seller is a limited company, a bankruptcy search if the seller is an individual and a planning search against the property which will disclose the planning history of the property. Generally searches are carried out by a recognized firm of law searchers who then have a certain level of indemnity insurance in the event of any errors being made. Searches are generally made by the buyer on the day of closing.

Key points that a seller should consider

The main items the seller needs to be aware of have been discussed above. However, in the purchase contract the seller needs to ensure that the price is stated correctly and there is no room for ambiguity. The date of payment of the deposit and the date that the sale is due to close should be clearly stated on the contract. Particulars of the property should be well defined in the contract and if possible a map should be drawn up by a surveyor with the dimensions of the property clearly marked. This is particularly important where a seller is retaining some of the property. The seller should also ensure that prior to selling the property he has all the necessary consents to effect disposal of the property within the time limits set out in the contract.

The seller or his solicitor needs to ensure that they have good title to the property so that it is the seller's to sell. In addition the seller has, of course, to keep in mind his obligations under the *Family Home Protection Act, 1976* in relation to the consent of spouses. Tax clearance certificates for capital gains tax may also have to be obtained by the seller before the sale can close. He should also ensure that any outstanding mortgage on the property is discharged as soon as possible after the closing of the sale.

The execution of a real estate purchase transaction

The buyer should always ensure that they pay only a booking deposit until the title to the property has been examined and verified. The fees payable to the various professionals involved are a matter of negotiation between the purchase/seller and the professional.

The buyer should engage a suitably qualified architect or civil engineer to carry out a detailed survey of the property to measure up and ascertain the nature and extent of the boundaries. A full appraisal of the structural condition of the property and a full planning search to ensure the property complies with current planning legislation and permissions are necessary. It should also be ascertained if there is to be any future interference from statutory road widening or other local government plans. With commercial property it should be ascertained that the building complies with all statutory requirements such as fire safety standards. The buyer should then rely on his/her solicitor to diligently carry out all of the necessary legal examinations of the title in order to complete the transaction. Permissions to build the house are obtained from the relevant local authority. The only permission which is essential for the building of a residential house is the Planning Permission to build. Every county in Ireland has its own local authority, whereas larger cities and places will have one or more local authorities.

Powers of Attorney

A solicitor may, with the correct authorization, sign a contract for sale in trust for his client. This is commonplace where the client lives abroad and is not in a position to travel to Ireland to sign documentation. Written authorization must be provided by the client detailing any conditions under which the solicitor can sign the contract for the purchase including the agreed price for the sale of the property. The form of the power of attorney is usually determined by the lawyer for the buyer and the bank which is involved. If the client creates the power of attorney as his residence outside of Ireland, normally the power will be drafted by an Irish solicitor in English and will be agreed as valid and sufficient if it is executed by the client in accordance with the laws of his own country in the presence of a local lawyer who witnesses the client's signature. Alternatively, the client can execute the documentation in the presence of a competent staff member of the Irish Embassy.

Under the *Enduring Powers of Attorney Act, 1996* a person may also provide authorization as set out in the Act to their solicitor or some other person they trust which provides that person with authority to sign documents on their behalf and contract for the sale or purchase of property on their behalf. This is commonplace in the case of people who lack the mental capacity to conduct their own affairs.

Financing

Most buyers obtain finance for the acquisition of a property by arranging a loan from a bank or lending institution and securing that loan by way of a mortgage over the property which is to be acquired. The standard procedure is that the buyer raises 10% of the purchase price himself as a deposit on the property. The lending institution may then provide the balance subject, of course, to on own terms and conditions and to the buyer's status. The loan cheque is released on the day the purchase is to be completed and the mortgage registered on the property along with the buyer's interest in the *Property Registration Authority*. Prospective buyers should also note that there are strict rules under the *Criminal Justice Act, 1994* for opening bank accounts in Ireland, and these must be complied with.

Purchase through a company

Real estate can be purchased by companies based in Ireland or abroad without any restrictions. If the company is located outside of Ireland and acquires a property in Ireland, the seller's solicitors will require proof that the execution of the contract by the company is in accordance with the law of the country in which the company is incorporated. This is usually achieved by way of a letter of confirmation from a lawyer of the country where the company is located or incorporated.

If a buyer wishes to acquire a property via the use of a company be it a limited company, public company or a company limited by guarantee the following considerations are important to note:

1. Some stamp duty reliefs available to an individual are not available to a company
2. There will be an annual cost in respect of filing accounts and completing all necessary forms particularly to satisfy Irish company law requirements

The preferred form of incorporation in Ireland is a Private Limited Company (Ltd). Public Limited Companies (PLC) are less common.

If there will be several owners, or if personal liability is to be avoided, then a corporation or other legal person is the preferred structure.

Warranty claims

Warranty claims are dealt with in detail in the section dealing with new buildings. There is a time limit within which such claims can be brought and buyers or their lending institution may request a report by a bonded surveyor prior to completing the purchase of a second-hand property.

Because of the wide scale independent guarantee scheme (the *Home Bond Scheme*) for structural defects operative in Ireland, separate guarantees are seldom contracted or given. However, warranties are often sought in respect of commercial buildings which are not covered by the *Home Bond Scheme* and these are the same warranties which are used internationally. Claims under the *Home Bond Scheme* for major structural defects must be brought within 10 years of the scheme being put in place for the property in question and if it is a minor defect within two years of the scheme being put in place. Claims against a builder for breach of contract must be brought within six years of the date from which the defect in the property became apparent.

In a case where a seller has a less favorable right in a property to that of a third party, but this is only discovered following the completion of the purchase, the matter must be decided by a court. Compensation could then be claimed as a remedy. The court must estimate the loss arising and determine the amount of damages and possibly vacate the registration of the new owner in favor of the third party.

24.4 New construction, rebuilding and renovation

The procedure involved in purchasing a new house in Ireland differs significantly from the purchase of a second hand house. It may be necessary to agree on several contracts between the parties, such as the agreement in relation to the transfer of the property, the sale agreement, the contract with the builder and possibly contracts with an architect and a solicitor. Generally it is normal for the buyer to enter into two agreements with the builder; one an agreement for the transfer of the site and the other a building agreement whereby the buyer is in fact employing the builder to build a house on the site. Often the seller in transactions involving new buildings will be a limited company and this also has to be taken into consideration by prospective buyers and their legal advisors. There is a standard set of documents which are normally sent to solicitors for the buyer at the start of the transaction which cover the fact that it is a new building.

Zoning law and construction permits

Buyers of new buildings and their legal advisors need to be more aware of Irish planning law and *Building Regulations* then they would be if purchasing an older property. The chief planning legislation in *Ireland* is the *Local Government (Planning and Development) Act, 1963.* All developments commenced after 1 October 1964 had to firstly obtain Planning Permission, unless they came within the definition of an "exempted development". A development is defined by the Act as *"the carrying out of any works on, in or under land or the making of any material change in the use of any structures or other lands".* Section 4 of the Act then lists a number of categories of developments which are exempt from the obligation to apply for Planning Permission. It is not proposed to go into detail on the list of exempted developments here. However, it would include developments which affect only the interior of a structure (e.g. putting up a partition wall) or works which do not materially affect the external appearance of the structure and would not make it inconsistent with the character to other buildings in the same neighborhood.

When buying a new property it may be assumed that Planning Permission will have been obtained. A copy of the decision by the local authority to grant permission, a copy of the actual grant of permission and the grant of approval should be furnished to the buyer together with the contracts. Generally when a local authority is granting Planning Permission for a new development it will impose financial or other conditions on the builder which must be complied with. For example, a certain amount of money may have to be paid by the builder as a bond or lodgment to the local authority before the roads and services in the development are taken into the charge of the local authority. Solicitors for the buyer will generally seek a letter from the local authority confirming that all financial conditions have been complied with. In the case of a new building the payments due to be made to the local authority may take some time and it is common practice for the local authority to state that all due payments have been made to date. The builder can then provide an indemnity to the buyer for any payments that remain owing.

The other chief legislation which affects new buildings in Ireland is the *Building Control Act, 1990.* This Act was followed by a series of regulations made under it and the Act and regulations are commonly known as the *Building Regulations.* The *Building Regulations* were targeted at improving the regulation of building standards and took account of the various issues at the time each regulation was made, such as access for the disabled in recent years or energy conservation in the past. Essentially, the Regulations regulate building works and provide minimum standards for design, construction, workmanship and materials used in the construction. The regulations are seen as a code of practice for building. Briefly they deal with matters such as structure, fire, site preparation, materials, sound, ventilation, hygiene, drainage and waste disposal, items that produce heat, stairs/ramps, energy conservation and access for the disabled. Essentially all works for the erection of buildings or the structural changes or change of use to buildings which commenced after 1 June 1992 must comply with the *Building Control Act.* The date for compliance with the various regulations made thereafter depends on the date the regulation was made.

In keeping with the *Planning Acts* certain classes of development are of course exempt. Again it is not proposed to go into these in detail. However, they include works commenced before 1 June 1992, alterations to buildings which do not affect structural or fire safety aspects and even building such as lighthouses. If a development is subject to the regulations a commencement notice must be submitted to the building control authority not less than 14 days and not more than 28 days before commencement of the development. Again there are certain exemptions to this rule. The Regulations also provide for the need to apply for a fire safety certificate before work can commence on the erection of a building. It must be accompanied by a detailed plan showing compliance with the *Fire Regulations* and state what the building is to be used for. It is an offence for a developer to carry out works without first obtaining a fire certificate. It should be noted that a building which is to be used as a domestic dwelling is exempt. However, if the development consists of a block of apartments, then a fire safety certificate will be required.

Under the *Building Regulations 1997 to 2012*, a Disability Access Certificate is required for new buildings other than dwelling houses and also for certain works on buildings such as shops, hotels, day care centres etc. since 1 January 2010. It is a certificate of compliance in respect of the requirements of the Building Regulations and its purpose is to ensure that non-domestic buildings and apartments are easily accessible to people with disabilities. This certificate is issued by the local Planning Authority and has to be obtained before the Commencement Notice is issued and before any works can start on the development.

There are strict penalties for developers who fail to comply with the *Building Regulations*. There is a five year time limit from completion of the development after which no enforcement notice can be served.

Architect's contract and building contract

In practice it is usual that the buyer of a new house will employ an architect to check that all Planning Permission conditions which relate to the house, including future developments and projects in the area and the structure of the house, are to a standard satisfactory to the buyer. The architect will normally assume a supervisory function during the course of the building project and will prepare a *snag list* of works and repairs at the completion of the building. Usually the architects for both the builder and for the buyer will meet to ensure that the matter completes.

The builder will normally build the house according to the plans of the buyer's architect, or the buyer will purchase the house which has been built according to the drawings of the builder. The architect will enter into a contract with the buyer in a standard form approved by the *Royal Institute of Architects in Ireland.*

The main two documents involved in the purchase of a new house are, as stated above, the contract of sale for the site and the building agreement. These will normally be executed at the same time at the start of the project. None of the contracts will be entered on any public register as this is a matter of private contract between the parties. The buyer will be one party to the contract and it will be necessary then to distinguish the seller of the land from the builder of the house. The builder may receive stage payments during the course of the building and the seller will be paid on completion of the house.

The contract for sale is in the form of the *Law Society Standard Contract for Sale*. It contains information relating to the physical location of the site, measurements, dimensions and boundaries and the title of the site. Normally this would include reference to a map drawn up by the site engineer or architect or a map approved by the *Property Registration Authority* in Ireland. A documents schedule in the contract will normally list the documents from which the builder deduces title, i.e. it will show how he is owner of the land. The contract then contains a list of general and special conditions which differ somewhat from those used for a second hand house.

The second document, the building agreement, is again a standard document drafted jointly by the *Law Society* of *Ireland* and the *Construction Industry Federation*. It is not used for second hand houses and is therefore widely believed to be the most important document in transactions relating to new houses. Briefly the agreement contains a covenant by the builder to build and finish the house in question to a certain standard and in keeping with the plans and specifications furnished originally to the buyer. Generally buyers employ their own architect to ensure that the house is being built in accordance with the plans and specifications. The agreement normally also provides a time by which the building work is to be completed together with details of how payment is to be made. The standard practice in Ireland is for 10% of the purchase price to be paid on signing the contracts and the balance to be paid on completion. Normally buyers pay a booking deposit to the auctioneer and the balance of the 10% is then paid when signing the contract and building agreement. The agreement then contains a set of general conditions which include conditions as to liability for any defects. When purchasing a new house the buyer is also provided with a *booklet of title* which is an indexed book containing documents evidencing the builder's ownership of the property. This is usually furnished with the contracts. An average *booklet of title* will contain documents such as:

- *Property Registration Authority* documents showing the registered owner
- Extracts from the memorandum and articles of association of the seller company which lists the powers of the company and in this case shows that they are authorized under their memorandum and articles of association to sell the company
- A certificate of incorporation of the company
- Planning Permission documentation which should show the approval from the local authority for the development
- Architects certificates which show that the development complies with all relevant regulations (which are discussed below)
- A letter from the local authority dealing with financial conditions which may be listed in the Planning Permission

The *booklet of title* will also contain various other documents such as the floor area certificate, as mentioned above, and an indemnity from the builder which states that he will construct the roads and footpaths in the development and maintain any services. A "document under seal" refers to a document which has the seal of a company on it. It would apply for example when a company is signing a *Deed of Transfer* for a new property to a buyer and the seal of the company is placed on the document.

In general it is now standard practice for buyers of a new property to seek a Certificate of Compliance with the planning acts and *Building Regulations*. This is generally provided by an architect, surveyor or engineer. It will generally specify the qualifications of the person providing the certificate, give details of the inspection of the building in question, confirm that the building is in compliance with planning acts and *Building Regulations* and be signed and dated personally by the person providing the certificate.

Completion of construction and formalities

On completion of the purchase of a new building there are a number of documents provided by the seller which might not be included if it were the sale of a second hand property. Most of these, such as the indemnity under seal in relation to financial conditions imposed by the Planning Permission have been discussed above. The final documents include a structural defects guarantee under seal and a *Home Bond* agreement which deal with protection for the buyer in the event of any future problems. No confirmation from the local authority is necessary and the buyer will normally accept a certificate from an architect certifying that the property has been built in compliance with *Planning Permission* and *Building Regulations*.

Deficiencies and warranty claims regarding new construction

The first protection for the buyer is generally contained in the conditions attached to the sales agreement. *General Condition 36 (a)* is a warranty that the Planning Permission in relation to the property is fully in order and states that where applicable, Planning Permission and building bye-law approval or building control approval have been obtained and all conditions have been complied with. Any planning irregularities must be disclosed in the special conditions of the contract. If any planning irregularities were not disclosed here it provides the buyer with a possible right of action against the seller for breach of warranty.

In the event of a buyer subsequently discovering structural defects in a property he has a number of options he may take to pursue an action against the builder. He may take an action in common law against the builder, an action against the builder for breach of contract and may go to the *National House Building Guarantee Company* pursuant to a *Home Bond* agreement.

Under common law the buyer of a new building would be entitled to have the building built in a proper workmanlike manner, using good and proper materials and the property should be fit for human habitation. Generally these rights are found in the building agreement signed at the start of the transaction. If the builder is found to be in breach of his obligations under the agreement the buyer may sue him under common law for negligence. There is a time limit of six years from the date the defect becomes apparent before which proceedings must be brought. In addition to an action under common law a buyer could also take an action for breach of contract against the builder as he failed to abide by the terms of the building agreement. The building agreement generally contains warranties to rectify any structural defects within a certain time limit. Obviously if this is not done then the warranty and therefore the contract is breached. In practice most such actions are actually a combination of both common law and breach of contract claims.

Finally a buyer may also have a right of action by virtue of what is known as the *Home Bond* scheme. The majority of builders in Ireland register with a company called the *National House Building Guarantee Company Limited*. This company provides a scheme known as the *Home Bond Scheme* which provides a guarantee against major structural defects for a period of 10 years and against water and smoke penetration for the first two years of the warranty period. If there are any major structural defects in the building then the builder is obliged to remedy them.

In addition, buyers should be aware that there are financial limits on the amount recoverable under the scheme. There is a limit of EUR 200,000 in relation to any one dwelling and EUR 2 million in relation to any one builder. Obviously these limits could fall far short of what would be necessary to repair major structural defects particularly where a builder has a number of houses with the same defects.

24.5 Rental and tenancy

Rental and leasing contracts

Renting property has become increasingly popular in Ireland in recent years as the cost of purchasing property has spiraled. However tenancies and leasing property have been part of Irish law in some form since the plantations of parts of Ireland by the English in the 17th Century. As the economy in Ireland was largely based on agriculture, at that point large estates were generally sub-divided between tenant farmers who had very little remedy against the landlords in the event of any dispute. It was not until the latter half of the 19th Century and the early 20th Century that legislation such as the *Landlord and Tenant Law (Amendment) Act (Ireland) 1860* (known as *Deasy's Act*) and the *Landlord and Tenant Act, 1931* was introduced to protect the position of the tenant.

Most tenancies in Ireland fall into two broad categories: a tenancy for a fixed term and a tenancy for a periodic term or year to year. Section 4 of *Deasy's Act* requires leases and tenancies to be in writing if they are to create a legal relationship of landlord and tenant. It is not uncommon in the Irish market to find leases which run for 999 years.

Residential tenancies can occur for either fixed terms or periodic terms though they are more commonly for short periods of time e.g. three years or one year. There is a standard form of letting agreement which is approved by the *Law Society of Ireland* which incorporates standard terms and any particular terms agreed between the parties. Generally, residential letting agreements would contain the name and address of both parties, the term of the tenancy, the agreed amount of rent and details of exactly how it is to be paid together with details of the value of the contents of the property.

The *Private Residential Tenancies Board* (PRTB) was established in 2004 by virtue of the *Residential Tenancies Act, 2004* to provide for a national tenancy registration system and for a dispute resolution mechanism between landlords and tenants. Landlords must apply to register the tenancy with the Board and penalties apply if he fails to do so. However, certain dwellings are exempt such as business premises, holiday lets or a dwelling let by or to a public authority. The Register is available for inspection to the public but the identity of landlord and tenant and the rent payable are not disclosed. Both landlords and tenants can avail of the dispute resolution service offered by the PRTB. It is to be noted however, that landlords who failed to register the tenancy have no entitlement to that service. Following a complaint to the PRTB the case will be dealt with by either a mediator or adjudicator before it comes to a tribunal hearing. The Board will then make a *Determination Order* which can, in case of non-compliance, be enforced through the courts.

Regulations on protection of tenants and rent control

In recent years the protection for tenants has grown and this has been reflected in standard letting agreements. However Section 12 of the *Housing (Private Rented Dwellings) Act, 1982* states that the landlord is deemed responsible for any repairs for which the tenant is not liable. In addition, the *Housing Act, 1966* states that a condition can be implied in a lease to state that at the commencement of the lease the house is fit for human habitation and the landlord will keep it that way throughout the duration of the lease. The *Housing Miscellaneous Provisions Act, 1992* contains provisions to state that it shall be the duty of the landlord of a house to ensure that the house complies with the requirements of any regulations made by the relevant Government department. If, for example, a law is passed which requires a particular standard for sanitary equipment in all rental accommodation, then it would be for the landlord to ensure that this regulation is complied with. Generally residential letting agreements contain covenants by the landlord to maintain the property in good condition and repair. Residential letting agreements can only be terminated on agreement between the tenant and the landlord, at the end of the duration of the letting agreement or if the tenant is in breach of one of the covenants of the letting agreement.

The *Landlord and Tenant (Amendment) Act 1980* as amended by the *Landlord and Tenant (Amendment) Act, 1994* also contains provisions to protect the tenant. The tenant has the right to compensation for improvements to the house and the Act specifically states that the tenant shall be compensated for every improvement by whomsoever made which adds to the letting value of the property and is in keeping with its character. The tenant may serve an improvement notice on the landlord in advance of the work and attach a statement of the proposed works, an estimate by an architect or surveyor and a copy of any necessary Planning Permission.

24.6 Succession and gifts

Applicable law and jurisdiction

A will executed in Ireland can dispose of property abroad and likewise, a foreign will can dispose of property in Ireland. The determination of the applicable law is dependent on the nature of the estate left by the deceased. Immovables (that is, land) are generally governed by the Irish rule of private international law that the applicable law is the law of the country where the property is situated i.e. *lex situs*. This is a common rule of private international law. The construction of that part of a will dealing with movables (like money), is generally governed by the domicile of the deceased, i.e. *lex domicilii*.

When a person dies intestate outside of the Republic of Ireland, leaving moveable property in Ireland, the applicable law is that of the domicile of the deceased. If the property is immovable, then Irish law applies. The Irish law is most complex in its definitions of "domicile" and local advice should be obtained to ensure validity and enforceability.

Fundamentals of the succession and gift/donation laws of Ireland

Inheritance law in Ireland is governed principally by the *Succession Act, 1965,* which also regulates gifts made by or to a person during their lifetime. These gifts are then taken into account by the administrator of the estate of the deceased person and by Irish tax law.

It is a comprehensive body of law and it is important to note that it sets out strict requirements of formality and capacity for the making of a will. If these requirements are not adhered the will can be rendered invalid. It is important therefore that anyone purchasing property in Ireland, particularly if they are foreign nationals, should have a will drafted by an Irish lawyer. A person is considered to have died testate if they made a valid will and intestate if they did not make a will or made an invalid will.

The Act also provides a number of important legal rights such as the right of the surviving spouse to a share of the estate regardless of whether the deceased died testate or intestate. Section 111 of the Act states that the surviving spouse of a deceased person with no children shall have a legal right to one half of the deceased's estate, or in the event that the deceased person had children, the surviving spouse shall have a legal right to one third of the estate. Significantly, it does not provide for any legal share for children. However, under Section 117 of the Act, if a child feels the parent did not fulfill their moral duty by making proper provision for them in the will they can make an application to the High Court to make such provision out of the deceased's estate as it sees fit. The court will take into account the circumstances of the child, the view that a prudent parent would take and the position of any other children in the family before reaching any decision on these matters.

Estates are normally administrated by executors named in the will of the deceased or in the case of intestacy the next of kin. The court may act as executor if no one else is available. The Estate is then administered subject to the approval of the Probate Court. Applications to the Probate court for a *Grant of Probate* allowing administration of the estate are normally made by Irish solicitors.

Beneficiaries under a will have certain tax free thresholds, as discussed below, within which no tax is payable. The administrator will normally collect details of gifts or inheritances received by the beneficiaries in the past as the amount of these will be added to their current benefit when assessing whether the beneficiary has exceeded the applicable threshold. In addition, an administrator will collect details of gifts made by the deceased person as these are also taken into account in the administration of the estate.

24.7 Taxes and charges

One-time taxes and charges on purchase

Real estate transfer taxes

There are a number of one-time charges in the case of acquisition or construction of a property. Again it must be pointed out that Irish tax laws can change on an annual basis and local legal advice should be sought. The position here applies as of October 2012. The main cost which arises for most buyers of property is that of stamp duty, which is payable to the Irish *Revenue Commissioner*. Stamp duty is, in essence, a tax on the legal documents used in the transfer of property. There are varying rates which can apply depending on the type of property involved.

The first distinction which applies in relation to stamp duty is between residential and non-residential property. Residential property is defined as a building or part of a building which at the date the deed is signed is used or is suitable for use as a dwelling. If a buyer buys a site with no building on it then it is classified as non-residential property even if it is possible to build on that land and at a later date a house is built on it.

The stamp duty rate for non-residential property is 2% on the full amount of the consideration.

The stamp duty rates for residential property are 1% on the first EUR 1 million of the consideration and 2% on the excess over EUR 1 million.

A number of stamp duty reliefs have been abolished such as the first time buyer relief. However, the transfer of property between spouses remains exempt from stamp duty. The new flat rates simplify the calculation of stamp duty significantly.

Stamp duty is a major consideration for any prospective buyer and should always be taken into account when considering a purchase price.

Sales tax (value added tax)

Value added tax (VAT) is charged at two rates in Ireland. The general rate is 23%, however in certain circumstances, e.g. for new houses, it is 13.5%. VAT is generally included in the purchase price quoted for a house, apartment or building unless a clause is set out in the special conditions to the contrary. It is not payable on second hand houses or on a site only.

Real estate registration and notary charges

There are of course other charges which buyers must be aware of when acquiring a new property. These include charges for the land registry and charges for the *Registry of Deeds*. The difference between the land registry and *Registry of Deeds* has been discussed above and the costs between the two vary. Both offices have a set list of fees which are chargeable when documents are being registered. As of 1 December 2012 the fees chargeable in the land registry for registration of ownership of a second hand house are as follows:

Price	Fee
Not in excess of EUR 50,000	EUR 400
In excess of EUR 50,000 and not in excess of EUR 200,000	EUR 600
In excess of EUR 200,000 and not in excess of EUR 400,000	EUR 700
In excess of EUR 400,000	EUR 800

First time registration in the Property Registration Authority of a property which was formerly registered in the Registry of Deeds costs EUR 130 regardless of the price of the property. Registration of a mortgage on a property costs EUR 175. Registration of ownership of any property or a mortgage in the *Registry of Deeds* costs EUR 50. There are also of course solicitor's costs which would generally be approximately 1% of the purchase price and fees for searches on the title of the property as discussed previously which costs about EUR 70 - EUR 100.

Annually recurring taxes and charges

Local Property Tax

Local Property Tax was introduced under the *Finance (Local Property Tax) Act, 2012* and formally commenced in May 2013. It is an annual tax on residential property with payment due in advance each November for the calendar year ahead (for example in November 2014, property owners will be asked to discharge the tax due for 2015). The tax is charged at 0.18% of the property value within certain bands set out in the Act. The values are placed in bands of EUR 50,000 and the tax is chargeable at the mid point of that band. For example if the value of the property is EUR 290,000 the relevant band would be EUR 250,000 - EUR 300,000 and the 0.18% is chargeable at the mid point being EUR 275,000.

Other Real estate tax

Residential Property Tax was an annual tax chargeable on the market value of residential property owned and occupied on the valuation date of 5 April annually at the rate of 1.5% on the excess of the value over a certain threshold. This tax was abolished in 1997. However, residential property tax clearance certificates may still be required from a seller if the value of the property exceeded the thresholds and they were in occupation of the property prior to 1997.

Income tax

Income tax is chargeable on all income arising in the State to individuals, partnerships and unincorporated bodies. In the case of individuals anyone who is resident, ordinarily resident or domiciled in Ireland is liable to income tax in respect of their total income wherever arising. An individual who is not resident in Ireland is normally liable to income tax in respect of income arising to them in Ireland only. The definitions of residence and domicile are discussed at a later stage. As of October 2014 the applicable rate of income tax for a single person is 20% on the first EUR 33,800 earned and 40% on the balance. Each person has a tax credit which for a single person is EUR 1,650 and this is deductible from the total amount of income tax payable per year. There are also a number of other exemptions and reliefs which may apply depending on individual circumstances.

In the case of real estate, income tax is only paid on any income deriving from property and therefore if there is no income deriving from the property or if the property is used personally then there is no tax payable on it.

Net wealth tax

There is no net wealth tax in Ireland.

Capital gains tax

Capital gains tax is chargeable on the gains arising on the disposal of assets after April 6 1974. A disposal of an asset includes a transfer by sale, exchange or gift. Again all persons who are resident or ordinarily resident in Ireland for a year of assessment are liable to the tax in respect of chargeable gains accrued in that year on the disposal of assets. This applies regardless of where the assets are situated. The tax is calculated on the chargeable gain which is the amount of the consideration reduced by what is called "deductible expenditure", i.e. the cost of acquisition and any improvements to the property. A system of indexation relief is used to adjust the deductible expenditure with the latest rates of inflation.

Once the chargeable gain is calculated the tax is charged at the rate of 30% for most disposals or 40% in certain situations. The 40% rate only applies in the case of gains on the disposal of foreign life assurance policies and/or an interest in certain offshore funds. Every other gain is chargeable at the rate of 20%. As with other Irish taxes there are certain exemptions and reliefs which apply. The first EUR 1,270 of any gain by an individual in a year of assessment is exempt and a gain on a dwelling house which has been used as the individual's principal private residence is also exempt.

Local advice should be sought for details of other exemptions or reliefs which may apply. Capital gains tax is payable by all persons whether they are resident in Ireland or not and whether they are Irish citizens or not. Those affected by capital gains tax should therefore look carefully at any double taxation issues which may arise.

Inheritance and gift taxes

Inheritances and gifts are taxable in Ireland by virtue of the *Capital Acquisitions Tax Act, 1976*. Section 4 of the Act charges gift tax on the taxable value of every taxable gift received on or after 28 February 1974 and Section 10 of the Act charges inheritance tax on the taxable value of every taxable inheritance received by a successor where the date of the inheritance is on or after 1 April 1975. It should be pointed out that Irish tax laws and rates change on an annual basis and the position reflected here is applicable up to October 2014.

The 1976 Act states that a person is deemed to take a gift or an inheritance where under any disposition they become beneficially entitled in possession either on a death (inheritance) or otherwise than on a death (gift) to any benefit otherwise than for full consideration in money or monies worth paid by that person. The taxable value of the disposition is arrived at by deducting from the market value of the property comprised in the gift or inheritance permissible debts and encumbrances and any consideration paid by the beneficiary. The market value is defined in Section 15 of the 1976 Act as the price which, in the opinion of the *Revenue Commissioners*, the property would fetch if sold on the open market on the date on which it is to be valued in such a manner and subject to such conditions as might reasonably be calculated to obtain the best price for the seller.

The Act also goes on to provide definitions for a taxable gift and a taxable inheritance. A taxable gift is the entire property comprised in the gift where at the date of disposition the disponer is resident or ordinarily resident in Ireland, or the beneficiary is resident or ordinarily resident in Ireland, or the property comprised in the gift/inheritance is situated in Ireland. The significance of this is that even if the gift consists of property outside of Ireland or partly of property outside of Ireland and partly of property in Ireland the entire gift is still chargeable to gift tax if the criteria are fulfilled.

A taxable inheritance is also the entire inheritance where the disponer is resident or ordinarily resident in Ireland at the date of the disposition under which the successor (i.e. the person receiving the inheritance) takes the inheritance. The date of the disposition is the date of the death of the disponer.

Inheritance and gift tax are chargeable at the rate of 30% on the market value of the property comprised in the gift. It should be noted that deductions may be made by the recipient for any consideration paid by them or any debts which have to be paid off before they receive the gift or inheritance. In the case of an inheritance these might be debts owed by the deceased, funeral expenses or solicitor's fees. Before the tax is calculated however there are a number of exemptions and thresholds which should be considered.

There are three tax-free thresholds within which tax is not chargeable. The threshold that a recipient falls into depends on their relationship with the donor. Again it must be pointed out that Irish tax rates can be adjusted annually and the threshold amounts can change accordingly. As of October 2014, the thresholds are as follows:

Class A: EUR 225,000:

This threshold applies to any gift or inheritance received where the beneficiary is a parent, a child or stepchild of the donor regardless of their age. It also applies where the beneficiary is a grandchild of the donor and the parent of the said grandchild is deceased.

Class B: EUR 30,150:

This threshold applies to any gift or inheritance received where the beneficiary is a brother or sister, nephew or niece.

Class C: EUR 15,075:

This applies to any beneficiary who does not come under either Class A or Class B.

These thresholds apply to all gifts or inheritances received by a recipient over a number of years and all gifts or inheritances received in that period are added together for the purposes of calculating the tax payable. It should also be noted that any gifts or inheritances between spouses are completely exempt from capital acquisitions tax. There are a number of exemptions which all beneficiaries should be aware of. Inheritances for public or charitable purposes, inheritances of a dwelling house taken after 1 December 1999 provided certain conditions are fulfilled, and inheritances of items which are of national, scientific or artistic interest are all exempt. There are also a number of exemptions from gift tax including the first EUR 1,250 of all gifts taken by the donee in any calendar year taken after 1 December 1999, a gift of a dwelling house taken again after 1 December 1999 in certain conditions, payments of support or maintenance, national lottery winnings and gifts for charitable or public purposes. No capital acquisition tax is payable where the beneficiary is a spouse of the donor.

There are also a number of reliefs which can apply in relation to agricultural or business property. Section 19 of the *Capital Acquisitions Tax Act,*

1976 states that if a gift or inheritance consists of agricultural property at the date of the gift or inheritance and at the later valuation date and is taken or inherited by someone who is on the valuation date a farmer as set out in the act, the market value of the agricultural property is replaced by the agricultural value in arriving at the taxable value of the benefit. In practice, this reduces the value of the gift or inheritance by about 90% and leaves it with a taxable value of 10% of its market value.

The *Finance Act, 1994* also introduced a relief in respect of business property comprised in a benefit taken by a beneficiary. Since the *Finance Act 1997* this has been a reduction of 90% in respect of a benefit taken on or after 23 January 1997. As distinct from agricultural relief in business relief it is the taxable value of the relevant business property which obtains business relief. Business property is defined by the 1994 Act as property consisting of a business (this includes a partnership or sole trader). It should be noted that one single asset out of a business on its own would not qualify for the relief.

There are a number of other criteria which must be fulfilled in order to qualify for both agricultural and business relief e.g. the property must be kept or if sold must be replaced by other agricultural/business property for a period of six years from the date of the gift/inheritance. There are also some smaller reliefs available to beneficiaries such as dwelling house relief (where the beneficiary occupied the dwelling house for three years prior to the gift/inheritance and does not have an interest in any other dwelling house).

There are also a number of smaller inheritance taxes such as probate tax which is discussed in further detail in the next section.

Other taxes and charges

Probate tax, which was charged at 2% on the value of the estate of the deceased person, was abolished in December 2000. However, it still applies for deaths prior to December 2000. Miscellaneous outlays not listed above include the fees for having a document such as a statutory declaration sworn (generally EUR 10 for each document). A buyer may also have to pay for a surveyor to examine the house if requested by the financial institution providing the mortgage.

Incorrect (lower) statement of sale price on the sales agreement

The practice of stating one price on a contract and then actually paying a higher price is illegal in Ireland and constitutes a revenue fraud. Any such contract would be void and both parties could face legal proceedings for fraud.

International taxation

Ireland has a comprehensive system of double taxation agreements in place with over 40 countries and is currently in negotiation with several more to implement agreements. Agreements in place include agreements with Australia, Austria, Canada, Germany, Japan, Switzerland, the UK and the US. The agreements generally cover income tax, corporation tax and capital gains tax. An agreement regarding capital gains tax is particularly important for foreign property owners who sell a property in Ireland and may be liable to pay capital gains tax on the profit. Where a double taxation agreement is in place and a person is paying tax in both countries, then that person has the facility to reclaim the tax paid in one country as a credit. Where a double taxation agreement does not exist with a particular country there are provisions within Irish tax laws which allow certain reliefs against Irish tax for tax that is paid in another country in respect of certain types of income.

24.8 Immigration law and tax residence

Entry, residence and settlement of foreigners

Entry into Ireland is open to any individual with a valid passport and in certain cases with a valid Irish visa. A list of countries whose citizens do not require a visa to enter Ireland was set out in the *Aliens (Visas) Order, 2003*. All countries within the European Union are included on the list as are most other European countries. The Order also lists countries whose citizens must have a visa to enter Ireland. There is an agreement in place between the EU and Switzerland which states that since 1 June 2002 Swiss citizens have the same rights as EU citizens with regard to living and working in Ireland.

Citizens of a European Union country can, of course, work and travel freely within the EU. All other persons, including citizens of non-EU states, whether they require a visa or not, may stay in Ireland for 90 days from arrival. Any person wishing to stay longer than the 90 days must register with the *Garda National Immigration Bureau* and show that they fall into one of three categories – student, worker with a legal work permit or retired person. Irish citizenship is available through birth, marriage to an Irish citizen or naturalization where a person has lived in Ireland for more than five years.

A work permit must be obtained for citizens from outside the European Union and European Economic Area who wish to enter employment here. The countries within the European Economic Area are the EU countries together with Norway, Iceland and Liechtenstein. Switzerland has a separate agreement with Ireland whereby its citizens can work here without the need for a permit. Only an employer can apply for a work permit to employ a person from a non-EU country or the EEA and the permit may last for up to one year. Therefore a person from an EEA or non-EU country must have an offer of employment in Ireland before they can obtain a work permit. Once they have a work permit it will then also be possible for them to obtain other work.

Tax residence

Residence for tax purposes is determined by the number of days an individual is present in Ireland during that tax year. Individuals will be deemed resident in Ireland for tax purposes if they spend 183 days or more in Ireland in one tax year. If they spend 280 days or more in

Ireland in two consecutive tax years they will be deemed resident in Ireland for tax purposes only in the second year. A day is counted when the individual is present in Ireland at midnight.

An individual may also choose to be deemed resident in Ireland for a tax year if they can show to the Irish *Revenue Commissioners* that they will be present in Ireland for the required 183 days in the next tax year. Once an individual is deemed resident in Ireland then that individual is liable to pay tax on his/her world-wide income to the Irish *Revenue Commissioners* during that year, subject however to the exceptions outlined below.

The term "ordinarily resident" which has been used in previous sections refers to an individual who is resident in Ireland as described above for three consecutive years. They will then be deemed as "ordinarily resident" in the fourth year. The individual must then be non-resident in Ireland for three years before they lose the classification of "ordinarily resident".

A person can be resident but not domiciled in Ireland for tax purposes if Ireland is not where they maintain their permanent home and if they are only in Ireland for a temporary period. Generally foreign employees working on a contract in Ireland may be living in Ireland but will not be domiciled in Ireland. Irish income tax applies only to Irish source income, i.e. money earned from working in Ireland. Any other income that a person earns outside Ireland is on a remittance basis and must be constructively remitted to Ireland in order for Irish income tax to be charged on it.

International double taxation for residents of Ireland

Ireland has a comprehensive network of double taxation agreements with over 40 countries. If an individual is tax resident in Ireland and has income which is taxable in another country as well, then, if there is a double taxation agreement in force, the Irish tax authorities will agree with the other country to exempt the income from tax in one country or allow credit in the other country for the tax paid to be in Ireland. Any income earned by the individual prior to becoming tax resident in Ireland will not be liable to tax if it was earned prior to the beginning of that tax year.

24.9 Checklist: Real estate in Ireland

- Prospective buyers should look at all hidden costs of buying a house before paying a booking deposit e.g. what stamp duty is payable, solicitors fees, registration fees, the cost of having a surveyor examine the house
- Prospective sellers should look at any taxes they might have to pay such as capital gains tax if they have not been living in the property for sale
- Auctioneers fees should also be agreed by the seller with his auctioneer before he places the house on the market
- The seller should also ensure that he will be able to pay the money owing on his mortgage from the sale price of the house. His solicitor should get a statement of the figures owing from the mortgage company
- Contracts and title documents to the property are inspected by the buyer's solicitors
- The buyer signs the contracts and pays a deposit of 10% of the purchase price
- Contracts and deposit cheque are forwarded to the solicitors for the seller
- One part of the contract signed by both parties must be returned to solicitors for the buyer
- A Draft *Deed of Transfer* and *Objections and Requisitions on Title* (a long document raising a series of questions about the property) are sent to the solicitors for the seller
- Replies to the *Objections and Requisitions* must be received and an appointment will then be made between the solicitors for both parties to close the transaction
- Law searches must be ordered to ensure there are no charges registered against the property and searches are also made against the seller
- Any stamp duty payable must be discharged within 44 days of the date of execution of the deed
- The buyer's interest in the property is registered by lodging the appropriate documents in the *Property Registration Authority*

24.10 Bibliography

Brady, James C.: Succession Law in Ireland, Butterworths, Dublin 1995

Corrigan, Kieran: Revenue Law in Ireland (Volumes 1 & 2), Round Hall Sweet & Maxwell, Dublin 2000

Laffoy, Mary: Irish Conveyancing Precedents, Butterworths Dublin 2007

Lyall, Andrew: Land Law in Ireland, Round Hall Sweet & Maxwell, Dublin 2010

Wylie, J.C.: Irish Land Law, Butterworths, Dublin 2010

Wylie, J.C.: Landlord & Tenant Law, Butterworths, Dublin 1998

25

Italy

Republic of Italy
Repubblica Italiana

by

Doris Reichel

Studio Legale Reichel
Via Roncaglia 14
20146 Milan
Italy

Telephone: +39 02 498 68 81
Facsimile: +39 02 498 42 98

dreichel@avvocato-reichel.com
avvocato-reichel.com

Doris Reichel founded The Reichel Law Firm of Milan in 1990. Through the years it has grown and established a name for itself, and now it counts three branches in Switzerland, Germany and Italy. The team, which over time has effectively combined a strong passion for law with that of different European languages, has become a firm and important point of reference for a multinational clientele thanks to their knowledge and use of various legal systems. The team's activity is heavily oriented toward real estate law, especially as regards litigation in a European framework, but also commercial, corporate, family, separation, divorce, information technology, bankruptcy, taxation, administrative, insurance, industrial, criminal law and much more.

25.1 Introduction

Italy is a country of important cultural and economic contrasts, if one takes into consideration firstly the northern parts, which belong to Europe's richest areas, and then, on the other hand, southern Italy and Sicily, which belong to Europe's least developed regions. As different as the mentality of people from northern and southern Italy, is the history of each of the Italian regions. The northern Italian regions were seized by Austrian conquerors. Naples was temporarily occupied by the French, while the south of Italy and Sicily had to endure Spanish occupation for some time. Italy has only existed within its present borders since its reunification that started in 1861 and lasted until 1919. Relics from those times of occupation can still be seen today. The regions of South Tyrol and Friaul-Julish-Venetia adopted the land register system introduced by Austria, differing from the system of other regions, which followed the principle of the person-related connection to the property.

After the monarchy was abolished in 1946 by referendum and the constitution was introduced in 1947, Italy became a democracy which transferred the legislative authority to the parliament as well as the authorization of control, to the executive authority. In accordance with the Italian constitution, the national territory is divided into regions, provinces and communities. Altogether, there are 20 regions with each one having its own regulations. The majority of the population speaks Italian or one of its dialects. In some valleys of Piedmont, the population speaks French as a language on a par with Italian, and in South Tyrol, German is spoken as an equivalent language to Italian.

25.2 Real estate ownership

Different forms and types of ownership

Sole ownership

The Italian law provides for several forms of ownership concerning real estate. Firstly, there is the form of sole property, in which the owner has the exclusive and comprehensive right to a property which has been recorded exactly in the cadastral and land register. Sole ownership can be a house, a plot of land or a condominium apartment.

Jointly owned property

Secondly, the property may be jointly owned, where two persons become co-owners of a property, for example, through inheritance. In this case, neither of the owners exclusively possesses the sole property, and the rights of each individual person refer to the whole property. Each one of the co-owners may enjoy the whole property or even parts of it but the other co-owners enjoy the same rights. In cases of a jointly owned property, a proportional share is assigned to each one of the co-owners of which he can dispose.

Apartment property – condominium

Thirdly, a special form of jointly owned property in Italy is the *condominio*. Usually, this is a certain number of different apartment units in one complex, each single apartment being the sole property of its owner. In addition to the sole ownership, the ownership comprises a co-ownership in the areas outside the said property. These areas can be the following: the soil on which the building stands, exterior walls, roof, stairways, entrance door or entrance gate, courtyard, gatekeeper's office or apartment, or central heating; and also any equipment serving a common use (elevator, drain pipes, electricity, gas, and water pipelines including the junctions into the separate apartment units). Thus, each co-owner can use the jointly owned property without having the possibility of changing its purpose. The common courtyard, for example, may not be used by a single co-owner to lay out a vegetable garden. In the administration of a jointly owned property, the costs of it will be apportioned on a "pro-rata" basis, referred to each share. This apportionment is effected by thousandth. As soon as there are more than 10 co-owners, the law stipulates that a *regolamento* (condominium regime) be established. That is why it is advisable when acquiring an apartment in an Italian *condominio*, to have a look at the *regolamento*. It will provide interesting information on the regulation of the common areas, restriction of usbility, apportionment of costs, as well as the rights and duties of individual co-owners. It can be important to inspect the *regolamento* where, for example, one intends to transform an apartment which, at present, is listed in the land register as living space into an office space. If the *regolamento* explicitly prohibits this, the intended alteration of the purpose of the apartment can only be realized by means of changing the *regolamento*, and that will require the consent of all co-owners.

Right to build

The *diritto di superficie* (right to build) is of little importance in Italy. It concerns the right to construct a building on the soil of a third party, the building remaining the property of the builder. The property of the third party, i.e. the plot of land the building was constructed on, remains unaffected. This leads to a severance of the property of the ground with the building constructed on it. The right to build is established by contract, which can either fix an exact period of time or provide that it will remain indefinitely.

Time sharing

There are still no specific regulations regarding time sharing in Italy. Time sharing is where a property owner gives a third party a right to a part of the real estate. This right gives the third party the possibility to use or to lease out that part of the real estate for a fixed period of time. The conveyance of time sharing is done by way of a notary deed.

Easements, charges, covenants, liens and mortgages

Under the Italian legal system, apart from property rights being established by law, no further additional property rights can be created. There exists a kind of *numerus clausus* of property rights. The property rights can be classified in terms of usufructuary property rights, including hereditary tenancy, real estate easements and usufruct, as well as a second group including the rights belonging to the collateral property rights, e.g. lien and mortgage. The effective creation of a property right requires written form, and the property rights must be registered in the land register to be asserted against any third parties.

With regards to easements, a connection between two different real estates is presupposed, whereas with usufructuary property rights, a direct connection between two legal entities related to the same real estate is presupposed. All property rights expire after a statutory period, unless the use has been extended by another 20 years (this concerns the deadline of acquisition by adverse possession).

Usufruct

The usufructuary has the right to use the property of somebody else, respecting, however, its economic purpose. As a rule, the usufruct is, unless otherwise defined, restricted to the lifetime of the usufructuary. The ownership of a right encumbered by usufruct limits the owner in such a way that he cannot draw financial advantages from the property until the usufruct becomes extinct. He only has the bare ownership of the property.

The usufruct can be acquired by law (e.g. usufruct of parents on goods of their minor children), acquired by adverse possession or by declaration of intent. The usufructuary can dispose of his right without ownership rights being affected. If a usufructuary leases the property on which he has usufruct to a third party, the tenancy contract will continue in case of the usufructuary's death for the term of the lease, at most, however, for five years from the death of the usufructuary.

Right of residence and utilization

The right of residence and utilization are two special cases of usufruct. Utilization is the right to use a property and possibly enjoy the usufruct of it, whereas the right to reside is the right to use real estate for one's own needs and the needs of one's family. The right to reside limits the holder to residing there, without changing the purpose of use. Neither the utilization nor the right to reside can be assigned or leased to another, since personal use is an essential element of them both and is expressly prohibited by law (see Article 1024 of the *Codice Civile).*

Easements

In an easement, a property (the serving property) is burdened to the advantage of another property (the dominating property). The following principles apply: the easement imposes only a negative obligation on the owner of the serving property. An easement can only be issued in the case of two different properties with two different owners. To create the easement, the properties do not necessarily have to be neighboring, but one property does draw an advantage from the other with regard to the object of the easement. The easement is created by legal transaction or acquired by adverse possession, by law or by court decision. If the owner of one property must by law grant an easement to the owner of the other property, the judgment of the court is required to create the property right. If the easement is based on a title establishing a right, the needs of the dominating property shall burden the serving property as little as possible. There are also statutory easements which are normally created to improve living conditions - for example, water pipes and electricity poles.

Liens on real estate / mortgage

A mortgage can be justified by law, by court order or by a legal transaction. A mortgage by law is created in the following cases: in favor of the seller of a property, if the purchase price was not paid in full at the time of the transfer of ownership (when the sales contract is concluded before the notary public, the parties expressly affirm having fully paid or received the purchase price); in favor of the heirs, the partners and other co-proprietors for the compensation payment for the real estates allocated to the co-proprietors; in favor of the State for property of a convicted person, pursuant to provisions of the penal code.

A mortgage ordered by the court is registered if a judgment regarding the payment of an amount has been made. This mortgage can still be registered even if the judgment is not yet final. Should the final judgment not confirm the preliminary judgment, the one in whose favor the mortgage was registered would have to agree to its cancellation and may be liable to pay damages.

A voluntary mortgage can be obtained either by way of a legal transaction or via a unilateral declaration of the person wanting to establish the mortgage. It will be registered at the property register of the town, in which the property is located. One has to show the document which is the basis for the permission to register the mortgage. The registration is valid for 20 years and has to be renewed after the term has expired. After expiration of the said term, the creditor will have to re-register the mortgage. However he may lose his original and perhaps advantageous rank.

The deletion of a mortgage will be effected if there are statutory reasons for deletion and in any case by the declaration of consent for the deletion by the mortgage holder. If the consent is refused, it can be obtained from the court.

Protection of ownership, proof of ownership and registration

The proof of ownership of real estate is obtainable from the registers of the Italian land registry, the *Conservatoria dei Registri Immobiliari.* The legal system recognizes, with the exception of the regions *South Tyrol* and *Friaul-Julish-Venetia*, a person-related connection when transferring real estate. Under this system, the land registers refer to persons involved in the transfer. Therefore, it only shows which transfers have taken place from one person to the other and not which transfers have taken place on a specific piece of real estate. Accordingly under the Italian system, the chronological priority of the entry and the continuity of the ownership register, as well as its declaratory character, are important. Because of the continuity of the ownership register and to ensure that one obtains property from the rightful owner, one would have to retrace all transfers of the past 20 years, since this would be the period for acquisition by adverse possession. The main real estate registers observing the principle of public disclosure are the following:

- The general register of application
- The register of transfers
- The register of entries
- The register of remarks

25.3 Purchase and sale of real estate

The sales agreement

When purchasing real estate in Italy, as a rule two contracts must be concluded: the preliminary contract and the notarized sales contract.

The preliminary contract is a contract which binds both parties by law to effect the subsequent transfer of ownership on the terms and conditions negotiated in the contract. In the preliminary contract, the contracting parties promise to observe and fulfill certain obligations, which have to be performed by the date of the notarized contract. An essential part of the preliminary contract is the stipulation of the purchase price and the terms of its payment. Another important aspect is the down payment, usually to be paid upon conclusion of the preliminary contract, which, depending on the contract, can have different legal effects especially where there is no notarized contract. In this case, the confirming down payment, known as *caparra (*Article 1385 of the *Codice Civile),* will be considered as a contractual penalty against the party breaching the contract. If the buyer prevents the transfer of ownership, he is prohibited from getting the *caparra* back. If the seller does not act in accordance with the terms of the contract, he will have to pay twice this amount to the purchaser, firstly as reimbursement of the confirming payment and secondly as a penalty.

The preliminary contract needs to be in writing. It is neither necessary nor usual to conclude this contract in the presence of a notary public. It is a private legal contract binding both parties and in which the actually paid purchase price is stipulated. The ownership is transferred upon the execution of the notarized contract. The notarized contract has priority over all other preceding contracts, including the preliminary contract, unless the preliminary contract contains a clause stating otherwise. The notarized contract can be affected as a public document or as a private document before the notary public.

To secure his rights, the buyer can have the preliminary contract entered in the land register. This ensures that the real estate cannot be sold twice. The registration of the preliminary contract provides protection for one year, if the parties have agreed on a deadline for the conclusion of the notarized contract. Otherwise, the protection will last for up to three years. However, private preliminary contracts can only be entered in the register if they are made by a notary public or if the parties' signatures have been certified by the notary public. The registration makes public the purchase price stated in the preliminary contract and so cannot be changed in the actual notarized contract. The disadvantage of this process is the costs. The registration itself causes a fixed tax of EUR 200 to be paid. If there was a *caparra* (confirming down payment) agreed upon, a tax of 0.5% is levied on this amount. If, however, an *acconto* (payment on account) was arranged, then a 3% tax is levied.

In Italy, it used to be quite common that a lower amount than the actual purchasing price was being stated in the notarized contract of transfer of property (under-recording). This was done to lower the calculated real estate transfer taxes, as the notarized purchase price was the basis for the calculation of the taxes to be paid. Although per the amendment of 2006 the transfer taxation is calculated no longer on the purchase price, but on the "cadastral value", illegal under-recording is still found (see 25.7 below).

With the signature on the notarized contract, the ownership passes from the seller to the buyer. The effective transfer of ownership does not require entry in the Italian land registry. The entry has a declaratory character and is used to make public a change of ownership so as to assert it against third parties. Should, therefore, a third party who is not the owner of the property, be registered by mistake as the owner, he could effectively transfer the ownership rights to a *bona fide* third party by notarized contract. However, this will be practically impossible, since he cannot furnish the necessary documentation with regard to the real estate. The notary public of the *bona fide* third party must satisfy himself as to the history of the property and as to the preceding transfers of ownership. Thus the notary public will notice that the non-entitled third party is not the owner of the real estate. It is different when the actual owner of the real estate sells it through a notarized contract, but his buyer does not make public the transfer of ownership. In this case, the seller named in the register as owner of the property could still sell it to a third party. If the ownership is transferred to a third party, the third party will have obtained the ownership legitimately and cannot be asked to return the real estate. Therefore, the buyer who obtained ownership in the first place would have to ask for compensation from the seller.

Restrictions on sale and acquisition

Restrictions under family law and matrimonial property regime

In general, in Italy, married couples are subject to the *comunione legale dei beni*, the system of community of property, which applies to the purchase of real estate. This means that both spouses obtain co-ownership of the real estate, even if the notarized contract is only signed by one of them. It is different if they declare in front of a notary public that the purchase is to be made exclusively from the personal funds of the purchasing spouse and that the other spouse waives his/her right to become a co-owner. If separation of property was agreed upon marriage, only the purchasing spouse can obtain sole ownership of the property. If community of property was optionally agreed upon marriage, the spouses will obtain ownership of the real estate in equal shares.

According to Italian law, it is not always necessary to have the consent of one's spouse when selling the property which is used as the family's main place of residence. However, consent is necessary if the real estate was purchased under the system of community of property and the spouse has become a co-owner under Italian law. Where there is separation of a property, i.e. that the property used as main place of residence is owned by one spouse only, the latter can generally dispose of it without restrictions. A problem could arise if during marital separation proceedings, a judge awards the real estate to the non-owning spouse as his/her residence.

If the buyer of the real estate is a foreigner, then the law governing the personal relationship between the spouses is applicable to questions of property rights. The couple can, however, stipulate that their property rights shall be regulated according to the law of the state of which at least one spouse is a citizen. The choice of matrimonial property regime will be valid if it is applicable to the law of the place chosen or pursuant to the law of the place where the agreement on the matrimonial property regime was concluded. The law also states that the personal relationship is governed by the law of the state of which both spouses are citizens. If they have different citizenships or more than one citizenship, their personal relationship is governed by the law of the state where the couple has their marital residence.

Options and pre-emption right

The contractual right of pre-emption means that a person will have, in case of sale, the contractual right to buy the real estate on the same conditions and price as another buyer would do.

If the owner wants to sell his real estate which is rented to a tenant, he has to consider the tenant's right of pre-emption to buy the said real estate. For example, if the owner wishes to sell an apartment, it has to be offered to the tenant at the same price as it would be offered to third parties. If the owner has offered it to the tenant and the tenant has refused to buy the apartment because the price is too high and the owner then sells it to a third party, the owner has to be careful that the official purchase price is not below that that was offered to the tenant. The owner has to have offered the apartment to the tenant at the same price as stated in the notarized contract. If the price in the notarized contract is below the price offered to the tenant, a legal right of repurchase can be exercised by the tenant. He can exercise this right of repurchase within one year from conclusion of the notarized contract. For commercial tenants, a compensation of 24 monthly rentals is to be paid in addition to their moving out. This right is embodied in the law. If the tenant exercises his right of repurchase, the new buyer will lose the property just purchased. The buyer is only entitled to the amount stated in the notarized contract. If the buyer has paid more than the price stipulated in the notarized contract, he may not be reimbursed the full purchase price, especially where the seller is not willing or not able to reimburse the difference.

In any case, the buyer of a property should ascertain whether such a right of repurchase was offered to the tenant and was refused by him before moving out of the property. The same applies, of course, if he is still living in the property. The buyer must, in particular, make sure that in the notarized contract, no purchase price is mentioned which is lower than that offered to the tenant.

It is possible that a tenant, who is informed about the ongoing negotiations between the owner and the potential buyer, agrees first of all to leave the property with compensation, and then, despite his agreement, does not move out and tries to get more compensation from the buyer. Neither the seller nor the buyer can do anything about this. In the interest of both parties, the property should be offered to the tenant so that all parties know where they stand after the term has expired. Where the tenant has not been formally informed about his right of pre-emption and is able to exercise it within 30 days from service of the offer, he could insist on his right of pre-emption. If he has not been formally offered the property or has not effectively waived his right, he could exercise his right of repurchase within one year after the conclusion of the notarized contract. The tenant cannot be forced out of the property if he relies on his right of pre-emption. If the buyer buys a rented property, it is his responsibility to get rid of the tenant. However, it should be mentioned that a property with a tenant may be about 20% to 30% cheaper than one without a tenant.

The right of pre-emption by the government may exist if the property to be sold is classified as particularly valuable for historical or cultural reasons. In this case and in order to prevent expropriation, the authorities need to be informed of the owner's intention to sell. The government must be given the opportunity to decide whether or not to purchase the property. The decision must be made within two months.

Agricultural real estate

There are no legal limitations or restrictions with regard to the acquisition of agricultural real estate.

In cases where agricultural land is being sold, the adjacent neighbors or leaseholders, (*azienda agricola* or *coltivatore diretto)* cultivating the areas to be sold have a right of pre-emption. In order to find out whether a neighbor is interested in exercising his right of pre-emption, the preliminary contract must officially be sent to him and he must be given 30 days from the date he received the contract to exercise his right. If the neighbor is not interested in buying the agricultural land, the notarized contract can be concluded after the 30 day term has expired, without running the risk of the right of repurchase.

Restrictions regarding acquisition of real estate by foreigners

According to the principle of reciprocity, foreigners can in general acquire real estate in Italy, establish companies and manage them with the same rights that Italians would have in the foreigner's home country, unless any special legal restrictions exist or the principle of reciprocity would prohibit it. The principle of reciprocity means that the foreigner is only allowed the same rights in Italy as those of an Italian in the foreigner's home country. These rights are pursuant to civil law and are not of a political nature.

In cases of the purchase of real estate in Italy by members of EU countries, the principle of reciprocity is given through the membership of the European Union. Due to Article 52 of the *Treaty of Rome*, the principle of reciprocity is no longer relevant. Therefore, there are no restrictions for European nationals and legal entities concerning the purchase of real estate.

The principle of reciprocity has to be taken into account when the purchasers of the property are non-EU nationals. It is different if a non-EU national takes residence (*residenza)* in Italy in the proper form. In this case, the foreign national has equal status with Italian nationals.

However, the property can only be resold or residence abandoned after a period of five years so as to prevent residence being established only as a way to obtain a tax-preferred status for the acquisition of the property and/or as an attempt to evade the principle of reciprocity.

Further important preconditions for buying real estate

Capacity to act and entitlement of the seller

Pursuant to Article 2 of the *Codice Civile*, the capacity to act is the ability to conduct legal transactions. The capacity to act is reached when a person comes of age (18 years). Minors or persons whose business activities are restricted by court order do not possess such capacity to act and cannot fully conduct legal transactions.

The entitlement of the seller to conclude the contract results from his status as owner of the real estate. A seller is capable to act if he is not restricted by his legal competence. The seller might be so restricted if he is not yet of age to perform the sale. In this case, the permission of his legal representative or an order of the judge of a guardianship court is needed. Another reason for not being able to sell a property would be the loss of legal competence through a penal conviction.

If, on the other hand, the seller is a legal entity, it needs to be shown that its legal representative is authorized and entitled to conduct the sale of the property. A legal representative may be restricted from acting on behalf of the company where the company becomes bankrupt. Then, the ability to conduct legal transactions on behalf of the company may be transferred to the receiver.

Third-party claims and unpaid taxes

Risks due to encumbrances with third-party rights and unpaid taxes can be quite extensive. This will not always be because of malicious non-disclosure on the part of the seller. Quite often, it has simply been forgotten or overlooked by him as agreements have often been concluded by the previous owners and the neighbors. Such encumbrances can be, for example, rights of way, pipelines, obligations not to build or restrictions on building, etc. If the real estate is burdened by an encumbrance, it normally means a decrease in value of the real estate or even a restriction on the planned future use.

Unpaid taxes are connected to each specific property and survive a sale. Therefore, new owners acquire the acquire the tax liability, and responsibility to pay the outstanding amounts. The legal basis for this is derived from the *Testo Unico delle Imposte sul Reddito.* Taxes on real estate have material character, which means that they are not connected to persons, and accordingly stay with the property. In order for the buyer to be protected, a declaration needs to be put into the notarized contract that all taxes have been paid up to the date of transfer.

Provisions for protecting the environment, nature and cultural heritage

To protect the environment and heritage of Italy, the Italian legislator has created a number of legal restrictions on the building of property, for example: protection of forests; declarations that the property is in an area of landslides, which would make building on the property impossible; regulations by authorities or local authorities having allocated a certain area to a certain use (agricultural areas, green belts); restrictions on real estate near to roads or cemeteries; restrictions on real estate near to an airport; restrictions on real estate near to railroad tracks; and restrictions on real estate falling under the *bellezze naturali*, i.e. an area of outstanding natural beauty, which makes building on it impossible or extremely difficult.

The examples listed above are restrictions on the building on real estate situated in areas which are protected in the public interest. These restrictions are to prevent any interference with nature and the landscape, which could change their character irretrievably. An unrestricted building could have a detrimental effect on the environment and thus destroy the balance of nature, for example if buildings are constructed too near to rivers, lakes or mountain slopes. The same restrictions apply to the protection of historical monuments. Constructions should not interfere with cultural monuments in such a way as to change or destroy their character. Examples are the buildings constructed without permission in the *Valley of the Temples* in Sicily.

Access to relevant records and documents

The timely inspection of relevant registers, mainly the land (*Conservatoria dei Registri Immobiliari*) and the land survey office *(Catasto Terreni* for pieces of land and *Nuovo Catasto Edilizio Urbano* for buildings) should be done at an early stage in order to get an overall picture of the legal situation. The land register shows the encumbrances and third-party rights mentioned above, as far as they have been registered. At the land survey office, one can verify whether the situation of the property according to the construction plans available reflects the real situation. If not, then the plans can be altered but as this could be very costly and time-consuming, the potential buyer needs to be informed as soon as possible.

The registers of the Italian land registry and land survey office can be inspected by individuals so the use of professionals is not compulsory. Nevertheless, it could prove to be difficult for a foreign individual to obtain the required information. Success depends on how the register is being kept, if it is up to date and if the person in charge is co-operative.

It could be useful to look at the copy of the original notarized contract, with which the seller at that time obtained the property. The identification of the plots of land to be purchased can be compared with the current entries in the land registry and land survey office.

Key points that a seller should consider

The seller is the contracting party carrying the smaller risk, if the property is being used in accordance with its specified purpose, under of the regulations of construction law, and if taxes and other charges have been paid on time. Therefore, the seller should not make any promises or accept conditions in the preliminary contract which cannot be fulfilled in time before the conclusion of the notarized contract. In this case, he would have to refund not only any down payments received by the buyer, but also pay double their amount. The buyer can also claim for damages. The seller must also make sure that the real estate is free from third-party encumbrances, for example, free from mortgages, unless otherwise agreed in the preliminary contract. After the actual sale has taken place, it is the seller's duty to notify the change of ownership within 48 hours to the appropriate authority. Failure to do so will result in a financial penalty.

The execution of a real estate purchase transaction

The purchase of real estate according to Italian law can be defined by three steps:

1. Usually, but not necessarily, the parties involved sign a preliminary agreement. The preliminary agreement constitutes an obligatory commitment between the parties. The parties commit themselves and promise each other to sign the subsequent purchase and sales agreement, with which the ownership of the property passes to the buyer. The buyer promises to buy the property on the conditions agreed upon, and the seller promises to transfer ownership of the property, free from encumbrances, according to the terms agreed upon, and to accept the agreed purchase price

2. The actual notarized agreement (the *atto di compravendita* or *rogito)* which has to be signed before a notary public with regard to the property, is carried out at a time agreed upon by the parties. Until that date, the parties will do what is necessary so as to complete the

notarized sales agreement. The obligations mentioned in the preliminary agreement are to be performed prior to the appointment with the notary public, since their realization is the basis of the conclusion of the notarized agreement. With the signature of both parties on the notarized agreement, the buyer will obtain ownership of the property

3 As a third and final step of the purchase of property, the notarized agreement will be entered into the different registers to make the purchase public. The entry will protect the buyer from any purchase by third parties, who have also concluded a notarized agreement, but whose entry was made at an earlier date into the Italian Land Register

Powers of attorney

In Italy, real estate can be purchased by power of attorney. The power of attorney can be executed in simple form by a notary public or can be a public document. It depends on how the purchase contract on which it is based is executed. It can be executed before a notary public as a private contract or as a public document.

The power of attorney for the execution before an Italian notary public may be an advantage where the purchaser is a foreigner and does not speak the Italian language. The notary public is bound by law to have a purchase contract executed in the form of a public document translated into the language of the other contracting party. Apart from the translated contract, the presence of an official interpreter and two witnesses is necessary, one of whom speaks Italian as well as the buyer's language. Since this will considerably prolong the procedure and also increase the costs, the contract can be executed before the notary public by power of attorney. The power of attorney has to be executed in the same form as the sales agreement. If the sales agreement is a public document, the power of attorney must also be a public document. If the sales agreement is a private contract, concluded before a notary public, the power of attorney needs to fulfill this lesser requirement.

Financing

It is possible in theory for a foreigner buying an Italian property to obtain financing through an Italian bank, but in practice it is difficult to achieve. Normally, an Italian bank is not able to judge whether the documents submitted by the foreign customer with regard to his income and financial status are correct. The Italian bank has to ensure that the repayment of the loan is guaranteed.

When financing is arranged through an Italian bank, the bank will have a mortgage entered as a real security against the property, when the notarized contract is executed. Therefore, a bank representative will usually be present when the contract is executed before the notary public. Since the seller will recieve the purchase price upon transfer of ownership, the bank should at this moment hand over the amount to the seller. However, as a rule, the bank will hand over the financed part of the purchase price to the seller only when it is certain that the mortgage has been entered. This will take about 10 to 14 days. For securing the bank's charge, it is common in Italy that the mortgage entered is for at least double the loan amount. The bank tries to guarantee that in case of utilization of the property, for which an execution action of many years would be necessary, all its claims are covered. The seller will, therefore, in the case of the buyer's financing through a bank, usually receive the full purchase price, when the mortgage has been registered in favor of the bank. If there is no agreement in the preliminary contract stating that the seller will receive part of the purchase price at a later date, the seller could refuse to sign because the buyer, in breach of the contract, did not pay the purchase price at the moment of signing the notarized agreement.

Purchase through a company

The purchase of real estate through a company still to be established will be an advantage if tax benefits outweigh the costs connected with this process. The form of company offering this advantage is normally a company with limited liability, abbreviated under Italian law as *Srl*

(Società a responsabilità limitata). The minimum capital for this form of company is EUR 10,000. The disadvantage is that the maintenance expenditure of such a company is quite high due to bureaucratic requirements. The services of an accountant are an absolute necessity. The *Srl*, like a stock corporation, is obliged to officially hold a general meeting at least once a year. The advantage of this form of company is the limitation of liability. Other, less formal ways to purchase through a company are, on the one hand, a *società in nome collettivo*, abbreviated to *snc* (general partnership), or a *società in accomandita semplice*, abbreviated to *sas* (limited partnership). Both forms are partnerships. In the first case, the individual partners are fully liable, whereas in the *sas*, there is limited liability of the partners. The *accomandatario* has full liability for the company's debts.

Purchase through a company can often be the only way to obtain ownership for a non-EU national who is limited by the principle of reciprocity. Reciprocity exists when an *Srl* is formed. However, the problem of reciprocity still exists when there is a partnership under Italian law, and all partners are non-EU nationals and have their residence in a non-EU country.

International property-holding structures via foreign companies are no longer common in Italy.

Warranty claims

Warranty clauses are seldom stipulated in the sales agreement with the consequence that statutory regulations apply. The rights of the buyer are set out in Article 1490 of the *Codice Civile*. According to this law, the seller warrants that the property is free of faults which would limit or prevent its use. According to Article 1495, the buyer is obliged to declare any faults within eight days after he has detected them. All claims will expire one year after the transfer of the property. The warranty is also valid for hidden faults, which were not visible at the date of transfer. In addition, there is a 10 year warranty for faults which cause complete or partial destruction due to poor soil or due to a deficiency of construction. These claims will become statute-barred one year after the faults have been detected.

Further warranties are stipulated by the law *No. 765* of *1967*, namely in cases where the seller is also the building contractor and he did not obtain a building permit to construct the property, and the absence of which was not expressly mentioned in the contract. The law allows claims for damages against the seller/ building contractor if, because of the unlawfulness of the building project, the buyer has lost tax benefits or other government benefits.

25.4 New construction, rebuilding and renovation

Zoning law and construction permits

The Italian legislator provides that every change from the point of view of urban development requires the prior approval by the community. Initially, the mayor of the community concerned was responsible for granting such approval. This responsibility was transferred in 1997 to local administrative officers. The application for a building permit or a permit to rebuild or to alter a building can only be filed by the owner of the building.

The procedure for granting a building permit was completely revised in 1995. It stipulates that after a building permit has been applied for, the office responsible for it must inform the applicant who will be the person in charge of his application. The applications are examined in the order of their receipt. Within 60 days after receipt of the application, the person in charge has to give his decision as to the application, taking into consideration the regulations for urban development and construction. This time period can only be extended once by the person in charge if he asks the applicant for further documents. In communities with more than 200,000 inhabitants, the time period is twice as long.

The decision of the person in charge has to be submitted to a building commission (*commissione edilizia)*, who has to furnish their report also within a set time period. If they do not furnish a report, the person in charge will notify the mayor, giving the reasons why the period could not be kept. If the applicant does not receive his permit because the authority and responsible division failed to act, the applicant can contact the president of the competent regional council (*Giunta Regionale)* who can appoint a commissioner. He can order that the applicant receives a decision on application.

Where new buildings are allowed to be constructed is determined in the zoning plan, the *piano regolatore*. This allows certain kinds of buildings to be constructed. It is up to the communes to determine, observing the general criteria specified by the regions, which of the building zones can be used for certain purposes.

The building permit (*concessione edilizia*) issued normally carries a time limit. This means that the building activity has to be started and completed within a certain time span. These time limits must be indicated in the building permit. The time up to the start of the construction must not exceed one year. The time up to the completion (i.e. the time within which the property must be fit for human habitation) must not exceed three years. The latter term can only by extended by decree. Circumstances outside the control of the owner must have existed that made it impossible to carry out the work on schedule. In order not to let the building permit expire within a year, the owner must start constructing the building within one year. It is not sufficient to just raise a fence around the property and put up signs. The owner must be able to clearly show the start of the building activity externally. This start is important for the expiration of the term, since the building permit will expire after one year if the building activity has not actually been started. If the building activity has not started and the term has expired, the term cannot be extended. A new building permit will have to be applied for. However, the legislator expressly provides for the possibility of extending the term if the construction was started within the term specified, but not completed because of factors outside the control of the owner.

To summarize, the building permit can be characterized as follows. The building permit, once issued, is in principle irrevocable, except for expiry or annulment. The holder of the building permit can assign it through declaration of intent to a third party. In case of death, it can also be transferred to the heirs. The building permit can only be obtained through the payment of a fee, and it needs to be published. This means that once issued it will be put up publicly by the authorities. The building permit carries a time limit.

The building permit is an irrevocable decree, i.e., once granted, it cannot be rescinded by the authority who issued it. This does not however exclude the possibility of annulment of the building permit, if the latter should never have been issued in the first place. The annulment can be effected in four different ways:

- Annulment by the authority having issued the permit
- Annulment by the higher regional authority
- Annulment by the government
- Annulment by the court

In the first case, the power to annul is used to cancel the following: an illegally granted building permit, or a building permit issued by an authority that was not competent to do it, or a building permit granted with too wide an ambit. The annulment is retro-active so that the annulment will be effective as from the moment the permit was granted. The annulment allows the state authorities to restore the statutory order which was violated.

The building zones, i.e. the areas where buildings are permitted to be constructed, are indicated in the *Piano Regolatore Generale* (PRG) or the *piano urbanistico*, a type of development plan established by the commune and which defines the kind of buildings to be allowed to be constructed in the area in question (e.g. industrial area, residential area, mixed area). It is the purpose of the development plan to regulate the building activity within the commune in such a way as to guarantee a consistent and uniformed approach to the development and to ensure the functionality of the buildings.

Architect's contract and building contract

In the building contract, a person undertakes to carry out any work, using his own required organizational means and at his own risk, against corresponding remuneration. Written form of the contract is not necessary, but is in every case recommended. The contractor is liable for non-fulfillment or delayed fulfillment of the work. Where a building contractor is obligated to construct a building, the contractor is allowed to use the help of third parties to carry out and to complete the work. The third party may even be an architect, if the buyer uses one. In this case, the architect represents the interests of the buyer and supervises the work to ensure that it is carried out in accordance with the buyer's wishes with regard to the materials used and the method of construction, etc.

The law provides the possibility to modify the price agreed upon in two cases: firstly, for unforeseen circumstances leading to an increase or reduction of the amount agreed upon; and secondly for unforeseen difficulties when erecting the building.

The contractor is liable for the fact that his work is free from deficiencies. Any defaults must be removed at their own cost and the price appropriately reduced. The Italian law presupposes that buildings by their nature have a long service life. Should, therefore, deficiencies show up within 10 years from the time of construction, which cause the collapse of a building, the contractor will be liable. The contractor has to be notified of the defaults within one year after their detection (see 25.3).

Completion of construction and formalities

If the construction work is not completed within the set time-limit, permission for the continuance of the building activity has to be applied for. This means, in essence, applying for a new building permit. A problem could arise where construction, which was previously allowed (especially when the building permit expired some years ago), would no longer be allowed today. This would mean that the construction could continue but only in a restricted way.

If a building permit was issued, all building activities have to be in line with that permit. Any deviation from the permit is considered an illegal act. In cases of violation against any building laws, the buyer has to verify that an application for a *condono* or an application for a *sanatoria* was filed in due time.

The amnesty for unlawful buildings or *condono* has been law since 1985 and was last used in 1999 as an instrument for a 'belated cure'. It allows for the subsequent granting of building permits for unlawful buildings, provided that in every individual case there exists the legal prerequisites for a belated permit. The law set out exactly which kind of violations of building laws could be 'cured', if an application was received within the statutory term and, in particular, if corresponding fines were paid, then a belated permit could be granted. Unless there is another amnesty (*condono*), then there is only one other possibility of a belated cure and that is through a *sanatoria* (law dated February 28 1985, *No. 47*). The *sanatoria* is more restrictive than a *condono*. It is essential that the statutory conditions for a *sanatoria* are met and these conditions are set out in Article 13 of the above mentioned law. These conditions are where real estate developments, subject to building laws, were undertaken without a building permit; where there are deviations from an existing building permit; or where alterations to the terms have been made. The person, who caused these violations of law, can apply for belated cure if at the date of the violations, the preconditions for granting the permit would have existed and still exist at the time when applying for the *sanatoria*.

The completion of a building has to be declared to the appropriate land survey office, which must receive the plans separately for each unit of real estate (e.g. apartment, garage, cellar, attic, etc.). The completed building must comply with the specifications of the building permit. Otherwise it will violate building laws and this will lead to administrative and legal consequences. When erecting a building in Italy, the authorities will not check whether the building is in agreement with the existing standards. It is, however, prescribed by law that each property, before being used for residential purposes, has to have a *certificato di abitabilità* (certificate of fitness for human habitation). This certificate can be applied for at the community. Violations of building laws will become apparent at the latest when the property is to be sold and there is no connection between the files of the land survey registry and the reality of the situation. This could eventually lead to making it impossible to sell the property.

Deficiencies and warranty claims regarding new constructions

Warranty claims and the terms involved were described above in 25.3. Should construction work result in a collapse of the building causing personal and property damage, the contractor will be liable unless he can prove that the collapse was not caused by faulty workmanship.

Deficiencies of new constructions are regulated by the Italian law, Article 1655 seq. of the *Codice Civile*. The contractor is liable for the fact that his work is free from deficiencies, unless the owner knows and accepts these deficiencies. Otherwise, the owner has to notify the contractor of the deficiency within 60 days. After expiration of this exclusive term, the deficiencies can no longer be asserted. The possibility of assertion of a deficiency will become statute-barred after two years from the handing over and acceptance of the building.

25.5 Rental and tenancy

Rental and lease agreements

On 1 January 1999, a new tenancy law came into force which replaced the former laws. The former laws will remain in force until the contracts concluded under them have expired. The main amendments of the new tenancy law are the following: the tenancy contract has to be made in writing; verbal agreements are null and void. The minimum term of a contract is four years; it can be renewed for another four years, unless the landlord gives at least six months' notice, indicating one of the reasons required by law. One reason could be for personal use by the landlord himself or his family. Further reasons could be heavy damage to the building, which make it necessary to renovate the property and the tenant remaining there would hinder the renovation; or it could be the necessary structural renovation of the whole building or planned additions to the building.

In certain cases, the change of use of property which was originally intended for residential purposes only, is possible if that change of use will serve certain social or cultural services (also if these services are exercised by legal entities). The renewal of the contract by the tenant and the notice by him must be declared in writing and by registered mail to the owner, observing the six months' notice period. Otherwise, the contract will automatically expire. Under certain circumstances, the law will grant fiscal advantages to those owners who can prove that the tenancy contract was registered, that the *ICI*-tax levied by the community was paid, and that the property has been duly covered by the annual tax return.

The leaseholder has the contractual obligation to use the property for the purpose for which it has been leased. The owner of agricultural land has the right to check whether the leaseholder is fulfilling this contractual obligation. If not, he may be entitled to terminate the contract. In this connection, the *coltivatore diretto* for agricultural land should be mentioned. This is normally a small farm, where the soil is cultivated by the leaseholder with his own means and with the help of his family. This agricultural "Entrepreneur" is not the owner of the means of production, namely the soil, but can only cultivate it against paying a rent. The law *No. 203 of 3 May 1982* was introduced, which has brought new regulations on lease holding. The leasehold contract runs for at least 15 years and the leaseholder can withdraw from the contract at any time. The owner of the soil can only terminate the contract if the leaseholder is acting in violation of the contract. Otherwise, he would have to take legal action and would have to apply for the annulment of the contract by court order. The statutory provisions are unilaterally to the advantage of the small farmer.

Regulations on protection of tenants and rent control

Under Italian law, there are regulations regarding the rent and any increase, which is to the advantage of the tenant. The rent can only be increased within the statutory contract term of four years by the index of the *Istituto Nazionale di Statistica.* This is an adjustment for the increase in the cost of living and the inflation rate. The tenant has the right to renew the tenancy contract for another four years, whereas the landlord can only give notice for one of the reasons already mentioned. If the property is sold, the tenant will have a legal right of pre-emption. The right of pre-emption has to be offered to the tenant by registered mail, stating the purchase price, terms of payment and possible take-over of loans. The tenant will have 60 days from receipt of the offer to agree to the offer or make a counter-offer, also by registered mail. The purchase of real estate does not affect an existing tenancy contract, i.e. the purchase does not cancel tenancy. The tenancy relationship is just transferred to the new owner.

25.6 Successions and gifts

Applicable law and jurisdiction

The foreign owner of real estate in Italy also needs to observe the Italian rules and regulations concerning the transfer of real estate upon death or by way of donation. This is set out in international private law, which is regulated in Italy by *law No. 218 of 1995,* Article 46. According to these regulations, in cases of inheritance, reference is made to the substantive national law of the devisor. Ownership of real estate by a foreign owner who has died will be handled, as far as the regulation of succession is concerned, according to the legal status of the deceased.

Article 51 of the same law deals with the transfer of the property itself. With respect to the procedural right of jurisdiction applicable in disputes concerning an inheritance, the Italian courts have jurisdiction for movable and immovable property, which is situated in Italy (see Article 50).

Foreign heirs must send a succession application to the competent registry in Rome. The registry in Rome is competent for those cases where a foreign owner has died and passed the property to his heirs. Foreigners with residence in a foreign country must file this application within twelve months. Its purpose is to enable the taxation of the inheritance in cases where the heirs are subject to taxation and to pay the taxes for clearance of the entries in the land register and land survey register. Notification is to be made on a form, which must be duly completed and accompanied by documents proving the succession (e.g. death certificate, data on the degree of relationship, birth certificates, certificate of inheritance or the will on which the heir bases his/her entitlement to inherit, documents on the property to be obtained from the land survey registry, etc).

Fundamentals of succession and gift/donation laws of Italy

Legal succession

Inheritance derives either from the legal succession or from the will of the deceased. Legal succession according to Italian law is bound to a hierarchy. It defines the persons who will be left a share of the wealth of the deceased. In the first place, these are descendants, legitimate and illegitimate, and the surviving spouse. If no child or spouse exists, then the next-closest relatives to benefit will be the parents and the brothers and sisters of the deceased.

In cases of a married couple with two children, the surviving spouse and the two children would each inherit one third (if there are more children; the estate will be divided into corresponding shares). If there is one child, the surviving spouse and the child will each inherit half of the estate.

According to the Italian law of succession, the person entitled to a statutory forced share (i.e. spouse and legitimate and illegitimate children) cannot be excluded from the inheritance, not even by a will. The statutory forced share is always equal to the legal claim of inheritance, i.e. there is no reduced statutory forced share, as provided in the law of succession in some other civil law countries.

Will

The will is a formal act and requires written form. The will can be handwritten or recorded by a notary public. The recording of a will can be public or private. A public will is drawn up before a notary public in the presence of two witnesses. However, the will can also be made as a secret document. The will must be written by the deceased and signed at the end. If a third party is called in for drawing up the will and if the will is typewritten, each half page must be signed by the deceased. Then the will is sealed and handed to the notary public in the presence of two witnesses. The deceased can, in general, freely dispose of his/her wealth. This freedom is restricted in as far as the law reserves a certain share (statutory forced share) of the wealth for certain persons, and these persons are entitled to their share even against the deceased's wishes.

Gifts

The Italian *Codice Civile* defines a gift or donation as a contract, in which one party voluntarily enriches another party, transferring one of his/her own rights or assuming one of the other party's liability. A donation is a formal contract, which has to be drawn up by public recording before a notary public. When the contract is to be signed, the contracting parties and the witnesses need to be present. The assets transferred by donation, no matter whether they are movable or immovable assets, must always be transferred by a public contract. The making of a donation requires full legal capacity. An exception to this rule is a donation in respect of a future marriage (*donazione abnuziale*). This is a donation between the future spouses or a donation of a third party to the future spouses. For such donations, the donation is perfected through the fact of the subsequent marriage. Moreover, the usual formality of recording before a notary public is not necessary.

25.7 Taxes and charges

One-time taxes and charges on purchase

Italian law offers, in certain cases, tax benefits for the purchase of real estate. These benefits are also applicable to foreigners if they fulfill the necessary requirements. To take advantage of such tax benefits, the real estate must not be a luxury property. The qualification of a property can be obtained from the land survey registry. The property has to be in the commune in which the buyer has his main residence (*residenza*) or in the commune in which the buyer will take *residenza* within 18 months after the notarized agreement. The notary public has to include a corresponding declaration to this effect in the contract. If the main residence is not taken in accordance with the declaration, the difference in tax will have to be paid. A sufficient place of residence is also the place where the buyer is gainfully employed or - if he works as an employee in a foreign country - the place where his/her company has its head office or a subsidiary. The tax benefit also applies to Italians having emigrated to a foreign country, but now wanting to take up their main residence in Italy.

Real estate transfer taxes

The tax levied on the purchase qualifying for tax benefits is 2% of the cadastral value (*rendita catastrale rivalutata*). The cadastral value is an officially fixed, average value of the property, which depends on the location and the use of the property. It may be lower than the appraised value of the property. For its calculation the officially given value is to be multiplied with a certain factor. The multiplication factors are specified by fiscal authorities too.

However, 11 categories and classes of real estate can be found, e.g. country residences A/8, castles and historic buildings A/9, well-kept flats A/1.

In addition to the latter tax, the mortgage and the land survey/cadastral tax are applicable, each to a fixed amount of EUR 50. However, the law stipulates a minimum amount being spent on taxes and that is EUR 1,000.

The purchase contract of the notary public and the annexes attached to the notarized contract will cost one fee stamp of EUR 16 for every four pages i.e. the exact amount of the cost depends on the number of pages of the contract.

If the purchase of the property is not subject to tax benefits or if it is not agricultural real estate, the following taxes are applied:

- Register tax: 9% of the cadastral value
- % of the cadastral value
- Mortgage tax and land survey/cadastral tax, EUR 50 each

Agricultural real estate is subject to a higher tax rate, namely 12% of the cadastral value. In addition, the mortgage and the land survey/cadastral tax are applicable to a fixed amount of EUR 50 each.

Sales tax (Value Added Tax)

Where a buyer intends to purchase a property which is still to be constructed, the contractor who is going to build and eventually sell the property will request the 10% of Value Added Tax (VAT) on the purchase price declared before the notary public. If the property is subject to tax benefits, then the contractor will require only 4% VAT. New properties which are built by a contractor and which, from the point of view of the land survey register, are deemed to be luxury real estate (i.e. more than 240m^2 living space, or properties with parks, swimming pool, sports grounds, high-quality furnishings, etc.) will be taxed at 22% VAT. It is not possible to buy such luxury property at a reduced VAT rate.

Real estate registration and notary charges

The notary's fees are due for payment at the moment of signing of the contract and are payable to the notary public, who, in turn, is responsible for passing them onto the fiscal authorities. The amount of the notary's fees depends on the purchase price fixed and is derived from the scale of notary's fees. To prevent the notary's fees, which are calculated on the purchase price, from becoming an obstacle in the fight against under-recording, the legislator has decided on a 20% fee reduction for notaries. The notary public has, however, a large scope of discretion for fixing his fees. In practice, the notary public will set his fees at his own discretion because there is a considerable difference between the amount usually charged by the notary public and the amount according to the fee scale. It is possible that for the same value, quite different fees will be charged as some notaries public are expensive and others are not. One should obtain a cost estimate from the notary public in order to have a precise assessment of the costs and so as to prevent unpleasant surprises later on.

The charges for the land register, which are also collected by the notary public, are low and not of any real significance to the total amount of costs arising from the purchase. A few examples, which are only estimates of the notary's fees, refer to the value of the property:

Value of property in EUR		Total notary's fees in % *
5,000 – 25,000	results in	7.66
25,000 – 500,000	results in	1.078
500,000 – 1,000,000	results in	0.440
1,000,000 – 3,500,000	results in	0.210
3,500,000 – 5,000,000	results in	0.140

* *empirical values/estimates*

Annually recurring taxes and charges

Real estate tax

Since 1993, the annual real estate tax was the *Imposta Comunale Immobiliare* tax (ICI) a local tax for the benefit of the commune in which the property is located. The amount of ICI varied from one commune to the other and used to be between 4 and 7 thousandths of the fictitious capital amount calculated via the *rendita catastale.* In 2012 the ICI was replaced by the *Imposta Municipale Unica* tax (IMU). This new tax replaces the ICI as well as the income tax for real estate's income. Like the ICI, it varies from commune to commune and is calculated via the *rendita castale,* but also on whether the property serves as a main residence or not. In the case of main residences, its amount varies between 0.4% (common taxation) plus/minus 0.2%, i.e. the minimum tax rate is 0.2% and the maximum tax rate is 0.6%.

The communes are enabled by the exchequer to increase the amount of the IMU.

The Italian tax system is subject to constant reforms. Changes must always be taken into consideration. Obtaining information about actual and current taxation is therefore recommended.

At present, the IMU is due in two instalments per year, in June and in December. In Italy, the owner of a property is responsible for paying the taxes. Usually there is no reminder to pay the tax by the fiscal authorities. The owner should use the services of an accountant or similar expert, who will calculate the IMU tax for him and who will complete the necessary paperwork.

Income tax

Real estate is also subject to income tax. Since 2012 the income tax for real estate's income is integrated in IMU tax.

For tax declarations that still have to be done with the ICI tax, the income tax is calculated as follows: for individuals, there is the *Imposta Reddito Persone Fisiche* tax (IRPEF), taxing the total income of an individual, independently of how it was earned. In principle, a fictitious income from the real estate is taxed. This income is calculated on the basis of the land survey data. The amount of tax depends on the individual's tax class, as this fictitious income is added to the other income of the individual. The total income determines the tax rate. The lowest tax rate is 23% for an income up to EUR 15,000, and the highest tax rate is 45% for an income over EUR 70,000. For persons subject to limited tax liability in Italy, there are no special tax rates. The same tax rates apply. For property acquired with tax benefits and used as main residence, tax concessions apply. In this case, no income is assessed for the property.

Net wealth tax

There is no net wealth tax in Italy. However, its re-introduction is sometimes discussed by politicians.

Capital gains tax

Since 1 January 2002 there is no longer any capital gains tax for individuals and legal entities. The tax (INVIM), was abolished as of 31 December 1992, with exceptions. Real estate which is part of the assets of a legal entity is still of fiscal relevance. Depending on the value of the property in the financial statement of the company and whether this value differs from the purchase price, the sale will be subject to the usual taxation for companies, the *Imposta Reddito Persone Giuridiche* (IRPEG).

Inheritance and gift taxes

On October 23 2001 the law *No. 383 of October 18th, 2001* came into force, which set out new regulations for inheritance and gift tax. Inheritance tax and gift tax were, in general, abolished. The abolition of the inheritance tax was valid for all heirs. Gifts were tax-free only for spouses and relatives up to the fourth degree (cousins). Gifts to other persons were tax-free up to an amount of EUR 180,759.91. In the meantime, inheritance and gift taxes were re-introduced. It distinguishes between unlimited income tax payers and limited income tax payers. To which group a person belongs depends on if the descendant was domiciled in Italy or not. The same holds true for the donor.

High tax free amounts are being provided for heirs and donee. Currently, the reduction of these tax free amounts is discussed and it is quite possible that they will be reduced in due course.

At present however, the following tax rates are being applied:

- Inheritances and gifts are tax-free for spouses and children up to an amount of EUR 1 million. If this exempt amount is exceeded, the tax rate will be 4%
- For transfers in favour of brothers and sisters there is no inheritance or gift tax up to an amount of EUR 100,000. If this exempt amount is exceeded, the tax rate will be 6%
- For transfers in favour of other relatives up to the fourth degree there is no tax-free amount. In those cases the rate of the inheritance and gift tax is 6%
- For all other transfers the rate of the inheritance and gift tax is 8%. In case of transfers in favour of disabled persons a tax free amount of EUR 1,500 exists

In case of a tax-free inheritance or gift, the transfer in the land survey registry from the deceased to the heir or from the donor to the benefactor will be subject to a tax. This could be a fixed amount of tax of EUR 200 for the mortgage tax and EUR 200 for the land survey tax, if the property is transferred as *prima casa.* In all other cases, the mortgage and land survey tax will amount to a total of 3% (2% plus 1%) of the land survey value of the real estate.

The declaration of succession, which has to be handed in within six months of death (for foreigners within 12 months), must still be filed with the registry in charge, despite the abolition of inheritance tax, because taxes are payable for the transfer of a property which is subject to a tax-free inheritance or donation (these are a mortgage tax of 2% and the land survey tax of 1%).

If, however, the prerequisites for a transfer as the main residence (*prima casa*) are satisfied, the two above-mentioned taxes will amount to only EUR 400.

Other taxes and charges

There are no further recurrent or one-time taxes for real estate. Additional costs to be considered might be fire insurance or a building insurance. These insurances are not compulsory under Italian law. Accordingly it is at the discretion of the owner to take out such insurances.

Since a condominium is part of a complex of apartments, in which many owners reside, the down payments to cover the condominium charges should be mentioned. These costs depend on the size of the condominium and on the expenses to be paid by them; they are apportioned to the individual owners by thousandth of share.

Incorrect (lower) statement of sale price on the sales agreement

Despite the fact that since 2006 transfer taxes are no longer calculated on the purchase price stated in the notarized contract but on the cadastral value, under-recording (indicating a lower purchase price than the real market price) still happens in Italy, even though it's illegal.

Until 31 December 2001, under-recording was also in the interests of the seller, who had to pay capital gains tax. The lowest possible value of the purchase price is the value registered in the land survey registry. Where a buyer purchases a property from a legal entity, and the price paid is lower than the market price, he could be taking a risk if the legal entity becomes bankrupt within two years after conclusion of the notarized contract. The receiver could, if the purchase price stated in the notarized contract does not correspond to the market value, challenge the purchase contract and reclaim the property. The buyer could then try to get his purchase price back from the receiver, but only for the amount stated in the notarized contract. The only other alternative would be to admit tax evasion because in reality he has paid a higher purchase price. This would then lead to an investigation by the fiscal authorities. The consequences are the following: a) if the amount evaded does not exceed EUR 51,645.69, then a person may have to pay a fine, the amount of which depends on the amount of tax evaded; and b) if the amount of tax evaded does exceed the above-mentioned figure, then a person will face a criminal prosecution. A conviction could lead to a prison sentence from six months up to four years, which will be published.

Another consequence of declaring a lower and incorrect statement of a sale price is that both the buyer and seller will have falsified the sales agreement, which could lead to criminal prosecution. If convicted of falsifying the documents, a person may be sentenced to up to two years of imprisonment. The sentence imposed will be towards the heavier side, if the buyer and seller have misled the notary.

The recording of an incorrect lower purchase price in the sales contract does in principle not affect the validity of the purchase contract.

However, time will show if the measures against under-recording (e.g. taxation calculated on the cadastral value, 20% notary's fee-reduction) prove successful.

International taxation

There are about 60 double taxation treaties in force between Italy and other countries, including all of the EU, Australia, Canada and the US. There are other treaties that are not yet in force. All of them, however, are based on the *Model Convention* of the *OECD* (*Organisation for Economic Development and Co-operation*).

According to the *Model Convention* and most of these double taxation treaties, a person who is resident in a contracting country may be taxed according to the law of another country by virtue of his/her residence, permanent stay, place of the management of his company or other similar characteristics. This means that a resident of one country, who derives income from or owns capital in another country, may be taxed according to the laws of the other country. Article 6 of the *Convention* provides that income derived by a resident of one contracting country from real estate situated in another contracting country, may be taxed in the latter.

To avoid double taxation on income derived from such real estate which has already been taxed in another country, the *Convention* provides exemption or credit methods for tax payers. According to the exemption method, the double taxation treaty signed between Italy and Germany, for example, provides that the Italian fiscal authorities can tax the income from the rental or leasehold of holiday property in Italy. The German fiscal authorities are not allowed to include this income in the basis of assessment of German income tax. Accordingly, the German authorities only have the right to tax the German income of the German tax payer applying the tax rate which would be applicable to the latter's income if the income earned in Italy had been added. The credit method, on the other hand, is when a resident or citizen of a country, such as the US, pays the amount of income tax to Italy as a credit against his income tax liability in the US.

25.8 Immigration law and tax residence

Entry, residence and settlement of foreigners

According to Article 5 of the *Schengen Treaty*, the entry of foreigners will only be allowed if they are in possession of a valid passport or an equivalent traveling document, as well as documents justifying the purpose and conditions of their stay in Italy, and if they can prove that they have sufficient financial means to stay in Italy and to return to their home country. A valid visa has to be presented, if prescribed, and there must be no contra-indications to bar the entry. The foreigner must not represent a danger to public order or national security to Italy or another member state of the *Schengen Treaty*.

Nationals of the member countries of the European Union as well as nationals of Iceland, Liechtenstein and Norway, are not considered foreigners.

Permanent residence in Italy requires a residence permit for the group of the extracomunitari, i.e. the nationals of non-EU countries. Members of EU countries may obtain a residence card (*carta di soggiorno*), but this is no longer obligatory. The application for a residence permit in *Italy* has to be filed within eight working days after entering into Italy at the police headquarters (*questura*) of the province in which the foreigner wants to take up his residence. The validity of the residence permit is normally limited in time, depending on the reasons for the visa.

Nationals of EU countries can receive a non-limited *carta di soggiorno* (residence card) for their stay or settlement in Italy. The conditions for permanent settlement are that an EU national has lived for at least five years in Italy with a duly granted residence permit or if the EU national is the spouse, minor or parent of an Italian national or another national of an EU country with *residenza* in Italy.

A bilateral treaty between non-member states such as Switzerland and the EU as well as the individual EU member countries with regard to the free movement of persons (*Treaty of Freedom of Movement*) aims to gradually introduce the freedom of movement of employed and non-employed persons. There will be a transitional term of 12 years until there is full realization of freedom of movement between Switzerland and the EU. For Swiss nationals seeking employment in Italy, access to the Italian labor market will remain regulated for the first five years after the treaty comes into force. During the first two years, the regulations will be similar to those for non-EU/EFTA nationals (agreement on residents) with the difference that Swiss nationals will enjoy preference over these foreigners.

Tax residence

First of all, two terms have to be clarified, the *residenza*, on the one hand, and the *domicilio*, on the other hand, which are defined by

Article 43, paragraphs 1 and 2 of the *Codice Civile.* A *domicilio* is the place where a person mainly pursues his business and activities and which is not necessarily the same as the *residenza.* A *domicilio* is not, generally-speaking, a person's permanent address. It is for example, a mailing address for a person who, whilst living and working in Italy, has not a permanent address in Italy. The *residenza* is the place where the person normally has his permanent residence/address. It is a fine distinction between both terms and it is, of course, possible for a person to have *domicilio* and *residenza* at the same address. However, the distinction becomes clear when considering that, for example, with *residenza*, a person is registered on the official electoral role, giving that person the right to vote, whereas with *domicilio*, there is no such right. Most foreigners often keep their *residenza* in their home country and establish a *domicilio* in Italy, by virtue of which they will pay taxes on their income earned in Italy according to the Italian tax laws. The take-up of residence, the *residenza*, in Italy means the person is considered a resident in Italy and so he can apply for an identity card or similar papers. Certain official certificates (e.g. on marital status) can also only be applied for at the authority of the place of one's *residenza.*

In cases where a foreigner keeps his main residence in his home country and only has a *domicilio* in Italy, but earns an income, he will be taxed according to the applicable double taxation treaty. Applying for a *residenza* would mean that he becomes fully taxable in Italy, even with income earned in a foreign country. For income earned in a foreign country, again, the respective double taxation treaties apply (see 25.7).

To voluntarily take up a fiscal status, namely to become an Italian taxpayer, a *domicilio fiscale*, pursuant to Article 1 of the *Testo Unico delle Imposte sul Reddito* in Italy mean that all income earned in foreign countries (taking into account any double taxation treaties) is taxed according to Italian law.

In recent years, there have been in Italy a series of changes in taxation, which led to the abolition of such relevant taxes as wealth tax, capital gains tax on property and reduction of the maximum tax rate. For example, on certain capital income, a withholding tax of 12.5% is now paid directly to the Italian fiscal authorities. Through this payment of the *imposta sostitutiva*, this type of income is taxed at a rate of 12.5% only.

The present general income tax rates in Italy are as follows:

	Tax rate
up to EUR 15,000	23%
above EUR 15,000 up to EUR 28,000	27%
above EUR 28,000 up to EUR 55,000	38%
above EUR 55,000 up to EUR 75,000	41%
above EUR 75,000	43%

International double taxation for residents of Italy

Taking up fiscal residence in Italy means that income earned in other countries will be subject to the respective double taxation treaty, depending on the kind, the amount and the source of income.

Accordingly, the double taxation treaties (see 25.7), provide that income derived by a self-employed resident of a contracting country (Italy) in respect of professional services or other activities of an independent character is taxable only in the country, unless he has a fixed base regularly available to him in another contracting country (for example the US) for the purpose of performing his activities. If he has such a fixed base, the income may be taxed in the other country but only so much of it as is attributable to that fixed base or if he is present in that other country for a period or periods not exceeding 183 days in any fiscal year.

With regard to salaries, wages and other similar remuneration derived by an employed resident of Italy, they are taxable in Italy, unless the employment is exercised in another contracting country (for example the US). Salary derived by an Italian resident in respect of employment performed in another contracting country is taxable only in Italy, if the resident is present in that other country for a period or periods not exceeding 183 days in any fiscal year and if this salary is paid by, or on behalf of, an employer who is not a resident of that other country, and the salary does not come from a permanent establishment or a fixed base which the employer has in that other country.

25.9 Checklist: Real estate in Italy

- Are there persons having right of pre-emption (i.e. tenants), who could prevent or cancel the sale?
- Do encumbering entries, such as mortgages, easements or rights of way, exist?
- Does the property comply with the valid standards of land survey registration and building law?
- In case of a purchase/sale by a married couple, how is the spouse who is not the owner of the property treated in the contract?
- Is the seller a legal entity and has the risk of bankruptcy been taken into account?
- What was the amount of the down payments in the preliminary contract? Normally they will amount to 10%. Is their possible re-payment secured?
- In certain regions of Italy (e.g. Sicily, Southern Italy, Umbria), the danger of earthquakes is quite high. Also other threats of nature (e.g. landslides, avalanches in the Alps, etc.) have to be taken into consideration
- The risks of an incorrect statement of sale price on the sales agreement (under-recording) have to be considered
- The total cost and taxes should be calculated in due time before entering into any real estate transaction

25.10 Bibliography

German-Italian Chamber of Commerce, Milan: "Der Immobilienerwerb in Italien" Practical help for the German buyer. 2. Edition, Milan 1998

Dossiers Internationaux: Italie, Editor Francis Lefebre, Levallois 2001

Galgano, Francesco: Diritto private, CEDAM, Padova 1996

McMahon, Barbara: The Complete Guide to Buying Property in Italy, Kogan Page, London 2004

Reichel, Doris: Ferienimmobilien in Italien, Erwerb, Besitz, Verkauf, Steuern, Deutsche Schutzvereinigung Auslandsimmobilien e.V., Freiburg i.Br. 2014

Rossi, Enzo: La Casa nel diritto privato, amministrativo, tributario, Utet, Turin 1998

Tamborrino, Francesco: Annuario Immobiliare 2002, Il Sole 24 ore, Milan 2002

26

Malta

Republic of Malta
Repubblika Ta' Malta

by

Adrian Camilleri*

Telephone: 00356 27015371/ 00356 79429655
Facsimile: 00356 27016571

adriancamilleri@gmail.com

Adrian Camilleri was born in Malta on 23 June 1980. He studied law at the University of Malta between 1998 and 2004 achieving his B.A Legal & Humanistic Studies (2001), Diploma of Notary Public (2002) and his LL.D. (2004). As part of his LL.D course he presented a thesis entitled 'The Preliminary Reference Procedure in EU, Maltese and UK Law'.

Adrian was called to the Bar in March 2005 and established a law firm as a sole practitioner specialising in litigation and extra-judicial legal work with special focus on matters relating to Company Law, Commercial Law, Property Law, Competition Law, European Law, Maritime Law, Civil Law, Criminal Law, and Family Law.

Adrian is also Chief Prosecuting Officer of the Malta Football Association (MFA) dealing with any disciplinary action which the Association takes against any persons within the Association's jurisdiction according to its statute and regulations;

Adrian has been appointed by the courts of Malta numerous times as a legal referee and arbiter in various civil and commercial cases and has also been appointed as a court expert in criminal inquiries and is currently a member of the Adoption Board and a Social Security Umpire.

*The author has taken over from the previous edition where the Malta chapter was written by Barry Woestenburg and Dr Josianne Cardona Gatt

26.1 Introduction

The Republic of Malta is an archipelago consisting of five islands, Malta, Gozo and Comino which are inhabited, Malta being the most populated, and two smaller islands, Cominetto and Filfla, the latter two being uninhabited.

The population counts more than 400,000 inhabitants and the official languages are English and Maltese. The mainstay of the economy is tourism; the secondary pillars of the economy are the financial services sector, manufacturing, the semi-conductor industry and the Freeport.

Malta became independent from Britain in 1964 after being a colony for nearly 200 years. It has been a Republic since 1974. It is a fully-fledged democratic country with respect for the rule of law. Malta has been a member of the European Union since 1 May 2004 and is a member of major international organizations including the United Nations, the Council of Europe and the International Monetary Fund. Malta adopted the Euro on 1 January 2008.

Malta has a sound infrastructure. Telecommunications, postal links, courier services, banking and all other services are efficient and of a high standard. The national airline, Air Malta, operates direct flight routes mostly within Europe and the Mediterranean regions and most major European airlines have frequent flights to Malta. There is a frequent sea link with Italy.

Malta traditionally is a civil law country and its laws are based on Roman law and on the Napoleonic Code. Its legal institutions and Courts of laws have long been established in Malta. Malta's legal system is on a par with other European countries and the rule-of-law is jealously safeguarded. Malta's laws are enacted by a freely elected Parliament and there is a strict separation of powers between Parliament, the Executive and the Judiciary, ensuring that Malta's Constitution reigns supreme over any law that Parliament enacts. However, after Malta's accession to the European Union, its laws are subject to the supremacy of the European Court of Justice and European Union's Legislation.

26.2 Real estate ownership

Different forms and types of ownership

There is only one type of ownership, outright title, but ownership can be limited in a number of ways; the more common limitations are the subjection of the ownership to the payment of ground rent (emphyteusis) or to the enjoyment of a particular person (usufruct). A property can be co-owned by several persons either because they have purchased the property together or because they have inherited the property from a common testator (or through intestate succession). A co-owner cannot be forced to remain in co-ownership with the other owners and can ask for the liquidation of the co-ownership, either through agreement or through judicial partition, however the latter is subject to there being the necessary elements required by law which may lead to such request for partition.

The administration of apartment blocks is regulated through *the Condominium Act* (*Cap 398* of the *Laws of Malta*) which has subjected most disputes to arbitration.

Every owner has the right to build on his property but this is subject to the planning regulations in force and not all property can be built on. The *Malta Environment and Planning Authority* has the function of issuing building permits.

Timesharing has spread in Malta; especially with regard to foreigners purchasing a right to a period of time for spending their annual holidays in Malta. The sector is subject to strict regulation under the *Timeshare and Timeshare-like Products Promotion (Licensing of OPC Representatives) Regulations 2010*. Companies active in the timeshare industry are required to deposit a EUR 2,500 guarantee bond with the *Malta Tourism Authority* for each sales representative employed. Heavy fines are imposed on companies infringing the law. In addition, in order to further protect buyers, the *Doorstep Contracts Act* stipulates that a purchaser of a Timeshare has the right to rescind (annul) the contract within 15 days of the agreement having been signed.

Easements, charges, covenants, liens and mortgages

There are a number of servitudes (easements) which can burden property; some are active and some are inactive and some depend on the location or situation of the particular properties. Therefore for example there might be a right of way over property, a lower roof may be subject to the receipt of rainwater from a higher roof, existing windows and doors cannot be blocked. Servitudes can be created by agreement between two parties; sometimes they can be created unilaterally by will or by the 'decision of the owner of two tenements' and at times servitudes are created by law. It is important to check whether property is subject to any servitude since some of them can be quite important and onerous and can limit considerably the enjoyment or development potential of property.

There is no right to *retratto* and once a property has been sold it can never be recovered from the buyer. This right used to exist in the older law but it has long been abolished. Therefore once a seller has sold his property, there is no way he can recover it from the buyer unless such property is purchased via a judicial sale by auction, in which case the debtor has the right to recover his property, which would have been sold to third parties, under certain conditions established by law.

The terms 'liens' and 'mortgages' do not exist under Maltese law. Causes of preference over immovable property are classified as being either hypothecs or privileges. A hypothec is usually voluntary and granted by agreement between the creditor and the debtor owning the property. A hypothec serves as security to ensure the repayment of a debt; the creditor holding a hypothec against a property will be able to claim payment of the debt in preference to other unsecured debtors. A property might be subject to multiple hypothecs which then rank according to their date of registration with an earlier hypothec enjoying preference over a later one. A privilege is a cause of preference granted by operation of law in particular circumstances where the law considers that a particular creditor should enjoy a right of preference over ordinary creditors.

In all cases these causes of preference constitute a privileged title against the property and the charge over the property will follow the property, independently of who the owner of the property is. A creditor enjoying a cause of preference over the property has the right to ask for the judicial sale of the property in satisfaction of his credit against the property. It is naturally very important to check that no hypothecs or privileges are registered against a property to ensure that no claims are entered against the property after it has been bought.

A property can be subject to the usufruct of another person; usufruct is the right to the enjoyment of the property by a person different to the owner, and the most common form of usufruct is that granted in a will to the surviving spouse over the estate of the deceased spouse. Other forms of usufruct are very rare today.

Property can also be subject to emphyteusis (payment of a ground-rent) which means that the buyer of the property, apart from paying the purchase price to the seller, will also have to pay an annual payment (see 26.3).

Protection of ownership, proof of ownership and registration

Ownership is proved primarily by notarial deed registered in the *Maltese Public Registry*. Every notarial deed of transfer of property is registered under the name of the seller and the name of the buyer; in order to prove ownership, a search is entered in the *Registry* on the name of the person alleging to be the owner and if the searches reveal a contract of purchase and no subsequent contract of sale, then the ownership is proved. Liabilities (hypothecs and privileges) are registered in the same way and therefore if a search on an owner's name reveals no liabilities it means that the property is not burdened by debts.

A land registry has been created which is creating a database of all property in Malta and is run by the Government. Eventually once all property has been entered into the database, the old registration system will be phased out and it will be possible to obtain details of ownership and liabilities by looking up the individual property, rather than having to search on the owner's name.

26.3 Purchase and sale of real estate

The sales agreement

The sales agreement is divided into two parts: the preliminary agreement and the final deed of transfer.

The preliminary agreement (*convenium*) is a private agreement between the seller and the buyer. It is recommendable that such is drawn up by a notary public or a lawyer. The preliminary agreement is an agreement between the parties whereby the seller promises to sell a given property to the buyer who promises to buy the property.

The price and all the other conditions of the sale are fixed in the preliminary agreement and these conditions are binding and cannot be varied on the final deed of transfer, unless both parties agree to the changes.

The preliminary agreement is binding on the parties and none of the parties can opt out of the agreement unless there is a valid legal reason for doing so. Such would usually be the discovery of a defective title of the seller, an unavoidable burden on the property or the discovery of defects in the property. A party who changes its mind can be forced through legal action to buy (or sell) the property.

It is common practice today for the buyer to pay 10% of the purchase price to the seller, which is usually held in escrow by a notary public. Should the buyer opt out of the agreement with no valid reason at law, instead of forcing the purchase through judicial action, the seller may have a right instead to retain the sum paid on account of the price.

The time for which the preliminary agreement remains valid is established between the parties on the deed. Such time may vary from three months to one year (or more) depending on when the parties wish to conclude the final deed. During such time the notary public will undertake researches in the *Public Registry* with the aim to collect enough information to satisfy the buyer that the seller has title to sell the property and that the property is not burdened by hypothecs, privileges or servitudes that have not been disclosed. Furthermore if a loan is being requested from one of the commercial banks in Malta to finance the purchase, during such time the bank will also conduct researches through its legal office in order to issue a sanction letter as an approval of the loan.

The law in Malta imposes on the parties the obligation to register the preliminary agreement with the Maltese Inland Revenue and 1% of the purchase price is payable to the Inland Revenue on account of the final transfer duty (5%). Preliminary agreements which are not registered will have no legal validity and will not be enforceable against a defaulting party.

Once the buyer is satisfied, then the notary public will publish a final deed of transfer which effectively transfers the title to the property once the deed is registered in the *Public Registry*. The notary must register the deed within 15 days from publication.

The only legal form of sales contracts are those published by a notary public. Any sales done by private agreement between parties, without being formalized before a notary public, have no effect at law.

Restrictions on sale and acquisition

Restrictions under family law and matrimonial property regime

Property purchased by a married couple who have been married in Malta or who have established themselves in Malta subsequent to their foreign marriage, is considered to belong to the spouses in equal portions, through the community of acquests. Although it is the practice to have both spouses appearing on a contract, a property bought in the name of one of the spouses is still presumed to belong to the community of acquests. However if the buyer can prove that he has used his own assets not belonging to the community of acquests to purchase the property, he would have a claim equal to the purchase price against the assets of the community. Husband and wife are prohibited from selling property to each other. Property is governed by the *lex situs* and therefore Maltese real estate will always be subject to Maltese law and it is not possible to change or choose the law which will govern property. Foreigners who purchase property after they have established themselves in Malta will become subject to the community of acquests regime; they can however opt out of this and exclude the community of acquests regime by entering into a public deed prior to their establishment in Malta and establish another matrimonial regime which is most commonly that of separation of estates. They can also opt out of the community of acquests if this has become already operational after marriage, but they would need the authorisation of the *Civil Court (Family Section)* to do so.

Options and pre-emption rights

It is possible to establish a right of first refusal for a property in which case, before selling freely on the market, a seller would be obliged to offer the sale to the person enjoying the right of first refusal. This right can only be granted contractually and there is no such right granted by operation of law.

Property can of course be rented out to third parties and rental agreements are private agreements that are not registered in the *Public Registry*. Therefore it might happen that a property that is sold is subsequently found to have been rented to third parties by a previous owner. Malta has very particular rent laws and one needs to be very careful, especially in cases where rent was agreed prior to June 1995. Rent laws were reformed in 2009, but far reaching protection of the tenant of residential properties still exists. It is therefore very important to ensure that the property being purchased is not leased or rented by the seller and in particular is free from any leases which began prior to June 1995. The sales contract will usually specify that the property is being sold 'with vacant possession' and if this is not found to be the case, then the buyer will have a right of action against the seller for rescission of the contract.

Agricultural real estate

There are no specific rules applying to the purchase of agricultural real estate. However, the acquisition of agricultural land by foreigners is restricted. EU citizens are allowed to purchase non-residential immovable property if that is required for their business activities. Non-EU citizens, however, are not allowed to purchase industrial or agricultural real estate, except for specific cases where it may be in the interest of Malta's economic development.

Restrictions regarding acquisitions of real estate by foreigners.

Chapter 246 of the *Laws of Malta* (*Immovable Property (Acquisition by Non-Residents) Act*) regulates the acquisition of real estate by non-residents. A fee of EUR 232.94 is charged in respect of any permit granted by the Minister. The law describes the instances when an *Acquisition of Immovable Property Permit (AIP Permit)* is required. Three categories can be distinguished:

1. Rules for EU citizens who have resided in Malta for at least five years. Citizens of EU member states who have lived in Malta for at least five years can freely acquire Maltese real estate (residential and non-residential) without obtaining an *AIP Permit*
2. Rules for EU citizens who have not lived in Malta for at least five years. This category of persons can acquire a primary residence or any immovable property required for business activities without obtaining an *AIP Permit*. A permit is required for obtaining immovable property for secondary residence and other purposes
3. Rules for non-EU citizens. These persons can acquire a primary residence for which an *AIP Permit* is required. The minimum purchase

price is EUR 104,486 for an apartment and EUR 174,143 for other types of property. These prices are subject to indexation. Immovable property for specific projects may also be acquired where a project may be in the interest of Malta's economic development. In these cases an *AIP Permit* is also required

There are certain areas in Malta, usually the more costly and up-market developments (called *Designated Areas*) where no AIP Permit is necessary and where there are no restrictions on the number of properties that can be purchased. In these areas, foreigners (EU and non-EU citizens) are allowed to buy more than one property and are entitled to rent the property to third parties. Rentals of other non-designated area properties are only allowed if government approval is obtained and if the property meets certain quality requirements.

Further important preconditions for buying real estate

Capacity and entitlement of the seller

Every seller and every buyer must have the legal capacity to act; therefore they must be capable of contracting under Malta's civil law and if they are acting on behalf of others, they must be duly authorised by a power of attorney. Although it is possible to have a verbal power of attorney, it is the practice to put this in writing and where it is executed outside of Malta, it is usually witnessed by a foreign notary public or Maltese consular office and though this is not mandatory it is recommended and always requested.

Third-party claims and unpaid taxes

Third parties cannot claim any rights against the property or against the new owners of a property unless their right has been registered and protected by a hypothec or privilege or unless they enjoy a servitude or usufruct (see 26.2). However tenants of property cannot be evicted just because there is a change in ownership of the property. There are no taxes on property in Malta and therefore there will never be unpaid taxes burdening the property; any personal tax owed by the seller will never have any effect on the property being sold, unless the unpaid tax has been registered and protected by hypothec or privilege.

Emphyteusis (ground-rent)

In Malta there is a particular legal institution called 'emphyteusis' which derives from Roman law and is very widespread. It can have very important consequences at law and must therefore be carefully considered. Emphyteusis can only be created by public deed and therefore will appear in the notarial searches.

Emphyteusis is a charge imposed on the property for an annual payment by the buyer to the seller of property; the payment is called ground rent. It is common to find that property is sold for 'x' Euro subject to an emphyteusis attracting a ground rent of 'x' Euro. This means that the buyer, notwithstanding that he has paid the full price to the seller, would still be bound in addition to make the annual payment of the ground rent. No matter how small the charge is in monetary terms (sometimes it can even be a few cents per year), the ground rent must be paid.

If the ground rent is not paid for three years, the person entitled to receive the ground rent can ask the Court to impose a term for payment on the debtor and if the ground rent remains unpaid, the Court may order the property to revert to the creditor of the ground rent. It is therefore very important, especially for foreigners, to make sure that they pay the ground rent annually. It has happened in exceptional cases that foreigners owning property subject to emphyteusis do not come to Malta for a number of years and forget to pay the ground-rent; and once they return they find that the Court has ordered the reversion of the property to the beneficiary.

Moreover, emphyteusis can either be temporary or perpetual and can be revisable. Where the emphyteusis is temporary, the property will revert to the beneficiary when the period of emphyteusis expires. Therefore the buyer will only be the owner for the specified period of time. Where the emphyteusis is perpetual, this does not arise.

Perpetual emphyteusis can be cancelled (redeemed) by the buyer by making a one-off payment to the beneficiary of the ground rent. The payment is calculated at 20 times the ground rent for one year unless agreed otherwise. Therefore if the ground rent is EUR 1, the payment due will be EUR 20 and payment of this sum will free the property from the emphyteusis.

Where the perpetual emphyteusis is revisable (that is, the ground-rent is revised from time to time depending on certain conditions), then it can only be redeemed after the first revision. It is important to ensure that the property one is buying is not subject to emphyteusis and if it is so subjected, it is important to make sure of the terms and conditions of the emphyteusis prior to acquisition of the property. These terms and conditions can be onerous and must therefore be investigated in detail prior to the acquisition.

Provisions for protecting the environment, nature and cultural heritage

Environmental protection, preservation of the countryside and protection of historical monuments are within the powers of the *Malta Environment and Planning Authority* (MEPA). Malta is divided into 'building' and 'green' areas and it is very difficult to obtain any form of permit to develop 'green' areas. Also, restrictions apply even within the building areas and not every kind of development is possible; certain properties are scheduled in varying grades and development is only allowed according to the scheduled grade of the property. Acquisition of historical monuments or houses of historical importance is restricted for foreigners.

Access to relevant records and documents

Registries and documents are not usually checked by the buyer but by the notary public who then passes on the collected information to the buyer's legal firm for vetting of title and liabilities. Although it is not always the practice for a buyer to engage a legal firm, it is not appropriate to solely rely on the notary's searches, since a notary has no right to give advice to either of the parties and moreover a notary public has no professional responsibility for interpreting the results of his searches in the Public Registry. Therefore it is recommended to engage the services of a lawyer besides those of a notary public.

A buyer would also do well to engage the services of an architect to inspect the building for structural problems and also to check with the *Malta Environment and Planning Authority* that the property has been built according to the proper permits.

Key points that a seller should consider

Although the law does not regulate how expenses necessary to formalise the contract are to be paid, the following practices have in time become consolidated, so that it will be very difficult to get parties to agree differently.

Transfer tax is paid by the buyer in addition to the agreed price, notaries' fees and researches are paid by the buyer, capital gains tax is paid by the seller, estate agent's fees are paid by the seller, lawyer's fees are paid by the party engaging the lawyer and architect's fees are paid by the party engaging the architect.

The execution of a real estate purchase transaction

The execution of the purchase contract must be done through a notary public who will, within 15 days, register the contract in the *Maltese Public Registry*. Any other form of execution is not valid and has no consequences. A deed of transfer which is not registered in the *Public Registry* by the notary will have effect between the contracting parties but will not bind third parties until it is registered. A notary who omits to register the contract will be liable for damages.

Powers of attorney

Powers of attorney, under Maltese law, can be verbal or written, and both versions are valid. However in practice, only the written form is used in contracts of sale and a copy of the power of attorney is usually attached to the original contract of sale. Powers of attorney executed outside Malta are usually witnessed by a Maltese consular officer or by a foreign notary public. Although this is not mandatory, it is advisable.

Spouses who sell property of the community of acquests are required to both sign the transfer deed. It is possible for one of the spouses to give a power of attorney to the other spouse for signing the transfer deed, without such spouse being actually present of the deed of transfer, however special statutory declarations which are to be included in the said power of attorney apply.

Financing

Financing can be carried out in three ways. The seller may accept to transfer the title of the property to the buyer although the full price has not yet been paid. In this case, the buyer would normally bind himself on the contract to make monthly (or other periodical payments) to the seller and to pay an agreed interest rate which cannot be more than 8% per annum. If interest is stipulated in excess of 8% the debtor can refuse to pay the excess and if the excess has been paid it can be recovered by the buyer. Where part of the purchase price is paid to the seller after the title of the property has been transferred, the seller on the sale contract would reserve in his favour a special privilege over the property being transferred and this privilege would be registered in the public registry. The effect of the privilege is that the seller's right of preference to recover his debt would follow the property, even if the buyer sells it to a third party. If the buyer or subsequent third party defaults on payment, the seller can bring a judicial action to have the property sold by auction and the seller would be paid from the proceeds of the judicial auction.

Alternatively, the buyer can seek financing from a private person. Where the foreigner contracts a loan, it would be the practice to register a special privilege in the lender's favour against the property to ensure repayment of the loan.

A third option is for the buyer to seek a bank loan from one of the commercial banks. These are easily available and banks would normally finance up to 75% of the purchase price. Banks protect their loans by also registering a special privilege against the property being sold.

Purchase through a company

It is allowed to purchase real estate through any entity, whether corporate or not. However, AIP Permit requirements cannot be circumvented by using these types of structures.

Defects and warranty claims

The Maltese civil code, by operation of law, imposes an obligation on the seller to guarantee the property sold against latent defects and peaceful possession. The two warranties can be excluded by the parties to a sales contract if they agree on this. Latent defects are defects in the property which the buyer could not have reasonably discovered for himself. Peaceful possession means that the buyer will not be molested or hindered in his enjoyment of the property by third party claims. In both cases the buyer has a right of action against the seller for restitution of part of the price or for rescission of the sale, however these kind of actions are to be instituted within certain periods of time established by law.

26.4 New construction, rebuilding and renovation

Construction zones and construction permits

All building or modification to buildings must be preceded by an application to the *Malta Environmental and Planning Authority* (MEPA). If building is undertaken without a permit, the authorities have the right to stop the works by issuing an Enforcement Notice and eventually they have a right to demolish illegal constructions with a right to be reimbursed for costs. MEPA is working on introducing a new system of penalties for illegalities in building property. Where an illegality is discovered by MEPA officials, fines will be imposed, which will be accumulative until such time that the illegality is removed. Buildings which are not built with the necessary permits will not be connected to water and electricity services.

It will be very difficult to re-sell buildings which are not covered by a regular building permit. Banks will not lend money to buyers if the property is not covered by a proper building permit. Therefore it is important that a buyer engages the services of an architect who can check that all the permits are in order.

Architect's contract and building contract

It is not very common in Malta to have a contract signed with the architect or builder because their responsibilities are regulated by law. It is obviously advisable still to engage a legal firm to draw up a contract with both parties. Malta is a civil law country which means that damages are automatically imposed on parties who default on their obligations, the main obligation being that agreements must be carried out in good faith and according to the necessary standards of diligence. Therefore both the architect and the builder are responsible for the stability of the building for a period of 15 years and any work they undertake must be completed satisfactorily, according to their art and trade. Independently of whether there is a contract their responsibilities cannot be avoided.

Completion of construction and formalities

When the construction is finished, a building inspector from the *Malta Environmental and Planning Authority* will visit the premises. If the building complies with the relative permit requirements the inspector will issue a certificate.

Deficiencies and warranty claims regarding new construction

This has already been covered in the previous sections and as stated, both the architect and the builders have a responsibility at law to guarantee the construction for a period of 15 years.

26.5 Rental and tenancy

Rental and lease agreements

There is no difference in Maltese law between renting and leasing agreements which both mean the same thing. Maltese rental agreements are especially complicated but the situation has become more stable since 1995. Prior to 1995, complicated rules made it nearly impossible to evict a tenant or to raise rents with the result that the rental market in Malta was practically non-existent. Since 1995, all new rental agreements have been liberalised and are free from the regulations of the old laws and the terms and conditions are now governed by an agreement signed between the parties. It is not necessary to register these agreements in the *Public Registry* and in theory they can be written by the parties and signed by them. However in practice rental agreements are drawn up by legal firms or by notaries.

In 2009 rent laws were reformed again and it is now possible to alter pre-1995 contracts under strict conditions. However, buyers who might suspect that the property they are purchasing has been leased to third parties before 1995 would be well advised to seek legal advice before proceeding further.

There is no restriction on rentals by foreigners and any foreigner can rent anything at any price and for any period of time. Foreigners renting property can, under certain conditions, re-rent it to third parties but this income must be declared to the Maltese tax authorities.

Regulations on protection of tenants and rent control

As stated above, prior to 1995, there were many rules which protected tenants and these applied mainly to Maltese tenants who used the rented houses as their ordinary residence. These have been abolished for agreements signed after 1995 and today all new rental agreements are regulated by the terms and conditions agreed upon in the contract, however, the latter agreement shall include the essential elements *ad validitatem* imposed by the law. Since 2009 it is also possible under strict conditions to alter the conditions of pre-1995 contracts.

26.6 Successions and gifts

Inheritance in Malta is regulated by the *Civil Code* and includes forced heirship provisions.

Applicable law and jurisdiction

As a general principle, the law of the country where the real estate is situated (*lex situs*) will regulate the way real estate is inherited. On the other hand, the succession to the movable estate of a foreigner passing away in Malta will be regulated by the law of his domicile.

Fundamentals of the succession and gift/donation laws of Malta

The *Maltese Civil Code* is the primary legislation regulating succession in Malta. Immovable property situated in Malta is subjected to Maltese succession law as the *lex situs*.

It is usually sensible to draw up a will in Malta to regulate the Maltese real estate. Wills are drawn up by a notary public. Spouses can leave each other as universal heirs. Also property can be left to the surviving spouse in the form of usufruct and the heirs will only enjoy the full ownership of the property once the surviving spouse is deceased.

To be recognized as valid under Maltese law, a will made abroad must follow the form prescribed by the law of the country where it is made. The rules regarding the reserved portion are considered to be public policy, and therefore any dispositions contrary to such rules contained in a will made outside Malta will not be given effect in Malta, if such a will is challenged.

If parties do not draw up a will, the property is inherited according to the rules of intestate succession in Malta.

- If the deceased was unmarried and without children, half of the estate devolves to the deceased's parents (or, if already deceased, to their descendants). The other half of the succession is devolved to the siblings of the deceased, and in the event that the siblings are already deceased, to their descendants
- If the deceased was unmarried and leaves children, the estate devolves upon the children – with equal shares for each child
- If the deceased leaves a spouse, and no children, the surviving spouse becomes the sole heir
- If the deceased leaves a spouse and children, the children – or their children if they are already deceased at the time of the death – become heirs in equal shares. They receive half of the succession. The other half of the succession is devolved to the surviving spouse. Maltese law also grants the surviving spouse the right to continue living in the principal residence of the deceased and the right of use over any of the furniture in the matrimonial home

As mentioned, Maltese law contains the right to a reserved portion to the benefit of the deceased's spouse and descendants. Under these rules the children receive a third of the estate. In an event where the deceased leaves five or more children, their reserved portion amounts to half of the succession. Along with the descendants of the deceased, the surviving spouse receives a quarter of the succession. In the absence of descendants of the deceased, the surviving spouse receives a third of the succession.

The *Civil Unions Act* (Cap 530 of the *Laws of Malta*) came into force in April 2014. In accordance with Article 3 of this Act, registration of a partnership as a civil union shall be permissible between two persons of the same or of different sex. Article 4(1) of the Act states that "save as provided in this Act a civil union, once registered, shall mutatis mutandis have the corresponding effects and consequences in law of civil marriage contracted under the Act". Therefore the above succession laws will also apply to the latter couples who are in a civil union and anything applicable to married couples in general would apply to couples who are in a civil union where applicable.

It is possible to donate real estate and this is treated as a transfer for all intents and purposes. Therefore donations must be done by deed published by a notary and registered in the *Public Registry*. Transfer tax at 5% must also be paid on donations. Reduced rates exist for donations to certain relatives.

26.7 Taxes and charges

One-time taxes and charges on purchase

Real estate transfer taxes

In principle the transfer of real estate attracts the payment of 5% duty paid to the notary when the transfer deed is published. The notary will pay the duty to the Inland Revenue. In case it concerns the buyer's sole ordinary residence part of the purchase price (currently EUR 116,468.67) is taxed at 3.5%, the rest at 5%.

Sales tax (Value Added Tax)

No Value Added Tax or sales tax is charged on transfers of real estate in Malta. However, Malta has a system whereby a final tax of 12% is charged on the transfer value of real estate. This final tax is payable by the seller.

Real estate registration and notary charges

The land registration and *Public Registry* fees are minimal and are of little concern to the parties.

Notaries will usually charge a fee of 1% of the purchase price, plus disbursements for copies, searches etc. The cost of searches has increased considerably in the last few years and it is normal to budget around EUR 1,000.

Lawyers representing either the buyer or the seller will usually charge around 2% of the purchase price.

Annually recurring taxes and charges

Real estate tax

There are no real estate taxes or rates.

Income tax

Income tax is not affected by the property's value except in the case of re-sale where capital gains tax can come into play.

Net wealth tax

There is no wealth tax in Malta. In addition, there are no recurrent taxes or fees due and once the property is bought, there is nothing else to pay. There are no local council rates, waste collection rates or similar.

Capital gains tax

As from November 2005, transfers of immovable property are, in principle, no longer subject to the capital gains rules but are subject to a final withholding tax of 12% on the transfer amount. Under the old system, a transferor would in principle be subject to a 35% tax on the gains made from the transfer. However, when a property has only been held for a period of less than seven years, the transferor may opt to have the actual capital gain taxed at 35%. In such case the transferor must inform the notary publishing the deed.

Non-residents may also opt to be taxed under the old system. To qualify, the non-resident must produce a statement signed by the tax authorities of the country of that person's residence confirming their residence in that country and certifying that he/she is subject to tax in that country on profits derived from the transfer of immovable property situated in Malta.

In order to secure the payment of capital gains, at the moment of signing the transfer deed, the notary will by law deduct 7% of the transfer price and pay this to the Inland Revenue on account of the tax liability.

An important exemption applies to the transfer of one's own principal residence. For the exemption to apply the law requires that the residence has been owned and occupied for at least three consecutive years immediately preceding the date of transfer and that the property is transferred within 12 months from vacating the premises.

Inheritance and gift taxes

There is no succession duty in Malta on movables but the transfer of real estate by inheritance attracts payment of duty at 5%. Duty is paid to a notary public who will then publish a deed transferring the property to the heirs. It is the notary public's obligation to pay the 5% duty to the Inland Revenue.

The same can be said for gift tax. Gifts or donations of immovable property are taxed at 5% but there are certain exceptions for donations to family members where the tax payable is reduced. There is no gift tax on movables.

Other taxes and charges

There are no other taxes or fees involved with the sales or purchase of property.

Incorrect (lower) statement of sale price on the sales agreement

If the transfer takes place through a sale at a price lower than the market value, the tax will be paid at 12% of the market value just the same. The Inland Revenue may appoint an architect to establish whether the value of the property shown on the deed reasonably reflects its market value. Where this varies by more than 15% the Inland Revenue may issue an order in writing requesting the difference in tax. Such order in writing may be issued within 12 months after the date on which the transfer is notified to the Inland Revenue. One would have to pay the difference in tax and relative penalties.

International taxation

Malta has negotiated more than 50 double taxation treaties. These are mostly based on the OECD Model treaty.

26.8 Immigration law and tax residence

Entry, residence and settlement of foreigners

Malta is a member of the European Union and a member of the Schengen Area. Any EU/EEA or third country national who resides in Malta for more than three months requires a permit from the immigration authorities, which is granted on specific grounds. The grounds on which EU/EEA nationals may become resident in Malta include economic self-sufficiency, employment, education and the opening of a business.

The qualifying criteria for Maltese residence in respect of third country nationals vary from those applicable to EU/EEA nationals. For instance, an employment licence is required in order for non-EU/EEA nationals to work in Malta. Such a license is granted upon satisfying certain criteria. Under certain conditions it is also possible for a third country national to become a resident by starting a business in Malta.

Tax residence

Tax residence in Malta is generally based on a variety of factors. Physical presence, intention and purpose are important factors in determining whether a person is considered a tax resident of Malta. All facts and circumstances of a specific case should generally be taken into consideration.

If a foreigner takes up residence in Malta he generally would not become domiciled in Malta. Such a person would become a non-domiciled resident tax payer in Malta. This may bring advantages from a Maltese tax perspective, as foreign income would not be taxable in

Malta if such income is not remitted to Malta. Foreign capital gains would also not be taxable, even if remitted to Malta. A tax resident in Malta is subject to income tax at progressive rates (up to 35%).

Recently a number of special tax regimes were introduced to attract high net worth individuals and retirees to Malta's shores: the *Global Residence Program* and the *Malta Retirement Program*. Tax residence can be obtained under these rules if specific requirements are met as regards real estate rental or investment value, remitted income, minimum tax and minimum stay..

Furthermore, in 2014 the Government of Malta introduced a Citizenship-by-Investment program. The Malta Individual Investor Programme (IIP), which was designed and implemented by Henley & Partners on behalf of the Government of Malta, is the most modern citizenship-by-investment program in the world. The IIP is the newest addition to the global citizenship-by-investment portfolio and offers investors the opportunity to gain Maltese, and therefore EU, citizenship. The Malta program includes three parts – a donation, an investment into stocks/bonds, and a property transaction. The combined minimum investment amount, including applicable government charges and citizenship application fees, is just under EUR 1 million.

International double taxation for residents of Malta

Malta has over 50 double taxation treaties. The double taxation treaties are mostly based on the OECD Model treaty and will generally mitigate tax considerably.

26.9 Checklist: Real estate in Malta

- Do not sign a preliminary agreement before you have taken legal advice
- With the preliminary agreement, expect to pay 10% of the purchase price as a deposit on account of the final payment and 1% on account of eventual transfer tax

- Do not under-declare the purchase price
- Appoint a notary of your own choice
- Get legal advice about the notary's researches before signing the final deed
- Taxes and charges are as follows:
    - 1% of the purchase price for the notary public
    - Up to 2% of the purchase price for legal advice
    - 5% of the purchase price as transfer tax
    - A small sum (a few hundred Euro) for researches in the *Public Registry*
    - Capital gains tax is always paid by the seller
    - Estate agents are paid by the seller

27

Monaco

Principality of Monaco
Principauté de Monaco

by

Donald Manasse

Donald Manasse Law Offices
4 Boulevard des Moulins
MC 98000 Monaco

Telephone: +377 93 50 29 21
Facsimile: +377 93 50 82 08

dmm@manasselaw.com
manasselaw.com

Donald Manasse has more than 20 years experience representing clients in international transactions with a particular emphasis on matters having a connection with Monaco and France. He is a lawyer admitted to practice in New York and Connecticut, USA, and since 1986 in Nice, France. His Monaco office was authorized as a legal consultancy in 1989, as foreign nationals are not admitted to the Monaco bar. His principal areas of work are financial regulation, multinational litigation, representation of victims in fraud cases, structuring and advising on multi-national investments; and languages include French, English, Italian, Russian, Flemish, Spanish and German.

27.1 Introduction

The Principality of Monaco is a sovereign state on the Mediterranean Sea, entirely surrounded by France. It is situated 22 kilometers from Nice and some 20 kilometers from the Franco-Italian border at Menton-Ventimiglia. The form of government is a constitutional monarchy, with strong executive powers reserved for the Sovereign Prince. The *Grimaldi* dynasty has ruled Monaco since 1297.

The country is one of the world's smallest states territorially (197 hectares). There are some 7,000 Monegasque citizens. Foreign residents comprise the remainder of the 32,000 residents.

Monaco's independence has been historically guaranteed by France, through a series of treaties concerning many aspects of political and financial life. Monaco is a member of the United Nations and of the Council of Europe.

Monaco is not a member of the European Union. However, a customs union exists with France, with the result that some of the advantages of the free exchange of goods apply to Monaco in the same way as they do to its neighbor. The currency is the Euro. Monaco's tax system is independent of France, although French nationals, with some exceptions, are considered to be residing in France for income tax purposes if they reside in Monaco. Similarly, Value Added Tax is applied in Monaco in an identical manner and with identical rates as in France, the standard rate being 19.6%.

The legal system is entirely independent of France, but the legal Codes (*Civil Code, Penal Code, Code of Civil Procedure, Code of Criminal Procedure, Commercial Code*) are based on the *Napoleonic Code*, with some important differences from France. The court system again is similar to the French system, and a number of the sitting magistrates are French judges seconded to the Principality, who however swear allegiance to the Prince. Money laundering legislation exists and is strictly enforced.

As regards real estate, the system adopted by Monaco is similar to the French system, but entirely independent. Monaco has its own estate registry. Taxation of real estate transactions is entirely established by Monaco law.

Monaco is divided into five areas: Monacoville, La Condamine, Moneghetti, Monte-Carlo and Fontvieille. The original part of Monaco is Monacoville, where the Palace of the *Grimaldi* family is situated, and La Condamine, where Port Hercule, a port known to the ancient Greeks, is found. Monte-Carlo was developed in the mid 1800s, when the famous casino was built. Moneghetti is a residential area bordering France on the west side of the Principality, with a number of older buildings. Finally, Fontvieille is a new town, built on 22 hectares of landfill into the sea beginning in the 1970s, which now houses a stadium, commercial center, a hotel and housing ranging from public housing to some of the highest cost buildings in the Principality.

27.2 Real estate ownership

Different forms and types of ownership

Ownership of real estate in Monaco can take a number of forms, but the general manner of ownership is the equivalent of *fee simple*, that is outright ownership of property. The most common form of ownership is the ownership of a condominium apartment. The cooperative form of ownership is unknown. In the condominium apartment, the owner owns the walls, and a percentage of the common areas. The relationship between the various owners in the building is regulated by a set of statutes adopted by the building co-owners, and binding on their successors. Ownership is perpetual and not limited in time.

While timesharing properties are not illegal they are not used in the Principality.

Easements, charges, covenants, liens and mortgages

Various ownership interests can be divided by an usufruct, so that one person may have the right to occupy the property during his lifetime (*usufruit*), with the other owners having a reversionary interest at death (*nue propriété*).

It is also possible to grant a long-term lease (*bail emphytéotique*) to a party, which is a ground lease, with the property reverting to the owner at the end of the lease. This form is most commonly used on government owned land leased for development purposes.

Property may have servitudes granted between private parties or with the state. The most common forms of servitudes are those relating to rights of passage of public utility facilities (cables, pipes etc.). It is also possible to obtain servitude on neighboring property which will preserve, for example, a particular view.

Property may also be burdened by liens and encumbrances, relating to debts of the seller, or financing by banks, or to undertakings made to third parties.

Protection of ownership, proof of ownership and registration

Only notaries (of which there are three in the Principality) may register a transfer of title to property at the Registry of Deeds (*Conservation des Hypothèques*), the property register. Proof of ownership is established by establishing an unbroken chain of title for 30 years, by the depositing of the "authentic act" of purchase in the notary's minutes *(au rang des minutes*), and by registering the authentic act at the *Registry of Deeds*.

The notary will then produce an *attestation* as proof of ownership by the buyer, and the certified copy of the act of purchase. In the case of the purchase of a company, ownership of the shares will evidence ownership of the company assets.

27.3 Purchase and sale of real estate

The sales agreement

The Monegasque *Civil Code*, as regards sales, considers an agreement between two parties to be "perfect" when there is an agreement as to the price to be paid and the thing to be sold. Because of this, a private agreement between a seller and a buyer as to the sale of real estate, where the property is sufficiently identified and the price is agreed, or can be determined by the contract, can be enforced at law.

The private sale cannot be registered at the *Registry of Deeds* without the intervention of a notary, but it may be registered at the tax office, to give certainty as to its date. Such a registration is very rare. Registration at the tax office will require payment of 4.5% registration tax, applied to the value of the contract.

In order for title in the property to transfer then to the buyer, a court order will be required, which means that without agreement to sign before a notary, a lawsuit will be necessary. Most sales agreements are accompanied by the deposit of 10% of the value of the purchase price, usually in escrow with the notary or with the lawyers charged with the sale in the event of a transfer of shares of a company owning property in Monaco. Thus, the sales agreement that results in a lawsuit (a rarity in the Principality) will put at risk the buyer's deposit, and the seller's title. In effect, if the buyer sues to enforce the private sales agreement, then the buyer will "publish" at the registry the fact that a lawsuit concerning title to the property is pending. All buyers will then be "on notice" and will purchase subject to that risk.

The more formal sales agreement, which may but does not have to be entered into in the presence of a notary, is known either as a *compromis* or as a *promesse unilatérale de vente*. The difference between the documents in Monaco law is similar to the difference in French law. With the *compromis*, there is an agreement on the price and the object of the sale, usually subject to conditions precedent. Once the conditions precedents are fulfilled, there is then a perfect sale. A court may order the transfer of title to a property if all conditions precedents are fulfilled, but one of the parties refuses to complete.

With the *promesse unilatérale de vente*, however, there is only an option to purchase, which may or may not be exercised. If it is not, the consequence is that the potential buyer's deposit is lost. But the title to the property will not be ordered transferred by the competent court, because there has not been an agreement of sale. In fact the *compromis* will state "Seller sells and Buyer buys..." whereas the *promesse unilatérale de vente* will state "Seller grants the right to purchase to the Buyer, who will exercise that right by ..." and specifies dates and the manner in which the option to purchase can be exercised. The sales agreement in either case can be as a private contract or a notarial contract. It can remain unregistered or be registered, in order to give notice to third parties.

It will also contain undertakings that the real estate to be sold will not have mortgages superior to the purchase price of the real estate, a precise description of the property, and a referral to all servitudes concerning the real estate, or to the fact that there are none other than those in the preceding sale documents.

In general, the initial sale agreement is an offer drafted by a real estate agent or lawyer (including foreign lawyers) in Monaco on behalf of one party, the buyer usually, and accepted by the other party. The parties may then enter into a more formal agreement, or may proceed directly to the notarial sale of the property. The *compromis* or *promesse unilatérale de vente* will generally be drafted by a notary or by other lawyers in Monaco, including foreign lawyers, where the transfer of property is concluded by transferring shares of a non-Monegasque company. The real estate agent is required to have a mandate either from the seller or from the buyer.

Completion of the transfer will always take place by notarial act, other than in those cases where property is held through a company. In those cases where property is held through a company, completion of the transfer will most frequently take place by private agreement and not by a notarial act.

Restrictions on sale and acquisition

Restrictions under family law and matrimonial property regime

Where married individuals are selling real estate, it is possible that because of the matrimonial regime to which they are subject, the spouse could possibly have an ownership interest, despite the fact that the property's title is in the name of one spouse only. This would be the case where spouses are considered married in the "community property regime". It is necessary in those cases to obtain the consent of the other spouse for the sale of property.

There is a requirement to obtain a spouse's consent to sell the matrimonial home.

Options and rights of pre-emption

Similarly, unless it is stipulated in the documents of purchase of the property, there is generally no statutory right to pre-emption on property. Tenants, for example, do not, unlike in France, have a first right to purchase the apartments they occupy, absent a clause to that effect in the lease, which is exceedingly rare. A right of pre-emption will only exist when stipulated in the *acte de vente*, and as a result few properties are so burdened.

A preemptive right generally exists in favour of the government, if the property was built or completed prior to 1 September 1947, and any such prospective sale must be notified to the appropriate government agency.

Agricultural real estate

There is virtually no agricultural real estate in Monaco, and therefore no special provisions exist in this regard.

Restrictions regarding acquisition of real estate by foreigners

There are no restrictions on the acquisition of real estate by foreigners in any part of Monaco. Certain apartments are reserved, for rental purposes, to persons having a certain length of residence in Monaco. Other apartments, owned by the state, are reserved for persons having special needs or special rights as regard their low income or their Monegasque nationality.

All properties on the market are freely purchasable by foreigners, either directly in their own name, or through companies. There is no prohibition to purchasing real estate through an off-shore company - as there will be no taxation in any event either of the ownership or of the resale. However, purchase of property through a foreign company or through a Monaco company held by a foreign company will be subject to a higher registration tax of 7.5%, whereas other transactions are subject to a 4.5% registration tax.

Further important preconditions for buying real estate

Capacity to act and entitlement of the seller

The notary, if the real estate is being sold, or the lawyer, in the event that a company holding property is sold, will verify the capacity of seller and buyer. If one of the parties is a physical person, then the verification will consider whether the party is competent to buy or sell, whether they are adults (in Monaco the age of majority is 18 years but foreigners are assessed in accordance with the age of majority in the country of their nationality).

As regards companies, the notary or the lawyer will verify that they exist, are in good standing in their jurisdictions, and that their directors or administrators have full capacity to act. For that purpose they will demand copy of the by-laws, certificates of incorporation, certificates of good standing and certificates of incumbency. For companies from civil law countries, extracts will be required from the corporate registries.

In the event that a company holding property is sold, additional guarantees are normally requested to guard against possible incapacity to act of the seller.

Third-party claims and unpaid taxes

The notary or a lawyer will verify with the *Registry of Deeds* that the property is not burdened with mortgages or other liens and encumbrances. It is rare to find a tax lien in the Principality because there are no property taxes and no occupancy taxes. More typically, there may be a lien to secure the recovery of common charges of the building that may have remained too long unpaid. In all instances a strict verification of the origin of the funds used by the seller to purchase originally, and by the buyer will be necessary to satisfy money laundering laws.

Heirs of a deceased owner may have a claim if there are ascendants or descendants – but potential heirs will not be entitled to interfere with a sale.

In addition, if the premises are the marital domicile of the seller, it will be necessary to obtain the agreement of the spouse.

Provisions for protecting the environment, nature and cultural heritage

There is no particular legislation for the protection of the countryside or as regards environmental protection. Building permits in general, and modifications of façades in particular will only be granted after the approval of the *Direction de la Prospective de l'Urbanisme et de la Mobilité*, which will take the aesthetic aspect of the building into consideration.

Key points that a seller should consider

The seller should inform the buyer of any hidden defects of which he is aware. The preliminary contracts and deed should relate any apparent defects in the property so that the buyer cannot deny having been informed.

It is not customary to subject a purchase to a satisfactory survey.

The seller will not be concerned regarding the taxation of the gain resulting from a sale, in the absence of capital gains taxation. However, he should preserve all invoices from works done on the property to ensure that his buyer may have recourse against the contractors. He should also be able to justify approval by the authorities of all modifications of the interior layout of the apartment as well as obtaining of a *certificat de récolement* which is the confirmation by the *Direction de la Prospective de l'Urbanisme et de la Mobilité* that the modification works have been executed in accordance with the approval by the authorities.

The seller needs to be concerned about the capacity of the buyer to pay and the source of funds used for the purchase. The source will be verified by the notary or the lawyer charged with the transaction. Nonetheless, the seller is not exempt from making a declaration of suspicion regarding the origin of the funds should any suspicious facts regarding the buyer come to his attention. Real estate commissions are usually charged to the seller, at 5% plus Value Added Tax. They may also be requested of the buyer, at 3% plus Value Added Tax.

The execution of a real estate purchase transaction

Because any modification of apartments or houses in Monaco requires the approval of the *Direction de la Prospective de l'Urbanisme et de la Mobilité*, it will be necessary to verify when purchasing real estate whether any works have been completed without such an authorization. The notary will do this by reviewing the last registered plan for the property and the current description.

The *Registry*, on the other hand, will record all modifications in the ownership, all liens and encumbrances. The *Registry* is very much up to date in the Principality with the result that it is possible to personally consult it prior to purchase to determine whether there are any pending transactions with regards to the same property.

Buyers normally pay the registration costs of the purchase. If the purchase is of real estate (rather than shares of a company) then the documentation will be by *acte authentique* which can only be signed before a notary. The notarial fees and registration costs are 6% of the purchase price. However, as indicated above, where a foreign company or a Monaco company owned by foreign companies is the purchaser, the registration cost will be of 7.5% to which must be added 1.5% for the notarial fee.

The transfer of shares of a Monaco property holding company in favor of individual(s) or a Monaco civil company owned by individual(s) is subject to a 4.5% registration tax, under legislation effective from 1 July 2011. The same transfer of shares in favor of foreign company(ies) or a Monaco civil company(ies) owned by foreign companies is subject to a 7.5% registration tax. For i) foreign property holding companies and ii) Monaco property holding companies owned by foreign companies or Monaco civil companies owned by foreign companies, it is now a requirement that a local fiscal representative be named who will vouch to the authorities whether the beneficial owner of a property company has changed during the preceding 12 months.

If there has been a change, the property holding company, through its fiscal representative, is required to pay the 4.5% registration tax. However, the fiscal representative is not required to disclose the identity of the shareholder, unless requested to do so by a demand from the authorities. If there has not been a change, the property holding company, through its fiscal representative, is required to pay a registration tax of EUR 10. Registration of the transfer of shares within 30 days of the execution is required if the company is a Monaco company (typically a Monaco *société civile immobilière*), regardless of how it is held. Transfers of Monaco company shares may take place by *acte authentique*, before a notary, but are frequently completed before accountants or lawyers. Transfers of foreign company shares take place by private sale and purchase agreements and are generally completed before accountants or lawyers.

Ordinarily, the purchase of real estate is executed before one of the three notaries of the Principality. The notary guarantees good title in the property and the absence of all liens and encumbrances.

The notary will have verified the prior ownership of the real estate (the *origine de propriété*) to ensure that there are no clouds on title during the period of 30 years (the statutory limitations period). Because of the small size of the Principality and due to the fact the *Registry of Deeds* has virtually no delay in the registration of documents, disputes as to title in property are rare in the courts. Real estate commissions are usually charged to the seller, at 5% plus Value Added Tax. They may also be requested of the buyer, at 3% plus Value Added Tax, but are freely negotiable.

Powers of attorney

Individuals selling or buying real estate must either be present or grant a power of attorney to a third party, often the local lawyer or a clerk in the notarial office, to execute the official transfer documents. The powers of attorney must be notarized, or registered before a consular officer. Monaco is a signatory of the Hague Convention on the execution of documents, and therefore an *apostille* will be recognized.

The same formality of the power of attorney will be necessary to register a mortgage on a property in favor of a lender, both for the borrower and lender's representative.

Where the entity being represented is a company, then a minute of the corporate meeting authorizing the purchase or sale or mortgage may specify the identity of the person who can represent the company to sign the act. In that event, the minute may replace the power of attorney, although more frequently the minute will authorize the issuing of that power, in which case, a formal power must be executed.

Financing

Real estate purchases may be financed by loans in whole or in part. The registration at the *Registry of Deeds* of a mortgage or lien to secure repayment must be done by a notary, unless it is a judicial mortgage ordered as a measure of protection for a creditor by the local court.

Local or foreign banks or companies may provide finance. The interest paid to foreign entities is not subject to withholding tax. One difficulty will be in obtaining a satisfactory evaluation of the real estate in order to ensure the lender of the safety of the security offered. The Monaco market is small, and unusual, and the experts that normally operate for lending banks on the Côte d'Azur may frankly say that they cannot evaluate Monaco real estate accurately.

Real estate is valued on a price per square meter basis, with opinions differing on how balconies and terraces are to be taken into account: they are often included at a third of their size.

Companies that are not regularly authorized financial institutions cannot habitually engage in real estate financing in the Principality without running the risk of being considered as illegally engaging in the banking business.

Purchase through a company

Foreign or local companies may purchase property in Monaco. While there are increased registration taxes at the outset and an obligation to name a fiscal representative concerning the foreign companies or local companies owned by foreign companies, with the ensuing costs, there is no counter-indication from a corporate tax point of view, as there could be in neighboring France. In fact, many Monaco apartments are held in either *sociétés civiles immobilières* created under Monaco law, or foreign on- and off-shore companies.

Warranty claims

In general, no warranties are given for apartments sold that are more than 10 years old. The purchase is usually made on an "as is" basis. However, if there has been renovation by the previous owner, then the intervening contractors may have residual warranties for the works, within a 10 year period of completion, depending on the nature of the work, and the date on which it was accepted by the owner. This is why it is important upon purchase of an apartment to request copies of all contracts with the contractors who participated in any works done.

27.4 New construction, rebuilding and renovation

Zoning law and construction permits

Any construction, and any rebuilding or renovation that requires the modification of a façade or exterior of a building, or the modification of inner walls of an apartment, whether or not they are bearing walls, requires a building permit. The permit is requested from the *Direction de la Prospective de l'Urbanisme et de la Mobilité* in Monaco, and will be presented by a Monaco architect. Foreign architects may and often do participate in the projects in the Principality, but must collaborate with a Monaco architect to do so.

Architect's contract and building contracts

The responsibilities of the architect are detailed under various articles of the *Civil Code* and under the *Code des devoirs professionnels des architects* which entered into force on May 20 2011, with regard to his or her client.

The architect's responsibility is for 10 years following receipt of the works by the client. The architect's contract will be based on a standard contract elaborated by the French architect's association. It is common that the architect's fees will be elaborated in accordance with the different aspects of his missions with payments being due once that aspect of the mission is complete. For example, the various stages of the architect's missions could be as follows:

- Preparation of plans with client's approval
- Preparation of the request for a building permit
- Obtaining of building permit
- Preparation of the *marché* or request from contractors to bid on the project

- Evaluation of the bids; choice of contractors
- Supervision of the works
- *Récolement* – or review of the works by the authorities, with a view to approval
- Receipt of the works by the client

The fee would be in this way compartmentalized, although being based on a percentage of the works. The *Code des devoirs professionnels des architects* which entered into force on May 20 2011 sets a minimum fee paid to the architect for a full project. The fixed minimum fee depends on the classification of the works:

- B1: simple conception design work that uses standard layouts and in which the work systematically uses identical elements and programs
- B2: works necessitating a thorough study because of the complexity of the program or because of connections or overlaps of different program elements, or because of the particular composition, structure, facilities, equipment or land
- B3: exceptional work involving research or a thorough specialized study

The percentages are as follows:

	B1	B2	B3
For works costing between EUR 225,225 and EUR 450,450	8.30%	9.40%	11.20%
For work costing between EUR 450,450 and EUR 1,876,873	7.60%	8.80%	10.60%
Above EUR 1,876,873	7.10	8.30%	10.00%

The amount of the architect's fee can be freely negotiated but cannot be inferior to the percentage mentioned above.

The contract clauses can be freely negotiated.

Completion of construction and formalities

The type of building contract will depend on whether the works to be done are a new construction of a multi-story apartment house, or the renovation of an existing building, apartment or indeed portion of an apartment. Where there are major works, such as construction or reconstruction of walls, roofs, electrical and plumbing systems, then the contractor will normally have insurance covering a 10 year period from the reception of the works. This is not a legal requirement in Monaco, but it is generally observed. For major building projects, a bank guarantee ensuring completion is normally required.

The building works must comply with the permits issued, whether on an individual basis, or a global (building site) basis. There is an inspection by the authorities upon the declaration that the works are complete. If the works are in accordance with the authorization obtained, the authorities deliver a *certificat de récolement*.

Deficiencies and warranty claims regarding new construction

The procedure for enforcing rights under warranty claims is a judicial procedure, which will require the nomination of an impartial building expert to review the works and evaluate the complaints concerned. The expertise process is generally lengthy and expensive, but is the only alternative where the contractor's insurance companies refuse to settle matters. Litigation is frequent, unfortunately.

27.5 Rental and tenancy

Rental and leasing contracts

For foreigners choosing to become residents in the Principality, the option exists to rent rather than purchase property. Legislation exists that limits certain apartment's availability to long-term residents and citizens. Such apartments, generally in older buildings built or completed before 1 September 1947, are subject to a form of rent control. It is important for the foreigner intending to purchase an apartment to know whether the property might be subject to such legislation. However, for the foreigner becoming a resident in a rental apartment, this is less important, because they will not have the option to lease such favorably priced properties.

Monaco law does not otherwise protect residential tenants. Expulsions for non-payment of rent are relatively easy to obtain from courts and to enforce with the assistance of bailiffs and the police. There is no prescribed length of time for which a residential apartment must be leased by an owner, unless the protective legislation applies. Leases are generally for either a one or three year period, with rental increases based on French construction indexes applying for the longer term leases. The owner may refuse to renew the lease, and may apply whatever lease increase the market will bear at the expiration of the contract. Similarly, there is no pre-emptive right to purchase allowed a tenant.

Typically, the lease agreement will contain a clause that automatically renews the lease for a period equal to the lease period, or for a period limited to one year, unless notice of the intention not to renew is given by either party at least usually three months prior to the lease's termination.

Tenants pay the condominial common charges on apartments in advance on a quarterly basis. Payments should be reconciled by the building managing agent at the end of each year with the actual expenditures. In principle the owners of the building should pay that portion of the charges which concern the general maintenance of the building (major works and renovations).

All tenants must have insurance to guarantee their neighbors and other third parties in the event of damages flowing from the use of the apartments (generally covering water damage and fire).

Tenants taking over apartments are sometimes asked by the prior occupants to pay the equivalent of "key money" for certain fixtures that may remain behind. This is not illegal, but the new tenant should not assume that they will be able to require the same amounts when they decide to leave, or are asked to leave, their apartments.

For residential tenants, a three month deposit is usually required. This deposit is kept either by the real estate agent or the owner, and it is not interest bearing. It should be returned at the end of the lease, and its purpose is not to guarantee the payment of rent, but the wear and tear on the premises, that will be determined by comparing the report of the visit by the owner and tenant at the beginning of the lease, with the same report made at the tenant's departure. This report, known in French as an *état des lieux* may be done in the presence of a bailiff (*huissier de justice*).

Regulations on protection of tenants and rent control

Rules protecting commercial tenants exist under *Law n° 490 of November 24th, 1948*. Commercial leases are, at the tenants' option, made for the duration of nine years, and the tenant may terminate every three years. The owner may not refuse to renew the commercial lease without paying the tenant an indemnity which is often equal to one year's turnover. The tenant may sell his commercial lease (residential tenants may not sublet without the owner's approval), but such a sale is subject to the landlord's preemptive right.

Certain types of apartments are subject to rent control, usually in older buildings built or completed before 1 September 1947, although the system is the subject of intense scrutiny and changes in its application are expected. Other forms of rent control exist, with a certain class of apartments reserved only for persons having resided in Monaco more than five years and having had an activity for more than six months during that period. Such tenants are entitled to a six year lease on the apartments available. Rents and terms and conditions of lease agreements are otherwise freely negotiable, and the legislation and case law is not protective of sitting tenants regardless of the length of time they have inhabited the premises or the cost of the improvements they may have made to the leased apartment.

27.6 Succession and gifts

Applicable law and jurisdiction

Monaco applies Monegasque law to all real estate situated in the Principality. Thus if a foreign national owns property in Monaco, at his death, the Monegasque *Civil Code* will apply as to how the property is bequeathed, which means that children will have a reserved right to inherit a portion of their parent's Monegasque real estate, and parents equally of their children.

The question of choice of law, as regards moveable property, in the event of death, is however very differently resolved. Monaco jurisprudence applies the law of the nationality of the decedent to his moveable estate. Monaco recognizes the principle of private international law known as *renvoi* so that the citizens of those foreign countries, whose law looks to the place of domicile of a decedent, will have Monaco law applied to their successions. Citizens of countries that apply the law of the nationality of a decedent to his estate will find that their national law controls their moveable or personal property at death.

Fundamentals of the succession and gift/donation laws of Monaco

The rules on inheritance under Monegasque law are that one child will inherit half of his parent's estate, two children will receive two thirds and three or more children will receive three quarters. The remaining part of the estate can be freely left by the person, by establishing a valid will, to whomever they feel should receive it.

Where real estate is owned by a company, then the shares of the company are considered moveable property, and the inheritance of those shares would not automatically be subject to Monaco law, and reserved heirship.

A foreigner may make a valid will in Monaco in one of the three Monaco forms – handwritten, authentic (before a notary) or mystic, (by turning over to a notary a sealed envelope containing the will). In addition, Monaco will recognize a will that is made in a form that is valid accordingly to the nationality of a testator, or valid in accordance with the law of the country in which the will is made. This means, for example, that while a joint will is radically invalid under Monaco law, it is valid for spouses of German nationality for example.

Monaco Law 214 of 1936 provides that foreigners whose national law allows the formation of trusts may validly create trusts in Monaco to arrange for their succession, either by a trust established during their lifetimes or at the time of their death through their will. The form required under Monaco law must however be respected, that is the trust must be created before one of the Monaco notaries (a foreign trust may be brought into Monaco). Any other form of trust created by will is invalid, and will render the will itself invalid, under current jurisprudence.

The matrimonial regime established by spouses at the time of their marriage and in the course of their first matrimonial domicile will be respected in order to determine rights of inheritance. Thus the estates of foreign spouses whose national law at the time of marriage, and the law of whose first matrimonial domicile was the community property regime, will take into account the surviving spouse's community property rights.

Similarly, Monaco will recognize the law of the nationality of a married couple as regards property rights in the event of divorce. Where the spouses are of different nationality, then Monaco will apply the Principality's regime which is the separate property regime.

27.7 Taxes and charges

One-time taxes and charges on purchase

Real estate transfer taxes

The transfer of title to property is subject to registration taxes and notarial fees.

Value Added Taxes

With regards to new buildings, Monaco follows the Value Added Tax regulations of France, and therefore the acquisition will be subject to Value Added Tax (VAT, French TVA) if the sale is the first transaction on the apartment within five years of the completion of the building. Notarial costs to be paid by the buyer will then be approximately of 2%, and any offer will be considered tax included (*toutes taxes comprises* or TTC) unless it is specified otherwise.

Real estate registration and notary charges

Registration costs at acquisition for purchasers who are individuals, or purchasing through a Monaco civil company owned by individuals, are 6%, of which 4.5% are the registration taxes and stamp duties and the remainder represent the notarial fees.

Acquisition costs are always borne by the buyer, not by the seller.

It is possible to purchase real estate with a lower acquisition tax, in a regime of *marchand de biens* or real estate dealer. The registration cost will be approximately 2%. However in that case, the property must be resold within four years, or a tax penalty will be applied. The capital gain earned in a *marchand de biens* transaction is subject to Value Added Tax. Fees for the purchase of shares of property owning companies are freely negotiated. Some lawyers will request a percentage based fee while others will bill either on an agreed capped fee or on an hourly rate basis.

Foreign companies, or Monaco civil companies owned by foreign companies, pay a registration tax of 7.5%, plus the 1.5% notarial fee.

Annually recurring taxes and charges

The only ongoing costs will be the condominial common charges, the annual insurance premium and utility bills, and for tenants, the rents and lease agreement tax (*droit au bail*, equal to 1% of the value of the lease and common charges upon registration and renewal).

Real estate tax

There is no land or real estate tax in the Principality. Following completion, there are no property taxes, habitation or occupancy taxes in the Principality. There is no withholding tax for the foreign company selling real estate and no requirement to file a tax return, unless the transaction is made under the *marchand de biens* regime.

Income tax

Monaco has no income tax on individuals. It applies a business profits tax to those businesses where more than 25% of the annual turnover is derived from clients outside of Monaco.

Net wealth taxes

There is no net wealth tax in Monaco.

Capital gains tax

There are no capital gains taxes in the Principality.

Inheritance and gift taxes

There is no inheritance tax between spouses, parents and children, regardless of the nature of the property, whether real or personal. The highest rate of inheritance tax, between unrelated persons, is 16%. Gift tax follows the inheritance tax.

Other taxes and charges

Real estate commissions are usually charged to the seller, at 5% plus Value Added Tax. They may also be requested of the buyer, at 3% plus Value Added Tax. However, commissions are subject to negotiation, and may be freely discussed by the parties concerned.

Incorrect (lower) statement of sale price on the sales agreement

The declaration of a false, low, price in an authentic act is a penal offence. Monaco retains the possibility of pre-empting properties by offering a price equal to the declared price, increased by 10%. However the use of this option is exceedingly rare.

International taxation

Monaco has entered into more than 25 treaties providing for the exchange of information or the elimination of double taxation treaties. The long-standing treaties with France only concern income tax and estate tax and are only applicable to Monegasque and French nationals.

27.8 Immigration law and tax residence

Entry, residence and settlement of foreigners

No customs or border controls exist on land between France and Monaco. Customs and border controls are situated at the Port of Monaco, for those entering by boat, and at the heliport.

Foreigners may freely come to Monaco. If they intend to settle in the Principality, they must make a request to the authorities within eight days of their arrival. If they do not intend to settle in Monaco, then a foreigner may remain for up to three months without having a residence permit.

The procedure to establish residence varies in accordance with nationality. All citizens of the European Community may apply for residence directly at the foreign police services in Monaco. Other nationals must apply at the French consulate at their current place of residence. France will in any case, even with EU nationals, be entitled to express its approval or disapproval of the application which will affect whether the foreigner is allowed to reside.

The procedure can take from six weeks to three months depending on whether the request is made directly in Monaco or through a French consulate. Once the *visa long séjour* (the visa allowing establishment in Monaco) is granted, and the foreigner arrives in Monaco, they must report and request the carte de séjour at the police.

Applicants must show they have either have gainful employment in the Principality or sufficient means to live without working, which is generally done by producing a letter from a bank in Monaco to that effect. The foreigner will be asked to show that they are of good moral character by producing copies of their police records or declarations from reputable professionals. They will also be asked to produce birth records, medical certificates and proof that they have appropriate accommodation in the Principality.

Once residence is granted, the foreign person is required to make Monaco their principal residence in order to maintain the residence permit. The foreign resident will be required to show proof of a residence, in the form of a lease or ownership documents, and to prove use of utilities (electricity, telephone and water) conforming to an actual residence, in order to be allowed to renew his residence permit.

Tax residence

Because the Principality has no income tax, it is not concerned with the fiscal place of residence of its residents. It is however very concerned, and enforces strictly, the requirement that the residence be a real and effective residence and not a sham.

Monaco will issue a certificate of residence for those individuals requiring it. It is not however a certificate of tax residence.

International double taxation for residents of Monaco

Again because Monaco has no income tax and no double taxation treaties, there is at present no incidence of double taxation for those becoming Monaco residents. But for the same reason, residents may find themselves subject to the highest withholding rates in the countries of origin of their income.

27.9 Checklist: Real estate in Monaco

- Determination of the type of real estate one seeks to find: residential or commercial; income generation or capital appreciation; price range determined on a Euro per-square-meter basis and section of Monaco; older building or newer building; with or without concierge; with or without parking; with or without view of the sea
- Selection of whether to purchase property or company owning property
- Determination of manner of purchase, whether through a company, trust or other entity, or whether in the individual's name
- Selection of appropriate real estate agent in accordance with the general market serviced (high end, middle range, low end or commercial)
- Visits to real estate
- Selection of notary and/or lawyer
- Offer to purchase accompanied by 10% deposit made to the name of a notary, lawyer or agent
- Signature of a preliminary contract (*promesse* or *compromis*) binding the parties and formalizing the deposit
- If condominium, review of the *règlement de copropriété* (Condominium Statutes) and annual running costs (*charges*) and works voted by the property owners that may be charged to new owners
- If company, same as above, but additional due diligence investigation of the company, the property and of its beneficial owners
- If works are required on the property, determination if the works will be authorized by the managing agent of the building and the *Direction de la Prospective de l'Urbanisme et de la Mobilité* of Monaco

- Conclusion of the transfer of ownership at the notary (or in the case of a company at the lawyer's office) and payment of the purchase price, fees and registration costs as applicable, following verification by the notary of the power of the buyer and seller to act, and of clear title on the property
  - If direct property ownership, registration of the transfer at the property registry (effected by the notary) and payment of registration fees within one month of signature
  - If ownership through a company, notification immediately to the company registered agent, administrators, banks etc., of the change in beneficial ownership, and change, if so decided of company administrators, contact numbers and addresses

27.10 Bibliography

Editions Francis Lefebvre, Dossiers Internationaux, Monaco 4th Edition

Editions Du Jurisclasseur: Principauté De Monaco, Monaco

Principauté De Monaco: Revue De Droit Monégasque, Monaco

EPI Communication: The Best of Monaco, Monaco 2004

28

Montenegro

Montenegro
Crna Gora

by

Dr. Wolfram Zeihe
Ivan Raičević

Prelevic Law Firm
Bulevar Sv. Petra Cetinjskog 130, 7th floor
81000 Podgorica, Montenegro

Telephone: +382 20 510 506
Facsimile: +382 20 510 507

office@prelevic.com

Dr. Wolfram Zeihe is a partner of Prelevic Law Firm in Podgorica and serves international investors as legal interface for their commercial undertakings in Montenegro. He focuses on real estate trades and developments and has a special expertise in the legal launch and the recovery of local residential and hotel projects as well as in the legal design of off-plan sales and maintenance concepts. His practice involves the setting up of joint venture relations, M&A, restructurings, loans and securities. He also serves as a trusted lawyer to the local Embassies of Germany and Austria. Dr. Zeihe has studied in Frankfurt, Paris, New York and Cologne and is a registered attorney with the BAR in Berlin.

Ivan Raičević is a Podgorica based attorney practicing with Prelevic Law Firm since 2011. He focuses on real estate transactions and developments, advises particularly in the local estate planning law and further involves in the creation of legal real estate sales and maintenance concepts for major residential projects in Montenegro. Mr. Raičević studied at the Faculty of Law of the University of Montenegro and is admitted to the BAR in Podgorica.

28.1 Introduction

Montenegro regained full national independence in 2006, after it had constituted part of former Yugoslavia for nearly 90 years. With a territory of less than 14,000 square kilometers alongside the western coast of the Adriatic Sea, it is home to 625,000 inhabitants. Although not part of the Eurozone, Montenegro has adopted the Euro unilaterally as a permanent foreign currency. The gross government debt of Montenegro amounted to EUR 2.02 billion in June 2014, 57.51% relative to the national GDP, which is below European average, but debts were accumulating rapidly in recent years.

Montenegro is member of the United Nations, the World Trade Organization, the OSCE and the Council of Europe. The political leadership, including main parts of the opposition, strives for EU membership. This is backed by a stable public acknowledgement. After concluding the *Stabilization and Association Agreement* in 2007, Montenegro gained official candidate status and on 29 June 2012 the EU launched the official accession negotiations. The talks initially focus on Chapters 23 and 24 of the *EU Acquis*, covering topics such as fundamental freedoms, judiciary, fight against corruption and organised crime. The *Montenegro Progress Report of 2014*, issued by the European Commission, is critical on the implementation of legislative reforms, notably as regards anti-corruption. Montenegro is also an official candidate state to join NATO. NATO membership is a short-term political goal of the Montenegrin Government.

Property investors choose Montenegro mainly for the construction of tourist facilities, such as resort hotels and second home developments. With an average flight distance of two hours from all main European capitals, Montenegro offers 250 kilometers of Adriatic coast, lined with beaches and historic sites dating back to Roman, Ottoman, Venetian and Austrian-Hungarian reigns. The Bay of Kotor, known as the southernmost fjord of Europe, is in its entirety a UNESCO World Heritage site. Along with Biogradska Gora, one of the oldest national parks worldwide, Europe's steepest canyon, Tara, and various other natural settings, Montenegro also possesses a uniquely untouched mountain region.

Montenegro earns 19.5% of its GDP in the tourism industry, although the country has still not reached the volumes of international tourism it had generated prior to the breakout of the Balkan wars. The real estate market in Montenegro was on a rise, until amongst other causes the global financial crisis of 2008 led to a major setback in both property trade and development. Meanwhile, the market shows clear signs of recovery and is now driven by institutional investors. Among those are *Dukley Group*, focused on the main coastal city, Budva, developing private residences, hotels and an improved marina; *Orascom Group*, which is building up a 7 million square meters site on the Luštica peninsula; *Porto Montenegro*, an already far realized project re-designating a former naval shipyard in the Kotor Bay to become a major luxury marina in the Mediterranean; and *Portonovi*, a future residential and tourist development, also in the Bay of Kotor, which is backed by the Azerbaijan state oil company *Socar* and is said to come to a total value of EUR 500 million.

28.2 Real estate ownership

Until recent years, the local laws still commonly assumed that private persons hold real estate through an exclusive usage right of principally state owned land. This conception changed in the political transition, which Montenegro is currently undergoing as a former Yugoslav republic. Upon the adoption of the *Constitution* in October 2007 and with the *Law on Ownership Rights* coming into force in March 2009, real estate ownership has now the unrestricted quality of freehold title ownership as the most comprehensive dominion over a particular property. Every owner is entitled to possess, use and dispose of its property within the limits determined by law.

Real estate may be acquired on the basis of the law, private agreements, decisions of judicial or administrative state bodies or by inheritance. Ownership rights are generally perpetual and not limited in time.

Expropriations are legal only to the extent necessary for satisfying of the public interest and require fair compensation. Real estates owned by the Montenegrin state or by a local municipality are commonly referred to as state property and are particularly regulated by the *State Property Law*. In contrast, private property is the real estate owned by legal and natural persons, for which solely the *Law on Ownership Rights* applies. Land, buildings and individual building units of one physical property may be owned by different persons and involve different legal positions.

Types of ownership

Types of ownership described by Montenegrin law are single ownership, co-ownership, joint ownership and common hold. A single owner has exclusive control over the property, including the right of disposal and the establishment of mortgages and liens.

Two or more owners sharing the freehold title to an undivided property are co-owners. The ownership relates to an ideal part of the whole property. If co-ownership parts are not defined, these are deemed to be shared equally. Each co-owner may possess and use the property together with the other co-owner/s in proportion to its ownership part without violating the rights of the co-owners. Co-ownership parts may be disposed of. Other co-owners, however, deserve a pre-emptive right. Costs of use, management and maintenance of a property and encumbrances shall be borne by the co-owners proportionally. Each co-owner has the right to require the division of the property.

Joint ownership evenly relates to undivided property, but unlike in case of co-ownership, the ownership parts are determinable, but not defined. Each owner is entitled to the use of the property and is responsible for managing it. Disposal and the establishment of encumbrances require the consent of all joint owners. The most common example is the joint ownership of spouses.

Common hold pertains to the ownership of common areas of a building and the land, on which such building is situated. This type of ownership applies in particular to residential or commercial buildings with more than one unit, where several owners share the property over common hallways, joint facility areas and similar. The common hold rights are accessory to the ownership over the individual building unit, and the transfer of the ownership of a unit automatically includes the transfer of the common hold rights over the common areas.

Easements, charges and mortgages

The Montenegrin law, similar to other jurisdictions, distinguishes between easements in favour of another property and private easements.

With the real easement in favour of another property, the owner of one property (dominant estate) is granted a right in respect of another property (servient estate), usually the performance of certain activities. Subject to the easement right may also be that the owner of the servient estate refrains from certain activities, which would affect the dominant estate. The Montenegrin *Law on Ownership Rights* does not give a final catalogue of real easements. The law does, however, regulate the most common types, such as the right of way, installation of utility lines, right to a window, the right to remain with a part of a building on the servient estate and similar. The real easement may be established by (i) legal transaction, (ii) court or administrative decision, and (iii) adverse possession. If the easement is established by court or administrative decision, the owner of the servient estate is entitled to compensation. If a dominant estate is being divided, the easement right remains for all parts of the divided property. However, the owner of a servient estate may request the termination of an easement, for which the encumbrance on its part is actually not required. Real easements may cease if the easement right is not exercised for a certain period of time, or if the requirement for the easement has vanished, or respectively, if circumstances, for which the easement right was established, have changed.

Private easements are established on real estate in favour of a particular natural or legal person. Private easements are not inheritable, and expire when the beneficiary dies or is dissolved. Private easements in favour of a legal entity expiry automatically after the lapse of 30 years. Regulated types of private easements are usufruct, right of use and right of dwelling.

Usufruct comprises the right to use and to collect the benefits from someone else's property with the obligation to preserve the essence of the servient estate. With the right of use the beneficiary may use another person's property and collect the benefits, within the limits of the beneficiary's personal needs and without violating the essence of the property. Benefits exceeding the needs of the holder of the right of use remain with the owner of the servient property. On the basis of a dwelling right, a beneficiary may exclusively use an apartment or apartment building along with members of its household, but only during the lifetime of the beneficiary.

Charges, meaning encumbrances on a property and restrictions of ownership rights, are registered with the land registry in accordance with the *Law on State Surveying and Cadastre of Immovable Property*. Encumbrances and restrictions that are not registered with the land registry do not affect a new owner of a property, if (i) such owner was neither aware, nor could have been aware of their existence, meaning that the new owner acted prudently and thoroughly checked the legal and factual state of the property prior to acquisition, and (ii) such encumbrances or restrictions are not directly established by law.

Neighbouring rights are legal authorizations of the owner of a real estate to use the neighbouring real estate, or to request from the owner of the neighbouring real estate to perform or to omit certain activities. Neighbouring rights exist *ex lege* and are not registered with the land registry. If construction activities on a property endanger a neighbouring building or similar construction, the owner of the endangered property may require the person who would be liable for the possible damage to take necessary precautions. A landowner may, for the purpose of irrigation, installation of pipes and performance of other activities, cross neighbouring lands, with the obligation to inform the neighbours in a timely manner. Owners of properties that are exposed to excessive emissions may require from the owner of the emitting property to remove the cause of the emissions and to compensate for incurred damages. Exceptionally, when excessive emissions are arising from activities permitted by a competent body, the owner of the exposed property is not entitled to request omission, but may require damage compensation and adequate measures to be undertaken in order to prevent or reduce future excessive emissions.

Mortgages are the most common means of security established on real estate in Montenegro. The subject of a mortgage may be any real estate property that can be monetarily valued and traded. Also, a co-ownership share of a property may be mortgaged individually. For mortgaging of a co-ownership share, the mortgagor does not require the approval of the other co-owners of the same property. In the case of joint ownership, all owners need to consent to the establishment of the mortgage, who, subsequently, become mortgagors.

A mortgage is established on the basis of (i) an agreement, (ii) a lien statement, which is the unilateral establishment of a mortgage in favour of a third person, (iii) a judicial decision, or (iv) by law. A mortgage agreement and a lien statement need to be concluded before a competent public notary in notary inscription form. A competent notary has its official seat in the court district where the relevant real estate is situated. A mortgage is deemed to be established upon registration with the responsible land registry.

Since the ownership over buildings and individual building units may be separate from the underlying land, mortgages over a construction land do not automatically extend to an apartment building and its units. Therefore, the legal institute of a mortgage over objects under construction provided by the *Law on Ownership Rights* has high practical relevance for lenders or financial partners of real estate developments in Montenegro. Accordingly, a mortgage over an object under construction, or parts hereof, such as apartment units, business premises, garages, or similar, may be registered for the construction land, even prior to the commencement of the construction works, provided that a final building permit has been issued.

Subsequently, when the newly constructed building along with its building units is registered with the land registry, the mortgage is *ex officio* registered for the building or individual units, respectively. The advantage of the mortgage over objects under constructions is that lenders, financial partners or plan purchasers are being secured by a priority rank mortgage over a newly constructed building or building unit, regardless of changes of the developer, land owner or owner of the building and the building units.

If the mortgagor defaults on the secured claim, the mortgagee may execute the mortgage either by judicial foreclosure or by extra-judicial sale. The judicial foreclosure is the usual manner of executing a mortgage. The mortgage agreement or the lien statement may, however, foresee an extra-judicial sales procedure, which avoids the involvement of local courts and enables the enforcement by the help of a public enforcer, a lawyer or a registered real estate agency.

A mortgage ceases when it is deleted from the land registry's entries. This will usually require that the mortgagee either waives its rights, the secured claim is entirely settled, or a court has finally decided on the cancelation of the mortgage. Unlike in other jurisdictions, a mortgage does not expire by the lapse of time, unless otherwise established by the mortgage agreement or the lien statement.

Protection of ownership and proof of ownership and registration

The data relevant to titles over a real estate are kept with the land registry, formally referred to as *Cadastre of Immovable Property*. The land registry records the factual details of the real estate, including cadastral maps plus respective property and obligation rights in accordance with the *Law on State Survey and Cadastre of Immovable Property*. The local land registries are regional units of the *Real Estate Administration of Montenegro*, and are part of the national administration under the Ministry of Finance.

The ownership over a real estate is regularly proved by an excerpt from the land registry, the Property Sheet (see 28.3). The Property

Sheet is a public document and the data contained within it is considered as accurate and true. However, a Property Sheet is not an undisputable proof of title rights. A third person providing a legitimate interest may initiate a court procedure with the aim to overrule the presumption of accuracy of the data contained in the Property Sheet.

The *Law on State Survey and Cadastre of Immovable Property* establishes the principle that the cadastral data may be relied upon. However, in the practice of the Montenegrin courts, a third person, who was not registered as an owner of a property may re-establish a registered ownership position even against a good faith buyer, if they serve sufficient proof that they are the real owner of the respective property. This exception follows the principle "no one can transfer to others rights more extensive than those that it possesses", meaning that by private transaction only an owner may provide title ownership. In such a situation, a buyer may acquire ownership only through the legal institute of adverse possession by holding the property as a good faith possessor for a period of 20 years.

The Montenegrin *Law on Ownership Rights* contains regulations protecting the owner against unjustified possession and other disturbances of the ownership right by another person. The right to file a complaint for the repossession of a property or to cease other disturbances is also granted to persons, who are still not the owners, but have a legal ground that is superior to a legal ground of a person, who is not the real owner and who is disturbing or is in unjustified possession of the property.

The registration of ownership or other property rights is initiated by submitting a request to the competent land registry. The rule of priority applies if more than one registration request is submitted for a particular real estate. Once a request for registration has been accepted, all other requests need to be denied, if in conflict with the new status created by the earlier registration.

28.3 Purchase and sale of real estate

The sales agreement

In a substantive sense, apart from detailing the contracting parties and the purchase price, a sales agreement needs to give a sufficient description of the sales object. This requirement has practical relevance in off-plan sales, where the cadastral details of the future property are yet unknown. Further, as a formal requirement, the sales agreement has to be concluded before a competent notary in notary inscription form. The recent introduction of notary offices is advantageous insofar as the notary is due to inform the parties on potential legal obstacles and legal risks.

The Montenegrin *Law on Ownership Rights* applies the legal institute of a *Clausula Intabulandi*. The *Clausula Intabulandi* is the written consent of the seller that the buyer may register its ownership title over a real estate with the competent land registry. The *Clausula Intabulandi* is made before the public notary. It may constitute a separate document or it may be included in the sales agreement. In practice, the *Clausula Intabulandi* is regularly issued by the seller subsequent to the payment of the purchase price. The public notary is not obliged but often volunteers to submit the *Clausula Intabulandi* to the responsible land registry to register the new owner.

The registration of priority notices is a legal possibility, but not often practiced. Instead, in order to ensure that the *Clausula Intabulandi* will be issued upon payment of the purchase price, the parties make escrow arrangements in larger transactions, with either a commercial bank, the notary or a local attorney serving as an escrow agent. In smaller transactions, the notary may be asked to transmit a previously executed *Clausula Intabulandi* independently to the land registry in the moment when the buyer has duly paid the purchase price to the seller.

Restrictions on sale and acquisition

Restrictions under family law and matrimonial property regime

Similarly to other jurisdictions, spouses may have individual and joint property. Consequently, spouses jointly manage and dispose of their joint property. Spouses may, however, regulate their property ownership differently by a marital agreement.

The Montenegrin *Family Law* presumes that in cases where only one spouse is registered with the land registry as an owner of a joint property, it is deemed that both spouses are registered, if such registration was not conducted on the basis of a written agreement between the spouses. This presumption may have significant implications in the establishment of various property rights. The *Law on Ownership Rights* prescribes that for the disposal and encumbrance of joint property the consent of all joint owners is required. Therefore, agreements of disposal or encumbrance of a joint property without the consent of all joint owners are null and void.

Exceptionally, on the basis of an agreement which was not concluded with all joint owners, a third party may nonetheless acquire ownership over the respective real estate, provided that the buyer is of good faith and that, in particular, the ownership right over the respective property was not registered in the land registry in the name of all joint owners. Although this exception is prescribed only for the transfer of title ownership, Montenegrin courts have extended this practice for cases in which joint property has been mortgaged by only one spouse. Such agreements are not declared null and void if the other spouse was aware of the mortgaging and did not object. This passive behaviour of a spouse is then deemed as acquiescence.

Pre-emption rights

A pre-emption right, meaning the obligation of an owner to offer real estate for sale to a certain beneficiary under the same terms and conditions agreed with a potential purchaser, may be based on contract or on law. A typical legal pre-emption right is the one of a co-owner of a real estate property. The contractual pre-emption right needs to be registered with the competent land registry in order to secure its effect against third parties. A pre-emption right based on law is unlimited in time and it is not registered with the land registry. A contractual pre-emption right expires after five years, unless it has been concluded for a shorter time period.

Agricultural real estate

Agricultural real estate is of common interest and enjoys special protection. The Montenegrin *Agricultural Real Estate Law* categorises agricultural real estate as fields, gardens, orchards, vineyards, meadows, pastures, swamps, ponds, marshes and other land with natural and economic conditions with the potential for serving general interest and agricultural production. Consequently, agricultural real estate may generally be used only for agricultural purposes, and only exceptionally for other purposes provided by law.

The intended use of a certain terrain is determined by the relevant planning documents. A building developer firstly acquires a copy of the plan for the respective land from the land registry, and then refers to the local municipality for the local planning documents or to the competent ministry for the state planning documents, in order to request the issuance of an excerpt from the relevant planning document.

Restrictions regarding acquisition of real estate by foreigners

Foreign persons, natural or legal, may in principle acquire real estate in Montenegro under the same conditions as Montenegrin persons. However, the *Law on Ownership Rights* stipulates a catalogue of exceptions. Foreigners may not acquire the ownership over (i) natural resources, (ii) goods in general use, (iii) agricultural land, (iv) forests and forest land, (v) cultural monuments of high importance and particular significance, (vi) immovable property within one kilometer of the national border and islands, and (vii) immovable property located in an area in which foreign ownership is prevented by law in order to protect national security interests. A significant counter-exception applies to agricultural land, forests and forest land. A foreigner may acquire such land of a ground area of up to 5,000 square meters, if it pertains to a residential building which constitutes part of the acquisition.

Apart from the restrictions pertaining to the acquisition of the title ownership, foreign persons remain entitled to short and long-term lease agreements; concessions; build, operate and transfer arrangements; and similar public-private concepts.

Foreigners originating from a EU member state have the right to claim equal treatment with Montenegrin citizens in respect to the acquisition of real estate. This follows from the *Stabilization and Association Agreement* that was concluded between the EU and Montenegro in 2007, even if the equal treatment is not yet reflected by the *Law on Ownership Rights*. In practice, EU citizens may trust that they will be treated equally when applying for a registration with the land registry.

A method often applied by foreign investors seeking to avoid restrictions for foreign persons is the establishment of a local limited liability company (d.o.o.), which enjoys the rights of a Montenegrin person.

Further important preconditions for buying real estate

Capacity to act and entitlement of the seller

Montenegrin citizens acquire full legal capacity for entering into binding contracts at the age of 18. Real estate property owned by minors or persons under custody is managed on their behalf by their parents or custodians. Regularly, parents and custodians need to obtain the approval of the local *Social Welfare Centre* before they dispose of or encumber a real estate on behalf of the minor or, respectively, the person under custody. In order to satisfy the needs of public trust in the land registry, possible limitations of the legal capacity of a property owner are required to be registered.

The authority of the natural person executing a sales agreement on behalf of a legal entity may generally be verified by an insight in the Company Registry, which lists the persons authorised for representing the entity. Accordingly, if the signatory acts on the basis of a power of attorney, such power of attorney would need to be issued by a person duly registered. In cases where a transaction appears essential to the overall business of a legal entity, the contractual partner should verify, if separate from a general authorisation for representing the company, the transaction is required to be backed by the board of directors or the shareholders' meeting. The public notary is obliged to verify in the individual case, if the natural person acting on behalf of a legal entity is duly authorised.

Third-party claims and unpaid taxes

The *Law on State Surveying and Immovable Property Cadastre* stipulates that the entire data registered in the land registry in respect to real estate, and the rights over such real estate, shall be considered as fully reliable. This means that no person shall suffer legal disadvantages from potential third party claims, if the ownership title or some other right over the real estate was established while relying on the records held with the land registry. Any new owner or acquirer of other rights is therefore legally protected from third party claims if such claims were not registered with the land registry, the acquirer did not have knowledge of such third party claims and could also not be expected to know of the discrepancy between the factual and the registered status. The level of caution that may be expected from an acquirer always depends on the individual circumstances. Generally, a person interested in acquiring a right to a real estate will inspect the entries held with the land registry and shall also verify the factual background, such as the existence of lease agreements and similar third party rights established for the property. Since an acquisition requires the notary inscription form, the public notary is obliged to warn the acquirer about existing third party rights.

Unpaid taxes may lead the Tax Administration to establish a security mortgage on one or more pieces of real estate owned by the tax debtor.

Such security mortgage will be registered with the land registry, but does in principle not hinder the transfer of the ownership title or other rights. The acquirer, however, has to fear the execution of the mortgage by way of a forced sales procedure, if the previous owner remains in default with its tax obligations. Should the registration of the security mortgage not be initiated prior to the title transfer, unpaid taxes cannot be settled from the respective real estate.

Provisions for protecting the environment, nature and cultural heritage

Certain undertakings require prior evaluation of their impact on the environment. This applies to projects in heavy industry, mining, energy, traffic, tourism, agriculture, forestry, water and communal management; and for any project planned in particularly protected areas. The evaluation may be conducted by a person registered for the performance of design, engineering and the development of respective studies and analyses.

Operators of facilities which are polluting the environment are required to monitor the emissions and other sources of pollutions. The operator is obliged to inform the *Agency for Protection of the Environment* if the pollution is determined to exceed the allowed limit. Further, any Entrepreneur performing activities which pose a risk to the environment or a health threat is required to maintain sufficient liability insurance.

The protection of cultural goods is regulated by the *Law on Protection of Cultural Property*. A cultural good may be subject to private ownership. The status of a cultural good is determined by the *Administration for the Protection of Cultural Property*. Anyone may initiate the protection of an asset as a cultural good by simple petition. The status of real estate as a cultural good is required to be entered in the land registry in the form of a notation. Once the private owner of a cultural good intends to sell a property, the State has a pre-emptive right to purchase it. Furthermore, ownership over a cultural good comes with certain obligations, such as proper use, regular maintenance and timely implementation of measurements for protection. Finally, the owner is obliged to report to the *Administration for the Protection of Cultural Property* every legal and physical change on the cultural good. In addition, if during construction or other works a property of archaeological significance is found, the person conducting such works is obliged to cease further activities and to report the findings immediately to the *Administration for the Protection of Cultural Property*.

Access to relevant records and documents

The local Land Registries are part of the *Real Estate Administration* of Montenegro. They hold the cadastral data on land parcels, objects, separate parts of objects, the rights over real estates, the persons holding such rights, encumbrances and restrictions. The Property Sheet is an excerpt from the registry, which gives the relevant information on a real estate in several parts:

- A sheet – land plot
- B sheet – right holder of land plot
- V sheet – structures and separate parts of structures and their right holders
- G sheet – encumbrances and restrictions

The Property Sheet is a public transcript and enjoys public trust. Anyone may acquire the issuance of a Property Sheet without having to prove a legitimate interest. The *Real Estate Administration* maintains an online data base, which is frequently updated. It appears, however, that the online entries are not always accurate. These may be used only as an indicator, but do not have the quality of a court proof.

Key points that a seller should consider

For securing the payment of the purchaser, the parties may involve a commercial bank as escrow agent. Also, payments may be deposited with the public notary. The notarial deposit has the same legal effect as a court deposit. Alternatively, it may be agreed that the public notary withholds the duly executed *Clausula Intabulandi* and transfers it to the land registry only when the buyer has paid the purchase price. The sales agreement may also be made in the form of an executive deed, giving it the function of a directly enforceable document. The seller is obliged to observe money laundry regulations established by the *Law on Prevention of Money Laundering and Financing of Terrorism*. Further, the seller is obliged to inform the buyer of any material defects or defects of title that the seller is aware of at the moment of transfer. While the property transfer tax will be borne by the buyer, the seller needs to bear in mind that the acquired purchase price may be subject to capital gains tax or personal income tax.

The execution of a real estate purchase transaction

The sales agreement and the *Clausula Intabulandi* are executed before a public notary in a notary inscription form. Following the conclusion of the sales agreement, the notary will *ex officio* report the agreement to the land registry and to the Tax Administration. Subsequent to the payment of the purchase price, the notary regularly volunteers for transmitting the *Clausula Intabulandi* to the responsible land registry for the title registration of the new owner. The title transfer is completed when the buyer has been registered as owner of the property.

Powers of attorney

The seller and buyer may each authorise a third person to act on their behalf on the basis of a power of attorney. In the case of a real estate transaction, the power of attorney needs to be made in a notary inscription form. The scope of authorisations given by the power of attorney may be determined at the discretion of the issuer.

Foreigners may issue the power of attorney before a public notary of their home jurisdiction, provided that reciprocity in the acceptance of foreign notarial acts can be assumed. Local notaries and courts do not require an Apostille. The foreign power of attorney needs to be translated by a sworn court interpreter admitted to the courts in Montenegro.

Financing

Typically, real estate acquisitions are financed in the way that a mortgage over the acquired property serves the financing institution as security. There are no limitations as to who may be the beneficiary of the loan. Apart from local commercial banks, a purchaser may also acquire a loan from a foreign bank. The buyer would then, apart from the loan agreement, which may be under foreign jurisdiction, conclude with the bank a separate mortgage agreement, or issue a lien statement, under Montenegrin law and the foreign financier may directly take the position of the mortgagee.

Purchase through a company

Legal entities may acquire ownership rights over real estate under the same terms as private individuals. The business form most commonly used as holding vehicles is the limited liability company, the *društvo sa ograničenom odgovornošću* (d.o.o.). The founder may be any foreign or Montenegrin natural or legal person. A d.o.o. may have up to 30 founders. The director of a d.o.o. needs to be a natural person. Foreign citizens may become directors, if they are at least temporary residents in Montenegro and hold a valid work permit. The seat of the company needs to have the status of a designated business space. Minimum capital for establishment of a d.o.o. is EUR 1. Apart from using local holding vehicles, a purchaser may equally buy through a foreign company under the conditions generally applicable to foreigners.

Defects and warranty claims

The seller is responsible for material defects existent in the moment of title transfer, regardless of whether or not the seller was aware of them. The same applies to material defects arising after transfer, if this is due to a cause previously existing. However, the seller is generally not liable for defects of which the buyer had positive knowledge or that the buyer could have noticed by regular inspection.

The buyer is obliged to inspect the property in a regular manner and to make any objections for visible defects within eight days, or immediately, if the sales agreement was entered between commercial parties. If the inspection is conducted in the presence of all contractual parties, the buyer is obliged to indicate visible defects immediately to the seller. Otherwise, the buyer loses his respective rights, such as removal of defect, price reduction or termination. If material defects appear subsequent to the handover that could not have been noticed by regular inspection, meaning hidden defects, the buyer is required to report the defect to the seller within eight days, or immediately, if the sales agreement was entered by commercial parties. The seller is not usually liable for material defects that occur more than six months after the handover, unless the parties have agreed otherwise. This timeline of six months does not apply if the seller had positive knowledge of the material defect, even if the buyer has failed to inspect the property or to timely notify the seller. The main secondary rights of the buyer (defect removal, termination, price reduction) expire one year after the buyer has notified the seller of the material defect. Accordingly, the buyer may be required to file a complaint to the competent court in order to avoid the lapse of legal deadlines.

28.4 New construction, rebuilding and renovation

Zoning law and construction permits

Spatial development and the conditions for construction of building structures in Montenegro are regulated by the *Law on Spatial Development and Construction of Structures*. Zoning is conducted through the adoption of planning documents, which regulate organisation, development and use of spatial areas, as well as measures and guidelines for protection and improvement of the same. The adoption of planning documents requires public participation and debate and the involvement of various competent state authorities and relevant institutions. Depending on whether these are adopted by the State or local municipal parliaments, planning documents are generally classed as state planning documents or local planning documents.

The *Spatial Plan of Montenegro* is the main strategic planning document on a state level and provides basic guidelines for the spatial organization of Montenegro. The *Special Purpose Spatial Plan* encompasses territories of one or more local municipalities with common natural or other features of special significance for Montenegro, such as national parks, maritime domain, natural reserves, cultural heritages, exploitation fields and similar. The *Detailed Spatial Plan* is adopted for regions where structures of interest for Montenegro or of regional significance shall be constructed, such as state structures of general interest, industrial areas, warehousing and free zones, tourist settlements, and similar. Finally, the *State Location Study* determines the requirements for construction and execution of works for areas of a *Special Purpose Spatial Plan.*

On local level, the *Spatial Urban Plan* defines the objectives and parameters of spatial and urban planning of a municipality. The *Detailed Urban Plan* then stipulates the requirements for the construction of structures for parts of the region covered by the *Spatial Urban Plan.* Alternatively, municipalities opt for the adoption of an *Urban Project*, a document generally similar to the *Detailed Urban Plan*, which is applied for specific areas with significant and complex construction projects. Finally, the *Local Location Study* applies to areas within the *Spatial Urban Plan*, for which it is not intended to adopt a *Detailed Urban Plan* or an *Urban Project.*

Construction projects in coastal areas in Montenegro fall under the regime of the *Law on Maritime Domain*, and further need to comply with the *Special Purpose Spatial Plan for the Maritime Domain*, which details the guidelines for construction and other interventions in coastal areas. If the *Special Purpose Spatial Plan* does not give all required planning details, a *State Location Study* needs to be adopted.

Classed under Maritime Domain are, in particular, the seacoast, harbors, marinas, bathing areas, cliffs and the sea bottom. Montenegro joined the *Convention for the Protection of the Marine Environment and the Coastal Region of the Mediterranean*, the so called *Barcelona Convention*. On this basis the Montenegrin Parliament adopted the *Law on Confirmation of the Protocol on Integral Management of the Coastal Region in the Mediterranean* in December 2011. Accordingly, Montenegro undertakes to determine an inland area where construction shall be prohibited. This zone shall not be less than 100 meter wide, measured from the seashore. This rule may however be adjusted if it is in the special interest of the State. A new law regulating the maritime domain is in the adoption process and it is expected that the requirements of the *Barcelona Convention* will be implemented in more detail.

Morsko Dobro is a public company established by decision of the Parliament of Montenegro on the basis of the *Law on Maritime Domain*. It manages the maritime domain and concludes individual agreements on the use of sites or facilities under maritime domain, such as the lease of beaches or the use of objects and land plots in coastal areas.

On the basis of the relevant planning documents, and upon the request of an interested party, the authority responsible for passing the construction permit issues the *Urban Technical Conditions* (UTC). The UTC are an excerpt from the detailed planning documents pertaining to a particular urban plot, or parts thereof, and summarize the necessary requirements for the technical documentation of the future development. Accordingly, the UTC give data such as purpose of the structure, number of floors, number of units, allowed usable area, boundaries and relations with neighboring urban plots, earthquake and environmental protection, connectivity matters and alike. The UTC are due to be issued within 30 days after the request has been submitted.

Prior to the development, the local municipality shall prepare the construction site for the equipment with communal services. This includes resolving of ownership relations through, for example, expropriation, the development of planning, technical and other documentation, measures for the protection of cultural or natural monuments, and similar. For equipment with communal services, the municipality further provides the connections of the urban plot for electricity and water supply, sewage system, telecommunication, road access and suchlike. The investor compensates the municipality for the connections for communal services with a respective communal fee. The connections with communal services may, alternatively, be constructed by the investor in accordance with the planning documents. In such cases, the question of connection charges is regulated by individual agreement between the investor and the municipality.

The Montenegrin Government currently considers dismissing the communal equipment fees in order to help improve the business environment in the real estate sector. The Municipalities strongly oppose this as they would suffer the loss in income.

The application for the construction permit needs to give the principal data for the envisioned building structure and needs to include the following documentation:

- Technical documentation, meaning the conceptual project or the main project along with the report on the respective review
- Evidence of the private legal rights for undertaking construction on the site and consents of all owners participating in the same urban plot, even if the building is constructed only on a part of the urban plot that is exclusively owned by the applicant
- Third party approvals, opinions, and other evidence related to the electric and water supply system and alike
- Evidence on payment regulations with regard to the communal services equipment
- Evidence of liability insurances for the investor and its technical consultants

The construction permit shall be issued within 30 or in some cases within 60 days upon the submission of the respective application. Subsequently, the investor is obliged to commence with the building works within two years.

The construction permit is normally issued by the local municipality. For some exceptions the *Ministry for Sustainable Development and Tourism* will be the issuing body, in particular, for state structures of general interest, hotels, religious, theater, cinema, sports and similar facilities exceeding a total area of 1,000 square meters, systems and structures to be built on the territory of two or more municipalities, various sorts of industrial facilities, and similar.

In order to simplify the procedure for issuance of the construction permit and for the avoidance of corruption gateways, Montenegro has recently introduced the system of *one counter window*. It removes the burden for the applicant of the construction permit needing to apply separately for subordinate approvals and consents of third party authorities and entities, and provides that the authority responsible for the issuance of the construction permit obtains *ex officio* such other data necessary for the development of the technical documentation.

Architect's and building contracts

An architectural contract is a type of service agreement and falls under the regime of the *Law on Contracts and Torts*. An investor enjoys all regular rights vis-à-vis the architect as service provider, such as for late performance, rectification of deficiencies, regulations for hidden defects, termination provisions and damage compensation.

The consultants responsible for the development of the technical documentation need to be registered with the local Company Registry for the development of such technical documentation. At least the leading designer needs to be a graduated engineer or have adequate technical experience with the development, supervision, revision or evaluation of technical documentation with a professional exam, and also needs to be a member of the *Chamber of Engineers of Montenegro*. The *Law on Spatial Development and Construction of Structures* establishes certain conditions if the technical documentation is being developed by a foreign professional.

The building contract between the investor and the main contractor is a type of a service contract, which is specifically regulated by the *Law on Contracts and Torts*. Written form is mandatory for the building contract. The local market is accustomed to optional turnkey clauses, whereby the main contractor is due to finalise the construction for a fixed fee. The building contractor is obliged to perform all construction works on the basis of the technical documentation. The building contractor is also obliged to allow the investor to perform constant supervision of the construction works and to control the quantity and the quality of the used materials.

Completion of construction and formalities

The construction of new objects usually has to be completed within three years after the issuance of the construction permit. In case of a reconstruction project, the investor will be given two years. Such terms may be prolonged upon the investor's request.

Prior to occupancy of a completed structure, the investor needs to obtain a use permit. The use permit is issued by the same authority that earlier granted the construction permit, and is granted if the constructed building is in accordance with the construction permit as well as with the applicable regulations, standards and norms of quality.

Deficiencies and warranty claims regarding new construction

The investor is obliged to inspect the new construction and to inform the building contractor on detected deficiencies without delay. Following the inspection and acceptance of the executed works, the contractor cannot be made liable for deficiencies that could be noticed by regular inspection. For hidden deficiencies, the investor may refer to the contractor within one month after detecting these. Following the lapse of two years after the acceptance of the building works, the investor can no longer claim deficiencies. However, if the building contractor knew of such deficiencies, and had not accordingly informed the investor, the contractor remains liable even after acceptance and even after the lapse of two years.

Separate from the rectification of deficiencies, the building contractor remains liable for the overall solidity of the building structure for as long as 10 years after the handover of the construction works. This liability includes defects of the land on which the construction was built, unless the contractor can refer to a qualified expert opinion, establishing the land as suitable for construction and if during construction no circumstances occurred which could raise doubt to such expert opinion. If the structural defect is caused by a flaw in the plans for the construction, the architect who developed the plan is liable towards the investor. The liability for the solidity of the building structure applies equally towards future acquirers of the building construction. Also, the liability for structural defects can neither be excluded nor limited by agreement.

28.5 Rental and tenancy

Rental and tenancy are governed by the *Law on Contracts and Torts*. The relations of lessor and lessee are organized materially similar to other European jurisdictions. Importantly, the Montenegrin law establishes fewer mandatory provisions for lease agreements with private tenants and widely allows contractual freedom also for lease agreements over housing space.

Rental and lease agreements

Lease agreements over any real estate need to be made in writing, and the signatories are required to have their signatures verified before a public notary. One copy of the notary's lease agreement will *ex officio* be sent by the notary to the competent tax authority. The lease fee accumulated by the lessor is subject to Personal Income Tax or VAT.

Unless otherwise regulated in the lease agreement, the lessor is obliged to maintain the real estate in mint condition and to rectify defects, while the lessee is obliged to cover minor repairs caused by the regular use of the property.

The *Law on Contracts and Torts* differentiates between the lease of housing space and commercial premises. If the lease agreement does not provide for a fixed lease term, the notice period for terminating the lease agreement is three months. When a lease of housing space is terminated, any person bearing a respective legal interest is entitled to request from the local authority body the eviction of the person occupying without legal ground the housing space or common parts of a residential building. Alternatively, a forced eviction may be reached upon a final court verdict.

According to the *Law on State Property*, real estate owned by the State or a municipality may be leased out by contract for up to 30 years subsequent to the decision of the Government of *Montenegro* or, respectively, the municipal administrations. A lease term of up to 90 years requires the decision of the Montenegrin Parliament upon the proposal of the Government. Regularly, public land may be leased out only following a tender procedure.

Regulations on protection of tenants and rent control

The Montenegrin law establishes no particular terms for the protection of tenants and does also not provide for capped fees of applicable rents.

28.6 Succession and gifts

Applicable law and jurisdiction

According to the *Law on Succession*, foreign citizens may, under the condition of mutual reciprocity, inherit real estates, other properties and rights like Montenegrin nationals, unless otherwise specified by international agreement. Reciprocity is presumed, unless a person with a legal interest in the matter proves the opposite. The Montenegrin jurisdiction is exclusively competent for the regulation of successions and gifts of real estates located in Montenegro.

Fundamentals of the succession and donation laws of Montenegro

With regards to legal succession, statutory heirs of the first order are children and the spouse inheriting in equal parts. If the deceased does not have descendants, the spouse comes in the second order with the parents of the deceased, each inheriting half of the decedent's assets. If the heir died prior to the deceased, the right of representation applies. This means that the part of the estate which would otherwise have been inherited by the already deceased heir, will be inherited by its children in equal parts, therefore, by the grandchildren, if a child of the deceased has already died, or by the brothers and sisters of the deceased instead of a departed parent. An unmarried spouse enjoys equal rights as a regular spouse. Also, adopted children and children born out of wedlock are treated as legally equal.

For succession by will, the Montenegrin *Law on Succession* distinguishes several forms of last will acts or testimonies. These are holographic testament, oral testament, witnessed testament, judicial testament, testament made on a Montenegrin vessel, testament made during war or mobilization and International Testament.

Foreigners intending to regulate their will in respect to real estate in Montenegro usually opt for the form of an International Testament. The International Testament is established irrespective of the testator's nationality, residence, location of the testator's estates or the place where the International Testament was made. When establishing the International Testament, the testator needs to comply with the provisions of the *Uniform Code of the Washington Convention*, which provisions are implemented in the local *Law on Succession*.

The testators cannot exclude obligatory heirs from the heritage. Obligatory heirs are the testator's progeny, spouse and parents. Progeny and spouse are entitled to one half of the part they would have inherited as statutory heirs. Other obligatory heirs deserve at least one third of the statutory heritage. Grandparents, brothers and sisters may become obligatory heirs if they are permanently incapable to work or lack the necessary means of living. Exceptionally, the testator may exclude an obligatory heir, if the heir has damaged the testator by violating legal or moral norms. The conditions for such exclusion are tight and may be accepted in cases where the heir has committed a severe criminal offence against the testator or its family members.

Gifts are donated by gift contract on the basis of the *Law on Contracts and Torts.* If the subject of the gift contract is the transfer of the ownership to a real estate, the gift contract needs to be made before a notary in notary inscription form. With a gift contract, the donor may withhold for itself or another person certain rights connected with the gift or order the beneficiary to perform or to allow certain activities. If the beneficiary does not comply with the order, the donor may terminate the agreement and require return of the gift. As in other European jurisdictions, the Montenegrin law regulates gifts *mortis causa,* meaning that a gift is made under the condition of the donor's death. The respective gift contract must also be made in notary inscription form.

The donor may terminate a gift contract or revoke a gift, if the beneficiary has shown grave ingratitude towards the donor or a donor's close person. Grave ingratitude is assumed if the beneficiary committed a criminal offence against the donor, or persons close to the donor, or if the beneficiary has gravely violated legal obligations towards the donor, or intentionally caused significant damage to its property.

28.7 Taxes and charges

One-time taxes and charges on purchase

Real estate transfer taxes

Each transfer of real estate – unless it relates to the first sale of a newly constructed object – is subject to Real Estate Transfer Tax. The Real Estate Transfer Tax is owed by the acquirer and amounts to 3% of the market value of the real estate as evaluated by the competent tax authority. Domestic and foreign legal and natural persons, resident and non-resident, are treated equally with regards to this tax obligation.

Tax exemptions apply, for example, to the acquisition of real estate by diplomatic representations, domestic state bodies and bodies of local municipalities, and to persons who acquire residential units for their housing needs for up to 20 square meters per household member. If the real estate is brought into a local legal entity by a shareholder as capital contribution, the Real Estate Transfer Tax does not fall due for the legal entity. The same applies in the case of company mergers and divisions. If real estate is inherited, a spouse, children or parents of the deceased owner are exempted from the Real Estate Transfer Tax.

Commercial banks in Montenegro do not pay Real Estate Transfer Tax for property acquired from a credit debtor in exchange for receivables, provided that such property is re-sold within three years following the date of acquisition.

Sales tax (Value Added Tax)

VAT is charged on the sale of goods and the provision of services, plus on imports to Montenegro. The regular VAT rate is currently 19%, while the reduced rate is 7%.

The first disposal of newly constructed objects is deemed as a sale of goods. The developer collects the VAT from the first purchaser along with the purchase price and reports and pays the collected VAT to the Tax Administration of Montenegro. The developer is required to specify the VAT either in the SPA or, if applicable, in invoices for the individual instalment payments. Each subsequent title transfer is subject to the 3% Real Estate Transfer Tax.

Real estate registration and notary charges

Any agreement on the disposal of a real estate, including preparatory documents, such as reservation or preliminary purchase agreements need to be concluded in a notary inscription form before the public notary. The notary fees depend on the transaction value and are currently determined by the *Notary Tariff*, as follows:

Real Estate Value in Euro	Notary Fee in Euro
0 to 5,000	70
5,001 to 20,000	120
20,001 to 40,000	170
40,001 to 60,000	250
60,001 to 80,000	300
80,001 to 120,000	350
above 120,000	*

**plus EUR 10 per each additional EUR 15,000 of purchase price.*

The notary fee for an individual notarization cannot exceed EUR 5,000. Regular sale and purchase agreements are charged with one whole fee, preliminary purchase agreements or reservation agreements are charged with one half of the applicable notary fee, while annexes are charged with 25%. The notary charges may increase depending on how many persons are parties to the transaction. Also, foreigners will likely be required to involve certified court interpreters. Any applicable fee will be increased by 19% VAT.

Once the agreement over the transfer of real estate is executed, the administrative procedure for the registration with the land registry may be initiated either by the public notary or by the acquirer. Currently, an applicant for title registration pays a fee of EUR 10 to the *Real Estate Administration* of Montenegro and an additional EUR 5 as State Administrative Tax.

Annually recurring taxes and charges

Real estate tax

The *Real Estate Tax Law* demands payment of a Real Estate Tax equally for domestic and foreign legal and natural persons, regardless of whether these are resident or non-resident in Montenegro. Anyone who owns real estate in Montenegro on 1 January will be liable for tax in that year. The tax base is the market value of the real estate on 1 January according to criteria such as purpose, size, location, quality of the real estate and other elements that may influence the market value. The Real Estate Tax rate may range between 0.1% and 1%. The actual rate is determined by the municipality where the real estate is situated. Exceptionally, the tax rate may be higher than 1%, in cases where the subject of taxation is:

- Uncultivated agricultural land
- Secondary housing
- An illegal construction object
- A hospitality facility situated in an urban zone with priority for tourist development
- Construction land that is not built-up in accordance with planning documents, or similar

The Real Estate Tax is calculated and determined for each individual taxpayer in an individual decision issued *ex officio* by the competent municipal tax authority. The local tax authority sends individual tax decisions with payment instructions to the residence address of the taxpayer by 31 May. The taxpayer may settle the Real Estate Tax in two equal instalments, the first of which is due on 30 June and the second on 30 November of the relevant tax year.

Income tax

The income tax of natural persons is regulated by the *Law on Personal Income Tax*. A taxpayer may be a resident or non-resident natural person, who generates revenues from:

- Personal earnings such as a monthly salary
- Self-employment activity

- Earnings from property rights, such as income acquired from leases
- Income on capital, such as interests
- Capital gains, for example, the positive difference between the purchase and the resale of an asset

Also subject to taxation for a resident natural person is the income personally generated inside and outside Montenegro. A non-resident natural person is taxed for the income generated from permanent business activity in Montenegro (see 28.8). Documented expenses may be set off from the tax base. The Personal Income Tax is regularly 9%, or 15%, if the personal earnings exceed a gross monthly amount of EUR 720. The taxpayer is required to calculate and declare their Personal Income Tax by submitting the special tax application form to the Tax Administration of Montenegro. The taxpayer is required to specify if income was generated outside Montenegro and if respective taxes were paid. If the taxpayer has generated income outside Montenegro, a proof of the tax payment in the foreign country, documented by the competent tax authority, should be submitted along with the tax application.

Local legal persons are obliged to pay Corporate Profit Tax on their income from inside and outside Montenegro. The Corporate Profit Tax is a flat rate of 9%. The tax base is the profit of the legal person reported in the Income Statement of the year the tax is determined for. Taxable profit is generally the revenues minus the expenses of the company, determined by the Montenegrin tax authorities in accordance with local accounting regulations and international accounting standards. The Income Statement and the Corporate Profit Tax Application should be submitted to the Tax Administration of Montenegro no later than three months after the expiration of a calendar year. The tax amount given in the Corporate Profit Tax Application is required to be paid within the same three month time period.

Net wealth tax

Net wealth is not levied in Montenegro.

Capital gains tax

The income tax of individuals and the Corporate Profit Tax of legal persons are subject to capital gains tax and may include the profit realized by the disposal of real estate properties, shared capital, securities, property rights or other. The tax rate is 9%.

Inheritance and gift taxes

The taxation of inheritance and gifts of immovable property in Montenegro is based on the relevant regulations of the *Law on Real Estate Transfer Tax*, and the tax amounts to 3% of the market value of the acquired real estate. Natural and legal persons acquiring real estate situated in Montenegro are also subject to taxation.

Remuneration for communal equipment of construction land

As one of several conditions for the issuance of the construction permit, an investor is required to obtain evidence that it has regulated the relations with the local authorities in respect to the remuneration for the equipment of the construction land with communal services. The remuneration is determined as a fixed compensation for the communal equipment of one square meter of the gross building surface and depends on the zone where the construction lot is situated, purpose of the future building, current equipment conditions on the respective construction land and the prospective participation of the investor in the communal equipment (see 28.4).

In addition to the remuneration for communal equipment of the construction land, investors in projects located in the coastal municipalities are obliged to pay the Regional Water Supply Contribution in view to support the development of the regional water supply network in the coastal area. According to the *Regulation on the Method of Calculation of the Special Contribution for Projects in Coastal Municipalities*, an investor pays 1% of the investment value determined in the respective project documentation submitted to the authority competent for the issuance of the construction permit.

Tourist tax

Tourist tax is payable by both residential and foreign natural persons who own secondary housing. The tourist tax is payable annually and is calculated on the basis of local regulations such as the real estate value, size and level of development. Secondary housing is defined as a residential facility that is not the permanent residence of the real estate owner, and which is used by the owner, its family and guests for recreation and vacation.

Incorrect (lower) statement of sale price on the sales agreements

The sale price declared in the notarial deed does not necessarily determine the remuneration of the notarial services or the tax basis of the Real Estate Transfer Tax. According to the *Law on Real Estate Transfer Tax* the declared sale price may generally serve as the tax basis. However, if the declared price does not agree with the market value of the respective real estate, the competent tax office is authorized to evaluate the market value. Further, if seller and buyer attempt to avoid taxes by stating a lower sale price than they have actually agreed, they expose themselves to criminal charges.

28.8 Immigration law, tax residence and naturalization

Entry, residence and settlement of foreigners

Foreigners, including those holding a temporary residence permit, are obliged to report to the competent police administration within 24 hours upon their arrival. Providers of accommodation are obliged to report the stay of foreigners to whom they provide accommodation within 12 hours upon arrival. These reporting obligations may be delegated to travel bureaus and similar agents.

The legal regime for residence in Montenegro is based on the *Law on Foreigners*. The law regulates the conditions for temporary and permanent residence in Montenegro. Other than as resident, a foreigner may reside in Montenegro for up to 90 days either on the basis of a visa for short stay (C visa), or without a visa but with a valid travel document if the foreigner is a citizen of a visa-exempted country. A long-term visa (D visa) applies to extended stays in Montenegro. It is issued for one, two or multiple entries to Montenegro, for a stay on the territory of Montenegro of more than 90 days but not exceeding six months, within a period of one year.

Foreigners intending to reside in Montenegro longer than 90 days or six months, for reasons other than those permitted on the basis of a visa issued for tourist, business related, personal or other reasons, must acquire a temporary residence permit. The temporary residence permit is issued for up to one year and may be extended for each individual occasion to a maximum of two years. At the latest 30 days before the expiry of the validity of the temporary residence permit, the foreigner may apply to the Ministry of Interior for its renewal. The law provides no limits as to how often a foreigner may apply for renewal of his or her temporary residence permit.

The temporary residence permit may be issued for one of the following reasons:

- Employment and work
- Performing business or entrepreneurial activities
- Seasonal work
- Participation in student exchange programs or other youth programs
- Specialization or professional training and acquisition of practical skills
- Scientific research
- Medical treatment
- Family reunification
- Humanitarian reasons and other justified reasons specified by law or international treaty

In practice, the residence reason of business or Entrepreneurial activity is rarely applied by the local authorities. A foreigner who has lived in Montenegro continuously for five years is entitled to apply for a permanent residence permit.

The Montenegrin parliament is currently discussing a proposal to add into the *Law on Foreigners* a further possibility to acquire a temporary residence permit by foreigners who use their own real estate in Montenegro. This property would have to have a certain – as yet undefined – minimum value. Unfortunately, the proposal suggests that the foreigner must regularly reside in Montenegro and provides restrictive requirements as regards time spent outside the country. Second home owners, who only visit occasionally – which is the vast majority of the foreign residential owners – could, therefore, not enjoy the benefits of the new regulation. Also, the temporary residence permit needs to be renewed annually and personally by the applicant. This is another inconvenience, making it less attractive to draw on this possible future option.

Tax residence and international taxation

Liability for paying taxes in Montenegro is determined by residence status or source of income. A tax resident may be defined as a natural person who has a domicile in Montenegro or maintains a center of business and pursues vital interests in Montenegro, as well as a person who is present in Montenegro for more than 183 days during a calendar year. Other persons who cannot be regarded as tax residents are liable to pay taxes on income generated in Montenegro. The applicable tax rate is 9%.

International double taxation for residents of Montenegro

A tax resident is assessed for their income generated worldwide. Personal income tax paid in another country may be claimed for a tax credit in Montenegro, if such country has concluded a double taxation treaty with Montenegro. Currently, Montenegro maintains double taxation treaties with over 40 countries, including France, Germany, Italy and the UK.

Economic citizenship

It is often enquired whether or not Montenegro offers an *Economic Citizenship Program*, whereby the Montenegrin State would grant citizenship to foreign individuals for certain forms of capital investment to the country. An initiative was undertaken by the Montenegrin Government in summer 2010 which sought to institutionalize naturalization for economic reasons under Montenegrin *Citizenship Law*. The plan, however, met harsh resistance, both nationally and internationally. In particular, Germany feared an abuse of the recent visa liberalization for Montenegrin nationals travelling to the Schengen area, disregarding the legal possibilities for excluding misuses of the intended naturalization practice through a restrictive regulatory set-up. The endeavors for implementing an *Economic Citizenship Program* have ceased.

28.9 Checklist: Real estate in Montenegro

- Due diligence on the real estate: verification of proper ownership title of the seller; identification of existing mortgages, registered litigations and other encumbrances; research of ownership history to exclude potential future claims of unregistered third parties; verification if subdivision is required; proof of existing use permit, if the property is a housing or commercial space
- Research of the zoning and planning status (for construction land): identification of building rights and parameters, plus restrictions imposed under the legal regime of *Morsko Dobro* for seaside properties
- Decision on whether to acquire privately, or through a foreign or otherwise local legal entity, depending on restrictions imposed for certain types of properties, the preferred tax structure and intentions of the buyer

- Research on applicable tax regime: regular acquisition tax of 3% (falls due upon execution of the sales agreement) or VAT (included in the purchase price) for newly constructed property; comparison of annual levies depending on acquiring person
- Conduct of acquisition: certified court interpreter required before the public notary for signatories that have no command of the Montenegrin language; securing of the *Clausula Intabulandi* with the acting public notary prior to the release of the purchase price; pre-registration if required with the land registry upon execution of the sales agreement; registration with the competent land registry as the final condition of ownership transfer after the obtaining of the *Clausula Intabulandi*,
- Particularities for off-plan sales: due diligence on the commercial and legal soundness of the seller (in particular property rights and building permits); verification that the acquisition object is duly identified in the contract; agreement on a fixed or at least determinable handover date; ideally registration of a mortgage over the object under construction; agreement on milestone structure for purchase price payments, in relation to fixed payment dates; handling of the danger of project fails or delays and the rectification of defects

29

Portugal

Portugal
Portuguese Republic
República Portuguesa

by

Cristina Dein

Text translated from the German original
by Francis Wallace and revised by David Willig

Dein Advogados

Rua Castilho 1, 5º Esq
1250-066 Lisbon
Portugal

Telephone: +351 213 884 095
Facsimile: +351 213 881 955

dein@dein.pt

Cristina Dein was born in 1967 in Germany. She graduated in Law from the University of Coimbra in 1993 and also attended law courses at the University of Konstanz (Germany). From early on, Cristina has been exposed to cross-cultural relations through first-hand experience. This represents a great asset in dealing with foreign clients and in providing international legal advice.

In 1996 she was admitted to the Portuguese Bar. In 2007 she took over the law office Jalles Advogados under her own name, where she had worked since the very beginning of her professional career. In 2009 she co-founded the DAV Portugal, an association of German and Portuguese lawyers, affiliated to the DeutscherAnwaltverein.

She attends to Portuguese clients but also to a very demanding German and English-speaking clientele with interests or aiming to invest in Portugal. She is the author of several publications and appears regularly as a speaker at conferences. The particularities of local bureaucracies and /or different social and cultural realities often cause complex legal problems. Addressing and solving these in a pragmatic way is her foremost interest.

29.1 Introduction

Portugal, a former seafaring nation and for over 800 years an independent nation state, lies to the west of the Iberian Peninsula, of which it makes up around one sixth. The island chain of the Azores and the island of Madeira also belong to Portugal. From a landscape and climatic point of view, the Portuguese mainland is very varied, with its coastline of almost 800 km in length. From the Spanish border the land falls gently away to the Atlantic, which guarantees abundant precipitation, and so Portugal appears as a garden, which is marked by the Atlantic and also by the Mediterranean climate. Apart from the mild climate the Portuguese are also held to be friendly and Portugal finds itself among the most peaceful countries in the world.

Since Portugal's accession to the European Union in 1986, strong socio-economic development has taken place in the country, including large investments in infrastructure. Portugal is in the Euro currency zone, and is a meeting point between Africa, America and Europe. The membership of Portugal in the EU led, moreover, to an increase in the demand among the foreign community for local properties, joined more and more in the recent past by investors from Asia, Africa and America.

The Portuguese property market is notable for a large quantity of newly built properties for sale and excellent tourist resorts and competitive prices. Also, the renovation of old buildings and old town centres is in full swing. Moreover, in the last few years the Portuguese government has succeeded in reducing bureaucratic obstacles and has created an investor-friendly climate.

29.2 Real estate ownership

The right to private property and to the transfer of property during life and on death is based on Article 62 of the Portuguese constitution. Property law and the various types of property are almost exclusively governed by the Portuguese *Civil Code*. The only real estate rights and restrictions are those which are set out expressly in the legislation. Portuguese civil law differentiates between rural and urban land (*prédios rústicos* and *prédios urbanos)*. A rural plot of land means a distinct part of the land together with the buildings situated on it, which are not economically independent of it. An urban plot of land means the buildings which are anchored to the ground, along with the areas which serve them.

Different forms and types of ownership

Sole ownership, joint ownership and collective ownership

The sole owner has comprehensive powers of ownership over his property.

If two or more persons own the property rights over a piece of property simultaneously, then Joint Ownership exists. Whilst the sole owner can avail himself of his property rights independently, in the case of joint ownership all the joint owners make use jointly of the rights in the piece of property, and take part according to their shares in the receipt of income and the payment of expenses.

The administration of joint property is carried out according to the principle of a majority of the joint owners, to whom at least half of the shares must belong. Every joint owner is free to dispose of his share in the abstract sense, or to encumber it. However, charging or disposing of a specific part of the property requires the consent of the remaining joint owners.

Every joint owner has the right to division of the property concerned, and can sue to enforce this right in the event of disagreements. Should a prohibition on division be agreed, this may not last longer than five years; a prolongation can be agreed after the expiry of this period. The co-owners have a legal right of pre-emption if the share of a fellow co-owner is disposed of, or if it is given to a third party by way of payment.

A further form of co-ownership is Collective Ownership. Types of collective ownership are specified as matrimonial collective ownership of goods, inheritance collective ownership, or collective bodies without legal personality.

In contrast to joint owners, the collective owner has no abstract share, of which he could dispose of freely. Collective ownership ends with the dissolution of the underlying legal relationship.

Tiered ownership

The institution of tiered ownership makes up a further form of property ownership. Each tiered owner has the sole property in his fraction, and is a co-owner of the common parts of the building. Existing buildings can retrospectively be converted to tiered ownership, with agreement from the responsible communal authority. Tiered ownership is established in the same way as normal property, via contract, possession for a prescribed period, or court decision. Disposal is governed by the general rules. There are many tourist resorts, predominantly on the Algarve, which have been established using the tiered ownership model. In a property acquisition of this sort, the contract of establishment and also the house and resort rules should be checked carefully, in order to avoid later surprises.

Building leases

Building leases consist in the fact that a building can be erected on another person's land, either for a period of time or in perpetuity. The property in the building and in the land fall under separate ownership. The lessee under the building lease has either to pay a once and final price or to meet a periodic ground rent payment.

Timesharing

The law of timesharing underwent a definite expansion in the 1990s, in particular in the strongly developed holiday areas of the Algarve and Madeira. The right to occupy by reference to time (*direito real de habitação periódica*) is regulated in legislation. The most recent *EU Directive 2008/122/EC* implements the protection of consumers in respect of certain aspects of timeshare such as long-term holiday products, resale and exchange contracts, transposed already into Portuguese law. Before entering into a contract or offer, the consumer has to receive exhaustive and accurate standard information regarding the timeshare from the seller. The timeshare contract must have a duration of not less than one year. The owner of a timeshare can, provided he observes his duties regarding maintenance, make use of the real estate as an owner during the agreed period of time. Timesharing is distinguished, moreover, by its simple transferability. Timesharing can only be set up by a notarized deed and since January 2009 also by a private document with recognition of signature. The legal owner receives a *Portuguese Land Certificate*, on which the constituent components which make up a timeshare, are based. The buyer must also be given a written completion document, which must contain further essential information and the component parts of the contract. The non-resident buyer must also be given an officially certified translation of the certificate (into one of the official languages of the *EU*) and a completion document. Timeshares can be transferred to third parties, and can be encumbered and inherited. Transfer is affected by endorsement on the certificate, with the signatures of both parties authenticated. The conclusion of a written preliminary contract, which must also be officially authenticated, is also possible. The buyer has a mandatory right of cancellation: he can cancel within a time limit of 14 consecutive days from the date of the preliminary contract or the transfer of the timeshare.

Easements, charges, covenants, liens and mortgages

As well as the law of property, which stipulates complete ownership over a piece of property, there are so-called limited property rights, which burden the property and grant the current owner rights of use, rights of guarantee (sale) or acquisition rights. Beneficial use, the right to use and reside, the right to grant a building lease, and rights of easement are among the limited property rights. Among guarantees over property are the mortgage, the assignment of income from real estate, the right of retention and the right to provisional satisfaction of certain state and municipal demands (land tax, purchase tax, gift and inheritance tax and court costs, which are a burden on the relevant pieces of land or the revenue arising from them, come under this category). Rights of pre-emption make up the tangible acquisition rights, which will be explored in the next section.

Beneficial use

Beneficial use gives the beneficial user the right to make various uses of the affected land during a specified period of time. Beneficial use rights can be established via contract, will, prescription or provision of statute.

Use and residence

Besides beneficial use, Portuguese law also recognizes the tangible right to "use and residence". When the right affects a residential building, it is categorized as right of residence. The provisions of beneficial use rights are used in a way that is subsidiary to the right of residence. The owner of the right of residence cannot encumber or lease out the right, however.

Building leases

The law of building leases also represents a type of servitude, which belongs to the above types of property, because it demonstrates characteristics that are similar to those of ownership.

Easements and administrative covenants

A burden is classified as an easement where it is imposed on a piece of land for the benefit of another piece of land with various owners. The commonest forms are rights of way, which allow access to a specified piece of land, and administrative covenants, for example the prohibition on building in the area bordering on streets.

Mortgage

The mortgage is a strictly accessory right, which is put in place over the land to give security for the claims of the mortgagor or of a third party.

The mortgage can be contractual or imposed by law or court order, and is extinguished, *inter alia*, when the underlying claim no longer exists. Urban and rural land, building leases and the beneficial use of tangible property and rights can be burdened with a mortgage. The voluntary mortgage arises under contract or unilateral declaration. It can also be established or modified by will. As an exception to the general rule that a simple declaration of the parties is needed to render a tangible legal right effective, to establish an effective mortgage this must be registered in the Land Register.

Portuguese law does not recognize the concept of underlying debt, which is not an accessory.

Protection of ownership, proof of ownership and registration

Under Portuguese law, property ownership passes at the time of conclusion of the sale contract. The contract has constitutive effect. Purchase contracts may be prepared not only by notaries but also by land registry officials and lawyers. Portuguese law does not recognize concepts such as the notarized property conveyance agreement under German law. On account of the fundamental rule of publicity and on account of legal certainty, the rights acquired must however be inscribed in the register, and only become valid against third parties when they are so registered. It is possible theoretically to transfer the same piece of land at different times to different purchasers. However, the only person who has an absolutely effective title is the purchaser in good faith who is the first to register his rights at the land registry, even if his title was acquired at a later date. The other buyers will only have the right to claim damages against the seller.

Proof of ownership should be provided exclusively by the production of an extract from the land registry. Cases in which a piece of land has not yet been registered are relatively rare, and are almost always confined to very rural areas in north and central Portugal. On account of the fact that most land owned there is in small plots, the division of land on inheritance, and also high emigration in the 1960s and 1970s, the parcels of land and their registered rights are only determinative of ownership to a restricted degree. It was not until the coming into force of the new *Land Registration Act* on 1 October 1984 that compulsory land registration for all land in Portugal was introduced. Until then, many rural pieces of land were exempted from the obligation to register.

In these regions, including a number of potential holiday areas in the coastal regions, the most up to date information about the legal relationships that exist can mostly be obtained from the responsible tax office. It issues a type of property tax register booklet (*caderneta predial*), for all urban and rural pieces of land, from which the nature of the land and the burdens affecting it, together with the priority order of the owners and the proprietary worth of the land can be determined. Moreover, every plot of land is allocated a number, under which it is dealt with by the relevant tax office. With the introduction of the geometrical Land Register in 1989 a national process of land valuation began – this did not include all areas - which has also led to the alteration of the plot numbers at the tax office. The rural plots, which are already included in the Land Register never have more than three numbers, and are allocated into various sections within a community. With rural plots that are not yet included in the Land Register, it sometimes happens that the effective areas of land do not correspond with the areas inscribed in the old Register. It is advisable here to carry out a valuation.

Within the framework of the *SIMPLEX Program* (Program for the abolition of bureaucratic obstacles) of the 17th Government, the *SINERGIC Project* was brought into being, which is progressing the complete inclusivity of Portuguese territory with the goal of creating a unitary land information system. In this should be included the title plan and Land Register information as well as the data in the land matrix, which is shared by all the tax offices, and which should be brought together electronically in a single Land Identification Number (*número de identificação predial, NIP*).

However, one must note the fundamental point that the proof of ownership can only be provided via an up-to-date extract from the register – the *caderneta predial* cannot be substituted for it.

29.3 Purchase and sale of real estate

The sales agreement

The purchase contract must be made the subject of a deed signed before the notary. Since 2009 it has also been possible to choose to draw up the purchase contract as a private authenticated deed. The authentication includes confirmation that the content of the contract is known to the parties and represents their intention. The parties are identified. Purchase contracts can also be prepared within the framework of the *Casa Pronta* services of land registry officials. A purchase contract which does not satisfy the formal requirements is null and void. This nullity means that the property cannot be passed and the purchase contract will not be registered in the Land Register. Property passes on the conclusion of the purchase contract. The parties can be represented by persons holding a power of attorney for this purpose. In Portugal the parties can have the purchase contract notarized by a Portuguese notary of their choice.

The authentication of a private purchase contract can be undertaken by a lawyer, a notary or a land registry official. The various possibilities regarding formalities allow the parties nowadays to conclude a purchase contract quickly and easily. The notarized deed containing the purchase contract is drafted in the Portuguese language and is read out aloud. The notary makes sure that each party has understood the contents of the purchase contract and that this reflects the will of the parties. Contracting parties who do not speak Portuguese must bring an interpreter with them. He translates the purchase contract simultaneously and will also appear in the purchase contract. The same applies to the purchase contracts issued by the *Casa Pronta* service.

Before binding oneself by contract, one should insist on having a copy of the text of the deed, so as to be able to check this through. This is advisable due to legal particularities or insufficient linguistic knowledge of the parties or the interpreter, in order to avoid later difficulties.

The risk is generally greater for the buyer than for the seller. The buyer should therefore have the documents that are relevant to the purchase checked over by a lawyer. It is also useful to enter into a preliminary contract with an enforcement clause, in order to bind the seller to carry out the contract, and also so as to be able to enforce his expressed obligations through the courts, should this be necessary. In order to protect the buyer's rights, one should also not dispense with a provisional registration of the purchase in the Land Register. The electronic Land Register allows an entry to be made in the Register almost simultaneously with the conclusion of the contract. This service is offered principally within the *Casa Pronta* framework.

In the case of preliminary contracts for the transfer of property in buildings or residences, or for the establishment of other property rights, the notarized signatures of both parties are required by law. Alternatively, the acknowledgement of the signature can be dealt with by a lawyer or land registry official. In the case of corporate entities, the authority to represent the party concerned is proved by provision of an extract from the business register or equivalent documents. Further, the permission to build or use the property should also be produced to the notary, and this will be appropriately certified in the purchase deed.

In general, the preliminary contract is only effective to create an obligation, so that the seller can, in theory, transfer the real estate to a third party, and the buyer can only bring a claim for damages against him. However, the buyer may register his acquisition provisionally, to have effect against third parties, at the land registry. This can be done either by a unilateral declaration of the seller or by registration of the preliminary contract. The provisional registration will remain effective for as long as the contractual obligation is supposed to be valid, and it can be prolonged for six months to a year after expiry of the original prescribed period, on application of the parties. On expiration of the prescribed period, the provisional registration expires automatically. When the promised contract is concluded and is entered in the Land Register, the provisional registration is converted into a final one.

In contrast to German law, Portuguese law has a governing principle of causality. For the establishment or transfer of a property right, the transaction, in which the willingness to transfer is declared, is sufficient. This means that on conclusion of the purchase contract the transfer of property takes place simultaneously. The purchase contract is therefore not only a causative transaction, which creates obligations, but also an actual disposal. The registration of the property in the land registry is not a new legal transaction. Nowadays, the entry in the land registry is dealt with directly by the notary, land registry official or lawyer, and is processed electronically. Extracts from the land registry can be obtained electronically. Third parties acting in good faith are protected in Portuguese law, on the one hand through a shortening of the periods of prescription and on the other hand by Articles 243 and 291 of the Portuguese *Civil Code*. The latter relates to errors in the concluded legal document. According to Article 243 of the *Civil Code*, the nullity that results from a fictitious transaction cannot be invoked against the purchaser in good faith.

In general, the purchaser in good faith is protected by Article 291 against the nullity or annulment of the prior legal transaction. Acquisition of a piece of land in good faith is only possible, according to this provision, when the registration of the purchase is carried out before the issue of proceedings for nullity or annulment of the previous legal transaction. This acquisition stands on an equal footing to the registration of the contract between the parties previously involved – however only when this does not take place in the first three years after conclusion of the void or voidable contract. In other words: after the expiration of three years from the challengeable or nullifiable legal transaction, the buyer in good faith can realize his rights fully, if his registration is made before the issue of proceedings for nullity or nullification of that transaction or of the contract connected with the unenforceability of the transaction.

Restrictions on acquisition and conveyance

Restrictions under family law and matrimonial property regime

The Portuguese conflict rules regarding the substance and effects of the legal or contractual property rights between spouses refer directly to the common law of the spouses at the time of the marriage. If there is no common nationality, the rules look to the law of the usual place of residence at the time of the marriage. If there is none, the law where the matrimonial home is situated is to be applied.

In the case where foreign law is applicable and one of the spouses has his usual residence in Portugal, the use of Portuguese property law can be agreed by contract.

Portugal has signed the *Hague Convention on the applicable law of matrimonial property* of 1978 but has not yet ratified it. In accordance with Article 2 of the *Convention*, this will also be applicable when the nationality, the habitual residence of the spouses or the law chosen by the contract is not that of a contracting state. The general point of application for the *Hague Convention* is the first usual place of residence of the spouses after the marriage, and – under certain conditions – the common nationality of the spouses, so that the results which follow from use of the Portuguese conflict of law rules can be altered as a result of the *Convention*, in cases where this is applicable.

If Portuguese law is applicable, the parties concluding the marriage can choose, by marriage contract within the legal limits, the property regime and its contents. Equally, the choice of a foreign governing law is allowed. This may not, however, take the form of a general reference to the foreign law concerned.

Portuguese law is governed by the principle of the immutability of the property regime, which only permits a few named exceptions.

The legislative Portuguese property regime, which is applicable where there is no marriage contract or an invalid contract, is that of the communality of property acquired during the marriage. In a few exceptional cases, the legislation makes the spouses subject to the property regime of separation of assets. Besides the property regime of communality of property acquired during the marriage (*comunhão de adquiridos*), Portuguese law recognizes separation of assets *(separação de bens)* and communality of assets (*comunhão geral de bens),* but these must be agreed by contract before the marriage.

The general regime of communality of property acquired during the marriage has effects on the property rights of the spouses. Property which is acquired by the spouses during the marriage becomes a part of the matrimonial property, unless it is acquired using one of the spouses' own assets. To address this, one must make an express choice of "sole property" in favor of the contracting spouse, in the relevant purchase contract. The other spouse must be in agreement, which will be documented by a declaration of his agreement. If a spouse subject to the communality regime has acquired a piece of land, without a simultaneous contractual agreement with the other spouse, then he can only dispose of the land jointly with the other spouse. A preliminary contract for the sale of real estate should therefore always be signed by both the vendor spouses, as the spouses can only dispose jointly.

Similarly to the property regime of communality of assets acquired during marriage, in the case of communality of assets the agreement of both spouses is necessary for the disposal of land. Only in the case of separation of assets can the spouse dispose of his real estate without the agreement of the other spouse. However, if the land in question is also the family home, the agreement of both spouses is necessary, even in the case of separation of assets.

For foreign purchasers, the exact stipulation of the civil and property regime in the sale contract is also important, possibly with the presentation of a marriage certificate and a consular declaration regarding the property regime, as this must always be stated in the case of married persons. The document must state correctly who has acquired property from the spouses, so that the correct entry is made in the Land Register and no problems arise when there is a further disposal or charge of the land.

Options and rights of pre-emption

The free disposability of real estate can be restricted, through agreed or legal rights of pre-emption, in favour of other persons. If such a right of pre-emption exists, the owner, who has decided to sell, is obliged to sell to the pre-emptor on the same contractual terms.

Options and rights of pre-emption can be agreed between the parties contractually and can also be established by will. In order to be valid, they must be in writing. As a rule, contractual pre-emptive rights are only effective to create a legal obligation between the parties, so in cases of enforcement or insolvency rights of pre-emption cannot prevail. The contractually agreed option, however, will then also have tangible effect, if the prescribed special requirements as to form are satisfied, and a corresponding entry in the Land Register will follow. A contractually agreed option with tangible effect has, however, no priority over the rights of pre-emption prescribed by law. The usual legal rights of pre-emption are stipulated in favour of co-owners, tenants and co-inheritors. Further, owners of servient pieces of land possess a legal right of pre-emption if the dominant land is disposed of. The owner of the burdened land has similar rights if a building lease is disposed of. On the disposal of rural properties, there are in certain circumstances legal rights of pre-emption in favour of the owners of neighbouring rural lands.

As an instrument of political control of land, the public administrative authorities are allowed a general right of pre-emption, which is transposed into many legislative provisions. On the acquisition of pieces of land or buildings, enquiries should be made of the responsible town authority as to whether a right of pre-emption in favour of the public authority, whether town council or other establishment, subsists (many historic town districts have a right of pre-emption in favour of the town). Legal rights of pre-emption are not entered in the Land Register.

Agricultural real estate

The law specially regulates the acquisition and use of rural pieces of land. In the tax office as well as at the Land Register, plots of land are designated as rural, agricultural (*prédios rústicos*) or urban land (*prédios urbanos*). A rural plot of land is as a rule also to be regarded as a piece of agricultural land – as such, it cannot be built upon.

In order to avoid the fragmentation of rural lands into uneconomic plots, Portugal has rules for the maintenance of productive minimum-sized plots, which vary according to region and type of cultivation between 0.5 ha and 7.5 ha. When acquiring rural land, one should ensure that the current minimum cultivable unit in hectares (*unidade mínima de cultura)* remains intact.

Should a rural piece of land be situated within an agriculturally protected zone (*reserva agrícola nacional – RAN),* the minimum cultivable unit is doubled automatically. Moreover, rights of pre-emption in favour of neighbouring land have to be borne in mind.

Restrictions regarding acquisition of real estate by foreigners

Since the introduction of the free movement of capital at the beginning of the 1990s, there are no longer any restrictions on the acquisition of land by non-residents, even if these are not nationals of EU member states. However, certain notification requirements which serve statistical or administrative purposes must be observed: capital transactions which qualify as foreign direct investment or as investment in land must be notified to the Bank of Portugal. For big investment operations made by national or foreign investors in the amount of more than EUR 25 million and complying with certain conditions, investment contracts with the *Portugal Global Trade & Investment Agency* (AICEP), a government business entity created in 2007 and focused in encouraging the best foreign companies to invest in Portugal, can be concluded.

In other respects there are no restrictions on the acquisition of real estate by foreigners who have their place of residence abroad.

If a foreigner wishes to hold a residence permit in Portugal, as the laws stand today, they may qualify by purchasing a piece of real estate to the value of EUR 500,000. Given the necessary paperwork and due diligence is concluded successfully for the applicant by a professional firm such as Henley & Partners, obtaining a residence permit may be possible.

Further important preconditions for buying real estate

Capacity to act and entitlement of the seller

The only person authorized to sell the land is the person who is entered in the Land Register as its owner. With joint property or property held in common, the latter brought about by inheritance, marriage or business association without legal personality, all the joint owners or common owners must agree to the sale. Natural persons of full age and capacity can conclude the purchase contract themselves or have their wishes represented by an attorney. Persons who lack capacity are minors (under 18 years old) and persons who are under the authority of trustees. Persons with limited capacity are natural persons who have been declared by court order to be without capacity to deal. In the case of persons who lack capacity absolutely, a legally authorized representative has to act; with persons of limited capacity, for example those without capacity to deal, the appointed trustee has to act alongside the person without capacity.

In the case of legal persons, it is necessary to check whether they are established according to law and therefore have capacity to deal. In trading companies this is established from the commercial register or from relevant documents (certificate of incorporation, certificate of good standing etc.). Legal persons act via their representatives according to law. The authority of the lawful representatives is established in the case of registered corporate entities from the commercial register. The Portuguese commercial register can be consulted online. An extract from the register remains valid for one year. Besides the obtaining of a current extract, it is however also advisable to examine the current constitution of the present corporate body, as the authority to deal in certain situations is often subject to the agreement of other representatives. Legislative restrictions also have to be borne in mind. Therefore, the transfer and mortgaging of real estate, which is owned by a limited liability company, is based on agreement by shareholders' resolution, if the bylaws of the company do not provide otherwise.

Third-party claims and unpaid taxes

In order to satisfy proven demands of creditors, the real estate of a debtor can be encumbered in the context of enforcement proceedings. The encumbrance is then only valid against third parties when it is entered in the Land Register. After entry of the encumbrance in the Land Register, the only rights that can be registered are those which do not conflict with the encumbrance.

Also, by way of a provisional measure, a piece of land can be affected by a freezing entry. After a judgment is obtained in the main action the provisional measure can be converted into an encumbrance in the context of ancillary enforcement proceedings.

On the grounds of unpaid taxes or national insurance contributions, there can be enforcement proceedings resulting in the land being encumbered. For this, the tax office of the debtor's place of residence or the location of the land is responsible. Charging in the context of enforcement proceedings by the tax offices has also to be inscribed in the Land Register. One can obtain information from the responsible tax offices regarding possible pending proceedings or the existence of tax debts on the part of the seller of the land.

Provisions for protecting the environment, nature and cultural heritage

Besides agricultural reserved areas, which have already been dealt with above, in the context of environmental protection and nature conservation there are also the national ecological reserves *(reserva ecológica nacional,* REN), the nature conservation areas, the coastal areas and the woodlands, where use and building activity are strictly regulated by various legislative texts. In the REN areas, which chiefly consist of sensitive areas as regards ground water reserves, all types of construction or destruction of the vegetation are forbidden. Similarly to the *reserva agrícola nacional* areas (RAN), the REN areas are also specifically identified in all town and country planning documents. The classification or declassification of REN areas is carried out via ministerial decision, which takes prior advice from the national REN commission. The ground protection zones of the coastal areas comprise a two kilometer wide strip, which extends from the highest tidemark into the interior. Its use and any changes of use are regulated in a legislative decree, which also regulates coastal town and country planning and all construction and building projects which are not comprised within a development plan.

For the protection of the qualifying wooded areas against arson, there is a general 10 year building ban on areas affected by forest fires, together with an obligation on the owner or tenant to replant trees. The felling of specified types of tree, including the olive tree, pine, cork and stone oak, is forbidden.

Every owner is responsible for avoiding pollution on his land, and in particular is responsible for ensuring that no damaging effects or dangers for neighbouring lands or for public health emanate from his land. The owner can be compelled by the public authorities to clean up pre-existing pollution at his own expense. An examination of possible pollution before the purchase is therefore called for.

The *Direcção-Geral do Património Cultural*, formerly *IGESPAR*, (DGPC) is responsible for the classification of real estate which is under historic site / listed buildings protection. If a piece of land is listed, the owners are under particular maintenance obligations and under a duty to present an appraisal to DGPC in the case of any plans to carry out alterations. The listing of buildings is published in the government's official journal as well as being registered in the Land Register. Listed buildings can also be consulted online. As compensation for the particular burdens which listed buildings carry with them, these buildings are exempt from land tax and from transfer tax on changes of ownership.

Access to relevant records and documents

As soon as the interested buyer has chosen a suitable property, the following points should be checked:

The entry of the property in the Land Register (*registo predial)* must be in the name of the seller. From an extract from the register one can check whether the property is the subject of adverse entries. It is also important to pay attention to the status of the entries.

The property must be registered at the tax office. The relevant local tax office provides a kind of property booklet (*caderneta predial)* for every urban or rural property, which nowadays is issued electronically and can be consulted online. From this, in similar fashion to a Land Register extract, the state and the owners of the property, as well as its value, can be established. When acquiring residential buildings that were erected after 1951, it is necessary to check, in addition, whether a dwelling permit or planning permission exists. This inquiry is made of the responsible local authority. When acquiring land for building purposes, the appropriate local plans should be checked at the responsible local planning authority. The existence of permits started to be noted in the Land Register.

For the purposes of consumer protection, dwelling houses which were newly built, reconstructed, enlarged or altered after 30 March 2004 must have a document (*ficha técnica de habitação,* FTH), in which the technical and functional particularities of the building as at the conclusion of the building works are described. The FTH also includes, among other things, details of the developer, building contractor and technical advice team for the build. Further, surface area details and a description of the materials used and of the equipment installed, as well as the manufacturers, will be recorded in it. The FTH is prepared by the building contractor, and a copy has to be deposited with the municipal authorities.

For old and new office and residential buildings, as from January 2009 an energy performance certificate *(certificado energético)* must be provided. The energy performance certificate is valid for 10 years.

Key points that a seller should consider

The seller has, as a rule, a more secure position than the buyer. The seller has to make sure that his property rights are entered in the Land

Register in accordance with the law, and that the property is also correctly described therein. The description of the property in the Land Register must correspond with the description of the property at the tax office or in the *caderneta predial.*

For buildings which require planning permission for residential or other use, this also has to correspond in content with the entries at the Land Register and tax office. Should this not be the case, then the entries must first be harmonized before the conclusion of the purchase contract. The seller also has to comply with the legally stipulated notification requirements towards those having rights of pre-emption. The seller has to further make sure that he is in the possession of the FTH and the energy performance certificate. The permission for residential or other use is noted in the Land Register.

The execution of a real estate purchase transaction

The search for a property or a buyer for a property takes place either via an estate agent or through direct contact between buyer and seller. If one instructs an estate agent, one should make sure that he is officially registered.

During the preliminary negotiations the relevant documents are checked and the requirements of the contract are agreed; as a rule these are set out in a preliminary contract. It is advisable to have the preliminary contract checked by an independent lawyer.

For a preliminary purchase contract in respect to real estate to be formally valid, the signatures of the parties have to be notarized. As an alternative the signatures can also be recognized by a lawyer; authorities to act and any powers of attorney are also checked by the notary or lawyer. The use permits must also be produced in case they are not yet noted in the Land Register. On conclusion of the preliminary contract, a down payment on account of the purchase price is due, which can amount to between 10% and 40% of the purchase price. Here it is important to know that if the buyer does not comply with the provisions of the purchase contract, he loses any instalments already paid towards the purchase price. However, if on the other hand it is the seller who does not fulfil the contract, he must pay back twice the amount of any instalments to the buyer.

In order to conclude the preliminary contract and to proceed further, both parties must have a Portuguese tax number. This can be requested on presentation of a passport or personal identity document at any tax office. Non-residents must appoint a Portuguese tax representative. This does not apply to EU citizens which are, following a decision of the European Court of Justice in 2011, allowed to register with an address in another EU country.

Before conclusion of the purchase contract, the transfer tax and stamp duty has to be paid at a tax office. The purchase contract itself can be executed at a notary of the parties' choice, at a Land Register with a *Casa Pronta* service or in the presence of a lawyer. A current extract from the Land Register has to be produced; the *caderneta predial*, proof of tax payment, as well as the construction or use permit and the FTH if applicable. The existence of an energy performance certificate must be mentioned. The parties also have to identify themselves by means of passports or personal identity documents, and if needed their marriage certificates. Furthermore, appropriate proof of authority to deal or power of attorney should be considered, together with the tax number. The buyer, as a rule, pays the fees and emoluments related to the purchase contract. The buyer and the purchaser have also to declare if a real estate agent was involved in the transaction. Nowadays the current extract of the Land Register and the *caderneta predial* might also be consulted online at the time of conclusion of the contract.

With a certified copy of the notarized deed containing the purchase contract or the private document with recognition of signature, the buyer can then apply for his name to be registered in the Land Register, as well as for the property to be transferred into his name with the tax office. The registration can also be done by electronic means. The

Casa Pronta service offers immediate registration in the Land Register; lawyers and notaries also offer this service.

Powers of attorney

According to Portuguese conflict of law rules, the existence, extension, alteration, validity, effect and cancellation of powers of attorney, which deal with the disposal, or administration of immovable property have to be dealt with according to the law of the state in which the property is situated. This law is also applicable in relation to the form of the power of attorney. A power that is to be used to deal with a property in Portugal has to, under Portuguese law, contain a certification of the signature and handwriting of the donor of the power. The power can either be drawn up as a notarized deed or as a private document with a certification attached. Should a foreign notary draw up the power, an apostille according to the *Hague Convention of 5 October 1961, Abolishing the Requirement of Legalisation for Foreign Public Documents*, must also be attached. The granting of a power of attorney can also be carried out directly, in Portuguese, at the local Portuguese consulate.

Financing

The usual financing of acquisition, refinancing or building and conversion works in relation to real estate is carried out by means of bank loans. As a rule, the banks will finance, according to the financial standing of the borrower, between 60% and 80% of the assessed value of the property. The interest rate will be agreed between the bank and the borrower. Until recently the maximum term of a loan was restricted by law to 30 years, but now the banks can set the term of the loan themselves, under the supervision of the *Bank of Portugal*. Loan contracts occur in practice with a term of up to 40 years, with instalments payable by the borrower up to the age of 70. Usually, however, contracts have a term of 25 to 30 years. As security for repayment, as a rule the banks require mortgages and life assurance. In general the banks are also willing to grant loans to owners who are not resident in Portugal. The conditions are however often stricter, as in addition to the usual mortgage and life assurance, guarantors and other additional forms of guarantee are required.

A land purchase can also be financed via leasing contracts. The landowner is or becomes the lessor, who devises the property to the lessee, in consideration for a payment. By this method, 100% finance can be obtained. In the case of leasing contracts affecting land, the legal minimum term is seven years, and the maximum term is 30 years. Leasing contracts for real estate have to be in writing. The signatures have to be certified, and the use or building permit has to be produced. A notarial deed is however not necessary. The leasing contract must be entered in the Land Register. Leasing contracts can be concluded with or without the option to purchase. In the case of a purchase option, the total of the purchase price that still has to be paid may not amount to less than 2% of the value of the leased property. The leasing rates, in which the amortization and finance costs are reflected, are normally payable in monthly or three monthly instalments. Main residences as well as second homes and holiday homes can be leased.

Purchase through a company

Natural or legal persons who are not resident in Portugal can invest freely in Portuguese companies, and can form companies. Among the most common types of companies is the limited liability company, which may also take the form of a one man company, and the joint stock company. The formation of a Portuguese company has been very much simplified within the framework of the *Simplex* Program. One should allow two to three weeks for the formation. Shelf companies with previously approved company names can be set up within almost one day. If one forms a real estate holding company, particular requirements have to be observed.

If a company with limited liability is used as the owner of a property, transfer tax becomes payable at the moment when 75% or more of the shares are acquired. The position with joint stock companies is different. The acquisition of properties via companies gives rise to additional costs, due to the need to prove the company's powers and obligations.

Therefore, in each individual case the financial risks should be checked, especially with regard to the taxation aspects. The purchase of a company is basically only worthwhile financially when the property will not be used permanently for one's own residence.

In many holiday areas on the Algarve, properties are frequently owned or purchased by offshore companies. The advantage is principally the fact that, on transfer, only the company's shares change hands; a purchase contract is not necessary, nor are transfer tax and stamp duty payable. On the purchase of an offshore company, it is advisable to carry out the legal checks on two levels: to check the legal status of the company, as well as that of the property.

One should also note that the tax rules for offshore companies in Portugal have been tightened. Which countries, territories or areas are classified as tax havens is ascertained from a list which is produced by the Portuguese Finance Ministry. The land tax on properties which are owned by offshore companies is automatically fixed at 7.5% of the value of the property (*valor patrimonial tributário*, fiscal property value), and is thus appreciably above the 0.3% to 0.8% tax rate for other properties.

Since 2008, there has been a uniform real estate transfer tax of 10% on the acquisition of real estate by buyers who have their place of residence or place of business in a state or area which has favourable tax treatment (according to a list published by the Finance Minister).

Because of intensified tax politics regarding offshore companies, together with a general reduction of inheritance tax and the tax exemption of close family members on inheritance and in the case of gifts, many pieces of real estate owned by offshore companies are changing their owners again.

Defects and warranty claims

Portuguese law distinguishes between legal defects and physical defects. The seller is obliged to sell the object free from defects. Legal defects are, under Portuguese law, the charges and burdens that exceed the normal legal limits of the current category according to law. Legislative or public law burdens are excluded from this. Only a buyer who at the time of the purchase had no knowledge of the burdens has a claim for protection, on the grounds that he entered into the contract as a result of a mistake or misrepresentation on the part of the seller. In these cases, the buyer can annul the contract and claim damages from the seller. In the case of deceit, the compensation will include the negative effect on the contract. If there has been a mistake, the compensation is limited to damage suffered. If mistake or deceit did not cause the contract to be concluded, but merely influenced the amount of the purchase price, the buyer can also demand a suitable reduction of the purchase price, besides the damages. A claim for annulment has to be commenced within one year after the purchase date.

In regard to liability for physical defects, the seller of an object is liable for defects which reduce the value of the object, or prevent the use of the object for a particular purpose. Furthermore, if the object lacks a particular characteristic which the seller claimed it possessed, he is liable; also where it lacks characteristics that are necessary for the stipulated use.

In the case of immovable property, the buyer has to start proceedings on grounds of a defect within one year of becoming aware of the defect, but in any event not later than five years after the transfer of the property. There is a debate about whether these time limits also apply to defects which are not serious – therefore, to be on the safe side, these defects should be notified formally within 30 days of becoming aware of them, and never later than six months after the transfer of the property.

The Portuguese legal system recognizes as claims for breach of contract a claim for annulment on the grounds of mistake or deceit, remedial works, a claim for repayment or reduction of the purchase price, as well as the award of damages.

An exclusion of liability is only possible if it is restricted to situations of minor carelessness.

29.4 New construction, rebuilding and renovation

Construction zones and construction permits

Building on land is only allowed in designated building zones. This designation as a building zone *(lote)* must be registered in the Land Register.

Zones where building is permitted, with the current reasoning and particular rules for building, can be established from the municipal local plans (master plans, urbanisation plans and detailed plans), as well as from the national classification of ecological and agricultural protected areas, nature reserves and historic listed buildings.

For building plans, including demolition, rebuilding or enlargement one must obtain a building license (*licença*), for which the town council or the mayor is responsible. A building license must also be obtained for the rebuilding, enlargement, conversion or demolition of listed buildings. Construction operations with less relevance in terms of urban planning are only subject to advance notice (*comunicação prévia*). If there is already a local detailed plan or an allotment operation (*operação de loteamento*), then an advance notice is also sufficient for building on a plot of land. No licence or advance communication is needed for maintenance or conversion works to the interior of non-listed buildings which do not involve an alteration of the structure, facade, roofline or foundations. Preliminary information can be obtained from the town council, concerning the likelihood of obtaining licences and concerning construction taxes, as well as about public law limitations, before a formal application is made.

Architect's and building contracts

In the case of contracts for works, there is a distinction between carrying out work for which permission is required, and other cases. Works contracts for the carrying out of work which require permission must be in writing. As well as the identification of the parties, the contract must contain the certification of the building company, the building project and its technical specification, the value of the contract, time limits and the method of payment. Registered or certified building firms must only carry out works requiring permission; the value of the building project must correspond with the building works valuation category in which the firm is certified. As regards architects' contracts, no particular form is required.

Completion of construction and formalities

After completion of the building, an application must be made to the local authority for issuance of a permit for use (*autorização de utilização*). In the course of the permission process, the local authority may arrange for its expert to inspect the site, in order to check that it corresponds with the approved building project. Further, the site book, which must be kept on site and must be maintained by the architect or engineer who is responsible for the works, can be inspected at any time. Completion of the building has to be reported to the local tax office, which will update the property tax register booklet and revalue the property.

Deficiencies and warranty claims regarding new construction

The person undertaking the works, who will often be the main contractor for the project, can be held responsible for defects in and damage to the works. Frequently however, the building quality standards cannot be compared with the high central European standards – particularly as regards noise and heat insulation – so in this regard claims for remedial works or damages are difficult to pursue, if specific and concrete quality standards have not been set out in the works contract. It is advisable in every case to require security for contractual performance from the builder.

The builder must check the works for defects, on handover, and must raise such matters without delay; such matters can give grounds for delaying handover or making it subject to conditions. Only hidden defects, that is, defects that are not immediately visible, may be notified within 30 days of acquisition of knowledge. The builder has the right to claim remedial works or rebuilding or a reduction of the works price. A withdrawal from the works contract is possible if because of the defects, the works are no longer suitable for the purpose envisaged. The above demands must be pursued within one year of refusal to accept the works, or acceptance subject to conditions, because otherwise they will become time-barred. In the case of hidden defects on handover of the works, the limitation period runs from the time of discovery of the defects, but in any event this may not be more than two years from the handover of the works.

The limitation period for serious building defects in building, conversion or renovation of buildings is five years, if no guarantee period has been agreed. The deadline for notification is one year after knowledge of the defects; the same applies for the deadline for requesting remedial works or compensation.

29.5 Rental and tenancy

Rental and leasing contracts

Portuguese law distinguishes between land and forestry lease contracts, as well as between rental contracts for permanent residential purposes and for commercial and professional use. General provisions on rental agreements and leases are set out in the Portuguese *Civil Code*, and these are particularly applicable to rental agreements for temporary purposes, holiday homes, garages and non-residential land.

Land and forestry leases must be made in writing. The minimum term for agricultural and forestry leases is seven years. The maximum term is limited to 30 years. Forestry leases also have a maximum term of 70 years.

Rental agreements for residential, commercial and professional purposes must equally be made in writing. The rental law has been subject to many reforms in the last years in order to reduce excessive protection of the tenant, facilitate eviction, allowing extraordinary raise of 'old' rents and increasing the dynamic of the rental market. The major reform took place in 2006 (*New Urban Lease Regulations approved by Law no. 6/2006, of 27 February*, NRAU) and the last modifications came into force in November 2012. The *New Urban Lease Regulations* apply to future contracts as well as contracts already in force, including a transitional period according to the respective date of celebration of the contracts and rental law applicable at that time.

In general the parties are free to set the duration of the rental agreements. If no duration is stated in agreements for residential use they are understood to have a minimum duration of two years. Rental agreements for non residential use have a minimum duration of five years if no duration is stated in the contract. The length of rental agreements which are effectively limited in time may not be agreed at more than 30 years. Agreement on the term is mainly important for determining the necessary notice period to be given by the lessor.

Regulations on protection of tenants and rent control

The lessee in a forestry lease can terminate this in writing at any time, subject to observation of a notice period of one year in case he abandons his activity or the land isn't economically sustainable. The lessor can only terminate the agreement on grounds of specified breaches of contract by the lessee. There is no automatic legally prescribed extension of the contract, if nothing to the contrary was agreed. The situation is different in the case of agricultural leases. These are extended automatically by seven years or the initial duration on expiry, if nothing to the contrary was agreed. The contract can be terminated in writing by the lessor and the lessee, at the end of either the original or the extended period, subject to the observation of a notice period of one year. Specific protection is granted to lessees older than 55 years and having had their residence or been working the land for more than 30 years. On the sale of agricultural or forestry land, the lessee has a legally prescribed right of pre-emption.

Rental agreements for residential use with an expressly set out effective duration are subject to an automatic extension but may terminated by both the landlord and the lessor observing the legally stipulated notice periods, which are varying in accordance with the duration of the contracts. Those contracts might further be terminated by the lessor by giving notice once at least one third of the duration stated in the contract has elapsed. Contracts concluded for an unrestricted time might be terminated by the lessor by giving notice once at least six months have elapsed. The landlord is allowed to terminate the contract based on own residence needs or demolition or undertaking of works. Apart from those reasons, subject to compensation for the lessor, the landlord may terminate the contract observing a notice period of at least two years.

The parties in a rental agreement not subject to residential use can freely agree on termination, notice period for termination and opposition against automatic extension. Where those issues have not been regulated in the contract, the legal provisions of rental agreements for residential use apply. The tenant has a right of pre-emption if the let property is sold and he has been a tenant for more than three years.

The landlord has to be responsible for normal maintenance of the property, and must carry this out. Exceptional maintenance work or improvements can only be required by the landlord if these are stipulated by the local authority or some other legal obligation or by an agreement between the parties. The tenant himself may only undertake work that alters the property with the agreement of the landlord.

The landlord, in accordance with an annually determined official formula which is related to inflation, can increase the rent annually. The updating of the rent does not take place automatically, however, but must be notified to the tenant annually in advance.

Extraordinary updates for rental contracts concluded before 1995 and 1990 are possible as well as negotiations concerning a new rent. In this respect the specific transitional dispositions of the last rental form entered into force in November 2012 must be observed.

29.6 Succession and gifts

Applicable law and jurisdiction

Portuguese private international law provides that on a succession the personal law of the deceased at the time of his death is applicable.

The personal law is the law of nationality of the person. In the case of stateless persons it is the law of the place of usual residence. Further, testamentary capacity is governed by the personal law of the testator at the time of a testamentary disposition. Dispositions on death are valid in form, if they comply with the local laws of the place where the disposition is made, or the personal law of the testator, whether it be at the time of the disposition or at the time of death; or if they comply with the law which the local conflict of law rules deems to be applicable.

Portugal has transformed into internal law the *Washington Convention of 1973 providing a Uniform Law on the Form of an International Will.*

Portugal has not yet ratified the *Hague Convention on the law applicable to the form of testamentary dispositions of 5th October 1961.* The most important starting point for the Convention is the applicability of the law of states in which the testator makes a disposition, or has his place of usual residence, or in which the real estate is situated. In the case of testamentary dispositions in respect of land situated in Portugal, the non-Portuguese testator, if he is a national of a member state of the above-mentioned Convention, should, to be on the safe side, comply with the form required in Portugal; especially as Portuguese law does not recognize holograph wills.

To succession of the estate of persons deceased on or after 17 August 2015 the *EC Regulation 650/2012* on jurisdiction, applicable law, recognition and enforcement of decisions and acceptance and enforcement of authentic instruments in matters of succession and on the creation of a *European Certificate* of succession shall apply. Article 21 of this *Regulation* establishes as a general rule that the law applicable to the succession shall be the law of the State in which the deceased had his habitual residence at the time of death.

Capacity to dispose of property (including gifts) in respect of real estate situated in Portugal is regulated by the personal law (law of the home country) of the person effecting the transaction.

However, as regards acquisition, transfer and loss of possession and ownership, and other property rights in respect of land, the applicable law is that of the place in which the property is situated (so-called *lex rei sitae).*

International jurisdiction over property rights over real estate situated in Portugal lies exclusively with the Portuguese courts.

Wills set up in Portugal under Portuguese laws and before a notary are centrally registered and can be accessed in case of death of the testator.

Fundamentals of the succession and gift/donation laws of Portugal

Portuguese law distinguishes between public and private wills. The public will is made by a public declaration, which is drafted by a notary. The private will is prepared and signed by the testator himself, and must be accepted formally and by the notary. The private will can be placed in the custody of a notary. Portuguese law does not recognize simple holograph wills. If the testator dies without having made a valid will, the legal provisions on intestacy come into play. The legal inheritors include the spouse, relations up to the fourth degree, and in default the state. The inheritance is apportioned per head except for a few exceptions.

Next of kin of the first degree are the spouse and the children; the spouse, however, has a guaranteed ¼ share of the estate. Next of kin of the second degree: should no children or their offspring be alive, the parents of the deceased inherit – however, in this case the surviving spouse is entitled to ⅔ of the estate. Siblings of the deceased are next of kin of the third degree. The other relations rank as next of kin of the fourth degree.

Spouse, issue and parents of the deceased have a claim to a protected share, which is to be borne in mind in dispositions on death or in lifetime gifts. The protected share of the spouse amounts to half of the estate, if neither issue nor parents are also living to inherit. The protected share of the spouse and the issue amounts to two thirds of the inheritance. If there is no spouse but surviving issue, the protected share is half or two thirds, according to whether there is one or more issue. If the only surviving next of kin are the spouse and the parents of the deceased, the protected share for these is also two thirds. The division is carried out according to the rules of the statutory next of kinship.

In Portuguese law, the term gift means a contractual disposition, with no value consideration, acting to reduce the property of the donor, of a piece of property or an entitlement in favour of the other contracting party. Gifts of real estate are only valid when they are the subject of a notarial deed. Pure gifts in favour of a minor produce their effects independently of an acceptance by the minor in everything benefiting the minor. A gift can be subject to particular conditions or the carrying out of particular actions, and is revocable at any time, as long as it has not been accepted. This also applies if the donee rejects the gift.

29.7 Taxes and charges

Once-time taxes and charges on purchase

Real estate transfer taxes

Real estate transfer tax, *imposto municipal sobre as transmissões onerosas de imóveis* (IMT), is payable on the transfer for valuable consideration of property or subsidiary rights. IMT replaced the former *SISA* - adapted from the French *assise* – at the beginning of 2004, as part of the reform of property taxation. The acquisition of land through purchase or exchange is therefore taxable. If the handover of the land to the future buyer takes place simultaneously with the conclusion of the contract, the transfer tax is due at that stage. Long-term rental contracts (more than 30 years) of rural properties are regarded as transfer value for fiscal purposes. The IMT is also due on the conclusion of irrevocable powers of attorney for the sale of real estate, or on surrender of contractual rights in a preliminary contract. The tax rate is 5% for rural properties. For urban properties, the maximum tax rate is 6.5%, whereas for buyers who have their residence or place of business in tax havens, a uniform tax rate of 10% is in force.

The tax is payable before conclusion of the purchase contract, at a tax office of one´s choice. There is a tax exemption in various cases, in particular on the acquisition of own homes or dwellings for permanent residence use, which serve exclusively residential purposes and which do not exceed EUR 92,407 in price. For prices over EUR 92,407 and up to EUR 574,323, reduced tax rates apply. If the price is over EUR 574,323, the uniform tax rate of 6% applies. In a case of no own permanent residence, reduced taxes apply until an amount of EUR 550,836 and the uniform tax rate of 6% if higher.

The acquisition of 75% or more of the shares of a limited liability company, which is the owner of the property, is also subject to real estate transfer tax.

Proof of payment or exemption must be made at the time of celebration of the purchase contract.

Sales tax (value added tax)

The Portuguese value added tax rate is currently 23%; the reduced rates are 13% and 6%. On Madeira the rates are 22%, 12% and 5%, and on the Açores 18%, 10% and 5%. The general rule is that any transfer of property or of subsidiary property rights in land, which is subject to real estate transfer tax, is free of value added tax. Value added tax at the normal rate of 23% is therefore only chargeable on contracts for works and the purchase of building materials for the construction of the buildings. Work contracts, which come within the meaning of specific local authority or national dwelling-house building or renovation programs, are subject to the reduced value added tax rate of 12%. Nevertheless certain entities are allowed to renounce to the exemption of value added tax in case of transfer of property or rental. Fees of private notaries and lawyers are also subject to the normal rate.

Real estate registration and notary charges

Land Register and notaries' fees are prescribed by law in the relevant fee scales. Under the new *Fees Order*, which was introduced at the end of 2001, the fees are no longer determined by the commercial value of the transaction, but according to a fixed value for types of transactions that are supposed to correspond to the relevant investment. A minimum fee of EUR 175 is payable for a notarial deed in respect of a purchase contract or gift contract. Nevertheless depending on complexity fees might be higher. Prices for Casa Pronta purchase titles are fixed at EUR 300 for each act. The fee for the registration of the purchase at the Land Register in favor of the purchaser is also EUR 250.

Recurring taxes and charges

Real estate tax

The person or beneficial user of a rural or urban piece of land on 31 December in any year is obliged to pay land tax, *imposto municipal sobre imóveis* (IMI). This is a municipal tax, which in the context of the property tax reform has replaced the former *contribuição autárquica* as from 1 December 2003. The amount of the IMI is determined by the fiscal property value (*valor patrimonial tributário)* of the piece of land concerned, which can be checked at the local tax office and which is also available from the *caderneta predial.* For rural land, the calculation of the value is based upon the revenue of the land; for urban land it is the average construction and square meter land area price, having regard to the area, designation, locality, quality and age. A real estate assessor, on the instruction of the local tax office, determines the fiscal property value. Should an owner not be in agreement with the first calculated value of his land, he can require a second valuation. The property values of land which was valued under the old system of the *contribuição autárquica* can differ very markedly. Fundamentally, newer buildings have a much higher property value than older buildings. The old property values (*valor patrimonial*) should progressively be brought into line with the new fiscal property values (*valor patrimonial tributário*) during the next few years. On the transfer of a property that was valued under the old system, a valuation according to the rules of the IMI takes place automatically. It is expected that the fiscal property value of a piece of land will amount to approximately 80% to 90% of its market value. In some cases they might be even higher as the market value. During the year 2012 an official evaluation according to the new rules of all urban properties took place with the aim to have all properties updated in their value by the end of 2012.

The IMI tax rate for rural land is 0.8% of its fiscal property value. For urban lands already attributed a new fiscal property value, it varies between 0.3% and 0.5%. The municipal authority is obliged to fix the annual tax rate within these margins: large cities tend to fix rates at the top end of the band. Properties which are held by offshore companies are charged a fixed tax rate of 7.5%.

Real estate which is acquired for one's own permanent residential purposes, can be exempted from land tax for a period of three years, on application by the taxpayer, if his taxable income is lower than EUR 153,300 and if the fiscal property value does not exceed 125,000. Exemption is also available for real estate touristic unit when a touristic use has been granted, as well as for urban property subject to rehabilitation.

Income tax

Persons who receive income from real estate situated in Portugal, towards which the profits from a land sale also count, are liable to income tax on that income. The obligation to pay tax also exists for persons who are not resident in Portugal. For the applicable tax rates, see 29.8.

Income from rental, leasing, parting with the right to use or with related facilities or services is taxable as well. For pieces of land, the maintenance costs as well as the land tax can be deducted. In the case of blocks of buildings, proven costs for maintaining the common parts are also deducted.

If the building is used for his own purposes, the owner only has to bear the land tax. The land tax can then not be deducted. No further tax is applicable.

Net wealth taxes

At present, there are no further taxes on real estate besides those mentioned.

Capital gains taxes

On a disposal of value of rights in land, or assignment of contractual options or other rights that derive from contracts regarding land, any capital gain (*mais-valia)* arising is taxable as income.

The taxable gain is determined by the difference between acquisition cost and the proceeds of sale. For persons resident in Portugal, the taxable gain is reduced by 50%. Proven costs which have increased the value during the last five years can be deducted. If the purchase and sale are separated by more than 24 months, the purchase value is also affected by an annual updating relief formula, which is determined by the Finance Minister. The tax rate is determined by reference to the total taxable income. For non-residents the capital gain is taxed at a uniform rate of 28%. Following a decision of the European Court of Justice, residents in an EU or EWR member state can meanwhile chose between the uniform rate of 28% or the Portuguese income tax rates, taking into consideration their global income.

The capital gain which arises on the sale of own homes or own residences, which are the elected main residence of the taxpayer or his family, is tax free if the total profit on sale, after deduction of any bank loans outstanding, is reinvested within three years after the sale in the acquisition of another own home, own residence or building plot situated in Portugal or another EU or EWR member state, or has been reinvested in the acquisition of another own home, own residence or building plot during the two years preceding the sale.

Inheritance and gift taxes

Within the context of the reform of property tax, the legislation on urban *SISA* tax, inheritance and gift tax is being completely abolished. From January 2004 the transfer for value of real estate is taxed within the framework of the IMT. Bequests and gifts are now subject to stamp duty (*imposto de selo*). The gratuitous transfer of land situated in Portugal, as well as its acquisition by prescription, is subject to stamp duty at the uniform rate of 10% of its fiscal property value. In the case of gifts, as well as the 10% charge, there is an additional charge to stamp duty of 0.8% of the fiscal property value. This additional charge does not apply to inheritance and acquisition by prescription.

Spouses, children and parents when beneficiaries of gratuitous transfers are exempted from stamp duty. Since 2009 the exemption is also extended to common law partners.

Stamp duty on gratuitous transfers is applicable only to natural persons. If the gift is to a company, the capital gain will be taxed within the framework of corporation tax.

The gratuitous transfer of shares in a company is not subject to stamp duty in Portugal, if the owner is not resident in Portugal.

Other taxes and charges

Stamp duty, which is applicable to contracts, certain deeds, books and papers, as well as on the transfer for value and gratuitous transfer of property or other tangible rights in real estate, has already been mentioned. In some districts sewerage rates may be payable in addition by property owners.

Incorrect (lower) statement of sale price on the sales agreement

With the introduction of the new property taxation legislation, the practice of understatement should officially be brought to an end. This objective will be pursued on the one hand by the application of lower rates of tax, accompanied by the adaptation of the obsolete property values to the real market values, and on the other hand by increased exchange of information as regards tax data.

In the case of an understatement of the value, one must reckon with not only the fiscal and/or criminal consequences, but also with possible difficulties on the later pursuance of claims by the buyer or seller in the event of non-fulfilment of the purchase contract. A purchase contract, in which the parties knowingly declare a purchase price that does not correspond with the price actually paid, is a void and sham transaction. The nullification can be brought about both by the parties to the transaction and by their heirs. An understatement can also have negative effects on the capital gains tax payable in the future. It should not be forgotten that the state, the municipalities and other public bodies, on assertion of a false or sham price, have a right of pre-emption, if it is proved that the taxable value is 30% (or EUR 5,000) over the value that has actually been taxed. The right of pre-emption must be subject of court proceedings.

An understatement of value can be pursued as tax fraud and on amounts of tax evaded of over EUR 15,000, a sentence of up to three years imprisonment can be the consequence.

International taxation

Portugal has concluded treaties for the avoidance of double taxation with many European states, among them Germany, Switzerland and the UK, as well as Canada and the US, in the area of income tax. Inheritance and gift taxes are not dealt with by any of the treaties.

Income from immovable properties, which is situated in Portugal and which belongs to a person resident abroad, can be taxed in Portugal. This also applies to profits that arise from the disposal of immovable property.

The incomes or profits, which are taxed at source in Portugal, are exempted from additional taxation in the state of residence of the taxpayer, but can be taken into account in determining the tax rate (tax rate reservation).

29.8 Immigration law and tax residence

Entry, residence and settlement of foreigners

Portugal is a member of the Schengen area. In order to travel to Portugal a valid passport or personal identity card from the country of origin, for the duration of the planned stay, is necessary; in some circumstances, a suitable visa is also needed. American, Australian and Canadian nationals can enter Portugal with a valid passport, if their stay for the purposes of tourism or business does not exceed 90 days.

Within the EU there is the right of free movement of persons, which Swiss nationals and nationals of EFTA member states can also make use of. For short stays of up to three months, EU, EFTA and Swiss nationals need no visa or permission to stay. In general, visas are granted for short stays, study and work purposes, temporary and permanent residence, and these are obtainable at the responsible Portuguese consulates.

For EU, EFTA or Swiss nationals to take up permanent residence in Portugal, a residence permit (*cartão de residente)* is necessary. The application has to be made within three months after arrival, at the foreign nationals' office that covers the place of residence. For the permit, sufficient financial resources for one's maintenance have to be demonstrated (contract of employment or declaration of commencement of activity for self-employed persons, together with first receipts for income), as well as a health insurance policy that is valid for Portugal, two photographs and a valid personal identity card or passport.

The conditions for grant of a residence permit for non-EU nationals or persons without equivalent status to EU nationals are appreciably stricter, as these persons do not enjoy freedom of movement. Before inward travel, a suitable visa for taking up residence should be sought at the responsible Portuguese consulate. Information will be supplied there about which documents are necessary. As a rule, however, necessary items are, *inter alia*, a doctor's certificate, an extract from central criminal records, information about type of residence in Portugal, declaration concerning the purpose of the stay and proof about available financial means. After entering Portugal, a residence permit should then be applied for.

Portugal has established a Golden Residence Permit Programme for Third State citizens involved in investment activities either individually or through a company. The investment operations considered for the residence permit were acquisition of real estate with a value equal to or above EUR 500,000, capital transfer equal or above to EUR one million or creation of at least 10 job positions.

The government has recently approved four additional options for investors:

1 Acquisition of properties, to be held for five years, in an amount equal to or higher than EUR 350,000 if they were built at least 30 years ago, or they are located in urban rehabilitation areas, as well as the rehabilitation of properties acquired

2 Transfer of foreign capital of at least EUR 350,000 to be applied in scientific research activities, developed by public or private institutions of scientific research, integrated into the national scientific and technological system

3 Capital transfer of at least EUR 250,000, to be invested in artistic production support, recovery and maintenance of national cultural heritage

4 Capital transfer of at least EUR 500,000 to invest in investment funds or capital ventures, oriented to the capitalization of small and medium companies, with a viable capitalization plan. The investor will be entitled to receive profit from its participation in the fund and to liquidate the asset at the end of the investment period

Encouraging investment into targeted areas

If the investment (excluding the investment in funds and in capital ventures) takes place in low-density areas (those with less than 100 inhabitants per km or with a GDP per capita below 75 % of the national average) the investment amount will be reduced by 20%. The same applies to the creation of employment, in a move designed to encourage investment into such areas.

Tax residence

On taking up residence in Portugal, one's entire income arising worldwide is subject to income tax in Portugal. Income arising during the course of the tax year is taxable. According to Portuguese law, a person has his residence in Portugal if he stays there for longer than 183 days, either continuously or with interruptions, during any period of 12 months, or even if he stays for a shorter period, if he has a place of residence which is intended as his usual residence. There is no wealth tax in Portugal.

The income tax rates for natural persons for the year 2014 are as follows:

	Percentage	
Taxable income (in Euros)	**(A) Normal**	**(B) Average**
up to 7,000	14.50	14.500
from 7,000 to 20,000	28.50	23.600
from 20,001 to 40,000	37.00	30.300
from 40,000 to 80,000	45.00	37.650
above 80,000	48.00	-

The provisions of the tax are governed by the following rules: if the taxable total exceeds EUR 7,000, it will be divided in two. In one part, which corresponds to the highest amount of this class of income, the relevant tax rate of Part B will be applicable. The remaining amount will be subject to the next highest rate of tax of Part A.

If the income is higher than EUR 80,000, this amount is taxed with an additional rate of solidarity of 2.5% or 5% if higher than EUR 250,000.

For the year 2014, taxable income exceeding EUR 6.790 is subject to an extraordinary surcharge of 3.5%.

Tax regime for non-regular residents

For the purpose of attracting non resident professionals qualified for activities with high added value, as well as beneficiaries of pension schemes granted abroad, Portugal has implemented a specific tax regime. The conditions to be met are regulated in the Investment Tax Code, created by *Decree-Law n. 249/2009*. One of the essential conditions is that the person has not been deemed resident in Portuguese territory during five years prior to the year in which he first intends to be taxed as a non-habitual resident. The tax scheme is valid for a period of ten years. The activities considered as high added value are fixed by law. Income obtained in Portugal from those activities by non-habitual residents are taxed at the special rate of 20%. Non-Portuguese investment income may be completely tax-exempt for the duration of eligibility.

International double taxation for residents of Portugal

For the avoidance of double taxation, Portugal has concluded treaties with almost all European countries, as well as with many countries outside Europe, among them Canada and the US. If a person is regarded by two contracting states as resident for tax purposes, this can have the consequence that both states apply the worldwide income principle for themselves. The double taxation treaty is then used to determine in which country the person has his place of residence and which country is to be regarded as the country of source.

Usually, the country of residence is the one where the person possesses a permanent place of residence; if the person has places of residence in both states, the place where the means of support is situated will be decisive. The usual place of residence stands in second place, and in third place is the country of nationality. If the responsibility for tax cannot be determined according to those criteria, the countries will negotiate this in a mutual agreement.

29.9 Checklist: Real estate in Portugal

- Checking the legal title of the property by obtaining extracts from the Land Register, Finance Ministry records (*caderneta predial*) and construction or use permit. Verification of existence of the *FTH* and energy performance certificate. Examination of the remaining authorizations of the buyer or seller
- Possible physical survey of the condition of the property, survey and examination of historic burdens and encumbrances
- Application for a Portuguese tax number
- Drafting and concluding a preliminary contract with an enforcement clause, having regard to the necessary formalities as well as to the provisional registration of the preliminary contract, or provisional registration of the purchase in the Land Register. First down payment towards the purchase price
- Payment of the transfer tax and stamp duty at the tax office
- After final examination of the relevant documents, conclusion of the purchase contract, and payment of the balance of the purchase price
- Registration of the purchase on the Land Register. Changing the record of the property at the local tax office into the name of the buyer, and possible application for exemption of the land tax
- Important: if there is a demonstrable non-compliance with the purchase contract on the part of the buyer, he loses the instalments on the purchase price, which he has already paid. If it is the other way round, the seller must refund the buyer with double the instalments that have been paid
- For the seller: Presentation of the income tax declarations for capital gains tax or exemption in the year following the sale

29.10 Bibliography

Dossiers Internacionaux: Portugal, Editions Francis Lefebvre, Levallois 2001

Hampshire, David: Buying a Home in Portugal, Survival Books Limited, 2002

Holtom, Harvey; Howell John: The Sunday Times Buying a Property: Portugal, Cadogan Books/Sunday Times, 2003

Postlethwaite, Justin (Editor): Portuguese Property Buying Guide 2004: The Ultimate Guide to Buying a Property in Portugal, Merricks Media, 2003

Sousa, Maria Constança Dias Urbano: das Timesharing an Ferienimmobilien in der EUR: eine rechtsvergleichende Studie unter Berücksichtigung der Timesharing-Richtlinie (94/47/EG), Nomos Verlagsgesellschaft, Baden Baden 1998

30

Spain

Kingdom of Spain
Reino de España

by

Philipp Kirchheim

Marimón Abogados
Passeig de Gràcia, 118, 5ª
E-08008 Barcelona
Spain

Telephone: +34 934 157 575
Facsimile: +34 934 158 311

kirchheim@marimon-abogados.com
marimon-abogados.com

Philipp Kirchheim, born in Munich in 1966, studied law at Freiburg i. Br. and Munich and in Seville. He lives and works as a lawyer in Barcelona and Seville (Spain) since 1998 and was admitted to the Munich Bar as Rechtsanwalt in 1998 and to the Barcelona Bar as Abogado in 1999. He is a partner with the firm Marimón Abogados.

Philipp specializes in real estate and related tax law and his expertise relates to both private as institutional clients and private and commercial real estate.

He has participated actively as a speaker in multiple congresses, seminars and has published numerous articles. Philipp is fluent in German, Spanish and English.

30.1 Introduction

Pursuant to the national constitution in force since 1978, the Kingdom of Spain (*Reino de España*) is a hereditary monarchy with a parliamentary democratic system of government. The King is Head of State. The legislative body is a bicameral parliament (*Cortes*) consisting of the House of Representatives (*Congreso de los Diputados*) and the Senate (*Senado*). The latter is the representative body of the 17 autonomous regional authorities (*Comunidades Autónomas* or *Autonomías*). Spain has a landmass of 505,990 square kilometers and approximately 47 million inhabitants. The principal urbanized areas are Madrid, in the middle of the country, and Barcelona. In addition, the coastal areas and archipelagos are, in the majority, densely populated. Climatically, the extremes are greater inland than on the southern and eastern coast, so that it can be noticeably cold inland, especially in winter, remaining mild nearer the sea. In summer, it is hot throughout Spain.

The Spanish real estate market, after experiencing a boom from the middle of the 1990s until 2007, and dramatically falling prices since then due to the implosion of such real estate bubble and the global financial crisis, is recently stabilizing and of increasing interest for investors, both institutional or private. Nevertheless, those substantial price falls now offer good opportunities to enter the market with potential for an interesting price evolution in the medium term. Consequently, today it is still possible to find great 'bargains' in Spanish real estate. Opportunistic investors have a great chance to enter into a very interesting market and destination, where factors such as political stability, population density and climate as well as the interesting and varied geography combine to make Spain an attractive investment location, and above all a strategic place to live within the framework of Europe or the Mediterranean region. Highly developed infrastructures make Spain also a very interesting place to live.

30.2 Real estate ownership

Different forms and types of ownership

Sole ownership

Article 33 of the *Spanish Constitution of 1978* guarantees the right of ownership, which is an absolute right limited only by the constitutionally guaranteed social function. In the *Spanish Civil Code* or *Código Civil* (CC), the right of ownership grants the (sole) proprietor the unique and exclusive right to use and dispose of his/her property without limitation except as established by law (Article 348, CC). The owner is thus able to use his property and its fruits, possess it directly or indirectly, dispose of or encumber it, enclose, demarcate and separate it, as well as to proclaim his ownership and ward off any interference to his property. Pursuant to Article 350, CC, the owner of any real estate has ownership over its surface as well as that which lies beneath. The right of possession and use of the airspace (*vuelo*) above a property, e.g. by building on it, is also derived from Article 350, CC. From this same right, the owner in turn accrues a temporarily transmissible building right (*Derecho de superficie*) that can be alienated or encumbered.

Co-ownership

Co-ownership exists when several legal or natural persons are jointly entitled to ownership of a property. At the same time each individual owner is entitled to a share (*pro indiviso*) of the undivided common property.

Although the configuration of joint ownership (*pro diviso*), whereby co-owners hold a property jointly without any assignment or division of the whole, is widespread in other jurisdictions, it does not exist under Spanish law. However, a statutory concept similar to joint ownership arises, where within the context of a co-ownership community, agreements are reached to jointly alienate or encumber portions of the co-owned property. Nevertheless, this is still not a form of common property in the sense of a collective ownership.

In the context of the co-ownership community, each co-owner has the full and exclusive ownership of his share. Nevertheless, each co-owner is entitled to use the whole of the property and to receive the fruits from the whole property that correspond to his ownership share. In return each one is obliged to bear the corresponding pro rata maintenance costs.

Alteration or transfer of the joint property may only be undertaken unanimously. Each co-owner may, however, encumber or alienate his own common share. No co-owner can be compelled to remain in the community, even though the law permits agreements on minimum affiliation for up to 10 years, which may be extended when they expire. The issue of potential preemption rights of co-owners may have to be considered.

Each co-owner has the right to demand the dissolution of the community, insofar as this does not render the intended use of the property impossible: the rights of third parties cannot thereby be affected. If the property is indivisible, which may be the case with a large number of properties, then it must be sold and the proceeds divided.

Condominiums

A particularly relevant form of co-ownership has its basis in the *Law on Horizontal Property* (*Ley sobre la Propiedad Horizontal*, LPH): According to this, the common elements of residential semi-attached or detached units or of an apartment building are co-owned by the owners on an individual basis by means of a so-called Declaration of Division (*Declaración de división horizontal*) of units, each one being owned individually. Therefore, within this physically connected space, private individual ownership and joint co-ownership exist side by side. These ownership communities govern themselves principally based on the will of the members as expressed in bylaws.

Please note that some autonomous regions have introduced some proper laws on the subject of co-ownership, so that the applying rules might vary in part from the general Spanish law LPH.

Timesharing (Part-time easement)

The part-time occupancy rights or time shares have been for many years a very relevant topic in Spain. As a consequence of the comprehensive, though late, implementation of the EU timeshare directive at the end of 1998, the ban on further designation of these rights as *Multipropiedad* (plural ownership) was highlighted as the most drastic and most exceptional change. These rights are now in fact designated as timeshare rights (*Aprovechamiento por turnos de bienes inmuebles*) in order to avoid any further suggestion that the rights correspond to ownership rights of the user. Rather, in the present framework of timeshare in Spain, it is a matter of an atypical, limited right *in rem* of the user. During the last decade, timeshare models have almost completely lost their importance and are now rarely an issue when talking about Spanish real estate.

The current legislation establishes that the easement must have a minimum duration of seven days per year; at the same time the relevant agreement may not give rise to an obligation of less than three or more than five years. Rights of users acquired prior to the introduction of the law remain in existence without a time limitation as long as other, strict, statutorily-determined standards are observed.

These standards obligate the owner of the timeshare property to observe a multitude of consumer protection regulations. In association with the operating company, the owner must create a system for use in the form of a public document, in accordance with legal requirements. The document must then be recorded in the Ownership Registry (*Registro de la Propiedad*). Furthermore, there are a number of provisions which strict ly regulate the conclusion of the contract.

Non-compliance with these provisions grants the user extensive grounds for termination of contract.

Easements, charges, covenants, liens and mortgages

The right of ownership of real estate is limited by easements, respective rights of occupiers of adjoining property, statutory rights of preemption or first refusal, or inalienability and other rights *in rem* of third parties. The latter basically serve to grant rights *in rem* in the broader sense such as the securing of liabilities or obligations as well as the securing of the acquired elements, i.e. unsolicited option or preemptive rights, through an interest in property.

Usufruct (beneficial use)

The legal right of usufruct (*usufructo*) conveys to the usufructuary the right to use and enjoy the fruits of a property without being owner. The usufructuary is obliged to maintain the property in form and substance.

Unless otherwise agreed upon within the grant of the usufruct, the authorized person can make use of the property, receive its fruits, e.g. from renting it out, encumbering it, or even assigning his/her right. On the other hand, the usufructuary is obligated to the absolute owner (*nudo propietario,* in Spain one speaks of the "naked" property, *nuda propiedad*) and is bound to preserve the property, to bear the brunt of its expenditures and encumbrances, as well as to return it at the end of the agreed period. The owner is obliged to bear the cost of extraordinary repairs insofar as they are required.

The right may expire: after a specific period of time; on the demise of the usufructuary; on the concurrence of the right of usufruct and the title to the "naked" property in one person; and, also, in the event of the destruction of the property subject to the usufruct.

The right of usufruct may be created by agreement of the parties or it may arise at law. Usufruct in favor of a legal entity is limited to a maximum of 30 years. The most common form of usufruct in Spain is the testamentary appointment of a surviving spouse as usufructuary of the deceased's estate, irrespective of whether the spouse acquires a statutory right of usufruct alongside descendants or heirs of a more distant rank. Furthermore, the right of usufruct is frequently employed in the acquisition of real estate where ownership is intended to pass to successor heirs but the testators-to-be are meant to maintain possession and control of the property by means of usufructuary right. When succession occurs, the usufruct simply expires and only this legal gain alone is subject to inheritance tax.

Right of use and right of residence

Spanish law recognizes the right *in rem* of use and residence (*Derecho de Uso y Habitación*) as a sub-form of usufruct. This right is strictly personal. Consequently, it cannot be transferred to another person in any way.

Heritable building right

By means of a heritable building right (*Derecho de superficie*), independent ownership is established on land belonging to another. The beneficiary of the heritable building right becomes entitled thereby to construct on or under the land of the property owner and, by paying an annual lease, has ownership of the building. The heritable building right is separate from the formal property right over the plot of land and thus the heritable building right breaches the fundamental principle of acquisition of ownership by accession (*Derecho de accesión*).

The essential characteristic of the heritable building right is that ownership of the constructed building erected is transitory in nature. The right terminates once the agreed time period lapses and ownership passes to the owner of the property, no payment being accrued as a result, although this can be negotiated. The duration of the heritable building right between private persons may not exceed 99 years. In the case of building leases arranged by municipal authorities, the maximum duration is 75 years.

An imperative condition for the validity of the heritable building right is its formal creation in a public deed. The heritable building right must be recorded in the Ownership Registry. In the case of the heritable building right, the entry in the Registry is the constituent act, in contrast to the fundamental principle of informality in the creation of rights *in rem* in Spain.

For the owner of the land, the principal advantage of the heritable building right is that he/she is titleholder of the appreciation in value of the property. In addition the owner gets a financial return and, in the long run, becomes the owner of a building. Real estate investors who do not wish to assume the risks of financing and constructing a building may find an effective and profitable alternative way with a heritable building right.

Leasehold (land rent)

The leasehold (*Censos*) constitutes land charges that are – systematically, in an inappropriate way – regulated within the framework of the contractual relationship rather than in the context of the property law regulations of the second book of the CC. Emphyteusis (*censo enfitéutico*) is distinguished from the land rent on the granting of capital (*censo consignativo*) and the land rent on conveyance of the property (*censo reservativo*). Today one frequently finds old, expired land rents recorded in the Ownership Registry that are canceled in the context of the first subsequent authorized amendment.

Land easements

Land easements (*Servidumbres*) are rights *in rem* to the benefit of a property of a third party. The easement encumbers a servient property in favor of a dominant property that benefits from the easement. Easements can arise either as a matter of law or based on the will of the parties, whereby the acquisitive prescription plays an important role. In principle, an easement agreement does not require any particular form; nevertheless only a public or notarized document or a judgment may be recorded in the Ownership Registry. Rights of way, water rights, easements for light and views, etc., are examples of statutory land easements. Voluntary land easements may be of many kinds, even including the right "to take part in local festivities from the balcony of a servient apartment". In addition to the usual grounds for the expiry of a right, the failure to exercise the easement for a period of more than 20 years should be noted.

Mortgages

Within the scope of encumbrances on real estate, Spanish law only recognizes the mortgage (*Hipoteca*), which is exclusively structured as a strictly accessory security right. In contrast to other jurisdictions, an agreement of a charge on the land is not possible. Neither a mortgage debenture nor a mortgage note exist in Spanish law; only registered mortgages are recognized.

A precondition of recording a mortgage in the Ownership Registry is, as with all entries, the presentation of a public or notarized document recording its creation, thus, precluding the entry of privately composed agreements. The entry of a mortgage in the Ownership Registry is the constituent act in the creation of the mortgage.

The commercial mortgage is the standard mortgage in Spanish law and includes a pre-existing demand for payment as well as interest, default payment interest and costs of judicial enforcement.

The maximum ceiling mortgage (*hipoteca de máximo*) guarantees claims for payment up to a specific amount or ceiling where the actual amount of the claim is either not yet known at the time the mortgage is created or changes during the period of validity (e.g. credit on a current account). The upper limit of liability of the real estate, the credit period, the extended periods, where applicable, as well as the due dates of the amortization on the credit account must be stated at the time of creation of the mortgage.

In principle, Spanish law does not recognize a consolidated mortgage (*hipoteca solidaria*), i.e. a mortgage that encumbers several properties equally as security for a specific claim. Nevertheless, in practice there is an important exception that can be implemented, especially when financing arrangements for property developers. A mortgage is first created on a single and usually large property. Later when the property is divided, a consolidated mortgage is deemed to exist, from the viewpoint of the protection of creditors, i.e. several properties respectively insure the entire claim.

The unilateral mortgage (*hipoteca unilateral*) alleviates the situation regarding the creation of mortgages in international legal relations. It is possible for the borrower to create a mortgage without the immediate participation of the creditor. The mortgage is thus then recognized in the place of residence or at the location of the creditor's office. If the creditor does not respond to the request of the borrower within two months, by presenting his/her declaration of acceptance at the Ownership Registry, the mortgage expires.

From a practical financial viewpoint, Spanish law regards a property encumbered with a mortgage as an economic unit. Consequently, the liability of the mortgage extends to all the component parts that are naturally connected with the property, including the improvements (*mejoras*), i.e. renovations, rebuilding, etc., but not to new buildings that are only included in the official documents of the mortgage by express agreement. Also, by law, liability does not extend to permanently installed furniture and fittings, fruits and revenues owed (*rentas)* but not yet collected (most notably, house rents). Therefore, if the mortgage is intended to extend to these items, they must be separately incorporated into the records documenting the creation of the mortgage.

The mortgage extends to the interest agreed upon within the scope of the credit contract and, in such case, to default payment interest and costs of judicial enforcement. According to Spanish mortgage law, except where limited by contract, interest accrued during the last two years as well as interest due and payable in the current year can be guaranteed by mortgage. This can be extended for up to five years if the parties agree. In addition, the mortgage guarantees the possible costs of judicial enforcement where this may be an additional claim in the future, up to a maximum of 20% of the secured principal claim.

There have been some cautious attempts to adapt the Spanish mortgage system to more flexible terms, but the essence is still a strongly accessory system and principle. The most innovative possibility was the so-called reverse-mortgage (*hipoteca inversa*), which allowed especially elder persons to mortgage their property either receiving one single payment from a bank, or a periodical or even lifetime monthly payment or rent. At the end of the mortgage, it is foreseen that the owners or –in case of lifetime structures, the heirs – have some time to sell the property and pay back the loan to the bank. Acceptance of this new mortgage model was not very significant, possibly due to the general economic and banking crisis Spain has suffered in recent years.

Following the reform of the Spanish civil procedure rules at the beginning of 2001, creditors now have at their disposal, in addition to the usual types of procedures i.e. recognition procedure and the general security enforcement procedure, a more effective summary mortgage enforcement procedure with shorter deadlines. The legislature has also incorporated an extrajudicial notarial enforcement procedure (*venta extrajudicial*) into the new civil procedure rules.

The breakdown of the Spanish economy during recent years has increased significantly the enforcement of mortgages. Due to the decrease in values and the high number of enforcements, prices that could be achieved through public auctions have frequently been below the current debt towards the mortgage bank. That, together with the fact that in the Spanish financing system the mortgage debtor not only guarantees payment of loan and interest etc through the mortgaged property itself, but also as a personal debtor, has led to dramatic consequences for many mortgage debtors that have lost not only their properties but are also left with a significant debt.

The problem has become a huge social issue within Spain, which can only be resolved with great difficulties in relation to older mortgages, as Spanish bank financing is based on the validity of those mortgages. Aside from 'good practice rules' that the government has established and requested the banks to observe voluntarily, it is very much under discussion if the so called 'giving in payment' (*dación en pago*) shall become a new legal principal for such cases. Recently the government has established rules in order to free debtors from enforcement temporarily when their social indicators justify such protection.

Still, there are many auctions taking place and due to little bidding interest, there is a good opportunity to purchase properties at very low prices.

When the claim secured by the mortgage expires, the property owner does not acquire any type of land charge that prevents subsequent encumbrances from rising in preference in the Ownership Registry. The mortgage is satisfied when a public document of satisfaction signed by the mortgage holder or mortgagee or a judgment with the force of law is recorded. In addition, as of recently, the owner has the option to file for satisfaction without the participation of the mortgage holder after the lapse of a specific period of time.

Statutory mortgages essentially protect the following groups in Spain: family members in family claims (e.g. for maintenance expense, inheritance, etc.); and insurance and ownership communities, insofar as their members fail to comply with their payment obligations, such as employees' wages, to a certain extent. Furthermore, claims of the state, the provinces and the municipalities are insured through statutory mortgages against their claims of the last two tax years, insofar as the corresponding acknowledgement of the debt is registered.

Protection of ownership, proof of ownership and registration

In contrast to other legal systems, Spanish law allows ownership of real estate to be established by means other than an entry in the Ownership Registry (*Registro de la Propiedad*). In fact, an acquisition that is completely detached from the Ownership Registry is possible. The entry in the registry is merely declaratory, i.e. as evidence of legality, but not the constituent act for the creation of the right of ownership.

Therefore, any qualified written or other type of document about the relevant acquisition of the property in its original form can be sufficient proof of ownership. Nevertheless, it regularly is the notarial contract of sale or deed, the *escritura pública*, that gives proof of the right of ownership.

Since problems in proving ownership are unavoidable because of the possible informality in the acquisition of ownership, Spanish legislation provides legal or notarial procedures by means of which a person's right of ownership can be established and, most importantly, subsequently entered into the Ownership Registry. In detail, this is a matter of the *Proof of Ownership Process* (*expediente de dominio*) or the notarial *Act of Disclosure* (*acta de notoriedad*), both of which are regulated in the Spanish mortgage law, *Ley Hipotecaria* (LH).

In spite of the informality, entry into the Ownership Registry has an importance that should not be underestimated since the principle of the bona fide effect of the Ownership Registry is stipulated in Article 34 of the LH, which reads: "A third party who, in good faith and in return for payment, acquires a right from a seemingly entitled person according to an entry in the Ownership Registry, is protected in his acquisition from the moment in which the right is recorded, even though, subsequently, the title of the transferor is annulled or terminated for reasons that did not themselves emanate from the Ownership Registry." This is one of the most important provisions of Spanish real estate law and unambiguously demonstrates the tremendous significance of the recording in the Ownership Registry.

The legal basis for the Ownership Registry is Article 605 ff of the CC, in conjunction with Article 1 ff of the LH. Pursuant to Article 1 of the LH, it is the task of the Ownership Registry to register or provisionally record those legal documents and contracts that affect ownership or other rights *in rem* in land. Formally, pursuant to Article 3 of the LH, rights may only be entered on the basis of public documents or notarial deeds (*escritura pública*), enforceable proof of indebtedness, court decisions or other official court documents. By contrast, the entry of privately drawn up contracts is categorically excluded.

The Ownership Registry is maintained in such a way that a separate sheet is created for every property. The Ownership Registry sheet is divided into three columns. In the right-hand column, every legal event connected with the corresponding property is entered in strict chronological sequence, whether a transfer of ownership, an attachment, a mortgage or an easement. The foregoing narrow column, the middle column, serves to consecutively number the entries. The column on the left contains the marginal notes *(notas marginales)*. The most diverse legal circumstances are entered in this column, which usually refer to the transaction recorded in the other two columns, such as tax liabilities of the property or the expiry of encumbrances on the property or the acceptance thereof, etc. In individual cases, the legal transactions to be recorded in the column on the left are specified by law.

Every document that is presented to the Ownership Registry is recorded in the *Registry Diary (Libro Diario)* specifying the precise date and time. Historically, documents received by ordinary mail were not considered by virtue of application of the principle of personal presentation. That changed at some point, so that documents could be sent by mail, later also by fax. However, the time of receipt was always deemed to be the moment in which the mail is opened in the Ownership Registry (pursuant to the mortgage regulation, *Reglamento hipotecario*, RH), which is a somewhat uncertain practice. This is of great significance, since, in Spanish law, a fundamental principle is that the earlier right has precedence over that which is established at a later time (*prior tempore potior iure*).

The Spanish legislator has now adapted all relevant proceedings to the modern technological possibilities and has specifically enabled a fast and direct communication between notaries and Ownership Registries via e-mail (*correo corporativo*) that mostly make unnecessary personal presentation to the Registry. This helps save time and gains legal certainty.

30.3 Purchase and sale of real estate

The sales agreement

Ownership of real estate is transferred in Spain according to the doctrine of *Título* and *Modo*. According to this doctrine, two elements are necessary for an effective transfer of ownership: an underlying transaction – the *Título*, e.g. a sales contract, a donation, or something similar, – and an act of transfer – the *Modo,* e.g. the handing over of the keys of a dwelling or the simple agreement to transfer possession of a property.

The buying of real estate in Spain is essentially informal: Article 1278 of the CC specifies the fundamental legal effectiveness of contracts, regardless of their form. Although Article 1280(1) of the CC establishes the obligation to notarially authenticate real estate transactions, the law nevertheless contains no rule of nullity in case of non-observance of this provision. In fact, Article 1279 of the CC grants both contractual parties the right to demand that the other party complete the legally required form, which implies that informal contracts are fully valid.

A further important difference between other jurisdictions and Spanish real estate law is the informality in the handing over of property. Under Spanish law, the transfer can be made by means of oral agreement or other type of implied action. A much-cited example of this is the act of handing over the keys. However, any other de facto granting of the power of disposal can also be regarded as a transfer of possession and therefore as procurement of ownership.

In addition, the issue of public sale contract documents is also tantamount to transferring possession, thus waiving the need for any other separate transfer of real estate. This would only cease to apply if special rules or clauses with regard to the granting of possession had been agreed in the notarial deed or *escritura.*

Usually, the process of Spanish real estate transactions begins with the signing of the privately drawn up sales agreement. This is not however to say that it would not also be possible to immediately sign a notarial deed or *escritura pública*, thus waiving the need for the private contract but this is not the usual practice in Spain. In contrast to many other jurisdictions, in Spain, the private contract binds the parties in exactly the same way as a notarial contract of sale.

An occasional practice is to take the property under consideration off the market for a short time prior to concluding the private contract in return for the payment of a small reservation fee. The idea is that the interested party investigates legal or technical aspects of the property during a short period of time. If the interested party then reneges on the acquisition, he usually forfeits the fee. This practice – very important in times of a booming real estate market – may have lost some importance during the lower demand of recent times and probably for the next few years. However, it is not recommended to pay any reservation fee, as it may be lost easily, if the purchase does not take place for whatever reason.

If the purchaser goes on with the purchase process – having paid a reservation fee or not – he would usually sign a privately drawn up contract. All the essential contractual conditions (agreement on the acquisition of completely unencumbered property, purchase price, manner of payment, date of transfer, fittings, etc.) should be determined without exception in this privately drawn up contract. Generally, a down payment for a maximum of 10% of the purchase price is agreed upon in this contract.

If this down payment is agreed upon as *arras penitenciales*, or deposit, pursuant to Article 1.454 of the CC, then this means that the parties can free themselves of the contract, which would, however, result in the following financial consequences: if the buyer fails to meet his obligations under the privately drawn up sales agreement (payment of the balance of the purchase price and attendance at the signing of the notarial document), then he would lose the down payment. On the other hand, if the seller fails to meet his obligations (attendance at the signing of the notarial document and granting of possession), then he is obliged to repay double the amount of the down payment to the buyer. This is probably the most frequently encountered arrangement in practice.

The privately drawn up contract can also refer to a simple purchase option instead of to a purchase. In that case, the party entitled to the option acquires the right to purchase a specific property at a specified price within the option period stipulated in the contract. Instead of a down payment, an option price is agreed, to which the option grantor is entitled just for holding the property in reserve in favor of the option taker. This differs principally from a contract of sale with an *arras* agreement pursuant to Article 1.454 of the CC in that the option grantor cannot be released from the contract simply by repaying the buyer double the amount of the *arras*. Thus, the buyer basically has a stronger position, for which he must, of course, pay the option price, which as a matter of principle is not offset against the purchase price, a frequent exception in practice being however that the offset is explicitly agreed upon. On the contrary, if the option is not executed within the agreed terms the option holder usually loses the paid option price.

This sort of a purchase option can also be agreed upon in notarial deed or *escritura pública* instead of by means of a private sales agreement and, in this case, even entered in the Ownership Registry. Article 14 of the RH nevertheless prohibits the agreement of an option period of more than four years. The advantage of agreeing on a purchase option in a notarial deed lies primarily in the legal security for the buyer, whereas the disadvantage lies in the additional costs incurred such as for taxes, notary and the Ownership Registry.

Once the privately drawn up sales agreement has been concluded, the notarial deed is usually executed within the timeframe foreseen for transfer of the property and for payment of the balance of the purchase price as agreed in the privately drawn up contract. All conditions and ancillary obligations in this connection effectively agreed upon in the privately drawn up contract should be fulfilled.

In summary, it should again be pointed out that the decisive step within the scope of acquisition of real estate in Spain is the conclusion of the privately drawn up contract of sale. This contract stipulates all those obligations of the parties, the partial fulfillment of which will already have taken place between the date of the conclusion of the private contract and the subsequent notarial document. The already fulfilled items from the private contract – e.g. renovation of an apartment – will no longer be mentioned in the subsequent notarial deed.

Nevertheless, the buyer should ensure that all the items still to be fulfilled are stated in the *notarial deed*. These can be, for example, taxes still to be paid, contract costs and other separate arrangements. This recommendation to incorporate the still unfulfilled obligations in the notarial deed is clear from the jurisprudence of the highest Spanish court, the *Tribunal Supremo*, on the relationship between two partially contradictory contracts: in order to resolve a conflict, it is determined that the later contract is always regarded as the final agreement between the parties, i.e. the *notarial deed*. None of the parties can rely on previous obligations concluded in a privately drawn up contract alone.

The issuance of the public document or notarial deed generally indicates the legal conclusion of the real estate transaction and it is a prerequisite in order for the new property owner to record the change of ownership in the Ownership Registry and thereby be appropriately protected against *bona fide* third parties. Moreover, anyone carrying out further business with this property, for example, creating a mortgage, will always wish to see the owner's notarial deed. On authenticating further dealings regarding the same property, the notary normally is accustomed to making a note of the later transactions this on the original deed so that neither multiple transfers nor encumbrances can be undertaken within a short period of time using one and the same document. This practice is still common and expected, although modern, technologically up-to-date-proceedings between notaries and Ownership Registries replace the original need to avoid multiple transfers etc.

Bona fide acquisition by unentitled persons: as already indicated, Article 34 of the LH is the principal rule regarding *bona fide* acquisition by unentitled persons as recorded in the Ownership Registry. Where the alleged titleholder challenges a successful acquisition by a third party in good faith, the titleholder must prove that the third party buyer knew about the inaccuracy in the Ownership Registry and consequently acquired the property interest in bad faith. This difficulty is of considerable significance in Spain since legal transfers can effectively take place without publication in the Ownership Registry, meaning that the Registry often does not reflect the legal reality.

Restrictions on sale and acquisition

Restrictions under family law and matrimonial property regime

According to Article 9 of the CC, the effects of marriage are governed by the law of the jurisdiction of which the married couple is citizens (the *lex patriae*). Consequently, any existing family law related limitations on real estate dispositions are to be determined in that way. The competence of each spouse to buy or sell depends on his or her individual matrimonial property regime.

The community of assets (*sociedad de gananciales*) is the default statutory matrimonial property regime in Spain. Accordingly, each spouse is entitled to half of all rights and accrued assets acquired during the existence of the community of assets. In addition, the law recognizes the community of accrued assets (*sociedad de participaciones*). As a third option, the married couple can agree to a separation of assets (*separación de bienes*).

Where the standard regime of the community of assets exists, sale by one of the spouses always requires the consent of the other spouse. If the matrimonial property regime is not obvious, authorities such as a notary or registrar will always presume that the regime of community of assets exists and will require express consent.

In practice, this presumption will frequently apply, contrary to legal necessity and requirement, even with regard to foreign matrimonial property regimes that are completely different and do not recognize any provisos for consent. Therefore one should always be ready to prove the seller's authority at the time of transfer.

Furthermore, it should be noted that numerous other applicable rules pertaining to the law of forum of individual autonomous regional corporations in matters of family and hereditary rights exist. Whereby, for example, in Catalonia, the standard statutory matrimonial property regime is the separation of assets. On the other hand, the transfer of the family home in Catalonia or Andalusia requires the consent of the other spouse, even if the property is solely owned by the transferring spouse.

In individual cases, it may be imperative that a lawyer performs a professional and detailed inspection of the prevailing situation in the respective region prior to the property transaction in order to avoid investing considerable sums of money in a real estate transaction that may be challenged at a later date.

Options and preemption rights

In addition to rights of preemption (*tanteo*), Spanish law also recognizes right of first refusal (*retracto*). However, the right of first refusal corresponds, from a practical standpoint, almost entirely to the right of preemption and thus both rights can be regarded as virtually the same. The contractual right of preemption can be agreed for a maximum period of 10 years and may be recorded in the Ownership Registry and thereby be enforceable *erga omnes*, that is, against every person.

Of greater significance than contractual rights of preemption, are the statutory rights of preemption in favor of tenants (Article 25 of the *Spanish Law on Municipal Tenancy*, *Ley de Arrendamientos Urbanos*, LAU), co-owners, adjacent owners of agricultural real estate and the transmittable long term leaseholder. Within these different rights of preemption, the right of a co-owner takes precedence over the right of a tenant or adjacent owner.

The most relevant pre-emption right in practice provides that the owner has to serve notice on the tenant of his intention to sell and of the essential contractual terms. Following notification, the tenant has 30 calendar days within which to exercise his preemption right, if desired. If the owner does not sell the property within a period of 180 days or the notified terms, the notification loses its validity and has to be reissued. If a conflict between contractual and statutory preemption rights were to arise, the former would only take precedence if it had been recorded in the Ownership Registry prior to the conclusion of the contract of sale.

In addition, rights of preemption in the public interest exist in favor of municipalities, for example, by virtue of the special historical and cultural significance of buildings. Each *Autonomía* regulates this issue in its own territory. Due to the numerous possibilities concerning the existence of such preemption rights, their application to a given situation should be studied beforehand.

Agricultural real estate

Traditionally, there have been three categories of land in Spain: urban land, land suitable for urban development and rural land (*Suelo Urbano*, *Suelo Urbanizable* and *Suelo Rústico*).

The concept of agricultural land is not governed by any special measure in Spanish private real estate law. Rather, the concept belongs exclusively to administrative law.

The transfer and acquisition of agricultural and rural land in general is not subject to any limitation in Spain. However, agricultural construction obligations may be partially attached to rural land (for example, due to subsidies previously granted), that are a charge on the right to use the property freely. Exceptional cases of this nature are definitely subject to a duty of disclosure by the seller. Otherwise, if circumstances so require, enquiries to the regional environmental minister can afford the buyer greater legal security.

The current text of the law designates rural land as "land unsuitable for development" (*Suelo no urbanizable*). This last category was seen as a catch-all category in earlier construction laws, that is to say, all land that was not urban or suitable for urban development was categorized as unsuitable for development. The *Land Law of 1998* (*Ley del Suelo*) amended this categorization to the effect that since then the catch-all category is land suitable for urban development.

Another legislation change in 2008 led to a new *Land Law*, which basically divides land into urban or rural, with the first one being suitable and the latter one unsuitable for construction.

Allocation to one of the three aforementioned land categories depends on the municipal development plan. To this end, and in particular with regard to plots of rural land that are being bought for construction, an enquiry should always be made to the municipality about the absolute minimum legal construction requirements for the construction site, such as the minimum size of the plot for construction, the permitted volume of construction, minimum clearances, building heights, number of floor spaces, etc.

Restrictions regarding acquisition of real estate by foreigners

The regulation governing foreign investment (*Normas en materia de inversiones extranjeras en España* of 1 July 1992) has liberalized all investments in Spain since 1992, meaning that investments no longer require permits. It should be noted that rules on investment are always linked to the place of origin of the investment and not nationality. EU citizens are exceptions to this rule, Swiss citizens are assimilated to EU citizens due to international treaties between the EU and Switzerland. Since 1999, foreign investments have only been considered as such at all if the amount has exceeded EUR 3,005,060.52. The previously mandatory process of prior government verification of the investment amount has now been replaced by a simple retroactive notice to the appropriate government office, which is merely for statistical purposes. In addition, there is now an obligation to report investments where the capital inflow originates from so-called tax havens prior to carrying out the investment. In this context very severe anti-money-laundering-legislation has been introduced in Spain, which requires a lot of registrations and information from foreign investors.

Special zones of interest for national security with limitation on acquisitions by foreigners were created by law in 1975. These primarily concern coastal zones and those islands in which the percentage of foreign ownership of property may not exceed certain threshold values. However, exceptional circumstances have had an important effect on these regulations. Thus, these provisions lapsed for EU citizens with Spain's entry into the European Union in 1986. Nonetheless, non-EU citizens are still requested to apply for specific authorization for their purchase transactions which may cause delay and consequently even threaten the success of the purchase process, as sellers might be under time pressure and authorization formalities can take some time. To avoid any problem, buyers should check applicability of national security rules as far ahead as possible. It is also worth noting that the same may apply to Spanish corporations that may predominantly be owned or governed by non EU citizens.

Further important preconditions for buying real estate

Capacity to act and entitlement of the seller

The seller's authority to dispose of property results from his ownership status. If applicable, the person entrusted with the sale may also be an agent, in which case the mandate does not need to be given in a particularly formal way, which is the situation frequently encountered when concluding a privately drawn up contract. On the other hand, an adequate notarial verification of the authority to dispose always has to be carried out on authentication of public documents.

The capacity to act and conclude a contract basically conforms to Spanish international private law according to the personal statute of the acting party, as determined by his nationality and thus dependent on his right of residence. In this context, the rule laid down in Article 10.8 of the CC is of importance. Contracts on immovable property situated in Spain, concluded for consideration, will be effective in Spain if concluded by a person who in fact lacks capacity to contract according to his right of residence, as the grounds for that person's incapacity to contract would not necessarily lead to incapacity to contract under Spanish law.

Under Spanish law, a person reaches his majority upon reaching his 18th birthday and is then entitled to undertake all functions of civil life.

Legal entities – in Spain this will mostly be a limited liability company, a *Sociedad de Responsabilidad Limitada* (*S.L.*) – are usually represented either by a manager (*administrador*) or by an authorized person (*apoderado*) that will prove their right to act on behalf of their company through a notarial deed of appointment of manager (*nombramiento de administrador*) or authorization (*apoderamiento*). Those deeds generally must be registered in the *Commercial Registry* (*Registro Mercantil*) to have full legal validity.

Third party claims and unpaid taxes

Encumbrances in favour of third parties only ever have an effect on the public if they are recorded in the Ownership Registry. This affects both the rights already mentioned and also possible provisional judicial attachments of the property as security for claims asserted in court (so-called *embargos preventivos*). These are comparable to a seizure *in rem* and are entered in the Ownership Registry by means of attachment notes (*anotación preventiva*). Furthermore, future claims based on succession rights that are registered in the Ownership Registry can also be in conflict with a clean purchase. However, provisions on encumbrance-free *bona fide* acquisition apply, that is to say, these should not be considered insofar as they are not recorded in the Ownership Registry and the buyer, in good faith, is unaware of their existence.

Liability of the property for tax liabilities of the prior owner can arise on the one hand from non-payment of current taxes such as local real estate tax (*Impuesto sobre Bienes Inmuebles*) or else from non-payment of non-recurring taxes such as the property acquisition tax (*Impuesto sobre Transmisiones Patrimoniales*, or ITP) or similar. While the former is directly attached to the property even without a corresponding annotation in the Ownership Registry (always ancillary to the delinquent taxpayer), in the case of ITP debts or similar, a *Notice of Tax Liability* (*afección fiscal*) must be entered in the Ownership Registry. In addition, there is an obligation of the property buyer to withhold 3% of the purchase price from non-residents and forward it to the tax authorities: this obligation also encumbers the property. According to article 66 of the *General Spanish Tax Law* (*Ley General Tributaria),* the general statute of limitations on tax obligations in Spain is four years from the end of the period of submission for the tax self-assessment form.

Finally, without the necessity of an annotation in the Ownership Registry the property is liable for debts owed to an ownership community.

Provisions for protecting the environment, nature and cultural heritage

Particularly in the case of rural properties, it should be verified whether the property is located in a specially protected area, whether for environmental reasons or forestry, species or landscape protection or as a nature reserve. There are regulations that can limit rights of use inherent in the right of ownership, such as building development plans, agricultural or hunting use, potentially even including access to private properties. Formal inquiries to the appropriate regional environmental minister, for example, can afford greater legal security.

In the case of real estate located near the sea, the possibility of any building development has to be studied in the context of the *Spanish Coastal Law* (*Ley de Costas*) of 1988. The *Coastal Law* has as its objective an orderly development of the Spanish coastal area, which is 7,880 kilometers long. Today, almost 40% of the Spanish population lives on the coast, although development on the coast is in fact even denser since tourist use is not included in this figure.

The law divides the strips of land immediately bordering the sea into various zones of protection, within which different types of development are possible: the national public maritime zone (*Zona de Dominio Público Maritimo*), the protection zone (*Servidumbre de Protección*) and the zone of influence (*Zona de Influencia*). In the protected zone, which is a strip that extends 100 meters inland from the water's edge at high tide, no buildings may be built nowadays for residential purposes, which include hotels. However, certificates of exemption do exist and also certain zones that had already been advertised as building land before the *Coastal Law* came into force are exempted. These advertised areas operate in non-compliance with the law under a variance or continuation permit. In recent years, the administration had put much emphasis in applying the *Coastal Law* after not doing so for decades, which led to protests from the affected owners. As discussed in 30.4, the *Coastal Law* has recently been revised by the legislator and will hopefully be less uncertain and conflictive in the future. Still, it is always strongly recommended to study profoundly the application of the *Coastal Law* when there is a possibility that it could affect a property or construction.

A general new requirement has recently been introduced to the acquisition process (and even lease) of any building as the *Energy Efficiency Certification* (*Certificación Energética de Edificios*) is now mandatory and must be obtained before formalising the transaction in a public deed.

Since the adoption of appropriate waste disposal standards in Spain, liability for contaminated sites has become a core problem in the area of environmental law. Article 27 of the *Spanish Waste Management Law* (*Ley de Residuos*) determines the principal liability of cause and ancillary liability of condition of all the owners of a property for the remediation of that property. The authorities are empowered to proceed directly against any liable person who fails to meet the relevant obligations. It must be emphasized that owners of contaminated properties are also responsible for remediation of sites contaminated before the standards pertaining to environmental law came into force. If the authorities detect pollution, they can demand the recording of an attachment note in the Ownership Registry and this encumbrance can have a direct effect on the property value.

In the case of listed buildings, it should be observed that on the one hand, prohibitions against modification or demolition may exist, which may however be offset against tax advantages, such as the exemption for owners of listed buildings from payment of wealth tax or real estate tax.

Access to relevant records and documents

In addition to verification of the Ownership Registry records, the interested party should request from the seller a copy of the most recent record of payment of real estate tax, a copy of the notarial deed, an extract of the cadastral registry and, if applicable, a certificate from the ownership community to prove that the seller is up-to-date with his payments. The *Energy Efficiency Certification* (*Certificación Energética de Edificios*) is now mandatory and should be asked for. In addition to these, some autonomous regions also oblige the seller to provide the purchaser a *Certification of Habitability* (*Cédula de Habitabilidad*), making it impossible to register the purchase at the land registry without such certification.

Key points that a seller should consider

In Spain, estate agents are scarcely regulated by law, which is why case law has had to define the essential issues. Since 2000, anyone is able to work as an estate agent. Notwithstanding, the seal of quality of the official estate agents (*Agente de Propiedad Inmobiliaria*, hereafter API) who are organized in professional chambers, provide these professionals with a degree of respectability. Since 2007, official APIs must follow specific sectorial professional rules, so some standards shall be observed from those professionals. Anyhow, it is remarkable that the number of estate agents and agencies has dropped dramatically due to the end of the real estate boom in recent years.

In Spain, the seller of real estate always bears the estate agent's commission, which is regulated only for the APIs and usually amounts to 3% to 5% of the purchase price. The seller should therefore include this in his calculations from the outset and should accordingly agree with the estate agent the amount and the due date of the commission. Thus, it should be clarified whether the commission is payable at the time when the contract is concluded (normally the private contract) or instead only falls due at the exchange of the respective actions of performance of the contract, that is, transfer of ownership against receipt of the total purchase price.

It should be considered whether the conclusion of an agreement in exclusivity with an estate agent is in the seller's interest in certain cases. In Spain, it is customary to commission several estate agents in order to achieve more exposure and consequently more offers.

The type of preliminary contract is another point to consider. While the unilateral option contract usually offers the buyer the greatest certainty that the purchase will take place, it may actually be more in the seller's interest to conclude the aforementioned *Arras* contract from which he can unilaterally release himself by repaying twice the amount of the down payment in the event that he gets a better offer. To ensure payment of the purchase price to the seller, the basic rule to be observed in Spain is that the balance of the purchase price to be paid after the down payment is usually paid with a certified bank check or in cash no later than but no earlier than the signing of the deed before the notary. Vehicles such as notarial escrow accounts, fiduciary accounts, etc. are unfamiliar and are thus difficult for notaries to accept. Insofar as the buyer is not required to pay part of the purchase price until a later date, it is advisable to agree on the inclusion of a resolutory condition or condition subsequent clause (*condición resolutoria*) in the notarial deed and thus recorded in the Ownership Registry.

In addition to the estate agent's commission, the seller should include the tax consequences of the sale in his calculations from the outset. Basically, the seller has to pay tax twice on the increase in value realized. On the one hand, the municipality should tax the objectively ascertained increase in value when a transaction of urban real estate is done, which is calculated on the basis of public municipal rates. On the other hand, the national fiscal authorities tax the subjectively generated increase in value, which is the difference between the original cost of acquisition and the proceeds of sale. Details of these issues can be found in the section on taxes.

The execution of a real estate purchase transaction

The standard sequence of reservation, private contract, and notarial deed – has been described above. The handling of a real estate purchase rests principally in the hands of a lawyer, as notaries in Spain essentially have a solely authenticating function.

It should be emphasized, however, that the role of Spanish notaries in improving legal security during the acquisition of real estate has increased significantly since the introduction of the statutory *Duty of Cooperation between Notaries and Land Registries* in 1992. Pursuant to article 175 of the *Spanish Notarial Regulation (Reglamento notarial)*, a preliminary inquiry at the Ownership Registry is a prerequisite for notarial authentication of the transfer of real estate. The notary makes the inquiry to the Ownership Registry by fax or by corporate e-mail, whereupon the registrar is obliged to communicate the current status of the register to the requesting notary within a maximum of three days. However, this inquiry does not prevent access to the Ownership Registry. Indeed, during the following nine days, the registrar is obliged to notify the notary of any interim recordings affecting the property on the same day as of their receipt at the Ownership Registry. This system ensures that the parties are always certain of knowing the current status of the register on the day of authentication.

As a complement to this procedure, the notary is obliged to immediately notify the Ownership Registry, by corporate e-mail or fax, of the authentication of any new deed relevant to the property. A party can renounce this obligation, which obviously is not recommendable in a normal transaction. On the basis of this notification, the registry gives the notice of receipt a rank of priority including the date of receipt of the notarial fax or corporate e-mail message. If the message arrives outside the opening hours of the Ownership Registry, which in Spain are 9a.m. to 2p.m., then the notice of receipt is dated as the start of the opening hours on the following day. The notice to the Ownership Registry produces a priority regarding the rank for 60 days, when the original deed is presented at the Ownership Registry within 10 working days of the date of the notice of receipt. If the deed is then not presented, the priority-ranked notice of receipt is deleted. If the procedure is correctly followed, the right accredited in the deed is recorded in the Ownership Registry. The 60 day period can be extended for periods of each another 60 working days up to an additional 180 working days, if the circumstances request such extension. The beneficiary is comprehensively protected in his ownership *erga omnes*.

A further prerequisite for the recording is the previous settlement of taxes arising from the purchase. By rule, this procedure is not normally handled by the notary but rather by the retained lawyer or by a *Gestoria*: these are agencies that specialize exclusively in the handling of administrative transactions and formalities.

After this whole process, the buyer of the property receives an *escritura pública* or notarial deed as title and proof of his ownership. It is furnished with all the stamps and tax receipts but more specifically with the original recording of the Ownership Registry concerning the completed recording.

Powers of attorney

Powers of attorney basically need to be in the form of a notarial deed and furthermore have to be certified and sealed with a *Hague Apostille* if issued by a foreign notary. Spanish powers of attorney are very detailed and frequently extend over several pages. This is due to Article 1713 of the CC, according to which the granting of full powers of attorney for anything other than purely administrative transactions requires express designation. Pursuant to Article 10(11) of the CC, the power of attorney for real estate transactions could in fact be subject to foreign law and thus to fewer and less restrictive provisions. Nevertheless, in practice, interpretative difficulties before Spanish notaries and Ownership Registry registrars are encountered frequently, meaning that an adjustment to Spanish custom in this area is practically required.

On the contrary to earlier legal situations, it is since a few years the notaries' obligation and responsibility to verify the sufficiency of powers of attorney that shall be used in any legal transaction. This was for years disputed between notaries and the Ownership Registries' judges, but has been decided as described by the Spanish legislator. It is therefore unavoidable that the notary states explicitly that he has been shown and considers sufficient any used powers of attorney.

If no notarial deed containing a power of attorney is available, then the authorized agent can act orally or in writing as a so-called "oral commissioner" (*Mandatario verbal).* The grantor of the power of attorney can subsequently remedy the formal deficiency by means of an official notarial declaration of ratification.

Financing

In Spain, foreign financing for mortgage secured bank loans is quite usual. Since loan contracts and mortgage securities are routinely joined in one single notarial deed, they are also referred to as "mortgage loans" (*préstamo hipotecario*).

It is characteristic to agree on a fixed interest rate for the first year followed by an annual adjustment to the variable and slightly higher European money-market interest rate (*EURIBOR*).

Due to the sustained period of low interest, banks now offer fixed-interest loans more and more frequently. While during the boom, banks offered in individual cases up to 100% and more of the value of the property to be financed, nowadays it is quite difficult to obtain bank financing at all. That is the result of the problems that have arisen from the crisis throughout the real estate sector and that tremendously affects Spanish banks, which now are very reluctant towards assuming risk.

Frequently, when buying a new construction directly from the developer, there will be an offer to assume the loan contract of the developer already in existence with his financing bank. Through that model the buyer and successor to the loan can save the cost of his own mortgage security by subrogating (*subrogación*) the existing mortgage. Finally, it should be noted that some foreign banks and financiers also grant loans for the acquisition of Spanish properties, securing such credit lines via mortgages on the Spanish property.

Purchase through a company

Tax motives usually lie behind purchases through a company. A practice in Spain has been to incorporate a standard stock or limited corporation that acquired, maintained and sold real estate, as if it was the company's commercial activity. In this way, property owners tried to take advantage of corporations' tax privileges, without strictly being entitled, which could have grave consequences, if a tax inspection discovered such irregularities. Due to the specific fiscal situation for non-residents in Spain, it was mostly members of this group that tried to save money through such constructions.

A purchase by a corporation does not in itself differ from the purchase by a natural person, as once property has been acquired the corporation also has to pay in full the property acquisition tax, ITP, or the Value Added Tax, *Impuesto Sobre el Valor Añadido* (IVA). On the other hand, as appropriate, tax advantages may be gained upon the acquisition of a corporation that itself already owns the property or upon the inheritance of the shares and thus the property.

In so doing, the acquisition may be made via a Spanish or foreign corporation, or an offshore corporation. Spanish law does not recognize any barriers to acquisition with regard to foreign companies, which means that a foreign corporation may acquire ownership of real estate in Spain at any time without limitation, as long as the required procedures for the acquisition of real estate by foreigners are respected. The mentioned strict anti-money-laundering-rules shall be noted again with respect to that.

The most suitable Spanish vehicle for such a procedure is the limited liability company, *Sociedad de Responsabilidad Limitada* (*S.L.),* which corresponds to a company with limited liability. Such a company can be easily incorporated with a small start-up capital of EUR 3,000, be maintained by a single shareholder and requires a chairman. There are undoubtedly a few tax advantages for companies, for example, companies are not subject to the wealth tax on assets and, if some requirements are met, can deduct input VAT.

However, if all the legal and especially all tax-related regulations are complied with, the savings, in the end, may not be such as to justify the effort of establishing and maintaining a standard company and its management aspects, such as the orderly keeping of books and the annual filing of reports and accounts with the Company Registry every year.

In contrast, a detailed examination of the applicable tax laws shows that, even with the *per se* tax-exempt transfer of corporate shares, the buyer cannot legally avoid payment of the Property Acquisition Tax, ITP, when buying property through a company set up solely for that purpose, as corporations with business assets of more than 50% in real estate are taxed as real estate when transferred. After some legal changes in recent years this does not apply anymore, when the property is subject to Entrepreneurial activity. The purchase can be subject to recoverable VAT in such case.

In addition, the seller will have to declare his gain on disposal, to the extent that the Spanish fiscal authorities establish the true value of the transfer.

Even the ability of conveying to the buyer the idea of buying a company instead of the real estate directly may be questioned. A possible construct for an economic structure using a corporation has thus not to be excluded but has to be examined on a case-by-case basis in order to withstand inspection by the fiscal authorities.

In general, it can be said that up until recent tax developments (see those mentioned immediately below), it did not appear to be cost-efficient to analyze the labor and other costs of a corporate structure unless the property had an appreciable value.

Foreign corporations, regardless of whether they are offshore corporations in a tax haven or corporations from other countries, are subject to an annual 3% special taxation for legal persons on the cadastral value of the property, meaning that an acquisition via a foreign company will scarcely be worthwhile. This may be appraised differently where a corporation has its registered office in a country that has signed a double taxation convention with Spain, including an information exchange clause, because corporations from these countries may be exempt from this specific taxation. Moreover, reference should be made to the prior duty of notification in the case of capital inflows from tax havens.

Defects and warranty claims

The law governing purchase guarantees protects the buyer with respect to the size of the land and contractually warranted characteristics of real estate. The system set out in Article 1469 ff. of the CC is of particular note: if the purchase price is agreed on the basis of a square-meter price and it is later apparent that the land is considerably smaller or larger than the parties had assumed, then the law provides for an equitable means of adjusting the purchase price. In practice, the property is then sold as *cuerpo cierto*, which roughly translated means "purchased as stands". In addition, the parties tend to agree that the buyer knows and accepts the physical and legal condition of the property. The buyer's rights of guarantee often revolve around hidden defects. The claim period expires six months from the transfer.

In the case of an acquisition from unentitled sellers, the rules on good faith apply first. However, in spite of this, *bona fide* acquisition can still result in the seller transferring the property to several *bona fide* buyers within a short time, the so-called double sale. In this case, Spanish law stipulates that the buyer who first registers his property right in the Ownership Registry is entitled to ownership. Additionally, the buyer of a third-party property is contractually entitled to claim damages against the seller.

30.4 New construction, rebuilding and renovation

Building and zoning law - Construction permits – Spanish Coastal Law provisions

According to the new Land Law (*Ley del Suelo*) from 2008 the different construction zones are basically divided into two, urban or building land *(suelo urbano)* and rural land *(suelo rural)*. In case of urban or building land, there is a need for access to or inquiry concerning local development and land use plans in order to evaluate the scope of the development potential. It should be pointed out that development costs are borne by owners with respect to urban or building land.

Particularly in case of purchase of building plots, it is highly recommended to check first if the seller paid all due development costs and if there are still other costs to be expected. In case of any doubts, the purchaser should try to withhold or deposit the corresponding part of the purchase price with a notary. Further information, including in relation to compliance with applicable building law regulations, can be obtained by means of a *certificate of non-objection*, issued by the local authorities.

Building projects require a building permit *(licencia de obra)*, which must be issued before the start of construction. The autonomous regional authorities have legislative powers in this area while the municipalities are usually responsible for administration. Practically, all new constructions and modifications require permits. Small building projects *(obra menor)* are subject to at least a duty of disclosure. On the contrary, big building projects *(obra mayor)* are always obliged to submit a corresponding application. The application procedure for the corresponding building permit is usually handled by an architect who submits the application together with his building project *(proyecto)* to the appropriate local authorities. The project includes a description of the construction, detailed plans, models for technical details and construction material, as well as any further documents required by the local authorities, as appropriate. The project requires an endorsement *(visado)* by the relevant professional chamber of architects. In addition, the total cost of the building scheme shall be specified, which is used as the basis for the calculation of administrative fees and construction taxes *(Impuesto sobre Instalaciones y Obras)*. Depending on the municipality, taxes may amount to a maximum of 4% of the construction costs.

The duration of the process strongly differs depending on the complexity of the development project, the relevant authority and autonomous region. A reasonable estimate would be between one and three months for the duration of the standard procedure, although this timeframe may be easily extended once the preliminary examination by the competent body determines small or formal but rectifiable deficiencies in the application. After major changes related to the legal effects arising from the inactivity of the administration *(silencio administrativo)*, the general rule nowadays is that the effective granting of applications cannot longer be a result of such inactivity, in particular in case of building projects that are incompatible with the applicable general plan for the development of local real estate or building code provisions. Once granted, the building permit has a limited period of validity which can usually be extended.

The responsible authorities are not deterred from ordering the demolition of illegal buildings in today's Spain. The limitation period for breaches of building regulations is usually four years at national level, but most autonomous regions have their own regulations that mostly provide longer periods. In Catalonia, e.g. the limitation period is six years. Nevertheless, in case of very serious breaches of building regulations such periods can be up to 10 years or exemptions from the limitation period may apply.

In recent years, due to its late effective application and partially opaque regulations, the *Coastal Law 1988 (Ley de Costas)* became an important issue in Spain. The starting point was the Spanish Coastal Law of 1969 which could not counteract the negative construction development and severe environmental impacts. On 27 July 1988, a new coastal law with broader protection legislation was enacted. The core of this new regulation was the division of the coastal area in basically three different protection zones:

- The seashore (zona de dominio público marítimo terrestre)
- The protection zone (zona de servidumbre de protección)
- The influence zone (*zona de influencia*)

As a result, the development potential and, even more important, the possible protection concerning already existing constructions depended on a complex and long-term measuring process of the complete Spanish coast line. Consequence of the sudden strict application of the Coast Law provisions, some two decades after its entry into force, was a storm of protest, particularly of non-resident property owners and investors. Later on, the government gradually modified several provisions by means of certain legal mitigations.

Finally, a new reform of the Coast Law came into force on 31 May 2013 by means of the *Law 2/2013* with the ambitious title "*Law on the protection and sustainable use of the coastal zone and change of the Coastal Law 22/1988 of 28 July*", followed by the *Royal Decree 876/2014 of October 10 concerning General Coastal Regulations* One of the main changes is the possible extension of usage permits from 30 to a maximum of 75 years with regard to buildings and private land bought before 1988, when seashore land became public land. Moreover, the reform introduces more flexibility when it comes to substantial maintenance or even modernizing works concerning construction legally built before 1988 in the protection or influence zone. Furthermore, a better coordination between the Ownership and Cadastral Registries with the Coastal Authorities shall guarantee a secure acquisition process with clearly marked properties in case of any non-compliance with coastal law provisions.

For now it remains to be seen whether the new coastal law will achieve its essential purpose: making the coastal regions more attractive again by increasing legal certainty for foreign investors in Spain and, on the other hand, a better protection of the Spanish coast line. For purchasers of potentially affected plots near to the coast line, it is highly recommended to apply for a *certificate of non-objection,* issued by the competent coastal authorities.

Architect agreement and contract for work

Architect agreements are not specially regulated in Spain and are subject to rules on works or mandate agreements, as applicable. On the other hand, architect agreements have been essentially defined by case law. The planning and management of the building project are the two essential contractual duties. It should be observed that only architects accredited in Spain may work on construction projects. In addition to the fully qualified architect *(arquitecto superior)*, in Spain, there is also the technical master builder or foreman *(aparejador or arquitecto inferior or técnico)*, who takes charge of the supervision of the construction and is a subordinate of the architect.

The actual construction agreement is categorized as a *contract for work and services* between the developer *(promotor)* or owner (*propietario* or *dueño de la obra*) and the contractor (*constructor*). The Spanish law regulating the building process (*Ley de la Ordenación de la Edificación*, LOE) was introduced in May 2000. The law concentrates on defining the multi-layered network of those persons involved in the construction and their rights and responsibilities concerning the building, the aspects of final acceptance and other associated formalities. Above all, questions relating to warrantee rights with respect to the building and their coverage through a system of mandatory insurance policies have been regulated which were previously non-existent or were developed only thanks to an increasingly extensive case law.

Notwithstanding the LOE, the actual construction contract continues to be a contract for work and services, within the scope of which the contractor has to construct the building on his own account, by his own means and at his own personal risk.

Building completion and formalities

Under Spanish law, the acceptance of the construction work is usually a two tiered process. In practice, at the end of the construction work, the contractor requests preliminary acceptance from the owner or developer of the building, whereupon, within the scope of a joint acceptance process, all elements requiring further work are recorded in a report. Once these defects have been rectified, a new and final acceptance or certificate of completion is given. This final acceptance triggers the statutory liability and warranty periods. Of particular note is the fictitious acceptance effect, insofar as the owner or developer does not comply with the formal request to accept the construction works within 30 days.

Numerous documents and records shall be handed over to the owner or developer in the course of the acceptance process. Depending on the autonomous region, these formal requirements can be subject to certain changes. In any case, the most important documents can be listed as follows:

With the *building book (libro de edificio)*, the owner or developer receives, among other things, an original copy of the planning documents, naming all those involved in the construction, the architect's *building completion certificate (certificado final de obra)*. The owner or developer requires these documents in order to notarially record the new building declaration *(declaración de obra nueva)*, by means of which the constructions works, in conformity with the law, may be recorded in the Ownership Registry. As a result, everyone can verify the legality of the development due to the notarially formalized and recorded construction work in the Ownership Registry. In addition, the owner needs the public declaration of approval for first occupancy *(licencia de primera ocupación)* and/or the public certificate of habitability *(cédula de habitabilidad)* that allows the building to be registered for electricity, water, gas and other utility connections.

With regard to the new building declaration, it has to be noted that the performance is, legally speaking, not mandatory and, accordingly, is voluntary. The most important law in this context to be observed is the *Royal Decree 1093/1997 of July 4*, which contains the provisions of the Spanish Mortgage Law that govern the recording requirements of the urban development projects in the Ownership Registry. The major advantages of the new building declaration, although associated with significant costs, show up regularly in the context of sale or financing of projects. By means of recording the construction, a simple inspection of the Ownership Registry enables a fast verifiability of the legality of the construction – as well as the payment of taxes and fees during the construction process - and thus provides legal certainty from the buyers perspective. Moreover, the confirmation of the economic value associated with such recording is a basic prerequisite required by banking institutions if a mortgage loan is planned. It should be stressed, however, that from a pure civil law perspective, already the physical connection of the building with the plot causes the acquisition of property concerning the construction. The recording of the new building declaration itself has a purely declaratory and thus a law confirming effect.

Construction defects and warranty claims

The tiered system of liability for construction defects, introduced by the LOE, leads to those involved in the construction being liable during differing periods of time for defects of varying importance. In general, those individuals involved in the construction, under whose responsibility a defect arose, are liable for their removal and/or damages. Provided the party causing the defect cannot be determined, a catch-all developer liability exists. In order to manage this wide spectrum of liabilities arising on grounds of consumer protection, there are statutory rights of recourse between those involved in the construction process.

The period of liability for building defects in weight-bearing parts, foundations, etc. (so-called structural defects) lasts 10 years. Those involved in the construction work are liable for three years for all defects affecting habitability (hygiene, health, noise abatement, technical equipment, etc.) and for one year for all other defects. A claim in respect of defects shall become statute-barred after two years from the date on occurrence of the damage.

In order to safeguard warranty claims, the law requires taking out compulsory insurance policies that, as proof of their existence, shall be handed over to the final consumer along with the building book.

If this is not done, the completion of the new construction cannot be recorded in the Ownership Registry. As a result, it is almost impossible for the buyer to take out a mortgage with a financing bank because within the scope of end-financing, banks only lend on "declared" new constructions and thereby making the transfer of the new construction significantly more difficult. However, hitherto only the insurance covering the 10 year liability for weight-bearing construction elements remains mandatory. Furthermore, those developers who build for themselves (*autopromotores*) are exempted from such obligation by law.

Without prejudice to these specific legal provisions, rights under civil law on sales and, as applicable, other further contractual warranty claims, remain unaffected.

In Spain, it is a very widespread practice to directly purchase a property as planned from the developer *(promotoras)*. This entails a series of consumer protection provisions. The most important is the safeguarding of instalment payments by means of bank guarantees as set out in the *Collateral Law of 1968*. According to this law, the repayment of advance payments of the buyer before or during the construction process shall be secured by the developer by means of the granting of a deficiency guarantee or an appropriate insurance policy. Furthermore, the amounts received are to be deposited in special accounts. In the case of breach of contract, the developer is obliged to return the full amount plus a 6% interest rate. Moreover, reference to such obligation shall be made in all advertising materials. In practice, the customer usually only receives such a guarantee if it is specifically requested and if the customer assumes the additional costs. In view of the frequent delays in construction completion and the practical impossibility of proper collateral security *(encumbrances)* for payments, it is strongly recommended to request these kinds of guarantees in any case.

Technical Building Regulations

In order to improve the often perceived as deficient quality of the Spanish housing construction in comparison to European standards, new technical regulations on construction were introduced in the liability regime of the LOE (*Código Técnico de la Edificación*, CTE) and came into effect in the spring of 2007. While the adoption of the LOE, according to the legislator approach, intended to particularly improve consumer protection aspects in construction, the aim of the CTE is to improve technical constructional issues, especially in the creation of technical quality standards.

These minimum requirements are regulated by basic requirements for improving the safety and habitability in the following areas: building stability, fire protection measures, general safety precautions; minimum requirements in the field of hygiene, health and the environment; minimum requirements with respect to noise impacts; energy-saving measures; solar thermal technologies for water heating and photovoltaics.

Thus, *inter alia* minimum requirements related to the building and construction materials to be used and overall building quality are determined to ensure the safety and indoor comfort of residents. In this area indeed numerous previous regulations existed, but these were not suited to the creation of modern and uniformly structured technical standards in a single legislated framework due to the diverse scattered legal standards and their often-outdated specifications. The CTE also incorporates a large number of European law requirements such as technical building energy-saving measures.

The CTE provides both in time and in terms of content for *provisional regulations* concerning the applicability of its provisions, in particular to minimize the economic impact on the construction costs. However, the scope of application covers all building measures that are associated with a building permit, i.e., construction modifications, refurbishment and redevelopment of buildings are also affected. Even the change of intended usage of a building may lead to the application of the CTE regulations. Exemptions are foreseen, if generally no risks for humans are to be expected.

There are basically two options for implementing the minimum requirements of the CTE: firstly, the respective construction works can be done according to the standard defaults *(Documentos Básicos)*.

Secondly, alternative options can be implemented under the responsible architect's guidance or project manager. In this case, the consent of the developer is required who has to capture any alternative implementations options of the CTE in writing in order to prove the comparability of its solutions with those of the *Documentos Básicos*.

In 2013, the legislator introduced the mandatory obligation to hand over an Energy Efficiency Certificate (*Certificación Energética de Edificios*) to the buyer or the tenant, in the event of rental agreements. The introduction of such obligation draws on the *Royal Decree 235/2013, April 5*. This law implements the EU Directive to increase energy performance and efficiency according to the Kyoto Protocol in Spain. Basically, it is a standard certificate of a technical expert, which for the moment identifies the energy efficiency of the property. There are significant fines in case of non-compliance with these regulations.

Another interesting aspect is the obligation to proceed with a *Technical Inspection of Buildings* (*Inspección Técnica de los Edificios*), now governed by the *Royal Law Decree 8/2011, July 1*, for buildings which are older than 50 years, that represents the general rule. The autonomous regions may provide shorter time limits and can introduce graduated procedure with different time limits and further details.

Finally it must be observed that in this area of Technical Building Regulations, the autonomous regions generally have a detailed regulatory competence that should be carefully studied in advance

30.5 Rental and tenancy

Rental and leasehold agreements

The basic regulation of rental law in the Spanish Civil Code is superimposed by the so-called *Law on Municipal Tenancy* (*Ley de Arrendamientos Urbanos*, LAU), which came into effect in 1995.

In 2013, a legislative reform of the LAU, mainly concerning rental agreements for residential purposes, was adopted by means of the *Law*

4/2013, June 4. The reform act introduces substantial changes after a long period with rather small improvements. The principle aim is that those Spaniards, who are in possession of second homes, deliver their properties on to the rental market. In the same direction, the reform pretends to strengthen the position of the landlord and, at the same time, configure rental agreements for residential purposes with more flexibility looking for the necessary balance between supply and demand due the fact that the strong housing market in the past had led to high vacancy rates. Furthermore, in litigation matters notice periods had been shortened considerably and express evacuation procedures may apply from case to case.

The most significant changes, by virtue of their importance, will be highlighted below. In any case, these changes are not applicable with regard to lease agreements which were signed before the reform came into force on 6 June 2013, unless it is agreed by the parties afterwards.

The LAU generally differentiates between rental agreements for residential purposes and those for other purposes (e.g. commercial lease agreements, seasonal rental agreements). Besides, in Spanish law there are no specific legal provisions governing leaseholds. Nevertheless, these legal relationships do of course exist as mixed-typical (*Arrendamiento de Industria*). The following remarks apply both to rental and leasehold.

Although an informal rental agreement is perfectly valid, and can even be concluded orally, each contractual party can request the other to formalize the rental agreement in writing. In practice, nearly all contracts are written agreements. The option of a notarial execution of the agreement might also be recommended, as this allows the agreement to be recorded in the Ownership Registry. This grants the tenant better protection and is of special interest in case of commercial lease agreement. As a conceptual change in conjunction with the reform, tenants of residential lease agreements only achieve full protection against third parties (*erga omnes*) if they record their contracts in the Ownership Registry, which is particularly relevant in the event of sale of the property.

The rent is basically freely negotiable. In case of rental agreements for residential purposes, an annual rental adjustment can be agreed. If there are no contractual provisions foreseen by the parties in that context, the rent will be adjusted to the consumer price index (*Índice de Precio al Consumo*, hereafter IPC). An increase in rent is also possible where renovations have been carried out. In contrast, with commercial lease agreements this *modus operandi* is often combined with different calculation and actualization methods due to the typically long-term binding contractual relationships.

A deposit is mandatory and shall not exceed one month's rent for residential rental agreements and two in the case of rental agreements for other purposes. The landlord can be obliged to pay the deposit at specific public offices, according to legal provisions of the autonomous regions. The repayment of the deposit in time is without interest. It should be noted that in addition to a deposit additional collaterals can be agreed upon that are mostly bank guarantees.

In the absence of written approval by the landlord, a prohibition on assignment and subletting exists in rental agreements for residential purposes. Rights of termination exist in particular in the case of the non-execution of necessary repairs by the landlord, severe disturbance by the landlord in regard to the dwelling and, its occupants, non-payment of the rent, unapproved subletting or assignment, willful damage to the rented property, disturbance or other dangerous or unlawful activities in the rented property as well as where the property is no longer primarily destined to be residential.

Tenant and leaseholder protection regulations

In case of rental agreements for residential purposes, only a few tenant protection regulations are essentially mandatory, insofar as most provisions can usually be waived. The duration of the rental agreement is basically freely negotiable; however, special regulations exist for rental agreements for residential purposes (not in the case of seasonal rental agreements, commercial lease agreements, etc.). With agreements of a duration of less than three years, the tenant can unilaterally extend the rental relationship for a maximum of three years and again, if necessary, for another year. On the other hand, the owner is entitled to a due ordinary notice of termination after three years, and then after four years. This automatic renewal within the first three years, however, does not apply if the tenant, up to 30 days prior to the annual agreement expires, unilaterally declines the respective auto-renewal modus. On the other hand, due to the rental law reform the tenant now is untitled to terminate the agreement after a minimum duration of six months and with a notice period of at least 30 days. In this context, a contractual penalty up to one month for each outstanding year, or the proportional amount in case the outstanding period is shorter than one year, can be agreed. Before the recent reform, the maximum auto-renewal modus implied a duration of maximum five years and afterwards a maximum of another three years applied, if so.

If no explicit term is agreed, a term of one year is deemed to have been initially agreed. Before the recent reform of the LAU, limitations with regard to the described contract extension modus were only possible in case of an explicit agreement on a personal use clause of the landlord. Now, after a minimum of one year of duration and without any explicit contractual provision in the lease agreement, the landlord is entitled to extraordinarily terminate the agreement in the event of a personal use. Nevertheless, such early termination is only possible if the landlord complies with a notice period of two months before such personal use is requested.

The tenant's heirs are likewise entitled to make use of such an entry right until the termination of the rental agreement as well as spouses, partners, and relatives of the ascending or descending line, siblings or handicapped persons provided that they have lived in the rented property prior to the death of the main tenant.

After the reform law, in the case of transfer of the dwelling, the buyer who acts in good faith only becomes a party to the rental agreement until the end of the contractual duration or the minimum term of lease if the lease agreement is recorded in the Ownership Registry. On the other hand, in that case the tenant has a statutory right of preemption, unless a contractually waiver is agreed. In such case, the landlord has to notify his intention to sell the property within at least 30 days before the formalization of the purchase agreement.

In contrast, with regard to commercial lease agreement, most protective provisions, except the deposit and procedural law provisions, are subject to the disposition of the parties and thus may be waived. Particularly in the context of rental agreements for residential purposes ensure that the tenant, according to the Spanish regulations concerning deficiencies of the rented property, shall not be entitled to claim rent reduction. Instead, the tenant has the right to claim the landlord for repair of deficiencies and only in cases of health hazards caused by the deficiency, e.g. mould formation, he is entitled to self-performance in the repair of defects and later set off his rent debt. A rent reduction is only applicable if the rented property due to maintenance or repairs made by the landlord - which the tenant is obliged to tolerate – is temporarily at least partially not usable.

30.6 Succession and gifts

Applicable law and jurisdiction

When determining the applicable law of succession, Spanish international private law adheres to the personal statute, which is in turn determined by the nationality of the testator. Thus, Spanish law does not adhere to the principle of residence or location. This principle has the following effects with regard to the German speaking countries.

As Germany and Austria follow Spain concerning the nationality principle, in general there are no conflict of law rules issues: Basically, the succession situation of the testator is determined by his national law. On the contrary, Switzerland follows the residence principal, so that in individual Swiss/Spanish cases it can come to split heirship or fragmentation of succession. The same rules as for Switzerland apply for the UK.

Spain is, along with Austria, Germany and Switzerland, one of the signatory countries to the *Hague Convention of 5 October 1961* on the *Conflicts of Laws Relating to the Form of Testamentary Dispositions*. Accordingly, a testamentary disposition in Spain is always formally effective and valid, if it is established pursuant to the legal provisions regarding the national law of the testator, of the place of establishment or the location of the property.

According to Spanish international private law, gifts and donations are subject to the national law according to the donor's personal statute, unless other provisions are made.

From an internal Spanish perspective, boundaries regarding conflict of law rules to the different *forum rights of autonomous regions* may be required.

In addition, from a *right in rem* perspective, it is particularly important to consider the point of intersection between the applicable substantive succession law in accordance with conflict of law rules - for example, Austrian law in case of an Austrian personal statute of the testator – and formal law aspects – e.g. formal registration requirements with regard to legal succession on a property in the Spanish Ownership Registry. In the latter case, and due to the location of the property, it is undisputed that Spanish or special *forum rights* take priority.

Not without difficulties, however, is the delimitation where substantive national succession law ends and formal Spanish regulations begin. From a practical point of view, this situation can be adequately resolved by determining the heir according to the conflict of law rules, whereas all formal questions should be implemented according to Spanish law. For example, under Spanish law often a *notarial inheritance acceptance deed* is a prerequisite for recording of legal succession in the competent Ownership Registry. There is a controversy whether such a corresponding notarial affidavit, which in an inheritance case settled under German substantive law becomes unnecessary, is dispensable or, as a formal condition for recording in the Spanish Ownership Registry, is essential. In any case, in practice it often represents the fastest and safest way to be recorded in the Ownership Registry.

Following Parliament's approval on 13 March 2012, the EU Council of the Ministries of Justice approved the *European Rules of Succession* on 8 June 2012. The rules should simplify the settlement of international successions within the EU when they go into effect in August 2015 in those countries which are a party to the agreement. Denmark and the UK will not join at the present time.

First of all, those issues that are not governed by these rules must be defined, e.g. the internal material succession law in participating countries will not be affected. In the case of Spain, it should also be determined whether or not the common law of the CC or any of the other *autonomous regions forum rights* applies in view of the major differences between these sets of regulations. Moreover, these rules will not affect the fiscal aspects of international successions which are always one of the crucial issues in wealth and succession legal advice.

The principal issue is currently the determination of whether or not the law applies to the full amount of the inheritance which shall be governed by the law of the last place of residence of the testator, except for those cases in which the testator had previously subject the taxation to their nation's laws. Said regulations are welcome in view of the tendency towards constant mobility and multiple residences. A fair amount of legal uncertainty is involved since the question of the last habitual residence can trigger legal consequences of enormous importance.

In cases involving individuals moving between various jurisdictions where there is any doubt, it would appear that the question of applicable law is open to debate between the heirs. To that end, it would be best if there was an official record of the deceased's choice of governing law for the succession, in addition to clearly and unequivocally drafted wills. This is of the utmost importance considering that the right of the rightful heirs – with all of the differentiations between jurisdictions – is governed by the law that applies to the entire succession. The considerable simplification entails, furthermore, the introduction of a *single succession certificate* that is intended to unify the various national regulations and forms, as has occurred with birth and death certificates. Such a standardized certificate would mean the elimination of *The Hague Apostille* requirement, as well as expensive translations involved in cross-border legal traffic.

The new *Rules of Successions* will be likely to entail the simplification of the processing and settlement of cross-border successions and inheritances, as long as the regulations are applied correctly. The truly important pending reform, the simplification of the tax rules for cross-border successions, has yet to be resolved. For now, from the practical point of view, it is advisable that individuals make a choice as regards the governing law for their wills and revise any previous wills to include the choice.

Fundamentals of the succession and donation laws of Spain

Under Spanish succession law, the possible applicability of rules pertaining to forum rights *(derechos forales)* of several Spanish autonomous regions must be noted. These are regional civil law regulations belonging to the Spanish autonomous regions, for example, Aragón, Catalonia, Navarra, the Basque region, Galicia and the Balearic Islands. Within the scope of this regional law, there are deviations from the generally applicable provisions of the CC, which, however, generally play no part in the scope of an international transaction to which the rules of the international private law apply.

The general Spanish inheritance law recognizes testamentary and statutory *(Sucesión ab Intestato)* legal succession. Within the scope of the testate succession, it should be observed that inheritance agreements or joint and/or mutual will and testaments are not permitted, but may be possible under regional law provisions. Wills and testaments in Spain can be either personally prepared in writing by holographic will (*Testamento Ológrafo*), or by a notary, with a distinction being made between the open and closed version (*Testamento Abierto* or *Testamento*

Cerrado). In addition, there is a central registry for wills *(Registro Central de Últimas Voluntades)* in Madrid, to which Spanish notaries must forward all wills executed before them. This registry is extremely practical because following the death of the testator, it is merely necessary to request the information regarding testamentary disposition in order to find out with which notary the testator executed his last will. One can then request a copy of the last will and testament from that notary's office. If no last will and testament is available, a *certificate of succession* should be requested from the relevant probate court in a complicated and time-consuming process.

Finally, a peculiarity of Spanish law is that the inheritance must be accepted and expressly declared as such. This can be accomplished either orally or implicitly but is usually done by means of a public document or notarial deed, the so-called *notarial inheritance acceptance declaration (Aceptación de Herencia)*, which enables the recording of the succession in the Ownership Registry.

Even if the testator has left a last will and testament, entitlements to the compulsory portions of the inheritance *(legítima)* must be observed: The children of the testator or their descendants are entitled to a portion of the estate in the amount of two thirds, one third of which is to be divided equally among them and another third of which is to be divided among the entitled persons at the testator's complete discretion. The final third is entirely discretionary. If no descendants exist, the parents and other ascendants are entitled to half of the estate, unless there is a surviving spouse, in which case the parents of the testator are entitled to a third. The beneficiaries of the compulsory portion represent a so-called *mandatory inheritance right* that generally grants the beneficiaries a direct heir position by law, i.e. *in rem* claim to the corresponding portion of the estate. In this respect, the Spanish obligations regarding compulsory portions are embodied much stronger than that kind of compulsory portion, which only grants a monetary compensation claim against the estate.

The surviving spouse has a *statutory lifelong right of usufruct* over a third part of the estate if there are descendants, to half the estate if there are ascendants and to two thirds of the estate in the absence of descendants and ascendants.

The intestacy or statutory succession provides first that descendants of the testator and, in the absence thereof, the ascendants shall receive equal portions. The surviving spouse inherits prior to the relatives of the collateral line. If the married couple were separated, siblings of the testator and other successive relatives in the collateral line inherit. The statutory succession law continues into the fourth generation, whereof the state inherits.

The Spanish law of donation stipulates *mandatory notarial authentication of donations regarding immovables*, otherwise the agreement is void.

30.7 Taxes and charges

Both the central Spanish state as well as the regional autonomies (*Autonomías*) and municipalities have tax levying as well as tax collection competences in various areas, meaning that, for example, an acquisition transaction can trigger diverse tax obligations and may require handling taxes before different tax authorities. In particular, reference should be made to the significantly different tax regulations that apply in the Canary Islands and also partially in the Basque Region and Navarra.

The terms or abbreviations NIF, CIF and NIE constantly come up in the tax administration of Spanish property:

- NIF (*número de identificación fiscal*) is the general taxpayer's account number for Spanish nationals
- CIF (*código de identificación fiscal*) is the taxpayer's account number for legal entities (thus, to be precise, the CIF is really a subcategory of the NIF)
- NIE (*número de identificación de extranjeros*) is the taxpayer's account number for foreigners, irrespective of whether they reside in Spain or not

A non-resident real estate owner in Spain is not obliged to appoint a tax representative. However, it is advisable and in certain cases compulsory to appoint a Spanish tax representative to effectively handle communications from the Spanish tax authorities.

Since the end of 2006 it is compulsory for foreigners to obtain a NIE number for any official act, such as the registration of a purchase to the Ownership Registry. This often complicates a quick execution of the transaction, as the application procedures usually are time-consuming and request either the presence of the foreigner before the Spanish police or the notarial signature of powers of attorney on that behalf. Timely coordination with competent advisors may help to mitigate the bureaucratic tasks. Private documents can normally be signed even before such NIE number has been obtained, even notarial deeds might be signed, but cannot be registered without the NIE. The same rules apply for foreign corporations. They need to obtain a CIF to act legally.

One-time taxes and charges on a purchase of Spanish real estate

Real estate transfer taxes

In the case of a purchase of real estate either value-added tax in the case of the purchase of a new construction (VAT) or the land acquisition tax in the case of the purchase of a second hand property (*Impuesto sobre Transmisiones Patrimoniales,* hereafter ITP, which is levied by the *Autonomías*), becomes due.

The ITP rate now stands in a range between 6% and 10% depending on the *Autonomía* where the real estate is located. In individual cases, according to the individual *Autonomía*, certain reductions of these tax rates apply, for instance, for social policy reasons in place at the time of acquisition if the property concerned is publicly promoted housing.

If the operation is subject to VAT, another Spanish tax, called stamp duty, is levied on notarial documents, which is known as stamp duty tax (*Impuesto sobre los Actos Jurídicos Documentados*, hereafter AJD) which lies typically between 0.5% and 1.8%, depending once again on the *Autonomía* in which the real estate is located.

Usually the buyer must pay ITP, VAT and AJD within, depending on the competent Autonomous Region, either one month or 30 working days of the authentication (Saturdays are considered working days) – to the relevant *Autonomía* in the form of self-assessment (*autoliquidación*). In the case of non-observance of the obligation, the property cannot be entered in the Ownership Registry. Furthermore, any delay will incur the legal interest rate on arrears during the whole delay period exceeding one year and additionally, a once-off surcharge on overdue payment of up to 20%, according to the duration of the delay.

Sales tax (value added tax)

Value added tax (*Impuesto Sobre el Valor Añadido*, IVA, VAT) is usually 21%. This does not fall due on the private sale of a property or on the second or subsequent transfers of the constructed property, subject to the ITP. However, the purchase of building land and corporate property is subject to the regular rate of 21%. However, the tax rate is reduced to 10%, insofar as the acquisition concerns housing as well as necessary fittings (such as garages, a limited number of storage rooms, etc.).

The tax is levied by the seller within the purchase price and paid by the seller to the tax authorities within the monthly or quarterly VAT tax returns.

In the case of second and subsequent acquisitions and insofar as the buyer is also a person subject to VAT, such as a corporation, the parties under certain circumstances can waive the statutory exemption from the VAT obligation, which applies to second and subsequent transmissions. In other words, the transaction is again subjected to VAT. The advantage is that VAT can be typically compensated in regular business operations due to input tax deduction entitlements. Moreover, in these cases VAT should not be charged by the seller because the VAT reverse charge system applies. However, reference should also be made to the fact that corresponding documents are then subject to AJD, whereby the corresponding tax rates of the *Autonomías* are usually then raised to 1.5% or even 1.8%, depending on the *Autonomía* where the real estate is located. The key to understanding this systematic taxation is the separation of taxes: while the VAT remains with the Spanish central state, ITP and AJD go to the *Autonomías*.

Real estate registration and notarial charges

In addition to taxes, fees for notarial authentication and for recording in the Ownership Registry burden the acquisition of a property. Statutory fee scales exist for professional groups, notaries and registrars (*Registradores*). As a rough guide, the costs of property acquisition (notary, Ownership Registry) amount to approximately 2 to 3% of the purchase price stated in the deed.

Annually recurring taxes and charges

Real estate tax

The annual municipal real estate tax (*Impuesto sobre Bienes Inmuebles*, hereafter IBI) is calculated based on the cadastral value of the property according to a municipal scale.

The legal basis for the determination of the cadastral value is Article 22 of the *Cadastral Law* (*Ley del Catastro Inmobiliario*) according to which the value of a property consists of the value of the land as well as its property development. According to the wording of the law, the cadastral value should be equivalent to the current market value, although in fact the cadastral value is typically lower than its market value.

Pursuant to the law on municipal taxes (*Ley Reguladora de las Haciendas Locales*, hereafter LHL), the real estate tax can amount to at least 0.3% up to a maximum of 1.3% of the cadastral value. The taxable person for IBI purposes is the owner of the property on 1 January of the respective year.

Income tax

Spanish law differentiates between the income taxation for residents (*Impuesto sobre la Renta de las Personas Fisicas*, IRPF) and for non-residents (*Impuesto sobre la Renta de los No Residentes*, IRNR). In Spain, the personal use of the property for second residential purposes is also taxed. The assessment basis for non-residents is the estimated economical value of use, which is calculated at a maximum of 2% of the cadastral value. A 24% tax, with no possibility of reduction, is imposed annually on this value. As for non-residents who rent out their properties, the realized gross income is also taxable at 24% with no possibility of reduction, unless the non-resident is tax resident in another EU member state. In this last case, the tax rate is 20% for 2015 and 19% for 2016 and subsequent years.

Wealth tax

In Spain, the wealth tax (*Impuesto sobre el Patrimonio*, IP) was abolished in 2008 although, due to the economic crisis, was then reinforced temporarily for the years 2011 to 2015.

IP applies equally for residents as for non-residents, both with an applicable allowable exemption of EUR 700,000 (some autonomies have driven down this exemption to lower amounts). The taxation is scaled and lies between 0.2% and 2.5% of the assessment basis, which is the highest of the following three values: the cadastral value, the purchase price or the officially determined value.

The tax rates are progressively scaled, the highest rate is applied to property assets that have a total net value of over EUR 10,695,996.06. Taxation may be avoided or at least lowered through reducing the net value of the wealth, for instance in the event that the acquisition has been financed with a mortgage loan. It has to be noted here that no net wealth taxation applies on companies, so purchase through a company can be a solution for non-residents to avoid the wealth tax. Some Autonomous Regions have not reinstalled the net wealth tax within their territories, so a specific investigation should be made from case to case.

Capital gain tax

In Spain, the profit generated when a property is transferred is first subject to income taxation for residents (IRPF) or non-residents (IRNR) and additionally, the municipalities levy a communal taxation on the appreciation in value of the land that has occurred during ownership of the property according to objective criteria. This is a taxation of appreciation in value of urban land (technically *Impuesto sobre el Incremento del Valor de los Terrenos de Naturaleza Urbana*, IIVTNU, but in general Spanish usage and hereinafter known for simplicity as Plusvalía Municipal). The two concepts are frequently confused, although they exist alongside each other and should be distinguished.

In the case of residents, the capital gain on disposal is subject to IRPF. However, the profit is not subject to tax, if and insofar as it has resulted from the transfer of the main dwelling used personally by the seller and if it is invested in a new dwelling within specific deadlines. Where the profit is taxable, the tax rate for residents scales between 19.5% and 23.5% for 2015 and 19% and 23% for 2016 and subsequent years. In the case of non-residents, the gain on disposal is taxed with a tax rate of 20% for 2015 and 19% for subsequent years.

The gain on disposal is calculated, for both residents and non-residents, from the difference between the purchase and transfer price, although the former was adjusted by multiplying it with an annually determined national coefficient for inflation purposes. Please note that the application of this coefficient for inflation purpose came to an end in 2014, which will increase taxation on a sale.

In order to secure the tax liability of the non-resident, which is often difficult for Spanish authorities following the transfer of the property, the Spanish legislator has developed the following system:

The buyer who acquires his real estate from a non-resident in Spain has to retain 3% of the purchase price and pay it directly to the Spanish tax authorities. The buyer has one month to pay the retained amount to the tax authorities, whereupon the seller has an additional three months to submit a tax return. In this tax return, the withholding tax (*retención*) is offset against the calculated overall tax liability of the seller pursuant to the above criteria.

In the case of non-fulfillment of this obligation, the property itself becomes liable, which implies that the buyer will endeavor to ensure that the amount is retained and paid to the Spanish tax office. There are certain exemptions to the withholding tax obligation for very specific cases.

Tax on appreciation in value of the land – Plusvalía Municipal

The person subject to tax in this instance is the seller of the property, although, in the case of gratuitous transfers, for example, by inheritance or donation, the beneficiary bears the tax burden. The *Plusvalía Municipal* is calculated by multiplying the cadastral value of the land (without buildings) by the number of years the seller has been in possession of the property, limited to a maximum number of 20 years. The value determined in this way is then multiplied by a maximum coefficient of 3.7%. The result of this calculation is the basis for taxation, which is then taxed at a municipal rate that cannot exceed 30%. In the case of two transfers within a year, the *Plusvalía Municipal* only becomes due once. It has to be noted that following recent legislation it is necessary to prove to the Ownership Registry fulfilment of the *Plusvalía Municipal* obligations, that is the payment and communication of such transmission to the competent Municipality.

Inheritance and Gift tax

Pursuant to the Spanish law on inheritances and donations tax (*Ley del Impuesto de Sucesiones y Donaciones*, LISD), it applies not only for residents but also for non-residents provided that the inheritance or the donation of a Spanish real estate is at hands.

For inheritances, the deadline for submission of the tax return is within six months of the succession. The statutory period of limitation is equivalent to the general fiscal statutory period of limitation contained in Article 66 of the *Spanish General Tax Act* (LGT), which is four years. It was, in particular in the case of non-residents, usual practice to allow the inheritance or gift tax to become time-barred. At all events, tax planning involving prescription periods is not only illegal but also extremely risky and therefore not advisable at all.

Due to enormous misuse, the statutory period of limitation since 2003 only runs, as a general rule, from the date on which any Spanish administrative authority is notified of the corresponding taxable event, i.e., that the succession or donation has taken place. This has made it since then more difficult for tax liability to become time-barred. It is however still under discussion why the person's death, as an objective event, should not justify commencement of the statutory period of limitation. Recent court decisions also underline that at least the inheritance cases must be considered time-barred, once the statutory period is finished.

Basically, all assets located in Spain are taxable, which includes bank accounts, motor vehicles and other movable property. In addition, the legislator adds a lump sum of 3% of the value of the legal estate for fittings and furnishings of the house of the testator (*ajuar doméstico*). Furthermore, the current market value of the property forming the real estate is taxable. The current market value is not easily determined. To prevent default application of this provision, at some Autonomous Regions, adjustment coefficients, which provide an approximation to the current market value from the point of view of the competent tax authorities, may be requested from the relevant tax authorities. This does not apply for all Autonomous Regions, nor for non-resident tax subjects.

Spanish law provides for a few allowable deductions in the case of inheritance taxation However, the *Autonomías*, which receive the corresponding tax income, can create additional deductions and exemption criteria, although they only apply to residents as a general rule. The most important of such exemptions is the reduction of the taxable value of the main dwelling of the testator by 95% up to EUR 122,606.47 per heir, insofar as it is transferred to immediate heirs and the property is nor sold by those heirs for 10 years as a general rule (said period of time will ultimately depend on the Autonomous Region legislation).

Inheritance and gift tax in Spain are regulated at both state level and at the level of autonomous communities. The autonomous communities' legislation grants residents a number of tax benefits that, in practice, allow them to pay much lower taxes than non-residents.

It should therefore be mentioned that in 2011 the European Commission decided to refer Spain to the EU's Court of Justice (ECJ) for discriminatory rules on inheritance and gift tax that require non-residents to pay higher taxes than residents.

In this regard please note that recently, on 3 September 2014, the ECJ made a decision in this case concluding that the *Spanish Inheritance and Gift Tax Law* contravenes the EU legislation by permitting the establishment of differences in the tax treatment of donations and inheritances between (i) beneficiaries and donees resident in Spain and those who are non-resident in Spain; between (ii) testators who are resident in Spain and those who are non-resident in Spain; and between (iii) donations and similar dispositions of real property located in Spanish territory and real property located outside of said territory. This decision has been recently incorporated in the Spanish Inheritance and Gift Law.

Those taxpayers who have been subjected to discriminatory treatment in the payment of the *Spanish Inheritance and Gift Tax* in recent years because they could not apply the more favourable legal provisions at the autonomous community level, can bring proceedings against the Spanish Tax Authorities to obtain a refund of undue amounts paid. For those cases where this type of claim would not be appropriate because it would be time-barred, another option which exists is to bring a claim of state responsibility against Spain within the year following the publication of the ruling.

Spanish inheritance and donation taxation is subdivided into the following tax classes:

Class 1	Direct descendants and adopted children under the age of 21 (inheritance allowable deduction of EUR 15,956 plus EUR 3,990 for every additional year under 21, up to a maximum of EUR 47,858)
Class 2	Direct descendants and adopted children as of 21 years or more, spouses and direct ascendants (inheritance tax allowable deduction of EUR 15,956)
Class 3	Siblings and distant ascendants and descendants (inheritance allowable deduction of EUR 7,993)
Class 4	All other heirs (no allowable deduction)

The tax scale is progressively structured and has a total of 16 grades ranging from 7.65% to 34%. The maximum rate applies to EUR 800,000. Finally, the sum of this calculation must be multiplied by a coefficient based on the net assets of the tax payers as per the following table:

Assets of the heirs (in Spain)	**Tax class**		
	I and II	**III**	**IV**
EUR 0 – 402,678	1.0000	1.5882	2.000
EUR 402,678 – 2,007,380	1.0500	1.6676	2.100
EUR 2,007,380 – 4,020,770	1.1000	1.7471	2.200
More than EUR 4,020,770	1.2000	1.9059	2.400

The interesting and, above all, unusual aspect of this system, from an international comparison, is the fact that for the overall tax burden, the existing assets of the heir receiving the inheritance are of significance.

The maximum tax burden is 81.6%. It should be noted that Article 23 of the LISD provides for the offsetting of inheritance tax paid overseas against the Spanish inheritance tax for those subject to unlimited inheritance tax (residents).

Of course, with such high taxation, ways are repeatedly sought to avoid or circumvent the inheritance tax. Individual advice and tax planning is imperative.

Finally, it should be borne in mind that the transfer of a property by means of an inheritance or donation also results in *Plusvalía Municipal* taxation on the beneficiary's estate.

Other taxes and charges

There is an extraordinary tax, to which non-resident legal persons that are tax residents in "tax havens", who are owners of or have rights of usufruct or use over property located in Spain are subject, the *Gravamen Especial sobre Bienes Inmuebles de Entidades no Residentes*.

The amount of the extraordinary duty amounts to 3% of the cadastral value. If no cadastral value is available the value is determined according to the provisions established in the wealth tax law.

Incorrect (lower) statement of sales price on the sales agreement

Under-declaration has been a crucial issue with regard to Spanish property until a few years ago: taxes are in the focus when talking about "A-" and "B-"money concerning real estate transactions ("A-money" is a commonly used term for the officially declared price, while "B-money" is the non-declared part of the purchase price). In a real estate market of decreasing prices and, generally speaking, transaction volume, with more difficult financing and stronger control mechanisms, under-declaration is no longer of such importance and meaning as in the years before. Still, it is important to know the traditional mechanisms to understand quite a few market habits.

The duplicity of contracts described in previous sections regarding the co-existence of a privately drawn up contract and the notarial deed, makes possible the most extensively used practice of under-declaration in Spanish real estate transactions. As there is initially no obligation to sign a privately drawn up contract, it is possible to immediately sign the notarial deed. Accordingly, buyer and seller are in a position to destroy the privately drawn up contract once the notarial deed has been signed. This in turn means that a higher purchase price can be agreed in the privately drawn up contract than in the notarial deed, which is then the only valid contract in existence and thus the "undeclared earnings" exist from the moment the privately drawn up contract is substituted by the notarial deed.

The under-declaration has several consequences and thereby distorts the contractual reality and the reality officially declared. Under civil law, the contract continues to be effective and under fiscal law, it is an actionable tax offence. The under-declaration does not endanger the purchase but both parties may be liable for claims by the defrauded tax authorities. Beyond certain limits, criminal actions may also be possible.

The Spanish tax authorities have four years to examine and, if necessary, to issue supplementary tax assessment notices for the amounts declared in the document and the tax assessment. These can of course be answered and challenged. Furthermore, in the case of tax fraud, interest and penalties will be levied and moreover the prescription period is extended to five years. In addition, recent legislative changes have significantly prohibited cash transactions. Depending on the case, cash payments from EUR 2,500 on might be considered illegal and be under penalty.

Moreover, on transferring the property at a later date, an under-declared acquisition can lead to a considerably higher taxable gain on disposal, which is usually more expensive than the cost of declaring the actual purchase price in the notarial deed. However, it is not uncommon that some sellers insist upon declaring a lower price in the notarial deed.

International taxation

The double taxation conventions signed by Spain adhere to the principle of taxation in the state of location as regards revenues from properties. The conventions, which are all similar in content, subject the gains on disposal of immovable assets to taxation in the state of the source. However, it is sometimes different in the case of a gain on the disposal of a right, even if this was linked to an interest in real estate, as for instance the sale of the shares of a company that holds Spanish real estate would be taxable in principle in the state of tax residence of the seller. In this regard, nevertheless, attention should be paid to the contents of the applicable, if any, convention to avoid double taxation because it can contain the so-called "real estate anti-abuse clause". In fact, this real estate anti-abuse clause is the general principle for Spanish tax purposes.

30.8 Immigration law and tax residence

Entry, residence and settlement of foreigners

There are no barriers for citizens of EU countries with regards to entry and residence in Spain.

The liberalization of the immigration rules extends to all citizens of the member states of the EU as well as the citizens of those states which belong to the European Economic Area and Swiss nationals. Certain family members, who live permanently with the entitled person, namely the spouse, children under 21 years of age or, in addition, the ascendants of the entitled person, are also included insofar as they receive maintenance payments from the entitled person.

The law grants the entitled person freedom of entry and exit, freedom of residence and freedom of movement within the national territory, as well as the right to assume an activity whether self-employed or for a third party. A valid identity card or passport is sufficient for entry.

Persons from non EU member states mostly require a visa, which can be refused on grounds of public safety, law and order or health. The visa then entitles the bearer to a stay of up to three months.

The following groups need no permit for a permanent residence: citizens of member states of the EU or the European Economic Area or Switzerland as workers, students or holders of a permanent right of residence and family members from Spain, as well as persons of the first group, who work in Spain, but are usually resident in another state.

To exercise an activity, service or a course of study, the internal national regulations apply in the same way as for Spanish citizens. A permanent right of residence is granted to all citizens of EU member states, who were economically active in Spain and fulfill one of the other prerequisites:

1 Ended working activity at retirement age with previous 12 months uninterrupted working activity and three year's residence in Spain
2 Ended working activity due to permanent disability and two year's residence in Spain (this time requirement is waived if a pension is being received from the state due to the disability)
3 Relocated the working activity to another state after three years while retaining normal residence in Spain

Thus, this regulation does not apply to retired persons, who were not previously employed in Spain. Nonetheless, retired or otherwise financially independent EU-citizens can apply for a residence permit as long as they prove their financial independence.

Even if they are family members, persons from non-member states of the EU still require a residence permit. A temporary permit is granted for a period of three months to one year. In the case of an intended residence of more than one year the applicant receives a five year permit, which is renewable. The permit for family members is dependent on the right of residence of the main person.

The application for a residence permit must be made within one month of entry. Exemptions are available where the applicant is unable to provide the visa necessary due to his own personal situation or the situation in his country of origin. The permit should always be granted within three months.

The entry or the residence permit can be refused for reasons of public safety, law and order and health.

Recently, Spain has been investigating the introduction of a new investment-based immigration program that would allow foreigners to obtain residence permits when acquiring real estate.

Tax residence

Anyone who lives for more than 183 days during the natural year in Spain or has his center of operations in Spain will be considered as a resident for tax purposes or tax resident. The 183 day time period can also consist of several and considerable interruptions. A tax resident's global income is subject to income tax in Spain. After a few tax increases during the recent economical crisis in Spain, the tax rate is currently still at a maximum of up to 48% (for instance, in Catalonia Autonomous Community). The tax rates have been gradually lowered from 2015 on.

In addition, where residence is taken up in Spain, the global assets of the tax subject are subject to net wealth tax, which may be considerable, with a maximum rate of 2.5%. There are of course wider options as regards a dynamic structuring of the income tax situation that should be analyzed carefully for each individual case. The personalized advice of a legal and tax consultant is indispensable in this context.

Within the scope of freedoms granted by the European Union, especially the Schengen Treaty, it is more difficult nowadays for the Spanish authorities to determine the fiscal residence of a person. The Spanish tax authorities try to prove that the tax subject is a tax resident, in order to be able to tax his global revenues. For that very reason, in the case of tax residence in tax havens and low tax countries, a certificate of tax residence is required. Notwithstanding this, the Spanish tax authorities may initiate an investigation to determine tax residence in Spain. An indication of tax residence is, for example, the permanent residence of the spouse and, if applicable, dependent children living in Spain. The tax authorities can draw on any imaginable indication of tax residence, such as the request for submission of the appropriate invoices for electricity, water, telephone, etc.

It has to be pointed out also that Spain has endured very much its antifraud mechanisms: the most significant measure is a new obligation for Spanish tax residents from 2013 on to report to the Spanish tax authorities all their overseas assets. Non-observance can be severely punished with important fines.

So, when acquiring a Spanish tax residence, a careful analysis should be made before to avoid later problems or tax burdens.

Special regime for impatriates for personal income tax purposes

The special tax regime applicable to workers posted to Spanish territory (also called "impatriates") has experienced important changes due to the adoption of the tax novelties regarding personal income tax (PIT) which were published in the Official State Gazette on 28 November 2014.

According to this regime, which has originally been intended for those workers who have been posted to Spanish territory due to an employment contract, is now extending its scope of application to those persons who are posted to Spain with the aim of acquiring the status of manager of a company. It is even allowed that these persons acquire shares in the company, but of less than 25%.

There are some other less important changes that have also been introduced, notably the fact that it is no longer required that the foreseeable remuneration under the employment contract may not exceed the amount of EUR 600,000 per year and that the work to be done must be realized for a company resident in Spain. In short, the scope and possibilities of application of this special tax regime have been extended.

With regard to the changes related to the contents of the regime, it must be pointed out that those impatriates who take advantage of this taxation modality will be subject to taxation in Spain from now on for the totality of the labor income, regardless of where it was generated.

A special regulation was also included in order to avoid the double taxation which could arise in those situations where the income is also subject to taxation abroad.

Apparently, those persons who benefit from this tax regime may obtain a certificate of tax residence in Spain from the Spanish Public Treasury for the purpose of those Double Taxation Agreements not deeming as residents those persons who are subject to taxation only for the income earned in their country of residence.

With regard to the tax rates applicable to the earned income, the applicable tax rate will be 24% up to the amount of EUR 600,000 paid to the tax payer and 47% (in 2015) and 45% (from 2016 onwards) from EUR 600,000 and above.

As regards the income derived from Spanish-sourced dividends or interests, among others, it will be subject to taxation in accordance with the tax scale set out for capital gains and investment capital earnings (between 20% and 24% for the income earned in 2015 and between 19% and 23% from 2016 onwards).

Furthermore, neither has the term of this special tax regime been changed, being applicable to the tax year where tax residence has been changed and to the five subsequent tax years, nor the requirement for the tax payer under this tax regime having to pay the Wealth Tax due to the possession of property or rights located or to be exercised in Spain.

Finally, regarding inheritance and gift tax for impatriates, due to the fact that these tax payers are Spanish tax residents, they will be subject to taxation like any other person being a tax resident in Spain for the totality of property and rights obtained, irrespective of where these are located or exercised.

Capital gains derived from a change of residence: the new exit tax

One of the most important novelties introduced by the Spanish legislator is the creation of an exit tax in the field of personal income tax (PIT). This taxation was traditionally foreseen in the field of corporate income tax, but never related to PIT. Historically, those taxpayers being natural persons and losing their tax residence did not experience any other adverse tax consequences except of those of losing certain tax benefits.

Due to the introduction of this new tax regime, all Spanish tax residents, having had this condition during at least 10 of the 15 tax periods previous to the last one where they have been subject to Spanish PIT, must declare the capital gain derived from the change of residence.

In the case of taxpayers opting for the application of this special tax regime for workers posted to Spanish territory, the term of the 10 tax periods would have counted from the moment of exhaustion of this special tax regime (one plus five years).

Only taxpayers who have had lasting bonds with our country will be required to pay these new taxable capital gains. In this sense, if a non-resident citizen temporarily establishes his/her residence in Spain and thus becomes a taxpayer during the course of several years, but loses his/her residence before the period of 10 years has elapsed, he/she will not have created sufficiently strong links with our tax system to be subject to this new tax regime.

Regarding assets subject to taxation, the new exit tax will not be applicable to the totality of the unrealized gains of the taxpayer losing his/her tax residence. In this sense, this new tax rate will only be applicable if (i) the taxpayer is the holder of shares in companies (irrespective of whether these shares are quoted shares or not) or in collective investment institutions, and the total value of all these shares exceeds the amount of EUR 4 million, and (ii) should this amount not be exceeded, if the taxpayer holds shares of more than 25% in either of the above-mentioned entities and the market value of the investment in that entity exceeds EUR 1 million.

As can be observed, this new exit tax, due to the fact that it is applicable to a closed list of assets, may have an influence in decision-making regarding an investment. As a consequence, a taxpayer who foresees a change of residence in the future will prefer to invest in fixed-income securities instead of investing in variable-rate securities or collective investment institutions.

These new capital gains will be applied to the taxable savings base in accordance with the following scale: from 20% to 24% (2015) and from 19% to 23% (2016).

If the person subject to the exit tax again obtains Spanish tax residence without having transferred the securities that gave rise to the exit tax, this person will have the right to request the return of all amounts paid at that moment of time, including the settlement of the interest for late payments in favor of the taxpayer from the date of payment of the exit tax.

If the posting is due to labor reasons, the taxpayer is offered the option of deferring the tax debt applying the rules regarding the accrual of interests and the provision of securities.

If the change of residence is made to other states of the EU or the European Economic Area and in order to comply with the Community regulations regarding the free movement of persons, the taxpayer must only communicate the capital gain arising from his/her posting to the Tax Administration, identifying the state where he/she is posted, as well as the maintenance of his/her ownership of the shares.

These capital gains must only be settled before the Spanish Treasury if the assets are transferred, the taxpayer is no longer deemed to be a resident of the EU or any of the abovementioned requirements are not met within the period of the 10 subsequent years to the one where the taxpayer has accounted for Spanish PIT.

International double taxation for residents of Spain

Spain has signed double taxation conventions with many states. These conventions govern the imputations of the various revenues. The content of most of the taxation conventions adhere to the structure of the model OECD convention. Clauses regarding the exchange of information with the authorities of the respective countries exist with all countries.

30.9 Checklist: Real estate in Spain

- The payment of a reservation fee should be avoided if possible, as the money is frequently not reimbursed in the event that the contract is finally not concluded, even though there may exist a legal right to reimbursement
- Examination of the proof of disposal of the seller. The latter can act on his behalf or on that of a third party. Where estate agents are used, the scope of representation and conditions should be thoroughly investigated
- Investigation of the entry in the Ownership Registry of the property and its encumbrances and at the Cadastral Registry
- Private contract: contains all the essential terms, both the framework points and the detailed individual matters. It is legally binding. The contracting parties should ensure that all undertakings and promises are in writing, that is, included in the contract
- Realistic time schedule, particularly in an international context. Organization of the financing aspects can take time, and generally the carrying out of formalities in Spain is often time-consuming. Application for the Spanish NIE tax number might take time
- Total costs: all handling and tax costs should be realistically planned from the outset
- Instalment payments should only be made in return for a guarantee
- In the case of an ownership community/condominium: Are larger investments planned? Is the seller up to date with his contributions?
- Coastal area, Balearic Islands, Canary Islands: is building allowed in these areas?
- Candor regarding the "official" purchase price. Should a contracting party wish to specify a lower price in the notarial deed than the effective purchase price, it may lead to a number of consequences that are not all favorable. Appropriate caution is essential

- Tax-optimized acquisition and transfer planning: A tax expert should be consulted before buying or selling properties in Spain to reduce the fiscal impact of any of these transactions because other opportunities for saving are not easily encountered

30.10 Bibliography

Various Authors:

Memento Práctico Fiscal 2014 y Memento Práctico IVA 2014. Editorial Francis Lefebvre. M. 2014.

Memento Práctico Inmobiliario 2012-2013. Editorial Francis Lefebvre. M. 2011.

Memento Práctico Civil Foral 2011. Editorial Francis Lefebvre. M. 2010

Memento Práctico Arrendamiento Urbanos 2001-2012. Editorial Francis Lefebvre. M. 2010

Memento Práctico Propiedad Horizontal 2014-2015. Editorial Francis Lefebvre. M. 2014

Arbeitsgemeinschaft Steuerrecht im Deutschen Anwaltverein: Steuerstandort Spanien. Immobilien – Unternehmen – Erbschaften, Richard Boorberg Verlag, Stuttgart 2001

Boothby Dan: Buying a House in Spain: Where and How to Do It, Vacation Work Publications, 2003

Carmona Fernández, Néstor: Manual Todo Renta No Residentes. Colección Todo, Editorial CISS, Grupo Wolters Kluwer. M 2011

Cordón Ezquerro, Teodoro (y otros): Manual de Fiscalidad Internacional. Instituto de Estudios Fiscales. CEF. M. 2007

Davey Charles: The Complete Guide to Buying Property in Spain: Buying, Renting, Letting and Selling, Kogan Page, London 2004

Derecho Mercantil Inmobiliario, Coordinator Álvaro Espinós Borrás de Quadras, Edition BOSCH, Barcelona 2009

Foster Anthony Ivor: The Complete Guide to Buying a Property in Spain, Property Search Spain, 2002

Gypps Emma / Hall Leonne: Spanish Property Buying Guide: The Ultimate Guide to Buying a Property in Spain, Merricks Media 2003

Juárez González, Javier Máximo: Manual Todo Sucesiones 2013. Colección Todo. Editorial CISS. Grupo Wolters Kluwer. M. 2013

Hortalà i Vallvé, Joan: Comentarios a la Red de Convenios de doble imposición. Editorial Thomson Aranzadi. M. 2007.

King Harry: Buy to Let in Spain: How to Invest in Spanish Property for Pleasure and Profit, How To Books, 2003

Lacalle Serer, Elena / Sanmartín Escriche, Fernando / Aparicio Urtasum, Carlos: Sucesiones y Herencias – Doctrina, esqemas, cuestiones, jurisprudencia y formularios, Edition Tirant lo Blanch, Valencia, 2008

Renouf Norman / Howell John: Buying a Property: Spain, Cadogan Guides, London 2002

Searl David: You and the Law in Spain: The Complete and Readable Guide to Spanish Law for Foreigners - Incorporating the Spanish Property Guide, Santana Books, 2004

Styles Joanna / Watson Jim: The Best Places to Buy a Home in Spain, Survival Books Limited, 2002

Süss Dr. Rembert / Various Authors, Erbrecht in Europa, 2nd Edition, zerb verlag, 2008

31

St. Kitts and Nevis

Federation of St. Christopher and Nevis

by

Andrew J. Taylor

Henley & Partners
R. L. Bradshaw
International Airport Building
Basseterre
St. Kitts, West Indies

Telephone: +1 (869) 466 0100
Facsimile: +1 (869) 466 0200

andrew.taylor@henleyglobal.com
henleyglobal.com

Jackie Hunkins

JHT Law & Consultancy Firm
Hunkins Plaza
Main Street, Charlestown
Nevis

Telephone: +1 (869) 469 7292
Facsimile: +1 (869) 469 7018

info@jhtlawfirm.com
jhtlawfirm.com

Andrew J. Taylor is a partner of Henley & Partners Group Holdings and is a leading authority in strategic international real estate advisory for private clients and developers. He is the co-editor and one of the co-authors of the International Real Estate Handbook – a standard reference in the field of international real estate advisory – as well as other publications, and for many years has produced various, highly regarded international market intelligence reports.

After finishing at the BC Institute of Technology for Business and Marketing Management, and forming a solid foundation with leading global real estate corporations, he lived in several countries and worked in many real estate markets before merging his own successful firm with Henley Estates, and later being appointed Vice Chairman of Henley & Partners Group Holdings.

Jackie Hunkins-Taylor is Managing Director of JHT Law, a Barrister-at-law, Solicitor and a Notary Public. Born in the island of Nevis, British West Indies, she was admitted to the St. Kitts and Nevis Bar in 2004. She studied at the University of the West Indies (LL.B Hons., 2002) and the Norman Manley Law School (Legal Education Certificate, 2004). Jackie is a member of the St. Kitts and Nevis Bar Association, the International Tax Planning Association and the Asia Offshore Association, and speaks English, French and Spanish. She has contributed to many publications.

31.1 Introduction

St. Kitts and Nevis is a democratic country with an economy that is driven primarily by tourism, and recently largely supported by a citizenship by investment program. Britain formed their parliamentary system and the Country is part of the Commonwealth, with the Queen of England as head of state. The official business language is English and the literacy rate is near 100%.

St. Kitts and Nevis was historically known as St. Christopher and Nevis and is still recorded as such in the country's constitution. Having secured independence in 1983, St. Kitts and Nevis is the only twin island federation which forms part of the Lesser Antilles; a group of islands located around 2,000 kilometers (km) to the southeast of Miami. The twin islands include St. Kitts with an area of 168.4 km^2 and Nevis with 93.2 km^2. The islands offer a perfect tropical climate and everything from sandy beaches to mountainous landscapes and rain forests. Differences in altitudes and in soil types also make it a paradise for tropical plants.

St. Kitts has an attractive championship golf course set between the Caribbean Sea and the Atlantic Ocean, and one 10 miles north at the new Kittitian Hill Resort which opened in 2014. One more golf course is set to open in the near future as part of the Christophe Harbour development, 10 miles south of Basseterre (the capital city). The most highly regarded and well known golf course in the country is found on Nevis at the Four Seasons Resort Nevis.

The truly appropriate motto of the local tourism authority is: 'Two Islands, One Paradise'. The tourism trend for St. Kitts and Nevis has been increasing since 1978. In 2014 there were 818,223 arrivals in St. Kitts compared to 547,561 in 2009. This growth represents a healthy average increase of almost 10% per year over five years. These 2014 tourism volumes makes St. Kitts and Nevis the second most visited Eastern Caribbean island, behind only St. Lucia, and just ahead of Antigua and Barbuda who welcomed 799,661 visitors in 2014. As tourism has grown the demand for vacation property has increased and the real estate market has greatly matured over the last five years. As of 2013, the majority of tourists staying overnight in St. Kitts and Nevis are from North America (71%), the Caribbean (17%), and the UK (8%). In 2012 St. Kitts and Nevis was ranked the third "Best Island in the World" by US News, beaten only by the Maldives (Indian Ocean) and Bora Bora (South Pacific). As St. Kitts and Nevis overcame the expected top Caribbean destinations such as the Cayman Islands (ranked 8th), St. Maarten (ranked 9th), and the US Virgin Islands, it is regarded by many as the number 1 island in the Caribbean.

St. Kitts and Nevis only recently diversified from the sugar industry to high-end tourism, and the landscape is seen as a blank canvas for sustainable and luxury development. Once the new high-end resorts and developments are completed, St. Kitts will offer everything from exclusive 5-star cottage retreats to a buzzing lifestyle around the cutting-edge super yacht marina. St. Kitts and Nevis is on its way to becoming the most luxurious and in-demand destination in the Caribbean. In terms of real estate, overall prices compared to other Caribbean Islands are still low, and therefore provides substantial room for capital appreciation.

Since 1983 the *Constitution and Citizenship Act of St. Kitts and Nevis* has legally allowed foreign investors, who pass intensive due diligence checks and are deemed suitable by the government's *Citizenship by Investment Unit*, to acquire Kittitian citizenship. As such St. Kitts and Nevis has become widely known for having the longest established and successful Citizenship-by-Investment program in the world.

The Federation is a member of the United Nations (UN), the Organization of American States (OAS) and, the British Commonwealth. The Eastern Caribbean Central Bank headquarters is located on St. Kitts and maintains the stability of the Eastern Caribbean Dollar (ECD). The ECD is the national currency of most eastern Caribbean countries and is pegged to the USD with a value of 2.7 ECD to the USD. The country is considered very tax friendly with no personal income tax, no capital gains tax, no wealth tax, no inheritance tax and no gift tax. Companies can easily acquire full tax exemption.

31.2 Real estate ownership

Land, as defined in the *Title by Registration Act* of St. Kitts and Nevis, has a similar meaning to the general term of real estate. Owning land in St. Kitts and Nevis means you own the land and all the fixtures and buildings thereon. The registered proprietors of real estate on St. Kitts and Nevis are the individuals or entities stated on the most recent certificate of title, issued by the *Registrar of Titles*, and the named parties are the absolute owner of the land with ultimate power to transfer the whole or part of the land.

When purchasing certain real estate in the country, an individual's immediate family and dependents of a certain age may acquire eligibility for the country's Citizenship-by-Investment program. These approved developments require special authorization from the government, and there are many real estate developments approved for the Citizenship-by-Investment program. When assessing citizenship-approved real estate, one must be personally diligent or work with a reputable company such as Henley & Partners, in order to ensure that fair market value is obtained and the developer is of sound reputation.

Different forms and types of ownership

Property in St. Kitts and Nevis may be owned in one of three ways, by a fee simple estate, a leasehold estate, or a life estate. A fee simple estate is also called freehold title, or share of freehold in connection to the condominium laws in St. Kitts and Nevis, and is the actual ownership of interest in land. It gives the right to use and enjoy the land for the duration of the life of the proprietor, his heirs and successors. A leasehold estate gives the right to possession for a definite period of time, for example for a month, a year or 99 years. A life estate is often found in family settlements where a person leaves property to a spouse for life and then to the children, although this life interest is often carved out of a fee simple estate.

Where two or more persons hold interest in property, a co-ownership is established and there are two types of co-ownership in St. Kitts and Nevis: joint tenancy and tenancy in common. A joint tenancy is where one title is held by more than one owner. The joint tenants have equal interest or rights such as the right to sever the joint tenancy. However, the most important feature of joint tenancy is the right of survivorship whereby on the death of one of the joint tenants, his interest automatically transfers to the surviving joint tenant so that he has no interest to transfer under a will or intestacy.

Tenancy in common arises where property is held by two or more persons and there is a distinct fixed share in the property. A tenant in common may dispose of his share by will or on intestacy. There is no right of survivorship.

Easements, charges, liens and mortgages

Any easement, right, liberty, or privileges with respect to land, or any part thereof, shall pass to the transferee; and he, and the persons deriving title under him, shall have use and enjoy the same accordingly. Any and all mortgages, incumbrances, liens or covenants will be included in the memorandum of transfer and later noted on the certificate of title. If the title has been transferred and issued to a transferee, it shall be implied that the transferee has accepted the land subject to such mortgages, incumbrances, liens or covenants. In the case of a mortgage, the transferee will be liable to pay the interest accruing thereon, and discharge the principal sums for which such mortgages and incumbrances have been granted, and indemnify the transferor from payment of same.

Protection of ownership, proof of ownership and registration

St. Kitts and Nevis has two different systems of transferring and showing proof of ownership for real estate. Under the British deed system inherited from the colonial period, title to property can be transferred with a deed in accordance with the *Conveyancing and Law of Property Act,* which requires an entry at the *Registry of Deeds* for upwards of 35 years in order to establish 'good root of title'. A second option is to acquire property by means of a *Certificate of Title* based on land surveying plans and subsequent entry in a title register on the basis of the *Title by Registration Act.*

The acquisition of title to property via a deed is less secure because the deed applies only to the seller and buyer and does not preclude a third party from asserting a better title. A valid property title can be acquired only if the basis of the current property title can be demonstrated to go back 35 years by submitting proof of an unbroken ownership chain. A *Certificate of Title* is preferable to a deed. A title certificate gives the buyer a government guarantee and a right *in rem* or title insurance, and such a title is valid with respect to everyone. A title certificate also displays all encumbrances, such as mortgages, on the property. If a property is acquired by means of a deed, the buyer or owner may subsequently request registration under the *Title by Registration Act* at any time by applying to the *Registrar of Titles.*

St. Kitts and Nevis is a small country in which lawsuits concerning disputes of ownership title to property are very rare. Before every acquisition, a lawyer will naturally check whether the ownership title is correct and unencumbered, and any problems will usually come to light in the course of these enquiries and can be resolved in advance.

31.3 Purchase and sale of real estate

The purchase and sale of real estate in St. Kitts and Nevis is straightforward. Typically in the case of a land purchase the property must first be surveyed, or existing plans must be confirmed by a surveyor and the result should be annexed in the sales contracts.

Once a purchase and sales agreement has been signed by both the buyer and seller, the property's title will be searched by the appointed lawyer to identify any encumbrances connected to the said title, and a *Memorandum of Transfer* (MOT) will be prepared for signature by both parties. The MOT, along with proof from the Department of Inland Revenue that all stamp duties have been paid, is then presented to the *Registrar of Titles* for registration in the land registry, as outlined under the *Title by Registration Act*. If the property is being transferred, a new certificate of title will be produced in favour of the transferee, and the previous (old) certificate will be cancelled and recorded as such in the Register. This process is straightforward although it can take several months before a certificate of title is available as proof of ownership. During this period of time, the signed memorandum of transfer is primarily used to show proof of ownership.

The sales agreement

There is no set, official, or government recommended sales agreement for St. Kitts and Nevis and in practice, sales agreements can be quite short and to the point. The critical points that should be in a sales agreement are of course the buyer and seller information; followed by specific details of the transaction such as price and any aspects included in the price (e.g. furniture); the party liable for covering stamp duty, closing fees, government fees or taxes; and most importantly a survey or exact plan of the property involved in the transaction; as well as your local attorney's advised standard general terms present in the local contract.

Typically the seller, or seller's attorney, produces the sales agreement. In this event the buyer should appoint a local attorney or professional to represent their best interests in the negotiation of contractual terms and the final agreement. As a rule, it is always important to identify all possible situations where you may be at risk, define how the risk is best alleviated or minimized and better yet, when at all possible, pass the risk on to the other party. It is always advisable to involve a local attorney to vet even the simplest sales agreement as in many cases, a simple agreement leaves you open to risks or sometimes worse, open to interpretation and therefore time-consuming litigation in the event of a dispute. Such a vetting service can cost as little as USD 1,000 in St. Kitts and Nevis although many also simply charge on an hourly basis.

In the event of disputes it is worthwhile knowing that contract law in St. Kitts and Nevis is based on the common law system and as such decisions will be determined accordingly.

Restrictions on acquisition and conveyance

Restrictions under family law and matrimonial property regime

By virtue of the *Married Women's Property Act*, every woman who marries shall be entitled to acquire, hold or dispose by will or sale, any real estate as her separate property, in the same manner as if she were in a legally un-married state.

Where property is owned as matrimonial property and the parties then divorce, they may apply to the courts for a determination of his or her property interest.

Options and rights of pre-emption

A contract for sale and purchase of property may provide terms such as an option to purchase or rights of pre-emption, that is, the right of first refusal should the purchaser desire to sell. Where there are such provisions, the contract should give specific conditions for the exercise of the option.

Agricultural real estate

Agricultural lands in St. Kitts and Nevis comprise mainly of cane fields, and are primarily owned by the Government. In the year 1775 there were 68 sugar plantations in the country and such lands were used to harvest sugar up until 2005. Following the closure of the fields and sugar factory, agricultural lands have become of new interest to the government who wish to diversify into the luxury tourism industry, and resort developers.

The restrictions imposed on the purchase include the standard *Alien Landholding License* as defined in the following section and, if the government owns the land, any specific government wishes for the area. In most cases, government lands would only be sold for developments of economic interest to St. Kitts and Nevis and most developers taking advantage of this are focused on housing, or the 4- and 5-star hotel categories.

Restrictions regarding acquisition of real estate by foreigners

A foreign national who wishes to acquire real estate on St. Kitts and Nevis may need to acquire an *Alien Land Holding License* as stipulated by the *Alien Land Holding Regulation Act Cap. 102.* The standard *Alien Landholding License Fee* is technically 10% of the property value although most major developments have a full exemption to this regulation. The details of exemptions vary slightly and for example, an *Alien Land Holding License* is not required at all for owning land or property at Kittitian Hill or in the Frigate Bay area of St. Kitts, and one only requires a license if owning over two acres of land in the Southeast Peninsula of St. Kitts. However, the Four Seasons Resort Nevis does require a license, although the 10% fee is waived.

A license can be acquired from the Government within a few weeks and should be applied for once an agreement has been made with the seller, and the exact property and price can be disclosed on the application form. The license, if required, will be needed prior to the formal closing and transfer of title taking place. In principal it is always recommended to obtain professional advice to ensure surprises are avoided during the closing period.

The *Alien Land Holding Regulation Act* also affects foreign nationals or foreign corporate entities who wish to become a director of a local company, hold shares in a local company, or to exercise votes in a local company. In any of these events a similar application must be filed and authorization granted before ownership may be issued.

Further important preconditions for buying real estate

There are two distinct real estate markets in St. Kitts and Nevis when considering potential buyers; the standard lifestyle market, and the citizenship-by-investment market. The standard real estate market in St. Kitts and Nevis includes both international tourists and permanent or temporary residents. International tourists mainly purchase property as a second home, vacation home, retirement destination, or an investment; whereas residents purchase for primary residence and investment. Such buyers are predominantly from the United States, Canada, St. Kitts and Nevis, the UK and other parts of Europe. These major countries send a high volume of tourists to St. Kitts and Nevis each year, and this helps fuel the appreciating property market.

Furthermore, there is a good long-term rental market connected to the three medical universities on the island. Teaching staff and medical students who reside on the island typically come from reasonably affluent families who can afford quality rental accommodation. These are all strong factors that attracts the standard market and overseas investors.

The citizenship market is made up of clients from almost every country in the world and who are primarily investing to acquire a second citizenship and passport. Investors looking for citizenship-approved property should choose projects that attract buyers from both the citizenship and lifestyle markets. For this reason, many recent purchasers following the citizenship program have been choosing the Four Seasons Resort Nevis; the most reputable resort in the country which has a strong historic track record of sales to the standard market and now also to the citizenship market.

Even if you do not plan to follow the citizenship program, selecting a property that is attractive to both markets will be a valuable asset at the time of resale. As the motivations for buying a specific property are vast, the sole deciding factor should not only be if the property is approved for citizenship however, it should be considered when making a purchase decision.

Once you have a list of potential properties, you may ask your appointed lawyer to verify that the properties are approved and qualify for the citizenship program. A few basic tests are also worthwhile knowing. If a property qualifying for the citizenship program was purchased before January 2012, but was not used for the citizenship program, and is being sold for the minimum qualifying citizenship investment level, there is a good chance it will still qualify the purchaser for citizenship. In the same scenario, if the property has had multiple previous owners there is a good chance one of the previous owners used it to acquire citizenship and, in this event, it would no longer qualify another investor.

If a property qualifying for the citizenship program was purchased after 17 January 2012, and is being sold for at least the minimum qualifying citizenship investment level five years later (must be after 17 January 2017) it should qualify in every case due to the new citizenship legislation implemented in January 2012 states "*...after January 17th 2017, where real estate that was already the subject of a Citizenship-by-Investment application and in respect of which, five years have passed since the granting of that Citizenship, then that property may be eligible for use in a subsequent Citizenship by Investment application.*" However while this is the full intention of the government and confirmed by them verbally, please note that the government used the words "may be" in their official written statement which leaves them sufficient room to change their mind without difficulty.

Capacity and entitlement of the seller

Under the laws of St. Kitts and Nevis the legal age of capacity is 18 years. An individual must be 18 years or older to enter into a contract to purchase property and must be mentally competent. A conveyance of a legal estate to a minor does not pass but rather is held in trust for said minor until he attains the full legal age.

A local company may also enter into a contract to hold, buy and sell property in accordance with the terms of its *Memorandum of Association* or *By-Laws*.

In terms of the citizenship program, Section 5 (5) of the *Citizenship-by-Investment Regulations, 2011* provides that companies established and maintained under the laws of St. Kitts and Nevis that are not exempt or offshore companies, may purchase real estate and qualify for the citizenship program.

Third-party claims and unpaid taxes

Where there are outstanding property taxes due on the property the vendor would not be able to pass clear title to any subsequent purchaser unless and until the taxes have been paid. To prevent such an eventuality prior to closing on a purchase, it is imperative for the purchaser's attorney to insist on the seller's attorney obtaining a tax receipt from the *Department of Inland Revenue* which indicates that there are no outstanding property taxes due.

The primary third party claim affecting the ability of a vendor to sell real estate would be the claim by a judgment creditor. In most instances, there would be a notice on the *Certificate of Title* in the form of a caveat on the property. In any case, the purchaser's solicitor should conduct a search at the *Supreme Court Registry* to ascertain if there are any judgments on record affecting the seller.

Provisions for protecting the environment, nature and cultural heritage

It is a pre-condition to every development of land that an environment assessment report be done by the *Department of Physical Planning* to protect and preserve not only the natural environment, but also historical and cultural value.

Access to relevant records and documents

There is a system of land recording and registration in St. Kitts and Nevis. Land searches can be conducted at the *Land Deed Registry* or *Registered Land Registry* at the Supreme Court in the St. Kitts Circuit as well as the Nevis Circuit.

Key points that a seller should consider

Prior to choosing a listing company or broker, an owner wishing to sell their property should confirm that it will (or will not) qualify a purchaser for the citizenship-by-investment program. This point is fairly unique to St. Kitts and Nevis (and other markets approving specific property for a citizenship-by-investment program) due to the two distinct real estate markets: the standard market, and the citizenship market. Targeting both markets at the time of resale will increase the liquidity and in turn, maximize the sales velocity.

It is worth discussing the pricing strategy with your local real estate professional as there are several strategies one can put in place to effectively attract citizenship investors. That said, several Caribbean Islands have seen how successful the St. Kitts and Nevis citizenship by investment program has been and, as natural as competition is, they have replicated it. In particular, Antigua and Barbuda's government instructed Henley & Partners to help design a near carbon copy of the program in St. Kitts and Nevis. Due to more competition entering the market, this could lead to a slower growth (or decrease) in price and qualifying requirements.

In every case an effective exit strategy should be considered and discussed with your advisor at the time of purchase and, in St. Kitts and Nevis, one should always consider property that will be easily sold to either the standard market or the citizenship market.

The execution of a real estate purchase transaction

Assuming the parties intend to proceed with the real estate purchase, the vendor's solicitor should draft in duplicate the sale and purchase agreement and forward to the purchaser's solicitor for approval. It is the responsibility of the purchaser's solicitor to investigate the title. Approval of the contract is dependent upon the result of the search and inquiries into any charges or third party interests. Once approved the contract can be executed and exchanged. At this point a security deposit which usually represents 10% of the purchase price is paid by the purchaser to the vendor. If the transaction is subject to approval of citizenship, frequently developers have started asking for a lesser amount of only USD 10,000. However it is standard that this is non-refundable in return for holding a property off the market for the duration of the citizenship process. As the program currently has a circa 90% success rate, the main reasons behind this deposit is that it covers the developer against some of the re-selling costs if someone is denied citizenship or decide to stop the citizenship process.

Thereafter the vendor will furnish a *Memorandum of Transfer* and produce a copy of his property title. If the investor has applied for citizenship and the contract is subject to approval of citizenship, the Memorandum of Transfer is typically processed once a citizenship approval in principal letter is received by the government and full payment is held in escrow or in trust. In any case a local lawyer will need to be instructed to execute the Memorandum of Transfer, and many charge the minimum fee set by the bar of 1%. The final step usually takes place at the office of the vendor's solicitor where the purchaser, upon paying the balance of the purchase price, becomes entitled to the title or deed of the property including the conveyance to him. Payment from an overseas person is typically made to the seller in the form of an international wire transfer and this is widely accepted in St. Kitts and Nevis. The currency of the transaction is primarily in USD, however, it is at the discretion of the seller and one may sometimes contract in ECD when working with locals and re-sale properties.

Funds may be transferred to the closing lawyer in trust or to an appointed escrow account. In most cases using an escrow account (with Grant Thorton in St. Kitts for example) is advisable for any large transactions as the transfer is connected to a large corporation rather than an individual's trust account and it therefore carries a lower risk. Local escrow agents typically charge 1% of the escrow value although in some cases a lesser fee can be negotiated for an easy transaction without staged payments.

It is widely recommended that a buyer inspects the property themselves or appoint a representative or professional to do the inspection on their behalf. Any discrepancies or problems should be alleviated before closing.

Powers of attorney

Powers of attorney must be signed by the grantor of the power and be proved by oath and affirmation by one witness. A full power of attorney requires two documents signed in front of a notary. First, one that states the basis and terms of the power of attorney and any parameters the appointed attorney must act within. The second document is a sworn statement supporting the validity of the power of attorney. Provision is made under the *Registration and Records Act* for the recording or registration of the power of attorney in the *Registry of Deeds* and records.

Financing

The primary source of real estate financing in St. Kitts and Nevis is typically from banks and money lending institutions such as Credit Unions and the *Foundation for National Development*. Most lending institutions require the following documents in order to process a loan application: employment letter, passport, driver's licence, bank reference, professional references, utility bill as proof of address, three to five years bank statements, executed agreement for sale, appraisal report on the subject property and security collateral.

As a foreigner, although possible, it is generally known to be difficult to obtain financing in St. Kitts and Nevis.

Purchase through a company

One may purchase real estate in the Federation through any entity, whether foreign, corporate, or not, as long as standard purchase conditions are met. Such conditions include those that typically affect foreigners and as such, these restrictions would also apply to foreign companies.

Those wishing to qualify for the citizenship program of St. Kitts and Nevis, by purchasing their selected and government approved real estate object through a corporate entity, must exclusively use a local company and further, the entity must not be classed as an exempt company for tax purposes. The government requires this to ensure ownership is not being transferred within the required minimum five year must-hold period imposed on citizenship investors. Furthermore, the main applicant of the citizenship application must technically be the sole owner of the shares. However, in practice multiple investors within the same company are successfully qualifying under the citizenship program when a real estate object is purchased at a value that would qualify all shareholders of the entity. Given of course each shareholder has and equal shareholding and all contributed the minimum required qualifying investment.

Warranty claims

Defects of a physical quality (referred to as patent defects) should be discovered by the purchaser as there is no obligation for the vendor to disclose these. The governing doctrine is *caveat emptor* (buyer beware). The conditions stipulated by the vendor that a property is free from defects would cause an action for breach of contract in the event the property is not free of defects.

As to legal defects of title there is an implied obligation that a seller would deliver a good marketable title to the property being sold.

31.4 New construction, rebuilding and renovation

Construction zones and construction permits

Construction in St. Kitts and Nevis is taking place throughout the islands as the citizenship program has recently sparked widespread development. The *Development Control and Planning Board* is the body that controls planning and construction in St. Kitts and proposals received by the planning board are primarily tourism related projects such as hotels or resorts, or single- or multi- family dwelling projects.

There is a *Building Code* that must be adhered to and all construction projects must pass through the control board. When in doubt, it is always best to acquire approval for all construction work to avoid costly adjustments or, in the worst case scenario, a court order to remove or destroy the work you have done. It is also important to note that there is no sewage system in St. Kitts or Nevis and so all planning should include septic tanks.

It is a pre-condition to every development or renovation of land that permission be sought by the *Department of Physical Planning.*

Architect's contract and building contracts

Professional architects and builders will submit general contracts for the design, producing working drawings and building for clients. Architects and builders would usually follow the Organization of Eastern Caribbean States (*OECS)* and the *St. Kitts and Nevis Building Code.* These codes provide guidance for site layout, electrical, structural and mechanical standards. The *St. Kitts and Nevis Institute of Architects* has been established to regulate and govern the practice of architecture in the Federation. There is a *Building Contractors Association* that provides continuous training and education to workers in the field.

Owners are free to utilize architects from any part of the world when building in St. Kitts and Nevis although it is wise to partner, at least jointly, with a local expert to ensure important considerations in terms of the build location and climate are taken into account throughout the design stage. For instance, certain materials should not be used near the ocean where salt corrosion is high or materials that can be quickly damaged by the tropical heat, roofs should all be bolted down, and all homes must be built to hurricane standards. Such specifics may not be understood by an architect without experience in the Caribbean.

Furthermore, many of the major developments impose architectural guidelines and rules that must be adhered to. This responsibility should be imposed on the contracted architect.

In all cases, a building contract will include staged payments that are connected to the building schedule and key milestones. When agreeing to the building schedule and milestones that trigger payments, it is crucial to ensure the developer does not take more than needed to build the property at an early stage of the build process. This would basically mean the building builder is taking their profit out early and may remove any leverage one would have over the contractor in order to complete the project if any difficulties arise.

Depending on the reputation of the builder and their financial stability a reasonable payment plan would reflect 20% on contract signing, 20% on completion of the foundation and ground floor slabs, 20% on completion of enclosing the property with roof and windows (sometimes called the core and shell), 20% on completion of interior plaster work, 10% on completion of the interior fittings and fixtures, and 10% on final completion and handover. However, even at completion, the contract should state payment will be held back until you have had enough time in the house to ensure all is perfect, and the developer has completed all outstanding work you have identified or any areas that need correcting or fixing. The moment the builder has all the money earned on the job, the job will become a lesser priority; it is thus important to ensure everything is done to a satisfactory level before any final payments are made.

Completion of construction and formalities

Prior to submitting a building permit application, both a *Land Usage Approval* and *Lot Approval* is required from the control board before an application for development is submitted. The Land Usage approval is basically an approval in principal that the control board provides on the project, and all projects must adhere to the building codes especially as St. Kitts and Nevis is technically in a hurricane zone. This initial process usually takes a few weeks, and once the building permit application is submitted, it may take another 30 days before receiving approval. This timeframe is determined greatly by the available resources and workload currently affecting the planning boards. Once a project is underway there may be random inspections by control officers to ensure the standards set by the control boards are being adhered to and the project is as approved. On completion an occupancy permit is also required and provided, again, by the local development and planning authority after their final inspection.

Deficiencies and warranty claims regarding new construction

Warranties are usually provided for in the construction contract. There are no laws which govern these. The parties to a construction contract must address the issue of defects and deficiencies in the contract by not only identifying possible defects but also making provision for possible remedies to such defects.

31.5 Rental and tenancy

Buy-to-let investment is common in St. Kitts and Nevis with rental properties widely available across both islands for both short- and long-term tenancy. Short-term tenants are typically tied to the tourism industry and the local long-term tenants are typically working professionals, medical students, and the general public. Many wealthy American families send their children to study in St. Kitts and Nevis due to the four successful universities on the islands; The University of Medicine and Health Sciences, The University of Veterinary Medicine, the University of Nursing, and the Medical University of the Americas. As the students and professors are typically quite affluent, they are primarily interested in renting or buying high-quality property, which together with a growing tourism industry, creates a strong and diverse rental market for such a small country.

Rental and lease contracts

Both residential and commercial leases in St. Kitts and Nevis are initiated once the prospective tenant identifies and selects a space available to lease. A lease agreement is to be made in writing and signed by the contracting parties only. Rental/lease agreements are not required to follow any government imposed standards however they should in principal always include all essential terms. Essential terms are considered a definition of the leased premises, details on the contracting parties, the terms surrounding rent and deposits, the commencement date and term of the lease, and all other material terms that can be identified as important to govern the relationship between the landlord and tenant. As there are no government policies or controls in place on such agreements, it is always recommended that a local lawyer (instructed with your best intentions in mind) review such agreements prior to binding yourselves to the terms.

Regulations on protection of tenants and rent control

There is no statutory regime established to protect tenants. Such protection exists mainly by virtue of the common law. Examples of the protections granted to tenants under the common law include the covenant for quiet enjoyment. There are a few exceptions however, where statutes reinforce common law principles created for the protection of tenants. An example can be found in the *Rent Restriction Act* where legislation affords some protection to tenants with regard to the amount of rent they may lawfully be charged. Tenants are also given some protection under the *Small Tenements Act* which provides the notice period which the landlord shall give tenants for repossession.

31.6 Succession and gifts

While there are succession laws in St. Kitts and Nevis, the beneficiaries are generally not taxed nor is there any succession taxes levied on the estate of a deceased person. There are no gift taxes levied in St. Kitts and Nevis.

Applicable law and jurisdiction

The *Wills Act (Cap. 84)* controls the disposal of immovable and movable property of a testator domiciled in the Federation at the time of death, when a legal will is in place. The *Intestates Estate Act (Cap. 36)* regulates the administration and distribution of estates when a person does not have a legally valid will. In neither act is there a tax imposed on the estate.

Fundamentals of the succession and donation laws of St. Kitts and Nevis

In the case of trusts, it is interesting to note that forced heirship does not exist in St. Kitts or Nevis and heirship rules in the settlor's or beneficiary's resident country cannot be legally forced.

31.7 Taxes and charges

The tax system on St. Kitts and Nevis is also financially interesting to those who wish to acquire real estate and/or become a legal resident. This is because income is not taxed and there are no wealth taxes either. From a tax perspective, the investment landscape is attractive and one can live very well on St. Kitts and Nevis.

One time taxes and charges on purchase and new constructions

Acquisition costs are payable when buying property and, depending on the seller, sometimes included in your purchase price. Accordingly, even if the charges are not visible, the total real estate acquisition costs range from approximately 6.2% of the purchase price to 13.2% unless the developer or seller has acquired a special stamp duty or tax exemption. These costs include real estate transfer taxes, the minimum legal transfer fee of 1% + 17% VAT, and the government assurance fund requirement of 0.2%.

Real estate transfer taxes

The government levies stamp duty of 5% of the property purchase price when condominiums are purchased, and 12% when land and detached or semi-detached properties are purchased. In many cases this stamp duty is paid by the developer or seller, or split 50/50 with the buyer and seller - although this is always negotiable.

Sales tax (value added tax)

With the *Value Added Tax* (VAT) *Act, 2010* a standard 17% VAT was established in St. Kitts and Nevis on 1 November 2010. VAT is not chargeable on real estate purchases and from a real estate perspective is only found on services relating to the purchase. This includes legal fees, local architects, valuations, or other 3rd party costs.

Real estate registration and notary charges

The preparation of plans, if required, cost approximately USD 500 depending on the size of the property and/or the land to be surveyed, and the closing lawyer must legally charge a conveyance fee of at least 1% of the purchase price + 17% VAT. Vendors are technically responsible for paying stamp duty on real estate although this is normally a point of negotiation and sometimes equally split between the buyer and seller.

At closing, before the government will issue a *Certificate of Title*, the purchasers of real estate must also pay a nominal registration fee of USD 2.68 and make a contribution to the national *Assurance Fund* equal to 0.2%. These are contributions to title assurance which is a legal requirement on St. Kitts and Nevis as defined in section 18 of the *Titles by Registration Act.*

If the real estate is exempted from an *Alien Land Holding License* (ALHL), on the island of St. Kitts purchasers are required to pay an exemption fee of USD 18.60. On the island of Nevis, there is no exemption fee for the ALHL but legal charges for the application will apply in most cases. Stamp duty and closing fees are typically included in the closing disbursements and invoiced by the closing attorney for payment to the *Comptroller of Inland Revenue.*

Recurring taxes and charges

St. Kitts and Nevis is widely known as a tax friendly country and this fact creates an attractive real estate market for investors. There are no high running taxes due other than the 0.2% land tax as described below, and if the property is rented, any rental income is tax-free for the owner. In the event of a sale, there is no capital gains tax to pay either.

Real estate tax

The *Property Tax Act of 2006* includes the legislation that outlines property tax in St. Kitts and Nevis. The *Comptroller of Inland Revenue* assesses the market value of each property and a set land tax is levied annually based on the class of property. The tax bands are as follows:

- 0.2% on residential
- 0.3% on commercial
- 0.3% on accommodation
- 0.0% on institutional
- 0.0% on agriculture

This tax was implemented in replacement of the 15% withholding taxes previously imposed on rental income exiting the country. The flat property tax of 0.2% applies to all residential properties in St. Kitts and Nevis and the government will typically invoice owners directly based on the address and contact details provided at time of the closing, and on the memorandum of transfer. It is therefore important to ensure your local representative or lawyer is aware of your current contact details or is properly authorized to pay such fees on your behalf from rental revenue.

Income tax

As mentioned above, the government previously levied a 15% withholding tax on the expatriation of rental profits from the country, if the property was rented. However any rental income is now tax-free for the owner and only the above property tax applies. Although there are no income taxes in St. Kitts and Nevis, in most cases it makes sense to maintain such proceeds within the country for local expenses or management or use on holidays.

Net wealth tax

St. Kitts and Nevis is proudly a tax friendly country and there are no wealth taxes of any kind in St. Kitts and Nevis.

Capital gains tax

St. Kitts and Nevis is an attractive investment destination due to the lack of capital gains taxes. In the event of a property sale, there is no capital gains tax payable.

Inheritance and gift taxes

No inheritance or gift taxes are applicable.

Other taxes and charges

The only other tax affecting the purchase of real estate in St. Kitts and Nevis is a stamp duty tax. Stamp duty is payable to the *Department of Inland Revenue* before the transfer of property title is processed, or simply due if the ownership of property is transferred to another person or entity.

The rate of stamp duty is typically 5% for the purchase or transfer of condominium or apartments, and 12% on the purchase of land and/or freestanding properties not classed as condominiums within the *Condominium Act*. Although this tax is frequently split between the buyer and seller (50/50), it is always a point of negotiation as it must be paid at the time of closing to complete a transaction. In the case of new-build developments or properties from developers, stamp duty is frequently included in the price although must still be considered at the time of resale. In some instances, developers have acquired special exemptions or concessions in relation to the selling stamp duty payable to Inland Revenue. Such exemptions typically benefit only the developer and are not passed on to the new owner if they were to re-sell a property.

Some may expect to avoid paying stamp duty on the re-sale by purchasing property through a company however, if the company's main purpose was to own property, the government recognizes this action as transferring ownership of the property and stamp duty is due. You are therefore unable to legally avoid this transfer tax in St. Kitts and Nevis by such practices. It would be understandably difficult for the government of St. Kitts to identify and tax the transfer of foreign shares, however this would still be considered a tax liable transfer if made aware. The government has full transparency on the transfer of local shares, and has full power to force payment of outstanding taxes on the new owner.

Import duties are very high in St. Kitts and Nevis and for example, importing a car without a tax exemption could incur over 100% of the value in various taxes. Therefore, in most cases it makes sense to purchase vehicles locally. Similar import duties also apply to the import of furniture and fittings, although if planning to reside in St. Kitts and Nevis one may be authorized to import such items duty-free under the *Movement of People Program*. *Customs Import Duties* are applicable according to the rates set out in the *Common External Tariff* of the *Caribbean Common Market*. The rates are applied based on the Cost, Insurance and Freight (CIF) and range from 0% to 45% with the majority of commodities attracting a rate of 25%.

Incorrect (lower) statement of sale price on the sales agreement

If the *Registrar of Titles* has reason to believe that the sum stated on the *Memorandum of Transfer* is not the true value of the property, they may try to agree on a new value with the person liable for payment of fees due to the *Assurance Fund*. If agreement cannot be made, then a Judge shall make a ruling after evidence to support the desired value has been presented by each party. As the *Assurance Fund* is only 0.2% it makes little sense to waste time making lower statements of sales price.

As stamp duty ranges from 5% - 12%, crafting a lower sale price into the sales contract may seem attractive although it is definitely illegal and not advisable. The pitfall from this practice is that the purchaser will face, on paper, an increased level of capital appreciation unless the next buyer also agrees to a lesser published price. At resale this normally risks a higher level of capital gains tax if the new purchaser does not agree. As there is no capital gains tax in St. Kitts and Nevis one may be tempted. That said, the problems that may arise from doing this far outweigh the potential benefits. Persons agreeing are likely to be of unsound character and you are then left facing various risks. Transferring money to someone without a contract or paper trail means there is no basis of refute in the event of a disagreement, or perhaps additional funds after closing will never arrive. Overall, the practice in St. Kitts, and elsewhere in the world, should always be avoided.

International taxation

St. Kitts and Nevis does not impose any tax on income derived from international sources. This applies to both local residents and citizens living abroad.

31.8 Immigration law and tax residence

The immigration law of St. Kitts and Nevis is unique due to the *St. Kitts and Nevis Constitution and Citizenship Act of 1983* which allows foreign investors to acquire Kittitian citizenship. This makes it the oldest existing Citizenship-by-Investment program in the world. Other countries such as Belize and Ireland used to have similar investment programs which allowed suitably qualified investors to acquire local citizenship however, they have all ceased, perhaps due to poor management or corruption. The Citizenship-by-Investment program of St. Kitts and Nevis is one of a few in the world, along with Malta and Cyprus, for example, to legally permit the acquisition of citizenship and consequently the right to carry a passport without a prior need to take up physical residence in the country.

This Act allows investors of sound character, who must currently pass both professional third-party due diligence and the local government's due diligence, to become a full citizen of St. Kitts and Nevis. The only difference between a citizenship investor and a born Kittitian is that their right to vote locally and hold a position of power in the local government is restricted. All citizens of St. Kitts and Nevis may pass their citizenship down by two generations.

Citizens of St. Kitts and Nevis are authorised to acquire and hold a blue Caribbean Community (CARICOM), St. Kitts and Nevis passport which at time of publishing allows visa-free travel to over 132 countries, including Canada, Singapore, Switzerland, the UK and much of Europe, and many others. This program is significantly attractive to wealthy and established individuals, international businesspeople that frequently travel worldwide, and people who wish to have a guaranteed and safe second home and nationality for their family in the event of unrest or political change in their current place of primary residence. Citizenship secures this right to move to one's second home at any time and set up one's main residence there. This is open to every citizen at any time, without the need for a visa or residence permit of any kind. In an unsettling, ever-changing world, acquiring an alternative citizenship is a wise decision and an investment for the future.

Acquisition of Citizenship-by-Investment

As of 2012 when the most recent regulation changes came into effect, in order to apply for citizenship as part of a real estate transaction, an investor must invest a minimum of USD 400,000 in citizenship approved real estate. This new citizenship legislation also outlines that a citizenship approved property purchased after 17 January 2012 may be eligible for a subsequent citizenship application once the five year must-hold period has passed. Prior years there was no possibility to re-sell property used for the citizenship program to anouther citizenship investors. Therefore the liquidity of citizenship investments, compared to previous years, has greatly improved. Since the inception of the real estate investment options, the minimum real estate investment has increased by approximately USD 50,000 every two years.

Due to more competition, from countries now offering similar citizenship-by-investment programs this trend may not continue.

A house or condominium unit must be acquired from a development which holds suitable written approval from the government. Most projects of interest to foreign investors have this approval, although only a few projects appear really attractive and make a corresponding investment advisable. One must expect to spend at least around USD 500,000 for a good quality-built apartment in a well-tended residential development. Like everywhere, prices have no upper limit, and if one is prepared to spend several million USD, a luxury property containing all conceivable comforts and conveniences may be acquired next to a golf course or by the beach.

Apart from the property investments, various other formalities still have to be satisfied. In addition to comprehensive application forms, other documents such as birth certificates, authenticated copies of identity papers, bank references and other letters of recommendation will be required. Also necessary is a police clearance certificate showing applicants have no criminal records in their home country or any other countries where they have established residence.

Government fees of USD 50,000 are payable for the main applicant as well as USD 25,000 for the spouse and each child under 18 included in the application. For children between the age of 18 and 25 who are still fully dependent on the main applicant, meeting set criteria such as being unmarried and attending full time education, the fee is USD 50,000 under both the real estate program and the *Sugar Industry Diversification Fund* (SIDF) program. The documents of all applicants are scrutinized carefully, a procedure known as due diligence, the cost of which is another USD 7,500 for the main applicant and USD 4,000 for each dependent 16 years of age or older. In addition to some minor charges (such as for issuing the bio-metric passports), there is also a fee for preparing, submitting and processing the citizenship application. The costs associated with acquiring the property depend greatly on the location of the property and the seller's willingness to cover the related purchase costs.

One may acquire citizenship through the real estate investment or a government donation/payment and both can be fully processed within four months. However, the only way to recover your investment and make a financial gain is through the real estate investment option. The SIDF program is based on a contribution into a national development fund, and you cannot recover any of these funds. The typical gross cost for a family of two to acquire citizenship under the SIDF program is USD 357,210 (USD 300,000 contribution and USD 57,210 in processing and government fees). The same family would only require an additional USD 175,000 to follow the real estate investment route (USD 532,210 in total, broken down to USD 400,000 personal property investment and USD 132,210 in processing and government fees). This extra USD 175,000 enables you to acquire a property valued at USD 400,000 rather than making a donation. Some of the best options available also reduce risk by providing guaranteed leasebacks on rental revenue on the full property value during this period.

Aside from the financial benefits you acquire through the real estate option, owning a residence in the country of your citizenship provides further advantages. Tax residence in a tax friendly country is extremely helpful for optimizing your tax structures. Having a residence in St. Kitts and Nevis with a mailing address and utility bills in your name provides the needed tools to enhance your tax planning capabilities, and provides the highest level of privacy with your international business and banking affairs.

There are over 50 citizenship approved projects in St. Kitts and Nevis, and great care in the selection is advised and professional advice is strongly recommended. Many of these projects were designed and built when the minimum qualifying investment level was USD 200,000, and such projects with leftover stock may now be selling for USD 400,000 to qualify the purchaser for the citizenship program. Further to this, these approved projects are at various stages of planning or construction and a wide range of financial situations exist due to the high number of developers wishing to leverage the citizenship program. Professionals such as Henley & Partners operate within this industry and can greatly assist anyone through this process.

A few of the larger developments are of particular interest to citizenship investors and include the Four Seasons Resort Nevis, Kittitian Hill on St. Kitts, and Christophe Harbour on St. Kitts.

The Four Seasons Resort Nevis is the only fully operating 5-star resort on Nevis and has been in existence for over 20 years. With the high quality construction, design and experience standards imposed by the Four Seasons brand, citizenship applicants frequently choose this project as their qualifying investment. The resort offers all the expected amenities of a 5-star resort, including an 18-hole golf course, a destination spa rated one of the best in the Caribbean, the finest sand beach and beach club on the island, several restaurants, tennis courts, games rooms and various daily activities for children. The resort provides private boats and drivers to transport guests from the main airport to the docks at the Resort, and there is a local airport on Nevis for private jets only 10 minutes away. Their villa and estate homes are all approved for the citizenship program and are surrounded by far-reaching views of the Caribbean Sea, the island of St. Kitts, the Four Seasons golf course, and a variety of private beautifully landscaped gardens. The Four Seasons Resort Estates makes every aspect of ownership worry-free, from design and development to year-round maintenance. The Four Seasons Villas are best suited for those who want a private residence without having to wait for amenities, or to live in a resort without visible ongoing construction. The properties available for sale are either custom home sites for personalized residences, or the "Villas at Pinney's Beach" that can be purchased through a fractional program for under USD 500,000. Qualifying investment options at this resort range from just under USD 500,000 to over USD 20 million.

Kittitian Hill soft-opened in 2014, is one of the newest locations on the island of St. Kitts and has several more phases of construction to be completed. Kittitian Hill is a hillside master-planned sustainable resort and community with views of the Caribbean Sea, and the islands of

St. Eustatius, Saba, St. Martin and St. Barths. Like the Four Seasons, Kittitian Hill will have an 18-hole golf course, destination spa, and they are also developing a village that includes commercial space, dining and entertainment options, duty free shops, a cinema, library and amphitheater. The real estate at Kittitian Hill includes detached cottages, village suites and luxury private villas. The architectural team is Bensley Design who focused on using the strong vernacular style of traditional Kittitian architecture. They have qualifying fractional investments from USD 400,000 up to around USD 4 million.

Christophe Harbour is the largest master-planned development on St. Kitts and will be in the construction phase for several more years. The area will provide luxury living, a super yacht marina, villages, 18 hole golf course, spa, club houses, and various fine dining restaurants. Christophe Harbour has approval from the government for 2000 residential dwelling units, primarily family homes and villas stretched across their 13 miles of coastline and seven distinct beaches and bays. They are primarily offering home sites (land) for people wishing to construct their own homes and, when investing in such, to qualify under the citizenship program you must invest at least USD 700,000. Land is available from around USD 500,000 to USD 2.7 million; construction companies can be engaged to build a home or you may hold onto the land for five years.

There are many investment options in St. Kitts and Nevis and the risk/reward ratio should be understood for each option before a decision is made. It is important to speak to the relevant experts and make an informed decision based on your expectations and requirements.

Entry, residence and settlement of foreigners

Foreign nationals and property owners have several options available for establishing the right to spend time in St. Kitts and Nevis. Foreign nationals may be granted the status of resident if he/ she can satisfy certain requirements specified in the *Immigration Act of 2002* and namely one of the following:

- Registration as a citizen: the easiest way to obtain full permanent residence in St. Kitts and Nevis is via the citizenship program. A citizen of St. Kitts and Nevis has the right to enter the country at any time
- Registration as a permanent resident: simply purchasing real estate does not automatically provide one the right to residence. However, property owners who desire to reside in retirement or who have resided in the country for over seven years may apply to the Minister responsible for immigration for permanent residence status which enables them to stay on the islands indefinitely
- Registration as a resident by virtue of employment: in this case the person may obtain work permit residence status
- A temporary residence status may be granted to spouses and minors of work permit holders
- An annual residence status may be granted to minors of permanent residents and persons who have become citizens

Outside of citizenship by investment, there are other methods of acquiring citizenship such as citizenship by marriage, citizenship by birth, citizenship by descent or citizenship by residence in the country for over 14 years. The latter applies to commonwealth citizens who own substantial assets or property in the country.

Tax residence

The tax system in St. Kitts and Nevis is financially interesting to those who wish to become resident there. This is because income is not taxed and there are no wealth taxes either.

International double taxation for residents of St. Kitts and Nevis

St. Kitts and Nevis imposes no tax on local or worldwide incomes of residents of St. Kitts. Local companies are taxed on their business performed locally, and *International Business Companies* are frequently used to conduct tax free business elsewhere in the world.

31.9 Checklist: Real estate in St. Kitts and Nevis

- Locate a knowledgeable professional to help educate you on the real estate market
- Decide between owning property on Nevis or St. Kitts
- Search and identify a desired property and identify:
    - Rental management possibilities and costs
    - Homecare possibilities and costs
    - Upkeep costs, insurance, and total holding cost of the property
    - Rental revenue possibilities and revenue potential if applicable
- Negotiate with the seller and agree on terms including:
    - Who pays the stamp duty?
    - Who pays the legal fees?
    - Who pays the other closing fees?
    - Is the furniture or any other movable property at the house included?
- Instruct a local lawyer knowledgeable in real estate matters
- Have the lawyer verify that the title is free and clear of title
- If applicable, have your lawyer confirm that the property is eligible for the citizenship program
- Have the lawyer draft a purchase agreement or vet the seller's agreement with your best interests in mind
- Ensure the transfer of property is done with as little risk (such as the use of escrow accounts)
- Sign paperwork
- Pay closing fees and transfer funds for closing
- Instruct lawyer to proceed with the transfer
- Acquire the keys

31.10 Bibliography

2012 The World Bank Group, Doing Business, Measuring Business Regulations in St. Kitts and Nevis, *http://www.doingbusiness.org/data/exploreeconomies/st-kitts-and-nevis/*

2014 Henley Estates St. Kitts and Nevis Market Intelligence

http://www.henleyestates.com/

2014 Annual Tourist Data, St. Kitts Statistics Office, Nevis Statistics Office, ECCB

2012 Article: "Best Island in the World" by US News" *http://travel.usnews.com/Rankings/Best_Islands_in_the_World/*

The top 10 destinations "where the best place to buy is now" by Robb Report, November 2008

St. Kitts Investment Promotions Agency, St. Christopher and Nevis *http://www.stkittsipa.org*

32
Switzerland

Switzerland
Schweizerische Eidgenossenschaft
Confédération suisse
Confederazione Svizzera
Confederaziun svizra

by

Christian H. Kälin

Henley & Partners Switzerland AG
Klosbachstrasse 110
8024 Zurich
Switzerland

Telephone: +41 44 266 22 22
Facsimile: +41 44 266 22 23

christian.kalin@henleyglobal.com
henleyglobal.com

Christian H. Kalin is an internationally well-known immigration and citizenship law specialist and the Group Chairman of Henley & Partners. He advises key clients as well as governments in those areas, is a frequent writer and speaker on these issues and is regularly quoted in the international media. He is the author of the Global Residence & Citizenship Handbook, editor and co-author of the Switzerland Business & Investment Handbook as well as numerous other publications.

After completing Zurich Business School and his training at a Swiss private bank, he lived and studied in several countries before graduating from the University of Zurich with a cum laude Masters degree in law. He is a member of the Governing Board of the Investment Migration Council.

32.1 Introduction

Switzerland, officially known as the Swiss Confederation, is a federal republic rooted in a long tradition. It comprises 26 cantons which are considered as sovereign (autonomous, politically independent) entities within the framework of the federal constitution. The approximately 2,700 Swiss communes also enjoy relatively broad autonomy. Although many branches of law are now treated uniformly throughout the country, there nevertheless remain many important domains which are subject to differing regulations between the cantons. This applies particularly to taxation, but also to other areas, so that in many cases there are several possible answers to a question about the legal situation prevailing in Switzerland.

In contrast, private law is laid down uniformly at federal level. It is of central importance to our concerns and is enshrined principally in two legal codes: the law relating to real estate is laid down in the *Swiss Civil Code* (German *Schweizerisches Zivilgesetzbuch, ZGB*, and in French *Code Civil Suisse*, CC), and the private-law regulations affecting real estate transactions are comprised in the body of *Swiss Code of Obligations* (in German *Schweizerisches Obligationenrecht*, OR, and in French *Code des Obligations*, CO). Together, these two legal codes contain the codified private law of Switzerland.

Switzerland has attracted foreign buyers of real estate for many years, not least because of its exceptional political and economic stability. The Swiss themselves, however, are a nation of tenants. Compared with other western countries, Switzerland has a very low rate of owner-occupation, only about 35%. Attempts to explain this circumstance have often pointed to the high cost of residential property in Switzerland. Real estate is generally regarded as being expensive, particularly because the country is densely populated so that little land is available, thus causing prices to rise. In reality, there is enough building land available but it is distributed very unevenly throughout the country. This situation is also confirmed by the fact that the rate of owner-occupation varies so greatly between the cantons. Relatively high prices (and low rates of owner-occupation) are found in and around the cities of Basel,

Zurich and Geneva, but many regions have enough reserves of building land which is often quite suitable and even attractively priced.

The immigration laws relating to citizens of the EU allow every financially independent holder of an EU passport to settle in Switzerland. Once resident here, EU citizens have the right to acquire property throughout Switzerland virtually without restriction.

32.2 Real estate ownership

In Switzerland, property is guaranteed by the *Federal Constitution*, whose Article 26 (1) states simply and unambiguously: "Private property is guaranteed".

Property law and thus the various types of property are regulated by the *Civil Code* (CC). The CC splits property rights up into two categories: firstly that of the comprehensive ownership right, and secondly that of restricted property rights (easements, usufruct and other servitudes, charges, liens and mortgages).

Different forms and types of ownership

Sole ownership

Real estate ownership refers to particular pieces of real estate, the independent and permanent rights recorded in the Land Register, as well as any mines and co-ownership shares relating to particular pieces of real estate.

The (sole) owner of a piece of real estate has the most comprehensive power of disposal and legal control over it which is possible within the scope of the prevailing legal and factual limits.

Co-ownership

A distinction is made between two types of collective ownership, namely co-ownership and joint ownership. Co-ownership is the normal case of collective ownership and is presumed unless otherwise established and in cases of doubt.

A co-ownership share in a piece of real estate is treated like a property, and co-ownership shares may be independently sold, mortgaged, or distrained (seized) by creditors. In contrast to joint ownership, co-ownership implies that the entire property is divided up into portions (quotas). Each co-owner possesses the rights and obligations of an owner with respect to his portion, which is correspondingly recorded in the Land Register.

Joint ownership / joint tenancy

Joint ownership presupposes one of the following legal relationships: community of property between spouses, community of property within a family as defined in Article 336 et seq. of the CC (*Gemeinderschaft, indivision)* or an ordinary partnership *(einfache Gesellschaft, société simple)*, general partnership *(Kollektivgesellschaft, société en nom collectif)* or limited partnership *(Kommanditgesellschaft, société en commandite)*. An individual joint owner has no independent right to the joint property and its disposal invariably requires the agreement of all joint owners. The individual share of a joint owner cannot be recorded in the Land Register.

Condominium ownership

Condominium ownership *(Stockwerkeigentum, propriété par étages)* represents a particular kind of co-ownership. In principle, the regulations relating to co-ownership also apply in this case unless any special legal stipulations pertaining to condominium rights take precedence over them. Every condominium owner has a special right to make exclusive use of specific parts of a building. In addition to the use of the premises, this in particular includes their internal fixtures and fittings. This special right may apply to entire stories or parts of them; the latter must comprise self-contained apartments or areas with their own access as well as separate arrangements for garages, cellar compartments, hobby areas etc. Ownership of a condominium is recorded by entry in the land register. The co-ownership shares designated as condominium ownership are listed on separate pages of the Land Register whereas the page for the entire property remains unchanged. In addition to describing the parts of the building, which must be precisely delimited and to which special rights apply, the instrument of establishment (condominium deed) must also contain the corresponding value quotas which define the extent of the entitlement of each condominium owner in the overall property. These value quotas form the basis for weighing the voting powers of the individual condominium owners at the condominium owners' meeting as well as for apportioning the communal expenditures for the administration and maintenance of the property. Each condominium owner is in principle free to sell his share. However, the instrument of establishment (condominium deed) or later agreements often include a preemption right in favor of the other condominium owners.

Right to build

The right to build *(Baurecht, droit de superficie)* represents an easement that gives a person the right to erect or retain possession of a building on a piece of land which he/she does not own. Such right to build is, unlike otherwise agreed, transferable and may be inherited, and can, as long as it is defined as an independent and permanent right (i.e. valid for at least 30 years), be recorded as a property in the Land Register. In the case of such a right to build, the ownership of the completed building remains with the person entitled to the right to build, i.e. ownership of the land and the buildings upon it are separate. An independent building right can be set up for a maximum period of 100 years. Also, the contract establishing an independent and permanent building right must be publicly authenticated to be valid. As a rule, payment of building-right interest is agreed and the land owner receives a lien to the building right to secure his claim.

Since 1 January 2004 it is also possible to establish an easement that gives a person the right to plant and retain possession of plants on a piece of land which he/she does not own *(Pflanzendienstbarkeit, plantations)*, similar to the right to build.

Timesharing (timeshares)

Swiss law does not actually allow ownership of property to be divided up into various periods of use calculated over the year. However, various arrangements to this effect in contractual and company law are possible. Thus participation in a company (for instance in the form of shares) or membership of an association may be acquired, and these in turn imply the utilization of property owned by the company or association.

In contrast to the EU, Switzerland makes no specific legal stipulations relating to timesharing. Thus purchasers of timeshares have no right of revocation after conclusion of an agreement. Swiss law offers only limited ways of withdrawing from a timesharing agreement despite the fact that this has far-reaching financial consequences for the purchaser. However, the Swiss Government is now planning to introduce regulations in line with the EU's timesharing directive.

Easements, charges, covenants, liens and mortgages

Easements, servitudes, usufruct, charges, liens and mortgages form what are known as restricted property rights. To be validly erected, they need to be entered in the Land Register. In contrast to the comprehensive property right of ownership, these imply only limited control over a property. Restricted property rights limit ownership to the encumbered property and to this extent take precedence over the property rights of the owner. If restricted property rights conflict with one another, then – with a number of legal exceptions – priority on the basis of seniority applies, i.e. a right established earlier has precedence over one established later. This arrangement is also associated with the principle of the precedence of easements, i.e. if a piece of land encumbered with an easement is mortgaged, the easement is included in the mortgage. Conversely, an existing lien has precedence over a later established easement, license or restrictive covenant. However, precedence of rights may be freely agreed when they are established; and for liens and mortgages there are even legal provisions for a corresponding setting of priorities.

Usufruct

Usufruct *(Nutzniessung, usufruit)* gives its beneficiaries the full right to possess and use a property (or part of a property) which they do not own. It represents a personal easement, i.e. it depends on the beneficiary and ends at the death of natural persons and after, at most, 100 years if the beneficiary is a legal person. Accordingly, usufruct may not be transferred to another person, although its exercise may under certain circumstances be granted to someone else. The beneficiary is responsible for the administration of the property, but the beneficiary may also let the property and retain the proceeds of the rental (in contrast to the right of residence). However, the beneficiary must undertake to treat the property with due care and is liable to compensate the owner for any damages. Usufruct of property requires an entry in the land register. If usufruct of a property is set up based on a contract, this contract must be publicly authenticated.

Right of residence

By analogy, the same conditions apply to rights of residence *(Wohnrecht, droit d'habitation)* as to usufruct. However, in contrast to the latter, the right of residence is restricted exclusively to dwelling at no cost. Their beneficiary may not let the apartment or house. If the dwelling right has been arranged by contract, public authentication and entry in the land register are also required. However, a dwelling right may neither be transferred, seized nor inherited, and can be drawn up exclusively in favor of an individual person.

Right to build

The right to build represents an easement which gives someone the right to erect or retain possession of a building on a piece of land which he/she does not own. As a building right also represents a kind of property ownership, it has already been discussed above.

Easements on property / servitudes

Whereas personal easements *(Personaldienstbarkeiten, servitudes personelles)* such as usufruct and rights of residence benefit a specific person, easements on property *(Grunddienstbarkeiten, servitudes foncières)* involve an encumbered and an entitled property. The respective owner of the encumbered property must tolerate certain interferences by the respective owner of the entitled property (such as right of way or right of passage) or restrict the exercise of his ownership right in a certain way (e.g. not build higher than one storey). Also, the owner of the encumbered property can only be obligated to refrain from taking action or to exercise tolerance, but not to take action on his own account. However, the CC does make provision for an easement on property to involve the obligation to take action, but only as an ancillary content, such as the obligation to maintain installations which serve the exercise of the easement or may otherwise be necessary. A written contract is sufficient to establish easements on property; public authentication is not required. However, the establishment of an easement on property also requires its entry in the Land Register.

Real estate charges

In contrast to an easement, a real estate charge *(Grundlast, charge foncière)* obligates the owner of the property to take action. However, the owner is not personally liable to perform, as liability is restricted to the relevant property. A real estate charge is a kind of half-way house between an easement on property and a lien or real estate security interest. As long as the services associated with the real estate charge are performed, it acts much like an easement, but if the services fail to be performed, the property becomes liable in the same way as for a real estate security interest. A special feature of real estate charges in Switzerland is that they can be redeemed, and the debtor is in any case bound to a real estate charge for a maximum of 30 years. To establish a real estate charge by contract, public authentication and entry in the land register are required.

Other easements

Article 781 of the CC defines a category of easement known as "other easements" which are positioned somewhere between personal easements and easements on property. For every easement which can be established as an easement on property, it is also possible to establish a personal easement according to Article 781 of the CC. However, easements of this kind do not represent an entitlement for the respective owner of the property but for a specific person and can as a rule be neither inherited nor transferred.

Liens and mortgages (real estate security interests)

Liens and mortgages (real estate security interests, *Grundpfandrechte, gages immobilières*) are used to secure claims and to mobilize the value of a property. In Switzerland real estate security interests can be established in the form of a simple mortgage *(Grundpfandverschreibung, hypothèque)*, a mortgage note *(Schuldbrief, cédule hypothécaire)*, as well as in the form of a real estate bond *(Gült, lettre de rente)* which is however virtually obsolete. All liens result from the conclusion of a publicly notarized agreement and entry in the Land Register. In the case of both the simple mortgage and the mortgage note, the debtor is personally liable.

The simple mortgage is for securing any kind of debts. Although the debtor is also personally liable in the case of a *Schuldbrief*, this most widely used debenture deed is a security which may also be used to mobilize the value of the property. A debenture deed may be transferred, ceded or mortgaged outside the Land Register in accordance with the law on securities. The creation and continued existence of a debenture deed is independent of the secured claim.

The claim secured by a lien must be exactly defined in its amount and recorded accordingly in the Land Register. The lien covers the entire property with all its parts and belongings. It is clearly apparent from the Land Register whether any liens or mortgages exist on the property and how high these may be. If the claim is for a specific sum, this must be entered and the security is then liable for the capital claim as well as for up to three due annual interest payments, collection costs and any default interest (known as the capital mortgage). A simple mortgage allows a claim to be secured even if its amount is not exactly defined. In such cases, the land register merely specifies a maximum amount for the demand, so that the liability cannot exceed this figure (known as a maximum mortgage).

Protection of ownership, proof of ownership and registration

The *Swiss Federal Land Register* (Article 942 of the CC*)* registers the existence and extent of ownership of private rights to real estate. Although it is called a *Federal Land Registry*, it is actually managed by the cantons. There is no centrally managed property register for the whole of Switzerland. The Land Register comprises a journal, a general register, a description as well as plans, supporting documentation and auxiliary registers. In addition, various types of land register are current in Switzerland. In addition to the *Swiss Federal Land Register* (managed by the cantons), cantonal Land Registries continue to exist, although these lack the full legal force of the federal register in some respects.

The federal government exercises general supervision over the land registry system via the *Swiss Office for Land-Register and Land Law (Eidgenössisches Amt für Grundbuch- und Bodenrecht)*. However, the cantons are responsible for setting up the land registry offices, defining the administrative districts, appointing and remunerating the officials as well as assuring cantonal supervision. They manage the Land Registers and are liable for all damages resulting from defects in this respect. The Land Registers in most cantons are now completely or or at least partially computerized.

Swiss Land Registers refer to individual properties. The properties entered in the Land Register include real estate, independent and permanent property rights, as well as any mines and co-ownership shares inclusive of condominium units. The owners of the properties are identified by means of an auxiliary register (or list) which is organized by municipality or land-register districts. As a rule, the entries in the Land Register are made by means of a written declaration by the owner of the relevant property (submission of registration). They are based on deeds (purchase, donation, easement-establishment and estate-division contracts) as well as on agreements and approvals. These deeds are kept by the land registry office as evidential records.

Anyone is entitled to inspect the land register without any special authorization. Those who credibly assert a relevant interest may inspect additional data forming part of the land register or obtain an extract of this data. The correctness of the entries in the land registry is presumed by law. The plea of being unaware of an entry in the land registry has no legal validity.

As a rule, an entry in the land registry is subject to the following requirements:

1. A valid sale, donation or exchange agreement
2. The seller or donor must be entered in the land registry as an owner
3. The seller or donor must be authorized to dispose of the relevant objects
4. The seller or donor must agree to the entry of the new owner in the land registry

The law relating to land registers is not fully covered by the CC. Supplementary regulations are found in the directives of the federal authorities, especially in the land registry *Ordinance of February 22, 1910 (Grundbuchverordnung, l'ordonnance sur le registre foncier)* as well as in official decisions of the cantons.

32.3 Purchase and sale of real estate

The sales agreement

Sales agreements, provisional agreements as well as agreements on purchase and repurchase rights which refer to real estate always require public authentication. The same applies to any changes in such agreements. Noncompliance with these stringent formal requirements renders the relevant agreement invalid. For the purchase of real estate, this means that neither the seller nor the buyer is bound by a written agreement unless it has been drawn up in the appropriate form by a public notary.

Swiss law makes a distinction between the contractual act creating an obligation and the actual transfer of ownership. The act of creating an obligation to ownership transfer and the actual transfer may take place concurrently or separately. However, the transfer of ownership depends on the existence of an effective act of disposal. This is known as the causality principle. In Switzerland (unlike, for instance, in Germany), this causality applies even after a disposal act has been concluded, and a defective or even invalid act creating an obligation is not remedied by an entry in the land register. This means that in such a case the Land Register can be subsequently corrected by a request for rectifying the Land Register. However, this does not exclude bona fide acquisition by an unauthorized party. The principle of the irrebuttable presumption of the accuracy of the contents of the Land Register means that a bona fide third party who acquires a real right on the basis of an entry in the Land Register can assume the correctness of the Land Register and that his acquisition can no longer be contested.

The conclusion of the sales agreement does not yet make the buyer an owner. The actual transfer of ownership only takes place when the seller has submitted his application to make an entry to the Land Register or when the new owner has been entered in the Land Register. When the contract has been fulfilled, the buyer pays the purchase price and the seller procures the property for the buyer by registering the entry in the Land Register. Ownership is transferred to the buyer only when the entry is made in the Land Register. In most cases, all rights and obligations as well as benefits and risks are transferred simultaneously with the entry in the Land Register. This must be noted particularly when acquiring real estate on the basis of a separate works contract.

Restrictions on sale and acquisition

Restrictions under family law and the matrimonial property regime

Before we can examine any existing restrictions of sale or acquisition on the basis of the matrimonial property regime, it must be clarified which property regime actually applies. This question is regulated by international private law (IPL). There are no state treaties which would have precedence in these matters. In Switzerland, the spouses may choose between the law of the country in which they have their matrimonial domicile and the law of the country whose citizenship one of them possesses. If one or both of them possess multiple citizenship, the law of one of the countries involved may be freely chosen. Although this choice of law may be made by a simple written statement, it is usually made in the form of a marriage contract. A choice of law may be made at any time and changed again at any time.

If no national law is chosen, the property regime is subject to the law of the country in which the spouses have their matrimonial domicile. If the spouses have never possessed simultaneous domicile in the same country, their common citizenship *(lex patriae)* shall be applied. Their common citizenship must already have existed before their marriage and not only as a result of it. If they never had a matrimonial domicile nor possess a common citizenship, then the matrimonial property regime according to Swiss law applies.

In Switzerland, most spouses have not concluded a marriage contract and are consequently subject to the legal property regime, which is the participation in acquisitions during marriage *(Errungenschaftsbeteiligung, participation aux acquêts)*. This property regime means that the spouses personally administer and use their respective assets during the marriage. When a marriage ends, a mutual settlement takes place on the basis of the prevailing property regime. In contrast to their own property, in particular assets which belong to a spouse at the beginning of the property regime or which are later acquired by him/her free of charge, for instance by inheritance, the mutual settlement includes the respective earnings from employment of the spouses, revenues from their respective estates, benefits from personal assurance schemes and similar assets. In principle, each spouse obtains half of the other's assets, corrected by specific deductions and additions.

The separation of property which applies both as a result of a marriage contract and, under certain circumstances, on the basis of the law, implies that each spouse administers and uses his/her assets him/herself without in any way requiring the consent of the other spouse. In principle, complete separation of their respective assets exists.

In cases of community of property, which is the only property regime that may be established solely by contract, almost all assets are held in joint ownership and administered jointly by both spouses. Apart from its regular administration, the spouses can obligate their common household or dispose of their joint matrimonial property only with the consent of the other spouse.

An important restraint on disposal concerns legal transactions relating to the matrimonial home. A spouse may perform such transactions only with the express consent of the other spouse, even if the disposing spouse is the sole owner of the family dwelling. The sale of agricultural land which is administered jointly by both spouses also requires the consent of both spouses.

Options and rights of pre-emption

Various legal rights of pre-emption must be considered. These may be neither inherited nor ceded and have precedence over contractual option pre-emption rights. A legal right of pre-emption applies mutually to co-owners, just as between the holder of a right to build and the respective landowner. In the case of agricultural land, additional pre-emption rights exist in favor of the relatives of the seller as well as in favor of the leaseholder.

Options to buy or pre-emption rights *(Vorkaufsrecht, droit de préemption)* or re-purchase rights *(Rückkaufsrecht, droit de réméré)* can be established contractually for a maximum duration of 25 years. The relevant contract must be officially authenticated, and a right of pre-emption can be noted in the Land Register. The note gives it a specific force with respect to any rights which may be subsequently acquired.

Agricultural real estate

A number of special laws and regulations apply to agricultural land in Switzerland. These are largely laid down in the *Federal Law on Rights to Agricultural Land (Bundesgesetz über das bäuerliche Bodenrecht, loi fédérale sur le droit foncier rural).*

Restrictions regarding acquisition of real estate by foreigners

The acquisition of property by non-resident foreigners has been greatly restricted in Switzerland since the early 1960s. This group comprises natural persons who are not Swiss and do not possess a required residence title in Switzerland, as well as legal entities domiciled abroad or foreign-controlled legal entities domiciled in Switzerland. On the other hand, citizens of EU/EEA and EFTA member states holding a residence permit B or C in Switzerland, as well as non-EU/EEA resp. non-EFTA nationals holding a residence permit C have the same rights as Swiss citizens and are consequently eligible to conduct all real estate business without restrictions. The citizenship of the acquirer's spouse is immaterial.

After relevant measures had initially been taken by means of an urgent federal resolution, the *Federal Law on the Acquisition of Real Estate by Non-residents (Bundesgesetz über den Erwerb von Grundstücken durch Personen im Ausland, Loi fédérale sur l'acquisition d'immeubles par des personnes à l'étranger)*, known as *Lex Friedrich*, came into force in the 1980s. This law was then revised on 30 April 1997, with few, but significant changes (the revised version is known as *Lex Koller*).

In principle, the revised legislation also makes the acquisition of real estate by foreign nationals subject to approval, and the cantons continue to be responsible for enforcing the law. However, the revised law of 1997 broadened the definition of the circumstances for an exemption. A check must therefore be made before every entry in the Land

Register or corresponding act of disposition to determine whether an exempting circumstance is present or not in the particular case.

All commercial real estate, i.e. premises used for business purposes, can now be acquired without approval. These premises do not need to be managed by the acquirer of the property. This means that foreign nationals can now invest in purely commercial properties without restrictions. However, purely non-commercial properties (such as dwellings, private houses, city apartments, tenements etc.) continue to be subject to approval, and in practice this approval is usually not granted.

Currently only one residential project in a Swiss mountain resort has been granted a special, rare exemption from the *Lex Koller* law. Due to this unique exemption, foreign (non-Swiss resident) buyers are able to acquire and transfer residential property at that project without authorization until the end of 2030.

There are demarcation problems in mixed premises. Depending on zone assignment, it may be specified that business premises must include a certain proportion of residential accommodation. Commercial real estate subject to such residential-share rules may normally be acquired without approval.

Private apartments and houses that are used by their owners as their principal residence are no longer subject to approval. Specific rules apply for non-EU/EEA resp. non-EFTA nationals holding Swiss residence permit B, however. The restriction on net living area has been lifted, although the area of the property must not exceed 3000 m². Further, the acquisition must be made in their own name. If the foreign national relinquishes his Swiss domicile again, he/she may nevertheless retain the property.

Secondary residences may also be acquired without approval under certain conditions. A foreign national who is a citizen of an EU or EFTA member state and works in Switzerland as a cross-border employee can acquire a secondary residence in the region of his workplace without approval. He/she must live in the dwelling himself/herself and is not permitted to let it. Note here that for the time being, special rules apply for citizens of the new member states which joined the EU on 1 May 2004.

Secondary residences are otherwise subject to approval. A foreign non-resident may be granted approval to acquire a secondary residence in a location to which he/she has exceptionally close links worthy of being upheld. Somewhat more than half the cantons recognize this as a valid reason for granting approval.

In contrast, vacation homes are invariably liable to approval. A quota system is applied to them. Each canton is allocated a specific quota within whose framework approvals may be granted. In addition, vacation homes may be acquired only in places specifically designated by the cantons as tourist resorts. Quota allocation and approval practice vary widely between individual cantons as well as between different communes within a canton. Both cantons and communes are also authorized to introduce more extensive restrictions by law. So it may well be the case that a vacation home can be easily acquired in one commune whereas the neighboring commune imposes an absolute ban on further approvals. It is consequently important to clarify in detail exactly before every purchase and every down-payment whether an approval exists or will be granted for the property to be acquired.

Very important in this regard is also a new law, referred to as *Lex Weber*. In March 2012, the Swiss people approved by vote a federal initiative which proposed a limit of 20% of secondary residences per municipality. The initiative entered into force on 1 January 2013.

If a foreign national acquires Swiss real estate from another foreign national, this acquisition is subject to approval in exactly the same way as an acquisition from a Swiss national.

Apart from the acquisition of full ownership, the obligation to obtain approval also extends to all other rights which grant the acquirer ownership-like status, such as options and pre-emption rights, usufruct, the conclusion of long-term rental and leasehold agreements, unusual financial arrangements which place the (domestic) property acquirer in special dependence on the (foreign) creditor, etc. The legislation also expressly covers changes of economic (beneficial) ownership. Whenever real power of disposal is acquired over real estate, an acquisition (which may be liable to approval) exists. The determining factor is always the economically authorized person standing behind an acquisition, so that fiduciary relationships are not relevant and always looked through.

Violations of the Swiss acquisition restrictions result in various sanctions under civil, administrative and criminal law. In the first instance, a violation leads to invalidity in civil law, and in most cases to nullity of the legal transaction liable to approval. An approval based on false information is revoked, and sanctions under immigration law may also be imposed. Evasion of approval obligation, giving of false information and the disregard of obligations may in addition be punished with fines and prison sentences. Because of the comprehensive scope of application of the acquisition restrictions and the corresponding sanctions, evasive legal transactions are not possible in Switzerland. In cases of doubt it is always wise to submit details of a planned acquisition of real estate to the relevant approving authority.

Other restrictions on acquisition

If the seller is himself also a non-resident and is merely liable to (restricted) tax in Switzerland on the property in question, the buyer of a property is not entered in the Land Register until the tax authorities have confirmed that all taxes have been paid. A corresponding confirmation must therefore be requested from the seller.

Further important preconditions for buying real estate

Capacity and entitlement of the seller

In principle, every acquirer must check the capacity and entitlement of the seller and (presumed) owner. This is because a sales contract concluded with a party who lacks entitlement or the capacity to act or conclude contracts may be completely ineffective or contestable, depending on the situation and circumstances. In Switzerland, those who are of age and capable of forming judgments are considered to possess legal capacity. A person is of age at 18.

The seller's entitlement must be verified by means of a current extract from the land register, or by means of an extract from the commercial register and corresponding powers of attorney depending on the situation (property of a company, agency).

Third-party claims and unpaid taxes

Every buyer should comprehensively check any existing claims of third parties which may encumber the property. Various easements, licenses and restrictive covenants as well as liens can have considerable impact on the value and potential resale of the property.

If the seller has not paid tradesmen's bills in connection with the building project, the tradesmen may enter what are known as security interests of craftsmen and contractors or building tradesmen's lien *(Bauhandwerkerpfandrecht, hypothèques des artisans et des Entrepreneurs)* in the Land Register. They must do this within three months of completion of the work. For the new owner, this lien means that his real estate is liable for payment of the outstanding bills. This must be considered when acquiring a newly built house or apartment and proof must be requested from the seller that no bills are outstanding.

In addition, the real estate is liable for any real estate gains taxes not paid by the seller. The buyer must consequently secure himself in this regard. He may do this by a bank guarantee or by withholding a corresponding sum via a notary.

Provisions for protecting the environment, nature and cultural heritage

Environmental protection and contaminated land

Environmental protection and the problem of contaminated land have acquired increasing importance in Switzerland in recent years. Swiss environmental law stipulates that the cantons are responsible for cleaning up landfills and other contaminated land if these lead to damaging or annoying effects or a real danger exists that such effects may occur. The *Directive on Contaminated Land* which came into force in 1998 regulates the uniform treatment of such areas throughout Switzerland and ensures the required legal security. Accordingly, clean-up of contaminated land may be required by the authorities not only within the scope of a building project but at any time. As a rule, the costs must be borne by the respective owner. Corresponding checks must be made before every acquisition of a piece of land, as the possible presence of hazardous substances both below ground and in the building materials affects the value and resale options of the property and may even render it unsellable. It can also incur major costs.

Protection of nature and cultural heritage

As a rule, nature protection regulations do not affect correctly zoned real estate. Nevertheless, it makes good sense to clarify the prevailing situation. The website *umwelt-schweiz.ch* (of the *Swiss Agency for the Environment, Forests and Landscape SAEFL, Bundesamt für Umwelt, Wald und Landschaft BUWAL, Office Fédéral de l'environnement, des fôrets et du paysage OFEFP)* gives a good overview of the topic. It should also be noted that bodies such as nature protection and environmental organizations (e.g. *WWF, Greenpeace*) as well as the *Swiss Heritage Society* (*Schweizerischer Heimatschutz, Patrimoine Suisse*, see *heimatschutz.ch*) have the right to object or appeal against building projects. This may lead to unexpected obstacles in certain cases.

More significant are the restrictions on historical buildings subject to monument protection. The federal government, cantons and communes invest in preserving historical buildings, and the authorities keep a record of this cultural heritage (see *kultur-schweiz.admin.ch*). Such restrictions are noted in the Land Register and mean that no changes may be made without approval by the authorities. However, the authorities may also intervene in a not (yet) classified building which may be deemed worthy of protection in the event of a building or renovation project. Thus for example in the city of Zurich, an owner will often not find out whether and to what extent his/her building is considered worthy of preservation until he/she enquires about a reconstruction or other building matter. So care must be taken when buying a historical building which may be classified as a protected monument. When considering a building project, it is wise to consult the relevant authorities as well as interested bodies (such as the *Swiss Heritage Society*) in advance in order to avoid undesirable surprises.

The other side of monument and heritage protection is that owners of protected buildings may be eligible for government funding to cover the costs of renovation and similar work. The buildings to be supported by the federal government are selected in close coordination with the cantonal departments of monument preservation. These pass the relevant applications to the *Heritage Protection and Monument Preservation Section* of the *Swiss Cultural Office (Bundesamt für Kultur, Office Fédéral de la Culture).* The federal government supports not only buildings of national interest, but also monuments of regional importance. In addition to federal grants, cantonal and communal grants may also be available.

Access to relevant records and documents

Swiss Land Registers provide definitive information about ownership. The Land Register must therefore be consulted in all real estate transactions. In addition, the documents which were used by the former owner, the seller, as a basis for entering his property in the Land Register must also be consulted.

Whoever buys a share in a condominium must request copies of all relevant minutes and documents concerning the condominium owners association, and especially a copy of the minutes of the last general meeting, a list of expenditures and the name of the administrator. In particular, he/she must check whether the meeting has decided on any building works which have not yet been carried out or other larger expenditures.

Key points that a seller should consider

From the seller's viewpoint it is particularly important that the full purchase price is paid in full or secured before or concurrently with the transfer of ownership. In Switzerland, this is usually secured by an undertaking to pay or handover of a certified bank check. In Swiss contracts dealing with the sale of used real estate, all liabilities are usually excluded. In addition, the seller must consider who is responsible for which fees and taxes. In many cases, notaries' fees and property-transfer taxes are split 50-50, but this distribution is ultimately a matter for negotiation. However, the seller is always liable to pay the capital gains tax on the property.

Broker commissions are normally borne by the seller and as a rule range between 1% and 5%, and for larger sales are usually set at not more than 2% of the purchase price. In the case of a property search commission, however, a brokers' fee may also be demanded from the buyer. Broker's fees can be freely negotiated between the parties concerned. They are subject to value added tax (VAT).

The execution of a real estate purchase transaction

In buying real estate, a distinction must be made between a purchase concerning a new and as yet undeveloped property still at the planning stage and a completed building.

The procedure for purchasing real estate can vary between cantons, depending on whether cantonal practice involves an official or a private notary. Where self-employed private notaries authenticate property business (as for example in the canton of Vaud), the procedure takes place via the notary's fiduciary account. The notary acts in practice as an *escrow agent* and receives the entire purchase price, which he/she does not transfer to the seller until the entry in the land register and thus the handover of ownership has been completed.

In cantons with state-employed notaries (such as the canton of Zurich), the land registry is usually on the same premises as the office of the notary who performs the authentication. Accordingly, the buyer and seller (or their representatives) are usually present together when the land-register application is checked and the land-register entry is signed by the seller, in response to payment by the buyer. Payment is usually made either by a certified bank check or an irrevocable undertaking to pay from a Swiss bank in favor of the seller.

In the case of a double sale, which is practically impossible in Switzerland in view of the country's secure land-registry system, whoever is first entered in the land register first acquires the property. In such a case, the other buyer merely acquires claims for damages.

In the case of new and not yet (completely) built properties it should be noted that the purchase price must usually be paid in several instalments in advance and in accordance with the progress of building so that the buyer incurs a risk – which may be considerable – depending on the building contractor. This may be secured with a corresponding bank guarantee. Unlike many other countries, however, Switzerland has no legislation in this domain to protect the buyer.

Powers of attorney

Special or general powers of attorney may be granted. Although powers of attorney require no specific form, those concerning real estate transactions usually require corresponding official authentication (signatures certified by a notary, i.e. notarized), which quite generally also makes good sense for important legal transactions. Powers of attorney concerning transactions with real estate and rights to land are invariably subject to the jurisdiction of the place in which the relevant property is located, and a choice of law is excluded in this regard.

Financing

In Switzerland, both banks and some life insurance companies grant mortgages against corresponding collateral of up to about 80% of the current market value of the property. However, this applies only to acquirers or owners of real estate who are resident in Switzerland and can produce proof of corresponding income. Foreign buyers of real estate often encounter considerable restrictions when trying to obtain local financing, unless they hold corresponding assets, such as securities or cash deposits at a Swiss bank. This may in most cases be used to finance the purchase of real estate. This kind of business is handled particularly by the two major banks, *UBS* and *Credit Suisse*, but also by the cantonal banks, the *Raiffeisen banks* as well as some smaller institutes such as the *Migros bank*.

Current interest rates for mortgages in Swiss francs are extremely low in a historical comparison, so it is worthwhile checking out the possibility of debt financing. In Switzerland, a mortgage may also make good sense from a tax viewpoint.

At the end of November 2002 the *Zurich Cantonal Bank* reduced its interest rate for first variable mortgages to 3.5%. This rate is used as the reference interest rate for calculating rents. The last time that interest rates as low as this were recorded was between 1946 and 1958. In March 2003, this rate was reduced by another 0.25% to a record low of 3.25%, and it has since fallen even further. Swiss mortgage rates are consequently at their lowest level ever.

Purchase through a company

In Switzerland, it is impossible for foreign nationals who count as non-residents (see the definition given above under *Restrictions regarding acquisition of real estate by foreigners*) to acquire residential real estate via a company, and that includes a Swiss company. This is in principle impossible even if the ownership relationships are disclosed.

In contrast, purely commercial real estate may be acquired without restrictions via Swiss or foreign companies, and interesting possibilities accordingly exist for tax-efficient structuring.

Warranty claims

In principle, the seller is liable for any defects of title and material defects. Any relevant warranty claims lapse within five years. For used real estate, however, any warranties are normally relinquished by the seller in the sales agreement. Only fraudulently concealed defects can justify warranty or damage claims. For newly built real estate, see the details further below under 32.4.

32.4 New construction, rebuilding and renovation

Zoning law and construction permits

The Swiss *Zoning Act (Raumplanungsgesetz, Loi fédérale sur l'aménagement du territoire)* obliges the cantons to define specific utilization zones, such as agricultural, industrial and construction zones. This is done in cantonal zoning laws that define the actual zones that exist and the way in which the land in these zones may be used. More detailed elaboration of these zones is left up to the individual communes. A glance at the commune's *zone allocation plan* will show in which (construction) zone the property to be acquired lies – and to what extent relevant restrictions may exist. In contrast, building restrictions based on private law such as easements are entered in the land register.

The communes are relatively free to issue building permits. It makes sense to start any planning work as early as possible and to submit a building application in good time. It is also recommended to discuss the building project in advance with the competent authorities of the relevant commune and to check out the legal situation and the required authorizations. There is no obligation to use an architect in Switzerland, and the profession of architect is not even protected. Nevertheless, architects, draftsmen and other experts are in most cases required to satisfy all the formalities and to prepare detailed plans. Any neighbors affected by the planned building work should also be informed at an early stage, and the neighbor's concerns should be taken into account as far as possible. Such precautions will preclude any lengthy legal proceedings due to their objections.

Architect's contract and building contracts

The architect's contract

In Switzerland, the architects' contract is based on the mandate of the Swiss contract law as set out in the *Swiss Code of Obligations*, although elements of a contract for work and services may also play a role. The *Swiss Society of Engineers and Architects (Schweizerischer Ingenieur und Architektenverband, Société suisse des ingénieurs et des architects,* SIA*)* has issued guidelines which have acquired great practical importance as "general terms and conditions of business" for the construction industry. SIA *standard 102* is of special interest with regard to architects, as it lays down their conditions of service and fees. Simple contracts are dealt with only in a relatively summary manner by the law, as they apply to many liberal professions. Special attention should be paid to fiduciary duty and the duty to take due care as well as to the stipulations that a commissioned party is liable for neglect of duty and that the contractor may revoke his order – in principle – at any time. As it is not uncommon for architects to have no liability insurance for construction damage, it is important to check that such cover is in place.

The professional designation of architect is not protected in Switzerland, so anyone may open an architect's office and call himself or herself an architect.

The building contract

In Switzerland, contracts regarding building/construction works are normally based on the (private) SIA *standard 118*, which is usually included in contractual agreements as a matter of course. However, it may make sense to adapt this standard to a specific building project. It is important for the person commissioning the building work (the principal) to insist that the building contract can be modified only with his agreement. This applies particularly to changes that involve financial obligations: these should be checked by the architect or builder but must not be carried out without the principal's approval. The same applies to the final account, which is checked by the builder but must be approved by the principal.

Completion of construction and formalities

The building must be constructed in accordance with the building permit and completed within the appropriate time. The local building authorities must be informed of the start of the building work and of its progress at regular intervals until the building is ready for occupation. They will then inspect the building. In addition to this official inspection, the principal must precisely record all defects at handover of the building, as the warranty and claim periods start from the day of handover.

Deficiencies and warranty claims regarding new construction

Almost every building has some defects. So it is important to proceed with great care at the handover of the building and to record all deficiencies. The builder is obliged to produce a defect-free building. If he fails to do so, the law grants the principal three defect rights in addition to the right to claim damages, namely the right of rescission, price reduction or rectification. In the building industry, however, the particular stipulation of SIA *standard 118* usually applies, which in the first instance grants the builder the option to rectify the work. Only if he fails to rectify the defect within the agreed time period do the other defect rights come into consideration. If the builder fails to rectify the defect, the principal may commission another tradesman with the rectification work as soon as the legal period has elapsed. The principal may also demand an advance from the defaulting builder to finance the replacement work.

In Switzerland, SIA *standard 118* normally makes provision for a warranty period of two years, which begins with the handover of the building. During the warranty period, the principal may give notification of defects at any time, with the exception of those which might give rise to further damage, which must be notified immediately. In most cases, however, no immediate notifications are made, but an initial defects list is prepared at handover of the building to the principal and a second defects list before the warranty runs out at handover of the keys. The builder's liability continues for what are called hidden defects and only lapses five years after handover of the building or 10 years in the event that the builder has deliberately concealed any defects.

32.5 Rental and tenancy

Rental and lease agreements

As mentioned at the outset, Switzerland is a "country of tenants". There consequently exists an extensive body of legislation and legal precedence concerned with rental law. The interests of the tenants are represented particularly by the *Swiss Tenants Association* (*mieterverband.ch*). The interests of the property owners are represented principally by the *Swiss Homeowners Association* (*hev-schweiz.ch*). The fundamentals of Swiss rental law are laid down in the country's contract law. In addition, regulations exist on renting and leasing residential and business premises, and the criminal code also contains articles which protect tenants.

Standard-form contracts are often used to conclude rental agreements. It is usual to pay a rental security amounting to between one and three monthly rents. This sum is paid into a designated bank account which is held in the tenant's name but can be disposed of only with the agreement of the landlord.

At the sale of a rented or leased property, the existing rental and leasing agreements are transferred to the buyer. The buyer can give notice of terminating the rental or leasing agreement by the next lawful termination date, but only under the condition that he/she can assert urgent personal need. However, this latter proviso does not apply if the rental is recorded in the land register.

Regulations on protection of tenants and rent control

In Switzerland, endeavors to protect tenants have led to government intervention for many decades. Free setting of rents on the residential market existed only between 1925 and 1936 as well as, after a decade-long phase of emergency regulations, for a year and a half in the early 1970s. Since then, tenant protection regulations have come into force, some of them with a broader impact, but tenants' protection is not as comprehensive in Switzerland as in some other European countries.

Legal restrictions cover protection against rent abuse and other abusive demands by landlords as well as regulations for protection against eviction. The increased eviction protection for tenants includes minimum legal periods of notice, the stipulation that all notices to terminate tenancy must be made on specific forms, the obligation to justify the notice, ways of contesting notice and extensions of the rental period.

32.6 Succession and gifts

In these domains, the *Swiss Private International Law Act (*PILA*)* covers the relevant international jurisdiction, the applicable law and the recognition of foreign decisions.

Applicable law and jurisdiction

The applicable law is based on the principle of habitual residence, i.e. it depends primarily on the country in which the testator had his last domicile. If no domicile may be determined on the basis of the PILA, usual residence takes the place of habitual domicile.

So if the testator had his last domicile in Switzerland, Swiss inheritance law will apply to his entire global estate (in line with the principle of indivisibility of an estate). However, if the testator has foreign citizenship both at the time of the choice of law as well as at the time of his decease, he/she may choose the law of the country of his/her citizenship *(lex patriae)* via a testamentary disposition or an inheritance contract. A partial choice of law is not permitted. Where a testator's last domicile was abroad, the Swiss provisions on the conflict of laws refer to the corresponding law of the country of domicile.

The *Hague Convention on the Conflicts of Laws relating to the Form of Testamentary Dispositions of 5th October 1961* applies to the form of testamentary disposition. Accordingly, a disposition of this kind is always formally effective and valid when it has been set up either in accordance with the stipulations of the *lex patriae* of the testator, the stipulations of the place of its formation or, in the case of real estate, of the place of its location.

Fundamentals of the succession and gift/donation laws of Switzerland

At the testator's death, the estate is transferred automatically and as a whole to the inheritors (in line with the principle of universal succession). Acceptance of the inheritance is not required. If neither a disposition in contemplation of death nor an inheritance contract exists, or if these are invalid due to defects in their form or content, then legal succession applies. Compulsory portions of the surviving spouse and close relatives should also be considered. Special stipulations apply to agricultural properties.

At the death of a married testator, the marriage is dissolved and the actual estate is determined as soon as the matrimonial property settlement has been concluded, i.e. the mutual economic claims on the basis of the matrimonial property regime have been determined and settled.

Legal succession

Swiss succession law is based on the *per-stirpes* system of the three generations of grandparents, parents and children. The closest inheritors of a testator are his/her descendants. Children inherit equal shares, and the place of any predeceased children is taken by their children (grandchildren of the testator) or their descendants. If the testator dies without issue, the estate passes to the parents. The mother and father each inherit half the estate. The siblings of the testator or their descendants (nephews and nieces) inherit in place of any predeceased parents. If there are no descendants on one side, the inheritance falls to the inheritors of the other side. If the testator leaves neither issue nor inheritors of the parental family, the inheritance passes to the grandparents' family. If the grandparents on the paternal and maternal sides survive the testator, each side inherits equal shares. Predeceased grandparents are succeeded by their descendants, i.e. uncles, aunts and cousins of the testator. If one grandparent is predeceased and also leaves no issue, the entire half of the estate falls to the inheritors of the same side. If there are no inheritors on the paternal or maternal side, the entire inheritance falls to the inheritors on the other side. The inheritance right of the relatives ends with the grandparents' family.

The inheritance right of the surviving spouse depends on the inheritors with whom he/she must share the inheritance. If he/she must share it with the testator's descendants, he/she receives half the inheritance. If he/she has to share it with parents, siblings, nieces and/or nephews, three quarters of the inheritance falls to the surviving spouse.

If the testator leaves no inheritors, the inheritance falls to the canton in which the testator was last resident, or to the commune to be designated by the legislation of this canton.

Testamentary dispositions

Testamentary dispositions are often also known as the "last will and testament". This is a unilateral declaration of a person's will, which becomes effective in law at the death of the declaring party. Whoever leaves a spouse, children or parents, may dispose freely of his/her assets after these have received their compulsory portion. The latter comprises three quarters of the legal inheritance right for children, a half for the spouse and a half for each of the parents. It is possible to favor the surviving spouse over their common children or those who issued from the marriage by granting him/her the right to the entire share to which these children are entitled.

Additionally, Swiss law makes provision for the institution of an inheritance contract or an inheritance renunciation contract. These are bi- or multi-lateral legal transactions. Whereas the testator may at any time supplement, replace, modify, fully or partially revoke, even destroy his will, an inheritance contract requires the cooperation of all those concerned if any changes are to be made.

Donations/Gifts

A distinction is made between immediate gifts and the promise to make a gift. In the case of an informal gift from one person to another, the conclusion and fulfillment of the contract take place concurrently, whereas they occur at different times in the case of a promise to make a gift. The latter must be made in writing to be valid. A purchase in which the purchase price is intentionally set very low is known as a mixed gift, a circumstance which may change the tax consequences. If the purchase price is purely symbolic, the contract must be considered a pure gift.

32.7 Taxes and charges

The federal structure of Switzerland is also reflected strongly in the country's tax system. Fiscal sovereignty is an entitlement of the federal government as well as of the cantons and their communes. Each canton has its own tax laws with its own tax rates, tax allowances etc. The relative independence of the cantons in the sphere of taxation ensures healthy competition, and the tax burden is accordingly moderate in an international comparison for both natural and legal persons. Another consequence is, however, that the tax burden may vary greatly between the individual cantons and communes, and the Swiss tax system is far from transparent.

One-time taxes and charges on purchase

Purchase / acquisition taxes

Most cantons levy a conveyancing tax on the transfer of real estate *(Handänderungssteuer, droits de mutation)*. The federal government levies no taxes of this kind. The remunerative transfer of ownership of property is normally taxable. As a rule, the basis for assessment is the purchase price or the taxable value of the property, the tax rates varying between 1% and 3% in the different cantons. In most cantons, it is usual for conveyancing taxes to be shared fifty-fifty between buyer and seller.

Sales tax (value added tax)

In Switzerland, value added tax (VAT) is levied at federal level. The standard rate currently stands at 8%. The actual sale of real estate is not liable to VAT. However, builders may opt to pay VAT. In addition, VAT is levied on all building work and materials.

Real estate registration and notary charges

The acquisition of property and the establishment of liens and mortgages to it are liable to Land Register and notary charges. Like conveyancing taxes, these are not regulated uniformly across the country and can vary greatly from one canton to another. Even payment is not the same everywhere. In most cantons, however, the following practice has become established: the costs (notary and land-register costs, conveyancing tax), are shared equally by the contractual parties. In some cantons (such as Vaud and Neuchâtel), these costs are usually borne by the buyer, whereas in others they are shared between buyer and seller. The costs associated with real estate security interests are normally borne by the buyer. In the end, however, parties are naturally free to apportion any costs among themselves.

Table 4. Acquisition costs and capital gains taxes in selected cantons[1]

Canton	Notary charges[2]	Land register fees[2]	Real estate transfer taxes	Establishment of liens and mortgages	Capital gains taxes
Berne	0.1-0.5%	CHF 100 to 500	1.8% (or 0.9% for purchase by descendants or spouse)	0.25%	2-8% (1) 2% reduction per ownership year, max. 70%; supplement for ownership under 5 years, max. 70%
Grisons	0.2%[3]	0.1%[3]	1 - 2%	0.3%[4]	5-15% 1.5% reduction for each ownership year over 10 years, max. 51% rebate
Lucerne	Max. 0.3%	0.2%[5]	1.5%[6]	0.2%	Tax 0.93 to 25.62% (profit-dependent) for short ownership supplement to 50%, for long ownership reduction by up to 25%. No tax on profits below CHF 13,000
Nidwalden	Max. 0.25%	0.1%	1% (purchase by issue or spouse tax-free)	0.2%, max. CHF 8,000	12 – 36% depending on duration of ownership
Schaffhausen[7]	0.1%	0.6%	-	0.3% incl. authentication fees	12 – 50% depending on duration of ownership. For short ownership supplement to 50%. 60% reduction for ownership over 17 full years. No tax on profits below CHF 5,000
Schwyz	0.09% + ca. CHF 350 copying fees	Depending on expenses	1%	0.12% of lien sum + ca. CHF 200 copying fees	9 - 33% depending very strongly on holding time and profit intensity
St. Gall	0.2% Max. CHF 12,500	0.2% Max. CHF 12,500	1-0.5%	0.3% total Max. CHF 6,000 per lien	Up to 33.5% for short holding supplement up to 5%, for long holding reduction by max. 40.5%
Ticino	CHF 200 + 0.01 - 0.05%	0.3% stamp duty, 1.1% land register or conveyancing fees	-	0.02 -0.7% lien 0.1 -0.3% for mortgages	Depending on ownership duration 3-30%
Thurgau	0.1% Max. CHF 5,000	0.4% Max. CHF 20,000	1%	0.15% Max. CHF 10,000	40% of profit on the property[8]

Canton	Notary charges[2]	Land register fees[2]	Real estate transfer taxes	Establishment of liens and mortgages	Capital gains taxes
Vaud	Max. 0.7% (for immediate transfer)	0.15%	3.3%	0.35% land register fees Max. 0.5% notaries' fees	7 – 30%
Zug	CHF 500 – 3300	Billing by services since 1.1.2008	- (As of 31 December 2007)	Billing by services since 1.1.2008	10-60%, depending on profit intensity and ownership duration
Zurich	0.1%	0.25%	- (As of 1 January 2005)	0.1% authentication fees, 0.25% land register fees	11-40% Supplement up to 50% if ownership < 2 years, reduction up to 50% if ownership over 5 years

Notes on the table "Acquisition costs and capital gains taxes in selected cantons".

Most cantons and communes charge handling fees and other ancillary charges of up to CHF 300.

The percentages refer to the purchase price, the sum of the lien or the profit obtained respectively.

Most cantons also charge minimal fees for issuing vouchers, publications etc.

1 This corresponds to "simple tax". The final tax rate depends on the tax schedule of the canton, the local commune and the parish. The "simple tax" is multiplied by the tax schedule of the canton, the local commune and possibly the parish

2 Notarial services are subject to 7.6% VAT, whereas pure land-register fees are non-VAT liable

3 Official registrars in Grisons are the patented notaries, the district notaries and the land-register administrators

4 The figures are: 0.2% for drawing up and authentication, and 0.1% for entry in the land register. An additional 0.1% is charged for preparing the title deed for a mortgage note

5 Of the cadastral value if this is higher than the sale price, otherwise of the sales price

6 Acquisition by spouse or descendants tax-free. Company conversion / merger / break-up tax-free

7 In the canton of Schaffhausen, all public authentications of property rights on properties are performed at the cantonal land-registry office

8 For holding periods under 3 years, +1% per month, for periods over six years, each additional year -4%, max. -72%

Recurring taxes and charges

Real estate tax

14 cantons (and in some cantons, the communes) levy a special wealth tax on real estate known as *Liegenschaftsteuer*, which is payable annually in addition to the general wealth tax. It is calculated on the market or taxable value of the property (excluding the debts encumbering it, i.e. any such debts are not deductible) and ranges between 0.05 and 0.2%.

Income tax

Both the federal government and the cantons levy taxes on income from real estate. In addition, a (hypothetical) income, known as the own rental value, is taxable even if the property is used by the owner. So a distinction must initially be made depending on whether the property is rented or used personally by the owner.

In the case of rental, the rental income is liable to income tax, although loan interest, administrative expenses and maintenance (value-preserving expenses, but not value-increasing investments) may be deducted.

In the case of owner use, fictitious rental incomes are calculated. Every piece of real estate is assigned an own rental value, which may be significantly below the market value, especially for older properties. This own rental value is subject to income tax, but here too the loan interest, administrative expenses and maintenance are tax-deductible.

The tax burden varies greatly between the individual cantons and communes. Income tax has a progressive structure throughout the country, with highest tax rates ranging between 12% for an annual income of about CHF 250,000 (cantons of Schwyz and Zug) and 34% for an income of about CHF 500,000 (canton of Geneva). In contrast, direct federal tax is uniform throughout Switzerland. It also has a progressive structure, reaching a maximum of 11.5% for an income of about CHF 800,000.

Net wealth taxes

In Switzerland, the cantons tax the assets of natural persons, whereas there is no wealth tax at federal level. Here too, differences between the cantons are considerable. The tax schedules are usually progressively structured. For assets up to CHF 250,000 the tax ranges between 0.2% and 0.4% in most cantons. For assets of CHF 1 million and more it is between about 0.4% and 0.7% per year.

Half the cantons also levy a special wealth tax on real estate, as mentioned above. It is calculated on the taxable value of the property (excluding any debts which encumber it) and varies between 0.05 and 0.2%.

Capital gains taxes

Switzerland imposes a capital gains tax on real estate at cantonal level. It is known as real estate gains taxes *(Grundstückgewinnsteuer, impôt sur les gains immobiliers)*. It is levied on the difference between the cost of procurement and the revenue obtained from the sale. It is payable by the seller and is independent of his income and asset circumstances. It is calculated on the basis of the tax rate applicable in the canton and the duration of ownership (the longer this duration, the lower the tax rate). In the case of a "normal" duration of ownership (from about four to six years), the maximum tax rate ranges from 30 to 40% in most cantons. This rate declines as the duration of ownership increases by about 50 to 70%, and increases for short durations by about 25 to 50%.

Only property transfers resulting from a sale are considered for capital gains tax. Property transfers based on gifts, inheritances or settlements of matrimonial property regimes are normally not taxable. However, in the event of a sale subsequent to a tax-free property transfer, the capital gains tax then payable is calculated on the basis of the original purchase value.

If an owner-occupied property is sold and the revenue from the sale is used within an appropriate period to acquire or build a replacement property for immediate occupation (known as a replacement acquisition), the capital gains tax is deferred.

Capital gains with regard to real estate are however taxed if they result from a business activity (i.e. if the real estate constitutes a business asset) or if the seller of the real estate falls within the definition of "professional real estate dealer" as developed by case law in the tax administration and the courts.

Inheritance and gift taxes

The federal government levies no inheritance or gift taxes, and a popular initiative which asked for the introduction of a federal 20% inheritance tax failed at the polls in June 2015. They are raised by the cantons, and more and more cantons are moving to exempting spouses and close relatives completely from these taxes. Spouses are now exempt in almost all cantons, and in most cantons descendants as well. Inheritance and gift taxes are levied on descendants only by the cantons of Appenzell Innerrhoden, Berne, Geneva, Glarus, Grisons, Jura and Vaud. There is also a growing trend to improve the treatment of cohabiting partners, who are in some cases already placed on an equal footing with spouses, i.e. completely exempt. The canton of Schwyz levies neither inheritance nor gift taxes.

Real estate is always taxed where it is located. If the testator or donor is domiciled in Switzerland, the canton of his/her domicile is responsible for taxing his/her movable assets.

Switzerland has also concluded several agreements on the avoidance of double taxation concerning inheritance and gift taxes.

Other taxes and charges

Considerable access charges must be expected for new buildings (e.g. charges for connection to the public sewerage system).

If the activities of a private real estate investor exceed the limits of "normality", he/she risks being regarded as a property dealer from the viewpoint of taxation. In that case, all income from real estate (gains from sales as well as current income from rentals) is regarded as earned income and is liable to regular income tax. Social security contributions of up to about 10% are additionally payable.

Incorrect (lower) statement of sale price on the sales agreement

The practice of stating a lower sale price than the actual price on the sales agreement in order to reduce the tax burden is encountered in Switzerland as elsewhere. In this way not only is a part of the conveyancing tax avoided, but the seller also "saves" taxes on the appreciation of the property. This procedure is also illegal in Switzerland. Such a lower statement invariably invalidates the sale agreement and incurs sanctions in tax and criminal law. It should also be noted that appeal by a party to the nullity of the agreement may in turn count as a misuse of rights.

International taxation

The double taxation agreements concluded to date allow Switzerland to tax domestic real estate as assets and any profits accruing from it as income to an unlimited extent. The contracting state must either exclude Swiss real estate from its own taxation or credit it against Swiss taxes. Most contracting states, such as Germany and the US, opt for the tax credit system.

The agreements do not cover the question of the international distribution of the debt and debt interest encumbering Swiss property. Because Switzerland does not simply – like all other countries – accept its "Swiss" debts and debt interest (with respect to each property), but only a share of its worldwide debts and debt interest (as a ratio of Swiss to the worldwide assets), it is obvious that double deductions or deduction gaps may occur.

Notes on the table "Overview of cantonal inheritance taxes".

The data given in the table constitutes no substitute for clarification of the details in an individual case.

Gift taxes may deviate from the figures given in the table.

The tax rate refers to the tax on taxable assets after deduction of allowances.

The diversity of cantonal practice precludes a transparent overall presentation.

Some cantons keep minor inheritances and bequests generally tax-free.

Diverse cantonal tax exemptions exist for disabled recipients or minors, or for designated uses (education, marriage, household effects).

Taxation of children in most cases also applies to other descendants (grandchildren, great-grandchildren). However, some cantons make a distinction between children and succeeding generations.

The assessment of the taxable assets, especially for real estate and business assets, is variable (tax value, market value, capitalized value or preferential assessment with subsequent equalization).

In most cantons, gifts and advances on inheritances by testators to inheritors are added variously to the accrual of the estate as regards tax allowances and tax progression.

Table 5. Overview of cantonal inheritance taxes

Accruals of inheritance	To children				To spouses			
	Allowance in CHF	% rate	Tax in CHF at accrual of inheritance: 100,000	Tax in CHF at accrual of inheritance: 500,000	Allowance in CHF	% rate	Tax in CHF at accrual of inheritance: 100,000	Tax in CHF at accrual of inheritance: 500,000
AG	-	Tax-free	-	-	-	Tax-free	-	-
AR[1,2]	-	Tax-free	-	-	-	Tax-free	-	-
AI[1]	10,000[3]	1	0	4,000	-	Tax-free	-	-
BL	-	Tax-free	-	-	-	Tax-free	-	-
BS[4]	-	Tax-free	-	-	-	Tax-free	-	-
BE[1]	-	Tax-free	-	-	-	Tax-free + civil union since 1.1.07	-	-
FR[5]	-	Tax-free	-	-	-	Tax-free	-	-
GE[6]	-	2 - 6	3,050	21,550	-	2 - 6 7 - 11 [6]	3,050	21,550
GL[4,7]	-	Tax-free	-	-	-	Tax-free	-	-
GR[8,9]	-	Tax-free	-	-	-	Tax-free	-	-
JU	-	Tax-free	-	-	-	Tax-free	-	-
LU[10]	100,000	1 - 2 (SRL 652 optional)	0	9,500	-	Tax-free	-	-
NE[11]	50,000[11]	3.0[11]	1,500	13,500	-	Tax-free	-	-
NW[12]	-	Tax-free	-	-	-	Tax-free	-	-
OW	-	Tax-free	-	-	-	Tax-free	-	-
SH[4,13]	-	Tax-free	-	-	-	Tax-free	-	-
SZ	-	Tax-free	-	-	-	Tax-free	-	-
SO[8,14]	-	0.8 - 1.2	800	4,000	-	0.8 - 1.2	800	4,000
SG[1]	-	Tax-free	-	-	-	Tax-free	-	-
TI	-	Tax-free	-	-	-	Tax-free	-	-
TG[15]	-	Tax-free	-	-	-	Tax-free	-	-
UR	-	Tax-free	-	-		Tax-free	-	-
VD[16]	250,000	0.024 - 3.5	0	14,295	-	Tax-free	-	-
VS	-	Tax-free	-	-	-	Tax-free	-	-
ZG	-	Tax-free	-	-	-	Tax-free	-	-
ZH[4]	-	Tax-free	-	-	-	Tax-free	-	-

Accruals of inheritance	To siblings			To nephews and nieces			To non-related persons		
		Tax in CHF at accrual of inheritance			Tax in CHF at accrual of inheritance			Tax in CHF at accrual of inheritance	
	% rate	100,000	500,000	% rate	100,000	500,000	% rate	100,000	500,000
AG	6 - 23	6,000	73,800	12 - 32	12,000	109,200	12 - 32	12,000	109,200
AR[1,2]	22	20,900	108,900	32	30,400	158,400	32	30,400	158,400
							Cohabiting > 5 years: allowance 10,000 / 12% rate		
AI[1]	6	5,700	29,700	9	8,550	44,550	20	19,000	99,000
							Cohabiting > 5 years: allowance 5,000 / 20% rate		
BL	0 - 16.5	11,800	76,091	0 - 27.5	19,667	126,818	0 -44	31,467	202,909
BS[4]	7.5 - 16.5	7,350	52,290	10 - 22	9,800	69,720	22.5 - 49.5	22,050	156,870
BE[1]	6 - 15	5,400	43,800	11 - 27.5	9,900	80,300	16 - 40	14,400	116,800
							Cohabiting > 10 years: allowance 10,000 / 6% rat		
FR[5]	5.25	4,987.50	25,987	8.25	7,837.50	40,837.50	22	20,900	108,900
GE[6]	6 - 11	8,390	51,390	8 - 13	10,380	61,380	20 - 26	23,760	127,760
GL[4,7]	4 - 10	3,600	39,200	7 - 17.5	6,300	68,600	10 - 25	9,000	98,000
GR[8,9]	10 7	10,000	50,000	10 7	10,000	50,000	10 7	10,000	50,000
JU	14	14,000	70,000	21	21,000	105,000	35	35,000	175,000
							Cohabiting > 5 years: 14%		
LU[10]	6 - 12	9,000	57,000	6 - 12	9,000	57,000	20 - 40	30,000	190,000
							Cohabiting > 5 years: allowance 2,000 / 6% rate		
NE[11]	15	15,000	75,000	18	18,000	90,000	45	45,000	225,000
							Cohabiting > 5 years: Tax-free		
NW[12]	5	5,000	25,000	5	5,000	25,000	15	15,000	75,000
							Cohabiting > 5 years: Tax-free		
OW	Tax-free	-	-	10	10,000	50,000	20	20,000	100,000
							Cohabiting > 5 years: Tax-free		
SH[4,13]	4 - 16	7,800	70,600	6 - 24	11,700	105,900	10 - 40	19,500	176,500
SZ	Tax-free	-	-	Tax-free	-	-	Tax-free	-	-
							Cohabiting couples: Tax-free		
SO[8,14]	4.8 - 11.2	9,799	54,100	9.8 - 23.7	20,822	113,300	12.8 - 31.2	27,495	150,800
SG[1]	20	18,000	98,000	30	27,000	147,000	30	27,000	147,000
TI	5.95 - 15.5	7,947	59,917	7.74 - 18.5	10,331	77,892	17.85 - 41	23,841	179,751
TG[15]	4 - 14	6,000	70,000	6 - 21	9,000	105,000	8 - 28	12,000	140,000
UR	4 - 10	7,000	50,000	6 - 15	10,500	75,000	12 - 30	21,000	150,000
VD[16]	5.28 - 12.5	8,118	62,500	7.92 - 16.5	12,177	82,500	15.84 - 25	24,354	125,000
VS	10	10,000	50,000	10	10,000	50,000	25	25,000	125,000
ZG	4 - 8	4,320	28,360	6 - 12	6,480	42,540	10 - 20	10,800	70,900
							Cohabiting > 5 years: Tax-free		
ZH[4]	6 - 18	6,750	67,500	10 - 30	14,000	117,000	12 - 36	16,800	140,400

1 Allowance for all other inheritors: BE, CHF 10,000; SG, CHF 10,000; AR, CHF 5,000; AI CHF 5,000

2 AR A cohabiting couple is treated the same as a married couple (Art. 3a StG AR; BGS 621.11)

3 Allowance raises up to CHF 200,000 if the beneficiary is under 35 years (Art. 100 Abs. 1a StG AI)

4 Allowances for siblings: BS, CHF 2,000; GL, CHF 10,000; SH, CHF 10,000; ZH, CHF 15,000. In the canton of ZH, cohabiting couples are taxed the same as a married couple in cases of gifts and inheritances

5 FR Allowance for every beneficiary is CHF 5,000 (Art. 24 EschG). The communes may levy taxes of up to 70% of cantonal tax

6 GE A spouse without children pays inheritance tax of 7–11 %

7 GL A building tax is levied as a supplement to the gross inheritance tax (currently +15 % of inheritance tax) to fund the canton's building program

8 Cantons which levy estate tax (tax on the estate, not on the individual accrual of the estate)

9 GR In addition to cantonal estate tax, the communes can levy tax on accrual of the estate (not included in the examples, as very diverse) and gift taxes. The cantonal gift and inheritance tax rate is 10%. Spouses and children are exempted from these taxes

10 LU Accrual of the estate to children: Canton tax free. However, the canton has granted the communes the competence to levy an inheritance tax of up to 2% for descendants. Virtually all communes have made use of this right. For descendants under the age of 14 or who are permanently disabled, a tax-free allowance of CHF 20,000 applies. Gifts and advances during the last five years before death are included in the calculation for determining the assets liable to inheritance tax, earlier gifts are generally tax-free

11 NE Allowance of CHF 50,000 applies only to descendants and parents

12 NW The allowance of CHF 20,000 is valid for all cases of death after 1 January 2007 and for all gifts made after this date. Everything above this allowance gets taxed following the tax rates for the different degree of kinship

13 SH There's a CHF 30,000 allowance applicable for parents. For all other beneficiaries (including siblings) it's CHF 10,000

14 SO The spouse and descendants pay estate tax of 0.8-1.2 %, but no tax on accrual of the estate. The other inheritors pay estate tax and tax on accrual of the estate. The table lists the overall tax. Gifts to spouses and descendants are tax-free; allowance for other gifts CHF 14,100

15 TG For inheritors who require permanent care and support: CHF 100,000 tax-free. For all other inheritors, usual every-day gifts and one-time bequests: CHF 5,000 tax-free

16 VD Spouses: tax-free. On accruals to the descendants CHF 250,000 is tax-free, for higher accruals the allowance is reduced. In addition to the canton, individual communes also levy inheritance tax

17 Partnership also applies to same sex couples

32.8 Immigration law and tax residence

Entry, residence and settlement of foreigners

Foreign nationals who need no visa to enter Switzerland as tourists or business visitors may remain in the country for up to three months without a permit as long as they pursue no gainful employment there. After three months, they must interrupt their stay for at least another three months. In such case, these three months must even be spent outside of the Schengen area, as since 2008 Switzerland has been part of the Schengen agreement. According to Schengen visa regulations, a visa-free stay as a tourist within the Schengen zone cannot exceed three months out of six. However, foreign nationals may enter Switzerland several times within any year and are under no obligation to register their presence there as long as they do not remain more than three months out of six in the country or in the Schengen zone, respectively, and not longer than six months in total in a year. The Schengen area essentially creates one borderless area throughout Europe, except those EU countries that are not yet part of this arrangement (Ireland, the UK and some of the new EU member states).

One often hears that it is exceptionally difficult to obtain a residence permit in Switzerland. This is incorrect in comparison with other western European countries or those of North America: for entrepreneurs, investors and financially independent persons at least it is often considerably easier to obtain a residence permit in Switzerland than in comparable countries.

However, acquisition of real estate in Switzerland is not associated with a residence permit, despite the fact that the acquisition of residential property itself requires authorization.

Types of residence permits

In Switzerland, there are different categories of residence permits available, with a distinction between permits for EU/EFTA and non-EU/EFTA nationals. Applications for residence permits are generally administered on a cantonal level, however, in case of applications for non-EU/EFTA nationals, final approval must be sought at the *Federal Immigration Department*.

For foreign residents who are gainfully occupied in Switzerland an application for a resident permit is usually combined with an application for a work permit. A resident permit will only be granted if the applicant has been granted working rights. This rule is not applicable to an applicant who is a student, retired, a family member, or a financially independent person.

The authorities have implemented a fixed annual quota system to regulate the number of first time residence permits available to non-EU/EFTA citizens. The cantonal labor authorities and *Federal Aliens Office* are given an annual quota to which they must adhere. A distinction is made between short-term residence permits (less than one year), annual residence permits (limited), and permanent residence permits (unlimited).

In order to become a permanent resident (Permit C), an application must be lodged with the specific *Cantonal Migration Office*, as each canton applies its own set of rules. Permanent residence is granted to an individual who has lived in Switzerland for a specific period of time. Once permanent residence status is obtained, it is granted for an unlimited period of time and there are no restrictions on employment, even a change of canton may be possible. However, if the person leaves Switzerland for a period of more than six months, the permanent residence status is forfeited.

EU/EFTA nationals

EU/EFTA nationals can obtain a residence permit easily. In addition, the EU/EFTA national is not subject to geographical restrictions within Switzerland and can acquire real estate without prior authorization.

The following resident permits exist for EU/EFTA nationals:

1 *B Permit* is a residence/work permit for resident foreign nationals who reside in Switzerland for a certain purpose, with or without gainful employment – the B Permit is valid for five years if the person is in possession of a valid employment contract with at least a 12 month duration

2 *C Permit* is a settlement permit for foreign nationals who have resided in Switzerland for an uninterrupted period of five years. This permit grants the applicant the right to settle in Switzerland without any restrictions or conditions on his residence (certain restrictions apply for citizens of Bulgaria, Cyprus, Malta, Romania and the EU-8 member states)

3 *G permit* is applicable to EU/EFTA nationals who are resident in a foreign border zone and are gainfully employed within the neighbouring border zone of Switzerland. The permit allows the national to work anywhere in Switzerland, on condition that the national returns to his/her place of residence in the EU/EFTA region once a week. The permit is valid for five years, provided there is an employment agreement of unlimited duration, or of more than one year's duration

4 *L Permit* is a short-term permit for EU/EFTA foreign nationals resident in Switzerland for period of usually less than one year

Non-EU/EFTA nationals

The process to obtain residence for non-EU/EFTA nationals is significantly more challenging.

Like most countries, Switzerland gives its nationals priority in the domestic labor market. A foreign national may acquire a residence and work permit to become gainfully employed in Switzerland if the Swiss employer can prove that he or she is indispensable for a specific function in the company, that he or she possesses the relevant qualifications for this function and that no suitable candidate can be found on the Swiss and European labor markets. Precedence is given to Swiss and EU/EFTA citizens. It is generally extremely difficult to obtain a permit under this category. Only a limited number of management level employees, specialists and other qualified employees are admitted from non-EU/EFTA countries.

If a foreign national establishes a company in Switzerland and is employed by it in a senior position, generally a residence and work permit will be issued within the scope of the economic promotion program. The rules vary between cantons but the compliance with the economic promotion program may be justified by economic reasons of sustained relevance to Switzerland. The criteria include the creation of new jobs for which domestic employees may be recruited, as well as the opening up of new markets, the securing of export sales and economically significant links abroad, and the creation of new tax revenue. The requirements fluctuate, depending on the canton in which the company is established.

To obtain a permit as a pensioner, the foreign national must be at least 55 years old, show close ties to Switzerland and have sufficient funds. The key condition here is the minimum age of 55 years. In many cases, it may also be difficult to fulfill the condition of close ties to Switzerland. However, despite these restrictive regulations, foreign nationals who do not meet the requirements under the retired persons category may still obtain a residence permit if they are financially independent.

Financially independent persons who are not gainfully occupied in Switzerland, but who agree to pay a certain minimum in net annual taxes, can usually acquire a residence permit regardless of their age, provided granting of residence to a potential taxpayer is considered being in the "fiscal interest" of the canton of residence. The minimum annual taxes that must be paid in order to qualify for this specific immigration category and these vary considerably from canton to canton. In order to avoid being taxed on the basis of worldwide income and wealth, the minimum tax payable is, in most cases, fixed in a lump-sum tax arrangement. This special taxation arrangement is negotiated on an individual basis and is decided upon by the cantonal authorities. This makes Switzerland an even more attractive place of residence for financially independent persons who wish to relocate to a milder tax climate.

The following permits are issued to Non-EU/EFTA nationals:

1. *Permit B* is a residence permit granted to a non-EU/EFTA national for a period of one year and can be renewed on an annual basis if the applicant has maintained the conditions upon which the permit was initially granted
2. *Permit C*, the settlement permit is granted to foreign nationals who have resided in Switzerland for a continuous and uninterrupted period of 10 years. US and Canadian nationals are subject to special regulations
3. A non-EU/EFTA national may also apply under the *Cross-border commuter permit (Permit G)*, if they are resident in a foreign border zone and are gainfully employed within the neighbouring border zone of Switzerland
4. Subject to the quota system, a *Permit L*, the short-stay permit, is granted to foreign nationals resident in Switzerland for a period of less than 12 months. Usually the terms and length of the permit will mirror the terms of the employment contract. However, if the employment period is less than four months, the application is not subject to the quota regulation

Tax residence

The legal basis of income, wealth, and lump-sum taxation in Switzerland is formed by the *Federal Direct Tax Act* (*Gesetz über die Direkte Bundessteuer*, DBG), the *Federal Tax Harmonization Act* (*Steuerharmonisierungsgesetz*, STHG), and – corresponding with the latter – the individual tax laws of the 26 cantons. Switzerland has a multi-layered tax system. Taxes are levied on federal, cantonal and community (municipal) levels, with the smallest percentage levied at federal level. Each canton determines its own tax rates with the maximum cantonal and municipal rate of approximately 35%. In addition, net wealth taxes are levied on cantonal and municipal level.

A person resident or domiciled in Switzerland is liable for tax on federal, cantonal and municipal level on worldwide income and net wealth, except on real estate situated abroad and income derived from a permanent business establishment. From the first day of residence an individual is liable for tax. A person is considered a resident if they hold a legal residence permit or intend to work in Switzerland for a period exceeding 30 days. Non-residents, however, are only liable for Swiss tax on certain income and assets, including from real estate or business interests in a permanent establishment in Switzerland.

Foreign nationals who fulfill certain requirements can avail themselves of a special tax arrangement whereby Swiss taxes are levied on the basis of expenditure and standard of living in Switzerland rather than on the usual worldwide income and assets. This fiscal arrangement is called lump-sum taxation (*forfait fiscal* in French) and is available throughout the country except in the cantons of Zurich, Schaffhausen, Appenzell Ausserhoden, Basel-Land and Basel-Stadt. In a referendum on 30 November 2014, the Swiss people decided with a clear majority to maintain the lump sum taxation system. The vote confirms Switzerland's reputation of continuity and stability.

The federal tax law and the relevant cantonal tax laws require that a foreign person wishing to benefit from this special tax regime must not have been resident in Switzerland during the last 10 years and may not carry out a gainful occupation in Switzerland. Under the lump-sum taxation regime, the Swiss tax authorities generally require the assessment of a minimum taxable income which must in general be equal to at least the tax resident's living expenditure. According to the now federally applicable tax regulations the taxpayer´s living costs are assessed to be at least five times the annual rental value of the apartment or house in which the foreign national resides in Switzerland. In some cantons this is even more, and from 1 January 2016 onwards will be at least seven times the annual rental value and in any case not less than

CHF 400,000 per annum. A grandfathering period of five years will apply to all existing lump sum taxpayers – for them, the new law will only apply as of the tax year 2021.

If spouses move to Switzerland and wish to benefit from the lump-sum tax option, both spouses must fulfil the requirements - unless one spouse continues to live abroad and does not obtain residence in Switzerland.

Besides offering a unique lump-sum tax system of taxation, which effectively caps income and net wealth tax for qualifying foreign citizens, Switzerland is also an attractive place of residence with regard to inheritance and gift taxes. The country has no federal inheritance or gift taxes. Instead, the cantons levy inheritance and gift taxes in their own competence, which means that there are 25 different inheritance and gift tax regimes, while the canton of Schwyz has neither inheritance nor gift taxes. Switzerland has entered into several inheritance tax treaties including treaties with Austria, France, Germany, the UK and the US.

Companies are taxed according to the canton in which they are established and the maximum income tax rate can be as low as about 14%. As tax planning through companies is permitted under Swiss taxation laws, dividends enjoy privileged taxation, which can significantly reduce the higher taxation rates applicable to individuals who are fully taxable (as opposed to individuals who opt for flat-rate taxation). Since January 2009, Swiss residents are only taxed on 60% of the dividend if the recipient owns at least 10% of the share capital of a Swiss company.

Individuals are exempt from capital gains tax from the sale of movable assets, but capital gains on immovable property will be levied on cantonal level. Furthermore, the Swiss tax treatment of trusts and the absence of controlled foreign corporation rules offer interesting pre-immigration planning opportunities for wealthy families.

Switzerland has close to 100 double-tax agreements. However, some of these agreements (e.g. with France, Germany and other European countries) are not applicable to individuals who reside in Switzerland on a flat-rate tax basis.

International double taxation for residents of Switzerland

Switzerland has concluded agreements to avoid double taxation with more than 50 countries. They apply to all natural and legal persons domiciled in Switzerland. Some agreements impose certain limitations for persons who are taxed on a lump-sum basis. Among the matters regulated by the double taxation agreements is the reduction of foreign withholding tax on dividends, license fees and interest. Depending on the double taxation agreement to be applied, this tax may be either reduced or completely waived. The non-recoverable share of foreign withholding tax can be completely or partially credited against Swiss taxes. Tax reduction is granted as long as double taxation agreements are not abused. Abuse stipulations of this kind form part of numerous agreements, but the *Swiss Federal Council* also took unilateral measures against improper claims on double taxation agreements concluded by the federal government. This is known in brief as the abuse regulations *(Missbrauchsbeschluss, Arrêté instituant des mesures contre l'utilisation sans cause légitime)* and is probably unique in the world. More information on it may be found on the website of the *Swiss Federal Tax Administration* (*estv.admin.ch*).

Various agreements contain special rules in particular as regards persons liable to lump-sum taxation in Switzerland. The agreement with Germany is of special relevance here. Germany has various tax policies which, in certain circumstances, make persons who leave the country liable to continued taxation even after leaving. The agreement with Switzerland includes certain rules to support these policies. The totality of the internal German regulations in combination with the agreement between the two countries obliges those who plan to leave Germany for Switzerland on the basis of lump-sum taxation to exercise great care. They may, for instance, no longer retain any relevant links (such as a secondary residence or similar) with Germany. There are similar provisions in some other high-tax countries and in the respective double taxation agreement they concluded with Switzerland.

32.9 Checklist: Real estate in Switzerland

- Tax rate of the commune: considerable differences in tax burden exist both between the various cantons and the individual communes within them
- Public transport and access: Switzerland is very well served by public transport. Nevertheless, the situation regarding accessibility by public transport should be clarified in each individual case. The same applies to the availability of local infrastructure (post office, schools, shopping facilities), as this can vary greatly. Practical help is available at *yourhome.ch*, which contains aerial photos and maps as well as information on all Swiss locations
- Purchases in the vicinity of Zurich airport must be approached with particular care in view of the still unclear situation regarding flight paths
- Contaminated land: check whether the land to be acquired is recorded in a register which lists such areas (see *altlast.ch*)
- Is approval for the acquisition mandatory (it is always mandatory for the acquisition of real estate by non-residents)? Is approval likely to be granted?
- Building zones and specifications: practice as regards building zones, building specifications etc is highly restrictive in some cases and can vary greatly between communes
- Will approval be granted for a possible extension/reconstruction?
- Are there any stipulations regarding heritage/monument protection?
- Have all duties and taxes been completely paid by the previous owner? In some cantons, the notary retains a certain percentage of the purchase price to secure payment of capital gains tax. Where this is not the case, the requisite assurance must be demanded
- Caution: for non-resident foreigners it is prohibited to use a company as an intermediary for purchasing residential property. Non-EU/EFTA foreign nationals – whether resident or not – acquiring

residential real estate in Switzerland must do so exclusively and directly in their own names. On the other hand, resident EU/EFTA nationals may acquire real estate without restrictions

- In the case of oil heating: is there an outside oil tank which may represent an environmental liability risk?
- Especially in Alpine areas: natural hazards (flooding, avalanches, landslides) may represent a risk
- When changing domicile: total tax burden? There are considerable differences in income and wealth taxation between the cantons as well as between the communes within the individual cantons
- Inheritance and gift taxes are levied on a cantonal basis in Switzerland. There are enormous differences between the cantons and taxes range from 0% up to 50%
- Capital gains tax: check the liability of the property, request assurances in this regard

32.10 Bibliography

Bundesamt für Justiz: Erwerb von Grundstücken durch Personen im Ausland, Info sheet, Berne 2002

Felder Daniel / Kaddous Christine: Accords bilatéraux Suisse – UE (Commentaires); Bilaterale Abkommen Schweiz – EU (Erste Analysen), Helbing & Lichtenhahn und Bruylant, Basle, Geneva, Munich and Brussels.

Gauch Peter / Tercier Pierre: Das Architektenrecht – Le droit d'architecte, 3rd revised and extended edition, Universitätsverlag, Freiburg 1995

Gauch Peter: Der Werkvertrag. Ein systematischer Grundriss, 5th revised edition, Schulthess Polygraphischer Verlag, Zurich 2011

Geiser Thomas / Münch Peter / Übersax Peter / Arnold Martin: Ausländerrecht. Ausländerinnen und Ausländer im öffentlichen Recht, Privatrecht, Strafrecht, Steuerrecht und Sozialrecht der Schweiz. Handbuch für die Anwaltspraxis Band VIII, Helbing & Lichtenhahn, Basle 2002

Geissmann Hanspeter / Huber Felix / Wetzel Thomas: Grundstückerwerb in Schweiz durch Personen im Ausland, Schulthess Polygraphischer Verlag, Zurich 1998

Guhl Theo / Koller Alfred / Schnyder Anton / Druey Jean Nicolas: Das Schweizerische Obligationenrecht, mit Einschluss des Handels- und Wertpapierrechts, 9th edition, Schulthess Polygraphischer Verlag, Zurich 2000

Hänseler Peter / Hochstrasser Daniel: Real Estate in Switzerland, Basel 1996

Hess-Odoni Urs: Bauhaftpflicht. Haftpflichtrecht des Grundeigentümers und des Bauherrn sowie der Planer und Unternehmer. Dietikon 1994

Kälin Christian H.: The Global Residence and Citizenship Handbook, 4th edition, Ideos Verlag, Zürich, 2014

Kälin Christian H.: Switzerland Business & Investment Handbook, Orell Füssli Verlag, Zürich, 2010

Koller Alfred (editor): Der Grundstückkauf, 2nd edition, Stämpfli, Berne 2001

Reber Hans J.: Rechtshandbuch für Bauunternehmer, Bauherr, Architekt und Bauingenieur, 4th edition, Baufachverlag, 1983

Schweiz. Verband der Immobilien-Treuhänder SVIT (editor): Schweizerisches Mietrecht, Kommentar, 2nd extended and updated edition, SVIT Verlag, Zurich 1998

Spescha Marc (editor) / Sträuli Peter (editor): Ausländerrecht, 2nd edition, Orell Füssli Verlag, Zurich 2004

Stoller Hans: Praxis-Ratgeber zum Hausbau. Vertragsklauseln – Bau-Garantien – Mängelrechte, 1st edition, Verlag Hauseigentümerverband Schweiz, 2003

Swiss-American Chamber of Commerce: Swiss Civil Code, Property Law, Articles 641 – 977. English Translation of Official Texts, Zurich 1999

Theiler Luzius: Worauf achten beim Erwerb von Wohneigentum?, 2nd edition, casanostra-Verlag, Bern 1998

Tuor Peter et al.: Das Schweizerische Zivilgesetzbuch, 13th edition, Schulthess Verlag, Zürich 2009

Wachter Thomas: Immobilien in der Schweiz – Zivilrecht und Steuerrecht in der Praxis, DSA – Deutsche Schutzvereinigung Auslandsimmobilien e. V., Freiburg im Breisgau 2001

Weigell Jörg / Brand Jürg / Safarik Frantisek J.: Investitions- und Steuerstandort Schweiz. Chancen und Risken von Investitionen und Wohnsitzverlegungen, 3rd edition, Verlag C. H. Beck und Stämpfli, Munich and Bern 2012

33

The UK / England and Wales

The United Kingdom of Great Britain and Northern Ireland / England & Wales

By

Nicholas Warr (International Head of Wealth), Elaine Dobson (Head of Residential Real Estate) Mustafa Hussain (Partner, Private Wealth)*

Taylor Wessing LLP
5 New Street Square
London
EC4A 3TW
England

Tel: +44 207 3007000
Fax: +44 207 3007100

n.warr@taylorwessing.com
e.dobson@taylorwessing.com
m.hussain@taylorwessing.com
taylorwessing.com

Taylor Wessing is a leading international law firm, advising clients in the world's most dynamic industries and with recognised expertise in the Private Wealth sector. Taylor Wessing advises families and high net worth individuals in the structuring of their investment transactions including succession planning, asset protection and risk mitigation. Both residence and tax consequences play a major role with respect to the structuring and allocation of investments. Real estate is a key asset class – including advising on the purchase, financing, occupation and sale of all types of residential, commercial and agricultural property. Taylor Wessing also advises on trusts, industrial investments, corporate governance, security and bespoke investment structures for Private Wealth clients.

*The authors have taken over from the previous edition where the UK chapter was written by Dr Reto Boehi

33.1 Introduction

The common law basis for English real estate law stems from a completely different tradition of jurisprudence from that which is the basis of most laws in continental Europe. The differences in concepts of ownership and rights relating to land are not just matters of detail, they are often differences based on fundamentally different ideas. These differences are further complicated by the rules of equity.

English law comprises a number of distinct elements:

- Common law: which has its origin in the unwritten laws of the middle ages
- Equity: a set of legal principles particularly associated with the law of trusts and having its origins in the function of the *Lord Chancellor of England* who was empowered to exercise the King's mercy in mitigating injustice which might sometimes be caused by the strict application of common law
- Parliamentary statutes
- Precedents set by judgments in Court

There is a clear distinction between rules relating to the creation of interest in real estate and the rules relating to chattels or moveable property. It should also be noted that English law applies only in England and Wales. Scotland has its own legal system which Scottish law firms advise on.

For tax purposes, England and Wales are incorporated within the UK. The UK has its own tax regime covering England, Scotland, Wales and Northern Ireland.

33.2 Real estate ownership

From 1925, English law recognised only two legal estates in land, namely freehold and leasehold estates. However a third legal estate, commonhold, was introduced by the *Commonhold and Leasehold Reform Act 2002*.

The most important legal interests, which exist in relation to both freehold and leasehold estates, are easements and legal charges. Most other interests and encumbrances take effect as equitable interests. The general principle is that legal estates and legal interests can only be created by means of a deed. There is an exception to this rule in the case of leases or tenancies with a term which does not exceed three years and certain other relatively rare exceptions.

Different forms and types of ownership

Under English law, real estate comprises not only the land but also all buildings erected on the land. The ownership of a house could either be freehold or leasehold but probably freehold and a flat will be leasehold.

Freehold

The freehold interest, generally, includes everything beneath the surface and all the air above, as well as all buildings and structures on the land. Freehold apartments are rare. In the case of long leaseholds, the buyer acquires his property on the strength of a long lease, with a term of, on average, 125 years. This long lease is generally granted for a fixed price or premium and usually there is a ground rent to be paid to the freeholder. The tenant can then sell the house or apartment in the open market, subject to the conditions contained in the lease.

The granting of long leases gives a certain control over an estate to the freeholder (for example a local authority or a family trust such as the *Grosvenor Estate*, the family trust of the Duke of Westminster). Family Trusts, which own large estates in exclusive areas of London (such as Mayfair and Belgravia) grant leases so that they can ensure that the facades and general appearance of buildings on the estate are kept in traditional style and they are therefore reluctant to, voluntarily, sell freeholds which would give buyers freedom to change the external appearance of buildings (see Enfranchisement below).

Joint Tenancies and Tenancies in Common

There are two forms of joint ownership in English Law: *Tenancy in Common* and *Joint Tenancy*. *Joint Tenancy* is the more common for married couples, while *Tenancy in Common* is more usual for parties who, for whatever reason, wish to retain the ownership in specific shares. It should be noted that the word "Tenancy" in this connection applies equally to the freehold or leasehold interest.

In the case of a *Joint Tenancy*, title to the property passes automatically on the death of one of the owners to the surviving owner.

In the case of a *Tenancy in Common*, each joint owner is regarded as owner of a separate share in the property and on the death of one owner, that share will pass in accordance with the provisions of that person's testamentary disposition or in accordance with the rules of intestacy, where there is no valid will relating to the property. The shares in a property belonging to tenants in common can be unequal but, in the absence of any express provisions to the contrary, they will be assumed to be 50:50.

Joint ownership, whether by way of joint tenancy or tenancy in common, creates a *Trust for Sale*, which means (in the absence of a contract to the contrary) that any joint owner can require sale of the house or apartment. As mentioned below, on completion of the sale, tenants in common would each receive a share of the net proceeds of sale in proportion to their specified interest in the property.

Commonhold, Right to Manage and Enfranchisement

Commonhold was brought into law on 30 September 2003 by the passing of the *Commonhold and Leasehold Reform Act 2002* and is a form of title to land.

Commonhold is sometimes compared with the American condominium. The detailed provisions are very complicated but the overall intention of this *Act of Parliament* was to provide the occupier of commonhold property with a measure of influence over how other properties within the commonhold estate are managed and used, for example to overcome problems of anti-social behaviour, or use or neglect of gardens. However the take-up has been limited to a few estates probably due to the reluctance of mortgagees to lend on commonhold units.

Right to Manage

The *Commonhold and Leasehold Reform Act 2002* also introduced some rights for long leaseholders, those with leases of over 21 years at the date of grant, to manage their buildings collectively subject to qualifying criteria. This is a useful resource to those tenants who are only interested in managing the building so as to have control over the finances of the service charges and how they are spent as opposed to owning the freehold asset.

Enfranchisement

Enfranchisement of Houses was introduced by the *Leasehold Reform Act 1967* and provided a mechanism for the tenants of houses to either claim a new lease or the freehold of the house from their Landlord, subject to certain qualification criteria. In the present day, the use of the legislation to claim the freehold is the favoured route. The criteria has been amended over the years between 1967 and 2002 but has produced a number of high profile Court cases including the most recent before the Supreme Court on what is "a house so called?" The legislation is very technical and expert legal advice should be sought.

Legislation introduced in 1993 by the *Leasehold Reform Housing and Urban Development Act 1993* introduced a right for tenants to claim an extended lease from their landlord or collectively with other tenants to acquire the freehold of their building. The qualification criteria for both is that to be a qualifying tenant the tenant must hold a lease of over 21 years at the time of grant. The landlord, subject to the qualification criteria being satisfied, must grant an extension of 90 years over the remaining term and the ground rent is reduced to a peppercorn rent but otherwise on the same terms as the existing lease. The landlord will be compensated as will every other landlord who has an interest in the reversion.

Should the tenants choose to collectively enfranchise the qualification, criteria includes whether the building qualifies, if the tenants qualify, and the number of flats in the building. As with the freehold claim of houses, the legislation is very complicated and expert advice should be obtained.

Rights to build

A freehold owner has an inherent right to build on land, subject to planning regulations and to rights of adjoining owners (for example rights of light and air) and to any restrictive covenants affecting the land. Rights to build for tenants will be controlled by the terms of the lease and may be excluded completely.

Easements, charges, covenants, liens and mortgages

Easements

English law has no equivalent to the concept of personal easements. It would be possible to create comparable rights by contract, lease or wayleave agreement (under which, for example, a telephone company or electricity supplier has the right to run cables over a private piece of land. Also, for example, a right to reside in a property does not exist as an easement, although a tenant for life under a trust would often have such a right and a wife may have a statutory right of occupation under the *Family Law Act 1996*. A tenancy for life may also be granted by a lease.

Easements are rights enjoyed by the owner or occupier for the time being of piece of land (the dominant tenement) to be enjoyed over neighbouring land (the servient tenement), for example easements for water supply, drainage, the use of drives and footpaths and, in the case of apartments, the use of entrance halls, passages and staircases in the apartment block.

Easements are not personal rights but rights attached to the land, as a benefit for the dominant tenement and as a burden on the servient tenement. Easements and restrictions, which affect title to land, are registered in the title registers of the land registry .

Covenants

Among other encumbrances which may affect land, the most common are positive covenants and restrictive covenants. Certain distinctions are made under English law. A positive covenant (for example, a covenant to keep a fence in good repair) is regarded as a personal covenant, which does not attach to the land but is binding only as between the parties who entered into that agreement. On the other hand, a restrictive covenant (for example a covenant not to build any new structures on the land without the consent of the neighbour) is said to "run with the land", so that it is binding on the owner for the time being of the land to which the restriction is attached. However, the right to enforce such restrictive covenants is an equitable right and not a legal right and it may lapse if the Court comes to the conclusion that, for example, the party seeking to enforce the right initially allowed the breach of covenant to take place without objection or if the Court is of the opinion that the circumstances of the dominant and servient tenements have changed so much that it is no longer appropriate to enforce the right. (This might be where the dominant tenement was originally another house but has been redeveloped for some other purpose, such as a shopping centre, and therefore no longer really benefits from the covenant).

Restrictive covenants appear in the *Charges Register* of the relevant title at the land registry. Positive covenants are not registered at the land registry but the presence of such may be indicated.

In summary, the burden of negative obligations or "restrictive covenants" affecting the relevant piece of land passes automatically to a new owner on the transfer of title, but positive obligations do not.

Local land charges

It should be noted that individual apartments or houses may be subject to local land charges, which are not registered at the land registry. For example it could be that a local authority has given financial assistance for the development of a particular plot of land where the grant of this assistance is subject to a condition that it should be repaid if the use of land is changed. The right of the local authority to repayment of the financial assistance in certain circumstances would be registered in the local land charges register of that authority. These rights and restrictions, which apply to the local area, will be researched by the lawyer acting for a buyer by means of standard enquiries (called "local searches") made with the local authority on behalf of the buyers.

Charges and mortgages

The law of mortgages was simplified by means of the *Law of Property Act 1925*. As a result of this statute, earlier forms of mortgage were replaced by an encumbrance known as a legal charge, which can be registered against the title to the property as security for a loan or other financial obligation. In the case of most mortgages for residential property, the legal charge is contained within the loan agreement but it is sometimes the case that the legal charge is given in a separate document to secure all of the owner's borrowings from a particular bank or building society. In any event the legal charge must be registered at the land registry.

The *Land Registration Act 2002* introduced new requirements and obligations and included a more open register such that the price paid and the actual documents can be seen by the public.

It should be noted that, in contrast to the law in some other European countries, the legal charge provides not only security for the payment of interest and repayment of capital but also secures other sums which may fall due to the bank under the terms of the loan agreement, for example the cost of carrying out repairs which should have been carried out by the borrower or legal and other costs incurred by the lender in enforcing the terms of the loan agreement.

Additionally, English law has a concept of the equitable mortgage which is rare and is usually seen where a charging order has been obtained at Court.

Charges and encumbrances affecting residential property are registered in the *Land Charges Register* for the relevant title at the land registry. If the property has not yet been registered at the land registry the charge will be registered at the *Land Charges Registry*, in accordance with the *Land Charges Act 1925*.

Licences, third party rights and overriding interests

The owner of land may grant licences to third parties, for example the owner of a country house may permit the grazing of horses or other animals in a meadow under an arrangement which gives rise to a grazing licence. It is possible that this arrangement is not recorded in any written document. If a grazing licence is valid for a period of less than 365 days, the licensee is not given "security of tenure", that is, the right to continue the arrangement beyond the specified period. However, if the contractual period is greater than 364 days, this will create an *Agricultural Holding* (not a grazing licence) with the result that there is an extended period of protection for the party grazing animals against termination of the arrangement.

Protection of ownership, proof of ownership and registration

Registration of real estate in England has existed since 1925.

However, because there was no general obligation to register title to real estate from 1925 and in most cases the obligation to register would only arise on the transfer of the particular title, the process of registering English real estate is not complete. Accordingly unregistered land ownership remains in a number of places in England and Wales. Transfer by gift, Assent or a transfer of an interest in land requires compulsory registration.

Every registered title has its unique title number, so that the freehold and leasehold titles for the same piece of land will have different title numbers. The registers kept by the land registry consist of the following:

- The *Property Register*, in which the piece of land is described and all easements noted as well as certain excepted rights (for example mining rights)
- The *Proprietorship Register*, in which the name and address of the owner is recorded as is, usually, the price paid
- The *Charges Register*, in which charges and encumbrances are either set out in full or briefly noted by reference to other documents

As mentioned above, local land charges are not recorded at the land registry but in the local land charges register of the relevant municipality.

Trusts

It should be noted that under English law there is a distinction drawn between legal ownership and equitable or beneficial ownership. Normally the buyer of real estate will be the legal owner but also the beneficial owner. However, for a variety of reasons (for example the wish to transfer the benefit of real estate to children under the age of 18) it is not uncommon for the legal title to be put in the name of two or more trustees. The trustees are "legal owners" but for the benefit of other persons who are "the beneficial or equitable owners". The land registry only registers the names of the legal owners (the trustees) and when a prospective buyer is in negotiation with trustees, no details of the terms of any trust are available in public registers. However it would be usual to see a "Restriction" on the title register to alert the buyer that the property is owned by a trustee and held on trust. The reason for this is that, under legislation passed in 1925, anyone buying from trustees acquires the property free of the interest of beneficial owners. The rights of beneficial owners simply transfer to the proceeds of sale and if the beneficial owners have any complaint about the transaction, their only claim is against the trustees. Accordingly the buyer of the property needs only check that at least two trustees are registered as legal owners.

33.3 Purchase and sale of real estate

The sales agreement

The provisions of Schedule 2, *Law of Property (Miscellaneous Provisions) Act 1925* require that every contract for the sale of land and buildings should be in writing. There is no requirement in English law for notarial attestation of the contract and indeed no legal requirement to use any lawyer at all. Nonetheless, because of the complexity of the rights and obligations associated with the transfer of land, it would be extremely unwise to buy or sell land without advice from a suitably qualified lawyer, normally a solicitor.

Although there is no compulsory form for the sale of property and the fundamental principle of freedom of contract applies, most S*ale Contracts* are based on a printed form, which is published as the Standard Conditions of Sale (currently 5th edition for residential properties and the 2nd edition for the Standard commercial conditions).

Standard Conditions of Sale are divided into three sections:

- Particulars of sale: this section contains a description of the property, the amount of the sale price, the amount of the deposit to be paid by the buyer on exchange of contracts and the date for completion of the transfer and payment of the balance of the purchase price
- General conditions: these appear as printed conditions, which set out the rights and duties of the parties for the period between the date of the contract and the transfer date. It should be noted that the effect of these general conditions can be modified or cancelled by provisions included under the section "*Special Conditions*", as for example, where the seller may be required to maintain insurance of the property until completion of the transfer
- Special conditions: these conditions can either deal with modifications to the general conditions or deal with other matters such as carpets, curtains and other furnishings. Similarly they may

provide that the seller may take with him certain things that the buyer might normally have expected to be left in the property.

It should be noted that ownership does not pass to the buyer upon signature of the contract but only on the execution and delivery of a further document called a transfer. *Form TR1* is used for the transfer of the whole of a registered title and *Form TP1* is used for the transfer of part of a title. These forms are applicable both to freehold and leasehold properties. Title to unregistered property used to be transferred by means of a document called a conveyance but there is now an obligation to register on the sale of unregistered land and therefore a form of a transfer will always be used. Where a short-term lease does not need to be registered (less than seven years) ownership is passed by means of a document called an "Assignment".

It used to be the case that title to unregistered land passed immediately on the date of a conveyance. However, in theory, title to registered land does not pass at the date of the transfer but only when registration is completed at the land registry. In practice, however, the transferee is treated as being the new owner from the date of the transfer, except in very limited situations.

Although title to a property does not pass to the buyer on the execution of the contract, the normal rule is that insurance risks will pass to the buyer when contracts are signed. Accordingly the buyer should make sure that he has insurance arrangements in place from that date. It is nevertheless possible for the buyer to negotiate a special condition in the sale contract, obliging the seller to maintain insurance until the transfer date.

Restrictions on sale and acquisition

English law has a fundamental concept of freedom of contract, which means that parties can agree to anything that is not forbidden or restricted by law.

Restrictions under family law and matrimonial property regime

If title to land is registered in the joint names of husband and wife, this creates what is known as a trust for sale where (as stated above) the rights of each individual are governed by one of two forms: joint tenancy or tenancy in common, as mentioned in 33.2.

Matrimonial Home Rights

It is sometimes the case that a home occupied by a married couple has its legal title registered in the sole name of one of the spouses. *The Matrimonial Homes Act 1967* gave a wife a right of occupation in cases where the property was registered in the husband's sole name. The concept of matrimonial rights has now been extended by Section 30 of the *Family Law Act 1996*, which creates "*Matrimonial Home Rights*" under which either spouse has a right to occupy the house where the other is the registered owner. This right only applies to what is described as the matrimonial home, so that in cases where one spouse owns more than one property, the rights of occupation would not apply to an apartment or house which had not been occupied as a joint home. The right only lasts so long as the marriage subsists.

Accordingly, in any contract for the sale of a property where one spouse occupies by virtue of matrimonial home rights, that spouse should be joined as a party to the contract to agree to the sale and release the rights. To avoid possible fraud by the spouse who is registered as an owner, the contract should contain confirmation that the other spouse has had separate legal advice before agreeing to the sale.

Release of matrimonial home rights

A spouse entitled to matrimonial home rights may, in writing, release those rights or release them as respects part only of the dwelling house affected by them (s32 and schedule 4 paragraph 5(1), *Family Law Act 1996*).

The legislation does not refer to any specific wording but a suggested form is given in *The Law Society's Conveyancing Handbook (*10th ed. edited by *F Silverman)*, to be inserted into the contract:

"In consideration of the buyer entering this agreement I [name of spouse] agree:

1 to the sale of the property on the terms of this agreement; and

2 that I will not register rights in relation to the property, whether under *FLA 1996* or otherwise, and that I will procure before completion the removal of any registration made by me; and

3 that I will vacate the property by the completion date."

Where there is any danger of a conflict of interest of the non-owning spouse that spouse should seek separate legal advice.

Where charge has been registered

Where a contract is made for the sale of an estate or interest in a dwelling house (or for the grant of a lease) and that dwelling house is affected by a duly registered charge, the matrimonial home rights constituting that charge are deemed to be released on the occurrence of whichever of the following events happens first:

1 an application by the spouse for the cancellation of the charge is delivered to the buyer or lessee or his solicitor, or

2 such application is lodged at the land registry

Where the charge has been registered and the rights are extinguished by the termination of marriage, the land registry will cancel that charge on the production of valid evidence of the termination (schedule 4, paragraph 4).

Options and rights of pre-emption

Freedom of contract principles allow parties to agree a wide variety of arrangements involving pre-emption rights or options to purchase but these rights must not infringe on the rule against perpetuities, so that these rights cannot subsist for an unlimited period of time. In most situations the absolute time limit for exercise will be 21 years but for certain rights a perpetuity period of 80 years applies. If a lease term exceeds 80 years an option for the tenant to take a reversionary lease after the end of the term would still be valid if exercised within one year following expiration of the lease. Pre-emption rights or options should be protected by registration, or they may be unenforceable.

Agricultural real estate

Although the acquisition of agricultural land is, in principle, similar to the purchase of any other piece of land, it requires extra care because of the special factors necessary for the conduct of a successful farming business.

The laws which parliament has passed in relation to agricultural land often provide more far-reaching rights to tenants of agricultural land than to tenants of residential or commercial properties. For example, there are special tax concessions for the occupiers of farmland. In recent years the trend has been to move towards closer harmony with guidelines applicable in the European Union and also to take greater account of environmental issues.

The sale and purchase of agricultural land brings the parties into contact with some of the more esoteric elements of land law, which often have a distant historical origin, for example laws relating to *Common Land.* Besides that, the use of agricultural land may be affected by other factors such as hunting and fishing rights, which may be of significant importance. The consequence of this is that the process of transferring agricultural land (of which a significant proportion is still not registered at the land registry but will now need to be registered for the first time) is more time consuming than other types of land purchase and it will often require the co-ordination of different areas of legal expertise.

Until 1995, the law provided considerable security of tenure for tenants of agricultural land. Of particular note is the fact that the rights could be inherited by family members on the death of a tenant. These tenancies were known as agricultural holdings, established by the *Agricultural Holdings Act 1986.*

Since 1 September 1995, tenants of agricultural land (with limited exceptions) are protected by the *Agricultural Tenancies Act 1995*. The tenancies are called *Farm Business Tenancies* (FBT). Under this statute, a lease of agricultural land with a term of at least two years will be automatically renewed from year to year. There are rules for terminating these tenancies and these involve fewer restrictions on the freeholder than apply for agricultural holdings under the Act of 1986. In particular, FBTs cannot be inherited. Accordingly, it is important that the buyer of agricultural land should check very carefully whether any part of that land is affected by an agricultural holding or an FBT.

Furthermore, the buyer should take account of the possibility that the seller has allowed a third party to graze horses or other animals on part of the land. Such agreements do not have to be in writing to be valid and are referred to as "grazing licences" if they exist for a period of less than 365 days. However, if such an arrangement has a term of 365 days or more it may be protected as an agricultural holding or as a FBT and therefore would be significantly more difficult to bring to an end. The buyer should check this carefully.

Restrictions regarding acquisition of real estate by foreigners

English law has no restriction on ownership of real estate by foreign corporations or individuals.

Further important preconditions for buying real estate

Entitlement and capacity of the seller

An individual acquires full contractual capacity on his or her 18th birthday, except in cases of mental impairment.

Children or adults suffering from mental incapacity may be given a guardian or administrator by record. Normally trustees will be appointed. Parents can be trustees for their children, often with a lawyer or other professional person acting as co-trustee. In these cases, as previously mentioned, the trustees are the legal owners of property and the children or mentally impaired persons will be the beneficial or equitable owners.

For individual sellers, it is appropriate to search the bankruptcy register of the *Land Charges Registry* to ensure the seller is entitled to transfer the property. If the seller is a company, the company must pass the appropriate resolutions, and directors be authorised to sign on behalf of the company.

Third-party claims and unpaid taxes

On purchasing land, whether freehold or leasehold, it is most important to check whether any third parties have rights over it. Where title is registered at the land registry the title registers may show easements and other rights in favour of third parties as mentioned above. Additionally, there are two categories of rights to be noted – overriding interests and minor interests.

Overriding interests include, for example, the rights of anyone in actual occupation of the property. Anyone purchasing a property acquires it subject to the burden of overriding interests, even as these may not be noted on the land registry title register. The *Land Registration Act 2002*, which mostly came into force on 13 October 2003, introduced a new obligation on the seller of real estate to disclose any overriding interests of which he is aware. This is not an absolute obligation to disclose all such interests and the buyer will in any event take the property subject to those rights which may exist. Any third party rights which exist, other than overriding interests, are minor interests and will only obtain protection for the third party if they are registered at the land registry. In cases where there is no note on the land registry of a minor interest, the buyer will take the property free from the third party rights.

In cases where title to a property is still not registered at the land registry, other rules apply to third party rights which should have been registered at the *Land Charges Registry* under the *Land Charges Act 1927*. If such interests are not registered, the general rule is that the buyer takes free from such interests. There is, however, a distinction to be made between "legal interest" and "equitable interest". Legal rights (for example a legal easement) bind all parties, regardless of whether the buyer had knowledge of the relevant interest. However a person who buys in good faith and for valid consideration will take the property free from equitable interests of which she has no knowledge. However the buyer may be presumed to have knowledge of those things which should have been revealed by ordinary prudent investigation.

A lawyer who is instructed to advise on the purchase of real estate will make the appropriate enquiries and investigations as to what third party rights exist over the property to be purchased and what rights exist over neighbouring properties. Nevertheless, it is still wise to make a visual survey over the property where this may reveal rights which would not be disclosed by documents. For example, if a path crosses the land to be purchased, it may be evidence that a public or private right of way exists across the land even though this right may not be recorded in any title document.

The buyer of land will not generally, under English law, be automatically burdened by any unpaid taxes relating to that land. There is therefore no obligation on the buyer to check the tax status of the seller and the buyer will have no obligation to meet any tax liability of the seller. As mentioned below, the tenant of a property owned by a landlord who is resident for tax purposes outside the UK may be obliged to deduct tax from rental payments, unless the Landlord is able to obtain a notice of approval from *HM Revenue & Customs* for such rental payments to be paid gross.

Provisions for protecting the environment, nature and cultural heritage

There are regulations for the protection of the environment which may affect certain landowners and require that they enter into a management agreement with a public environmental body. However this would seldom relate to the owner of a house unless it was attached to a large acreage of land. The management agreement would provide that the landowner would make a fixed financial contribution to the cost of measures for environmental protection within the area. The apportionment of these payments at the time of sale and the question of whether the buyer of the property will become subject to these financial charges can involve lengthy negotiations before the contract is settled. This situation is particularly applicable to purchases of farms and other large estates.

It should also be noted that certain localities are designated as being areas of *Outstanding Natural Beauty* or as being areas of *Special Scientific Interest,* for example for the purpose of protecting rare plants, birds insects etc. Localities so classified have a specially protected status and in these areas the owner is unlikely to obtain planning permission to erect new buildings, even for agricultural use.

There are green areas around the outskirts of London, which are collectively known as *The Green Belt.* Until recently, it has been difficult to obtain planning permission for new buildings within the *Green Belt*, so that existing residential buildings have had an enhanced value. However, because of a huge demand for houses in the south east of England, the Government is reconsidering its policy for new construction within the *Green Belt* and it may be that in future years significant housing development will be permitted.

In the case of larger building developments, there may be additional requirements imposed on the developer, for example an obligation to produce an *Environmental Impact Study* and a *Traffic Impact Study* with his application for planning permission.

Buildings which are officially registered as being of historical or architectural interest (*Listed Buildings*) have special statutory protection which restricts the freedom of the owners to undertake alterations and the freedom of the planning authority to agree to such alterations. *Planning Policy Guidance Note 15 (PPG15)*, under the title *Planning in a Historical Context*, now requires the responsible planning authorities to look more flexibly at the use of historical buildings and to reach balanced decisions in individual cases which would allow the use of the relevant building for purposes which fit contemporary needs so as to promote the continued maintenance of their historical character. It has been found that excessively strict policies rendered certain buildings unmarketable and hence they fell into ruin.

Listed Buildings (a term which may include just part of a building, such as a historical staircase) are those that form an integral part of the urban environment and were not built more recently than July 1 1948. Listed buildings fall into the following three categories:

- Grade I: buildings of exceptional interest (approximately 2% of listed buildings)
- Grade II: particularly important buildings of more than special interest (approximately 4% of listed buildings)
- Grade III: buildings of special interest which warrant every effort to be made to preserve them

It is now generally recognised that a change of use for old buildings can be a catalyst for restoration and future preservation. In certain circumstances the restrictions associated with the listing of a building can be relaxed where this is necessary to keep the building in prolonged use. It is unquestionably considered ideal if a building can continue to be used for its original purpose. This should be done wherever possible.

Alterations to or demolition of listed buildings requires the consent of the local planning authority or of the *Secretary of State*. However, work to repair the building using materials which are the same as the original requires no consent.

Application for consent for works on a listed building should be made to the relevant planning authority which has eight weeks in which to consider the application. This time limit can be extended with the agreement of the applicant or in the event that any element of the application is changed.

It is important to note that retrospective permissions obtained in respect of works which have already been carried out are invalid. It is therefore most important that the necessary permissions are obtained for works on a listed building before construction commences.

Access to relevant records and documents

As a result of the *Land Registration Act 2002*, there has been a dramatic change in *Land Registration Rules*. The new rules took effect on 13 October 2003. From that date the land registry ceased to issue certificates of title in paper form and title to land depends only on what is recorded electronically within the land registry's computer database. This database can be accessed online and this is part of a general government programme to ensure that titles are easily available for public inspection.

There has also been a dramatic increase in the numbers of documents which are to be available for inspection on the register, for example leases and mortgage documents, which were referred to previously, but not available in full text. There has been concern that confidential information may now be accessible to the public. To meet these concerns, the land registry has created a procedure whereby an applicant may request that parts of a document be excluded from the copy to be shown in the public register. The basis of the request is that the information to be excluded is "prejudicial information" that is personal information likely to cause substantial or unwarranted damage or distress or information likely to prejudice the commercial interests of the applicant. (It should be noted that price information is not considered to be commercially sensitive.) If an application to exclude some information from the register is granted, the record will nevertheless show that some information has been omitted from the register.

In the event that a piece of land has not yet been registered at the land registry, title can only be established by means of inspection of deeds and documents, generally held by the owner's bank or lawyers. Nevertheless some public information is kept at the *Land Charges*

Registry in which certain encumbrances are registered, for instance an option to purchase or a restrictive covenant. If the seller is a corporation, investigations should be made at the *Companies Registry* which will have details of mortgages registered against that company. If a seller is an individual, it is also normal and appropriate to make a search with the bankruptcy register of the *Land Charges Registry* to ensure that the seller is entitled to transfer the property. On completion of any transaction for such a property, registration at the land registry is compulsory.

Key points that a seller should consider

If someone proposes to sell a house, he will generally be looking to acquire a new residence at the same time. It is therefore important to check that there are no impediments which will stop the transaction proceeding to the planned timetable. Accordingly it is advisable to ask whether the buyer himself has a house to dispose of and how that sale is to proceed. In England, this is referred to as a "chain" of buyers and the ideal situation is to find a buyer who is "chain free", that is someone who can buy without needing to sell a property.

It is particularly important in chain transactions, but also in other cases, to check whether the intending buyer has arranged satisfactory finance before marketing or sale negotiations with other possible buyers are discontinued.

As mentioned elsewhere, there are no restrictions on foreigners acquiring real estate in England but all those involved in a land transaction must be aware of strict duties to report any suspicion of money laundering.

The execution of a real estate purchase transaction

A purchase transaction generally commences with the intending buyer making a written but non-binding offer to purchase the property "subject to contract". A person unfamiliar with the local market will often use a chartered surveyor to advise on the terms of the offer and to make that offer on his behalf. If this initial offer is accepted by the seller, the buyer will not be contractually bound to purchase until "exchange of contracts", that is, when both parties have signed and exchanged their copy of a written contract.

In the interval between the offer and exchange of contracts, the solicitor will generally carry out the following investigations on behalf of his client:

- He will check the title to the property and investigate whether any other party has a right of pre-emption or whether there are boundary disputes. He will establish the extent of the owner's rights and what easements, charges or other encumbrances exist
- He will check any lease affecting the property and its associated documentation
- He will check the ownership rights relating to fixtures and fittings within the property
- Where the property has been recently constructed, he will look at the construction documentation, building permits etc. and ensure, where possible, that all guarantees are transferred to the buyer
- He will make appropriate enquiries with the relevant local authority such as the town authority or county authority, (which is often the responsible highway authority). His investigations may also reveal any possible difficulties with building permits or permissions to change use of the property or even a threatened compulsory acquisition of the property for municipal works or road construction

In the light of the results of these investigations, and any tax considerations, he will negotiate the terms of the purchase contract.

When all the due diligence is satisfactorily completed, finance for the purchase arranged and agreement reached on all points within the purchase contract, the parties will proceed to exchange of contracts. At this point, the buyer will pay a deposit, normally 10% of the purchase price. This deposit may be paid to the seller but it is generally preferable that it is paid to the solicitors acting for the seller to be held by them as stakeholders until completion of the sale.

The parties typically agree a period of four weeks between exchange of contracts and transfer of the property (to allow for all appropriate removal arrangements to be made). During this period the lawyers will settle the terms of the transfer documents and check with the land registry that no new encumbrances have been registered against the property and any necessary finance or mortgage documents will be signed and executed and a title report given to the lender so that the money is available before the completion date.

Stamp Duty Land Tax (SDLT) is a tax on land transactions, described in more detail below, under which the buyer generally has to submit a self-assessment form to *HM Revenue & Customs* for SDLT purposes, together with payment of the SDLT due, within 30 days of the transaction. This is usually facilitated by the lawyer acting as the buyer's agents and submitted online.

If *HM Revenue & Customs* is satisfied with the completion of the self-assessment form, they will issue a certificate of receipt. This is an important document, as it must be submitted to the land registry with the application for registration of the transfer to the buyer. No registration will take place without this certificate.

It will be noted that there is a time lag between completion of the transfer and the application to register the transfer at the land registry. The buyer's lawyer will ensure that the buyer has priority over any new encumbrances by lodging a search form at the land registry to check what entries are on the title prior to completion of the transfer. The certificate of search returned by the land registry will state a priority period of 30 working days and so long as the application to register the transfer is lodged with the land registry within this priority period, the buyer will have priority over any other applications which might be received by the land registry.

Real estate is normally sold, but where real estate is to be transferred by gift and not by way of sale, it should be remembered that legal ownership can only pass by means of a written transfer, registerable at the land registry. Handing over the keys to the house will not pass legal ownership, but in certain circumstances, where the intention to make a gift is clear, the legal owner could become in equity a trustee of the property and the receiver of the keys become the beneficial owner. The tax considerations are mentioned below.

Powers of attorney

Documents relating to the sale and purchase or mortgage of real estate may be executed on behalf of one or more parties by a person acting under a valid power of attorney. A power of attorney may confer a "general power" to conduct transactions in general or a "special power" to execute documents for a specific purpose, for example, the purchase of a house.

- *Powers of Attorney Act 1971* is an Act relating to the creation of powers. It contains guidance as to execution of powers and effect of a 'general power of attorney'
- *Trustee Delegation Act 1999* is an Act to amend the law relating to the delegation of trustee functions by power of attorney and the exercise of such functions by the donee of a power of attorney; and to make provision about the authority of the donee of a power of attorney to act in relation to land
- *Enduring Powers of Attorney Act 1985* allows the donor to confer powers to a donee via a valid instrument (prescribed form). These powers will survive any subsequent mental incapacity by the donor. There is an obligation on the donee to apply for registration of the power if it is apparent that the donor is becoming mentally incapacitated. When applying for registration the donee must comply with certain notice requirements (i.e. towards family members). Power granted can be general authority or a more limited authority (similar to the restricted 'special power'). Where an instrument is

expressed to confer general authority on the attorney it operates to confer, subject to the restriction imposed by Subsection 5, and to any conditions or restrictions contained in the instrument, authority to do on behalf of the donor anything which the donor can lawfully do by an attorney. Limited authority is expressed as the 'power to do specified things'. Both types of authority are subject to whatever additional restrictions and conditions are in the instrument. Under both types of authority (subject to conditions or restrictions) the donee may act in ways to benefit himself (Sections 3, (4) and (5))

There are no statutory provisions that relate to automatic expiration of an enduring power after a certain time limit and there is apparently nothing in the Acts imposing an obligation to check if a power has been revoked.

Once an enduring power is registered under the *Enduring Powers of Attorney Act 1985*, the donor may not revoke it without the court's confirmation. Under the same Act the court has powers to revoke a registered power (i.e. under the provisions of the *Mental Health Act* part VII).

Any power granted overseas with the express intention of being effective in England would comply with English execution requirements, if it includes a straightforward jurisdiction clause that it is to be governed by English law.

Financing

Many banks in England offer mortgage finance but, for buyers whose normal residence is in another country, the formalities associated with the prevention of money laundering may be time consuming. If speed is necessary, it may be appropriate to arrange the necessary finance with a bank at home. If a person who is not resident in the UK takes up a loan facility to invest in UK real estate, he can set off the interest against his taxable income in the UK, regardless of whether the lender has its place of business in the UK. If a loan is granted by a family member or some other close acquaintance, it is not possible to offset more than a normal commercial rate of interest against taxable income.

Purchase through a company

Real estate may be purchased by a company, which it will normally hold beneficially for itself, but may hold as nominee for another. In the first case limited liability should be available, but not in the latter situation. If the company is non UK incorporated, it will be treated as UK resident for tax purposes if its central management and control takes place in the UK. Holding property through a company may also lead to a double capital gains tax liability if the company sells the property and the money is then extracted from the company.

Warranty claims

The normal rule in a sale of any property is *caveat emptor* i.e. buyer beware. However the sales agreement normally imposes some obligations on the seller which would include an unlimited title guarantee. This means that the seller gives the buyer a guarantee against adverse claims of title to the property. This guarantee does not include any rights or encumbrances which might be discovered by making appropriate enquiries with the land registry or other public authorities.

It should also be noted that the guarantee does not relate to the physical condition of the property. A buyer can usually only take action against a seller in the case of the seller making a representation about the condition of the property which then proves to be false. It is therefore normally advisable to have properties inspected by a professional surveyor and to make prudent enquiries about such things as flooding in bad weather and the nature of any building work which the seller has carried out in the house.

33.4 New construction, rebuilding and renovation

Construction zones and construction permits

Building control is exercised at a variety of levels and through different statutory bodies.

The general rule is that new buildings require building permits known as "planning consents" issued by local authorities under parliamentary statutes known as the *Town and Country Planning Acts* or, more briefly as the *Planning Acts*. These laws relate to every kind of "development", an expression which includes not only new construction but also particular changes in the use of a building, for example the conversion of a single family house into two or more self-contained apartments. There is also a *General Development Order* (GDO) which allows certain minor works to be carried out without the need for any application for planning consent, for example an extension of a living room. Even where the GDO is applicable it is still necessary to obtain approval of plans and specifications under the *Building Regulations*. These regulations are dealt with in a separate section of the local authority's building control department and focus more on the engineering aspect of construction to ensure that that the regulations for structural stability, security, drainage and environmental regulation are complied with.

It should be noted that the GDO does not apply in the following two instances, namely where the house is situated in a neighbourhood which is classified as a *Conservation Area* in official local plans; secondly, the GDO does not apply where the house itself is a listed building.

Planning permission is required for all new construction to the exterior of the building. This does not include repair of the existing structure so long as the same materials are being used. Where work is to be carried out on a listed building, it is not only necessary to obtain planning permission but also separate building permit known as *Listed Building Consent*. In such cases, the local authority will be looking to monitor compliance with the outlines laid down by statutory consultees for such works, for example, *English Heritage*. Even where listed building consent is issued, it will frequently contain strict stipulations and conditions relating to the building materials and construction matters to be permitted. Breach of these conditions will attract sharp penalties.

Architect's and building contracts

It is naturally possible for an individual to engage his own architect and appropriate consultants for the building of a new house; however this method of procurement requires experienced legal advice to ensure that the individual contracts for architects and consultants are not only appropriate in themselves but fully co-ordinated to avoid contradiction or gaps in responsibility.

It is much simpler to buy a newly constructed house from a developer who is a member of the *National House Builders Council* (NHBC) or other recognised supervisory body for the house building industry. A certificate issued by the NHBC gives the buyer a 10 year guarantee, up to a certain limit, against certain structural defects (such as inadequate foundations), and a two year guarantee against more minor building defects. The rights attached to these guarantees can be transferred to a subsequent buyer, insofar as the relevant time limits remain unexpired. However, the maximum coverage is GBP 1 million, although other products may provide higher coverage.

In the case of renovation works or alteration works, an *NHBC Certificate* is unlikely to be available unless the house is almost entirely reconstructed (for example everything except the original façade). Nevertheless, certain insurance companies will offer limited guarantees for renovation works or building alteration works. In other cases, where no such guarantees can be obtained, the owner might simply look to the relevant trade contractors, such as electricians and roofing specialists for specific guarantees relating to the work and perhaps also engage a project manager who will accept responsibility for adequate supervision of works.

Completion of construction and formalities

A contract for the purchase of a house or apartment to be constructed by the seller usually provides that the buyer will pay the balance of the purchase price within 14 days following the date on which completion of the property is certified by the seller. The buyer would be well advised to have a provision entered into the contract allowing the buyer to inspect the property for defects when the property is certified, so that he can either contest the obligation to make the payment in the event that there are serious defects or reach an agreement that a certain sum is to be retained until smaller defects are put right.

Additionally, all completed buildings should be inspected by a representative of the local authority *Building Control Department*, who should certify that it has been completed in accordance with the relevant planning conditions and building regulations. The buyer should insist on this being done before payment of the purchase price.

The buyer of an apartment should also ensure that the obligation to pay the money does not arise only when the apartment itself is completed, but when other communal facilities are also ready for use, such as lifts, car parks and communal swimming pool.

Additionally, he should check that any conditions imposed by a bank or other lender before the loan can be drawn down are satisfactorily dealt with in the purchase contract. It may be that the bank will wish its own surveyor to inspect the completed building before the loan is granted.

Deficiencies and warranty claims regarding new construction

As mentioned above, the NHBC provides "*Buildmark Cover*" guaranteeing against building defects where the builder is a member of the council. This cover falls into three parts:

- Problems before completion of the building, for example where the builder becomes insolvent before the property is finished
- Defects arising in the first two years, a free independent resolution service to deal with problems arising in the first two years
- A problem arising during year's three to ten. In this case, such building defects will need to be the subject of formal claim with the *NHBC* who will provide the necessary claim documentation (*nhbc.co.uk*)

33.5 Rental and tenancy

Rental and leasing contracts

Under English law, a lease is not only a contract between landlord and tenant but it creates an "interest in land". The landlord can sell on his interest in the land without terminating the lease. The buyer from the landlord takes the land subject to and with the benefit of the lease terms. Similarly the tenant can assign its lease, subject to any contrary provisions that may be included in the lease contract.

In principle, every occupier who pays a weekly, monthly or yearly sum of money for the exclusive use of a house or apartment has a tenancy under English law. The rights of the tenant are mainly governed by the terms of the lease contract (in accordance with the concept of freedom of contract) but they are also materially influenced by relevant statutes.

English law makes a difference between fixed term tenancies and periodical tenancies (for example, a lease for a term of seven years as opposed to a yearly tenancy). All lease contracts with a fixed duration of more than three years must be created by deed. Since 13 October 2003, there is an additional requirement that all leases granted for a term of seven or more years, or assigned at a time when seven or more years of the term remain unexpired, must be registered at the land registry . If the title of the landlord is already registered at the land registry, the tenant may be registered with *Title Absolute*. In the absence of proof of the landlord's title, the tenant may be registered with *Good Leasehold Title*.

As to the influence of statute, laws created between 1950 and 1990 had provided so much protection for tenants that landlords became unwilling to grant residential tenancies. In recognition of this, the government passed various *Housing Acts* and created new tenancies known as "shorthold tenancies" and "assured shorthold tenancies" which allowed landlords to lease properties on the basis that they could recover possession of the property at the end of a fixed term, for example, three years. The tenant does not have an automatic right to renew the lease and the landlord (after giving appropriate notice) may either re-let the property at the end of the term or occupy the property for his own use.

Regulation on protection of tenants and rent control

Care should be taken about the notices to be given to terminate a tenancy. Under English law, a tenancy does not necessarily terminate automatically at the end of a fixed term of, say, two years. Where a landlord intends to terminate a tenancy he must consider any express provisions contained in the lease or tenancy agreement relating to the service of notice on the tenant. Secondly the landlord must have regard to the statutory provisions which are relevant to the particular type of tenancy. The landlord must comply both with the contractual arrangements in the former and the statutory obligations in the latter. For example under the *Housing Act 1988*, a tenant of an assured shorthold tenancy must be given at least two months prior notice in writing before the end of the tenancy. If the tenancy agreement provides for three months' notice, the landlord must comply.

In the case of an agricultural tenancy, the *Agricultural Tenancies Act 1995* requires notice to be given at least 12 months but no more than 24 months before the date of expiry of the tenancy.

The present law states that assured shorthold tenancies have a minimum of six months duration but in November 2003 the Government's Law Reform Agency, the *Law Commission*, announced changes which will introduce a tenancy form with no minimum duration. It is expected that necessary legislation will be passed through parliament during 2004. The proposal nevertheless provides for a minimum period of two months' notice to terminate such a tenancy.

33.6 Succession and gifts

Applicable law and jurisdiction

Under English law, when someone dies leaving a valid will, then their property will pass according to that will. If someone dies without leaving a valid will dealing with all of their property the *Administration of Estates Act 1925* applies.

With regard to conflict laws, in the case of intestacy the rule is as follows:

1 Where the property is movable, the applicable law is that of the country in which the intestate was domiciled at their time of death
2 Where the property is immovable, the applicable law is that of the country where the property is situated

Fundamentals of the succession and gift/donation laws of the UK

In English law there is no general obligation on a testator to leave any part of his estate to any particular person.

If someone dies leaving a spouse and children, that spouse is entitled to personal chattels, a statutory legacy of GBP 125,000 and a life interest in half of the remainder of the estate. The other half will go to the children, who inherit the remaining half on the death of the surviving spouse.

If there are no children then all personal chattels and GBP 200,000 goes to the surviving spouse, and a half share in the residue. The remainder goes to the deceased's parents equally if more than one, or if there are none then on trust for the deceased's brothers and sisters, nephews and nieces.

If there is no spouse then the property will be distributed as follows:

- Natural and adopted children, but if none
- Parents, but if none
- Brothers/sisters (whole blood), but if none
- Brothers/sisters (half blood), but if none
- Grandparents, but if none
- Aunts/uncles (whole blood), but if none

- Aunts/uncles (half blood), but if none
- The Crown (bona vacantia)

If a person is aggrieved because they have been left out of a will, have not benefited from the intestacy rules or is dissatisfied with any benefit received, they may apply to the court under the *Inheritance (Provision for Families and Dependants) Act 1975*, provided they fall within a certain category of persons (a spouse, a child or someone treated as a child, a dependant or cohabitee). The court has discretion to vary the effect of the will or intestacy rules to reflect the legitimate claims of a dependent person.

It is generally desirable to have a will drawn up in the UK if UK property is owned by an individual. This avoids the necessity of a resealing of a foreign grant of probate in the UK in order to deal with the administration of a property owned by the deceased. Property owned by companies or trusts are not generally required to go through the probate procedure.

However, the courts will recognise in particular circumstances that certain family members or other dependants had a legitimate right to expect a reasonable provision from the estate of the deceased person. If any person feels that they have been wrongly omitted from a will or that the intestacy rules have not made adequate provision for them they may apply to the court under The *Inheritance (Provisions for Families and Dependants) Act 1995* if they fall within certain categories of persons – a spouse, a child, someone treated as a child, a dependant or co-habitee. The court may in its discretion vary the effect of the will or the intestacy rules to reflect the legitimate claims of such dependant person.

33.7 Taxes and charges

One-time taxes and charges on purchase

Purchase / acquisition taxes

Stamp Duty Land Tax (SLDT) is a tax chargeable on land transactions with effect from 1 December 2003. *Stamp Duty* historically applied to transfers of freehold and leasehold land, but since 1 December 2003 has only applied to transfers or other dealings with stock or marketable securities.

Unlike *Stamp Duty*, SDLT is not a tax on documents. The tax is therefore chargeable whether or not the transaction is effected by means of a document (or instrument) – and the place of execution of any document, and residence of the parties to a transaction, have no bearing on the charge to tax.

Some of the key SDLT concepts and terminology are set out below:

- Land Transaction: the acquisition of a chargeable interest in land
- Chargeable Interest: an estate, interest, right or power in or over land in the UK, or the benefit of an obligation, restriction or condition that affects the value of any such estate, interest, right or power
- Effective Date: if a transaction is completed without previously having been substantially performed the effective date of the transaction is the date of completion; if a contract is substantially performed without having been completed, the effective date of the transaction is when the contract is substantially performed
- Exempt Interest: a security interest (held for the purpose of securing the payment of money or the performance of any other obligation), a licence to use or occupy land and a tenancy at will
- Substantially Performed: a contract is substantially performed when (a) the buyer or a person connected with the buyer takes possession of the whole (or substantially the whole) of the land that is the subject matter of the contract; or (b) the whole, or substantially the whole, amount of the consideration is paid (which in the case of a rack rent lease includes the first payment of rent)
- Major Interest in Land: any fee simple or term of years absolute – so it includes all freehold and leasehold interests
- Notifiable Transaction: most land transactions, including the grant of a lease even if it is exempt

- Linked Transactions: transactions forming part of a single scheme, arrangement or series of transactions between the same parties or persons connected with them

The basic rules governing the charge to SDLT are as follows:

- SDLT is payable by the buyer on land transactions and is calculated by reference to the chargeable consideration provided by the buyer (which includes any Value Added Tax payable on the consideration). The liability to account for SDLT is triggered by reference to the effective date of the transaction
- If there is a contract for a land transaction that is completed by a conveyance, the contract and conveyance are together treated as a single land transaction that has an effective date on the day of completion. For these purposes, "contract" includes any agreement and "conveyance" includes any instrument. The terms thus include a contract to sell a freehold followed by a *Land Registry Transfer*, or an agreement for lease followed by the grant of the lease itself
- If the contract is not completed with a conveyance, but is instead substantially performed, the land transaction is treated as having an effective date that is the date of such substantial performance
- If there is substantial performance of a contract, giving rise to a liability to notify and pay SDLT, and there is a subsequent conveyance, both are notifiable transactions. However, SDLT is only paid on the conveyance to the extent that the SDLT due exceeds the SDLT chargeable by reference to the contract
- For leases, SDLT is payable by reference to (a) any premium payable for the grant of the lease (using the percentage figures from the tables below); as well as (b) the total net present value (NPV) of rents payable over the life of the lease (at 1%, for residential after deducting a GBP 125,000 threshold) and 1% after deducting GBP 150,000 for mixed use or commercial.
- Rent changes after five years are to be left out of account when calculating the NPV of the lease for SDLT purposes when it is granted

- Even after five years, if the rent is reviewed and the result is an "abnormal increase" in rent (as calculated under the relevant SDLT rules), this will be treated as the grant of a new lease and SDLT will be payable by reference to the NPV of the increase for the balance of the term
- Where a lease with an uncertain rent, such as a turnover rent, is granted the rules provide for a "reasonable estimate" to be made for tax purposes at the outset. SDLT is paid by reference to the estimate. If the rent is still uncertain at the five year point, then an additional return will be required for which the NPV is recalculated. If the rent becomes certain before the five year point then the additional return will be required at that time. The new NPV calculation will be based on the highest rent in any period of 12 months in the previous five years. Depending upon the NPV calculated by making a "reasonable estimate" at the outset, this may lead to a payment of further SDLT or a repayment of all or some of the tax originally paid

The amount of SDLT payable in respect of a chargeable transaction is calculated as a percentage of the chargeable consideration. The percentage is progressing as of 4 December 2014 for contracts entered into.

Table 6. SDLT, non residential or mixed use

Non residential or mixed	
Up to GBP 150,000 and annual rent under GBP 1,000	0%
GBP 150,001 - GBP 250,000 up to GBP 150,000 and annual rent is GBP 1,000 or more	1%
GBP 250,001 - GBP 500,000 up to GBP 150,000 and annual rent is GBP 1,000 or more	3%
Over GBP 500,000 up to GBP 150,000 and annual rent is GBP 1,000 or more	4%

Table 7. SDLT, residential

Residential	
Up to GBP 125,000	0%
Over GBP 125,000 - GBP 250,000	2%
Over GBP 250,000 - GBP 925,000	5%
Over GBP 925,000 - GBP 1,500,000	10%
Over GBP 1,500,000	12%

Sales tax (value added tax)

The purchase of real estate is generally exempt from VAT (currently at 20% in the UK) unless the seller (or the landlord, in the case of a lease) has validly opted to tax the land and buildings in question, which will often be the case with commercial property. VAT is not normally payable on the purchase of dwellings, but will normally be payable on the cost of home improvements made. There are other VAT considerations where commercial property is converted to residential use.

Real estate registration and notary charges

Fees payable to the land registry depend on the value of the property and if the registration is submitted online. The maximum fee is currently GBP 910.

There is no requirement for a notary to be involved in UK land transactions.

Annually recurring taxes and charges

Real estate tax

There are no annual real estate taxes currently payable in the UK, other than rates and council tax payable to the local authority. Since April 2013, there has been annual tax charge for residential properties valued at over GBP 2 million owned by certain non-natural persons, called the *Annual Tax on Enveloped Dwellings* (ATED). The amount of ATED will depend on the value of the property on 1 April 2012 (until April 2017) (or its subsequent purchase price). The bands and charges (which are index-linked) are shown in the following table.

From 1 April 2015 a new band came into effect for properties valued at over GBP 1 million and up to GBP 2 million, with an annual charge of GBP 7,000. From 1 April 2016 a further band will come into effect for properties valued at over GBP 500,000 and up to GBP 1 million, with an annual charge of GBP 3,500.

From 1 April 2015 the charges for all of the bands above GBP 2 million increased and are:

Table 8. Annual tax on enveloped dwellings

Property value	ATED (from 1 April 2015)
Over GBP 2m to GBP 5m	GBP 23,350
Over GBP 5m to GBP 10m	GBP 54,450
Over GBP 10m to GBP 20m	GBP 109,050
Over GBP 20m	GBP 218,200

Income tax

If the foreign resident or domiciliary is simply using the property as a home then there should be no income tax as the property will not be generating any income.

If the property is being rented out then the foreign owner will be taxable on the rental profits and must submit tax returns every year. If the owner is non UK resident then there is an obligation on the tenant or property agent to deduct basic rate tax (2014/15: 20%) before sending the net rents abroad.

It is possible for non-resident landlords to apply for approval under *HM Revenue & Customs' Non-Resident Landlord Scheme* where, in return for a commitment on the part of the landlord to submit annual UK tax returns, *HM Revenue & Customs* will allow the rents to be sent abroad gross of tax. This is a cash flow advantage only: income tax will still be payable on the net profits of the letting business.

There are various methods of minimising the income tax payable on the rents and the most common is to use borrowings, as an arm's length amount of interest payments should be deductible against the rental income when calculating the tax payable, provided that the loan was taken out 'wholly and exclusively' for the purposes of the letting business; this is often a trap.

It should be remembered that if a UK property is directly owned by a foreign domiciliary, upon his death (even if he is non-resident) there is a requirement that UK probate is obtained. This can be particularly irritating if the foreign domiciliary has no other UK assets.

If the property is rented out by a company the income tax position is broadly the same as for personal or direct trust ownership, except that the company's liability to income tax is restricted to the basic rate (20% for the tax year 2014/15). If any back-to-back arrangements are used to reduce the company's liability to income tax on rents then transfer pricing needs to be considered.

If the company allows the property to be used to provide the foreign domiciliary with rent free accommodation then there may be an assessment on the foreign domiciliary's occupation as a benefit in kind under the UK's income tax regime.

Net wealth tax

There is currently no wealth tax in the UK.

Corporation tax

Corporation tax (the main rate is 21% for the corporation tax year 2014/15) is payable by a company in respect of income received or gains realised on roughly the same principles as income tax and capital gains tax for individuals. It can also be payable in respect of foreign companies that become tax resident in the UK by virtue of their central management and control being in the UK.

Capital gains tax

Subject to the five year temporary non-residence rules, certain non-resident owners may at present dispose of UK property without any liability to capital gains tax (CGT). CGT is only payable if the taxpayer is actually resident in the UK during the year of disposal. An individual who is not resident in the UK may nonetheless be taxed on certain gains if they are carrying on a trade in the UK through a branch or agency. From April 2015 non-residents will be subject to CGT on gains arising on the disposal of UK residential property.

From a CGT perspective, direct ownership of owner–occupied property can be particularly effective as, if the property is the taxpayer's main or sole residence, it will be exempt from CGT by way of the main residence exemption. New rules as to how this relief will operate in respect of a property located in a jurisdiction in which the owner is not tax resident will be brought in from April 2015.

Ownership through a company

A non-UK resident company (by virtue of being incorporated, controlled and managed outside the UK) will not suffer corporation tax on its capital gains. However, if the company has been controlled and managed in the UK, it will be liable to pay tax on its capital gains.

Since April 2013 the scope of CGT has been extended to also include non natural persons (including both non-UK resident and UK resident entities) that are within the scope of ATED (as described above). Where applicable the potential charge to corporation tax is replaced with a charge to CGT.

Inheritance and gift taxes

The major problem with direct ownership is that the property is a UK situs asset and as such is always subject to inheritance tax (IHT), regardless of the taxpayer's foreign domicile or residence. Thus, when the taxpayer dies, IHT will be payable at the rate of 40%, insofar as the value of it and any other UK assets exceed the prevailing nil rate band (which for the tax year 2014/15 stands at GBP 325,000).

However, there are various estate planning techniques which can be used to mitigate the IHT exposure on UK assets.

One technique is for the taxpayer to give the property away to a younger member of the family. The gift will be a 'potentially exempt transfer' and as long as the donor survives the gift by seven years there should be no IHT payable by him. However, there are various anti-avoidance measures which can defeat the purpose of the gift.

Other taxes and charges

Other than SDLT, VAT, IHT, corporation tax, capital gains tax and income tax there are no relevant taxes and charges apart from Council Tax and business rates, which are payable by the owner or occupant to the *Local Authority* depending on the value of the property.

Incorrect (lower) statement of sale price on the sales agreement

It is strictly illegal to state a lower price than the real price in the sale agreement. It is sometimes done to reduce the SDLT band, but will normally be discovered when the tax return is submitted.

Contracts for the purchase of land and transfers of title of land must be in writing. If the price shown in the transfer document understated the true price being paid by the buyer, lender and buyer and their respective legal advisers could be guilty of fraud on the *Inland Revenue.*

As mentioned above, SDLT is a tax on transactions relating to land and not a document tax. Accordingly, the provisions of the contract and all related documentation may be brought into assessment and duty payable by reference to the consideration disclosed. As before, any failure to disclose the true consideration being paid could result in prosecution by the *Inland Revenue*. It should be noted that it is the buyer's personal responsibility to submit an accurate SDLT return to the *Inland Revenue* following completion of the transaction.

International taxation

Double tax treaties are relevant to ascertain the prevailing residence for tax purposes in respect of individuals if the individual is resident in the UK for UK domestic tax purposes, and in a treaty country for domestic tax purposes of that country. The double tax treaty will set out rules for ascertaining the country in which the tax payer resides for the purposes of payment of tax.

The rules in the majority of treaties follow the *OECD Model Convention*, the general rules of which are:

- If the individual has a permanent home available to him in one of those countries then he will be treated as resident in that country
- If he has a permanent home in both countries, he will be treated as resident in the country with which his personal and economic ties are closest
- If he does not have a permanent home in either country, or the closeness of his personal and economic relations is inconclusive, he will be treated as resident in the country where he has a habitual abode
- If he has a habitual abode in both or neither countries, he will be treated as a resident of the country of which he is a national
- If he is a national of both or neither countries, the residence ultimately will be determined by mutual agreement between the taxing authorities of each country

In respect of planning with the use of offshore trusts and companies, treaties are not normally very relevant, as most low tax jurisdictions do not have any treaty with the UK. Guernsey and Jersey do have restricted treaties, but they are not in the form of the *OECD Model Convention.*

In respect of high tax countries, treaties will be rather more relevant. If an individual is resident in a foreign country by virtue of the tests set out above under the treaty, the treaty will generally only allow the UK taxing rights over UK source income and gains. The latter will not be relevant for non-residents in many cases.

33.8 Immigration law and tax residence

Entry, residence and settlement of foreigners

Under European Union (EU) law, EU citizens and citizens of countries within the European Economic Area (collectively known as EEA nationals) are entitled to free movement within the EEA. Such citizens entitled to this include workers, self-employed, providers and recipients of services, students, financially independent persons, retired persons and family members. They are entitled to a conditional right of residence, rights of entry, access to employment, self-employment, study and social security.

Immigration for EU/EEA and Swiss nationals

Nationals of countries in the EEA, which besides the EU includes nationals of Iceland, Liechtenstein and Norway, have been given the same rights as EU citizens to enter, live and work in the UK.

From 1 June 2002, by virtue of the *Immigration (European Economic Area) Regulations 2000*, Swiss nationals and their family members have the same rights as EEA nationals to enter, live and work in the UK.

For convenience, EEA nationals and Swiss nationals are referred to as "EEA nationals" in this summary.

Family rights

If an EEA national has a right to live and lives in the UK, his or her family (whether or not they are EEA nationals) may join him or her.

Family members who are EEA nationals have the same 'freedom of movement' rights as the EEA national they are accompanying or joining. Non-EEA nationals do not have these rights (but may have other immigration rights of their own). Non-EEA national family members will need to apply for an EEA Family Permit prior to travelling to the UK.

Family members living in the UK as the family members of an EEA national may lose their right to stay if the EEA national leaves the UK permanently or no longer has a right to live in the UK.

Rights as to working

With the exception of Croatian nationals in certain circumstances, an EEA citizen in the UK does not need a work permit to accept offers of work, or to work in employment, self-employment or in business.

Documentation

An EEA national with a right to live in the UK is not required to obtain a residence permit or register with the police. However, he or she can apply for a residence permit if they wish. The permit confirms that the applicant has the right to live in the UK. If the EEA national does obtain a permit, it will usually be valid for five years.

Staying in the UK indefinitely

EEA nationals (apart from students) may apply for Indefinite Leave to Remain in the UK (i.e. with no time limit or conditions upon their stay) if:

- They have been working or supporting themselves financially in the UK for at least five years and are still doing so (this may be evidenced through a residence permit); and
- They still have the right to live in the UK

EEA nationals who are now of pensionable age and retired or permanently incapable of work due to injury etc may qualify to live in the UK indefinitely in certain circumstances.

Non EU/EEA nationals only have the right to live in the UK if they have the appropriate right of abode, visa or work permit.

Tax residence

Domicile for UK tax purposes is generally where an individual has his permanent home. Every person is born with a *Domicile of Origin*, but can change this by choice if he settles in another country or state with the intention of doing so permanently or indefinitely. It is distinct from residence for tax purposes. A non-UK domiciled and non-UK resident person will pay no inheritance tax (except on UK assets), capital gains tax (except on UK residential property from April 2015) or income tax (except on UK source income). A non-UK domiciled but UK resident person will be treated on the same basis except that he will be taxable on income and capital gains remitted to the UK or earned or realised in the UK (this remittance basis treatment is not automatic and it is necessary to make a claim, including in certain circumstances payment of a GBP 30,000, GBP 60,000 or GBP 90,000 remittance basis charge, depending on the number of years the individual has been resident in the UK). For inheritance tax only, a non-UK domiciled person will be treated as domiciled in the UK once he has been resident in the UK for 17 out of any 20 tax years. The payment amounts quoted are as of 6 April 2015.

Prior to 5 April 2013 the rules on residence were primarily case law based. Since 6 April 2013 a statutory residence test has been in operation. There are two limbs to the test and if either is met then the individual is resident in the UK for the tax year in question. If neither is met then the individual is not resident in the UK for that year. The two limbs are an 'automatic residence' test (broadly day count related) and a 'sufficient ties' test (looking at the strength of certain ties to the UK such as family, work and accommodation).

The consequence of being UK resident is that all UK source income and capital gains, together with any income and capital gains remitted to the UK from abroad (if remittance basis taxation is available, and any relevant charge has been paid), will be taxable, possibly at a top rate of 45% (2014/15). The remittance rules are attractive for non-UK domiciliaries (i.e. whose permanent home is abroad) who are resident in the UK. This means that foreign source income and gains not remitted to the UK are outside the UK tax net in certain circumstances. Non-domiciliaries are also not liable to UK inheritance tax (except on UK assets) unless they have been resident in the UK for 17 out of any 20 year period, or been domiciled in the UK within the last three years.

International double taxation for residents of the UK

Where a UK resident suffers tax in another country, provided there is a double tax treaty in force with the UK, usually only the primary taxing country will tax. This, however, needs to be considered in each case.

Some UK residents will be taxable in their home country as well as the UK. In this situation if there is a double tax treaty, and the UK has a large network of treaties, then their liability to double taxation is likely to be relieved. Most treaties have a tie breaker provision which will determine which country has principal taxing rights, which will normally depend upon where the individual's main centre of existence actually is. Treaties are also useful in situations such as becoming non-resident to avoid capital gains tax. Whereas normally an individual has to be non-UK resident for five years for to avoid a capital gains tax charge, if the individual becomes tax resident in a country with an appropriate double tax treaty, then provided he becomes resident in that other country under the tie breaker rules, he would not need to be outside the UK for five years but could potentially achieve this in a shorter period depending on the rules of the other country.

Where liabilities to UK tax arise, it may be necessary to consider whether any double tax treaty relief applies.

33.9 Checklist: Real estate in the UK

- In the light of the principle of *caveat emptor*, a professional survey and valuation (normally by a chartered surveyor) is strongly recommended
- It is essential that the title, possible encumbrances and terms of the purchase contract be checked by a suitably qualified lawyer
- Planning permissions and building regulations: it should be remembered that there may be very tight restrictions in relation to building works, especially for historic or architecturally interesting buildings or for buildings within a conservation area

- Where a leasehold property is being acquired, check the tenancy conditions carefully to see that no restrictions conflict with your lifestyle and to check whether you need landlord's consent for any proposed alterations to the property or to sublet
- Third party consents for extensions and alterations: check whether you will need consent of neighbours to alterations which you plan
- Acquisition costs (for example, SDLT, legal and surveyor's costs) and the annual outgoings and local taxes should be checked
- Easy rail connections and other transport links can have a significant impact on the long-term value of a property. Similarly, the suitability of other local amenities for the buyer, such as schools, shopping and leisure facilities should be carefully checked, as there are very significant variations on the qualities of these facilities from place to place

33.10 Bibliography

Lennon Alan: Agricultural Law, Tax and Finance, Sweet & Maxwell, London 1990 (Loose leaf with updates)

Aldridge Trevor M: Aldrige's Residential Lettings (11th Ed), Sweet & Maxwell, London 1998

Bridge Stuart: Assured Tenancies, Blackstone Press, Cambridge 1999

Driscoll James: Butterworths Residential Landlord and tenant Handbook, Butterworths Law, London 1998

Williams Del. W: Landlord and tenant Casebook, Estates Gazette, London 2002

Clarke David: Leasehold Enfranchisement and Right to Manage, Jordans, London 2003

Fancourt T.M: Megarry's Assured Tenancies, Sweet & Maxwell, London 1999

Lewison Tim / Brock Jonathan: Woodfall; Landlord and tenant (28th Edition), Sweet & Maxwell, London 1978 (4 volumes plus index loose leaf).

O'Grady Sarah: The Complete Guide to Buying & Selling Property. How to get the best deal on your home, Kogan Page, London 2004

34

The US / State of Florida

United States of America

by

Claudio Riedi

Lehtinen Schultz Riedi Catalano dela Fuente PLLC
1111 Brickell Avenue
Suite 2200
Miami, FL 33131
US

Tel: +1 305 760 8544
Fax: +1 305 536 5720

criedi@lsrcf.com
lsrccf.com

Claudio Riedi is a partner in the law firm of Lehtinen Schultz Riedi Catalano dela Fuente, PLLC, who focuses his practice on real estate, business, and banking transactions, commercial and land use litigation, and administrative proceedings.

He was born and raised in Zürich, Switzerland, and attended the University of Zürich, and earned a BA Degree from Florida International University (high honors) and a law degree from the University of Miami (magna cum laude). He has lived in Florida since 1986.

34.1 Introduction

The history of real estate in Florida, much as the history of Florida in general, is relatively brief. Particularly in South Florida, where much of Florida's population is concentrated today, trade in real estate did not become important until the 1920s.

But since the 1920s, the real estate market in Florida has boomed. Real estate in Florida, and the sale and purchase thereof, has always depended on the weather and on "foreigners." In Florida, "foreigners" are "non-Floridians." If the US is considered a country of immigrants, Florida is the state of immigrants in the US. Until a few years ago, Florida followed the general rule that more land for development could be found at any time and that growth had no limit. Only since the 1980s has it been recognized that growth has its price: water supply, protection of the environment, services for an ever-growing population and quality of life suddenly have become important issues. This does not come as a surprise if one considers that Florida has surpassed dozens of other states in population growth and that Florida is now the 4th most populous state in the US.

The real estate market in Florida is subject to highs and lows unknown in other parts of the world. Particularly since 2007, the housing market in Florida has undergone drastic changes.

Median home prices for Miami-Dade County:

2007	USD 330,000
2012	USD 150,000
August 2014	USD 226,000

source: zillow.com

Particularly in the higher-priced marked, such as luxury condominiums, the price fluctuations were even more extreme, and the recovery has been healthier, which prices abve 2007 levels in some cases..

The lessons to be learned from the recent convulsions in Florida's real estate market are:

1. While the current real estate market shows solid gains, there is no such thing as a sure investment in Florida real estate. Real estate investments are always speculative
2. Banks have tightened their lending requirements as a result of extreme numbers of defaulted loans between 2008 and 2010

It appears that the fundamentals in the real estate market are now stronger than they were before the bursting of the real estate bubble after 2007. While prices are expected to rise more slowly than in the run up to 2007, a repeat of the price collapses is not expected in the foreseeable future.

34.2 Real estate ownership

Different forms and types of ownership

Ownership in Fee Simple

The most common and simplest kind of real estate ownership in Florida is ownership in *fee simple*. Ownership through *fee simple* has no end in time. There are four subcategories of fee simple ownership:

- Fee Simple Absolute
- Fee Simple Determinable
- Fee Simple Subject to a Condition Subsequent
- Fee Simple Subject to an Executory Limitation

Fee simple ownership can be transferred through a deed or a will, as long as the deed or the will contain the required formalities. Without indications to the contrary, it is assumed that fee simple ownership has been transferred. However, if the document contains sufficient indications to the contrary, it is assumed that the ownership that has been transferred is not fee simple. For example, if the transferring person determines that the property should be held only during the life span of the receiving person, it is then assumed that ownership is a so-called "life estate" (see below).

Fee Simple Absolute

Ownership through *fee simple absolute* has no limitations that would restrict or reduce the duration of the ownership. For this reason ownership through fee simple absolute is the most common and valuable form of property ownership. In case of doubt, it is preferable to hold ownership through fee simple absolute. The words *fee simple* and *fee simple absolute* are generally synonymous.

Fee Simple Determinable

Fee Simple Determinable is ownership held as *fee simple* which ends automatically when a predetermined condition occurs. Ownership through *fee simple determinable* is identical to *fee simple* ownership, except that the period of time ownership is held through *fee simple* is limited. Ownership through *fee simple determinable* can be sold, gifted or inherited, but the successor owner is always bound by the condition.

Fee simple determinable is often expressed with sentences such as "until ...... occurs", "as long as .....", or "during the existence of ......". Because there is always the possibility that an event in the future may terminate the current ownership of a *fee simple determinable* title, there is a corresponding ownership interest which is called a *reverter*. According to Florida law a *reverter* must be limited to 21 years. If the condition of the *reverter* has not occurred within 21 years, ownership automatically becomes *fee simple absolute*. A *fee simple determinable* differs from a *fee simple subject to a condition subsequent* (see below) in that a *fee simple determinable* ends automatically when a predetermined condition occurs. On the other hand, a *fee simple subject to a condition subsequent* gives the transferring party the right to take back the property when a predetermined condition occurs. A *fee simple determinable* differs from a *fee simple subject to an executory limitation* (see below) in that ownership through *fee simple determinable* reverts to the transferring party, whereas ownership through *fee simple subject to executory limitation* reverts to a third party.

Fee Simple Subject to a Condition Subsequent

Ownership in *fee simple subject to a condition subsequent* is property ownership which can be taken back by the creating party if a certain set of circumstances occurs. The right of the creating party to step in and take back the property is called *Power of Termination*. Just like *reverters*, powers of termination are limited in Florida, with certain exceptions, to 21 years from the date of creation of the property interest.

A *condition subsequent* is normally created through expressions such as "conditioned upon that ....", "on the condition that .....", or "but if .... occurs, then ....". A *fee simple determinable* will not terminate automatically when the predetermined condition occurs. The creating party has to become active and assert her power of termination. Until the creator of the estate asserts this power, nothing changes in the property rights of the new owner after the condition occurs. Furthermore, if the creator/transferor does not exercise her rights within a reasonable period of time, the right can be lost.

Fee Simple Subject to Executory Limitation

Ownership in *fee simple subject to executory limitation* is similar to the property interests described above with the distinction that the ownership does not revert to the previous owner but to a third party when the condition occurs. This transfer of ownership to a third party occurs automatically without the third party having to become active and assert his rights.

Life Estates – Lifetime Ownership

A *life estate* is a time-limited property interest, limited either to the life span of the receiving party or the life time span of a third party. If the duration of a *life estate* is limited to the life span of a third party, the ownership is called *life estate pour autre vie*. A *life estate* ends with the death of the measuring life. If the creating document (deed or will) does not state anything to the contrary, it is assumed that the measuring life is that of the receiving party. With few exceptions, *life estates* are not inheritable, because they end with the measuring life. *Life estates* can be sold or gifted during the measuring life, but their value is greatly reduced by the fact that the receiving party does not know how long the ownership will last.

Because in case of doubt Florida law always assumes property is held in *fee simple absolute*, a *life estate* has to be described very carefully and precisely. The owner of a *life estate* is the absolute owner of the property during the existence of the *life estate*. He is entitled to all income generated by the property during his tenancy. However, the owner of a *life estate* does not have the right to squander the value of the property, so that the successor owner receives a property of reduced value. This means that an owner of a *life estate* must pay property taxes and maintain the property in acceptable condition.

Timesharing

Timesharing or timeshares are a special variety of fee simple ownership in Florida for "less than one year in a calendar." Florida was a pioneer for timeshare ownership. In 1976, Florida enacted the first timeshare law in the US, and the legal provisions have been revised and adjusted several times since then. A timeshare interest is usually purchased through transfer of 1/52 of an undivided interest in a vacation apartment, together with rights of use that can apply to a special type of apartment, e.g., a two bedroom apartment, or a specific season (high/low season). Such rights of use create a *floating timeshare*. Florida law also permits exchange programs, where an owner first books a week, and then contributes this week to a pool out of which all contributors can take a week in other parts in the world. Offers of timeshares have very broad disclosure obligations. Offerors have to create and provide to interested parties a *public offering statement,* which explains the risks of the purchase and clearly informs the prospective buyer that he has a 10 day right of cancellation.

Concurrent Estates

All the above-described property interests can be held in the name of one or several persons. If the property is held at the same time in the name of more than one person, the estate is called a *concurrent estate* or *co-tenancy*. The joint owners are often referred to as *co-tenants*. Florida generally recognizes three different types of concurrent estates: *joint tenancy*, *tenancy in common*, and *tenancy by the entireties*.

Joint Tenancy

A joint tenancy exists when two or more persons have the undivided ownership of real estate with the automatic right of survivorship after the death of a co-tenant. Whenever real estate is held by two or more persons, it is assumed that a *tenancy in common* has been created without an automatic right of survivorship for the surviving party. Therefore, this right of survivorship after the death of a co-tenant has to be expressly provided for in the will or deed creating the tenancy. The sole distinction between a *joint tenancy* and a *tenancy in common* is that the *joint tenancies* provide for this automatic right of survivorship after the death of a co-tenant. If a *joint tenant* transfers her ownership to a third party, the *joint tenancy* is automatically dissolved and a *tenancy in common* is created. In other words, the person who takes ownership from the transferring co-tenant in a joint tenancy does not become a new *joint tenant*, but rather a *tenant in common* (see below).

Tenancy in Common

The most common type of joint ownership is a *tenancy in common*. Florida law assumes that a *tenancy in common* is created when two unmarried persons jointly take ownership in real estate. All *tenants in common* have the right to own and control the entire property, which does not necessarily mean that all co-tenants have to be in possession of the real estate. Where a co-tenant controls ownership of a real estate under this form of ownership, it is assumed that she holds the property for herself and her co-tenants.

Where title to a property is transferred to two or more persons without further indications, the resulting interest is a *tenancy in common*. Property of a *tenant in common* can be freely transferred to a third party.

The new owner will again become a new *tenant in common* together with the other *co-tenants*. A *tenant in common* cannot, however, transfer only a certain portion of a real estate (e.g., the southeastern quarter of the property). A *tenancy in common* can be divided by the co-tenants at any time *(partition)*. A *tenant in common* can also demand the partition of a property or, where partition is not possible, can force the sale of a property and distribution of the proceeds among the co-tenants.

Tenancy by the Entireties

A *tenancy by the entireties* is similar to a *joint tenancy* with the limitation that a *tenancy by the entireties* can be created only between married persons. When a deed in the name of a married couple does not contain any contrary indications, it is assumed that a *tenancy by the entireties* is being created. When a property is transferred to several persons, two of which are married to each other, it is important to ensure that the respective rights are carefully described. For example, there can be a *tenancy in common* in part and a *tenancy by the entireties* in part. When one of the married owners under a *tenancy by the entireties* dies, their ownership interest automatically transfers to their spouse.

It is important to understand that a spouse cannot transfer her portion in a *tenancy by the entireties* without the consent of her spouse. Even a lease held in an *estate by the entireties* cannot be extended without the consent of both parties. Ownership in a *tenancy by the entireties* cannot be partitioned or transferred by inheritance, because the surviving spouse automatically takes the undivided ownership interest upon the death of her spouse.

Condominium

A condominium is a form of ownership in which the owner of a property, usually an apartment, owns a certain fraction of the common areas of an apartment building, together with one of the apartments. This form of interest is created by a so-called *declaration of condominium* to which all owners within the condominium are legally bound.

Future Interests

All of the above-described forms of ownership can either be current or in the future. A future ownership occurs when the transfer does not occur immediately by way of deed. This is normally the case by transfer through a will. A discussion of all forms of future ownership would exceed the scope of this chapter. An attorney wishing to create a future ownership has to consider, however, that the future interest must vest within 21 years of the death of a currently living person. This rule is called *rule against perpetuities* and is strictly enforced.

Easements, charges, covenants, liens and mortgages

Florida recognizes a variety of legal encumbrances on real estate, including easements, licenses, restrictive covenants, liens and mortgages.

Easements

Explicit Easement

An easement gives another person the right to use the property of another person to a limited extent. An easement right can be enforced against third parties. Easements can be sold or gifted. The property on which the easement is located is called the *servient tenement*. The property that benefits from the easement is called the *dominant tenement*. An *easement appurtenant* is an easement that benefits another property independent from the owner. An easement can be either positive, i.e., it entitles an owner to limited use of the servient tenement; or it can be negative, i.e., it may prohibit the owner of the servient tenement from undertaking specific activities.

An easement can either be explicit, by implication or created through adverse possession. If easements are to be enforceable it must generally be recorded in the public records.

Because an easement is a property right, it is covered by the *Statute of Frauds*, which requires a written form. An easement can either be created in a deed or with a separate document. If the easement is on a separate document, it requires the same formalities as a deed.

Easement by implication

An implied easement can only be created if it derives from an explicit *easement* in written form, or if it is a legal necessity. The former can apply if, e.g., certain necessary rights in a deed are not explicitly mentioned. The latter case can apply if a property that is part of a larger property parcel is transferred to a buyer who, without the easement, would have absolutely no access to a public road.

Easement by adverse possession

An easement by adverse possession is created in some cases where a servient tenement has been used for 20 years without interruption. The alleged owner of the easement must prove that she has enjoyed the easement right for an uninterrupted period of at least 20 years; that she has done so openly and with the knowledge of the owner; that she has not been granted these rights with the explicit approval of the property owner; and that she has enjoyed these rights according to a clearly defined route. An example is a situation where a *dominant tenant* has continuously been driving over a neighboring property to get to his own property for at least 20 years. If the neighbor (*servient tenant*) has had knowledge of this activity and has neither protested nor given his explicit approval, the *dominant tenant* may be entitled to an easement by adverse possession.

Charges

Florida law does not recognize the concept of "charges," but instead refers to "encumbrances," all of which limit to some degree the ownership rights to real estate to which they apply.

Restrictive Covenants

A *restrictive covenant* can either be public or private. Public *restrictive covenants* are created by the legislature to protect the public interest (e.g., designation of a historic neighborhood and corresponding zoning restrictions). Private *restrictive covenants* are created by private persons or corporations. An example is the rules and regulations of a condominium, which bind all members of the condominium. Other examples are age restrictions of the owner in a building, e.g., owners must be 50+ years of age, or architectural restrictions through *restrictive covenants*, e.g., the color of the paint of the house, or restrictions concerning the type of house or construction in a given area.

Liens

Liens are easy to create and correspondingly common in Florida. They often arise from construction work and services. For instance, an architect or engineer in Florida can have a lien recorded on a real estate to secure payment for his services that benefit the property. He must adhere to certain formalities, and the lien can only be recorded in the correct amount of the services rendered. Recording an amount that is intentionally higher than the actual amount is illegal.

Particularly with new constructions, it is imperative to have all existing liens released by the closing date. The property owner must secure and record so-called *lien waivers* or *satisfactions of liens* so that the title is not clouded by additional demands. Title insurance will ensure that no liens that would cloud the title are discovered after closing. Even if disagreements over certain liens are pending, it is possible to transfer a clean title if a security deposit is made in the court registry in the amount of the lien.

Mortgages

A mortgage secures some sort of obligation, usually the requirement to repay a loan made for the purchase of real estate (purchase money mortgage). Without a mortgage, a lender would have no priority over other creditors of the borrower in case of non-payment. The mortgage enables the lender to assure repayment of the loan over all other creditors of the borrower by taking regress to the property on which the mortgage is recorded. The mortgage must be recorded in the public records to create priority as against subsequent lenders or trade creditors of the borrower. Mortgages remain an encumbrance of the respective property until a "satisfaction of mortgage" has been recorded, which cancels out the mortgage.

Licenses

A license is the right to use the property of another person in a restricted manner. An example is the use of a property for logging purposes. Because a license is a personal right, it is not required to be in writing. A license usually cannot be sold, given away or transferred with a property. A license can be revoked by the licensor at any time. Thus, a license cannot confer a permanent right of residence.

Construction Law and Building Lease

A discussion of construction law and building leases would go beyond the scope of this chapter. Suffice it to say that construction law is heavily litigated in Florida.

Protection of ownership, proof of ownership and registration

Evidence of ownership of real estate in Florida is established by a *deed*. The deed document can be a *warranty deed* (guaranteed title) or a *quit-claim deed* (transfer of an existing title including possible restrictions). The deed must be recorded in the public records to provide evidence of ownership to third parties. The public records are kept on the county level and contain property ownership records that can be traced back to the very first owner of a given piece of land in the distant past.

If several claims to the same real estate are recorded, the claim that has been recorded first has priority over those recorded at a later date. Therefore the buyer of a property has an incentive to have the deed recorded in the public records as soon as possible after the sale. Once the deed has been recorded in the public records, it is assumed that all members of the public have been informed of the new ownership right. It is therefore imperative for a subsequent buyer to carefully check the public records for potential claims against the property. This record search is normally conducted by the *title agent* and is part of the transfer formalities.

The main function of the public property ownership records is to protect a buyer against property claims of earlier owners that have not been recorded. It must be stressed that even the recording of a deed in the public records does not provide complete protection against competing claims. Just because a document has been recorded in the public records does not mean that it is automatically legal. If, for instance, the recording officer made an error, the incorrect recording does not create legally enforceable rights in the party recording the instrument.

It should further be noted that property deeds are not the only records recorded in the public records. For instance, court judgments against a judgment debtor can also be recorded in the public records of a county, thus creating a lien on real estate of the debtor. If a certified copy of the court judgment is recorded in the public records, claims from this judgment take precedence over other claims recorded subsequently. If real estate, however, is held by a married couple as *tenants by the entireties* (see above), even the recording of a judgment lien in the public records does not give the creditor the right to execute against the real estate.

Florida law determines which types of documents can be recorded by the clerk in the public records. Most clerks will record almost any document, provided that it is notarized (by a notary public) or certified (as a correct copy by a court). Every document to be recorded must show the name and address of the person who prepared the document.

Requirements for a valid deed

The most important document for the transfer of real estate is the deed. The following are the minimal requirements for a valid deed in Florida:

- Exact legal description of the property to be transferred as well as the *property ID number*

- Name and social security number of the transferring person (*grantor*). The marital status of the grantor (married or single) should be stated
- Name of the new owner (*grantee*). If the property is to be held by several persons, the document should state the future ownership relation between the parties
- Date of the deed
- The signature of the *grantor* must be clearly legible
- The signatures of two witnesses who witnessed the *grantor* signing the deed are required. If the *grantor* is a corporation, the business owner, the president or chief executive officer, or another authorized officer of the corporation may sign the deed, which signing must also be witnessed by two witnesses. The names and addresses on the document must be legible. The corporate seal is sufficient in lieu of the two witnesses
- Notarization: a deed should be notarized by a notary public so that the document can later be recorded in the public records. Non-notarized documents cannot be recorded in the public records
- The name and address of the person who prepared the document must be on the deed, together with instructions to the clerk of court concerning what to do with the deed after the recording
- There should be a 3"x3" empty space in the upper right-hand corner of the first page of the document where the clerk will affix the recording information. The clerk generally records on what page and in what book a particular deed has been recorded (e.g., *Book 1045, Page 375*)

34.3 Purchase and sale of real estate

The sales agreement

Basic requirements

Contracts for the purchase and sale of real estate are enforceable only if they are in writing and signed by the party against whom the contract should be enforced; if they contain a clear mutual promise – called consideration; if the parties have agreed on all basic conditions of the contract; and if the terms of the contract, including the description of the property and the parties, are clearly defined.

Written contract

The written form of a valid contract is an absolute requirement for a real estate transaction in Florida. This can consist of several written documents, as long as these are all signed by the party against whom they are to be enforced. For instance, several letters and fax documents may constitute a valid contract. The *Florida Association of Realtors*, together with the *Florida Bar Association*, have developed a standard purchase and sales contract for real estate in Florida, which is periodically updated according to the latest legal requirements. This *FAR/Bar* contract is used for the overwhelming majority of real estate transactions in Florida. An attorney who would like to familiarize himself with the modalities of a real estate transaction in Florida should carefully review the *FAR/Bar* standard contract because it contains most of the important details of a transaction. Separate additional documents may be added to the *FAR/Bar* contract as *addenda* or *riders,* which contain additional specific agreements. The use of prepurchase contracts is not customary.

The only exception to the written form requirement of a contract for real estate exists when one of the parties has partially performed under an agreement.

Mutual promise of consideration

Mutual consideration is an absolute requirement for every contract in Florida. A purchase and sales contract is a mutual agreement containing the promise of the buyer to pay a certain amount of money or exchange another item of value to the seller, and the promise of the seller to transfer the title of the real estate to the buyer. Both promises must be backed by an appropriate consideration. The buyer's promise of payment and the seller's promise to transfer the property are normally sufficient.

Agreement on all basic conditions

A purchase and sales agreement for real estate is not enforceable if the basic terms and conditions of the contract are unclear or ambiguous. A purchase and sales agreement is clear and unambiguous if the contracting parties have actually reached an agreement concerning the terms and conditions that constitute the necessary requirements for a valid purchase agreement.

Description of the real estate

One of the most important parts of a valid purchase agreement is the property description. An adequate property description identifies the real estate without further proof. A description is adequate if a land surveyor can clearly identify the property using the description.

Signature of both parties

The buyer generally makes an offer by completing and submitting a full purchase and sales agreement, dated and signed unilaterally. The seller then has a certain number of days to countersign, or to make changes and then countersign the agreement. In the latter case, the contract with the changes is considered a counter-offer and must be accepted in writing by the buyer. Only when total agreement exists has a valid contract been created.

Preparation of the purchase agreement

In most cases use of a standard agreement is recommended, together with *riders* and *addenda*, if necessary. The contract most often used since 1973 is the above-described *FAR/Bar* standard contract. Hundreds of thousands of real properties have been legally transferred with this contract. Although a preprinted contract may not be appropriate for every transaction, the *FAR/Bar* contract is suitable for the vast majority of residential real estate transactions, and often for commercial transactions. Fillable FAR/Bar contracts can be found online, but it is advisable, to have an attorney review completed contracts before execution.

Contracting parties

The name of the seller must appear in the purchase contract exactly the same way it appears in the existing title document. If, for instance, the title is held by Mr. and Mrs. X, a married couple, then the sellers must be listed as such in the contract. It is therefore advisable to consult the old deed prior to the completion of the purchase contract. It should be ascertained whether or not the property is the primary residence (*homestead*) of the seller. If this is the case, both spouses must be listed as the sellers.

Real estate is often held in the name of a corporation or partnership. If the real estate is owned by a partnership, the partnership agreement should be reviewed to ensure that a person authorized by the partnership signs the contract. In case of a limited partnership, all general partners must co-sign the contract. In case of a limited liability company under *Florida Statute* section 608.425, the by-laws determine who can sign agreements. If the transferring party is a corporation, the exact name of the corporation and the state in which it is registered must be shown on the contract. The contract must be signed by the president or vice president of the corporation and, if possible, the corporate seal should be affixed to the contract. Information concerning all Florida corporations can be searched via the Internet. It is highly advisable to review the corporate structure prior to signing a purchase and sales agreement with a corporation. (*sunbiz.org/search.html*).

If title is held in the name of a trustee, the trust document should be reviewed to determine if the approval of the trust's beneficiary is required for a valid transaction.

The name(s) of the buyer in the purchase contract must be shown exactly the same way the title for the property is to be held. An exception exists where the buyer plans to assign the agreement before closing to a yet to be founded corporation or partnership. In that case, the words "*or his/her assigns*" should appear after the name of the buyer. Contracts made in good faith with persons who are not authorized to sign them are not enforceable.

Legal description and survey

If real estate is located in a *platted subdivision* or is part of a *condominium*, the legal description must contain the precise name of the subdivision or the *condominium*, as well as the book and page number where it is recorded (e.g., *OR 523 P. 1056*) and the recording information of the official condominium declaration.

An attorney who prepares the contract should never assume that a certain item is part of the property (e.g., washer/dryer). If there is any doubt, it is better practice to list the item specifically in the contract to make it part of the transaction.

If the property to be transferred is developed, the attorney must determine whether the improvements are a fixed part of the property, or *personal property*, i.e., items that can be removed from the property. In the latter case, the contract must clarify which items are included and which are excluded. The legal description must be carefully reviewed. An attorney should never trust the legal description of the previous deed, because the smallest mistakes can make it into a document and may not be discovered over decades. Although the *title insurance* offers some protection in such cases, an attorney should never rely on insurance to replace careful drafting.

Purchase price and payment

The contract must clearly set forth the purchase price. If a down payment is made, it should be noted in the contract whether payment is to be made directly to the seller or into an escrow account. It should also indicate whether such a down payment is to be deposited in an interest-bearing account and who should collect the accrued interest. Sometimes, a second down payment is required before the closing. The same considerations apply for a second down payment as for the first.

The contract must state precisely how the balance of the purchase price is to be transferred at the time of closing. The *FAR/Bar* contract provides that the amount must be paid in cash or with a cashier's check. It is advisable for the attorney to determine early how the final payment will be made, and prepare the contract accordingly. *Official checks* (guaranteed checks) have recently become a popular option. A buyer should verify whether his bank can issue such an *official check* for the closing.

Contingencies

The *FAR/Bar* contract contains detailed descriptions of the most common contingencies in Florida real estate purchase contracts. These contingencies can be included with simple checkmarks next to the specific contingency. After signing the contract, the seller has a due diligence period, in which he can carefully inspect the property. Some properties are transferred *"as is"* - generally an indication of deficiencies. In such a case, it is particularly important that the buyer has the property immediately inspected by a professional inspector. If the inspection shows deficiencies, the contract can be cancelled within a certain period of time, usually 10 days.

There are numerous companies in Florida that specialize in inspections of real properties. For a few hundred dollars, a buyer can have some certainty that the property satisfies minimum requirements. An inspection can also determine why a property is sold *"as is"*. The vast majority of properties are sold with a simple right of inspection, and the rights to have the seller repair the deficiencies. This right for repairs is often capped at a certain percentage, e.g., repairs to be made by the seller cannot exceed 5% of the purchase price. The inspection must be undertaken expeditiously and thoroughly. Problems that are not discovered within the inspection period usually cannot be claimed later by the buyer. Particularly, banks insist that the property is checked for termite and roof damage before making home loans.

It is good practice to include a representation from the municipality's zoning authority that the property can be used for its intended purposes. While this is generally not a concern with residential purchases, it is important to obtain confirmation where the buyer intends to use the site for commercial or mixed use purposes.

Clear title

One of the most important requirements for a successful transaction is timely evidence by the seller that he has marketable title to the property. This should not be taken for granted. Because a property's title can be clouded for a variety of reasons, the purchase contract usually contains a clause that requires the buyer to make payment only if the seller can provide evidence of clear title. Although the seller in most contracts has the burden of proof for a clear title, it is the parties' decision who will pay for the costs associated with a title search. A title insurance company is generally retained early on to search title and issue a *title commitment*. The *title commitment* confirms that the title insurance company will issue a title insurance policy once certain requirements have been met, e.g., a deed to the buyer has been executed and unpaid taxes and/or potential liens have been paid off. The parties then must comply with all these requirements prior to the closing date, so that a clear title is available on the closing date.

If a property is acquired with third-party financing, the financial institutions, such as banks or savings and loan institutions, usually require a title insurance policy issued in their name. It is of utmost importance that a separate policy is issued in the name of the buyer, without which the buyer would have no regress should title problems arise. A separate policy for the buyer is often less expensive if issued by the same title insurance company that issued the bank's policy.

Unless the contract states otherwise, the seller has a reasonable time to provide clear title and to remove potential title problems. If title problems are found, the *FAR/Bar* contract states that the seller has 30 days after notice to remedy them. If these problems have not been removed, the buyer has the right to either buy the property in its existing state or to cancel the contract. The seller is legally obligated to make a good-faith effort to remove the problems.

Pro-rated costs

Because the exact closing date is not known at the time the purchase and sales agreement is signed, and because certain costs accrue until the day of the closing, the contract usually contains a clause for pro-ration of these costs. This cost pro-ration is actually calculated when the closing date has been determined. The most common examples for pro-ration are property taxes, home owner's insurance (the property must always be insured), rental income, maintenance fees to the *condominium association* and prepaid maintenance costs.

Disclosure

In recent years, a clear trend has developed to require disclosure of certain information about a real estate prior to the sale. In most cases, the principle of *caveat emptor* no longer applies. In particular, in the case of condominiums, any information that could negatively affect a property, and which is not readily apparent to the buyer, must be disclosed. It is therefore advisable that all potential problems are disclosed early.

Condominiums are particularly sensitive to this disclosure requirement. Even for resales, the law requires that extensive information must be disclosed to the buyer, including the *condominium association*'s declaration, by-laws, rules and regulations, a valid copy of the *Declaration of Condominium*, and a list of frequently asked questions and answers. These documents are usually made available by building management so that a buyer and seller can inspect them at any time.

Restrictions on sale and acquisition

Restrictions under family law and matrimonial property regime

Generally, any restrictions on the sale of real estate in Florida depend on the entity in whose name the property is held. If the property is held by a person (or a corporation), only the consent of that person (or corporation) is necessary for the sale of the property. If the property is held in the name of several persons, the consent (signature) of all the owners listed in the title is required. This means, for example, that for the sale of a home owned by *tenants by the entirety*, the signature of both spouses is required for a legally enforceable agreement. If the real estate is held in the name of one of the spouses, the spouse's ability to transfer legal property depends on whether the property is a *homestead*, i.e., the primary residence of the married couple. If this is the case, the consent of the other spouse is required, even if that other spouse is not shown as an owner on the deed. If this is not the case, the owner listed on the deed can transfer the property without consent of the spouse. If there is any doubt, both spouses should sign the purchase/sale agreement and the deed.

Real estate and restrictions on its conveyance under Florida law are generally subject to the marital property regimes of the state of Florida. The only exception is the case where a married couple has a prenuptial agreement that provides for application of a different law, which is generally enforceable in Florida.

All marriages, in which at least one of the spouses has resided for at least six months in Florida, are subject to Florida matrimonial property law, including the worldwide properties owned by the spouses, regardless of the spouses' citizenship or place of marriage. Accordingly, in case of a divorce both partners are entitled to *equitable distribution* of marital property, which means that both parties will receive one half of the property created during the marriage (including real estate) and one half of the debt accrued during the marriage. Real estate owned in the name of only one spouse, but purchased during the marriage with marital funds is to be equitably distributed as well. Foreign property (i.e., property not within the US) can be distributed by the court in case of a divorce, but the judge has no direct jurisdiction to enforce the distribution for such properties as provided in the final divorce judgment. In cases where a divorced party refuses to distribute foreign property as decreed by the court, the Floridian judge may compensate the spouse residing in Florida with a correspondingly higher share (of up to 100%) of the marital assets located in Florida, and may in addition award a money judgment. Such a money judgment can usually be enforced and domesticated abroad.

According to *Florida Statute* a spouse cannot be entirely disinherited. Each spouse has an *elective share* of the net value of the estate of a person who died as a Florida resident. This *elective share*, however, has to be elected within a certain period of time, and is considered waived if not so elected. In most cases the surviving spouse waives the *elective share*, so that the executor of the estate can freely sell the properties to be liquidated.

An additional complication arises if a property that represents a *homestead* is to be devised to non-heirs in a will. If the deceased leaves behind a spouse or minor child, the will cannot be executed as such. In such cases it is advisable to consult an attorney specializing in the field.

Options and rights of pre-emption

Preemptive rights generally exist in the form of options, which are legally enforceable in Florida provided that a separate *consideration* was paid for the option. As a matter of law, no preemptive rights can be implied or derived from a rent or lease agreement. There are no preemptive rights of the government, e.g., for historic buildings. The government has, however, the right to take property for public purposes against payment of fair market price *(eminent domain proceedings)*.

Agricultural real estate

Agricultural property is subject to special rules. Particularly where undeveloped property is purchased, the buyer must be mindful of applicable zoning. The zoning determines, among other things, the development envelope and permitted uses of any given real estate. *Zoning variances* (deviations from the existing zoning) can be applied for, but are often hard to obtain. If such a variance is requested, neighbors usually have the right to object and decisions by the planning authorities are often more political than legal in nature.

Additionally, in most jurisdictions, the applicant must demonstrate a legal hardship to justify a variance. This is an extremely high burden, as the applicant must show that he will be deprived of all reasonable beneficial use of the property without the variance. Property zoned as agricultural is usually taxed at considerably lower levels than developed property. Owners holding property for speculative purposes therefore often let some cattle graze on the property to assure lower taxation of their undeveloped property.

Restrictions regarding acquisition of property by foreigners

Foreigners generally have the same right to purchase real estate in Florida as do Florida residents. Foreigners have certain tax disadvantages (primarily estate tax) and limitations on liability (no *homestead-exemption* protection from creditors), but they are in no way restricted in their right to own or convey real estate in Florida. Mere ownership of real estate in Florida (as well as the entire US) does not provide a basis for entitlement to a specific visa or residence status in the US.

Further important preconditions for buying real estate

Capacity to act and entitlement of the seller

Once it has been determined who the title owner of a given real estate is, the legal capacity and entitlement of the seller to convey a specific property is practically a given. In a normal case the seller/buyer is an adult (older than 18 years) and has absolute ability to transfer or acquire property. Married persons are subject to special rules. Children under age 18 and persons under guardianship can only act through their guardian. Florida law distinguishes between guardians for a person and guardians for a property. Only a guardian for property can sell real estate of a minor child. The *circuit court* with jurisdiction has to approve any sale of property owned by a minor through a guardian.

In the case of death of a real estate owner, only a *personal representative* with the consent of the probate court has the ability to sell the property. However, if real estate is owned by a married couple as *tenants by the entirety*, or by two or more persons as *joint tenants with right of survivorship*, title of the real estate is transferred to the surviving owner by operation of law upon the death of the other owner (the co-owner). If that surviving person wishes to sell the property subsequently, a notarized (and recorded) certificate of the *personal representative* is necessary, which waives all entitlements of the estate to the specific real estate. Without such a waiver by the personal representative, the personal representative can later take regress to the real estate, now in the name of a bona-fide third party, for payment of debts of the estate.

A trust generally acts through its trustee. Accordingly, if real estate is held in the name of a trust, the consent of the trustee is absolutely required for a sale of the property. Additionally, the trust instrument should be reviewed to determine whether the trustee truly has the legal ability to sell the property and that he is not subject to legal limitations. The basis for the legal capacity of the trustee to act (i.e., trust instrument) must be recorded together with the deed in the property records to give a buyer good title in a purchase of real estate from a trust.

Corporations/Partnerships

A Florida corporation has capacity to sell real estate if there is no provision to the contrary contained in the articles or by-laws of the corporation. The same is true for Florida partnerships, where the partnership agreement is the determining document. This is not automatically the case with foreign corporations and partnerships, and the applicable law in the jurisdiction of the foreign corporation/partnership must be consulted (see also *Purchase through a company* below).

Third-party claims and unpaid taxes

Competing claims or liens of third parties can generally be avoided by purchase of a title insurance policy by and for the buyer. The title insurance company, in the process of issuing the title insurance, generally reviews the public property records, from the present time back to the Florida land grant, and guarantees, with virtually absolute liability, that no claims or liens of third parties exist. If this review turns up existing liens, e.g., for unpaid taxes, the necessary amount for payoff of the taxes is withheld from the purchase sum at closing and forwarded by the closing agent directly to the taxing authorities. Only with this proof of payment will the title insurance company issue its title policy.

It should be noted that all title policies contain certain exceptions and qualifications that have to be observed.

Certain obvious prescriptive rights of third parties and non-payment of certain taxes at time of closing are usually not insured. Unpaid property taxes generally lead to the issuance of a *tax certificate*. A *tax certificate* is offered for sale to the general public. In essence, the *tax certificate* provides that a member of the public has stepped in and paid the tax for a certain real estate. The seller has to pay off all *tax certificates* including substantial interest if she wants to regain and sell good title to the property. If a *tax certificate* has not been paid off by the owner within three years, the person who purchased the *tax certificate* can force the sale of the real estate for repayment of the tax debt.

Provisions for protecting the environment, nature and cultural heritage

Environmental considerations in Florida have become a very important aspect in every real estate transaction. It helps to remember that environmental problems in Florida have to be remedied primarily by the owner of the property and not by the party causing the problems. It is therefore particularly important for commercial properties that the property is carefully inspected for environmental problems prior to the purchase. This is normally accomplished through a *Phase I Environmental Assessment* (EA), which costs approximately USD 3,000. If no problems are discovered, no further testing is necessary. If however, contamination is found (e.g., oil or gas leaks from an old tank), a *Phase II EA* or even a *Phase III EA* needs to be undertaken, which are considerably more expensive. Environmental testing prior to purchase is the only true insurance against unpleasant surprises. Properties in environmentally sensitive areas and waterfront properties are subject to additional strictures.

Historic preservation in Florida is far less advanced than in other countries. However, certain areas (e.g., Miami Beach and the City of Miami) designated as historic have far more extensive *Historic Preservation*

Regulations. In those areas, even properties barely older than 60 years are subject to historic preservation regulations, so that even the slightest modifications require the approval of the local preservation board, which are sometimes withheld for the most obtuse of reasons. *Historic Preservation Regulations* add another layer of approvals for development of a site. In addition to meeting zoning regulations, the application must satisfy the often subjective criteria imposed by the preservation regulations. Indeed, demolition is often forbidden; accordingly, a buyer should confirm whether a property is located in a historic district before purchase.

Access to relevant records and documents

The single most important source of information for the purchase of real estate is the public property registry, which is maintained in the county where the real estate is located. The recorded property information generally consists of photographic scans of the relevant documents, such as deeds or lien documents, together with a computer record as to where those photographic records can be found. Anyone can view and copy the records, but copies are relatively expensive. The property records are normally reviewed by the title insurance agent (often the attorney closing the real estate deal) because lay people invariably miss important entries in the records. Only notarized or court-certified documents can be recorded in the property records. More information is available at each county's recorder's office, e.g. *miami-dadeclerk.com/library/county_recorder/985-Web.pdf*

The most thorough course of action would be to order a property's complete building permit history. While limited records are usually available online, a complete search typically involves a microfilm search conducted by the municipality. A requester should allow several weeks for a municipality to fulfill this request.

Key points that a seller should consider

The seller's prime objective in real estate transactions is to ensure that all legal impediments (hidden or obvious defects) to a sale are disclosed prior to the sale. Moreover, the seller has the obligation to present good and unencumbered title for closing. Ultimately, the main objective of the seller in a real estate transaction is to ensure that he received the purchase price. Accordingly, the seller or his attorney has to ensure that at closing, payment of the purchase price is made in cash or cash equivalent. A seller should pay particular attention that the sale and purchase agreement does not contain any guarantees for which compliance cannot be met. The simplest form of a contract is an "as is" contract, in which the seller makes no promises concerning the condition of the real estate. However, an "as is" sale may affect the value and therefore the purchase price of the property negatively. Most contracts have standard representations by the seller and give the buyer 30 days to inspect the property.

The execution of a real estate purchase transaction

The sale and purchase of residential real estate in Florida typically involves four separate steps (commercial properties are generally more complicated).

1. The seller enters an agreement with a real estate broker for the marketing of the property. The real estate broker enters the property in a so-called *multiple listing service*, a computer system that contains the overwhelming majority of available properties. As soon as the property has been entered into the *multiple listing service*, every broker in Florida has access to information concerning the property, and the assumption is that the broadest possible spectrum of potential buyers will thus see this property. The *multiple listing service* can be searched by specific criteria, such as number of bedrooms, price range, and location.

2. An interested buyer finds a property for sale either through a private search or through a real estate broker and submits an offer of purchase. This offer of purchase is normally made through a unilaterally signed standard purchase and sale agreement and a modest down payment (*earnest money*). The unilaterally signed contract is then

presented to the seller, who can either accept the offer by countersigning or modify the offer in a number of ways. If the seller accepts the offer and countersigns, the contract becomes legally enforceable. If only the slightest changes are made to the offer, the document becomes a counteroffer, which in turn has to be accepted or changed by the buyer who originally submitted it. The contract only becomes legally enforceable when complete agreement has been reached between the parties.

3 In many cases, the buyer requires financing for the purchase of the real estate. Loans are generally available through commercial banks or saving and loans institutions and in rare cases through an agreement for payment over time with the seller. Banks normally require an appraisal of the real estate, an exact survey, a roof and termite inspection, a qualification of the credit worthiness of the borrower, as well as income verification for the borrower. It is generally the bank who determines who will be the title agent for a transaction, i.e., the agent who supervises and conducts the formalities of the property transfer. In simple transactions, the buyer and seller often agree to transact the entire transfer through a title agency, but it is generally advisable for each party to hire their own attorney. The title agency does not represent the interest of the buyer, but those of the bank.

4 The transaction is closed through the delivery of the executed deed and entry of the deed in the public records of the county where the property is located. At the same time, any unpaid portions of the purchase price are paid to the seller or distributed by the title agency to any third parties who must be satisfied to ensure clear title. Prior to the closing, the title insurance company presents to both parties a *title commitment*, which indicates exactly which steps have to be undertaken and which documents have to be provided to enable the title insurance company to issue its policy. This *title commitment* in some way becomes the blue print for the entire transaction. After the closing, the title insurance company issues its title insurance policy if all these conditions have been complied with. The buyer is protected by this title insurance policy, if problems with the title to the property should arise after the purchase. If any unforeseen claims are made by third parties, the title insurance company is usually required to pay them off. Although purchase of a title insurance policy is not legally required for a transaction in Florida, it is absolutely recommended. Banks without exception require title insurance policies in their name as a condition to financing real estate purchases.

Powers of attorney

The validity of a power of attorney is generally judged by reference to Florida law, but it is advisable that the law of the jurisdiction in which the power of attorney is issued is respected as well. A power of attorney that is valid under Florida law generally has to be signed by the party issuing the power of attorney, and must be notarized by a notary public. Because a Florida notary public can only notarize documents within the political borders of the state of Florida, powers of attorney to be executed abroad generally require signature before a consular representative of the US. All powers of attorney must be in writing and the legal qualification of the issuing person has to be demonstrated. The power of attorney has to expressly authorize the actions to be taken by the beneficiary of the power. According to Florida law, a person can also issue a *durable power of attorney,* which gives another person, e.g., an attorney, the power of representation until further notice.

Financing

Financing for a real estate purchase in the US is usually obtained directly from a bank or savings and loan institution, or indirectly from a mortgage broker. A mortgage broker collects the necessary information and documentation from the client (the party seeking financing), and searches for the most favorable interest rates and loan terms for the client. A mortgage broker is usually compensated for her services with a percentage (e.g., ¼%) of the amount financed. Because mortgage brokers can often find a ½% to ¾% more favorable interest rate for their clients, it is worthwhile for a prospective borrower to work with a mortgage broker.

The mortgage payment in the US generally is applied in part to principal and in part to accrued interest. In most cases, the mortgage is repaid over 15 or 30 years, so that the real estate is owned free and clear after payoff. In the middle of 2012, the fixed interest rate for a 15 year mortgage was approximately 3.0% and that of a 30 year mortgage approximately 3.5%. However, borrowers can negotiate even more favorable interest rates if they are willing to pay *points* at closing (i.e., 1 *point* equals 1% of the loan amount) or if they are willing to accept a variable interest rate.

Purchase agreements often contain a clause according to which the buyer is required to close the transaction only if suitable financing is available. The parameters for such financing are often spelled out in the purchase and sale agreement, for example "a 6% fixed-rate mortgage for 30 years". The purchase and sale agreement also determines how soon the buyer has to apply for financing, by when he has to have obtained a loan commitment, and how he has to inform the seller if he is unable to obtain the financing he seeks. The buyer has to make a good-faith attempt to secure financing, and he runs the risk of losing his down payment if he fails to do so.

Foreign buyers are generally expected to provide a down payment of 20%-40% of the purchase price from their own funds. Interest rates for foreign buyers are usually slightly higher than for Florida residents, given the higher risk of default. Non-residents also have to expect to present voluminous information and documentation to support credit worthiness, such as an appraisal of the property to be financed, a US credit report, bank references, credit references, corporate documents, reference letters from tax advisors, copies of the passport with the necessary visa, etc. If ownership of the prospective property is not to be held in the name of an individual, but of a foreign corporation, that must be disclosed at the initial meeting with the lender because many banks are not willing to lend to a foreign corporation, and most require a personal guarantee from a private person with sufficient credit worthiness.

At the time of the loan application, the lender must provide to the borrower a *good-faith estimate* of the costs and expenses expected to be incurred in connection with the loan.

The most important documents required for third-party financing are the mortgage and the *promissory note*. The *promissory note* is proof of the existing debt the borrower is required to repay to the lender. The mortgage gives the lender regress to the real estate if payment under the *promissory note* is not made as required.

The *promissory note* contains the promise of the borrower to repay a sum certain at a certain time at a certain interest rate. *Promissory notes* are usually negotiable papers. In contrast to payment notes in other countries, *promissory notes* in the US can contain a variety of repayment provisions and can require repayment over long periods of time in a single document (a 15 to 30 year term is common). Almost every *promissory note* provides that if payment is not made as required, the lender can immediately demand payment of the entire loan amount and can, according to the mortgage, take regress to the real estate.

The mortgage document is a contract between the borrower and the lender to secure the payment obligations in the *promissory note*. The mortgage forms the basis of a lien on the real estate. The mortgage must be signed by the borrower/debtor and must be recorded in the public records of the county in which the real estate is located.

Purchase through a company

The purchase of real estate in the US through a company offers certain advantages and is advisable in many cases. The main reasons for the purchase of real estate through a company are limitations of liability and certain tax advantages. Particularly in cases where the buyer intends to rent out the real estate or use it commercially; there is always a considerable risk that third parties could be injured on the property.

Because owner liability in Florida is relatively strict for injuries occurring on the property, ownership through a corporation offers some protection. Because shareholders of a corporation in Florida, with very few exceptions, are protected against debt or liabilities of the corporation, liability claims as a result of injuries on a property can only be made against the owner of the property, i.e., the corporation. In most cases, the only asset of the corporation is the real estate itself. Therefore, liability for injuries on the property is limited to the net value of the property itself. With private ownership, a person injured on the property could take regress to all assets of the property owner.

Real estate ownership through a corporation can also offer certain tax advantages to non-Florida taxpayers. In those cases, it is advisable to own the Florida real estate through a foreign corporation. In contrast to direct real estate ownership, the shares of a non-US resident in a foreign corporation are not part of the taxable estate in case of the death of the foreign shareholder. Therefore, if a non-US resident owns the shares of a foreign corporation, which in turn owns the Florida real estate, the death of the foreign shareholder will not bring the real estate into the taxable US estate. Structures with foreign corporations have to be planned carefully, because even the slightest variations can have drastic tax consequences.

Warranty claims

Warranty claims in Florida must be distinguished between claims related to title and claims related to physical property. Claims related to title in Florida by and large are covered by the title insurance. Claims against inadequacies of the real estate itself generally depend in Florida on the purchase and sale agreement or the general contractor agreement. The law does provide additional remedies in case of intentional misrepresentations by the seller.

The constitution of the state of Florida provides that the homestead of a Florida resident (US citizen or permanent resident) cannot be taken to satisfy judgments of claims by creditors. Over time, Florida has come to be known as a "debtor's paradise" because even investments of millions of dollars in the primary residence cannot be taken to satisfy claims. The sole exception to this rule are claims against the real estate itself, e.g., through mortgages where the real estate has been pledged as a security. This protection of the primary residence (homestead exemption) will not prevent a lender from executing against a real estate pledged as a security. Because mortgages are generally secured through the real estate itself, the bank can take regress against the real estate even if it is the primary residence of the debtor. A filing for bankruptcy by the debtor will stop any and all execution efforts by third parties (*automatic stay*), but the existence of the mortgage creates the basis for the creditor to obtain relief from the automatic stay to proceed against the real estate even during the pendency of the bankruptcy.

34.4 New construction, rebuilding and renovation

Construction zones and construction permits

Construction permits from county authorities are required for all new construction and renovation work. Generally, construction permits will only be issued if the intended construction complies with existing zoning and comprehensive plan regulations. In cases where the intended construction is not in compliance with existing zoning and comprehensive planning, a *zoning variance* must be obtained, which is often difficult. Most jurisdictions require the applicant to demonstrate a legal hardship in order to justify a variance. This is an extremely high burden. The applicant must show, among other things, that the property is deprived of all reasonable beneficial use without the variance.

The importance of understanding applicable zoning is particularly important if undeveloped land is purchased. To obtain a permit for any construction or renovation, the construction plans must be signed by a licensed architect (and/or licensed professionals relevant to the intended construction/renovation) and must be submitted together with the application for the construction permit. All deviations from approved construction plans during the process of construction are again subject to approval by the *Building Department*, and must often obtain approvals from other agencies (e.g. *Water* and *Sewer*), depending on the nature of the project.

Commercial projects are subject to payment of impact and/or concurrency fees. These fees are designed to off-set the impact of the project on the municipality's resources (i.e. roads, schools, fire department, parks, etc.). These fees can be substantial and must be paid prior to the issuance of a building permit.

Architect's contracts and building contracts

In many new construction cases, the owner enters an agreement with a *general contractor* (and sometimes separately with an architect) for the construction of the intended building. In contrast, a builder or developer usually offers all-inclusive pricing for a model home that can be viewed prior to construction. When an owner does not want to buy an existing model from a developer, separate contracts have to be entered into with various specialists, which all have to be carefully coordinated. Because these agreements differ for each construction phase, and because such construction requires daily supervision, inexperienced owners should think twice before attempting to supervise their own construction. An owner in any case should only work with licensed and insured general contractors and architects and under no circumstances with unlicensed professionals, who need to have plans signed by another licensed contractor/architect. An architect's or general contractor's contract defines the terms of planning, construction supervision, technical control and execution of construction, as well as the deadlines and costs. Contracts with unlicensed persons/companies for work requiring a licensed professional are generally not enforceable; further, unlicensed professionals cannot obtain permits to perform the construction.

Completion of construction and formalities

Timely completion of construction as provided in any agreement is the exception rather than the rule in Florida. Courts rarely penalize developers and general contractors for delays, even in extreme cases. Construction quality often leaves much to be desired and only meticulous supervision during the construction ensures decent construction quality. After completion of construction, the general contractor has to obtain a C*ertificate of Occupancy* (CO) from the *Building and Zoning Department*. Payment obligations in construction contracts are often tied to the builder obtaining the CO, but the certificate itself does not indicate that the work has been completed perfectly. A CO is often issued even if there are still substantial cosmetic deficiencies in new construction.

Deficiencies and warranty claims regarding new construction

After completion of construction, and prior to acceptance, the buyer and the general contractor usually conduct a walk-through, where all construction deficiencies are entered in a *punch list*. Because it is often difficult for lay people to discover deficiencies, it is advisable to conduct the walk-through with a licensed construction inspector to be paid by the buyer. The builder must remedy all items on the *punch list* within a "reasonable period of time". Regrettably, there are often disagreements as to what constitutes "reasonable period of time" and courts offer little assistance. It is advisable to consult with an attorney early on if it appears that the builder is not conscientious in remedying punch list items. The warranty period for a given construction object is set forth in the agreement, and there are no legal or customary warranties.

34.5 Rental and tenancy

The residential lease statutes in Florida differ from commercial lease statutes. In general, Florida Landlord and Tenant law gives the owner (lessor/landlord) far greater rights than the renter (lessee/tenant). There is always the assumption that if rent is not timely paid, or if the lease expires, the lessor/landlord has the almost absolute right to have the lessee/tenant removed from the property. Even decade-long tenancies do not entitle lessees to any special legal right to extend an expired lease.

Rental and lease agreements

The legal rights of residential tenants are somewhat broader than those for commercial tenants. They are set forth in *Florida's Residential Landlord and Tenant Act*. Condominium units are not covered by this law, and are subject to additional legal rules and protections. Lease agreements generally must be in writing, but a *tenancy-at-will* may be created through an oral agreement. The duration of a *tenancy-at-will* depends on the lease payment interval; for monthly leases, *tenancies-at-will* have a 30 day termination notice requirement. For shorter lease-payment periods, shorter termination notices apply. Contrary to the customary rule in the US, a prevailing party in residential lease litigation is entitled to attorney's fees from the losing party. In Florida, it is customary to make three monthly rent payments at the commencement of a lease: first month's rent, last month's rent and one month security deposit. At the time of lease termination, the landlord must return the security deposit to the tenant within 15 days after the lease expires, or give notice within 30 days why the landlord is retaining a portion or the entire security amount. The tenant's obligations include the requirement to keep the property clean and to maintain the facility. He must not disturb the quiet enjoyment of his neighbors or recklessly or intentionally destroy any part of the property. The landlord, on the other hand, is legally required to maintain the structural portions of the property, ensure that the property complies with all applicable laws and regulations, and pay for maintenance of locks, pest control, garbage disposal, water, sewer and, if necessary, heating. However, the landlord can shift the cost for those services to the tenant in a lease agreement.

Regulations on protection of tenants and rent control

Generally, Florida recognizes only very limited tenant protection regulations, mainly certain minimum termination notices. For those unfamiliar with US law, it should be stressed that a tenant does not acquire any rights as a result of long-term lease relations with the landlord. If the lease expires, or is legally terminated, the tenant must vacate the property immediately. Note that some cities, e.g. Miami-Beach, do not permit short-term rentals of less than six months.

34.6 Succession and gifts

Applicable law and jurisdiction

The legal succession regime depends on the conflict rule of law of the applicable countries. Customarily, the legal succession laws of the country in which the decedent resided at the time of death or the law of her country of citizenship apply. This rule also applies to foreign properties of the decedent, e.g., shares of a foreign corporation owned by a decedent with last place of residence in Florida.

Fundamentals of the succession and gift/donation laws of Florida/US

The following information only applies to real estate owned by a natural person, and not to property owned by a corporation. Separate legal requirements apply to the latter.

Wills

Florida has extremely strict rules for the validity of wills. Wills in Florida must be in writing, but not necessarily machine-typed. In addition to the testator, at least two witnesses have to sign the will, and have to confirm that the testator and the witnesses signed the will in each other's presence. Florida law does provide for recognition of foreign wills, but only if those foreign wills were executed in accordance with the foregoing formalities. In particular, *holographic wills*, signed only by the testator without witnesses, are invalid in Florida.

Without a valid will, Florida law provides for application of the legal succession rules, which can lead to entirely different results than those intended by the testator. For testators with a will valid in another jurisdiction but invalid in Florida, the solution is a separate *Florida will* in which the testator makes specific decisions for the devise of property located in Florida and executed with the necessary legal formalities.

Legal succession

If a property owner dies without a valid will, and his estate falls under Florida law, real estate is divided according to the legal succession laws of Florida. If a decedent was married at the time of death, the following rules apply:

- If no surviving children are alive: 100% to the surviving spouse. If biological children of both spouses survive, the first USD 60,000 plus one half of the remainder goes to the surviving spouse. If biological children of the decedent are alive which are not biological children of the surviving spouse, one half of the estate goes to the surviving spouse, the rest to the biological children of the decedent
- If the decedent was not married at the time of death: 100% to the biological children. If no biological children survive, 100% to the father and the mother of the decedent. In cases where there are neither biological children nor parents, the property goes in equal parts to the siblings of the decedent or their successors. In cases where there are neither biological children, parents nor siblings/ successors of siblings, the property goes in equal part to the parental or maternal grandparents or their successors
- In cases where neither of the foregoing is alive, the estate goes to the relative of the last pre-deceased spouse, as if that spouse had survived the decedent. Within those categories, the succession is generally *per stirpes*, i.e., the distribution to children generally is in equal parts. If a child predeceases, that child's share goes to the successors of that child in equal parts. If the predeceased child has no successors, her portion goes to the surviving siblings

Gifts/Donations

The record owner of a property can freely give away or donate her property rights at any time. Obviously, the owner can only give the specific rights she owns, e.g., a life estate or similarly limited property rights. Moreover, gifts have similar tax consequences as inheritances (see below).

34.7 Taxes and charges

Because Florida does not impose state income taxes on individual tax-payers, Florida's state income consists primarily of *sales taxes, real estate taxes, and fees.*

One-time taxes and charges on purchase

Purchase/acquisition taxes

Deeds and other documents used to transfer real estate in Florida are subject to Florida's *documentary stamp tax*. This tax is currently set at USD 7 to USD 10.50 for each USD 1,000 of the purchase price of the property, i.e., documentary stamp taxes for a USD 200,000 property is USD 140 in most cities. If buyer and seller do not agree otherwise, this tax is to be paid by the buyer. The tax is normally paid at the time of recordation in the property records by submitting a separate form and a corresponding check. Because the amount of *documentary stamp tax* is listed on the document in the public records, and because the tax rate is generally known, the purchase price for a given property can be calculated from the recorded documents.

Value Added Taxes

Florida has a *sales tax*, which is one of the most important and imposing taxes in Florida. With some exceptions, sales tax is applied to all products or services rendered to end-users in Florida. The tax is usually not relevant in real estate transactions, but if a foreign purchaser of real estate intends to ultimately live in the Florida property, she should expect this tax to be applied to virtually every purchase. As of October 2014, the *sales tax* for Miami-Dade County, Florida is 7%, and for Broward County (Fort Lauderdale), 6%. Certain luxury products are taxed only on the first USD 5,000.

Real estate registration and notary charges

All documents to be recorded in the public records are subject to recording fees. Currently, the *recording fees* in Miami-Dade County are USD 10 for the first page and USD 8.50 for each additional page. Other counties have comparable fees. A notary public in Florida has one main function, to notarize signatures. This service is often entirely or nearly free of charge.

Recurring annual taxes and charges

Real estate tax

Annual *real estate taxes* are, next to *sales taxes*, the most important source of revenue for the state of Florida from private individuals. Property taxes vary from municipality to municipality. For example, in Miami-Dade County alone, taxpayers are subject to dozens of varying tax rates, depending on the location of the particular property. If an owner has owned and lived in the same property for a long time, he may pay as little as USD 800 in annual property taxes, whereas the new neighbor may pay as much as USD 3,000 for a comparable property. This is so because the law limits yearly increases of property taxes, whereas the entire increase in market value is assessed at the time of sale to a new owner. To calculate property taxes, the market value of the real estate is estimated and multiplied by a particular "millage rate".

There are a number of exceptions to this rule. First, the property is almost always appraised at 10 – 20% below actual market value, in particular at times of rapid increases in property values. Secondly, the first USD 50,000 of the value of the primary residence of a citizen or Florida resident is not taxable according to the *Florida homestead exemption* laws (not to be confused with the *homestead exemption* laws previously discussed in connection with owner liability and legal capacity). Third, the annual adjustments to market value are limited, so that real estate that has been owned by the same owner for a long time is often taxed at a low rate. Conversely, real estate purchased recently or expanded in size by the owner is often drastically reappraised, which can lead to a doubling or tripling of real estate taxes overnight. A buyer of real estate can therefore not rely on representations of the previous owner as to the tax amount paid in the past. The exact calculation of real estate taxes for a particular property is rather complicated and often hard to understand (even for experts). Owners may challenge overly aggressive reappraisals of real estate, and the assistance of an attorney is often advisable. The county government issues real estate tax statements around September for the current year, and payment before the end of November entitles the owner to a rebate.

Income tax

Income tax for individual US residents is assessed uniformly at the federal level, and depending on the state, additionally on a state level. Unlike many other states, Florida taxes the income of certain corporations, but not of individual taxpayers. All US citizens and permanent residents must pay income tax on their worldwide income. For all other persons residing in the US the following rule applies: if the actual presence in the US exceeds certain time limits, those persons may also be subject to US income tax with their worldwide income (see below, tax residence). For foreign residents residing in the US for less than the legal time limit, only income actually earned in the US, e.g., from rentals of real estate in Florida, is subject to US income taxation.

Net wealth tax

The net wealth or estate of a living US taxpayer is not separately taxed in Florida.

Capital gains taxes

Capital gains taxes in the US are a political hot-button topic. Capital gains are generally taxed similarly to simple income. The tax is to be paid by the seller of taxable assets at the time of the sale of the taxable asset directly to the tax authorities. The capital gain is the difference between the original purchase price of the taxable asset and the sales price, minus expenses necessary for the maintenance of the property during ownership, as well as additional investments in the property during the time of ownership (e.g., additions improving the value of the real estate, legal expenses, documented repairs and certain costs in connection with the original acquisition). US taxpayers enjoy a substantial life-time exemption from capital gains taxes, which apply to foreigners only to a limited extent.

Real estate transactions in the US are subject to the *Foreign Investment in Real Property Tax Act* of 1980 (FIRPTA), and the direct taxation related thereto. FIRPTA presumes that every seller of real estate is a foreign person, subject to direct taxation on any capital gains. Therefore, a US taxpayer has the legal obligation to prove at time of sale of the real estate that he is not a foreign taxpayer. Every seller has to report his FIRPTA status to the tax authorities on Form 8288 and Form 8288-A, and if appropriate, pay the withheld FIRPTA tax to the tax authorities within 10 days. Because non-payment of the FIRPTA tax can lead to a lien on the real estate, the buyer has to insist that all FIRPTA taxes are either paid immediately to the tax authorities at time of closing or that written proof of tax-free status is provided, usually in the form of a "non-foreign affidavit".

FIRPTA provides that 10% of the sales price of the real estate has to be withheld as a direct tax, unless one of several exceptions applies:

1. If a buyer is purchasing the property for his own use and the purchase price does not exceed USD 300,000
2. If the seller has obtained a tax exemption certificate from the tax authorities according to which he is not subject to the tax or subject to a reduced tax
3. If the seller provides an affidavit at time of closing that he is not a foreign tax payer

Some modest income tax increases became effective 1 January 2013 (a person with USD 100,000 to 200,000 in annual income will pay about

USD 2,000 more in annual income taxes), but further increases appear unavoidable to deal with the looming fiscal cliff in the United States.

Inheritance and gift taxes

In civil law countries, the entire estate of the testator passes to her heirs at the time of death (principle of universality). Therefore, the heirs are the debtors and responsible for the payment of inheritance taxes. In contrast, Florida law (and US law in general) provides for the creation of a separate tax entity at time of death, the decedent's estate. Inheritance taxes are assessed to the entire value of the estate, and paid by the estate to the tax authorities. Disbursements by the estate after payment of estate taxes to the various heirs is no longer subject to additional taxation. American taxpayers enjoy a USD 1 million lifetime exemption (the exemption is unlimited between spouses).

To what extent a foreign citizen is subject to US estate tax depends on whether the person is considered a limited or unlimited US taxpayer. A foreigner is considered an unlimited taxpayer, meaning his worldwide estate is subject to US estate tax, if the testator is domiciled in the US for estate tax purpose at his time of death. A foreign natural person is considered domiciled in the US if he has his residence or presence in the US with the intent to live permanently in the US. The right of taxation belongs to the state in which the decedent had his center of life. A US resident foreign citizen therefore is subject to the unlimited US estate tax.

In contrast, a person not domiciled in the US is taxed only to a limited extent. This generally means that estate taxes are applied only to that portion of the estate that is actually located in the US, e.g., real estate in Florida. Because non-domiciled taxpayers have only very limited tax exemptions, most of the value of a Florida real estate falls under this tax.

Because non-US residents are subject to different estate tax rules than US taxpayers, proper planning of real estate acquisition can lead to substantial tax advantages. For countries without a double taxation agreement with the US, foreign testators who own US real estate in their individual names are subject to the full US estate tax. Unlimited spousal exemption is available for the surviving spouses only in cases where that spouse is a US citizen.

In stark contrast, shares in a foreign corporation owned by a non-US resident at the time of his death are not subject to US estate taxation. Accordingly, if Florida real estate is owned by a foreign corporation, which in turn is owned by a non-US taxpayer, US estate tax does not consider a transfer of the shares of that foreign corporation to the heirs to the decedent as a taxable transaction. However, the transaction may be subject to taxation in the decedent's country of citizenship.

Because the estate tax in the US can be as much as 55% of the value of the estate, it is usually advisable for a non-US taxpayer to own Florida real estate valued at more than USD 300,000 through an off-shore entity, or through a Florida entity wholly-owned by an off-shore entity. Real estate brokers should advise such clients to contact an attorney prior to signing a purchase and sale agreement for real estate. If this is not feasible for any reason, the purchase agreement should at least contain the words "and/or assigns" after the name of the purchaser, i.e., the contract can later be assigned to a third party, such as a foreign corporation.

In cases where a foreign investor has already purchased the Florida real estate in his own name or together with a spouse or family member, a correction of this problem is usually difficult and expensive. When the foreign corporation is formed after the purchase of the real estate, and the real estate is to be shifted into ownership of that foreign corporation, the transfer to the foreign corporation creates FIRPTA obligations which can be rather substantial. Additionally, transfer taxes, documentary stamp taxes, title insurance fees and accounting costs are to be added, leading to a substantial expense.

Other taxes and charges

There are no other substantial taxes or fees relevant to real estate in Florida.

Incorrect (lower) statement of sales price on the sales agreement

An incorrect statement of the sales price for real estate for the purpose of evading taxes is illegal in Florida and extremely unusual. For every purchase of real estate a *Housing and Urban Development statement (HUD)* has to be signed by the parties, which documents all money flows at the time of closing. Stating a lower than actual purchase price is tantamount to tax fraud, and exposes the involved parties to substantial penalties, including jail.

International taxation

Many countries have double taxation agreements with the US. As a result, US taxpayers are entitled to a credit for income and estate taxes they have already paid in their country of citizenship, and in turn foreign taxpayers are entitled to a credit in their country of citizenship for taxes they have already paid in the US. In the case of Florida real estate ownership by a resident from a country with a double taxation agreement, this means that the Florida home owner who is not a US tax resident can claim a tax credit in her home country for US income taxes paid. If, for example, the foreign owner of a home in Florida earns income in Florida from the rental of the Florida home to third persons, that income is taxable income in the US and possibly also in the foreign country of citizenship of the owner.

If both the country of citizenship of the home owner and the US are signatories to a double taxation agreement, taxes on the income earned in the US from the rental of the home must be paid only once, either in the home country or the US, as provided in the double taxation agreement. Similarly, estate taxes paid after the death of a foreign owner of Florida real estate must not be paid again in the home country of the deceased property owner if the two countries have a double taxation agreement. Of course, such estate taxes for property owned in the US by a non-US taxpayer can be entirely avoided in many cases with proper tax planning.

34.8 Immigration law and tax residence

Entry, residence and settlement of foreigners

Every foreigner who intends to work or be commercially active in the US, including foreigners intending to purchase US real estate for investment purposes, must observe US immigration laws. US immigration law contains detailed requirements for the immigration of non-US citizens. Immigration and visa approvals are now handled by the *Department of Homeland Security.* Outside the US, immigration applications are handled by US consulates and embassies.

It is important to note that real estate ownership in the US does not automatically confer the right of residence in the US. However, US immigration laws allow foreign investors to structure their immigration status in such a way that they obtain the right of staying in the US for their intended purpose through a number of non-immigrant visas, and in some cases ultimately obtain the unlimited residence right (*green card*). Every non-US citizen is considered a "foreigner". Non-immigrants are foreigners who intend to stay in the US for a limited, determined period of time. Immigrants are foreigners who wish to remain permanently for unlimited duration in the US.

The following visa classifications may be available for foreign investors. Non-immigrant visas are usually issued by the US consulate in the home country of the foreigner. In certain cases it is possible to change the non-immigrant status of a foreigner after entry into the US.

B-1 Visa

The B-1 visa is a business visa for foreigners who remain in the US temporarily and who have a permanent residence abroad. The holder of a B-1 visa may engage in business activities, e.g., prepare contracts, search for real estate, review commercial investments, etc. The B-1 foreigner may not work in the US for a salary. Until April 2002, the B-1 visa was issued automatically for six months. Since then, travelers have to explain why they want to stay for up to six months. If a period of less than six months is justified, less than six months of a stay is approved. Real estate ownership in the US may in certain circumstances be sufficient reason to justify a six month stay.

H-1B Visa

The H-1B visa allows US corporations and other organizations to temporarily hire foreign persons who, based on their education, qualify for certain positions requiring the hiring of foreigners. There are two categories of persons fulfilling the requirements for an H-1B visa:

1. holders of university degrees and professionals
2. persons who have attained exceptional reputation or skills in their field of expertise

Foreigners wishing to invest in US real estate can possibly qualify for an H-1B visa if the intended investment is structured as a corporation, and offers the foreigner a professional position (e.g., investment advisor) and if the necessary requirements and/or professional experience is adequate and fulfilled. H-1B visas are usually issued for three years, but extensions of up to six years in total are possible.

L-1 Visa

The L-1 visa is intended to enable foreign companies to transfer employees to the US. The foreign employee has to have been employed by the applying company for at least one year prior to application, and must have held an executive or managerial position, or must have special skills or abilities. The holder of an L-1 visa first receives authorization to stay in the US for one year for a new corporation or up to three years for an older existing corporation. The holder of an L-1 visa can apply for an extension and is also permitted to bring his spouse and his unmarried minor children to the US.

E-Visa

The E-visa category authorizes foreign business owners, managers and employees to stay in the US for an extended period of time to set up and manage a trading company (E-1 Visa). The requirement is that the majority of the corporation's trade must be between the US and the foreigner's home country. This visa can also be obtained by foreigners from countries participating in the E-visa program, who make a substantial investment in the US (E-2 Visa). The duration of the work authorization of an E-visa is between one and five years, and an unlimited extension can be obtained if the foreigner provides adequate proof that he will leave the country after expiration of the current stay.

Permanent residence and immigration visas

In addition to regular visas, some 10,000 permanent residence visas are annually available to investors fulfilling the following requirements:

1. The new business must have been formed by the foreign investor
2. The foreigner must have irrevocably invested at least USD 1 million (or at least USD 500,000 in a special economic development area) in the new business after 29 November 1990
3. The new business must benefit the US economy and must create at least 10 full-time jobs for US employees (the jobs of the visa applicant, her spouse and children are not counted for this purpose)

The foreigner must hold a managing position within the new company. Visas in this category are issued initially for a period of two years. After two years, the immigration officials determine whether the foreigner has indeed created a commercially successful business, which conforms to the requirements of this visa category before issuing an unlimited and permanent residence permit (known as a green card).

Each year the US conducts a so-called visa or green card lottery, in which 50,000 permanent residence authorizations are awarded to the winners. The odds of winning a green card in the lottery depend on the number of applicants from a given country, but are between 1:20 and 1:25 for most European countries. More information is available at *usa-green-card.com*

Tax residence

A non-US resident, who resides in the US for more than 183 days in any given calendar year, becomes a tax resident in the US unless the taxpayer proves that he has a closer personal and economic connection to another country. To be exempted from US taxpayer status under these circumstances, the taxpayer must make a timely application to the tax authorities. The economic ties of such an applicant are presumed to exist where the individual is conducting his primary commercial businesses, or where the individual has his primary residence. Similar factors are considered on the personal side. The application has to be submitted no later than the due date for the personal income tax return, e.g., for the tax year 2012 no later than 15 April 2013.

Even persons residing for fewer than 183 days in a calendar year in the US can become US tax residents. Tax law provides that residence days of the preceding year (1/3 of the days counted) and the pre-preceding year (1/6 of the days counted) are also taken into consideration in calculating the residence days for a year. If the total sum of those days is 183 days or more, there is the presumption that the foreigner is a US tax resident. As a result of this formula, a foreigner who resides in the US for less than 120 days in any given calendar year will not fall under this presumption.

As indicated above, once an individual is a US resident for tax purposes, the entire worldwide income of that person is taxed on a federal level. Income tax for private individuals in the US is taxed in the US uniformly on a federal level, and depending on the state, also on a state level. Florida has no personal income tax. On a federal level the following personal income tax rates applied in 2014 for individual taxpayers:

Annual Taxable Income	Tax Rate
USD 0 - USD 9,075	10%
USD 9,076 - USD 36,900	15%
USD 36,901 – USD 89,350	25%
USD 89.351 - USD 186,350	28%
USD 186,351 – USD 405,100	33%
USD 405,101 - USD 406,750	35%
Over USD 406,751	39.6%

International double taxation for residents of Florida

With the above-described residence in the US (residence of more than 183 days in a given calendar year), even a foreigner without legal immigration status can become a US taxpayer. This can lead to the result that a person is taxed both in his home country and in the US. To avoid this situation, the US has entered into double taxation agreements with numerous countries. According to these agreements, such individuals must be granted tax credits in their home country for taxes paid in the US. These agreements also determine which country has jurisdiction over a taxpayer.

34.9 Checklist: Real estate in Florida

- Search for properties only with licensed brokers; request printout from the *Multiple Listing Service*; ask broker for a Comparative Market Analysis (CMA)
- Consult with an attorney prior to execution of a Purchase and Sale Agreement. Caution: the unilateral signing and submission of a Purchase and Sale Agreement often is tantamount with the outright purchase of the property given that the seller can accept the submitted contract, thus creating a valid final agreement
- Is the purchaser an individual person or a corporation? Can the purchase agreement be assigned by an individual buyer to a company?
- For third-party financing: immediately request from the bank a good-faith estimate of the expected closing costs, including sales price, property tax prepayment, legal costs (settlement fees), document preparation fees, abstract and title insurance, recording fees and inspection fees
- Due diligence: retain a specialist to carefully inspect the house for termite and roof damage, and other potential problems; order appraisal; order credit report for buyer; order title insurance commitment and begin assembling required documents; prepare documents for closing; review whether the property has all the

necessary hook-ups, such as water and sewer; transfer cable, telephone, electrical, gas and water services from the old owner to new owner for the day of closing. Obtain zoning confirmation from the municipality, confirming that the property can be used for its intended use. Confirm that there are no liens or other penalties recorded against the property

- Review the HUD Financing Statement prior to closing and thoroughly understand all financial transactions shown on the HUD financing statement. The law requires that all financial transactions have to be listed on this statement with precision. Ensure that sufficient witnesses are available for the closing. Documents can be pre-executed by the seller prior to the closing, if necessary, abroad
- After the closing immediately send deed to the recorder's office; withhold FIRPTA taxes and send to tax authorities; submit tax return the following year to obtain a partial or complete refund of FIRPTA taxes. For US residents or green card holders, apply for homestead exemption

34.10 Bibliography

Alpert, Jonathan L.: Florida Real Estate, Lawyers Cooperative Publishing Co., Rochester N.Y., 1982, Rev. 1999

Ballinger, Kenneth J.: Florida Real Estate Handbook, Michie Corp, Charlottesville Va. 1979

Florida Real Property, Probate & Trusts, Collected Cases & Subject Matter Index, Judicial & Administrative Research Associates, Inc., Tallahassee, FL 1999

Florida Bar: 1995 Real Estate Update and Certification Review Course, Florida Bar CLE, Tallahassee, FL 1995

Florida Bar: Basic Real Estate, Florida Bar CLE, Tallahassee 1997

Gibson, Paul C.: Florida Real Estate Transactions, D & S Publishers, Clearwater FL 1982, 1997

Stuart, Don W. / Guttmann, Louis B. / Awerbach, Martin S.: Examining and Evaluating Title to Real Property in Florida, Professional Education Systems, Eau Claire, Wisc., 1990

Thompson, Marvin / Harwood, Bruce: Florida Real Estate: An Introduction to the Profession, Reston Pub. Co., Reston, Va., 1980

Rich Neysa / Brady James C.: Florida Real Estate Closings, Settlement Procedures in Residential Transactions, Harrison Co, Norcross, GA 1982

Various Internet Resources, including publications of the Internal Revenue Service

Henley & Partners Group Offices

For a complete and up-to-date list of all Henley & Partners group office locations worldwide, visit *henleyglobal.com*

Antigua and Barbuda

Henley & Partners Caribbean Ltd
Jolly Harbour
PO Box 262
Antigua
St Mary's

Tel	+1 869 465 6220
Fax	+1 869 465 6221
Contact	Gaye Hechme
Email	*gaye.hechme@henleyglobal.com*

Belgium

Henley & Partners Belgium bvba
Henley Building
Lange Klarenstraat 22
2000 Antwerpen, Belgium

Tel	+32 3 288 43 43
Fax	+32 3 293 46 87
Contact	Leon van der Heiden
Email	*leon.vanderheiden@henleyglobal.com*

Canada

Henley & Partners Canada Ltd
2020 University St., Suite 1920
Montreal, H3A 2A5, Canada

Tel	+1 514 288 1997
Fax	+1 514 284 6258
Contact	Daniel Perron
Email	*daniel.perron@henleyglobal.com*

Henley & Partners Canada Ltd
885 West Georgia Street
Suite 1030
Vancouver, BC, V6C 3E8
Canada

Tel	+1 604 239 2170
Fax	+1 888 702 6945
Contact	Jon Green
Email	*jon.green@henleyglobal.com*

Croatia and Montenegro

Henley & Partners Croatia
Mihovilova Sirina 3
HR-21000 Split, Croatia

Tel	+385 21 321 027
Fax	+385 21 321 028
Contact	Marko Jug-Dujakovic
Email	*marko.jug-dujakovic@henleyglobal.com*

Cyprus

Henley & Partners Cyprus Ltd
9, Spirou Kiprianou Avenue
Suite 301, 3070
Limassol
Cyprus

Tel	+357 2531 1844
Fax	+357 2531 1770
Contact	Yiannos Trisokkas
Email	*yiannos.trisokkas@henleyglobal.com*

Dubai/UAE

Henley & Partners Middle East DMCC
Reef Tower, JLT, Suite #1301
P.O. Box 213757
Dubai, UAE

Tel	+971 4 392 77 22
Fax	+971 4 392 77 33
Contact	Marco Gantenbein
Email	*marco.gantenbein@henleyglobal.com*

Hong Kong

Henley & Partners Hong Kong Ltd
1002A, Tower 1, Admiralty Center
18 Harcourt Road
Admiralty
Hong Kong

Tel	+852 3101 4100
Fax	+852 3101 4101
Contact	Jennifer Lai
Email	*jennifer.lai@henleyglobal.com*

Jersey

Henley & Partners Ltd
Henley House
9 Hope Street
St Helier
Jersey, JE2 3NS
British Isles

Tel	+44 1534 514 888
Fax	+44 1534 514 999
Contact	Hugh Morshead
Email	*hugh.morshead@henleyglobal.com*

Malta

Henley & Partners Malta Ltd
Aragon House
Dragonara Road
St. Julian's
Malta
STJ 3140

Tel	+356 2138 7400
Fax	+356 2138 6401
Contact	Stuart MacFeeters
Email	*stuart.macfeeters@henleyglobal.com*

Philippines

Representative Office of
Henley & Partners Singapore Pte. Ltd.
Unit 10A, Net Lima Tower
5th Avenue, corner 26th Street
Bonifacio Global City
Manila, Philippines

Tel	+632 669 2771
Fax	+632 651 5902
Contact	Diego Vivas
Email	*diego.vivas@henleyglobal.com*

Portugal

Henley & Partners Portugal Lda
Palácio Alagoas
Rua da Escola Politécnica 183A
1250-101 Lisboa
Portugal

Tel	+351 213 970 977
Fax	+351 213 970 982
Contact	Emi Silva
Email	*emi.silva@henleyglobal.com*

Russia/CIS

Representative Office of
Henley Estates International Ltd.
Sechenovsky pereulok, 6
Moscow, Russia

Tel	+7 495 774 1501
Fax	+7 495 769 9253
Contact	Mechislav Polozov
Email	*mechislav.polozov@henleyglobal.com*

Singapore

Henley & Partners Singapore Pte. Ltd
36 Robinson Road
City House, Level 14-06
Singapore 068877

Tel	+65 6438 7117
Fax	+65 6438 7227
Contact	Dr. Juerg Steffen
Email	*juerg.steffen@henleyglobal.com*

South Africa

Henley & Partners South Africa (pty) Ltd
4 Niblick Way
#9, Fairways Office Park
Somerset West
South Africa 7130

Tel	+27 21 850 0524
Fax	+27 21 850 0596
Contact	Andrew Taylor
Email	*andrew.taylor@henleyglobal.com*

St. Kitts and Nevis

Henley & Partners Caribbean Ltd
Sugar Bay Club
Zenway Boulevard
P.O. Box 2505
Frigate Bay
St. Kitts, West Indies

Tel	+1 869 465 6220
Fax	+1 869 465 6221
Contact	Christopher Willis
Email	*christopher.willis@henleyglobal.com*

Switzerland

Henley & Partners Switzerland AG
Henley Haus
Klosbachstrasse 110
8024 Zurich
Switzerland

Tel	+41 44 266 22 22
Fax	+41 44 266 22 23
Contact	Dr. Peter Krummenacher
Email	*peter.krummenacher@henleyglobal.com*

Turkey

Henley & Partners Turkey
Louis Vuitton Building
Abdi Ipekci Caddesi
Bostan Sokak No. 15, 5th Floor
Nisantasi, 34367 Istanbul, Turkey

Tel	+90 212 373 9588
Fax	+90 212 373 9589
Contact	Tolga Habali
Email	*tolga.habali@henleyglobal.com*

United Kingdom

Henley & Partners UK Ltd
20 Grosvenor Place
London SW1X 7HN
United Kingdom

Tel	+44 207 823 1010
Fax	+44 207 235 4489
Contact	Hakan Cortelek
Email	*hakan.cortelek@henleyglobal.com*

Vietnam

Representative Office of
Henley & Partners Singapore Pte. Ltd
Harbour View Tower
35 Nguyen Hue Boulevard
Ben Nghe Ward, Dist 1
Ho Chi Minh City
Vietnam

Tel	+84 8 3821 7582
Fax	+84 8 3821 7592
Contact	Gam Ha
Email	*gam.ha@henleyglobal.com*

Index

www.ingramcontent.com/pod-product-compliance
Lightning Source LLC
LaVergne TN
LVHW052010200926
848481LV00005B/1458